ENCYCLOPEDIA

OF

NEEDLEWORK

BY

THERESE DE DILLMONT

D·M·C LIBRARY

ENCYCLOPEDIA

OF

NEEDLEWORK

BY

THERESE DE DILLMONT

New Edition, revised and enlarged

CRESCENT BOOKS
NEW YORK

This edition published 1987 by Crescent Books
Distributed by Crown Publishers, Inc.
225 Park Avenue, South
New York, New York 10003

Copyright © BRACKEN BOOKS 1987

ISBN 0-517-63180-6

Printed and bound in Hungary
h g f e d c b a

TABLE OF CONTENTS

TABLE OF CONTENTS

TABLE OF CONTENTS

TABLE OF CONTENTS

TABLE OF CONTENTS

TABLE OF CONTENTS

COLOURED PLATES WITHOUT TEXT

TABLE OF THE COLOURS AND SIZES
of the cotton, flax and silk articles bearing the D.M.C
trade mark.

D.M.C LIBRARY
List of the illustrated works published thus far.

Preface.

The want till now of any complete work on the subject has induced me, in the serviceable form of an Encyclopedia of needlework, to sum up the knowledge and experience which years of study and actual practice have enabled me to accumulate. Careful workers will be able by its help to instruct themselves in every branch of plain and fancy needlework therein described.

The patterns given, even the simplest, were all worked specially for the book and are accurately reproduced and clearly explained.

Not to limit my readers to dull directions and theory the book has been copiously illustrated with designs taken from the artistic productions of countries and periods famed for skill and taste in different branches of needlework.

At first sight some of the designs may appear rather difficult to execute but when the directions are accurately followed all difficulty will disappear.

That I was able to make such an interesting selection is owing in great measure to the kindness with which certain private collections were placed at my disposal from which I have drawn extensively and I desire to take this opportunity of thanking the generous owners for the free use they allowed me to make of the artistic treasures in their possession.

The choice of colours and material — a difficult matter to many — will be found comparatively easy, if the notes affixed to the illustrations are attended to; and here I may observe, that a satisfactory execution of the patterns will always be greatly facilitated, by the use of the D.M.C cottons, silk and flax thread, for long experience has convinced me of the superlative excellence of all articles bearing the mark of that distinguished firm.

In conclusion I may express the hope that this volume will be favourably received by the public to whom it is specially addressed; this will be my best reward for the care and trouble that have been expended upon it.

THERESE DE DILLMONT.

Note of the editor.

The hope expressed by the author at the end of her preface has been fully realised. The Encyclopedia of needlework has found a place in most women's libraries and its success has exceeded all anticipation

Numerous editions have been issued ; it has been translated into four different languages and hundreds of thousands of copies are in circulation. At the Chicago Exhibition it figured as one of the 40 French books reputed most useful in women's education.

These results have encouraged the editor further to improve and perfect the work. It has been more or less re-cast in the later editions ; the several chapters have been revised and extended ; new engravings introduced and a fresh attraction added in the shape of 12 full-page coloured plates, without text. Thus enlarged and embellished, the Encyclopedia of needlework will, we are confident, find ever-growing favour.

PLATE I

FLAT STITCH EMBROIDERY ON VELVET
worked with D.M.C Persian silk (Soie de Perse).

PLATE II

RAISED SATIN STITCH EMBROIDERY ON CAMBRIC
worked with D.M.C Floss embroidery cotton, special quality
(Coton floche à broder, qualité spéciale).

PLATE III

STRAIGHT STITCH EMBROIDERY ON TAMMY-CLOTH
worked with D.M.C Pearl cotton (Coton perlé).

PLATE IV

EMBROIDERY ON LINEN
worked with D.M.C Floss flax or flourishing thread (Lin floche).

PLATE V

TAPESTRY IN HALF CROSS STITCH
worked with D.M.C Pearl cotton (Coton perlé).

PLATE VI

APPLIQUÉ EMBROIDERY ON DAMASK GROUND
worked with D.M.C Persian silk (Soie de Perse).

PLATE VII

CORNER FOR CHAIR-BACK IN CROCHET
worked with D.M.C Crochet cotton 6 cord (Cordonnet 6 fils).

PLATE VIII

EMBROIDERY ON LACIS OR NET CANVAS
worked with D.M.C Persian silk (Soie de Perse).

PLATE IX

PLATE X

CUT STITCH AND EMBROIDERY ON LINEN
worked with D.M.C Embroidery cotton (Coton à broder).

PLATE XI

FIGURE STITCH EMBROIDERY
worked with D.M.C Pearl cotton (Coton perlé).

PLATE XII

LACE EMBROIDERED ON NET
worked with D.M.C Floss flax or flourishing thread (Lin floche).

Stripe showing running-stitching, button-holing and herring-boning.

Plain Sewing

Many, on opening the *Encyclopedia of Needlework* will be disposed to exclaim as they read the heading of this first chapter : What is the use of describing all the old well-known stitches, when machines have so nearly superseded the slower process of hand-sewing? To this we reply that, plain sewing being the foundation of every kind of needlework should be most thoroughly learned to begin with. Those who have their work done for them by others, should at least know how to distinguish good work from bad, and those in less fortunate circumstances, have to be taught how to work for themselves, and the hand that can do good plain sewing will soon learn to do any sort of fancy-work.

Position of the body and hands. — Before describing the different kinds of stitches, a word should be said as to the position of the body and hands when at work. Long experience has convinced me that no kind of needlework necessitates a stooping or cramped attitude.

To avoid this, see that your chair and table suit each, other in height, and hold your work so that you hardly need to bend your head at all. Never pin your work to your knee, it obliges you to stoop over it in a way that is both tiring and ungraceful.

Needles. — These should always be of the best quality. To test a needle, try to break it between your fingers; if you feel it resist and then snap clean in two, the steel is good : if it bend without breaking, or break without any resistance, it is bad. Never use a bent needle, it makes ugly and irregular stitches, and see that the eye, whether round or egg-shaped, be well-drilled, that it may not fray or cut the thread. Short or half-long needles are the best for white work, long ones for dress-making, and longer ones still, with long eyes, for darning. The needle should always be a little thicker than the thread, so as to make an easy passage for it through the stuff.

To preserve needles from rust keep a little powdered stone alum in the packets, and a little box of it will be found useful in case of damp hands for powdering them with. Rusty needles can be polished by passing them backwards and forwards through a fine emery cushion.

Scissors. — Scissors are a very important accessory of the work-table, and two kinds are indispensable; a pair of large ones for cutting-out, with a blunt and a sharp point the latter to be always held downwards; and a pair of smaller ones with two sharp points.

The handles should be large and round; if at all tight, they tire and mark the hand.

Thimble. — Steel thimbles are the best; bone are very liable to break, and silver ones are not deeply enough pitted, to keep the needle from slipping. A thimble should be light, with a rounded top and a flat rim.

The thread. — Except for tacking, your thread should never be more than from 18 to 20 inches long. If the thread be in skeins, it does not matter which end you begin with, but in the case of reeled cotton, thread your needle with the end next to the reel, when you cut it; as the other end is apt to split, and unravel, when twisted from left to right, as is generally done, to facilitate threading. The cotton should always be cut as breaking weakens it.

Knotting the thread into the eye of the needle (fig. 1). — When the thread becomes inconveniently short, and you do not want to take a fresh one, it may be knotted into the needle, thus : bring it round the forefinger close to the needle, cross it on the inside next to the finger, hold the crossed threads fast with the thumb, draw the needle out through the loop thus formed, and tighten the loop round both ends.

Materials. — For tacking, use cheap cotton, on reels and in balls, slightly twisted and specially made for the purpose known as D.M.C Tacking thread (Coton a bâtir). (*)

For plain work, use D.M.C Alsatian thread (Fil d'Alsace) sold in black and white. As a coloured material we recommend D.M.C Alsa, a brilliant cotton thread, on reels, a good substitute for an inferior quality of silk.

Position of the hands when a weighted cushion is used (fig. 2). — The stuff, fastened to a cushion must be held with the left hand, which should neither rest on the table, nor on the cushion, the needle must be held between the thumb and forefinger of the right hand, and the middle finger, protected by the thimble, pushes the needle far enough through the stuff, for the thumb and forefinger to be able to take hold of it and draw it out; the thread will

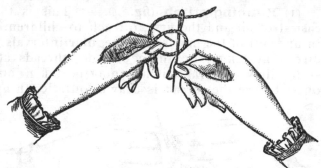

Fig. 1. Knotting the thread into the needle.

Fig. 2. Position of the hands when a weighted cushion is used.

then lie between the fourth and fifth fingers in the form of a loop, which must be gradually tightened to avoid its knotting.

Position of the hands without cushion (fig. 3). — When the work cannot be fastened to a cushion, it must not be rolled

---

(*) See at the end of the last chapter the tables of the sizes and colours of the cotton, flax and silk articles, mark D.M.C. — The French names, in brackets, are those stamped on the labels of the D.M.C articles.

over the forefinger of the left hand, but should merely be held between the thumb and forefinger and allowed to fall easily over the other fingers. Should the stuff need to be slightly stretched, draw it between the fourth and fifth fingers, this will prevent it from getting puckered or dragged.

Stitches. — Plain sewing comprises 4 varieties of stitches. (1) running, (2) back-stitching, (3) hemming and (4) top or over-sewing.

(1) **Running-stitch** (fig. 4). — This is the simplest and easiest of all and the first to teach to children. Pass the needle in and out of the material, at regular intervals, in a horizontal direction, taking up three or four threads at a time. If the stuff allow, several stitches may be taken on the needle at once, before the thread is drawn out. Running-stitch is used

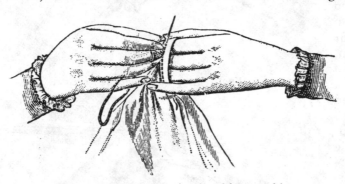

Fig. 3. Position of the hands without cushion.

for plain seams, for joining light materials, and making gathers.

(2) **Back-stitch** (fig. 5). Working from right to left take up six threads of the stuff on the needle and draw it out, then carry your thread back, from left to right, and insert the needle three threads back from the point at which it was last drawn out, and bring it out six threads beyond. This back-stitching as well as stitching, can be done better and more quickly by machine than by hand.

Stitching (fig. 6). — The production of a row of back-stitches that exactly meet one another without any intervening threads as in back-stitching, constitutes what is called stitching. Only one stitch can be made at a time and the needle must be put in, exactly at the point where it was drawn out to form the preceding back-stitch, and brought out as many threads further on as were covered by the last back-stitch. The beauty of stitching depends on the uniform length of the stitches, and the straightness of the line formed, to ensure which it is necessary to count the threads for each stitch, and to draw a thread to mark the line. If you have to stitch in a slanting line across the stuff, or the stuff be such as to render the drawing of a thread impossible, a coloured tacking thread should be run in first, to serve as a guide.

Stitched hem (fig. 7). — Make a double turning, as for a hem, draw a thread two or three threads above the edge of the first turning, and do your stitching through all three layers of stuff; the right side will be that on which you form your stitches.

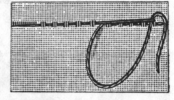

Fig. 4. Running-stitch.

(3) **Hemming and plain hem** (fig. 8). — To make a good hem, your stuff must be cut in the line of the thread. Highly dressed stuffs, such as nainsouk and calico, should be rubbed in the hand, to soften them, before the hem be laid. Turn in the raw edge with a double foldover not more than an eighth of an inch wide.

Only hems that are more than half an inch wide need to be tacked, and the first turning has only to be just wide enough to prevent the edge from fraying. In hemming you insert the needle and secure the thread under the edge of the fold, and directing the needle in a slanting position leftwards, take up two or three strands of the stuff below the fold, bringing the needle out through the edge of the fold.

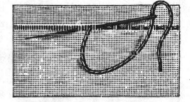

Fig. 5. Back-stitch.

Make a continuous succession of fine regular stitches thus, two or three threads apart, like teeth, which confine the fold closely to the rest of the material. To ensure the hem being straight, a thread may be drawn to mark the line for the second turning, but it is not a good plan, especially in shirt-making, as the edge of the stuff, too apt in any case to cut and fray, is thereby still further weakened. Hems in woollen materials, which will not take a bend, can

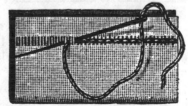

Fig. 6. Stitching.

only be laid and tacked, bit by bit. In making what are called rolled hems, the needle must be slipped in, so as only to pierce the first turning, in order that the stitches may not be visible on the outside.

Hems with ornamental stitches (figs. 9 and 10). — In underclothing where something more decorative than an ordinary hem is wanted "hem-stitch" may be employed, as shewn in figs. 730 and 731; or the edge of a plain hem may be overcast with stitches of different kinds, worked in colour. Make the hem first, as in fig. 8. For the overcasting choose bright colours to heighten the effect. For a stout material we advise D.M.C Embroidery cotton (Coton à broder), D.M.C Pearl cotton (Coton perlé) and D.M.C Floss flax or flourishing thread (Lin floche); for fine transparent stuffs D.M.C Special stranded cotton (Mouliné spécial), D.M.C Persian silk (Soie de Perse) (*), which can easily be separated and used in single or double strands as desired.

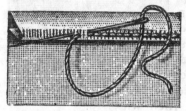

Fig. 7. Stitched hem.

Fig. 9 is worked thus: hold your stuff, in the left hand, the right side towards you, the hem turned upwards, and starting on the left, insert the needle exactly into the edge of the fold and bring it out on the right side, skip six threads, take the needle over to the back and bring it out in front, skip six threads and so on to the end. In this way your hem will be overcast with slanting stitches, slanting from left to right. The second row must be set the reverse way, from right to left, in the same holes as the first row, so that the stitches cross each other at the edge of the fold and look the same on both sides of the hem.

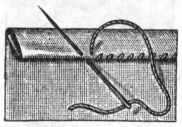

Fig. 8. Hemming and plain hem.

In the case of fig. 10, hold the stuff as before, the right side towards you and begin on the left. Insert the needle into the edge of the fold and make three button-hole stitches (see figs. 36 and 37) meeting in the same hole at the bottom; skip eight threads and make your second group of three stitches and so on.

These little clusters of three are fan-shaped as seen in the figure.

_____

(*) See at the end of the last chapter the tables of the sizes and colours of the cotton, flax and silk articles, mark D.M.C. — The French names, in brackets, are those stamped on the labels of the D.M.C articles.

Flat seam (fig. 11). — Lay your two edges, whether straight or on the cross, exactly even, tack them together with stitches ¼ of an inch long, ¼ of an inch from the edge, and then back-stitch them by machine or by hand, following the tacking-thread. Cut off half the inner edge, turn the outer one in, as if for a hem and sew it down with hemming-stitches.

Smooth the seam underneath with the forefinger in working to make it lie quite flat. Beginners should flatten down the seam with their thimbles or with the handle of the scissors, before they begin to hem, as the outer and wider edge is very apt to get pushed up and bulge over in the sewing which hides the stitches.

Rounded seam. — Back-stitch your two edges together, as above directed, then cut off the inner edge to a width of four threads, and roll the outer one in with the left thumb,

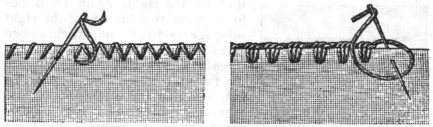

Figs. 9 and 10. Hems with ornamental stitches.

till the raw edge is quite hidden, hemming as you roll. This kind of seam, on the wrong side, looks like a fine cord laid on, and is used in making the finer articles of under-clothing.

Fastening threads off and on (fig. 12). — Knots should be avoided in white work. To fasten on in hemming turn the needle backwards·point upwards, make one stitch and stroke and work the end of the thread in underneath the turning. To fasten on, in back-stitching or running, make one stitch with the new thread, then take both ends and lay them down together to the left, and work over them, so that they are wound in and out of the next few stitches.

(4) **Another kind of sewing-stitch** (fig. 13). — For dress-seams and patching; sew from right to left, inserting the needle first into the selvedge nearest to you. It is advisable to tack or pin the two edges together first as above, and hold them tightly with the thumb and finger to keep them perfectly even.

Top or over-sewing-stitch (fig. 14). — This stitch is used for joining selvedges together. To keep the two pieces even, it is best, either to tack or pin them together first. Insert the needle, from right to left, under the first thread of the two

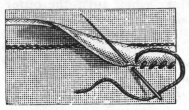

selvedges and through both edges and sew from right to left, setting your stitches not more than three threads apart. The thread must not be drawn very tight, so that when the seam is finished and flattened with the thimble, the selvedges may lie, side by side and not overlap.

Fig. 11. Flat seam.

Antique seams (figs. 15 and 16). — Tack or pin the selvedges together as above, then pointing the needle upwards from below, insert it, two threads under the left selvedge,

then on the right, again from below, under two threads of the right selvedge, setting the stitches two threads apart. In this manner, the threads cross each other between the two selvedges, and a perfectly flat seam is produced. We find seams of this kind in old embroidered linen garments, where the

Fig. 12.
Fastening threads off and on.

stuff was too narrow to allow for any other.

In making sheets the widths of linen are sometimes joined in a similar way, the only difference being that the stitches are set slightly slanting instead of straight, fig. 16.

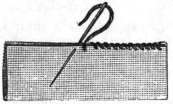

Openwork seams (figs. 17, 18, 19). — These are used, like figures 15 and 16 in making bed and table-linen, for joining together widths of stuff that are too narrow to allow for a close seam. Here the stitches require a strong twisted thread, such

Fig. 13.
Another kind of sewing-stitch.

as D.M.C Flax lace thread (Lin pour dentelles). (*)

Lay the work straight before you so that the two selvedges lie parallel : fasten your thread on the left, insert the needle

(*) See at the end of the last chapter the tables of the sizes and colours of the cotton, flax and silk articles, mark D.M.C. — The French names, in brackets, are those stamped on the labels of the D.M.C. articles.

on the right, two threads from the edge, bring it out above the thread, make a little loop and in drawing up the thread you close the loop, thus forming a knot. Then returning to the left side, make a similar stitch there, at a distance of three threads from the starting-point, pass back to the right, skip three threads, make your knot as before and so on. The stitches on the right are thus the counterpart of those on the left.

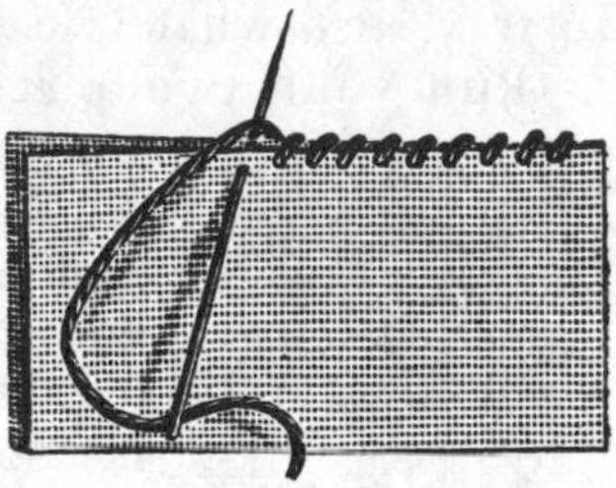

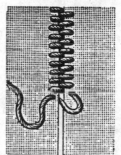

Fig. 14.
Top or over-sewing-stitch.

The seam shewn in figure 18 is formed of groups of three button-hole stitches, placed alternately, first on the edge of one width and then on that of the other. The first and the third stitch are worked over two threads, the middle one over four; the groups are five threads apart from each other.

The seam represented in figure 19 is particularly suited for trimming coloured under-linen. The width of the insertion may be increased at will by the addition of two or more bands of coloured stuff to the edges of the white material. These may be made of a coloured ribbon or a strip of stuff, taken double and folded in at the edges and joined to the selvedges or the material by two rows of little bars of overcasting-stitch, for which it is best to use D.M.C Alsatian thread (Fil d'Alsace), D.M.C Alsa or D.M.C Flax lace thread (Lin pour dentelles). It is advisable to tack hem and insertion very carefully parallel to each other on waxed cloth to avoid one or the other getting puckered in the working. The rows of bars should be begun on the left in the edge of the material and not in the edge of the band that is to be inserted. The needle must enter the insertion two threads from

Fig. 15. Antique seam.

Fig. 16. Antique seam.

the edge and come out to the right of the thread, then pass once over the stretched thread, thus forming a bar of overcasting-stitch, and come out through the edge of the material on the right, three threads distant from whence the first stitch issued.

The bars must be at equal distances from each other and quite vertical.

French double-seam (fig. 20). — For joining stuffs liable to fray, use what is called the French seam.

Run your two pieces of stuff together, back to back, the edges perfectly even, then turn them round close to the seam, so that the right sides come together inside and the two raw edges are enclosed between, and run them together again. See that no threads are visible on the outside. This seam is used chiefly in dress-making, for joining light fabrics together which cannot be kept from fraying by any other means.

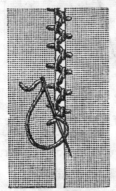

Fig. 17.
Openwork seam.

Hemmed double-seams (figs. 21 and 22). — Turn in the two raw edges, and lay them one upon the other, so that the one next the forefinger lies slightly higher than the one next the thumb. Instead of upwards from below insert the needle first into the upper edge and then slightly slanting, into the lower one. This seam is used in dress-making for fastening down linings. Figure 22 shews another kind of double seam, where the two edges are laid together, turned in twice and hemmed in the ordinary manner, with the sole difference that the needle has to pass through six layers of stuff.

Gathering (fig. 23). — Gathers are made with running-stitches of exactly the same length set in a straight line; alternately, take up and skip three or four threads, and instead of holding the stuff fast with your thumb, push it on to the needle as you go, thus forming the gathers and only draw out your needle every five or six stitches.

Fig. 18.
Openwork seam.

Stroking gathers (fig. 24). — When you have run in your gathering-thread, let it go and holding the work between the thumb and forefinger of your left hand take a strong needle and stroke it down vertically between the gathers so as to fix them evenly side by side, in doing so push each under your left thumb to keep it in its place, whilst you support the stuff at the back with your other fingers.

Running in a second gathering-thread (fig. 25). — To fix the gathers after stroking them run in a second thread ⅔ of an inch or so below the first, according to the kind of stuff and the purpose it is to serve : take up five or six gathers at a time, and draw your two threads perfectly even, that the gathers may be straight to the line of the thread.

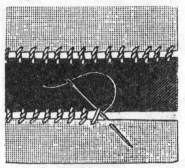

Fig. 19.
Openwork seam.

Sewing on gathers (fig. 26). — To distribute the fulness equally, divide the gathered portion of material, and the band, or plain piece, on to which it is to be sewn, into equal parts, and pin the two together at corresponding distances, the gathered portion under the plain, and hem each gather to the band or plain piece, sloping the needle to make the thread slant, and slipping it through the upper threads only of the gathers.

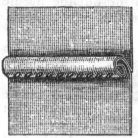

Fig. 22.
Open hemmed double-seam.

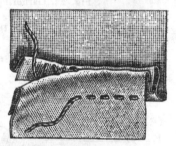

Fig. 20.
French double-seam.

Decoration of the gathers, known as "Smocking" (figs. 27 and 28). — This kind of work occurs in the national costumes of the Hungarians, as well as in England, where it is still in great vogue. "Smock" is an old English name for shift or chemise, hence the term "smocking" came to be applied to the ornamental gathering of the necks of those garments. A great variety of patterns exists but they are all executed in the same way so that one explanation will suffice for all.

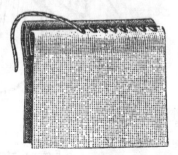

Fig. 21.
Hemmed double-seam.

Prepare your stuff as described in figures 23 to 25. After the first row of gathers, make as many subsequent rows as the pattern selected requires, leaving rather less than ½ an inch of the material between. For the embroidery use a strong thread, such as D.M.C Embroidery cotton (Coton à broder), D.M.C Pearl cotton (Coton perlé) or D.M.C Floss flax (Lin floche). (*)

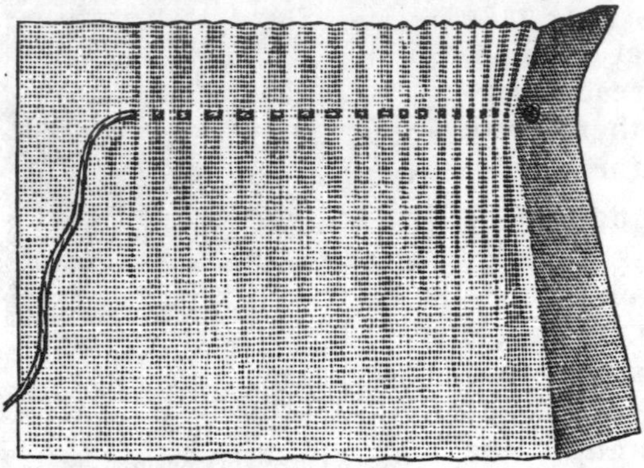

The three horizontal rows which form the heading of the pattern are worked from left to right. Begin with the third row from the top, carry the thread over two gathers and bring it back under one gather, carry the thread again over two, and back under one, taking care to bring out the needle above the stitch just made, so that the stitches may be slightly slanting.

Fig. 23. Gathering.

Following upon these three rows or stitches, comes the so-called "smock-ing", done from right to left. At the first auxiliary thread which follows, you slip the needle under two gathers, and return once again with a back-stitch;

Fig. 24. Stroking gathers.

then, $\frac{3}{16}$ of an inch above, you again take up two gathers — the first of which has already been secured below by the first

(*) See at the end of the last chapter the tables of the sizes and colours of the cotton, flax and silk articles, mark D.M.C. — The French names, in brackets, are those stamped on the labels of the D.M.C articles.

back-stitch, whilst the second was still open — you secure them both by a back-stitch, descend to the first line, make a back-stitch and so on.

The thread you are embroidering with remains all the time on the right side of the work. The second row is made quite close to the first, the third to the second, and so on. From the second row on, you leave out the back-stitch on the side touching the finished border. In the last row, you make the scallops, which

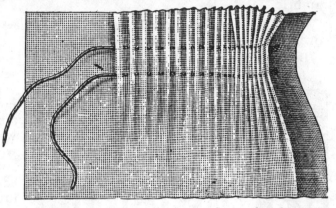

Fig. 25. Running in a second gathering-thread.

must be placed at regular intervals along the whole length of the embroidery. They are made to and fro, without the course of the stitches being interrupted as figure 27 shows.

The auxiliary threads which held the gathers at starting, must be drawn out and removed when the embroidery is finished.

Whipping (fig. 29). — Whipping is another form of gathering, used for fine materials. With the thumb and forefinger of the left hand, roll the edge over towards you, into a very tight thin roll, inserting the needle as you go on the inside of the roll next the thumb,

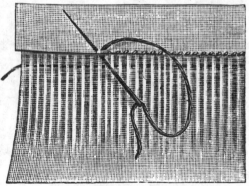

Fig. 26. Sewing on gathers.

and bringing it out on the outside next the forefinger, at regular distances as in running. Draw up the thread every few stitches only. By pushing the stuff slightly on to the needle with the left hand as you go along, the gathers form quite naturally.

Scalloped hem (fig. 3o). — In order to utilise a hem as a trimming or ornament, fold over the edge to a depth of about an inch and run in a thread with small running-stitches up and down, as shewn in figure 3o. By slightly drawing the thread, little scallops form themselves, especially in calico and cambric.

Sewing on round cord (fig. 3i). — For sewing on round cords, use strong thread.

Be careful not to stretch the cord but to hold it in as you sew, because it invariably shrinks more than the stuff in the first washing. Hem it with small close stitches to the edge of the turning, taking care that it does not get twisted.

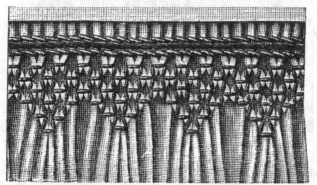

Fig. 27.
Decoration of the gathers known as "Smocking".

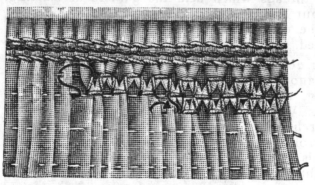

Fig. 28.
Decoration of the gathers, known as "Smocking".

Sewing on braids or tapes (fig. 32). — These should be back-stitched on to the right side of the article they are to be attached to, quite close to the edge, then folded over in half, and hemmed down on the wrong side. Like the cord, the braid or tape must, in the back-stitching be eased with the left hand to allow for its shrinking in the wash without puckering the article it is sewn to. Though the back-stitching could be more quickly done by machine, it is better done by hand, as the easing cannot be done by machine. To save time, however, the first stitching is often done with the machine, or the

braid or tape is folded in half, the material to be bordered
with it placed between and the two machine-stitched together.

Sewing on tape-loops
(figs. 33 and 34). — These, in
the case of the commoner articles of house-linen, are generally fastened to the corners.
Lay the ends of your piece of
tape, which should be about
6 inches long, side by side,
turn in and hem them down,
on three sides ; the loop should
be folded so as to form
a three-cornered point,
as shewn in the illustra-
tion. Join the two edges
of the tape together in
the middle with a few
cross stitches, and stitch
the edge of the hem of
the article to the loop,
on the right side.

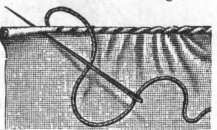

Fig. 29. Whipping.

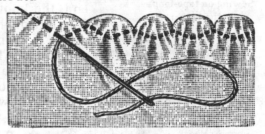

Fig. 30. Scalloped hem.

Figure 34 shews how to sew
on a loop in the middle of an
article, the two ends separately,
one on one side, the other on
the other.

**Strings and loops for fine
underclothing** (fig. 35). — Sew
these on, likewise, on the wrong
side of the article, hemming
down the ends, and fastening
them on the right side, with two
rows of stitching
crossing each other
diagonally and a third
row along the edge.

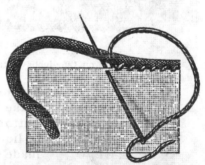

Fig. 31. Sewing on round cord.

**Button-hole
stitch and button-
holes in linen** (fig.
36). — Cut your hole

Fig. 32. Sewing on braids or tapes.

perfectly straight, to fit the size of the button, having previously marked out the place for the slit, with two rows of

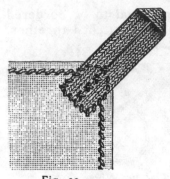

Fig. 33.
Sewing on tape-loops
to the corner.

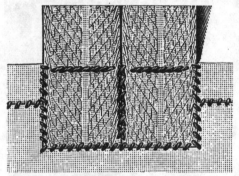

Fig. 34. Sewing on tape-loops in the
middle of the article.

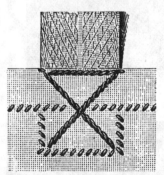

Fig. 35. Strings and loops
for fine underclothing.

running-stitches set contrariwise, two or three threads apart. Put in your needle at the back of the slit, and take up about three threads, bring the working thread round, from right to left, under the point of the needle, and draw the needle out through the loop, so that the little knot comes at the edge of the slit, and so on to the end, working from the lower left-hand corner to the right. Then make a bar of button-hole stitching across each end, the knotted edge towards the slit. For button-holes in house-linen and underclothing use D.M.C Alsatian thread (Fil d'Alsace) (*) and D.M.C Alsa, both very strong and firmly twisted.

Button-holes in dress-materials (fig. 37). — Mark out and cut them as above described; if however, the material be liable to fray, wet the slit as soon as you have cut it, with liquid gum, and lay a strand of strong thread along the edge over which to make your stitches. The end of dress button-holes where the button comes to lie must be round, the stitches being made to diverge round it like rays from a centre.

Here the stitches must be very slightly tightened; a good plan is to lay two threads of coarse silk or a very fine cord along the edge to make your stitches over, and draw it up slightly when the button-hole is finished to straighten the edge. This gives it

(*) See at the end of the last chapter the tables of the sizes and colours of the cotton, flax and silk articles, mark D.M.C. — The French names, in brackets, are those stamped on the labels of the D.M.C articles.

firmness and strength and prevents the stitches from getting stretched in buttoning, close the button-hole with a straigth bar of stitches across the other end, as in figure 36. As material we specially recommend D.M.C Alsa made in a great variety of shades.

Sewing on buttons (figs. 38 and 39). — To sew linen, or webbed buttons on to underlinen, fasten in your thread with a stitch or two, at the place where the button is to be; bring the needle out through the middle of the button, and make eight stitches, diverging from the centre like a star, and if you like, encircle them by a row of stitching, as in figure 39. This done, bring the needle out between the stuff and the button, and twist the cotton six or seven times round it, then push the needle through to the wrong side, and fasten cff.

Binding slits (figs. 40, 41, 42, 43). — Nothing is more apt to tea than a slit whether it be hemmed or merely bound. To prevent this, make a semicircle of button-hole stitches at the bottom of the slit, and above that, to connect the two sides, a bridge of several threads, covered with button-hole stitching, fig. 40.

Figure 41 represents a slit backed with a narrow piece of material cut on the cross; figure 42 a slit backed with a wide straight piece.

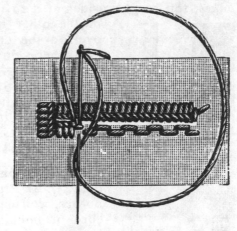

Fig. 36. Button-holes in linen.

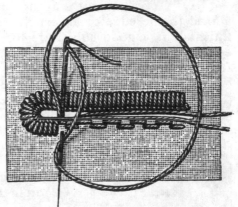

Fig. 37.
Button-holes in dress-materials.

Fig. 38. Sewing on
linen buttons.

Fig. 39. Sewing on
webbed buttons.

2

When two selvedges form the slit, it is unnecessary to back them but take a small square of stuff, turn in the raw edges, top-sew two sides of it to the selvedges of the slit, turn

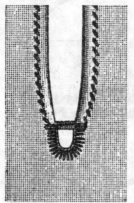

in the other two, fold over on the cross, and hem them down over the top-sewing, as shewn in figure 43. Such little squares of material, inserted into a slit or seam, to prevent its tearing, are called gussets.

Sewing on piping (fig. 44). — Piping is a border, consisting of a cord or bobbin, folded into a stripe of material, cut on the cross, and

Fig. 40. Binding slit with hem.

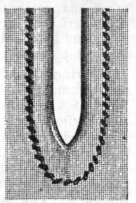

Fig. 41. Binding slit with piece on cross.

affixed to the edge of an article to give it more strength and finish. It is a good substitute for a hem or binding on a bias edge, which by means of the cord, can be held in and prevented from stretching. Cut your stripes diagonally, across the web

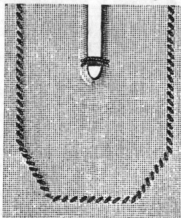

of the stuff and very even ; run them together, lay the cord or bobbin along the stripe on the wrong side, $\frac{3}{16}$ of an inch from the edge, fold the edge over and tack the cord lightly in. Then lay it on the raw edge of the article with the cord towards you and with all

Fig. 42. Binding slit with broad band.

Fig. 43. Strengthening slit with gusset.

the raw edges turned away from you. Back-stitch the piping to the edge, keeping close to the cord. Then turn the article round, fold in the raw outside edge over the others, and hem it down like an ordinary hem.

Herring-boning (fig. 45). — This stitch is chiefly used for seams in flannel and for overcasting dress seams and takes the place of hemming for fastening down the raw edges of a seam that has been run or stitched without turning them in. Herring-boning is done from left to right and forms two rows of stitches. Insert the needle from right to left, and make a stitch first above and then below the edge, the threads crossing each other diagonally, as shewn in figure 45.

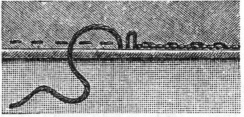

Fig. 44. Sewing on piping.

When this stitch is made in a lining, the thread must never shew on the right side of the work itself. The same stitch is often used in fancywork as an ornament and is then done in colours.

Ornamental stitches for underlinen (figs. 46, 47, 48, 49). — A plain surface may be rendered more attractive by embroidering it with one or other of the stitches described below, either in white or in colours. We recommend for this purpose, D.M.C Pearl cotton (Coton perlé), D.M.C Flax lace thread (Lin pour dentelles). (*)

Figure 46 illustrates single coral stitch, worked vertically; the width of the stitch may be varied at will but must

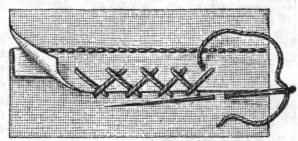

Fig. 45. Herring-boning.

be kept uniform throughout. Bring the needle up in the centre line, hold the thread down with the left thumb ⅛ of an inch beneath where the needle came out. Insert the needle on the left of the line, level with where it came up but a short distance off and bring it out in a slanting direction, so that it comes up in the centre line and over the held down thread. Tighten, and repeat this stitch to the right of the line and continue working left and right like this to

(*) See at the end of the last chapter the tables of the sizes and colours of the cotton, flax and silk articles, mark D.M.C. — The French names, in brackets, are those stamped on the labels of the D.M.C articles.

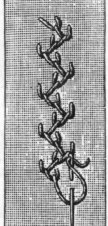

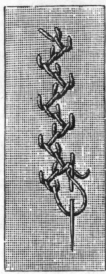

Fig. 46.
Ornamental
stitches for under-
linen.

Fig. 47.
Ornamental
stitches for under-
linen.

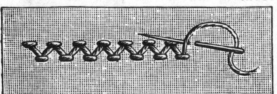

Fig. 48. Ornamental stitches for underlinen.

Fig. 49. Russian stitch with interlaced stitches.

the end. Fasten off with a back-stitch.

Figure 47 illustrates double coral stitch, which is the same as single only worked twice to left and twice to right as seen in the figure.

The stitch in figure 48 is worked horizontally. Begin on the left with a horizontal stitch over four threads then go two threads back to the left — bringing out the needle that is in the middle of the last stitch made — make a slanting stitch to the right over four threads, then, passing the needle under two threads, make the bottom horizontal stitch; come back to the middle for the second slanting stitch upwards and repeat the first horizontal stitch already described.

The stitch in figure 49 is made in two rows. The first row is in Russian cross stitch, see figure 45, over eight threads in height and four in width. The second row to be worked in coloured thread as a contrast to the first consists of horizontal stitches, interlaced between the threads of the Russian stitch, as shewn in the engraving.

Border worked in chain stitch.

The Sewing and Embroidering Machine

Machine Sewing and Embroidering

The Sewing-machine. — The first attempts to construct a sewing-machine were made in the middle of the eighteenth century.

In 1755, an Englishman, F. Weisenthal, took out a patent for an apparatus furnished with a double-pointed needle, the eye in the middle, which was made to work backwards and forwards through a material without having to be turned round. From 1755 to 1846, Thomas Saint, J. Duncan, J. A. Dodge, B. Thimonnier and Walter Hunt severally, contributed to the development of this elementary device and took out patents for their inventions without arriving at any very practical results. It was not until 1850, that the sewing-machine, in the hands of Elias Howe, a mechanic of Massachusetts, and I. M. Singer after many vicissitudes, became a practical thing and began to come into general use.

Since that time it has undergone numerous modifications and improvements, which have made it, in its present perfected form, an indispensable article in daily use.

We shall not stop to describe the differences often quite insignificant between the systems adopted by different makers, but merely give a brief description of the machine and its different accessories.

Every sewing-machine consists of two essential parts:

The upper one comprising the needle-holder and the mechanism which gives it its vertical movement; the lower comprising the shuttle and its action. The thread, winding off from the reel, runs through the eye of the needle, after receiving the necessary tension by means of a small but very important accessory, called the "tension". The needle, in descending, passes the thread through the stuff and conducts it in front of the shuttle, where a little vertical movement causes it to form a loop into which the shuttle runs with its thread; the needle in re-ascending makes the stitch, whilst a little claw "feed-point" pulls the work on, and regulates its length.

The first machines worked with only one thread without a shuttle and produced the so-called "chain-stitch", fig. 5o, which has the great defect of coming undone so easily if one stitch happens to break.

These machines without shuttle are hardly ever used now, excepting for certain special kinds of embroidery or provisional seams which have to be unpicked afterwards.

Modern machines work with two threads; they are provided with shuttles containing a thread which with the needle-thread produces lock stitch.

There are two kinds of shuttles: the long and the circular or central: The former contains a small oblong reel, on which the thread is wound; a horizontal movement to and fro drives the shuttle and thread through the loop formed under the stuff by the needle-thread and at each passage of the needle a stitch is made. The long shuttle is still much used but the circular one which has a round reel, big enough to hold a quantity of thread is preferred. Being fixed on an axle on which it moves round, it allows a more regular tension of the shuttle thread.

Attachments. — As the sewing-machine became more and more perfect, its uses increased and various very ingenious appliances were invented to facilitate such preparatory work as the laying of hems, basting on braid, &c. These attachments are fixed on to the machine in the place of the presser and with a little practice very good results are **obtainable**. Those in most general use are :

The hemmer, which folds down the stuff mechanically. There are non-variable hemmers for wide and narrow hems and variable hemmers which can be adapted to any width in removing at will a plate of regulation.

The binder, by means of which a material can be bound with a braid or ribbon : these are placed, folded in the binder, and the edge of the material to be bound placed well between the fold ; then the stitching is done, careful attention being paid to the material remaining within the folded binding.

The braider, for laying down a braid on a piece of stuff on which a pattern has been traced. The braid is fixed into the braider and stitched along the lines of the drawing, whilst you hold and turn the stuff about so that you have the part to be braided always before you.

The gatherer, which enables you without any preliminary work to gather a material and fix it on to a band or crossway piece. Place the material to be gathered under the gatherer, and slip the band into its horizontal slit and then proceed with the stitching. There are various other attachments, for darning, quilting, &c., but they are in less general use, unless it be by the trade.

Sewing-machines can be worked by hand or by treadle and by one or both feet, or by mechanical power. Hand-worked machines are no longer much used, those with treadles being more practical as they leave the worker's hands free. Machines moved by mechanical power are chiefly used in business work-rooms.

Machine sewing. — Without entering on a complete course of instruction in sewing-machine work, some general indications and practical advice may not unlikely be useful to our readers, seeing that bad work, due in reality to lack of experience or forgetfulness of certain principles, is often attributed to the machine or to the materials employed.

The stitches. — As said above, two different stitches can be produced by the machine : chain stitch, fig. 50, and lock stitch, fig. 51.

Chain stitch (fig. 50). — This stitch is on the whole little used because it comes undone too easily. Certain kinds of embroidery and ornamental seams are done with it. On the right side of the stuff, chain stitch looks the same as lock stitch, it is only on the wrong side that it bears out its name. When it is used for embroidery or for an ornamental seam or hem, the pattern must be traced and the stitching done on the wrong side of the material that the chain may show on the right side.

Chain stitch is very elastic which is an advantage in the case of certain materials that are elastic in themselves.

Fig. 50. Chain stitch.

Lock stitch (fig. 51), is done with two threads, and looks the same on both sides. It is used in dress-making and for underlinen and also in flat-stitch embroidery.

On some machines lock stitch must be worked with two threads or different sizes, the

Fig. 51. Lock stitch.

finer one for the shuttle, on others the two threads may be of the same size.

To produce good work, it is essential to have :

A clean and well oiled machine ;
Good materials ;
A correctly-adjusted tension.

How to keep the machine in good condition. — A good machine if kept in proper condition should work easily and noiselessly; a machine that works with difficulty and noisily tires the worker and wears out quickly : it is therefore very important to keep it in perfect condition.

To that end it must be regularly oiled. The little holes visible on its surface are the oil-holes, and lead to those places subject to friction.

The quality of the lubricating oil is important and only one specially intended for the purpose, to be had at any druggist, should be used. When the machine is not in use it should be kept covered up and free from dust.

Whilst in use and particularly with certain stuffs a fluff is produced which by degrees gets into the different parts of the machine and prevents its running easily; it also happens that after long disuse the oil becomes thick and impedes the motion and then a thorough cleaning is advisable.

Begin by dropping a little turpentine or paraffine into the oil-holes, then work the machine both backwards and forwards rather quickly, clean the driving gear thoroughly with the turpentine or paraffin (which dissolves all dirt), wipe and lubricate afresh with the usual machine oil.

Needles. — These should be well finished and quite free from any particle of rust. Those you keep in stock should be kept slightly greased to preserve them from rust.

The size must be carefully adapted to the stuff and thread.

Fig. 52. Bobbin-thread being too tight.

Materials. — Thread wound on reels is generally used for machine work. The usual kinds are D.M.C Best 6 cord sewing-

Fig. 53. Bobbin-thread being not tight enough.

machine cotton (Câblé 6 fils) (*) or D.M.C Three cord twist (Retors 3 fils); the former made of 6 single strands twisted together 2 and 2, then united and twisted the reverse way, the latter made of 3 single strands, twisted one way. The best 6 cord is very superior to the 3 cord twist on account of its regularity and greater strength and is preferable for all seams which demand a regular and strong stitch.

With regard to the exterior appearance of the thread, we have unglazed and glazed; the former is most used, as being more pliant and more adaptable to every kind of seam; the glazed is stiffer and more adapted for stuffs with a great deal of dressing in them.

(*) See at the end of the last chapter the tables of the sizes and colours of the cotton, flax and silk articles, mark D.M.C. — The French names, in brackets, are those stamped on the labels of the D.M.C articles.

We particularly recommend the D.M.C Best 6 cord sewing-machine cotton (Câblé 6 fils). The coloured thread we should advise is D.M.C Alsa, a very brilliant cotton thread to be had in fast dyes and which, thanks to its fastness and silky aspect resembles in many cases sewing silk.

In machines with two threads you should always use the same quality of thread for the bobbin and the shuttle, but taking generally a finer number for the shuttle.

The tension (figs. 52 and 53). — The tension of the thread demands especial attention because on it and on its not breaking the perfection of the seam depends. The tension is regulated by a special screw placed on the side of the machine. In a stitched seam the two threads should meet in the middle of the thickness of the two layers of stuff, see fig. 51 ; the seam then presents a good appearance, is elastic and strong. If the bobbin-thread be too tight, fig. 52, or not tight enough, fig. 53, the seams will be irregular and loose.

If the tension of the thread be properly adjusted, breakages which are so troublesome and so often attributed to the quality of the thread, will rarely occur.

Embroidery and machine darning. — Sewing-machines with circular reels can be used for embroidery and darning. All that is wanted is the addition of certain accessories.

We shall not give a lengthy description of machine embroidery and darning as any one can get the needful explanations from the firm that supplies the machine.

We limit ourselves to a few directions to be completed later on in subsequent chapters.

How to adjust the machine for embroidery and darning. — Remove the presser and raise the bar of the presser as much as possible that it may not intercept your view in working, unscrew the handle and replace the needle-plate by the special embroidery-plate.

With the help of the machine thus prepared you can make all the different kinds of laces and embroideries worked in back-stitch ; the length of the stitch being regulated according to the pattern you are working from.

Different kinds of embroidery and lace that can be made with the machine. — Almost every sort of work can be made with the sewing-machine.

We may mention the patterns done in darning stitch on net and tulle and openwork on linen and tammy-cloth; also the different kinds of embroidery on white stuff, shaded and unshaded satin stitch embroidery, and knotted stitch embroidery.

Some things may be worked with a right and a wrong side, others both sides alike; but the work itself is always done in the same way; the result depends only on the choice of material.

Excepting in the case of small rows of openwork, all stuffs destined for embroidery must be mounted on a special frame, very much like the Swiss tambour, fig. 91; it consists of two thin wooden hoops, between which the stuff is held; the frame resting on the plate of the machine is without any support.

Materials. — These should be selected according to the kind of embroidery or lace you intend making. D.M.C Alsatian twist (Retors d'Alsace), on reels, and white and écru D.M.C Alsa should be used for work done in darning stitch and for openwork; D.M.C Embroidery cotton (Coton à broder), (*) on reels, is best for embroideries on white stuff; D.M.C Alsa and D.M.C Alsatian twist (Retors d'Alsace), in colours, for satin stitch embroidery and knotted stitch, &c.

The above mentioned threads will serve as the superior thread (the bobbin thread) for embroideries that have a right and a wrong side; as the inferior thread (the shuttle thread) use D.M.C Machine thread (Fil pour machines) No. 150.

Embroideries that are the same on both sides use the superior threads throughout.

Hygiene. — Much has been said and written on the subject of the injuriousness of treadle-machines to health. On the one side the dangers have been exaggerated, on the other they have been taken too little count of; we on our part are convinced that, as in the case of many other exercises, if it be not abused, far from being injurious to health their use is salutary; only if practised to excess will it have bad results.

(*) See at the end of the last chapter the tables of the sizes and colours of the cotton, flax and silk articles, mark D.M.C. — The French names, in brackets, are those stamped on the labels of the D.M.C articles.

To work a sewing-machine for two or three hours a day cannot possibly harm a healthy person, but in workrooms where people sit at a machine day after day without intermission we should welcome a more general application of mechanical power as the motive power and the great advances made by electricity for the conveyance of power admit of installations of this kind at no very great cost.

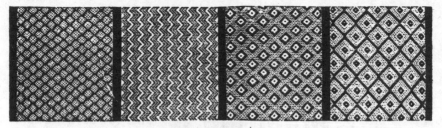

Specimens of pattern darns.

Mending

The mending of wearing-apparel and house and under-linen, though often ungrateful work is yet a necessity, to which every female hand ought to be carefully trained. How best to disguise and repair the wear and tear of use or accident is quite as valuable an art as that of making new articles.

Under the head of mending, we include the strengthening and replacing of the worn and broken threads of a fabric, and the fitting in of new stuff in the place of that which is torn or damaged. The former is called darning, the latter patching.

Darning. — When only a few of the warp or woof threads are torn or wanting, a darn will repair the mischief, provided the surrounding parts are in good condition. When the damage is more considerable the defective piece must be cut out.

Needles. — There are needles specially made for darning, with elongated eyes, to receive the loosely-twisted strands or darning thread used for the purpose.

Materials suitable for mending. — In some cases the warp of the stuff itself can be used for darning, otherwise thread as much like the stuff as possible should be chosen. D.M.C Darning cotton (Coton à repriser) or D.M.C Stranded darning cotton (Coton mouliné doublé) are used for most kinds of darning. D.M.C Darning cotton (Coton à repriser) can be had in 18 different sizes, from Nos. 8 to 100, white and unbleached, and in all the colours of the D.M.C colour-card, in No. 25. D.M.C Stranded darning cotton (Coton mouliné doublé) is made in Nos. 1 to 10, white and unbleached, the latter is best for darning the coarser articles of house-linen.

These are but very slightly twisted and can be split or used double, if necessary to suit the material. For darning damask linen D.M.C Floss flax or flourishing thread (Lin floche) in Nos. 25 to 150 should be used. D.M.C Superfine embroidery cotton (Coton à broder surfin) No. 100 is particularly suitable for darning cambric and other fine transparent stuffs.

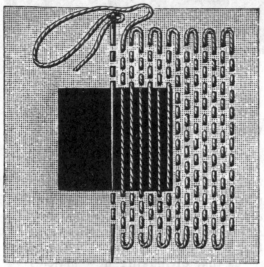

Fig. 54. Linen darning.
Drawing in the warp threads.

Different kinds of darns. — These are four, (1) Linen darning, (2) Satin or Twill darning, (3) Damask darning, and (4) Invisible darning, called also Fine-drawing.

(1°) **Linen darning** (figs. 54, 55, 56). — All darns should be made on the wrong side or the stuff. The longitudinal running, to form the warp, must be made first. The thread must not be drawn tightly in running your stitches backwards and forwards, and be careful to leave loops at each turning, to allow for the shrinking of the thread in the washing, without its pulling the darn together.

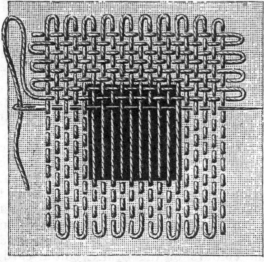

Fig. 55. Linen darning.
Drawing in the woof threads.

Run your needle in, about ⅜ of an inch above the damaged part, take up one or two threads of the stuff and skip as many, working straight to a thread; on reaching the hole, carry your cotton straight across it, take up alternate threads beyond, and proceed as before.

Continue the rows backwards and forwards, taking up in each row, the threads left in the preceding one. Turn the work round and do the same for the woof; alternately taking up and leaving the warp threads, where the cotton crosses the hole. The threads must lie so close both ways, that the darn, when completed, replaces the original web. The threads are only drawn so far apart in the illustrations, for the sake of clearness.

Darns are sometimes begun from the corner, see fig. 56, so as to form a diagonal web, but they are much more visible done this way and therefore not to be recommended.

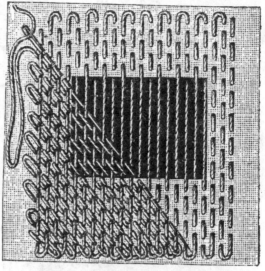

Fig. 56. Diagonal linen darning.

Darning linen with the sewing-machine. For coarse household linen we prefer machine-darning which is both even and strong and saves both time and eyesight.

For filling up holes in moderately coarse linen and calico, use D.M.C Alsatian twist (Retors d'Alsace) No. 100 or D.M.C Embroidery cotton (Coton à broder) No. 120, on reels; D.M.C Alsatian twist (Retors d'Alsace) No. 80 and D.M.C Embroidery

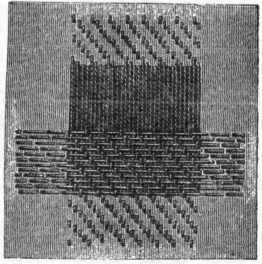

Fig. 57. Satin or twill darning.

cotton (Coton à broder) No. 100 will be best for piqués and stout linen and D.M.C Alsatian twist (Retors d'Alsace) No. 60 and D.M.C Embroidery cotton (Coton à broder) No. 80 for coarse damask and soft thick flannel (molleton). The darning itself is done in horizontal and vertical lines as in hand-darning.

(2°) **Satin or twill darning** fig. 57). — By twill darning, the damaged web of any twilled or diagonal material can be restored.

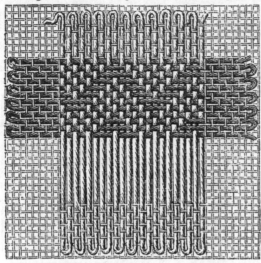

Fig. 58. Damask darning. Wrong side.

It would be impossible to enumerate all the varieties of twilled stuffs, but the illustrations and accompanying directions will enable the worker to imitate them all.

Begin, as in ordinary darning, by running threads across the hole to form a warp, then make the cross-runnings, passing over three threads and taking up one. In every succeeding row, advance one thread in the same direction. Or, miss one thread of the warp and every succeeding row advance one or two threads. The number of threads to be skipped and taken up, depends on the web the darn is to imitate.

When the original is a coloured stuff, it is advisable to make a specimen darn first, on a larger scale, so that you may be more sure of obtaining a correct copy of the original web.

(3°) **Damask darning** (figs. 58, 59, 60, 61, 62, 63). — A damask darn is begun in the same way as the above; the pattern is formed by the cross-runnings and will vary with the number of warp threads

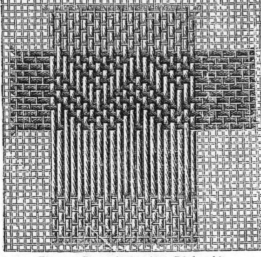

Fig. 59. Damask darning. Right side.

taken up and skipped, in each successive running. The woven
design that is to be restored by means of the needle should
therefore be closely examined first.

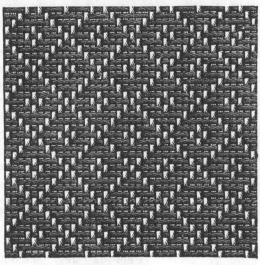

Fig. 60.
Damask darning. Covered ground.

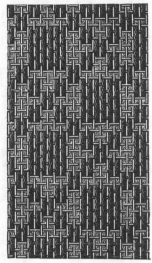

Fig. 61. Damask darning on
needle-made ground.

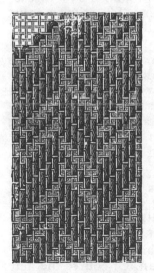

Fig. 62. Damask darning
on needle-made ground.

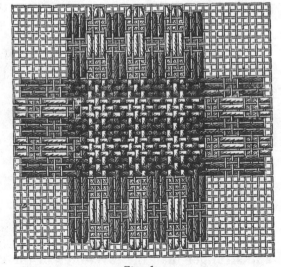

Fig. 63.
Damask darning with coloured thread.

Figures 58 and 59 shew the wrong and right sides of a damask
darn, in process of making. Figure 60 represents a completed one.

In the case of coloured webs, a light shade of cotton is generally used for the warp, and a coloured one for the woof.

Figures 61 and 62 illustrate two specimens of the darning, formerly done in the convents: the warp and the woof were first drawn in with rather fine thread, and the pattern then reproduced on this foundation with coarser, or, coloured thread.

The darn shewn in figure 63 is done in white and in a bright colour. By following the indications given in the figure you will be able to imitate a checked material.

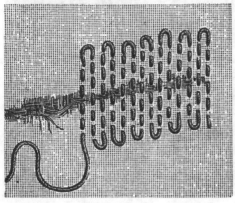

(4°) Darning lost in the ground (fig. 64). — A kind of darn used for repairing rents, the edges of which fit exactly into one another. Neither the torn threads of the material nor the rough edges must be cut off; the torn part is first tacked upon a piece of oil-cloth,

Fig. 64. Darning lost in the ground.

wrong side uppermost and the edges drawn together by a thread, run in backwards and forwards across them. The stitches must be set as closely together as possible, and regularly inverted, as in every other darn.

Fine-drawing (fig. 65). — The art of making invisible darns in cloth, though so invaluable is all but unknown. It is a tedious

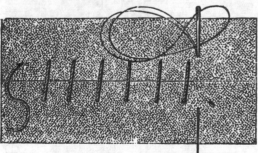

process and though easy enough to understand, is one requiring great patience and care in the execution.

Use as fine a needle as possible and thread it with hair, instead of silk or any other kind of fibre. Red and white hair is the strongest,

Fig. 65. Fine-drawing.

and stronger than the ravellings of the stuff. Of course the hair must first be carefully cleansed from grease. Pare the edges of the rent on the right side quite clean and even, with a razor, so that rent and stitches are entirely lost in the hairy surface of the cloth. Scissors do not cut so clean, and are liable moreover to disturb the nap and render the darn more visible. When this is done, fit the edges exactly together and overcast them with stitches wide apart. Then thread a needle with a hair by the root and slip it in, $\frac{1}{8}$ of an inch from the edge into the thickness of the cloth, not letting it come out at the back. The hair thus remains embedded in the nap. The needle traverses the overcast stitches and reappears on the other side of the seam, $\frac{1}{8}$ of an inch from the second edge. In bringing the needle back it must be inserted just where it came out: it must then be run in slightly slanting to give it a different direction from before so as not to interfere with the last stitch. The hair must be given a little play in working.

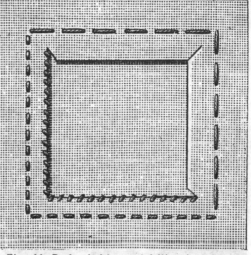

Fig. 66. Back-stitching and felling in a patch.

When the seam is finished, iron it on a bare board, laying a damp cloth on the wrong side of the darn. The sharpest eye will fail to detect a rent carefully darned in this manner.

Fine-drawing with the machine. For this you begin by fixing the piece to be darned on to tracing paper, then you join the two edges of the stuff by a very close zig-zag seam.

For coloured stuffs use D.M.C

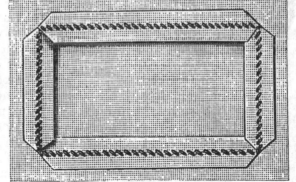

Fig. 67. Top-sewing in a patch.

Alsatian twist (Retors d'Alsace) No. 5o, on reels, or D.M.C Alsa.

Patching. — When a piece of a garment or other article is too torn to bear darning it must be cut out and replaced by a new piece. In the case of underlinen the new piece should be of a lighter material than the garment itself. Cut the patch to the line of the thread, and about 1 inch larger each way than the piece it is to cover or replace and turn in the edges all round. Cut the edges of the hole to be filled, to a thread, as in all patching and fix in the patch with a flat seam (running and felling) or top-sewing.

Back-stitching and felling in a patch (fig. 66). — Tack in the new piece, so that its edges over-lap the edges of the hole. The back-stitching must be done on the article itself, it being easier then to do the corners neatly. The hem is turned down on to the patch. Make a little snip at the corners with the scissors to prevent puckering. The back-stitching should meet at a right angle at each corner.

Top-sewing in a patch (fig. 67). — To do this, the edges of the hole and of the patch must first be turned in and either over-

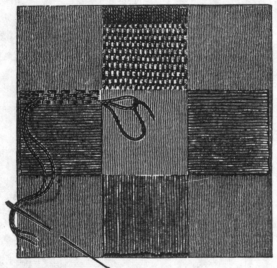

cast or hemmed, to prevent their fraying, after which, sew the two edges together. The raw edges may also be turned in with button-hole stitches, fig. 69, or herring-boned as in figure 45, or both edges may be hemmed before they are top-sewn together.

Drawing in a patch (fig. 68). — Take a square piece of the original stuff, 2 or 3 inches larger each way, than the hole to be filled, draw out threads on all four sides, till the piece exactly matches

Fig. 68. Drawing in a patch.

the hole and tack it into its place. Thread a very fine needle with the two ends of a thread of silk, run it in at the corner of the stuff, and draw it out, leaving a loop behind. Into this loop, slip the first of the threads, which as it were, form a fringe to the patch und tighten the loop round it, and so on with each thread, alternately taking up and leaving threads in the stuff as in ordinary darning.

To put a patch this way into a thin material, you must darn in the threads a good long way into the material, in order that the double layer of threads may be less visible.

Stripe in flat and raised satin stitch, and Madeira embroidery.

Embroidery upon White Stuff

Formerly the kind of embroidery we are going to describe was only known by the name of "white embroidery". The term is no longer correct now that it is done in colours quite as often as in white: We have therefore headed this chapter "Embroidery upon White Stuff".

Exclusively used for trimming underlinen and articles of dress the different kinds are distinguished by the different modes of working. We shall begin with the simplest, which is the raised embroidery done in button-hole and satin stitch (French plumetis); then go on to describe the so-called Swiss embroidery with its openwork groundings; Madeira, Renaissance and Richelieu work and Venetian embroidery, an imitation of Venetian lace, which is certainly the most artistic kind of embroidery upon white. At the end of this chapter we shall introduce our readers to a kind of Danish embroidery, called "Hedebo"; and to "Piqué" embroidery, much used in the last century for trimming underlinen and dresses.

Preparatory work. — Embroidery is generally done either on a backing of oil-cloth, or in an embroidery frame, called "tambour frame". Only skilful workers can dispense with one or other of these aids, for an untrained hand can hardly avoid puckering. If you work without a foundation, the material must be held quite smoothly over the forefinger so that the threads lie perfectly straight, otherwise, the pattern is very apt to get pulled out of shape in the working. With the three other fingers you hold the material fast, the thumb resting on the work itself, beyond the outline of the pattern, which must be turned towards the worker. It is always the outside edge of a pattern, drawn in double lines, that should be turned towards the palm of the hand.

Tracing patterns. — Patterns are generally to be had ready traced, but as they have often to be repeated, enlarged, or reduced, several ways of doing so, are described at the end of the last chapter.

Materials. — The different kinds of embroidery on white stuff require different materials and we cannot do better than recommend those bearing the D.M.C mark, distinguished for their smoothness and strength and the great variety of fast colours in which they are made. Raised embroidery should be done with D.M.C Embroidery cotton (Coton à broder) and D.M.C Special embroidery cotton (Coton à broder spécial); in certain cases D.M.C Floss embroidery cotton (Coton floche à broder) may be used, it is less twisted than the former, and whilst it covers the stuff quickly, gives a perfectly smooth surface. For underlinen and childrens' clothes sometimes embroidered in colours use D.M.C Embroidery cotton (Coton à broder), made in a great number of shades; this, in white, is best for embroideries with raised work and ornamental stitches, as in letters and monograms, &c. For kitchen cloths and such like, generally marked in a plain stitch, take D.M.C Floss flax or flourishing thread (Lin floche) or D.M.C Marking cotton (Coton à marquer). All the Swiss embroidery is done with very fine thread, the raised parts with D.M.C Superfine embroidery cotton (Coton à broder surfin) and the lace stitches with D.M.C Alsatian thread (Fil d'Alsace) or D.M.C Flax lace thread (Lin pour dentelles).

For the padding of the raised embroidery, take D.M.C Darning cotton (Coton à repriser) the colour of the embroidery.

Renaissance, Richelieu and Venetian embroideries, consisting of detached figures, outlined with button-hole stitches and connected by button-hole bars, require several kinds of thread. The outlining should be done in D.M.C Embroidery cotton (Coton à broder), the bars and the ornamental stitches, in D.M.C Alsatian thread (Fil d'Alsace). For Madeira work, a special thread is made called D.M.C Madeira Embroidery cotton (Coton à broder Madeira), of a greenish-blue tint to imitate the real Madeira work.

"Hedebo" embroidery should be done in linen thread; D.M.C

Floss flax or flourishing thread (Lin floche) for the raised parts and D.M.C Flax lace thread (Lin pour dentelles) for the openwork. "Piqué" embroidery can be done in cotton or linen thread. For the fillings we recommend a loose thread such as D.M.C Darning cotton (Coton à repriser), D.M.C Special stranded cotton (Mouliné spécial) or D.M.C Floss flax (Lin floche); for the outlining on the contrary, a very twisted thread, either, D.M.C Knotting cotton (Fil à pointer) or D.M.C Flax lace thread (Lin pour dentelles).

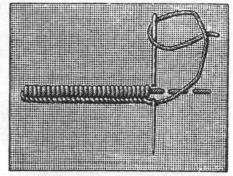

Fig. 69. Blanket, or button-hole stitch.

Outlining and padding.
The outlining of a pattern is a very important preliminary. A want of precision in the ultimate effect is often due merely to careless outlining. This part of the work should be done with rather a coarser cotton than the embroidery itself. Fasten in the thread by a few running stitches, never with a knot, a rule to be observed also in embroidering, except in very rare cases. Finish off your thread

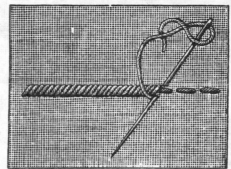

Fig. 70. Slanting overcast.

by drawing it through the tracing stitches, or through some part of the pattern that is already finished. Fill in the spaces between the lines with a padding of threads, loosely run in so that they lie thickly and solidly in the centre, and

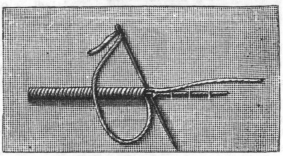

Fig. 71. Straight overcast.

shade off on both sides. The fulness and roundness of embroidery depends on the firmness of this substratum of threads. This preparatory work is clearly explained in figures 81 to 85.

Blanket, or button-hole stitch (fig. 69). — Work from left to right; run in a foundation line, hold down the working thread below the run line with the right thumb; insert the needle above and bring it out below the run line but above the working thread; tighten the loop thus formed, without drawing up the stuff, and continue in this manner, setting your stitches closely and regularly, side by side.

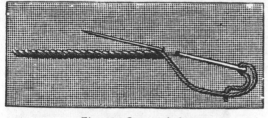

Fig. 72. Stem stitch.

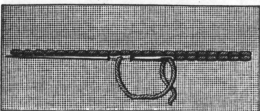

Fig. 73. Back-stitching.

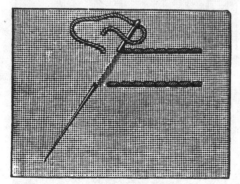

Fig. 74. Crossed back-stitch. Right side.

Slanting overcast (fig. 70). — Work over a single run thread from left to right in a slanting direction. Insert the needle above the run thread and bring it out below. If the lines of stem stitches are to be very fine and neat the needle must only raise the threads under the running.

Straight overcast (fig. 71). — This is also worked from left to right over a single run thread. To give the stitch more relief, a round twisted thread is lain on the run thread and covered with vertical stitches set closely together. This kind of stem stitch is used chiefly for embroidering letters and monograms.

Stem stitch (fig. 72). — This is done without a foundation thread. Pass the needle under one or two horizontal threads and under four or six vertical ones so that the last stitch extends half its length beyond the preceding one. The outlines of monograms, initials, numbers and designs for table-cloths, napkins, &c. are generally done in this stitch.

Back-stitching (point de sable) (fig. 73). — Back-stitching, that is small, even stitches set closely together, is done from right to left, along a straight line and is chiefly used for filling in the centres of letters, leaves and flowers. As represented in the engraving it is called back-stitch; it is known as *point de sable,* when the stitches are not so close together.

Crossed back-stitch (figs. 74 and 75). — Used, generally speaking, only on very thin transparent stuffs: it forms a close seam of cross stitch on the wrong side and two straight rows of back-stitching on the right. To work, insert the needle as if for an ordinary back-stitch, pass it under the stuff, sloping it a little towards the second outline of the pattern, and draw it out almost in front of the first stitch. After making a back-stitch, pass the needle up again under the stuff and bring it out at the spot where the next stitch is to come.

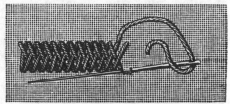

Fig. 75. Crossed back-stitch. Wrong side.

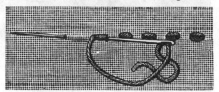

Fig. 76. Simple knot stitch.

Fig. 77. Knotted knot stitch.

Figure 75 shews the interlacing of the threads, and another way of doing the stitch; the wrong side of which may, in many cases serve as the right.

Simple knot stitch (fig. 76). — This is nothing else but two back-stitches, side by side, covering the same threads.

Knotted knot stitch (fig. 77). — Knotted knot stitch consists of one chain or tambour stitch and one back-stitch and produces much the same effect

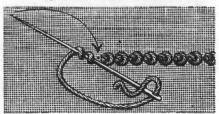

Fig. 78. Twisted knot stitch.

as twisted knot stitch. Having inserted the thread into the stuff you put the needle in again at the same place and bring it out a little further on so that the little loop of thread is under the point of the needle. This little loop is then secured by a small back-stitch.

Twisted knot stitch (fig. 78). — To work hold the working thread down with the thumb close to the spot where you first brought it out, twist it twice round the needle, turn the

needle round from left to right, following the direction indicated by the arrow, pass it through the fabric at the place
which is marked by a dot, and draw it out at the place where
the next stitch is to be.

Post stitch (fig. 79). — Similar to knot stitch and much
used for patterns, composed of little flowers and leaves, where
it often takes the place of raised satin stitch. The illustration represents five leaves
finished and the sixth in
process of being worked.
Insert the needle at the
point of the leaf then slip
it under the stuff near the
stalk and bring it out
there to the half of its
length. Place your left
thumb on the eye of the
needle and twist the thread
with the right hand round
the point as often as is
necessary to cover the space under which it has passed. Then
advance your left thumb on to the spirals thus formed, and
draw the needle with the remainder of the thread through them;
then carry the point of the needle back to the end of the leaf
and bring it out at the place indicated for the next stitch.

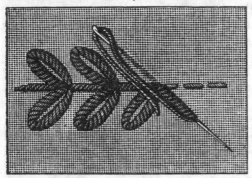

Fig. 79. Post stitch.

Button-hole bars (fig. 80). — When a pattern is ornamented with openwork bars, begin by tracing the outside
parallel lines. Then
button-hole the whole
lower line and the up-
per one, till you come
to the place where the
first bar is to be;
then carry your thread
across and bring up
the needle from below
through one of the
loops, as shown in the figure; lay three threads in this manner,
inserting your needle, the third time, one loop further on.
Then cover the three threads thickly with button-holing. When
the work is finished cut away the stuff between the bars.

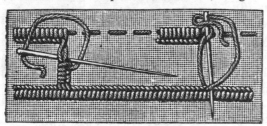

Fig. 80. Button-hole bars.

Different kinds of scallops (figs. 81, 82, 83). — The outlining, padding and button-holing of these scallops is executed

in the manner already described. Be careful to adapt the length of the stitches to the shape and size of the scallops. If they are pointed, figs. 82 and 83, the stitches will have to be set more

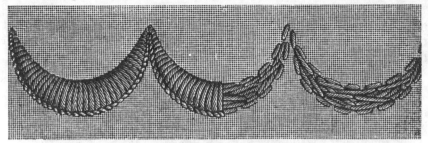

Fig. 81. Large round, button-holed scallops.

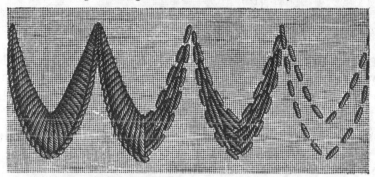

Fig. 82. Large pointed, button-holed scallops.

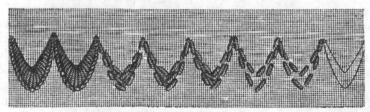

Fig. 83. Small pointed, button-holed scallops.

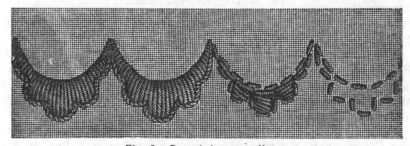

Fig. 84. Rounded rose scallops.

closely together on the inner line, and a little play allowed them on the outer, to come exactly to the point, which should be very carefully shaped.

Rose scallops (figs. 84 and 85). — These are large button-holed scallops with indented edges, in the one case, rounded at the top and sharply pointed at the join; in the other, pointed at the top, and joined at the bottom by a straight bar of button-holing.

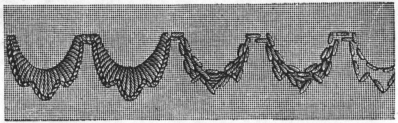

Fig. 85. Pointed rose scallops.

Eyelet-holes (figs. 86, 87, 88). — Outline the eyelet-holes very carefully first by running a thread round them, then cut out the enclosed stuff with a pair of sharp finely pointed scissors, and edge the hole with plain overcasting-stitches, worked from left to right.

When you have a long row of eyelet-holes to make, outline the upper and lower halves alternately, first on one side and then on the other, using two threads, and then overcast them in the same way. The double crossing of the working threads between the eyelet-holes makes them much stronger than if each hole were finished off separately, and the thread passed underneath from one to the other.

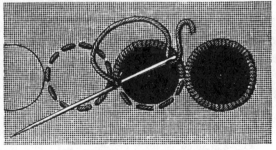

Fig. 86. Overcast eyelet-holes.

The lower halves of shaded eyelet-holes, see figs. 87 and 88, are covered with very short stitches and the upper halves with long ones ; they may be edged entirely, either with button-holing or overcasting, or half with one and half with the other, as in figure 88.

Six ways of working the leaves (fig. 89). — After tracing the pattern, fill the inside with as many stitches as you

can get into the space; begin to embroider the leaf from the
top, letter A, covering it with flat stitches, very close together,
worked from right to left. After tracing the outline of the design,
fill in the centres with a padding of long, close stitches. B illustrates a leaf, divided through the middle by a line of overcasting
and embroidered in straight satin stitch. Leaf C, divided like
the preceding one, by a vein done in overcast. Leaf D is em-

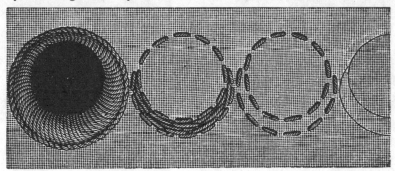

Fig. 87. Button-holed shaded eyelet-holes.

broidered in rather wide slanting satin stitch; leaf E in slanting
satin stitch, but very narrow, with a vein in overcast stitches
and leaf F is embroidered, half in straight satin stitch and
half in back-stitch, outlined with overcasting-stitches.

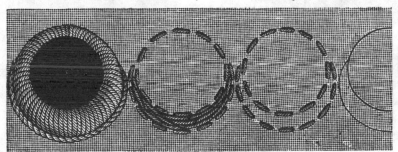

Fig. 88. Shaded eyelet-holes half overcast, half button-holed.

Leaves and flowers of all descriptions can be executed in
any of these stitches and in different combinations of the same.

Six ways of making dots (fig. 90). — Dots, when they
are well made, are exceedingly effective in white embroidery,
particularly if they are worked in a variety of stitches. Dot A
is worked in raised satin stitch; B, in raised satin stitch,
framed in back-stitch; C, in raised satin stitch, framed in twisted
knot stitch; D is composed of several post stitches of different

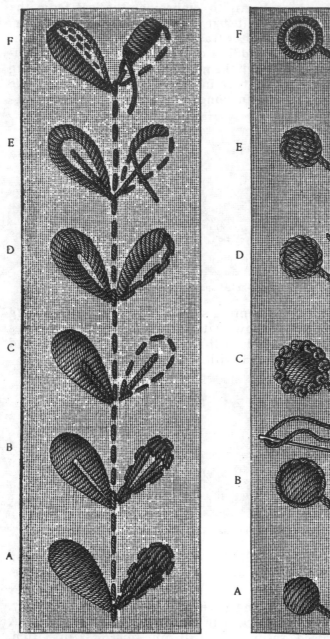

Fig. 89.
Six ways of working the leaves.

Fig. 90.
Six ways of making dots.

lengths, set in a frame of stem stitches; E is worked in back-stitch outlined with overcast, and F consists of a small eyelet-hole which forms the centre, framed with overcasting-stitches.

Embroidery frames (figs. 91 and 92). — Initials, mono-grams, crowns and all designs with fine, delicate lines, which

Fig. 91. Swiss embroidery rame.

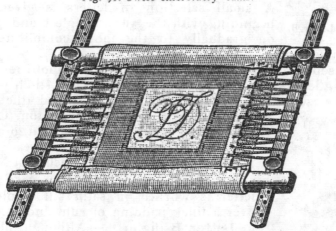

Fig. 92. Ordinary embroidery frame.

require very accurate execution can only be really well done mounted in a frame. The Swiss frames, which are round and known as tambour frames, are the most generally used. They consist of two wooden hoops, one of which is fastened to a circular support, which can be fixed to the edge of a table by a wooden screw. The other hoop is loose. Place your stuff on the hoop which you fasten to the table, so that the pattern comes in the middle, then press the loose hoop down on to the stuff so that it is firmly held between the two.

Tambour frames can only be used for embroidering pocket-handkerchiefs and other small articles; bigger articles have

Fig. 93. Letter X.

to be done in an ordinary frame. Sew a piece of strong stuff into the frame, stretch it as tightly and evenly as possible, and cut out a square in the middle the size of the pattern. Then tack your work in underneath, straight to the thread, dividing it out carefully with pins first, to ensure its being set in perfectly even. Roll or fold up the rest of the stuff over the edges of the frame and secure it with a few stitches or pins, to keep it out of the way of your hand as you work.

Fig. 94. Letter B.

Letters and monograms. Raised embroidery. — Embroidery in raised satin stitch (plumetis), is, as we have already said, much used for letters and monograms on underlinen. These may be infinitely varied according to taste and the time the worker has at her disposal. A small selection of letters is given here, beginning with the very simplest and passing on gradually to the more complicated and decorative ones.

Raised embroidery done with the machine. — In working letters and monograms in raised satin stitch with the machine, see also p. 26, take for the top thread (the bobbin

Fig. 95. Letter C.

thread) D.M.C Embroidery cotton (Coton à broder), on reels, in Nos. 80 to 120 and for the bottom thread (the shuttle thread) D.M.C Machine thread (Fil pour machines) No. 150.

Letter X (fig. 93). — This very simple letter is worked in satin stitch (plumetis) over a thick padding of run stitches.

Letter B (fig. 94). — Although this letter is not much bigger than the preceding one, it lends itself to a greater richness of execution, the wider parts being worked in satin and stem stitch.

Letter C (Fig. 95). — Letters of this size admit of the use of several kinds of stitches, by dividing, or "splitting", the shading or dark parts of the letter. The engraving shews a specimen of this so-called split embroidery, done in three different stitches, satin stitch, back-stitch and overcasting.

Letter P (fig. 96). — This letter, Italian in character, lends itself to execution in two colours; the lighter for the principal lines in satin stitch, the darker for the flourishes in straight overcasting-stitch.

Vignette with the monogram HB and a crown (fig. 97). — This figure shews how monograms may be enriched by means of vignettes. The floating ribbon and the letters are all done in satin stitch without any ornamentation, we had this subject executed as a specimen of what may be done in this way.

Fig. 96. Letter P.

Letter O (fig. 98). — Letters of this kind are more difficult to execute than the preceding ones. When you have come in the plain part to the place whence the ornament starts, carry your thread to the point, and beginning with small stitches, work back increasing their length to the main stem and join on to it so that the stitches merge together.

Letter A (fig. 99). — The embroidery is "split" so as to form little squares in the

Fig. 97. Vignette with the monogram HB and a crown.

division, which are filled in with simple knot stitch, fig. 76. Here two colours may be introduced, unless the letter is to be altogether white.

Letter D (fig. 100). — The outlines of this letter are in straight overcasting-stitch; the wide parts are filled in with triangles in flat stitch and back-stitch (point de sable, fig. 73).

Monogram F V (fig. 101). — In the days of Holbein, paintings and gobelins,

Fig. 98. Letter O.

were signed by the authors with their initials, seldom with their whole names. The monogram reproduced here, consisting of

Fig. 99. Letter A.

the letters F and V, is taken from documents dating from that time. To suit the stiff character of the letters they are worked in straight satin stitch, shaded, and straight overcast-stitch.

Letter E (fig. 102). — Letter E, plain English in its character, is worked on a richly ornamented, bright coloured foundation. The letter is in satin stitch, in a light colour, the foundation in straight overcast-stitch, in a dark one.

Monogram U G (fig. 103). — Of the same origin as figure 101, this monogram is handsomer and richer as regards the style of

Fig. 100. Letter D.

work. The letter U is done in split embroidery, whilst the outlines of letter G are in stem stitch, the fillings in back-stitch.

Letter J (fig. 104). — This letter is embroidered in the Swiss manner, the fillings in open stitches. After doing the outlines in very close overcast-stitch, cut out the stuff between and fill in the space with the little insertion, fig. 886. Be careful to make the dots very round and to give a graceful turn to the tendrils that adorn the letter.

Letter R (fig. 105). — The grounding which forms the body of this letter is composed of fine lace stitches, see figs. 890 to 924. When these are done, work the outlines in straight overcast-stitch, and cut away the stuff at the back of the openwork.

Fig. 101. Monogram F V.

Letter K (fig. 106). — This letter may also be classed amongst the manuscript letters. The ground is left blank in the engraving; for the double outline in overcasting-stitch, a fancy stitch or crossed back-stitch may be substituted.

Letter J (fig. 107). — Here letter and ornaments are done in overcasting-stitch. In the letter and the framing the stitch must be thicker and stronger than in the ornaments. If worked on white stuff, unbleached cotton or Tinder grey 386, may be used for the foundation in back-stitch; the rest should be white.

Letter N (fig. 108). — Here it may be seen how, by means of auxiliary stitches and finely executed designs richness and beauty may be added to the simplest letters. The starred effect of the ground of letter N is produced by little eyelet-holes, where the pattern seems

Fig. 102. Letter E.

to indicate satin stitch. Although the work demands greater care and patience if executed by means of eyelet-holes, we strongly recommend that it should be done in this manner, rather than in plain satin stitch, because the solid letter will stand out in much better relief on the openworked ground.

Letter M (fig. 109). — This letter with ornaments in the Holbein style

Fig. 103. Monogram U G.

can be worked in white on a dark ground, just as well as in the colours reproduced in the model, either a very delicate pink, Geranium red 353 for the letter, a dark red, Cardinal red 347, for the little twigs, the bar and the frame, and a light blue, Indigo blue 322, for the ground.

Letter J (fig. 110). — Letters of this size are generally only found in ecclesiastical books, missals, &c. Given the richness of the design, the execution

Fig. 104. Letter J.

Fig. 105. Letter R.

Fig. 106. Letter K.

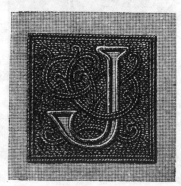

Fig. 107. Letter J.

may be quite simple. Our engraving shews the letter worked in satin stitch and stem stitch.

Letter R (fig. 111). — The outlines of the letter are worked in straight overcast-stitch and the inside filled with diagonal lines of the same stitch. A frame consisting of a double line encloses the letter; the ground is covered with little stars in satin stitch.

Letter O (fig. 112). — In letter O, the dark outlines are done in straight overcast-stitch, the ornaments in satin stitch, the filling quite flat in encroaching satin stitch, in white, see figs. 274 and 276, which stands out effectively on a ground covered with back-stitches.

Alphabets for monograms (figs. 113, 114, 115, 116, 117, 118). — It is often difficult to find monograms for marking underlinen. We therefore present our workers here with two alphabets which will enable them to make their own, whatever their initials may be.

These alphabets are of medium size. The letters can be made larger or smaller at will.

We again take this opportunity of advising our readers to be guided in all such modifications by the indications given in the last chapter.

The three first plates represent letters, intentionally stunted in height, and rather massive, intended to frame the taller and more attenuated letters of the fourth and fifth plates.

The interlacing of the letters needs some attention; the specimens on the subsequent pages with the accompanying directions as to the most appropriate stitches for the purpose will be found useful by our readers.

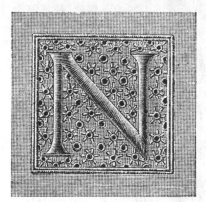

Fig. 108. Letter N.

Fig. 109. Letter M.

Monogram composed of letters A and D (fig. 119). — Here letter A is embroidered in blue and shaded with red ; letter D is embroidered in cross stripes, the left part in light blue and white, the right in light blue and dark blue.

For the little ornaments, the two latter shades can be used indifferently.

Monogram composed of letters V and S (fig. 120). — For deep and half mourning when white handkerchiefs cannot be used, these two letters have been worked in mourning shades that their use may be shown. Both are embroidered in grey set with black.

Fig. 110. Letter J.

Monogram composed of letters R and C (fig. 121). — The distinction between these two letters is marked by the

different working. Letter R, embroidered in satin stitch, the setting in slanting overcast-stitch, whilst C has no setting and

Fig. 111. Letter R.

the wide part between the two edges of very close overcast is worked in slanting stripes done in back-stitch (point de sable, fig. 73) and satin stitch.

Monogram composed of letters G and E (fig. 122). — For letter E, worked in satin stitch, white embroidery cotton was chosen; for the fancy stitches of letter G, D.M.C Superfine embroidery cotton (Coton surfin), which, owing to its ivory tint, makes the G stand out from the E, moreover it somewhat softens the red of the setting.

Crowns. — We append to the letters and monograms a few examples of embroidered crowns to go with the letters in the preceding pages.

In these examples will be seen the different ways of embroidering crowns from the simplest to the most ornamental, making use of all the stitches hitherto described.

Fig. 112. Letter O.

All the small details in the crowns must be worked with the greatest accuracy, especially those representing pearls and

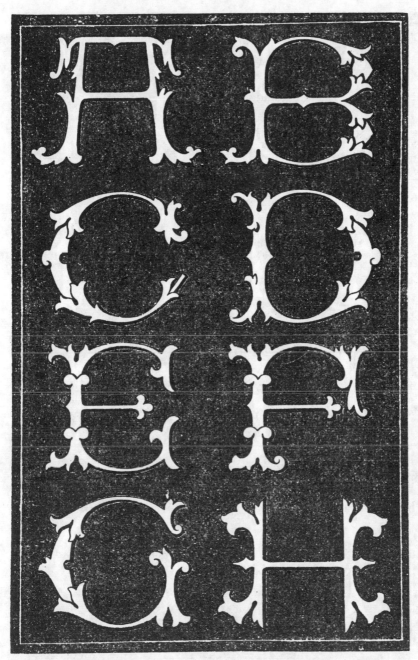

Fig. 113. Alphabets for monograms. Outside letters A to H.

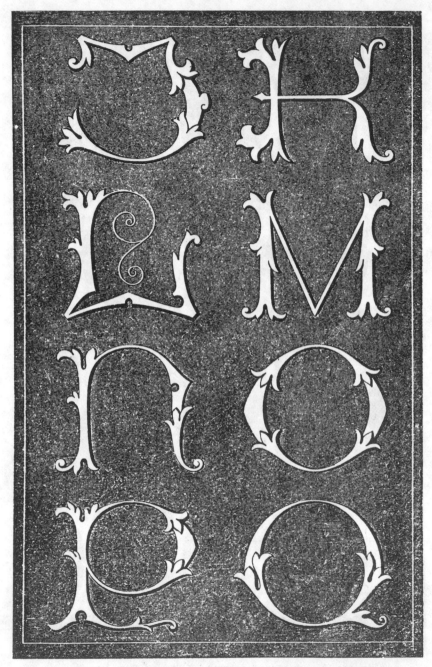

Fig. 114. Alphabets for monograms. Outside letters J to Q.

Fig. 115. Alphabets for monograms. Outside letters R to Y.

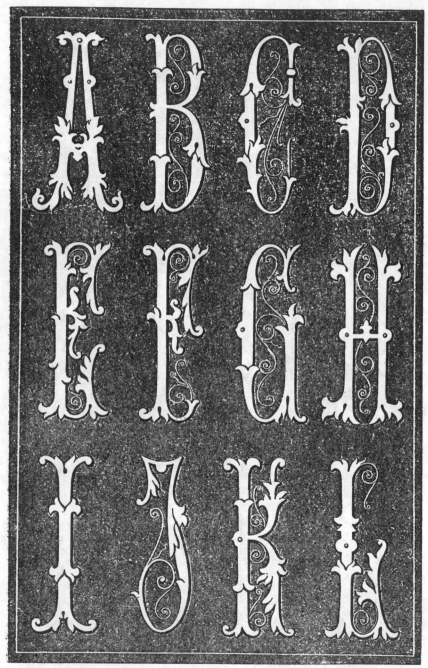

Fig. 116. Alphabets for monograms. Inside letters A to L.

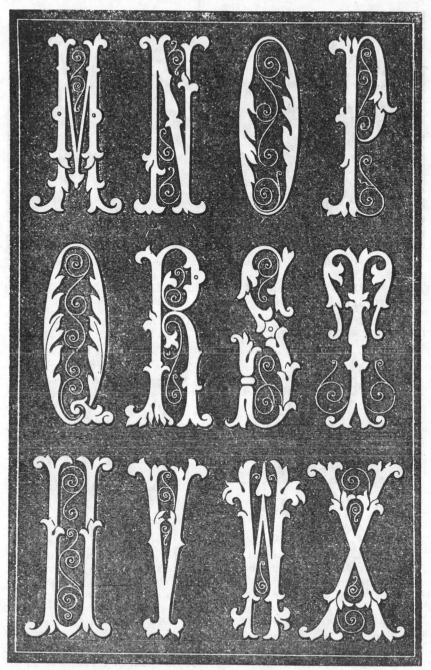

Fig. 117. Alphabets for monograms. Inside letters M to X.

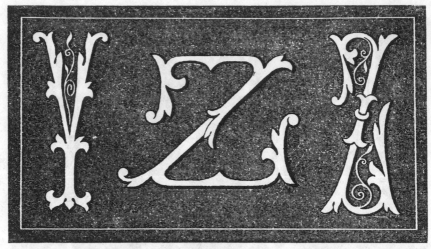

Fig. 118. Alphabets for monograms. Last inside and outside letters.

gems. Colours must only be introduced when the monogram is embroidered in colours.

Nobleman's coronet (fig. 123). — This is worked in white. The balls must be thickly padded so as to stand out in high

Fig. 119. Monogram composed of letters A and D drawn from the alphabets of monograms.
Materials : D.M.C Embroidery cotton No. 100. — Colours : Blue fast dye 797, 799, Turkish red 321 and white. (*)

Fig. 120. Monogram composed of letters V and S drawn from the alphabets of monograms.
Materials : D.M.C Embroidery cotton No. 100. — Colours : Ash grey 318 and Black fast dye 310. (*)

(*) These numbers refer to the colours on the colour cards of the articles stamped with the D.M.C trade mark. These cards can be consulted at all the mercers' and needlework shops.

relief like beads. The part beneath from which they spring is filled in with back–stitch.

Baron's coronet (fig. 124). — This is all worked in satin stitch in two strongly contrasting colours.

Fig. 121. Monogram composed of letters R and C drawn from the alphabets of monograms. Materials : D.M.C Embroidery cotton No. 120. — Colours : White and Cardinal red 347.

Fig. 122. Monogram composed of letters G and E drawn from the alphabets of monograms. Materials : D.M.C Embroidery cotton No. 120, white and Turkish red 321 and D.M.C Superfine embroidery cotton No. 100, écru.

Count's coronet (fig. 125). — This is worked in satin stitch and straight overcast, all in one colour ; the space between the circlet and the balls is filled with openwork stitch.

Royal crown (fig. 126). — The whole series of these royal crowns is classical and common to all countries. They may be worked in white or in se-

Fig. 123. Nobleman's coronet.

veral colours, according to the object they are to adorn. The ground on which the ermine tails rest may be covered with single or double back-stitch or with encroaching flat stitch, see figs. 274 and 276.

Letters and monograms in fancy embroidery. — Plain letters to be worked quickly can be done in chain, stem, or cross stitch, or with soutache according to taste. For bed and household linen and all such ordinary purposes, quick and inexpensive marking of this kind will be found useful and practical.

Letter J (fig. 127). — When time is an object and you have no embroidery frame at hand this can be worked in ordinary chain stitch, see figs. 229, 254, 255. The finer your cotton and

Fig. 124. Baron's coronet.

the smaller and more regular your stitches the better the effect of this kind of marking will be, particularly if done in colours.

Letter G (fig. 128). — This is a specimen to shew how big letters may be executed in a variety of lace stitches. After making the outline with a double row of stem stitch, fill in the interior with little wheels, see figs. 673 and 674, made with D.M.C Alsatian thread (Fil d'Alsace).

Fig. 125. Count's coronet.

Monogram G W (fig. 129). — As regards composition and execution, all the letters of this series are extremely simple, yet when reproduced in embroidery, are most effective. We recommend plain chain stitch, fig. 229, or chain stitch with overcast-stitches, fig. 230, for monograms of this kind.

Letter A (fig. 130). — This roun-

Fig. 126. Royal crown.

ded letter is worked entirely in crossed back-stitch, see fig. 75, with coloured thread.

Letter M (fig. 131). — This is an example of modern gothic letters worked in crossed back-stitch and stem stitch.

Letter A (fig. 132). — This is one of the old gothic letters; it is worked in two colours; the stem stitch and the crossed back-stitch which fill in the body of the letter are done in the lighter colour, the back-stitches which are set in the crossings of the crossed back-stitch are done in the darker colour.

Letter A (fig. 133). — Soutache shews to great advantage here, for the big lines of this letter. A light coloured one should be taken for the outline and a dark one for the Arabic interlacings which fill in the empty spaces; for the plain net stitch, fig. 890, between the two lines of soutache use D.M.C Alsatian thread (Fil d'Alsace). Letters like this are very suitable for table-cloths, sheets, &c., because they are clear and distinct, and if done as described, take much less time than if they were to be reproduced in embroidery.

Fig. 127. Letter J.

Alphabet in Soutache (figs. 134, 135, 136, 137, 138, 139). — This alphabet which is one of the best of its kind, was taken from a work published in Venice in 1562, by Giovan' Antonio Tagliente, secretary and calligraphist to the Republic. The letters of this alphabet do not lend themselves to raised embroidery, but can be executed in soutache.

Fig. 128. Letter G.

The sewing on of the braid is done with very small running stitches and the interlacing with a tapestry needle, into which the braid is threaded; both operations are shewn in figures 136 and 137. The embroidery of the connecting bars and the small leaves and tendrils in satin stitch, that complete the letter are explained by figure 138,

Fig. 129.
Monogram G W.

whilst figure 139 represents the letter in its finished state. For sewing on the braid, use D.M.C Alsatian thread (Fil d'Alsace) and for embroidering the details, D.M.C Embroidery cotton (Coton à broder).

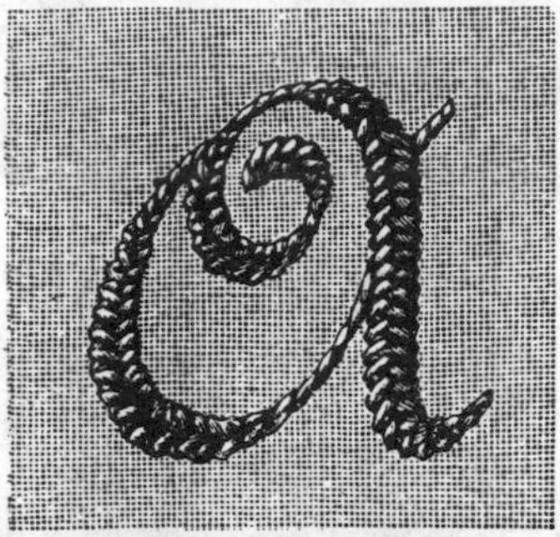

Fig. 130. Letter A.

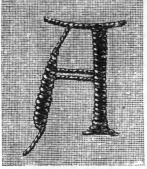

Fig. 131. Letter M.

Fig. 132. Letter A.

Small insertion in satin stitch with row of openwork (figs. 140 and 141). — Begin by the leaves in satin stitch, and then do the stalks in slanting overcast.

The two lines which border the openwork are done in straight overcast, see fig. 71. When all the embroidery is finished, begin the openwork, for which no threads need be drawn. It is formed by the drawing together of certain parts of the stuff. As seen in figure 141, the openwork stripe takes six threads in height; beginning on the right, at the bottom, make two back-stitches from left to right, over six threads of the stuff, then follow two stitches over six vertical and three horizontal threads sloping towards the right, after which you make two more horizontal back-stitches at the top, to return to the first line with two slanting stitches over six vertical and three horizontal threads, sloping to the right. Continue in this manner drawing the stitches very tight, and the openwork comes of itself.

Border in satin stitch and back-stitch with openwork spiders (fig. 142). — In spite of the fineness of the pattern, this border, suitable for pocket-handkerchiefs, is not difficult. The little flowers with six petals which encircle the openwork spider, are done in straight satin stitch, the flowers with five petals, in the sprays, in slanting stitches with veins between. The leaves are outlined in straight overcast and filled in with back-stitches. The empty spaces in the big flowers are also filled in with back-stitches. For the working of the spiders, which are bordered in overcast we refer our readers to the chapter on "Needle-made Laces". Little clusters of eyelet-holes in overcast are strewn over the ground. For the embroidery we recommend D.M.C Embroidery cotton (Coton à broder) No. 80; for the spiders, D.M.C Alsatian thread (Fil d'Alsace) No. 120, in white.

Flower in satin stitch with openwork centres (fig. 143). — This kind of embroidery in satin stitch with openwork centres is known as "Swiss embroidery".

Before beginning the satin stitch make the openwork centres, for which directions are given in the chapter on "Open-

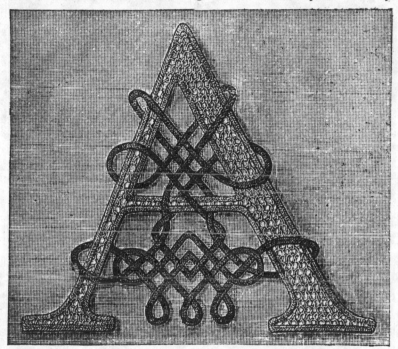

Fig. 133. Letter A.

work on Linen" figures 772 and 774; then do the eyelet-holes in straight overcast, and next the padding of leaves and petals for the satin stitch. For the openwork, use D.M.C Alsatian thread (Fil d'Alsace) No. 150; for the padding, D.M.C Floss embroidery cotton (Coton floche à broder) No. 35 and No. 70 for the satin stitch.

Three English embroidery patterns (figs. 144, 145, 146). Embroidery consisting chiefly of eyelet-holes formerly known as English embroidery is now generally called Madeira work

Fig. 134. Alphabet in Soutache. Letters A to N.

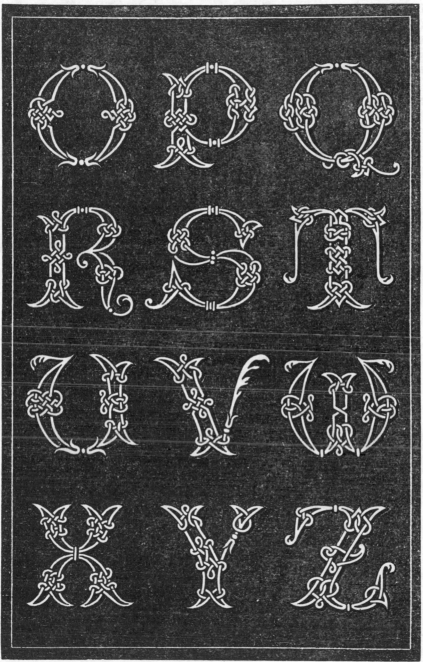

Fig. 135. Alphabet in Soutache. Letters O to Z.

from the island where it originated: worked like the English in plain overcast it surpasses all other in the regularity of the stitches and the firmness and neatness of the workmanship. The edges of the stuff are well covered and enclosed by the stitches, so that they never fray or wear out with use.

The scallops of figures 144 and 146 are edged with shaded eyelet-holes, whilst those of figure 145 are button-holed.

Fig. 136.
Letter T of the alphabet in Soutache.
Mode of interlacing the Soutache.

Fig. 137.
Letter M of the alphabet in Soutache.
Mode of sewing on the Soutache.

Fig. 138.
Letter W of the alphabet in Soutache.
Mode of placing the bars and embroidering the leaves.

Fig. 139.
Letter A of the alphabet in Soutache in its finished state.

These three patterns are particularly suitable for trimming pillow-cases and underlinen.

Openwork embroidery done with the machine. — To do English, scalloped embroidery, Renaissance, Richelieu and Venetian embroidery with the machine, all the outlines must be closely overcast over a strongly twisted thread.

D.M.C Special crochet cotton (Cordonnet spécial) in Nos. 3o to 5o should be overcast with D.M.C Embroidery cotton (Coton à broder), on reels, in Nos. 8o to 12o or with D.M.C Alsatian twist (Retors d'Alsace) Nos. 3o to 6o for the top thread (the bobbin thread) and D.M.C Machine thread (Fil pour Ma-

Fig. 140. Small insertion in satin stitch with row of openwork.
Materials: D.M.C Embroidery cotton or D.M.C Floss embroidery cotton, in white.

chines) Nos. 15o for the bottom thread (the shuttle thread).

Renaissance embroidery (figs. 147 and 148). — This is the term applied to embroidery worked entirely in button-holing and connected by button-hole

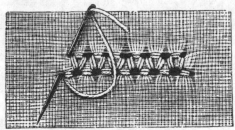

Fig. 141. How to do the openwork.

bars without picots as shewn in the accompanying figures. The button-holing is done over a single tracing thread and of the same width throughout, excepting on the outside edge where it may be made a little wider, fig. 147. The flowers and leaves in figure 148 are ornamented, on the outside edge, with picots in dot

Fig. 142. Border in satin stitch and back-stitch with openwork spiders.
Materials: D.M.C Embroidery cotton No. 8o, and D.M.C Alsatian thread No. 12o, in white.

stitch (point de poste), as described in the chapter on "Needle-made Laces", fig. 870.

Richelieu embroidery (fig. 149). — The name applied to embroidery of a similar kind to the Renaissance but in which the connecting bars, as well as the outside edge, are ornamented with picots.

Fig. 143. Flower in satin stitch with openwork centres.
Materials : D.M.C Floss embroidery cotton Nos. 35 and 70 and D.M.C Alsatian thread No. 150, white.

It is used, like the Renaissance, for trimming bed and table-linen, and, in many cases is a very good substitute for pillow Lace.

Fig. 144. English work.
Materials : D.M.C Madeira cotton (Special cotton for English embroidery).

Fig. 145. English work.
Materials : D.M.C Madeira cotton (Special cotton for English embroidery).

Venetian embroidery (fig. 150). — This is work resembling Venetian lace in appearance, hence its name. The stuff

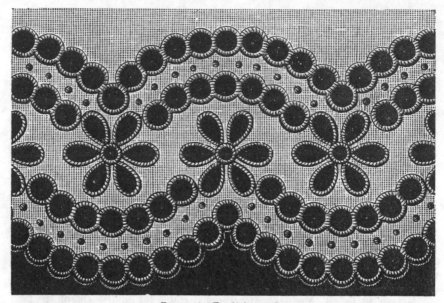

Fig. 146. English work.
Materials : D.M.C Madeira cotton (Special cotton for English embroidery).

Fig. 147. Renaissance embroidery.
Materials : D.M.C Embroidery cotton, D.M.C Floss embroidery cotton,
white or écru.

on which it is done takes the place of the needle–made grounds
in lace. The button–hole outlines are worked in high relief,
the connecting bars with or without picots, these are described

Fig. 148. Renaissance embroidery.
Materials : D.M.C Embroidery cotton, D.M.C Floss embroidery cotton,
white or écru.

Fig. 149. Richelieu embroidery.
Materials : D.M.C Embroidery cotton, D.M.C Floss embroidery cotton,
white or écru.

in detail in the chapter on "Needle–made Laces", see figs. 866
to 871. The ground, rarely left plain, is embroidered with fancy

stitches, as shewn in our engraving. The thick padding over which the button-hole stitches are made is an important part of this work and should be done as follows: take from six to eight threads of D.M.C Darning cotton (Coton à repriser) No. 25 and fasten them down on the traced line of the pattern with overcast stitches, set a little distance apart, the threads forming as it were a thick round cord laid upon the tracing. In the wider parts of the outlines the number of padding threads may be increased, and may be lessened where the

Fig. 150. Venetian embroidery.

scallops narrow. Having finished the whole of the embroidery, cut away the material underneath the bars. Use a sharp small pair of scissors and cut with the utmost care.

Insertion in Venetian embroidery (fig. 151). — Herewith we present our readers with an insertion suitable for trimming bed and table-linen, &c. A fine linen but one of which the threads can be counted should be selected for this work. The padding for the raised parts should be done with D.M.C Darning cotton (Coton à repriser); the button-holing with D.M.C Embroidery cotton (Coton à broder); the bars and

Fig. 151. Insertion in Venetian embroidery.
Materials : D.M.C Embroidery cotton, D.M.C Darning cotton
and D.M.C Alsatian thread, white.

Fig. 152 Border in Danish embroidery in white, called "Hedebo".
Materials: D.M.C Floss flax or flourishing thread and D.M.C Flax lace thread.

the fillings with a twisted thread, such as D.M.C Alsatian thread (Fil d'Alsace).

A description of the different stitches will be found in the chapter on "Embroidered Laces".

Fig. 153. Border in "Piqué embroidery".
Materials: D.M.C Knotting cotton or D.M.C Crochet cotton 6 cord, D.M.C Darning cotton or D.M.C Special stranded cotton and D.M.C Alsatian thread, écru.

Border in Danish embroidery "Hedebo" (fig. 152). — The Danish peasants decorate their linen with rich openwork

embroidery in white called "Hedebo" work. This embroidery
is little known elsewhere, and designed exclusively for the
personal use of those who make it, has not yet found its way
into the open market.

Our engraving, fig. 152, is taken from the border of a towel.
It would do also for small table-cloths, table centres, &c. Begin
with the little openwork squares, which divide the whole stripe
into squares and triangles, and are made on counted threads,
then trace the pattern for the figures that have to be embroidered. The openwork grounds of these, a great choice of which
is given in the chapter on "Embroidered Laces", figs. 802 to 817,
have to be done first, and then, lastly, the embroidering of the
figures, in satin stitch, after padding them. A little openwork
border all round completes the whole.

Border in "Piqué embroidery" (fig. 153). — This kind
of work is done in white on strong firm stuff, on which the
outlines are traced by a cord, or in overcast and the fillings
are made with different stitches to imitate a figured material.
It is now generally used for trimming bed and table covers of
all kinds, childrens' clothes, &c. In the engraving the different
parts of the pattern will be seen to be filled with damask
stitches, of which a description will be found in the chapter
on "Embroidered Laces", figs. 794 to 801.

The cords which outline the subjects are made in crochet
chain stitch. The material used for our model is plain molleton; the damask stitches are done in D.M.C Special stranded
cotton (Mouliné spécial) No. 25, écru. The crochet cord is made
with D.M.C Knotting cotton (Fil à pointer) Nos. 20 and 30; sewn
down with D.M.C Alsatian thread (Fil d'Alsace) No. 100, écru.

Patterns of needlework. — Besides the different kinds of
work described above a great choice of patterns for embroidery
on white stuff will be found in the following publications of
the D.M.C Library : *Alphabets and Monograms, The Embroiderer's Alphabet, Motifs for Embroideries V* and *Works
of various kinds.* (*)

(*) See at the end of the volume the list of the albums
of the D.M.C Library.

Border in cross stitch. — Pattern reserved.

Linen Embroidery

Linen embroidery may be classed under two heads: one comprising all the embroideries done on counted threads, after a pattern drawn on checked paper, or embroidered; the other, embroidery done on a pattern transferred to the linen by means of tracing paper and worked with a free hand without regard to the threads of the stuff. (*)

The embroidery never covers the whole ground but leaves blank spaces of linen between.

Linen embroideries of this kind have for centuries been a domestic industry amongst the rural population of different lands. The country of their origin is easily recognisable by the character of the pattern and the colours in which the work is executed. The Italian, Greek and Spanish embroideries of the 15th to the 17th century are mostly done in one colour, a purple red; whilst the oriental ones are characterised by the great variety of colours introduced, mixed with gold and silver thread. The embroideries of the Slav, Hungarian and Swedish peasants are alike distinguishable by their richness of colouring, red, blue and yellow being the predominant notes. In our day linen embroidery adapted to modern taste is in great

(*) See at the end of the volume the list of the albums of the D.M.C Library, that relate to embroideries on counted threads.

favour owing to the variety of stitches and patterns and their comparatively easy execution.

Stuffs. — Most old embroideries especially the Italian ones are on very fine linen. Such minute work demands more time and perseverance than · people in these days care to spend on fancy work. To meet the exigencies of the times stuffs have been produced with round distinct threads which can be easily counted to facilitate the counting of the stitches and the copying of the patterns.

The linen stuffs can all be had either in white, cream or écru.

Cotton and linen materials are also now made in every variety of colour, and for cushion and table-covers, panels and blinds worked in stem and line stitch, &c., are often preferable to the white or cream.

Preparatory work. — Small pieces of linen embroidery done in simple short stitches, can be done in the hand; but larger pieces worked in more elaborate stitches with fillings on big surfaces, or bars of stretched threads, overcast, must be mounted in an embroidery frame, see fig. 92. The work will always be neater and the stuff will not get puckered or crumpled.

To mount a piece of work in a frame proceed as follows : stitch a tape or a strip of stuff to two opposite sides of the work, turn down the edges of the two other sides about half an inch and sew them to the webbing nailed on to the two bars of the frame, stretching the stuff tightly as you sew.

Then mount the frame, by slipping the two "stretchers", bored through with holes, into the slits at the two ends of the bars, stretch the material firmly and fix the "stretchers" by running the metal or wooden pegs through the holes to fasten the four sides of the frame together. Then stretch the material in the other direction, in the following manner : take a piece of twine or strong cord, thread it through a packing needle and brace the material with it to the stretchers. At each stitch pass it over the stretcher and into the material, and make the stitches close together. Brace both sides of the material in this way and then draw the twine up upon each side evenly and quite tight.

Marking out the ground for linen embroidery on counted threads (fig. 154). — Before beginning a piece of embroidery on counted threads, take a coloured thread and mark out the stitches. This is generally done, as shewn in figure 154, by alternately over and under ten threads, along two sides at least, in the length and breadth of the stuff. Then, having counted the number of stitches both ways divide them in two, and starting from the middle stitch, trace two lines, one horizontal, the other vertical, right across the stuff. The point of their intersection will be the central stitch. This

Fig. 154. Marking out the stitches.

sort of ground plan will be found most useful and the two intersecting threads should not be pulled out, until at least, half the work is finished. If furthermore, you have corners to work or a pattern to reverse in the angle of a piece of embroidery, trace diagonal lines besides, from the corners to the centre.

Materials. — As embroidery on linen is chiefly used for articles that need frequent washing, the thread that will best

bear washing should be used. In this respect the first in order
are the D.M.C cotton, linen and silk threads.

For work done in cross stitch, square stitch and stroke
stitch on a harsh stiff stuff their moderately twisted threads
are best, such as D.M.C Embroidery cotton (Coton à broder),
D.M.C Pearl cotton (Coton perlé). For work on linen or
canvas, soft and supple stuffs, in cross stitch, plaited stitch
and flat stitch, a loose thread is preferable, we recommend
D.M.C Special stranded cotton (Mouliné spécial), D.M.C
Floss flax or flourishing thread (Lin floche) and D.M.C Persian
silk (Soie de Perse) (*). These, all composed of six strands,
can be used double or more at will, according to the coarseness
of the stuff to be embroidered.

Stitches. — Plain cross stitch, as shewn in figure 155, is the
most common, but it is inferior to the stitch that is the same
on both sides and is so attractive in the beautiful old embroideries still to be met with here and there from which we
draw many of our best inspirations to this day.

Besides cross stitch and all its varieties, stroke stitch and
square stitch alike on both sides, known as Holbein stitch are
much used.

Cross stitch patterns are now often worked in straight stitch,
or "point lancé". This latter which is carried over several
threads of the stuff at once, is quicker to do than· plain cross
stitch and is therefore much used for fancy work.

As will be seen from subsequent engravings a pattern is
seldom executed in one stitch only. Combinations of stroke
stitch and gobelin stitch, star stitch and plait stitch, &c. in the
same piece of work are frequent and such combinations
enhance the beauty of the pattern.

Plain cross stitch (fig. 155). — Plain cross stitch is formed of two oblique stitches, placed one across the other,
crossing each other in the middle. If the material admits of
your counting the threads, you can work your stitches directly
upon it, if not you must cover it with an auxiliary canvas
upon which you work the pattern, and which you draw out
thread by thread when the work is finished. It is perhaps as
well to add that when an auxiliary canvas is used it must be
most carefully tacked upon the stuff following the thread of the

(*) See at the end of the last chapter the tables of the sizes and colours of
the cotton, flax and silk articles, mark D.M.C. — The French names, in brackets,
are those stamped on the labels of the D.M.C articles.

same and a sufficient margin left to allow of the drawing out of the canvas threads when the work is finished.

To make a neat cross stitch, you must insert your needle and draw it out at the same hole.

Two-sided cross stitch (fig. 156, 157, 158, 159, 160). — Straight lines of cross stitch, alike on both sides, can be worked in two journeys to and fro. Working from left to right, begin by fastening in your thread, never with a knot, but by two or three little running-stitches, which are hidden afterwards by your first cross stitch. Directing your needle to the right, pass it diagonally over a double cross of the warp and woof of the canvas or material, and so on to the end of the line.

Having come to the last stitch, draw out your thread in the middle of it, make an auxiliary diagonal stitch downwards to the right, bring the needle up in the middle of the last stitch, take it thence upwards to the left, across two threads and begin the return journey from right to left, crossing and thus completing the first row of stitches. In the auxiliary stitch with which you begin the backward journey the thread lies double on both sides.

Often the two auxiliary stitches are covered by a long stitch, as shewn in figures 157 and 158. After the last stitch of the first

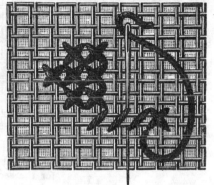

Fig. 155. Plain cross stitch on auxiliary canvas.

return journey, you bring the thread back again to the right for the second row of stitches, which fills by a half cross the spaces left empty by the two first rows of stitches.

Figure 158 shews how you pass to the row beneath. The above mode of working two-sided cross stitch cannot be applied to letters or patterns in broken lines, which both are made up chiefly of isolated stitches.

Figures 159 and 160 explain the course of the stitches in embroidery of this kind.

The working detail A, fig. 159, indicates the spot where the thread should enter the stuff, and the position of the needle for the first stitch; detail B the first half-stitch of the cross completed with an auxiliary stitch to the right, the thread issuing on the right and the position of the needle for

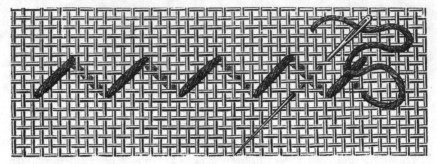

Fig. 156. Two-sided cross stitch worked in four journeys to and fro.
First journey and auxiliary stitch for the return.

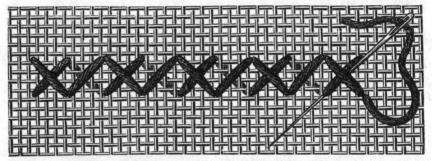

Fig. 157. Two-sided cross stitch worked in four journeys.
First and second journey and first return completed. Auxiliary stitch
for the second return.

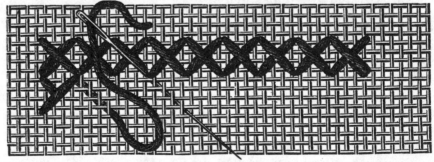

Fig. 158. Two-sided cross stitch worked in four journeys.
Two journeys and two returns completing one row. Beginning of a new row.

the third stitch which completes the cross; detail C shews the stitch begun in B, in its finished state and the position of the needle to reach a stitch on the right : detail D, a cross stitch finished and the beginning of another stitch beneath.

In figure 160, detail E shews how to work stitches to the left ; detail F, an auxiliary stitch to reach an isolated cross stitch on the right, detail G, auxiliary stitches between two isolated cross stitches and detail H, a second and last auxiliary stitch to complete the cross.

It requires both care and practice to do this two-sided marking-stitch so as not to disfigure the stuff by superfluous stitches.

Two-sided Italian cross stitch (figs. 161, 162, 163, 164). — Two-sided Italian stitch consists of cross stitches, alike back

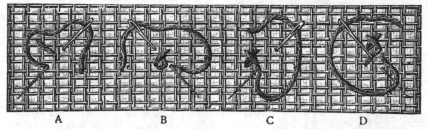

Fig. 159. Different positions of the needle for isolated stitches
in two-sided cross stitch.

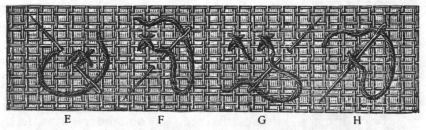

Fig. 160. Different positions of the needle for isolated stitches
in two-sided cross stitch.

and front, divided from each other by horizontal and vertical stitches. The upper and lower stitches should all slope one way as in plain cross stitch. Italian stitch is worked in one journey to and fro. Figure 161 shews how to fasten in the thread and place the needle for the first stitch from right to left ; figure 162, the position of the needle from left to right to form the cross at the back and the vertical stitch to the left, on the right side ; figure 163, the position of the needle for a two-sided horizontal stitch at the bottom of the cross, where upon you proceed as in figure 161. Figure 164 explains the return of the thread which completes the double crosses and the lines between. The vertical lines, not made on the first journey are completed by the stitches of the return journey.

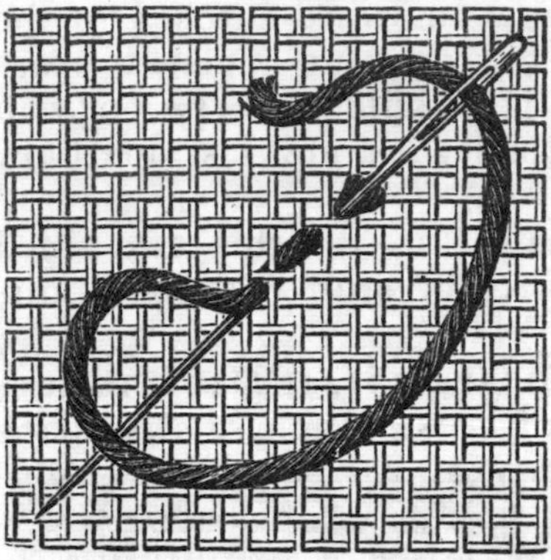

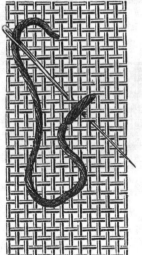

Fig. 161.
Two-sided Italian cross stitch.
Introduction of the thread and position of the needle for the first stitch.

In the next row the horizontal stitches form the top of the stitches of the row below.

To make a last row, pass the needle from left to right under and over the threads of the foundation, starting from the last cross stitch, before passing it under the vertical stitch, shewn in figure 164. This embroidery stitch on a thin stuff, produces an extremely pretty transparent effect, provided only the thread be tightly drawn in the working.

Montenegrin cross stitch (two-sided) (figs. 165, 166, 167). — The Slavs of the S. district of E. Europe, and especially the Montenegrins have a great predilection for this stitch which has been rarely described, till now in books on needlework.

Fig. 162.
Two-sided Italian
cross stitch.
Position of the needle
for the second stitch.

Here again we have cross stitches divided by vertical ones but made on the right side over two oblique threads, whilst on the wrong side we have ordinary cross stitches divided, as on the right side by intermediate vertical ones. Coarse cotton should be used for this work; it produces a richer effect, it covers the threads of stuff better and also the vertical stitch which in the Slav embroideries is entirely hidden between the cross stitches.

Begin, as letter A indicates, in figure 165, with a long slanting-stitch from left to right across 4 horizontal and 8 vertical threads, then, bringing your needle back from right to left under four threads, draw it out, and stick it in again from left to right under the four first threads of the canvas, as shewn in the engraving. These two stitches finished, proceed to the third, indicated by letter B; it crosses the first stitches vertically, after which recommence with the first stitch.

On the wrong side the threads form cross stitches separated by vertical ones and the regular variation in the inclination of the stitches, one cross leaning to the right, the other to the left, produces a charming effect on the wrong side.

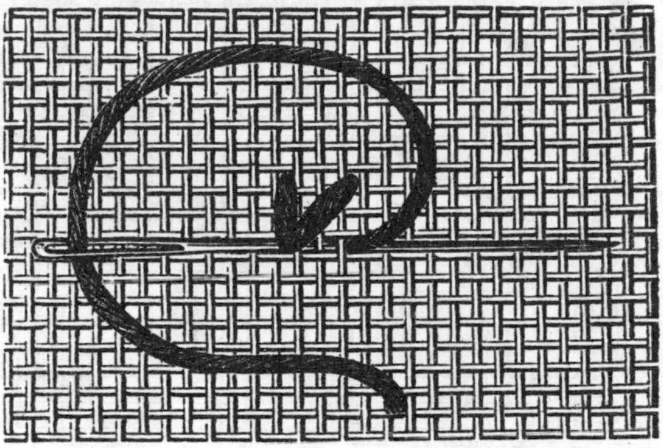

Fig. 163. Two-sided Italian cross stitch. Position of the needle for the third stitch.

Plaited Slav stitch (figs. 168, 169, 170, 171, 172, 173, 174, 175). — Plaited Slav stitch is very like Montenegrin stitch but is easier, and requires less time and attention than ordinary cross stitch. It is generally worked over three and six threads, as seen in figure 168; but if it is to be rounded it must be worked from the outset over an equal number of threads.

For a straight row, the first stitch should be carried over eight vertical threads; but to round the stitch, you must carry your thread over only four threads of the stuff both ways, fig. 169, thus establishing after that, the first setting stitch to the left; which is followed by a half stitch, after which the needle returns to the starting point of the first stitch. In figure 170 the half-stitch is finished and hidden by the next stitches; the fifth stitch which stops at the fifth thread is

Fig. 164.
Two-sided Italian cross stitch.
Second row completing the cross stitch.

begun and the needle is directed obliquely from left to right under three threads of the stuff. In figure 171 the needle comes back to the left in a horizontal direction under four threads

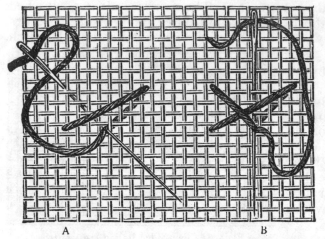

Fig. 165. Two-sided Montenegrin cross stitch. First and second oblique stitches and transverse stitch. Right side

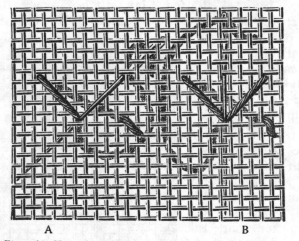

Fig. 166. Two-sided Montenegrin cross stitch. First and second oblique stitches and transverse stitch. Wrong side.

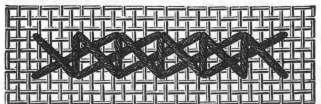

Fig. 167. Two-sided Montenegrin cross stitch. Series of finished stitches.

so that the right setting-stitch is finished as you pass to the stitch above. In figure 172 the needle passes vertically downwards under four threads, then, following the direction indicated by the arrow, it passes in an oblique direction over two threads and comes back under two. Figure 173 shews the position of the needle for the vertical setting-stitch and the dotted line marking one cross stitch and one long stitch to form the plait.

Figure 174 shews a circle completed, with setting-stitches all round.

Plaited Slav stitch can also be worked obliquely and can then be adapted to waved broken lines and stalks of leaves and flowers.

Figure 175 shews how this stitch is worked obliquely over two threads.

Plaited Algerian stitch (fig. 176). — The distinguishing feature of this stitch is that it only advances one or two threads at a time. It should be begun on an uneven number of threads and like the Greek and Slav stitches looks best

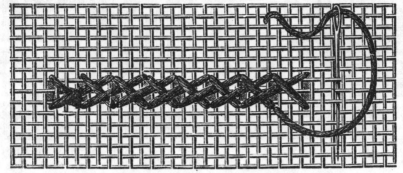

Fig. 168. Plaited Slav stitch.
Worked in horizontal line.

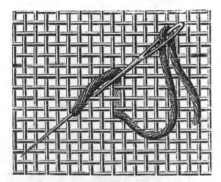

Fig. 169. Plaited Slav stitch.
Left setting-stitch.
The half-stitch for the return and po-·
sition of the needle for the next stitch.

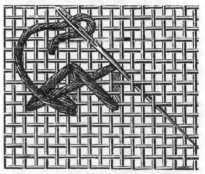

Fig. 170. Plaited Slav stitch.
Position of the needle
for the half-stitch and for the right
setting-stitch.

worked with coarse cotton. The rows may touch either at the top or the bottom of the stitch, so long as you keep to one plan throughout.

Two-sided plaited Spanish stitch (figs. 177 and 178). — This stitch has the advantage of being not only very effective, but also very quickly executed and is therefore to be recommended where the object is to produce a certain effect with a relatively small expenditure of trouble and time.

It is worked in two rows forwards and backwards. All cross stitch patterns can be worked in Spanish stitch, only the gaps left by the long stitches have to be filled in with short ones. In itself, the stitch consists of slanting-stitches

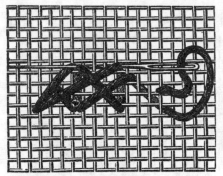

Fig. 171. Plaited Slav stitch.
Setting-stitch to the right and position of the needle for a setting-stitch at the top.

Fig. 172. Plaited Slav stitch.
Position of the needle for returning to the lower row and dotted line marking the right half-stitch.

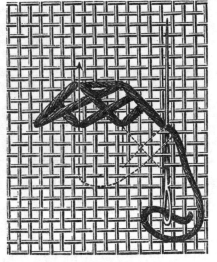

Fig. 173. Plaited Slav stitch.
Right setting-stitch and beginning of a second row of stitches.

Fig. 174. Plaited Slav stitch.
Berry encircled with setting-stitches.

over five and three threads, three threads apart. Figures 177 and 178 explain the manner of working this stitch, which will be found both pleasant and easy to do. In certain imitation Oriental carpets worked on coarse linen we meet with this stitch, only the threads are much closer than in Spanish stitch proper (see the chapter on "Tapestry", knitting stitch, fig. 375).

Two-sided line stitch (figs. 179 and 180). — Square stitch, Holbein stitch, line or stroke stitch as it is sometimes called, and setting-stitch, are all worked on similar principles.

Though all these two-sided stitches are related to each other and by no means difficult of execution, any one new to the kind of work will find a little practice necessary to make the stitches follow in their proper order.

Figure 179 explains how the needle has to pass alternately and step by step over and under the threads of the stuff and figure 180

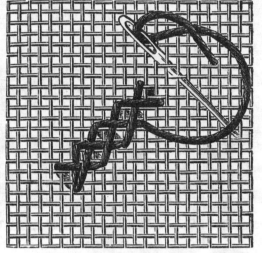

Fig. 175. Plaited Slav stitch.
Worked in oblique line.

how, the threads left uncovered in going, are successively covered in returning.

The great difficulty is how to place your first row of stitches so as to ensure an unbroken course back. You will do well before setting out to study what will be the most direct course back so that you may not come to a stand-still, or be obliged to make extra stitches on the wrong side. If you have to pass obliquely across the stuff, as patterns often

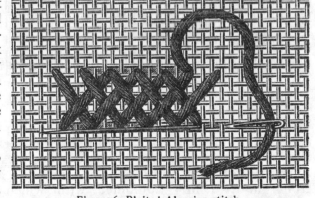

Fig. 176. Plaited Algerian stitch.

necessitate, pursue the same course as though you were covering the straight threads of a material.

Triangular two-sided Turkish stitch (figs. 181, 182, 183, 184, 185). — Amongst the many pretty stitches which distinguish the Turkish embroideries, there is one in particular, apparently very difficult but really not at all so. Although it resembles line stitch upon straight threads, in the Oriental embroideries we find it generally worked in diagonal lines and each row requires two journeys to and fro.

In the first, fig. 181, the needle always passes over and under two vertical and two horizontal threads in a diagonal line. Returning you pass the needle under the stuff and the stitch on the right, bring it out at the bottom of the stitch, make a slanting back-stitch upwards, over two horizontal and two vertical threads, pass the needle horizontally over two threads to the left, bring it out again near the upper stitch, re-insert it near the

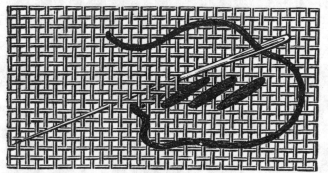

Fig. 177. Two-sided plaited Spanish stitch.
First row.

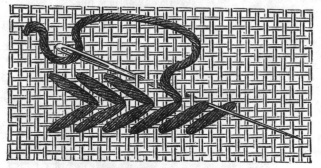

Fig. 178. Two-sided plaited Spanish stitch.
Second row.

lower stitch thus forming a second slanting-stitch, when you carry your thread to the bottom of the vertical stitch. Four threads always meet in the hole made by the needle. The third and fourth round should be worked in a different colour from the two first combined with which they form one complete row of stitches.

Figures 183 to 185 illustrate the same stitch worked in straight lines.

In figure 185 the dark thread shews the two first rounds, the light one the third and fourth.

One-sided insertion (figs. 186, 187, 188, 189, 190). — Beginning with a plain cross stitch, made over three threads both ways, direct your needle upwards and pass it, three threads above the first stitch, under the same number of threads of the stuff, fig. 186. Then, returning to the line of the first stitch, pass the needle under six threads, fig. 187, and make another cross stitch, after which add another stitch downwards, figs. 188 and 189, followed again by a cross stitch, after which you begin the series of stitches over again, as in figure 186.

Fig. 179. Two-sided line stitch.
First row.

Figure 190 shews a piece of the insertion in its original size, worked in D.M.C Special stranded cotton (Mouliné spécial). (*)

Two-sided insertion with the wrong side in square stitch (figs. 191, 192, 193, 194, 195, 196, 197). — Figure 191 explains the first stitch and the passage

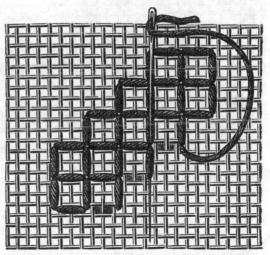

Fig. 180. Two-sided line stitch.
Second row.

(*) See at the end of the last chapter the tables of the sizes and colours of the cotton, flax and silk articles, mark D.M.C. — The French names, in brackets, are those stamped on the labels of the D.M.C articles.

of the thread from left to right, under three vertical and three horizontal threads, as well as the second stitch to the left over six threads, and the position of the needle for beginning the third stitch. Figures 192 and 193 shew the second and third stitch finished, the course of the fourth and the return of the needle for the next one; figure 194, the first horizontal stitch below over six threads and the return stitch under three, figure 195, the eleventh stitch finished and the next step for the twelfth. Figure 196 shews a series of stitches on the right side, and figure 197 the same on the wrong side, presenting quite a different appearance from the right side, but which goes quite well with any two-sided embroidery.

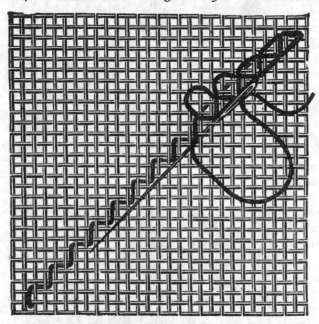

Fig. 181. Triangular two-sided Turkish stitch
worked diagonally.
First journey forward and first return forming a half-row
of stitches.

These insertions can be worked on any kind of stuff, only the stitches require to be made both ways over a number of threads divisible by three, for instance, over six, nine or twelve threads, you will find it impracticable over eight, ten or fourteen.

Insertion in button-hole stitches (fig. 198). — Begin by making a button-hole stitch upwards, over four threads, and distant six threads from the point where the needle came out, and draw it up right; then make a similar stitch downwards, so that the two meet in the same hole. After making five such stitches upwards and downwards, jump six threads of the stuff, and begin another group of button-hole stitches like the first.

Different hems for embroideries (figs. 199, 200, 201, 202). — Coloured embroideries can be finished off not only by openwork hems, but also by hems ornamented with various kinds of stitches, and even when the stuff has a good selvedge the stitches can be made over that.

If you wish to copy the two kinds of stitches shewn in figures 199 and 200 along a cut edge, prepare a rolled hem in a fine material and a flat hem in a coarser one. This done, make three button-hole stitches at a little distance from each other — in figure 199 they are two threads apart. — Then jumping twice the number of threads you left between the stitches, make the next group. In figure 200 the ornamentation of the hem consists of two stitches the width of the hem — if there be one — both in the same hole, and two longer ones four threads apart from the others and followed by three pair of the shorter stitches, four threads apart as before.

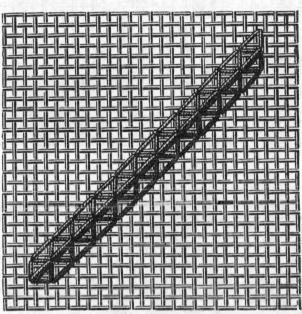

Fig. 182. Triangular two-sided Turkish stitch
worked diagonally.
Two journeys to and fro, forming the complete row.

Another hem, quite as original and pretty is shewn in figures 201 and 202. Begin by rolling up about ⅔ of an inch of the edge as tightly as the stuff will allow, then bring your thread forward from the back and skipping nine threads make nine stitches one thread apart from each other, drawing up each tightly and making them lie quite close side by side. It is advisable to draw out a thread along the hem so as to get the stitches in a perfectly straight line. The stuff must be entirely covered by the stitches, this will

be best attained by using a loose thread, such as D.M.C
Special stranded cotton (Mouliné spécial), D.M.C Floss flax
or flourishing thread (Lin floche) or D.M.C Persian silk
(Soie de. Perse). (*)

Gothic border in cross stitch (fig. 2o3). — We are in-
debted for this pretty pattern quite Gothic in character to
a visit we paid to the National museum at Munich, where we discovered it amongst a heap of old things thrown aside on one side as rubbish.

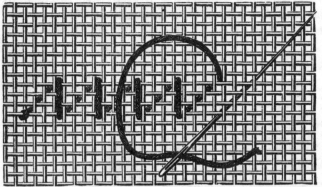

Fig. 183.
Triangular two sided Turkish stitch worked horizontally.
First journey.

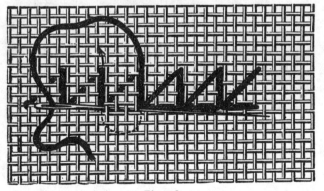

Fig. 184.
Triangular two-sided Turkish stitch worked horizontally.
First journey back.

Its simple graceful out-lines renders it peculiarly suitable for the decoration of table covers, bed spreads, curtains, towels and such like. It should be finished off with a deep fringe, made with the threads of the stuff itself or with a heavy knotted fringe. (See chapters headed "Macramé" and "Needlework Trimmings".

The design may be worked in one shade of colour or in

(*) See at the end of the last chapter the tables of the sizes and colours of
the cotton, flax and silk articles, mark D.M.C. — The French names, in brackets,
are those stamped on the labels of the D.M.C articles.

two, as in figure 203, where all the outside cross stitches are in the darker shade.

Cross stitch border. Chinese subject (fig. 204). — This which formed the border of some richly embroidered Chinese hangings is an

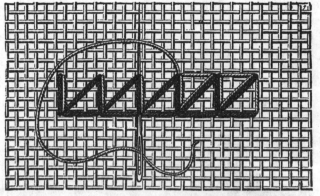

Fig. 185. Triangular two-sided Turkish stitch worked horizontally.
First and second forward journeys and first return journey completed and second return in course of execution.

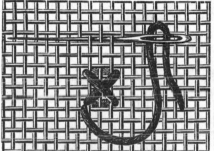

Fig. 186. One-sided insertion.
First cross stitch and position of the needle for the upper stitch.

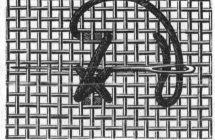

Fig. 187. One-sided insertion.
Position of the needle for finishing the upper stitch and returning to the cross stitch.

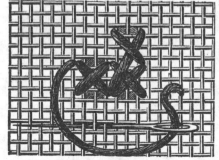

Fig. 188. One-sided insertion.
Second cross stitch finished and position of the needle for the lower stitch.

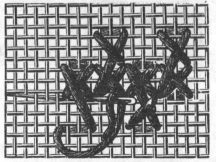

Fig. 189. One-sided insertion.
Series of stitches finished and position of the needle for returning to the cross stitch.

interesting subject sure to be appreciated by our readers. For
want of space this pattern is given in two pieces; see the
points of junction at A and B. We recommend it as very
suitable for chair backs and the like. It should be worked on
slightly tinted canvas in three distinct shades of blue. The
work may be edged with a narrow pillow lace.

**Powdering and border in cross and line stitch.
Albanian subjects** (figs. 205 and 206). — These two pretty

designs, of
Albanian ori-
gin, are dis-
tinguished for
their harmon-
ious colouring
and the charm-
ing distribu-
tion of shades.

Fig. 190. One-sided insertion.

A purple red is the leading note, sub-ordinate to it are a
dark blue and a pale green, interspersed with single stitches
here and there in bright yellow and old gold colour.

In the powdering, fig. 205, the flowers of every alternate
diagonal row are worked in red, with decorative stitches in green

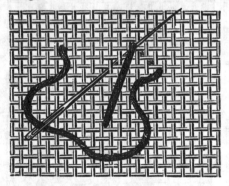

Fig. 191. Two-sided insertion with
the wrong side in square stitch.
First stitch finished and position of the
needle for the second stitch.

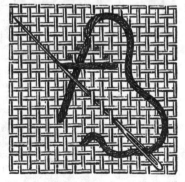

Fig. 192. Two-sided insertion with
the wrong side in square stitch.
Second stitch finished and position
of the needle for the third stitch.

or blue. In the rows between the flowers are alternately worked
in green or blue, the decorative stitches in red and throughout
four stitches of a bright yellow form the centre of the flower.

In figure 206 which serves as border to the above foundation, yellow and old gold are only introduced into the stalks

of the conventional flowers which, with the cross between them, form a square.

These squares are separated from the lower border by a narrow insertion three cross stitches in height, which may also be re-placed by long vertical stitches, over a corresponding number of threads. This straight band is bordered top and bottom by a row of back-stitches. The colours used for the powdering alternate in the band, and above and below is a waved line of stroke stitches.

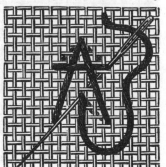

Fig. 193.
Two-sided insertion with the wrong side in square stitch.
Third stitch finished and position of the needle for the fourth stitch.

These two patterns seem intended for a table-cover trimming. The border with the sprays, fig. 206, should go all round the cloth and the centre be filled with the powdering, fig. 205.

To simplify the work the centre may be divided from the border by a stripe of dark velvet or silk and another stripe of the same added to the outside border instead of the worked border of sprays.

Cross stitch border. Greek subject (fig. 207). — Plain and compact figures such as the plait stitch, figure 207, lend themselves best to this design. All the dark lines are worked in Black fast dye 310; the leaves in the form of steps, up to the beginning of the stalks, marked by the change in the direction of the stitches, are worked one in light red, the other in dark, with the result that two light leaves and two dark ones always face each other. In the original the cross bars that connect the leaves are in yellow, whilst the detached figures that separate them, are in pale blue.

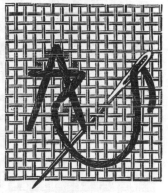

Fig. 194.
Two-sided insertion with the wrong side in square stitch.
Fourth stitch finished and position of the needle for the fifth stitch.

The outside part of the figure is filled in with yellow stitches, only the double cross stitches, should all be worked in plain gold, or, if preferred, in Gold chiné green and gold. The S S in the narrow outside border should be worked in two shades of blue; the outside stitches in dark blue and light blue for filling in. The little figures with transverse bars that unite the S S should be alternately set in black and filled in with light red, and set in dark red and filled in with yellow. Owing to the limited choice of types at our disposal the dark red and dark blue are represented by the same kind of cross, that is to say by medium ones.

We can recommend this pattern as spe-cially suitable as a trimming for articles of dress; in which case it should be worked

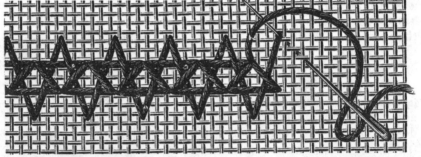

Fig. 195. Two-sided insertion with the wrong side in square stitch.
Series of stitches finished and position of the needle for the twelfth stitch.

Fig 196. Two-sided insertion with the wrong side in square stitch.
Right side.

Fig. 197. Two-sided insertion with the wrong side in square stitch.
Wrong side.

on a linen braid or a stripe of canvas, as being so much more convenient to handle.

Corners in stroke stitch (figs. 208 and 209). — These pretty little subjects can be used for the decoration of ladies and childrens' collars, fine pocket handkerchiefs and finger napkins for afternoon tea, and may be worked in one or two colours, according to taste. If two colours be preferred the

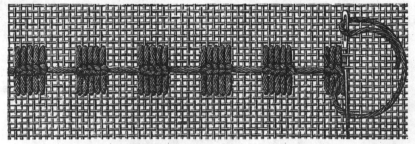

Fig. 198. Insertion in button-hole stitches.

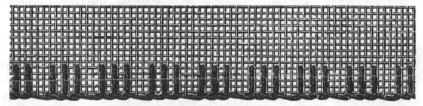

Fig. 199. Selvedge or hem ornamented with single button-hole stitches.

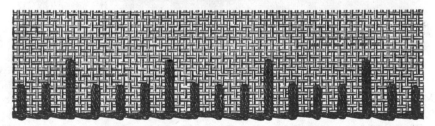

Fig. 200. Selvedge or hem ornamented with double button-hole stitches.

inside should be done in the lighter, the little outside edge in the darker shade, as shewn in the engravings.

Border in stroke stitch (fig. 210). — This is copied from a charming piece of Italian work, though, judging from a resemblance in the different subjects to the rose, the thistle and the shamrock it might have been supposed to be of English origin. The original must evidently have been worked in a most brilliant purple red, toned down by time to the

colour of Rust yellow 3o8, or Rust brown 3314 of the D.M.C
colour card.

Seeing the harmonious effect produced by the faded red
on the white linen, we specially recommend one or other of
the above mentioned shades as being the only ones which
will give the new work anything like the refined distinguished
appearance of the old embroidery. If this pattern be used as
a border for a side board or dresser cover it would look well
finished off with a wide border of openwork chosen from the chapter on "Open-
work on Linen".

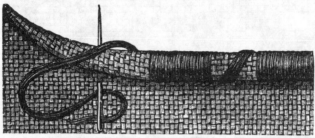

Fig. 201. Rolled and ornamented hem.
Detail magnified.

**Grounding in
diagonal lines
worked in
back-stitch** (fig.
211). — This
pattern can be
worked in two-
sided stroke
stitch, or in plain
cross stitch.

The original
piece from which
our pattern is
copied is done
in back-stitch
in a very loose
thread. As this
pattern, worked
on a stouter
stuff will work

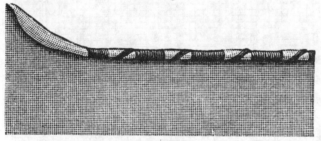

Fig. 202. Rolled and ornamented hem.
Natural size.

out rather large it can only be reproduced on objects of some
size such as cushions and panels and should be worked all in
one colour.

It may be varied by the addition of a second row of
sprays on the upper sides of the diagonal stalks, like those
on the lower sides, turned different ways, so that a leaf
comes above a flower and a flower above a leaf.

Powdering in cross, stroke and star stitch (fig. 212). —
This is a charming combination of cross, stroke and star
stitches, which can be made use of wherever embroidery is
available as a form of decoration.

The cross stitches in which the close parts of the pattern

Fig. 203. Gothic border in cross stitch.
Materials : D.M.C Embroidery cotton, D.M.C Pearl cotton
or D.M.C Floss flax or flourishing thread.
Explanation of the colours : ▓ Blue fast dye 797 or Rust brown 3310,
▧ Blue fast dye 799 or Rust brown 3313. (*)

(*) These numbers refer to the colours on the colour cards of the articles
stamped with the D.M.C trade mark. These cards can be consulted at all the
mercers' and needlework shops.

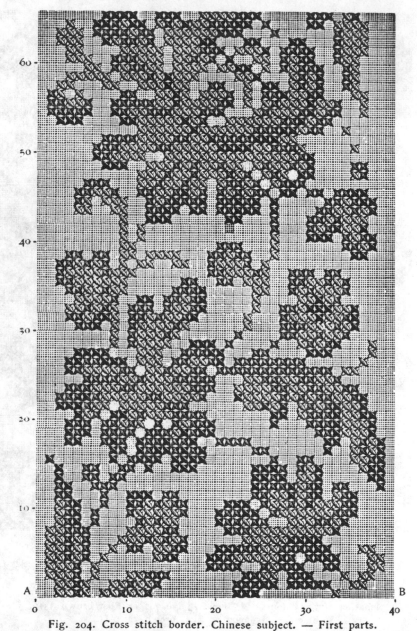

Fig. 204. Cross stitch border. Chinese subject. — First parts.

Materials : D.M.C Embroidery cotton, D.M.C Pearl cotton or D.M.C Floss flax
or flourishing thread.

Explanation of the colours : ✖ Indigo blue 312 or Solid blue 824, ✖ Indigo blue 334
or Solid blue 826, ✖ Azure blue 3325 or Solid blue 827.

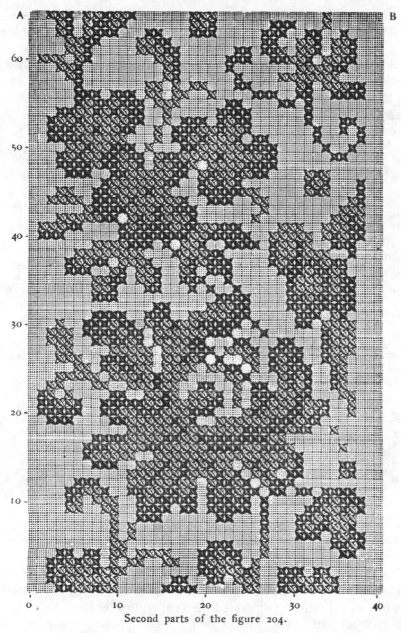

Second parts of the figure 204.

are worked should be in one colour only, the stroke and star stitches in D.M.C Gold chiné (Chiné d'or).

This design can be used as a grounding for a small carpet

or cushion; it should be finished off by a small embroidered border or a band of stuff. For dessert d'oyleys, a single subject only should be used, which should be repeated in each corner.

Border in cross, square and stroke stitch. Wallachian motive (fig. 213). — A piece of Wallachian needlework, exe-

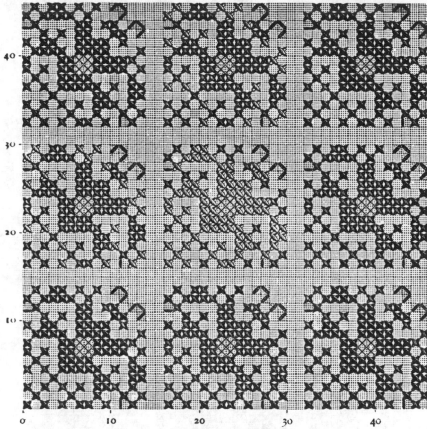

Fig. 205. Powdering in cross and stroke stitch. Albanian subject.
Materials : D.M.C Pearl cotton or D.M.C Floss flax or flourishing thread.
Explanation of the colours : ⊠ Blue fast dye 798, ⊠ Cardinal red 347,
⊠ Moss green 470, ⊠ Saffron yellow 725. (*)

cuted on rough hand-woven linen, and uncommon both in colour and design, suggested the charming embroidery here represented. In place of the somewhat crude colours of the

(*) See at the end of the last chapter the tables of the sizes and colours of the cotton, flax and silk articles, mark D.M.C.

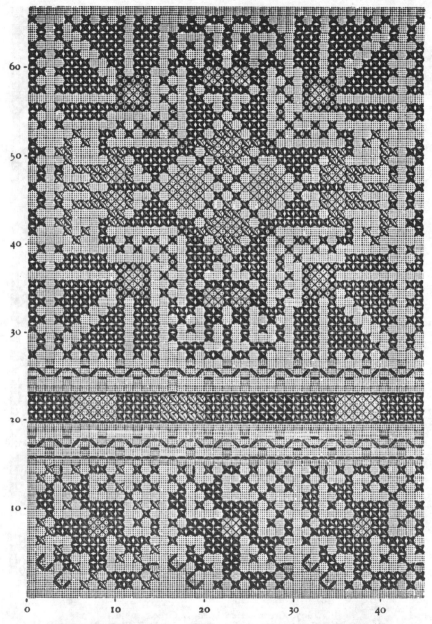

Fig. 206. Border in cross and stroke stitch. Albanian subject.
Materials : D.M.C Pearl cotton or D.M.C Floss flax or flourishing thread.
Explanation of the colours : ⬛ Blue fast dye 798, ⬛ Cardinal red 347,
⬛ Moss green 470, ⬛ Old gold 728, ⬛ Saffron yellow 725.

Fig. 207. Cross stitch border. Greek subject.
Materials : D.M.C Special stranded cotton or D.M.C Floss flax and D.M.C
Embroidery gold thread.
Explanation of the colours : ✕ Black fast dye 310, ✕ Geranium red 349 and
Indigo blue 312, ✕ Geranium red 352, ✕ Rust yellow 308, ✕ Azure blue 3325,
✳ D.M.C Embroidery gold thread or D.M.C Gold chiné, green and gold.

original, indicative of an uneducated taste we have substituted softer and more refined shades.

The setting in square and stroke stitch is worked in dark red, Cardinal red 346 and green, Yellow green 734.

The fillings in cross stitch should be done alternately in Indigo blue 311, Garnet red 309, Yellow green 734 and Old gold 680.

In our engraving the pattern is worked in cross, square and stroke stitch, and is so easy as to be within the capacity

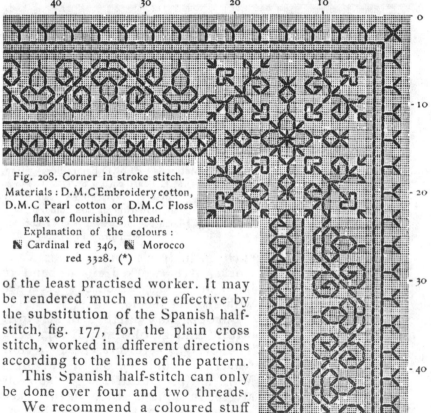

Fig. 203. Corner in stroke stitch.
Materials : D.M.C Embroidery cotton,
D.M.C Pearl cotton or D.M.C Floss
flax or flourishing thread.
Explanation of the colours :
Ⅳ Cardinal red 346, Ⅳ Morocco
red 3328. (*)

of the least practised worker. It may be rendered much more effective by the substitution of the Spanish half-stitch, fig. 177, for the plain cross stitch, worked in different directions according to the lines of the pattern.

This Spanish half-stitch can only be done over four and two threads.

We recommend a coloured stuff for this pattern — red or dark brown — in stripes, which can then be used for trimming curtains or portières, table-covers, panels, &c. These should be made of cloth or plush, the bands of embroidery laid on and bordered, if approved of, by a fancy fringe.

(*) See at the end of the last chapter the tables of the sizes and colours of the cotton, flax and silk articles, mark D.M.C.

Border. Italian design in "point lancé" (fig. 214.) —
The beauty of the Italian designs, worked in "point lancé"
(straight stitch) on fine linen, consists in a happy selection of
colours for the embroidery. In our model the waved line is
worked in golden yellow and the little flowers along it in
ivory white. The little crosses and the little trees are done
alternately in red, green and blue.

We recommend this pattern for trimming articles of dress,

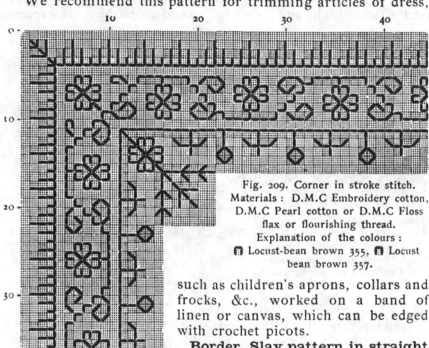

Fig. 209. Corner in stroke stitch.
Materials : D.M.C Embroidery cotton,
D.M.C Pearl cotton or D.M.C Floss
flax or flourishing thread.
Explanation of the colours :
▣ Locust-bean brown 355, ▣ Locust
bean brown 357.

such as children's aprons, collars and
frocks, &c., worked on a band of
linen or canvas, which can be edged
with crochet picots.

**Border. Slav pattern in straight
stitch and stroke stitch** (fig. 215).
The design here presented to our
readers is copied from a cuff of a
Moravian peasant dress. The subjects
are set in square stitch openworked
— explained in the chapter "Open-
work on Linen", fig. 742 — or stroke stitch filled in with
horizontal or vertical "point lancé". The embroidery is worked
in counted stitches on cream linen; the material to be used
is D.M.C Persian silk (Soie de Perse) in yellow and cream.
This may be advantageously replaced by D.M.C Special stranded cotton (Mouliné spécial) and D.M.C Floss flax or flourishing
thread (Lin floche). When this pattern is used to trim articles

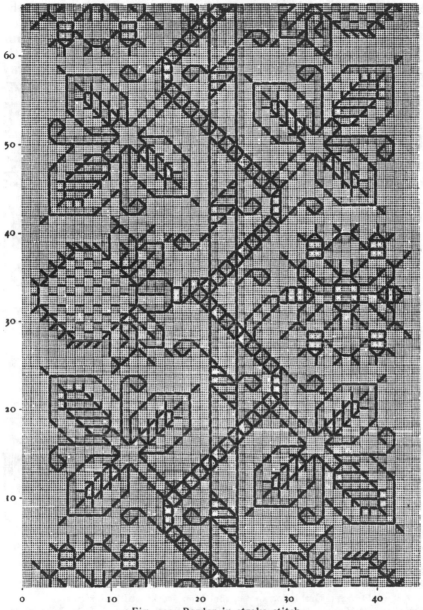

Fig. 210. Border in stroke stitch.
Materials : D.M.C Embroidery cotton, D.M.C Pearl cotton or D.M.C Floss flax or
flourishing thread, in Rust yellow 308, or Rust brown 3314. (*)

(*) See at the end of the last chapter the tables of the sizes and colours of
the cotton, flax and silk articles, mark D.M.C.

of dress, the embroidery should be done directly upon the article itself and not on a band of stuff.

Ground and border in triangular Turkish stitch and "point lancé" (fig. 216). — This pattern which seems particularly suitable for the ornamentation of dessert and tray

Fig. 211. Grounding in diagonal lines worked in back-stitch.
Materials : D.M.C Embroidery cotton, D.M.C Pearl cotton or D.M.C Floss flax
or flourishing thread, in Morocco red 3329 or Lilac grey 314. (*)

(*) See at the end of the last chapter the tables of the sizes and colours of
the cotton, flax and silk articles, mark D.M.C.

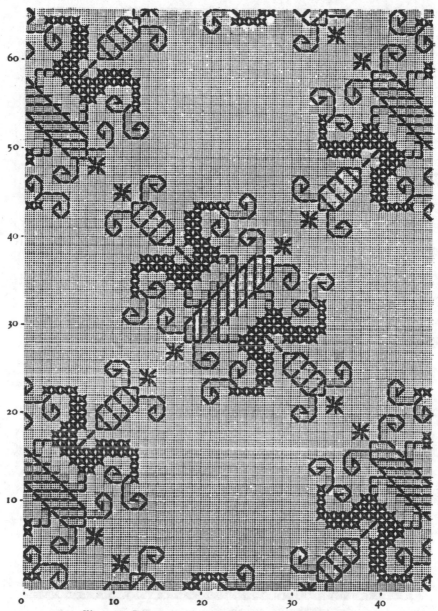

Fig. 212. Powdering in cross, stroke and star stitch.

Materials : D.M.C Pearl cotton, D.M.C Embroidery cotton or D.M.C Floss flax
or flourishing thread and D.M.C Gold chiné.

Explanation of the colours : ✖ Garnet red 326 or Old blue 930, ✳ D.M.C Gold
chiné, blue and gold, or D.M.C Gold chiné, red and gold.

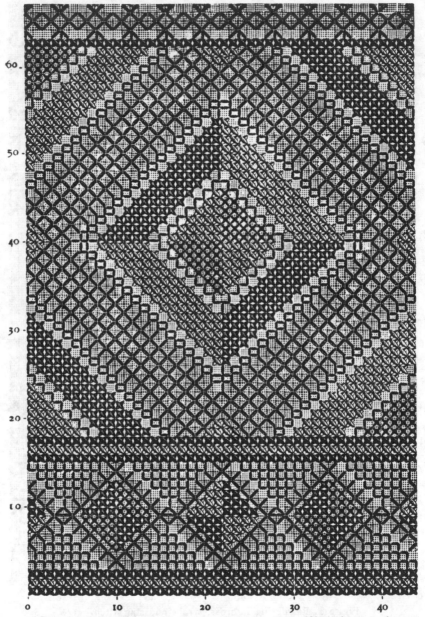

Fig. 213. Border in cross, square and stroke stitch. Wallachian motive.
Materials : D.M.C Special stranded cotton or D.M.C Floss flax.
Explanation of the colours : ✖ Indigo blue 311, ✖ Garnet red 309, ✖ Old gold 680, ✖ ⁄ Yellow green 734, ✖ Cardinal red 346.

d'oyleys, little pincushions and chair-backs of all kinds was copied from an old Turkish shawl, embroidered entirely in gold. The diagonal lines are all worked in D.M.C Gold chiné, gold and blue and gold and red. The triangular Turkish stitch, described in figures 181 to 185 is particularly effective when combined with other kinds of embroidery, as shewn in figure 216 where the Turkish stitch and "point lancé" meet.

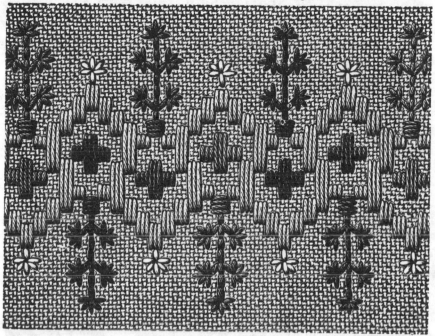

Fig. 214. Border. Italian design in straight stitch.
Materials : D.M.C Persian silk, in Golden yellow 1318, Maize yellow 1069, Moss green 1129, Indigo blue 1011 and Crimson red 1185, or D.M.C Special stranded cotton or D.M.C Floss flax, in Old gold 680, Maize yellow 579, Moss green 470, Indigo blue 334 and Garnet red 326. (*)

The ground is divided into oblique squares; the lines that define them, illustrate the use of the triangular Turkish stitch, worked as explained in figure 182, in two colours, in D.M.C Gold chiné, gold and red and gold and blue.

The insides of the squares number each nine stitches, a tenth is added which is covered by the first stitch of the next side and set behind it. The stalk which separates the two little

(*) See at the end of the last chapter the tables of the sizes and colours of the cotton, flax and silk articles, mark D.M.C.

leaves and is surmounted by a small lozenge, must be begun above the fifth of the nine stitches; you make five stitches, but so as to end above the five stitches with the stitch going obliquely over the threads, turned towards the interior of the stalk, so that the last stitch of the first row forms with the first stitch of the second row a triangle at the top of the stalk.

Taking the two shades of D.M.C Gold chiné, frame a whole row of squares inside with Red chiné and the next with Blue chiné. As regards the lozenges in D.M.C Gold chiné, gold

Fig. 215. Border. Slav pattern in straight stitch and stroke stitch.
Materials : D.M.C Persian silk, in Straw yellow 1262 and Old gold 1168;
or D.M.C Floss flax or D.M.C Special stranded cotton, in Cream yellow 712
and Golden yellow 782.

and écru, which fill the corners and those at the end of the stalk make the first stitch over three threads of the stuff, then increase by two threads at a time, until you reach eleven, and then decrease in the same manner. Coming then to the leaves in D.M.C Gold chiné, gold and green, which rest on both sides against the stalk, you again make a first stitch over three threads of the stuff, increase by one stitch along the stalk, and keep a straight line on the opposite side. After the ninth stitch, over eleven threads of the stuff, you decrease again by one thread at a time on the side kept straight in the first instance; then you add four stitches over three threads only and in the opposite direction to the first part of the leaf.

The border of little dots and zig-zags, which makes such

Fig. 216. Ground and border in triangular Turkish stitch and "point lancé". Materials : D.M.C Gold chiné, in gold and red, gold and blue, gold and écru, gold and green. (*)

a good finish to this pretty pattern, is done in D.M.C Gold chiné, gold and red.

Table-cover in Morocco embroidery (figs. 217, 218, 219, 220). — This kind of work named after the country of its origin, belongs both to the class of darned and damask embroidery.

In working the pattern of the table-cover, represented in figure 217, you skip five threads and take up the sixth; and coming back you take up the third of the five threads, skipped in going, and so on over the whole surface of the

Fig. 217. Table-cover in Morocco embroidery.
Materials: D.M.C Pearl cotton, D.M.C Embroidery cotton, D.M.C Special stranded cotton or D.M.C Floss flax, in Morocco red 3327, Cardinal red 347 or Geranium pink 891. (*)

work, unless the lines of the pattern necessitate a departure from this rule, as, for instance in certain parts of figure 218, where you will notice, the stitches are carried over seven or eight threads; also in the borders figures 219 and 220, where the stitches are arranged in a somewhat arbitrary manner, merely in order to bring out the pattern more clearly.

(*) See at the end of the last chapter the tables of the sizes and colours of the cotton, flax and silk articles, mark D.M.C.

Figure 218 represents a quarter of one of the subjects of which figure 217 is composed.

Four such, joined together, form one of the squares and beginning to work from the middle, you go on to the point where you wish to add one of the two little borders, fig. 219 or 220; for the ground can be enlarged to any size by the addition of more than the four squares shewn here.

Fig. 218. Morocco embroidery.
Quarter of one of the subjects of figure 217.

Most of the linen and cotton stuffs can be used as a foundation for this charming embroidery; the materials must be adapted to the stuff. D.M.C Pearl cotton (Coton perlé) is only suitable for coarse fabrics, whilst D.M.C Special stranded cotton (Mouliné spécial) and D.M.C Floss flax (Lin floche), single strands of which can be used if desired, are better suited for the finer fabrics.

Border in Persian embroidery (figs. 221, 222, 223, 224). — Persian embroidery, executed in several colours on a foun- dation of fine linen is always characterised by dark outlines in square and stroke stitch. The insides of the figures are covered with filling stitches which give the effect of a coloured

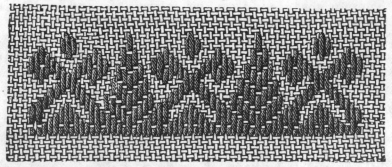

Fig. 219. Morocco embroidery.
Small outside border of figure 217.

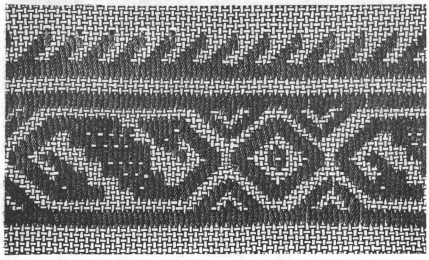

Fig. 220. Morocco embroidery.
Border and insertion suitable for bordering figure 217.

stuff. Embroidery of this kind requires infinite care and minute- ness but when finished the effect amply repays the worker for the trouble bestowed upon it.

For the border, fig. 221, begin by making the outlines in black silk, and then fill in the foundation with the stitch explained in figure 222.

Fig. 221. Border in Persian embroidery.
Materials : D.M.C Persian silk, D.M.C Special stranded cotton or D.M.C Floss flax
or flourishing thread.

This stitch is worked in one round to and fro. Begin by a horizontal stitch over five threads of the stuff, take up the sixth thread, skip five and so on. Coming back finish the stitch by making in the same way horizontal stitches over five threads with one thread between, only they must be set inversely.

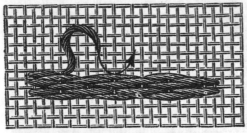

Fig. 222. Filling stitch used for Border figure 221.

Note further that in coming back you must insert the needle quite close to the stitches of the first row. Having finished the first double round, miss one thread upwards of the stuff and begin the next round, and so on until the whole figure is filled.

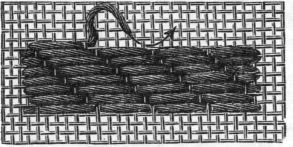

Fig. 223. Another filling stitch with horizontal stitches in oblique lines.

As may be seen from the engraving of the border, the filling stitch is worked sometimes in horizontal sometimes in vertical lines, according to the spaces to be filled.

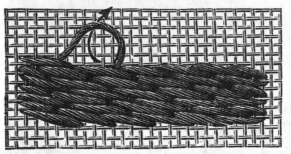

Fig. 224. Filling stitch with oblique encroaching stitches.

For the colouring we recommend Bronze green 1094 and Cinnamon brown 1152 for the big dark figures or the border and Greenish grey 1178 and Old gold 1168 for the centres of these figures; the four little squares inside the intermediate figures are filled in with Greenish grey 1178 and Havana brown 1081, the light triangles above and below with Maize yellow 1069, the little detached leaves in Scabious violet 1230.

The ground of the wide middle border is worked in Indigo blue 1010, the ground of the narrow borders at the edge in Old gold 1168. The little figures in these narrow borders are worked alternately in Scabious violet 1230, Greenish grey 1178 and Bronze green 1094.

This kind of border with a less elaborate ground is very suitable for trimming carpets, cushions or panels.

In figures 223 and 224 we give two other filling stitches, met with likewise in Persian embroideries.

The stitch, fig. 223, is composed of horizontal stitches over five threads of the stuff, with one thread between ; in the next

Fig. 225. Border embroidered in straight stitch with rows of openwork between. Materials : D.M.C Pearl cotton or D.M.C Floss flax, white. (*)

rows, the stitch advances to the right by one thread, so that the ground forms a pattern composed of oblique stripes.

Figure 224 entirely covers the stuff of the foundation. It consists of horizontal rows of oblique encroaching stitches. It is worked like the other in horizontal rows over six vertical and one horizontal threads, then you come back diagonally under two threads and repeat the stitch above described.

(*) See at the end of the last chapter the tables of the sizes and colours of the cotton, flax and silk articles, mark D.M.C.

Stitches of the same kind are described in the chapter on "Netting", see figs. 725 to 727.

Border embroidered in straight stitch with rows of openwork between (fig. 225). — This border, of Hungarian

Fig. 226. Border in Bulgarian embroidery in straight stitch.
Materials : D.M.C Pearl cotton, D.M.C Special stranded cotton or D.M.C Floss flax, in Cardinal red 304, Solid blue 826, Beetle green 3347 and Rust brown 3314. (*)

(*) See at the end of the last chapter the tables of the sizes and colours of the cotton, flax and silk articles, mark D.M.C.

origin, formed the trimming to an unbleached linen sheet; the embroidery itself was worked in white linen thread. The square openwork stitch, which divides the band into squares and triangles, is described in the chapter on "Openwork on Linen", see fig. 743.

The triangles, are filled with a half-star in straight stitch and a band of little squares left blank.

Inside the squares is a star in straight stitch, with the rays done in double back-stitch; whilst the space round the stars is filled with eight little squares.

To complete the band, add above and below a little row of openwork, chosen from the chapter already referred to.

Worked in white on white, this kind of embroidery is used for trimming bed-linen; in white on a unbleached or yellowish ground, for table-linen.

Border in Bulgarian embroidery in straight stitch (fig. 226). — The Bulgarians make the aprons and bags which form part of their national costume of a coloured stuff, handwoven by themselves. The charming patterns of these handwoven stuffs can easily be reproduced in embroidery. Figure 226 represents one of these borders, copied from a bag, and reproduced in embroidery in straight stitch on linen. It may be used to trim bags, cushions, hassocks, &c. Our model is worked in vertical « point lancé », over four threads of the stuff, in four colours.

The darkest shade in the engraving represents dark blue, the medium one, red, the light one, green, and the lightest of all, yellow.

Embroidery on linen done on a traced pattern. — For embroidery done independently of the threads of the stuff which forms the foundation, the pattern must first be transferred to the stuff.

According to the character of the design the outlines alone may be embroidered, or the different subjects filled in, or both.

In the case of merely outlining the pattern, one or other of the stitches most resembling a cord or a braid should be selected, unless a crochet or knotted cord or woven braid be preferred.

If the pattern is to be entirely covered you have a large number of stitches to choose from, all fitted for the purpose, namely, flat stitch or straight stitch, the varieties of cross stitch, known as Russian stitch, or Mossoul stitch, Roman stitch, fish-bone stitch, &c.

The patterns with embroidered outlines and fillings combine every kind of stitch as the following engravings will show.

Quite a different kind of embroidery is that known as Maltese, where the pattern is formed by a succession of little tufts or balls.

Materials. — For raised stem stitch and chain stitch, &c., use a moderately twisted thread, such as D.M.C Pearl cotton

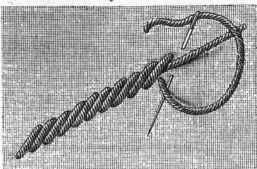

Fig. 227. Raised stem stitch.

(Coton perlé), D.M.C Embroidery cotton (Coton à broder), in some cases, as for instance, for pearl stitch, D.M.C Crochet cotton 6 cord (Cordonnet 6 fils), or D.M.C Knotting cotton (Fil à pointer). For flat stitch, crossed back-stitching and other filling stitches take loose thread, such as D.M.C Special stranded cotton (Mouliné spécial), D.M.C Darning cotton (Coton à repriser), D.M.C Floss flax (Lin floche) or D.M.C Persian silk (Soie de Perse). (*)

Rich patterns sometimes require the introduction of metal threads; in this case use either the D.M.C Embroidery Gold or Silver threads (Or et Argent fins)

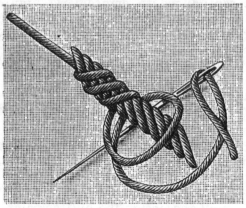

Fig. 228. Another kind of raised stem stitch.

and D.M.C Gold chiné (Chiné d'or).

Stitches. — The stitch most often used in linen embroidery, on a traced pattern, is flat stitch, done like white embroidery — embroidery in raised satin stitch — with the only difference that it is done without any preliminary padding.

(*) See at the end of the last chapter the tables of the sizes and colours of the cotton, flax and silk articles, mark D.M.C. — The French names, in brackets, are those stamped on the labels of the D.M.C articles.

In the chapter on "Embroidery upon White Stuff", fig. 72, we described raised stem stitch. The same chapter contains a description of crossed back-stitching, see figs. 74 and 75.

We subjoin here an explanation of a series of stitches which may be used either for outlines or fillings.

Raised stem stitch (figs. 227 and 228). — Take a very thick thread, such as D.M.C Pearl cotton (Coton perlé) No. 3, or the coarser numbers of D.M.C Crochet cotton 6 cord (Cordonnet 6 fils), lay it as foundation thread along the line of your pattern and work over it wide slanting stem stitches, fig. 70, either in the same number of thread used for the

  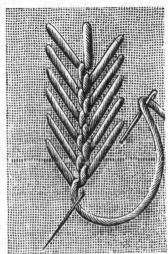

Fig. 229.	Fig. 230.	Fig. 231.
Chain stitch.	Chain stitch overcast.	Fish-bone stitch.

foundation thread, or a finer one, according to the stuff you are embroidering upon.

You may overcast the same stitch in the manner shewn in figure 228; using a coloured thread for the second layer of stitches; this produces an agreeable variety.

Chain stitch (fig. 229). — After bringing out your thread at a fixed point, insert the needle again at the same place, leaving a little loop on the right side of the stuff, and bring it out 3 or 4 threads distant from the first stitch.

Hold the loop of thread with the left thumb and slip it under the point of the needle, then draw up the thread and the stitch is finished. You next re-insert the needle at the hole where the thread last came out, form the loop and so on; the last loop is secured by a back-stitch.

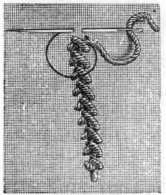

Fig. 232.
Beaded or knotted stitch.

This stitch is used in place of stem stitch for small subjects which are merely outlined, or for outlining bigger ones filled in with flat stitch or in some other way.

We shall have frequent occasion to revert to this kind of stitch.

Chain stitch overcast (fig. 230). — After finishing the chain stitch as just described overcast it with a coloured thread at each loop of the chain without taking up the stuff beneath, see fig. 230. The effect produced is that of a round cord.

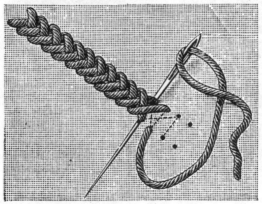

Fig. 233. Basket stitch on linen.

Fish-bone stitch (fig. 231). — This stitch is very like feather stitch, see fig. 46, consisting also of two button-hole stitches, one to the right and one to the left; only the stitches are much longer towards the outside, and the inside threads form a vertical vein instead of an undulating line. In linen embroidery this stitch is most often used as a filling for leaves, which it is particularly well adapted for because of the veining obtained.

Fig. 234.
Roman stitch.

Beaded or knotted stitch (fig. 232). — This is a stitch often met with in old church and house-linen embroidery.

Contrary to most stitches, it is worked upwards, the needle is put in horizontally under the stuff, the thread tightly drawn, then laid from left to right and drawn through underneath the first stitch following the direction of the arrow and a tight knot made. We meet with the same stitch, worked in a variety of ways, according to the taste and skill of the worker; for instance, the knots may be set slanting, or else straight and very close together when they present the appearance of a close string of beads, or again wide apart.

All these ways are admissible but care must be taken in each case, to make the stitches perfectly regular. It is only the direction which is given to the stitch and the number of threads taken up with the needle that changes the appearance of the stitch.

Basket stitch on linen (fig. 233). — This stitch has some resemblance with plait stitch, fig. 168, and with the Montenegrin, fig. 167, only that it is not crossed by a vertical stitch like the latter. Basket stitch can be worked on all kinds of stuffs, on counted threads, or on a wide or narrow tracing, with fine or coarse thread, and more or less closely, according to taste.

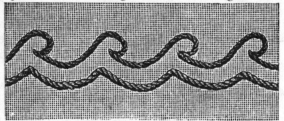

Fig. 235. Border in stem stitch. .
Materials: D.M.C Pearl cotton, D.M.C Embroidery cotton or D.M.C Floss flax or flourishing thread, in Turkish red 321 and Black fast dye 310. (*)

Fig. 236. Border in single chain stitch.
Materials: D.M.C Pearl cotton, D.M.C Embroidery cotton or D.M.C Floss flax or flourishing thread, in Locust-bean brown 303 and Cornflower blue 792.

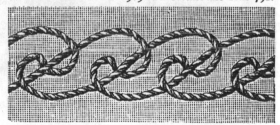

Fig. 237. Border in chain stitch with overcast stitches.
Materials: D.M.C Pearl cotton, D.M.C Embroidery cotton or D.M.C Floss flax or flourishing thread, in Locust-bean brown 303, Cornflower blue 792, and Rust brown 3314. (*)

You insert the needle, make a slanting-stitch downwards from left to right, and according to the stuff and material

(*) See at the end of the last chapter the tables of the sizes and colours of the cotton, flax and silk articles, mark D.M.C.

you are using, passing under 3 to 6 threads of the stuff, then coming back to the right, make at the line a second slanting stitch upwards of the same width as the first, then a third starting from the same hole as the first stitch downwards to the right, then a stitch upwards and so on. The dotted line in the engraving indicates clearly the course of the stitches.

Roman stitch (fig. 234). — This consists of stitches that are worked in the width of the stuff, intersected by back-stitches set slightly slanting.

Fig. 238. Flowers in flat stitch.
Materials : D.M.C Embroidery cotton, D.M.C Pearl cotton, D.M.C Floss flax or flourishing thread, in Scarlet 815 and Saffron yellow 725.

Though the engraving is so clear as to render it hardly necessary we subjoin an exact description of the way the stitches should run.

Bring out the needle on the left, 2 or 3 threads beyond the line your embroidery is to take, letting yourself be guided with regard to the number of threads you take up by the quality and nature of the stuff and the material you have selected : put the needle in on the right, the same distance in advánce

of the line as before and bring it out in the middle of the
width of the stitch, then passing the needle over the first
stitch, put it in again one or two threads in advance of the
hole where it came out, and draw it out close to where the
first stitch began.

Three little borders in different stitches (figs. 235, 236,
237). — We give here three little borders intended for trimming

Fig. 239. Border and flower in flat stitch, stem stitch and chain stitch.
Materials : D.M.C Pearl cotton, in Black fast dye 310, Scarlet 498, Golden
yellow 783, Indigo blue 322 and Maize yellow 579.

small tea-napkins, aprons and dresses, which represent the
kind of pattern called line designs.

Figure 235 represents a small band executed in stem
stitch in two shades of colour, figure 236 another design
in single chain stitch and figure 237 the same in overcast
chain stitch.

Flowers in flat stitch (fig. 238). — This flower represents the kind of embroidery known as Hungarian. The Hungarian peasants use it to ornament their clothing and their house-linen.

The foundation is of fine linen, the embroidery bright red with occasional leaves in gold colour. The direction of the stitches is clearly shewn in the engraving, the embroidery needs no further explanations.

This kind of flower, repeated along a waved line, or used as a corner ornament, is specially adapted for the adornment of table or house-linen, but it can also be used for cushion covers, aprons, &c.

Fig. 240. Border in Servian embroidery.
Materials: D.M.C Pearl cotton No 12, in Indigo blue 311, Cardinal red 347 and Pistachio green 319, and D.M.C Embroidery gold thread No. 20. (*)

Border and flower in flat, stem and chain stitch (fig. 239). — This is a specimen of the kind of embroidery by the Moravian peasants used for trimming their cuffs, shawls and caps; it should be worked in red, black, yellow, blue and cream, the characteristic colours of the embroideries of that country. The work is done on dark blue linen.

You begin with the overcast eyelet-holes done with yellow thread, then you do the petals of the flowers in flat stitch in red, the up-turned scalloped leaves and the two small leaves at the bottom of the stalk are worked in cream. In the border blue flowers with black centres alternate with red flowers with blue centres and yellow leaves with cream. Having finished the flat stitch you do the fillings.

The apple itself as well as the heart below are framed

(*) See at the end of the last chapter the tables of the sizes and colours of the cotton, flax and silk articles, mark D.M.C.

with, alternately, run and chain stitches, in red; the inside of the apple in black; all the other parts in run and chain stitch of the flower and the border are embroidered in yellow, excepting the veins of the yellow leaf in the border which are in blue.

The eyelet-holes in the flowers are encircled by three rows of chain stitches in black. Two rows of chain stitches — blue and black — finish off the border at the top and three rows — blue, yellow and black finish it off at the bottom. For working the chain stitch, see fig. 229.

Border in Servian embroidery (fig. 240 . — The peasant women of Croatia often weave their aprons of coloured threads mixed with gold and silver thread. As a specimen of design we give the border figure 240, which was worked with D.M.C Pearl cotton (Coton perlé) in red, blue and green, and with gold thread and gold spangles. The setting of each lozenge consists of two lines in stem stitch, in coloured thread, with a gold thread between, laid down with overcast stitches.

Fig. 241. Border in Persian stitch.
Materials: D.M.C Pearl cotton or D.M.C Floss flax or flourishing thread, in Black fast dye 310, Moss green 469 and 471, Cardinal red 347, Old gold 680 and Mauve violet 315.

Inside are eyelet-holes in gold thread, ornamented with a
double back-stitch. Finally, the oblique bands are filled with

Fig. 242. Flower in Mossoul stitch.
Materials : D.M.C Gold chiné, in black and gold, green and gold, red and gold,
blue and gold, écru and gold, and D.M.C Gold cord.

little gold spangles secured by three stitches in D.M.C Pearl cotton (Coton perlé) gold colour.

The width of this band may be varied at will; either by the addition of scallops, or by using it as an insertion it will always make a handsome trimming for summer dresses or other fancy articles of dress.

Border in Persian stitch (fig. 241). — This kind of embroidery, of Persian origin, is very like the stitch explained in figure 75.

Instead, however, of bringing the needle out, as indicated in figure 75, take it back as you see in the engraving, to the space between the outlines of the drawing and at the back of the thread that forms the next stitch.

Before filling in the different spaces in the pattern, trace the outlines with short stem stitches, or a fine cord, laid on, and secured with invisible stitches.

Fig. 243. Border in flat stitch set two ways and stem stitch.
Materials : D.M.C Persian silk, in Black 1187,
Myrtle green 1138, Orange yellow 1115, Indigo blue 1010, Copper
red 1133 and Maize yellow 1069,
or D.M.C Special stranded cotton or D.M.C Floss flax, in Black
fast dye 310, Pistachio green 367, Saffron yellow 725,
Azure blue 3325, Locust-bean brown 357 and Cream yellow 712. (*)

This graceful design which can be applicable to various uses, is composed of 7-lobed leaves, worked alternately in dark

---

(*) See at the end of the last chapter the tables of the sizes and colours of the cotton, flax and silk articles, mark D.M.C.

and light green, of flowerets of 3 petals, worked in Cardinal red and the centres in Old gold, and of small leaves, in Mauve violet. The setting or outlining, throughout, is done in Black fast dye.

Flower in Mossoul stitch (fig. 242). — For this stitch follow the description attached to figure 75 in the chapter on "Embroidery upon White Stuff"; the stitches must be set far enough apart for the stuff to shew between.

As material take D.M.C Gold chiné (Chiné d'or).

Gold chiné, red and gold and black and gold is used for the eight petals of the big flower at the top, Gold chiné, blue and gold for the three-leaved buds on both sides of the stalk. The little pointed leaves are in Gold chiné, green and gold, and the heart of the flower and of the buds in Gold chiné, écru and gold.

All the chief figures are outlined with D.M.C Gold cord (Cordonnet d'or) laid on and secured with invisible overcast stitches.

This kind of flower is suitable for covering large surfaces, such as are required for panels, cushions, chairbacks, &c.

Border in flat stitch set two ways and stem stitch (figs. 243 and 244). — This shews the character of the Servian

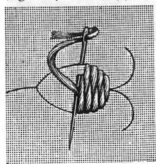

Fig. 244. Flat stitch set contrariwise.

embroideries, which are executed on fine linen in coloured silk and are mostly used for the decoration of the peasant women's shawls. The figures are filled in with flat stitches set contrariwise, the way this is done is explained by figure 244. The outlining and the stalks are done in plain stem stitch.

The darkest shade represents black; the lightest, white. The big petals of the flowers are alternately red and green. Blue, yellow, red and green are equally distributed throughout the other parts of the flower. This kind of flower like the preceding figure, is suitable for grounding.

Border in Roman stitch (fig. 245). — This border is worked for the most part in Roman stitch, fig. 234. The original, in very good preservation, notwithstanding its age, is worked in rather bright red thread on a slightly tinted stuff.

By using D.M.C Pearl cotton (Coton perlé) in Rose fast

dye 3350, for the embroidery, a good imitation of the old work will be secured.

Roman stitch is used wherever the lines of the pattern are widest apart; there where they narrow, as in the inden-

Fig. 245. Border in Roman stitch.
Materials: D.M.C Pearl cotton, D.M.C Special stranded cotton or D.M.C Floss flax or flourishing thread, in Rose fast dye 3350. (*)

tures of the leaves the twists of the stalks and the scalloped edges of the flowers, flat stitch predominates.

By the repetition of the detached figure this pattern may be made to serve either for a stripe or for a grounding; if you

(*) See at the end of the last chapter the tables of the sizes and colours of the cotton, flax and silk articles, mark D.M.C.

use it for a stripe the centre flower of the principal subject, with the stalks lengthened, will look very well worked as a separate subject between the big bouquets.

Worked in a double row base to base, these large figures form a very handsome border, which makes an effective trimming for furniture and hangings.

Fig. 246. Bird in mediæval embroidery in figure stitch.
Materials: D.M.C Floss flax or flourishing thread or D.M.C Special stranded cotton, in white or écru. (*)

Bird in mediæval embroidery in figure stitch (figs. 246 and 247). — In the middle-ages a particular kind of embroidery was practised in Switzerland and in Southern Germany done in a kind of stroke stitch with long overcast stitches,

---

(*) See at the end of the last chapter the tables of the sizes and colours of the cotton, flax and silk articles, mark D.M.C.

which, owing to the subjects represented by the embroidery (biblical personages, animals, birds, figures of saints) was called figure stitch.

Such embroidery was mostly used for hangings. It was done on linen with white or unbleached linen thread, little differing in shade from the foundation; the effect of the work is only seen against the light, when the figures stand out dark on the more or less transparent ground.

This kind of embroidery lent itself advantageously to compositions in the Romanesque style, in which detached figures of animals or birds are framed in rich ornamentation. It has now been adopted for the embroidery of panels and table-covers for verandahs and dining and smoking rooms.

The bird in figure 246 is a specimen of this ancient work.

The stitch itself is done in two rounds, and a coarse loose thread should be chosen for the purpose.

You stretch a thread over the whole surface to be embroidered, then cover it with long slight-

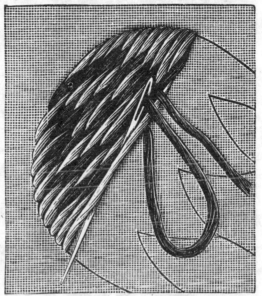

Fig. 247. Figure stitch.

ly slanting-stitches, making only very short ones at the back. To shew the course of the stitches more clearly, we have given the engraving in two shades. The long thread stretched across the whole surface — first round — is light-coloured, and the slanting overcast stitches — second round — dark, see fig. 247.

The first and the last of these stitches must never touch the outlines. When the first series of stitches is finished, stretch a second thread quite close to the first, cover it with slanting-stitches and so on till the whole figure is filled. In surfaces of a certain size, such as, the wings and breast, the stitches may be made longer; the head and the claws on the other hand

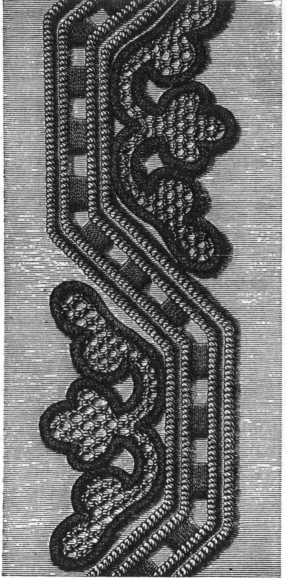

Fig. 248. Border with outlines in beaded or knotted
and basket stitch and fillings of various kinds.
Materials — For tne knotted or beaded stitch: D.M.C
Crochet cotton, 6 cord No. 2, in écru. — For the basket
stitch: D.M.C Special stranded cotton No. 25, in Indigo
blue 312. — For the Gobelin stitches: D.M.C Special
stranded cotton No. 25, in Morocco red 3327.
For the lace stitches:
D.M.C Flax lace thread No. 20, in white.

require short stit-
ches. The effects
of light and shade
are produced solely
by the different di-
rection and length
of the stitches.

We advise our
readers frequently
to consult the en-
graving so as to
give the stitches the
right direction in all
the different parts
of the bird.

**Border with
outlines in beaded
or knotted and
basket stitch and
fillings of various
kinds** (fig. 248). —
The stitch, shewn in
figure 232, is used
here for marking
the lines which en-
close the little sub-
jects worked in Go-
belin stitch, D.M.C
Special stranded cot-
ton (Mouliné spé-
cial), in red, whilst
the detached subjects
are worked in basket
stitch, fig. 233, D.M.C
Special stranded cot-
ton (Mouliné spécial)
in blue.

The insides of
the figures are to be
filled in with one or
other of the lace
stitches (see the
chapter on "Needle-

Fig. 249. Border in which the outlines are executed in braid and the fillings
in different kinds of stitches.
Materials: D.M.C Superfine braid, D.M.C Alsatian twist No. 50 and D.M.C
Embroidery cotton No. 20, in Garnet red 335.

made Laces", figs. 890 to 929, which can be worked either so that all the stitches enter the stuff, or so that they form a network over it.

The work may be simplified by sewing D.M.C Superfine braid (Lacets superfins) or a crochet braid along the straight lines instead of embroidering them in basket stitch.

This kind of embroidery is mostly used as a trimming tor ladies' and childrens' articles of dress.

Embroideries executed in braid. — The two following subjects may be classed amongst work in which a small braid takes the place of needlework.

In the border figure 249, the braid takes the place of embroidered outlines, whilst the bouquet, fig. 251, shews the use of braid in making flowers and ears of corn.

Border in which the outlines are executed in braid and the fillings in different kinds of stitches (figs. 249 and 250). — Sew down D.M.C Superfine braid (Lacet superfin), between the outlines of the traced pattern, with small back-stitches, with D.M.C Alsatian twist No. 50, set in the middle of the braid, and made as invisible as possible. At the curves in the pattern, sew the braid on the outside line, and

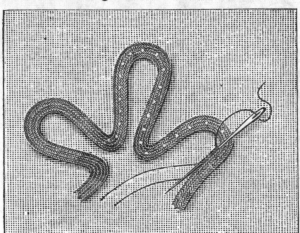

Fig. 250. How to gather the braid for forming the curves.

gather it on the inside so that it may lie quite flat, see fig. 250.

When you have done all the outlines in this manner, embroider the filling stitches with D.M.C Embroidery cotton (Coton à broder) No. 20.

The insides of the flowers and leaves are filled with fishbone stitches, fig. 231; the stalk is covered with crossed back-stitch, fig. 75, and spiders in darning stitch form the centres of the flowers.

This kind of work, which should be done in colours, is to be recommended for trimming table-linen, toilet-covers, table-cloths and panels, which are exposed to frequent washing, &c.

Flowers in braid and embroidery (fig. 251). — In the bouquet here represented, braid forms an excellent substitute

Fig. 251. Flowers in braid and embroidery.
Materials: D.M.C Superfine braid, in white, écru, Rust yellow 308, Indigo blue 322
and D.M.C Embroidery cotton No. 35, in écru,
Orange yellow 444, Indigo blue 311, Lime-tree grey 391, Mignonette green 750,
Pistachio green 319, 320, 369, Morocco red 3328.

for satin stitch embroidery, as it involves an expenditure of much less time and labour.

For the ears of corn, fig. 251, use D.M.C Superfine braid (Lacet superfin), écru and Rust yellow 308; for the marguerites white braid and for the cornflowers, Indigo blue braid 322.

As regards the execution, nothing could be simpler than the mode of making these flowers.

Fig 252. Thimble for crochet work on a frame.

Thread a tapestry needle with the braid and draw it into the stuff from the wrong side out to the right, at the bottom of one of the petals of the flowers. Thread an ordinary needle with a thread to match the braid in size and shade and draw it through from the wrong side to the right at the right place for the point of the petal; bring the braid there and secure it by two stitches made over it; then take the braid back to the bottom of the petal and fasten it down by a stitch, draw it through the stuff and bring it out at the place for the next petal. The natural irregularity of the petals of a flower can be imitated by using braid of different widths, folding it over more or less closely and laying it down in shorter or longer lengths as required.

Each petal requires only 3 or 4 stitches to keep it in its place.

You will observe that the points of braid are wider apart in the marguerite than in the cornflower, where it suffices to

Fig. 253. Crochet needle or crochet work on a frame.

fold back the braid without drawing it through the stuff, and to secure it by a stitch top and bottom on the right side.

The ears of corn are still more quickly done; a single stitch in the braid imitates the beard, and small stem stitches hide the junction of the ends of the braid and are continued along the stalks.

The stamens of the marguerites are worked in twisted knot stitch, fig. 78, with yellow cotton and those of the corn-flowers with dark blue cotton.

The other little details of the pattern are executed in flat and stem stitch in the colours indicated beneath the engraving. With this to go by the distribution of the colours for the different parts cannot possibly present any difficulty. We need only point out that the Morocco red 3328 is intended for the little knot of ribbon tied round the stalks of the flowers.

It is a pretty subject which takes very little time to do, and may serve as decoration for all sorts of articles such as book-covers, sachets, pincushions, lamp mats, &c.

Fig. 254. First position of the hands for crochet work on a frame.

Crochet on a frame (figs. 252, 253, 254, 255). — Big pieces of work, requiring a great assortment of colours are executed in chain stitch with a crochet needle instead of an ordinary needle.

The size of the frame must be adapted to the article the work is intended for.

The loops or chain stitches which are made with a small hook require a special tool, shewn in figure 253, where the hook

is screwed to the handle, as in the case of the stitching needle
to which we shall allude later on.

A sort of thimble, fig. 252, is worn on the forefinger of
the right hand, made of a small plate of sheet brass, rolled
up, but not joined, so that it will fit any finger; it is open at
the top, like a tailor's thimble and has a little notch on the
side, which is placed above the nail, and in which, when you
are working, you lay the needle. From the thimble being cut

Fig. 255. Second position of the hands for crochet work on a frame.

slightly slanting at the top, the part which covers the outside
of the finger is a little longer than the inside.

This thimble greatly accelerates the downward and upward
movements of the needle necessary in this work.

After fastening on the thread you pass the hook through
stuff stretched on the frame keeping it in the notch in the
thimble, the screw turned towards your thumb, you throw the
thread, held by your left hand on the frame, on to the hook

and bring the hook back to the surface of the work, pressing down the stuff, as you do so, with the thimble on your fore-finger so as to prevent its being raised up by the hook in re-turning and bringing with it a chain stitch, figs. 254 and 255.

Fig. 256. Spray worked in crochet on a frame, in the Turkish style.
Materials: D.M.C Embroidery gold and silver threads No. 40, D.M.C Gold chiné, in black and gold, red and gold, blue and gold, green and gold. (*)

(*) See at the end of the last chapter the tables of the sizes and colours of the cotton, flax and silk articles, mark D.M.C.

A little practice is necessary to acquire the right action or the hands, there being always a tendency, as in tatting and macramé to confuse the movements of the right and the left hand. As soon as you realize that the upward drawing of the

hook and the downward pressure of the stuff with the thimble have to be simultaneous you will find that you can work with great rapidity and with charming results.

Thread with a very strong twist, which the hook cannot split is the only suitable kind for this work. Of the D.M.C threads, Alsatian thread (Fil d'Alsace); Alsa, the Embroidery gold and silver threads (Fils d'or et

Fig. 257.
Working of the ear of corn.

d'argent fins) and Gold chiné (Chiné d'or), are the ones to be specially recommended.

Spray worked in crochet on a frame, in the Turkish style (figs. 256, 257, 258). — This spray, composed of leaves

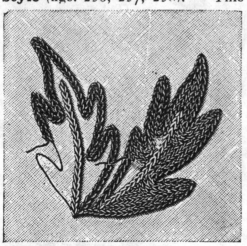

and ears of corn was taken from a copy of a modern Turkish veil, worked in gold and silver.

We have just explained the way to do crochet work on a frame, we have only to add, that the outlines must be done first, then the veining, if there be any, and lastly, the filling.

Figure 257 shews part of an ear of corn, and the filling has been begun.

Figure 258 shews the manner of doing the scalloped leaves; the right

Fig. 258.
Mode of working the scalloped leaves.

half of the right leaf is finished, in the left half you see the filling in process of being done in two rounds and a zig-zag following the outside lines. In the left leaf you again see the outlines and the shaded filling in course of being worked. The big leaves outlined in gold, with the veining in silver are filled in with Gold chiné green and blue, the small leaves with Gold chiné green and black; the ears of corn shew alternately outlines in gold with Chiné red and outlines in silver with Chiné black.

This kind of crochet on a frame, worked in gold and silver thread, is only used for very rich and handsome articles.

Fig. 259. Border with grounding in single Malta stitch, also called tassel stitch.
Materials: D.M.C Special stranded cotton, D.M.C Alsatia
or D.M.C Floss flax or flourishing thread, in Old blue 931, Golden green 580,
Golden yellow 781 and Maize yellow 579. (*)

Little borders of it are used for the ends of veils, neck-ties and collars; and larger ones for trimming scarves, fans and fronts of dresses, &c.

(*) See at the end of the last chapter the tables of the sizes and colours of the cotton, flax and silk articles, mark D.M.C.

Malta embroidery. — The natives of Malta make a special kind of embroidery which they use for the decoration of their rooms and furniture. The pattern is formed by little tufts or tassels, made in two different ways : single and double ones.

We present our readers with two patterns with the two different kinds of stitches, adding all the details and explanations necessary.

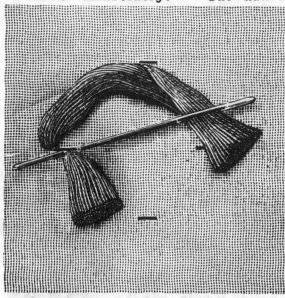

Fig. 260.
Single Malta stitch, called also tassel stitch.
How to make the little tassels.

Fig. 261.
Single Malta stitch, called also tassel stitch.
Four little tassels finished.

Border with grounding in single Malta stitch, also called tassel stitch (figs. 259, 260, 261). — We recommend this kind of work with pendent tassels, for panels and curtains, and hangings of all kinds. It can be so easily and quickly made, that it seems specially suitable for covering large surfaces. The stuff on which it is worked must be very strong and firm; one of a slightly yellow or pink shade is preferable to the unbleached stuffs.

After tracing the pattern, marking by a horizontal line the place for each tassel, begin the embroidery at the bottom.

The stitch, which recalls the single Smyrna stitch — see the chapter on "Tapestry", figs. 376 to 378 — is very easy ; you count, according to the coarseness of the stuff, four to six threads in width for each stitch. The direction of the stitch, which secures the tassel at the top, is always vertical.

As material use D.M.C Alsatia or a loose thread, such as D.M.C Special stranded cotton (Mouliné spécial) or D.M.C Floss flax (Lin floche), of which take six to twelve threads for a needleful. Begin the stitch in the middle of the horizontal line traced on the right side of the work where you leave a cluster of threads about one inch long lying on the surface of the work, then bring out the needle 2 or 3 threads further on

Fig. 262. Malta stitch.
First detail.

Fig. 263. Malta stitch.
Second detail.

to the left, lay the thread over the cluster and put the needle in again a few threads distant from the centre of the stitch

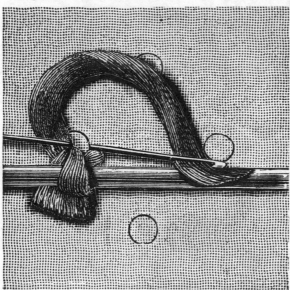

Fig. 264. Malta stitch.
Third detail.

on the right, and finally come back to the middle of the stitch where you cut the thread the length of the first little cluster, and the stitch is completed.

Our engraving, fig. 260, shews how to make the little tassels; in figure 261, four little tassels are shewn finished. The border with the little exterior triangles is worked in green and cream, the straight lines which border it, in blue and yellow.

In the grounding, the squares are done in blue, the lily flowers in yellow and green and the little lozenges in the middle of the empty spaces, in cream and green.

Border in double Malta stitch (figs. 262, 263, 264, 265, 266). — To make this stitch, take a big cluster of D.M.C Special stranded cotton (Mouliné spécial), pass it under two or three vertical threads of

Fig. 265. Malta stitch.
Four stitches finished.

the stuff, from right to left, fig. 262. Come back and pass the needle under the two or three threads in front of the first stitch. The threaded cluster of threads thus passes under the one you had reserved; the stitch must be drawn rather tight.

Repeat the first stitch, making a loop in the middle over a spool and of the same length as the cluster of threads you had reserved, fig. 264. Repeat the second stitch, passing over the loop, and cut the threaded cluster the length of the loop.

In figure 265 our stitches are shewn finished in their actual size.

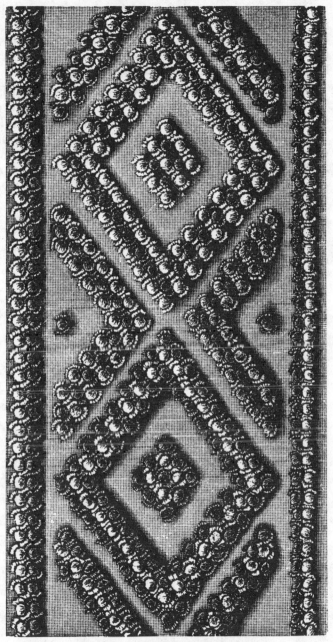

Fig. 266. Border in double Malta stitch.
Materials : D.M.C Special stranded cotton, D.M.C Alsatia or D.M.C Floss flax or flourishing thread.

Figure 266 represents the border of a curtain embroidered on a loose fabric ; the horizontal lines which terminate the border, in Beetle green 3346 and Golden yellow 781, the big lozenges in the border, in the same colours, the angles in Indigo blue 312 and Cardinal red 347.

Patterns of needlework. — Besides the different kinds of work described above a great choice of patterns for linen embroidery will be found in the following publications of the D.M.C Library: *Albums for Cross-Stitch Embroidery I, II and III, Cross-Stitch · New Designs I, II and III, Marking Stitch I, The Embroiderer's Alphabet, Motifs for Embroideries I, II, III, IV and V, Works of various kinds, Motifs for Coptic Embroidery I and II.* (*)

(*) See at the end of the volume the list of the albums
of the D.M.C Library.

Border in satin stitch. Louis XVI style.

Embroidery on Silk and Velvet

In view of the rich silken fabrics, such as velvet brocade and plush, with their warm and changing tints and soft effects, or the many beautiful stuffs interwoven with raised gold and silver designs, one is inclined to think that nothing can be done to add to their richness and beauty. And yet at all times, the exigencies of worldly luxury and those of ecclesiastical display and ceremonial have encouraged every endeavour to enhance the value and splendour of these costly fabrics by rich embroidery.

This chapter comprises the various kinds of work most used for coloured embroidery on silk and velvet. They are, it may be observed, not very different from those already described in the preceding chapter.

To begin with the most familiar kind, namely, flat or satin stitch embroidery, which may be subdivided into unshaded, shaded, two-sided (that is, the same on both sides), called also Chinese flat stitch and needle-painting. Next come knot stitch and chain stitch and lastly Arabian embroidery.

Though all these stitches are here included under the term "Embroidery on Silk", they may equally well be worked on the newer linen, cotton and woollen stuffs now made:

only materials must in each case be selected that will best harmonise with the stuff.

Stuffs. — All the originals of our patterns are executed on a silk or velvet foundation.

We recommend specially all the thicker silk fabrics, such as satin, reps and velvet with a short nap. Thin stuffs, liable to stretch in the working, should be avoided, as also plush because the stitches unless thickly padded are lost in the fleecy surface.

Embroidery for ecclesiastical purposes is often done on gold and silver brocade ; but we cannot recommend these stuffs as the metal threads are so apt to injure the embroidery threads with which the work is done. If however a gold and silver brocade is to form the ground we advise the embroidery being executed on a linen foundation and then cut out and appliquée on to the brocade. (See the chapter on "Appliqué work".)

Materials. — The choice of materials must depend absolutely on the kind of embroidery and the delicacy of the design. Thus embroidery in flat stitch, Chinese embroidery and needle-painting require a loose thread, such as D.M.C Persian silk (Soie de Perse) (*), which can be used in single strands, if desired. Again, knot stitch and chain stitch work, on the other hand, require a strongly twisted thread.

In working on cotton or linen instead of silk use D.M.C Special stranded cotton (Mouliné spécial) or D.M.C Floss flax (Lin floche) ; D.M.C Embroidery cotton (Coton à broder), D.M.C Pearl cotton (Coton perlé) and D.M.C Alsa are best for knot stitch and chain stitch embroidery.

Frame and mounting. — Preparatory work. — A good strong frame, made after the pattern shewn in the accompanying engraving, fig. 267, is indispensable for embroidery on silk and velvet. The bars or rollers should be round and well polished so as not to mark the stuff, when, as in the case of large pieces of embroidery which have to be done length by length, it has to be rolled up upon them.

A piece of stout white or unbleached stuff has to be sewn into the frame in the manner described in the preceding chapter.

(*) See at the end of the last chapter the tables of the sizes and colours of the cotton, flax and silk articles, mark D.M.C. — The French names, in brackets, are those stamped on the labels of the D.M.C articles.

On this tightly stretched foundation lay the stuff which you are going to embroider, and hem or herring-bone it down, taking care to keep it perfectly even with the thread of the foundation and, if possible, more tightly stretched, to prevent it from being wrinkled or puckered when you come to take it off the backing.

For directions how to transfer the pattern to your stuff and prepare the paste with which the embroidery should be

Fig. 267. Embroidery mounted in the frame.

stiffened before it is taken out of the frame see the chapter "Miscellaneous directions".

Before beginning the embroidery it is advisable to provide yourself with a coloured sketch from which to work. This is essential for all unskilled workers and prevents them from making great mistakes in the arrangement of the colours.

Satin stitch embroidery done with the machine. — All kinds of satin stitch embroidery can be done with the machine. For single-faced embroidery, use for the top thread (the bobbin thread) a strand of D.M.C Persian silk (Soie de

Fig. 268. Border in unshaded flat stitch.
Materials : D.M.C Persian silk,
in Indigo blue 1009, 1010, 1011, 1012 or D.M.C Floss flax,
in Indigo blue 334, 322, 312, 311.

Perse), D.M.C Embroidery cotton (Coton à broder) No. 80 or D.M.C Alsatian twist (Retors d'Alsace) Nos. 30 and 50; with D.M.C Machine thread (Fil pour machines) No. 150 for the back thread (the shuttle thread).

For double-faced embroidery, use for the back thread also D.M.C Persian silk (Soie de Perse), D.M.C Embroidery cotton (Coton à broder) or D.M.C Alsatian twist (Retors d'Alsace).

Border in unshaded flat stitch (figs. 268 and 269). — This pattern is done in ordinary flat stitch and slanting stem stitch. Each figure should be begun at the point. The leaves must be done in two parts, one half after the other, and the vein must be a carefully traced line between the two. Generally the stitches are set more or less slanting as may be seen from the explanatory engraving, fig. 269.

If it should be necessary, little by little, to change the direction of the stitches so as to suit the shape ot the subject you are copying, it is advisable to make a few little auxiliary stitches starting from the exterior outline and leading to the middle of the subject. These stitches which

Fig. 269. Detail of figure 268.

will always be partly hidden by the stitches of the correct length to follow, will enable you to reproduce curved shapes, without the stitches over-lapping each other in the inner outlines.

Fig. 270. Border in Chinese embroidery with a right and a wrong side.
Materials : D.M.C Persian silk,
in Mignonette green 1020, 1024, Ivy green 1416, 1182, 1184, Yellow green 1276,
Old pink 1002, 1004, 1006, 1008 and Peacock blue 1221. (*)

The dots must be begun exactly in the centre. You finish one half first, then the other ; by this means you will best succeed in making them quite round.

Our border is worked in one colour, but in four shades ot the same. The slanting stem stitch, described in figure 72, is

(*) These numbers refer to the colours on the colour cards of the articles stamped with the D.M.C trade mark. These cards can be consulted at all the mercers' and needlework shops.

in very dark blue, the three following blues are used simultaneously for the flowers and leaves in flat stitch, as the engraving shews.

This pattern is very suitable as a border for small rugs and table-covers on which you do not wish to expend much

Fig. 271. Bouquet in Chinese embroidery with a right and a wrong side.
Materials : D.M.C Persian silk in Old red 1035, 1037, 1040,
Greenish grey 1177, 1179, 1180, Mignonette green 1018, 1021, 1024. Beetle green
1199, 1223, Golden green 1261, 1145 and Snow-white 1219.

time. In this case it is best to work it on a separate stripe or a different stuff from the article itself. (*)

Border in Chinese embroidery with a right and a wrong side (fig. 270). — This is done entirely in unshaded

(*) We here refer our readers to our album "Flat-stitch embroidery" which contains a series of 27 patterns with explanatory text and tracings for the same.

flat stitch ; the direction of the stitches is shewn in the engraving. As regards the arrangement of colours, it is enough to say that the big flowers are done in four shades of pink, the leaves in dark blue and yellow and in five shades of bright green, evenly distributed.

Worked on a silk ribbon, this border may be used as a trimming for articles of dress.

Bouquet in Chinese embroidery with a right and a wrong side (fig. 271). — Here the work is the same as for figure 270. The chrysanthemums are embroidered in three reds, as also the little round flowers with five petals. The big

Fig. 272. Border in Chinese embroidery — both sides alike.
Materials : D.M.C Persian silk, in Indigo blue 1009, 1010, 1011, 1012,
and Blueish white 1186; D.M.C Special stranded cotton or D.M.C Floss flax,
in Indigo blue 334, 322, 312, 311 and white. (*)

flowers resembling campanulas, are executed in three shades of greenish blue the calyx is in red.

The leaves are covered with Mignonette green and Golden green, some of the points are embroidered in dark Beetle green. Various other shades are distributed amongst the little leaves and stalks.

The light pendent branch is worked in white.

This bouquet can be used for a small pincushion, a sachet, or a blotting-book ; four of them placed each in a cornet forms a pretty ornament for cushions and small table-covers; a big powdering of bouquets can be used for panels and

(*) See at the end of the last chapter the tables of the sizes and colours of the cotton, flax and silk articles, mark D.M.C.

hangings ; in the latter case the bouquets should be worked on a bigger scale. See the chapter entitled "Miscellaneous directions", for the way to enlarge a pattern.

Border in Chinese embroidery — both sides alike (fig. 272). — Before turning to embroidery in shaded flat stitch, we will give here a specimen of Chinese embroidery, the same back and front. This kind of work comes from China and Japan, where it is used for the trimming of garments. The original of our engraving is worked on a dark thick silk ground ; nevertheless for this embroidery that has no wrong side, that is to say, is alike back and front, one may, without inconvenience use transparent stuffs. The work is less difficult than would appear at first sight. Fill in all the shapes with flat stitch, only taking care that the stitches follow each other very regularly. In any case you should try to avoid coming back into the parts already finished and jumping from one figure to the other without fastening off the thread.

When you begin the embroidery, you first fasten on the thread by a few stitches in the inside of one of the subjects to be covered afterwards this last being done, the thread is fastened off in the finished embroidery without the stitches being interfered with.

The border is worked with D.M.C Persian silk (Soie de Perse (*) divided into single strands, in four shades of Indigo blue ; only a few very small light lea es are done in white.

This embroidery, alike back and front, lends itself wonderfully well to the adornment of articles of dress, where embroidery with a wrong side to it would have great disadvantages. Scarves, neckties, collars, cuffs and fans are all suitable objects for it.

Border in shaded flat stitch (figs. 273 and 274). — The most usual flat stitch embroidery is the shaded kind in which the most complicated subjects, conventional as well as those imitating nature, can be reproduced.

Our engraving represents a border of conventionalised flowers embroidered on silk of a fine grain, with a slightly twisted thread, in encroaching flat stitch.

The working of the embroidery is shewn by the explanatory

(*) See at the end of the last chapter the tables of the sizes and colours of the cotton, flax and silk articles, mark D.M.C. — The French names, in brackets, are those stamped on the labels of the D.M.C articles.

Fig. 273. Border in shaded flat stitch.
Materials: D.M.C Persian silk, D.M.C Special stranded cotton or D.M.C Floss flax.

figure 274. You always begin with the lightest shade, and following the outlines exactly, you cover a part of the figure which has to be filled with flat stitches, directed towards the interior of the figure.

These stitches must be of different lengths. The next row of stitches worked with a darker thread "encroach" on the light stitches of the preceding row, so that the shades melt into each other. In this manner you add shade upon shade until the figure is entirely covered.

We recommend beginners to consult the engraving frequently, so that they may learn to place the stitches very exactly, as the engraving indicates; this will largely contribute towards a successful result.

Fig. 274. Detail of figure 273.

The stalks and foliage are worked in slanting stem stitch. As regards the colours, take Cherry red for the big flowers, Indigo blue for the calyx, and Bronze green and Ivy green for the stalks and leaves.

Shaded flat stitch embroidery is mostly used for big rugs, table-covers, panels and hang'ngs.

Japanese Bouquet in needle-painting (figs. 275 and 276). Needle-painting is the name applied to that kind of shaded flat stitch embroidery by which birds and flowers and all sorts of ornaments can be as faithfully reproduced as by brush-painting.

The bouquet, fig. 275, is copied from a Japanese painting, and worked in encroaching, flat and plain flat stitch, in D.M.C Persian silk (Soie de Perse), divided into two strands.

Beginning with the lightest shade, — white in this case — add, as previously explained, one shade after another, bringing out the thread from the part already embroidered and inserting

Fig. 275. Japanese Bouquet in needle-painting.
Materials : D.M.C Persian silk, in Steel blue 1105, 1106, 1107,
Indigo blue 1011, 1012, Golden green 1144, 1145, 1146, Cachou brown 1014,
Rust brown 1155, Old red 1036, 1038 and Blueish white 1186 ;
D.M.C Special stranded cotton or D.M.C Floss flax, in Blue grey 594, 593, 592
Indigo blue 334, 322, Golden green 582, 581, 580, Cachou brown 437,
Rust brown 3314, Geranium red 352, 349 and Cream yellow 712. (*)

(*) See at the end of the last chapter the tables of the sizes and colours of the cotton, flax and silk articles, mark D.M.C.

it in the stuff not yet covered, until the figure is quite filled. To give the stitches the proper direction it is best to begin each figure from the middle and then finish the sides one after the other. The stamens are worked in twisted knot stitch, see figure 78 in the chapter on "Embroidery upon White Stuff". The big centre flower is shaded in red. The flower, growing up, in white and green, with blue and red calyx. The buds are worked in blue and yellow, the stalks in a dull blue and the leaves in bright green.

This bouquet can serve the same uses as the one represented in figure 271.

Bouquet of wild flowers in needle-painting (fig. 277). — This charming design, specially adapted to the adornment of sachets and bonbonnières, is worked with D.M.C Persian silk (Soie de Perse) divided into two strands.

Fig. 276. Detail of figure 275.

The poppies are embroidered in violet, the pinks in pink, the big leaves in mignonette green, the grasses and stalks in bright green; the ears of corn are shaded in yellow.

Butterfly in needle-painting (fig. 278). — Here the whole work is done with one strand of D.M.C Persian silk (Soie de Perse) (*), which makes it easier to produce a fine gradation of shades.

The two big wings of the butterfly are almost entirely tinted in blue, from the lightest to the darkest shade, with a white stripe, running round the outer edge, interspersed with black stitches. Set close to the body are a dark red dot and a few triangular spots in pink, edged with white.

(*) See at the end of the last chapter the tables of the sizes and colours of the cotton, flax and silk articles, mark D.M.C. — The French names, in brackets, are those stamped on the labels of the D.M.C articles.

Fig. 277. Bouquet of wild flowers in needle-painting.

Materials : D.M.C Persian silk, in Scabious violet 1201, 1230, 1202, 1203,
Old pink 1001, 1002, 1003, 1004, 1005, 1006,
Mignonette green 1206, 1207, 1425, 1018, 1019, 1020, 1021, 1022, 1023, 1024, 1025,
Rust brown 1154, 1229, 1155, Ivy green 1314, 1181, 1182, 1183, 1184,
Bronze green 1093, 1096, Cream white 1220 ;
D.M.C Special stranded cotton or D.M.C Floss flax, in Mauve violet 377,
316, 376, 315, Tender pink 3326, Garnet red 335, 309, 326, 3367,
Lime-tree grey 393, 392, Mignonette green 750, 751, Saffron yellow 727,
726, 725, Golden green 583, 582, 581, 580, Yellow
green 731, 730, Cream yellow 712.

The small lower wings, worked in a complete scale of red, are streaked with black lines, with white stitches and green crescents, set close to the edge.

The body of the butterfly is white with horizontal black lines across it, the feet are white, the eyes black, the proboscis red and the antennae white dotted with black. Close attention should be paid to the engraving in order to give the stitches the right direction, so important in needle-painting.

This butterfly can be used as a detached ornament for

Fig. 278. Butterfly in needle-painting.
Materials : D.M.C Persian silk, in Indigo blue 1009, 1010, 1011, 1012, 1013, Cherry red 1059, 1060, 1210, 1439, 1061, 1321, 1062, 1063, Ivy green 1314, 1182, 1184, Black 1187 and Blueish white 1180.

little fancy articles, work-bags, bonbon-bags, sachets and so forth.

Bouquet in knot stitch embroidery (figs. 279 and 280). — Knot stitch is to be met with mostly in Chinese and Japanese embroideries ; it lends itself admirably to shaded work and the gradual merging of colours into one another.

In Japanese embroidery we generally find the design worked in knot stitch, outlined with a gold thread laid on with either visible or invisible overcasting-stitches of a colour that contrasts with the gold.

Fig. 279. Bouquet in knot stitch embroidery.
Materials : D.M.C Alsa, in Blue fast dye 799, 798, 797, Golden green 583, 581,
Cachou brown 435, Drab green 692, 691, Tender pink 3326, Garnet red 335, 358,
Pistachio green 319 and D.M.C Embroidery gold thread No. 20. (*)

(*) See at the end of the last chapter the tables of the sizes and colours of
the cotton, flax and silk articles, mark D.M.C.

Directions for working twisted knot stitch will be found in the chapter on "Embroidery upon White Stuff", fig. 78.

After tracing all the outlines in D.M.C Embroidery gold thread No. 20 (Or fin à broder), laid down with overcasting-stitches in dark green thread, you fill in the design with knot stitch, making the stitches all the same way.

Where two shades touch each other, make one dark stitch and one light alternately, so that the change of colour may be less apparent. See the explanatory engraving, fig. 280.

The two big fruits are done in yellow, one light, the other darker, the leaves in different greens and blues mixed, the stalks and tendrils all in pale blue.

This kind of embroidery is suitable for ornamenting glove

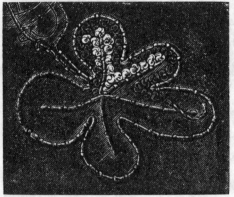

Fig. 280. Detail of figure 279.

and jewel boxes and caskets, where it rests on a cardboard or wooden foundation.

Imitation of knot stitch with the machine. — To imitate knot stitch with the machine you make rows of back-stitches in a spiral. As top thread use D.M.C Alsa, D.M.C Alsatian twist (Retors d'Alsace), or one strand of D.M.C Persian silk (Soie de Perse), and as back thread D.M.C Machine thread (Fil pour machines) No. 150.

Bouquet worked in chain stitch (fig. 281). — Oriental embroidery, especially the Turkish, Persian and Indian, remarkable for theirs fineness of execution and beautiful colouring, is very often done in chain stitch.

Our pattern, from a piece of Persian embroidery of the 18th century, shews how well chain stitch lends itself to shaded work. The foundation is dark yellow silk, the embroidery presents a rich scale of colour, red, green, brown, blue and violet. The colours must be uniformly distributed throughout the different subjects of the design, so that none should predominate. The essential thing is to take careful note of the lines and the movement of the rows of stitches; on which account you should always work inward from the outer edge.

As to the colouring, we can only give general directions. The big leaves are shaded in brown and green, with red veins and blue leaflets. Blue, red and violet alternate in the flowers. For directions how to do the chain stitch with the help of a crochet needle, we refer our readers to the chapter on "Linen Embroidery", figs. 252 to 255, where the necessary explanations will be found.

Chain stitch embroidery, being very elastic, is used by

Fig. 281. Bouquet worked in chain stitch.
Materials : D.M.C Alsa, in Geranium red 353, 352, 351, 350, 349, Pistachio green 320, 367, 319, Drab green 692, 691, Indigo blue 334, 312, Raspberry red 3686, 3684, Scabious violet 396. (*)

preference for articles of dress, fronts of dresses, collars, cuffs, scarves, &c.

Oriental stitches (figs. 282, 283, 284). — We have called the three following stitches Oriental stitches, because they are

(*) See at the end of the last chapter the tables of the sizes and colours of the cotton, flax and silk articles, mark D.M.C.

met with in most Oriental embroideries, and it is more than probable that we owe them to the Asiatics, who from all times have excelled in the art of embroidery.

These stitches are only suitable for large bold designs and are done on a big scale. Worked in one colour and very boldly outlined, this kind of embroidery is styled "Arabian embroidery". If, on the contrary, these stitches are worked in subdued colours and if the subjects of the design are not outlined, the embroidery is better known as "Renaissance embroidery", which however must not be confounded with Renaissance embroidery on white.

Set the vertical stitches first. In working with a soft, silky material, to economise it and prevent the embroidery from

Fig. 282. Oriental stitch.

becoming too heavy, you can begin your second stitch close to where the first ended. But if you use a strongly twisted thread, or one liable to twist, take it back underneath the stuff and begin your next stitch in a line with the first, so that all the stitches of the first layer, which form the grounding are carried from the top to the bottom. The same directions apply to figures 283, 284, 285, 286.

Having laid all your vertical threads, stretch threads horizontally across, and fasten them down with detached stitches, set six vertical threads apart. The position of these stitches on the transverse threads must alternate in each row, as indicated in figure 282.

For figure 283, make a similar grounding to the one above described, laying the horizontal threads a little closer together than in figure 282, and making the fastening-stitches over two horizontal threads.

In figure 284 the second threads are carried diagonally across the foundation threads and the fastening-stitches are given a similar direction.

Plaited stitch (fig. 285). — After laying the vertical stitches, a kind of plait is formed in the following manner. Pass the thread three times alternately under and over three of the foundation threads. To do this very accurately, you must take your thread back, underneath, to its starting-point, and consequently always make your stitch from right to left.

Mosaic stitch (fig. 286). — In old embroideries we often meet with this pretty stitch, employed as a substitute for plush or other costly stuffs, appliquéd on to the foundation.

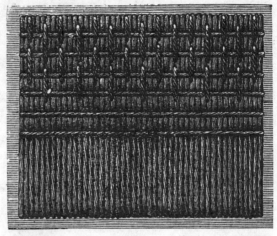

Fig. 283. Oriental stitch.

It is worked in the same manner as the four preceding stitches.

Each stitch must be made separately and must pass underneath the foundation, so that the threads which form the pattern are not flat as in the preceding examples, but slightly rounded.

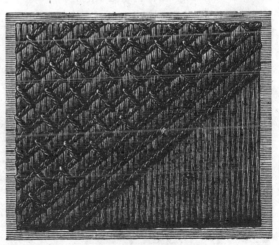

Fig. 284. Oriental stitch.

Border in Arabian embroidery fig. 287). A modern Caucasian design inspired us with the idea for this border. The embroidery is worked in two different oriental stitches and the plaited stitch, see figs. 283, 284, 285. The ornament placed on a dark blue velvet ground is embroidered in D.M.C Persian silk (Soie de Perse) and outlined with gold and silver thread.

The filling stitches, illustrated in figures 283 and 284, are worked with three strands of silk, covered with D.M.C Embroidery gold thread (Or fin à broder No. 40, secured by back-stitches in D.M.C Embroidery silver thread (Argent fin à broder) No. 40.

The plaited stitch, see fig. 285, is worked entirely in silk.

For the arrangement of the stitches, consult the engraving.

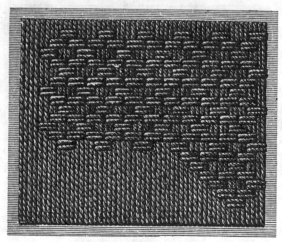

Fig. 285. Plaited stitch.

Fig. 286. Mosaic stitch.

The colouring is as follows : in the little border the big leaves are in yellow green, the little ones in rust brown and the two narrow bands in pink. The narrow braid, which twines over the wide border, is in yellow green, the second braid which comes back upon itself, in rust brown, the small leaf inside in dark green, and the big drooping leaves in light green. The up springing leaves are to be embroidered in pink and the little figure above them in light green ; the calyx in white silk, placed beneath the pink leaves, rests on a figure in dark green.

After filling all the different parts of the design, do the lattice work with D.M.C Gold cord (Cordonnet d'or), and the ornaments on it with a silver cord, which you can make yourself with threads of D.M.C Embroidery silver thread (Argent fin à broder) No. 20, with the help of a wheel for the purpose

(see the chapter "Needlework Trimmings"). The little stalks
are done with D.M.C Gold cord (Cordonnet d'or). To finish
all the subjects are outlined with D.M.C Gold cord (Cordonnet

Fig. 287. Border in Arabian embroidery.
Materials: D.M.C Persian silk, in Beetle green 1223, Bronze green 1094, Drab brown
1270, 1123, Olive green 1222, Snow-white 1219, D.M.C Alsa, in Golden yellow 782,
D.M.C Gold cord, D.M.C Embroidery gold and silver threads Nos. 20 and 40. (*)

d'or), fastened down with invisible overcasting-stitches with
D.M.C Alsa, in Golden yellow 782. (See also the chapter on
"Gold Embroidery", fig. 292, for directions how to sew on the
cord.)

This extremely beautiful design, with its scalloped figures,
is specially suitable for lambrequins of all kinds. The narrow
border should come at the top, so that the scallops may hang
downwards.

Patterns of needlework. — Besides the different kinds of
work described above a great choice of patterns for embroidery on silk and velvet will be found in the following publications of the D.M.C Library : *Flat-stitch Embroidery, Motifs
for Embroideries I, II and V.* (*)

(*) See at the end of the volume the list of the albums
of the D.M.C Library.

Border embroidered in gold and silver thread with purl and spangles.

Gold Embroidery

Comparing the different kinds of needlework from the point of view of the effect they produce, embroidery done with gold or silver thread, usually called "Gold embroidery", unquestionably holds the first rank.

In the 17th and beginning of the 18th century it was cultivated chiefly in Spain, Italy, France and Germany, where it was adopted at that time for the decoration of ecclesiastical ornaments and vestments.

Since the 18th century it has mainly been in the hands of those who made it a profession.

It was rarely to be found in private houses, for every one shrank from attempting work which used to be considered, as requiring an apprenticeship of nine years for proficiency to be attained in it

But as, for some time past, it has become usual to introduce many different kinds of embroidery into one piece of work and to use gold, the same as other materials, a greater interest has come to be taken in gold embroidery even amongst those who are not professional workers.

We hope that thanks to our illustrations and accompanying directions, our readers will be able to dispense with the five years apprenticeship, which even now experts in some countries consider necessary.

In gold embroidery the effect is produced by the different ways of covering the design, after it has been padded in more or less relief, with metal threads. Besides the actual gold and silver thread, a shot thread is now very much used, made of a thread of gold and a thread of colour — écru, blue, red, green and black, which varies and enhances the effect of gold embroidery.

Stuffs. — Gold embroidery requires a strong and firm foundation. It is generally done on silk, velvet or brocade, but cloth and leather also make good substitutes, according to what the work is intended for.

Materials. — For gold embroidery the materials most to be recommended are the D.M.C Embroidery gold and silver threads (Or et Argent fins), which are made in Nos. 20, 30 and 40. To obtain a good firm outline, surround all the different figures of the design with D.M.C Gold cord (Cordonnet d'or); D.M.C Gold chiné (Chiné d'or) (*), to be had in five different colours, can be used when you wish to heighten the effect of the gold embroidery by introducing colour.

A special material, D.M.C Turkish gold cord (Ganse turque) Nos. 6 and 12, is specially suitable for the imitation of the Turkish embroideries.

According to the stitch you work in, besides the gold or silver thread, you will need a coloured thread to fix it. Use D.M.C Alsa, in Golden yellow 782 or Ash grey 762. The same article should be used for overcasting the metal threads with a colour contrasting.

Implements. — The first and most needful requisite for gold embroidery is a strong frame, on which to mount the work, see fig. 267.

Besides this you want a spindle on which to wind the thread, a very small pricker or stiletto and a tray to hold the materials.

The spindle (fig. 288). — The spindle is an implement made of hard wood, about 9 inches long, for winding the metal threads upon, and directing them as you work, so that they should not suffer from contact with the hand. Cover the round stalk and part of the prongs with a double thread of D.M.C Pearl cotton (Coton perlé), yellow or grey, ending

---

(*) See at the end of the last chapter the tables of the sizes and colours of the cotton, flax and silk articles, mark D.M.C. — The French names, in brackets, are those stamped on the labels of the D.M.C articles.

with a loop, in which you fasten the gold or silver thread which you wind round the stalk. The thread is generally wound double on the spindle.

The pricker or stiletto (fig. 289). — This is needed for pricking the holes for the needle to go in and come out of. It consists of a metal handle and an ordinary sewing needle, fixed into the handle by a screw.

In very soft supple stuffs it is not necessary to prick holes for the needle, but in brocade, plush, skin and leather, where every mistake shews, the place for the stitch must be marked beforehand.

Tray for the materials. — Cut out as many divisions in a thin piece of wood or stout cardboard as you will require materials for your work, for these include not only gold and silver threads, but likewise, beads and spangles of all sorts and sizes, as well as bright and dead gold and silver purl, or bullion as it is also called.

For the pieces of purl alone, which should be cut ready to hand, you should have several compartments, in order that the different lengths may be kept separate. The bottom of the tray ought to be lined with coarse unmilled cloth, as the materials will not slip about upon it and can be picked up with the needle more easily than from a smooth hard surface.

Preparatory work. — Whatever the kind of gold embroidery and the stuff on which it is to be worked may be, the first thing to do is to fasten a piece of stuff into the frame as a lining. On this sew the stuff to be embroidered, stretching it as tightly as you can. After tracing the pattern, you can begin the embroidery at once, unless it be of a kind that requires preliminary padding, which, for all the different sorts of flat stitch embroidery is not needed.

In the case of raised work, the padding should be done according to the directions given in the chapter on "Embroidery upon White Stuff", for Venetian embroidery, fig. 150.

Use for this a soft loose thread, such as D.M.C Embroidery cotton (Coton à broder) or D.M.C

Fig. 288.
The spindle.
In reduced
size.

Special stranded cotton (Mouliné spécial), yellow or grey. (See also fig. 295.)

Instead of a padding of stitches you may use pieces of cardboard or leather the shape of your pattern but as the cutting out of these pieces and the fixing them on requires great care and precision we cannot recommend it; the padding of stitches will be found much less difficult and troublesome.

The different kinds of gold embroidery. — These are distinguished by their different mode of execution.

    1° Chinese embroidery;
    2° Embroidery on a foundation of cords;
    3° Embroidery in back-stitch;
    4° Embroidery on couched threads;
    5° Fancy embroidery with spangles and purl.

Chinese embroidery includes all embroidery in which the subjects are covered with gold or silver thread couched side by side and fastened down either visibly or invisibly with overcasting-stitches made with a thread either of the colour of the metal thread or of a different colour.

Fig. 289. The pricker or stiletto. Natural size.

Embroidery on a foundation of cords. — In this kind of embroidery the metal threads are laid down over a padding of cord and secured with overcasting-stitches, the same as in Chinese embroidery. These two kinds of embroidery do not take much gold or silver thread as they only form a layer on the right side of the work.

Embroidery in back-stitch. — Here the whole design is covered with flat stitches made through the stuff.

These three kinds of gold embroidery can be done with or without preliminary padding, according to the requirements of the pattern.

Embroidery on couched threads. — This always requires padding. The thread is taken backwards and forwards over it, and secured at each turn by a back-stitch at the bottom of the padding. The spindle on which the thread is wound should be used here, as it will enable you to direct the thread better.

Fancy work with spangles and purl. — Gold embroideries over which much time cannot be spent, are worked

Fig. 290. Border in gold embroidery with cord and spangles.
Materials : D.M.C Gold cord and D.M.C Alsa, in Golden yellow 782
and Cardinal red 346. (*)
Spangles, purl and red stones, see figure.

(*) These numbers refer to the colours on the colour cards of the articles stamped with the D.M.C trade mark. These cards can be consulted at all the mercers' and needlework shops.

with spangles and purl; often even imitation pearls and precious stones are introduced. Fancy work of this kind is sometimes to be met with in the genuine gold embroidery. When this occurs in any of our patterns we give an explanation of the different stitches in question.

Border in gold embroidery with cord and spangles (figs. 290, 291, 292). — Copied from an 18th century piece of work, this border is a type of those gold embroideries in which the effect is produced by a thick cord laid down on the foundation with invisible stitches and which may. be looked upon as the easiest kind of gold embroidery. The beauty of the work depends here on the choice of the pattern.

Fig. 291.
Detail of figure 290.

The outlining must be done without any break, as in our pattern, for the frequent passing of the thick cord through the stuff is liable to deface it and spoil the appearance of the whole.

After tracing the pattern, outline the whole with D.M.C Gold cord (Cordonnet d'or), fastening it down between every turning with an invisible overcasting-stitch with D.M.C Alsa, in Golden yellow 782. At the beginning and end or each round, thread a tapestry needle with the cord and draw it through the stuff.

Fig. 292. Detail of figure 290.

After all the outlines have been covered in this manner with Gold cord, ornament the insides of the little flowers with single spangles fastened down by a little piece of purl through the middle, as shewn in the engraving figure 291.

The veins of the leaves require rather more care. After

fastening the first spangle by a back-stitch, bring out the
needle close by, thread a second spangle and a piece of purl
and stick it again into the hole of the first spangle. In this
manner the second spangle will half cover the first. Do the
same with a third and a fourth thus forming the veins entirely
of spangles half overlapping each other as figure 292 clearly

Fig. 293. Butterfly in gold and silver embroidery, in the Chinese style.
Materials : D.M.C Embroidery gold and silver threads No. 20 and D.M.C Alsa, in
Scabious violet 397, Indigo blue 322, Pistachio green 319, Chesnut brown 405,
Black fast dye 310, Cardinal red 347 and Mandarin yellow 740. (*)

(*) See at the end of the last chapter the tables of the sizes and colours of
the cotton, flax and silk articles, mark D.M.C.

shews. The red stones placed singly in all the different parts of the border are fastened on with two back-stitches in red cotton through holes pierced in the stones. (See fig. 291.)

This handsome wide border is suitable for chasubles and copes, altar-cloths and other church decorations.

Butterfly in gold and silver embroidery, in the Chinese style (fig. 293). — This butterfly, both in design and manner of working, is a type of the Chinese gold embroideries. All the various portions are embroidered with gold or silver thread, used double, and laid down with overcasting-stitches

Fig. 294. Border in stitched gold and silver embroidery.
Materials : D.M.C Embroidery gold and silver threads No. 20, D.M.C Special stranded cotton and D.M.C Alsa, in Golden yellow 782 and Ash grey 762. (*)

in different colours, which tones down the brilliancy of the metal threads and gives them a peculiar reflection.

For the execution of the work we refer our readers to figures 296 and 304, where all the explanations and details are fully given, and confine ourselves to pointing out the colours to be used.

The body, the antennæ and the feet are worked in gold and brown, the eyes, in gold and black.

The chief parts of the big front wings are also in gold and red, the small portion of the right wing in gold and orange

---

(*) See at the end of the last chapter the tables of the sizes and colours of the cotton, flax and silk articles, mark D.M.C.

yellow, the light part of the left wing in silver and green.

The bottom left wing is in silver and green, the right one in gold and orange yellow. The tail-like continuation of the wings is in gold and silver and violet. The round spots in the gold wings are in silver and green, those in the silver wings in gold and orange yellow. Before beginning to work this butterfly you should examine the engraving carefully so as to see how to give the gold and silver threads the proper direction.

This butterfly can be introduced into any embroidery in the Chinese style as a separate ornament or scattered over a large surface as a powdering; it may be used singly as an ornament on a small blotter, cigar-case, pincushion or fan.

Border in stitched gold and silver embroidery (figs. 294, 295, 296). — We took our idea for this border from an old piece of 17th century work which is a good specimen of stitched gold embroidery.

As was already said in the introduction to this chapter, this is flat stitch embroidery, worked in gold thread, generally over thick

Fig. 295.
Detail shewing padding of figure 294.

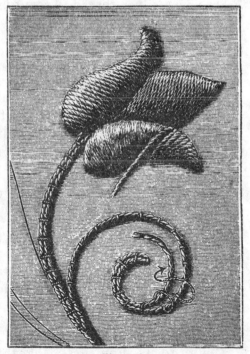

Fig. 296.
Shewing how the stitched embroidery and the stalks for the border are done, fig. 294.

padding, which padding is done with coarse loose thread. We used for it D.M.C Special stranded cotton (Mouliné spécial) No. 14, which is secured by overcasting-stitches made with a single strand of this cotton. After covering the pattern with several layers of thread, graduating them down at the sides and ends, fill up all the irregularities with two threads of straight stitches in D.M.C Special stranded cotton (Mouliné spécial), and then cover the whole with flat stitches set the opposite way to that of the subsequent gold embroidery, see fig. 295. The fine parts of the pattern are only padded with two threads of D.M.C Special stranded cotton (Mouliné spécial). Over this padding the gold embroidery is done in the same way as the unshaded flat stitch, see fig. 296. It is advisable to use very coarse needles which make a big enough hole for the metal thread to pass through without injuring the stuff, in some cases rather fragile.

In our border, fig. 294, the small leaves, the buds and the thicker parts of the undulating line, are worked in D.M.C Embroidery silver thread (Argent fin à broder) No. 20, the big leaves and calices in D.M.C Embroidery gold thread (Or fin à broder) No. 20. As the engraving shews the stitches are all set slanting, excepting in the top and bottom lines where they are straight, worked in gold thread. In order to make these lines quite straight it is best to substitute pieces of stiff cardboard pasted on, for the padding of stitches.

The stalks and the tendrils are formed of two parallel gold threads held down by overcasting-stitches with D.M.C Alsa No. 40, in Golden yellow 782. There where a little branch or stalk separates from the main stalk, you carry a single thread to the end of the stalk, then bend it round at the point and bring it back close to the first, so that it looks as if the embroidery had been done with a double thread, as the engraving, fig. 296 shews. The stitches that fasten down the gold threads must be set in coming back even with those over the first thread.

This border can be used for blotting-books, lamp-mats, &c.

Border in back-stitch embroidery, chiné d'or (fig. 297). With the exception of the rings that unite the different parts of the figures, all the subjects of this border are worked in back-stitch with D.M.C Gold chiné (Chiné d'or).

Owing to its suppleness, this thread lends itself admirably to this kind of gold embroidery, as the coloured threads interwoven with the gold thread add richness to the general effect of the work. Our border, the design of which is taken from an old embroidery of the 17th century, comprises all the colours of the Gold chiné. The big turned-back leaves are worked alternately in green and blue, the ombelles in écru, and the small leaves in red. Only the dark lines which border the pattern are worked in black.

The small details may be worked alternately in one or other of the five above-named colours.

The entire embroidery is done without padding ; the stitches are set more or less slanting, according to the space to be

Fig. 297. Border in back-stitch embroidery, chiné d'or.
Materials : D.M.C Gold chiné, in écru, black, red, green and blue, D.M.C Special stranded cotton No. 25 and D.M.C Alsa, in Golden yellow 782, and Gold purl. (*)

filled in. The little rings in relief, on the other hand, must be very thickly padded, and then embroidered with purl in the way described in figure 305.

This kind of embroidery, owing to its being much less stiff and unyielding than the previous patterns can be applied to articles of dress and domestic furniture.

Ornament in gold and silver embroidery done with couched threads on a cord foundation (figs. 298, 299, 300, 301, 302). — This is a specimen of embroidery with couched

(*) See at the end of the last chapter the tables of the sizes and colours of the cotton, flax and silk articles, mark D.M.C.

Fig. 298. Ornament in gold and silver embroidery done with couched threads
on a cord foundation.
Materials : D.M.C Embroidery gold and silver threads Nos. 20, 30 and 40, D.M.C Alsa,
in Ash grey 762 and Golden yellow 782, and D.M.C Knotting cotton No. 15, in écru.

threads on a cord foundation. This method uses less material than the stitched gold work, because the metal threads are not taken through to the wrong side of the work.

The three-pointed leaves are done with couched threads, in D.M.C Embroidery silver thread (Argent fin à broder) No. 3o, used double ; the mode of working is explained by figure 299. This kind of embroidery is done over cardboard shapes, which you can prepare yourself. Transfer the pattern on to white cardboard, or stout cartridge paper, cut it out with a very sharp knife so as to ensure smooth clean-cut edges, and then stick it on to the stuff with stiff paste. If the embroidery is to be done with gold thread, use yellow cardboard.

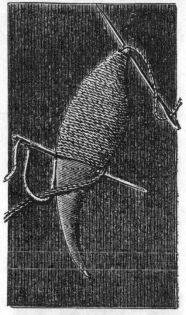

In the case of long stripes of cardboard, it is well to fasten them down at intervals with overcasting-stitches ; the small details, the little leaves, for instance, need only be secured with one stitch at each point. (See figs. 299 and 3oo.)

Take the silver thread and wind it double upon the spindle, then thread a coarse needle with a thread of D.M.C Alsa, waxed to make it still stronger. After fastening on the silver thread and the Alsa at the end of the leaf, begin the embroidery by couching the silver threads across the figure and securing them on the opposite side by a back-stitch ; continue to lay it backwards and forwards in this manner — by means of the spindle — securing it with a stitch at each

Fig. 299.
Detail of figure 298.
Worked with a double thread.

Fig. 3oo.
Detail of figure 298.
Worked with a single thread.

turn, until the whole figure is covered, as shewn in figure 299. The little fine points are embroidered in flat stitch, also explained by the engraving. Where the leaves touch a stalk, you finish these points when the stalk is finished, so as to be able the better to hide the junction of the stalk and leaf, both embroidered in different ways. In our pattern, the petals are worked in D.M.C Embroidery gold thread No. 40 with a single thread, with couched threads over yellow cardboard shapes. (See fig. 300.)

The thick stalks of the flowers and the leaves attached to them are worked in D.M.C Embroidery silver thread (Argent fin à broder) No. 20 ; the connection between the two branches in D.M.C Embroidery gold thread (Or fin à broder) No. 20, with a double thread over cords. For this work, before beginning the gold embroidery, you cover the whole pattern with horizontal stitches, placed a little distance apart, or coarse string, or cord, over which comes the embroidery. Figure 301 shews how these cords are placed ; the best material for this purpose being D.M.C Knotting cotton (Fil à pointer) No. 15 which should be thoroughly waxed before using, to make it stiffer. When you have laid this cord backwards and forwards, as shewn in the engraving, you take gold or silver thread double and lay it to and fro, lengthways over the cords, fixing it at every alternate cord stitch by a very tight back-stitch made in D.M.C Alsa of a corresponding colour. When you have got to the end of the figure, you come back with the thread, placing the stitches in each row between those of the one before. In order to fill in the shapes properly, it is best to begin the embroidery exactly in the middle of the cords and to fill in one side after the other. (See also the explanatory engraving figure 302.) In bigger designs you can make pretty grounds by different ways of placing the back-stitches.

Fig. 301.
Detail of figure 298.
Laying the cords.

Fig. 302.
Detail of figure 298.
Fixing the cords.

A detached ornament is often used for decorating pincushions

Fig. 303. Ground with border in gold and silver embroidery, in the Chinese style,
on cord foundation, with couched threads and purl.

Materials: D.M.C Embroidery gold and silver threads No. 20, D.M.C Embroidery
gold thread No. 30, D.M.C Gold cord, Dead gold and silver purl, D.M.C Special
stranded cotton No. 25 and D.M.C Alsa, in Golden yellow 782 and Ash grey 762
and D.M.C Knotting cotton No. 15, in écru.

Fig. 304. Detail of figure 303.
Filling in a leaf.

Fig. 305. Detail of figure 303.
The purl embroidery.

or blotting-books, and a powdering of them produces a very good effect for panels and carpets, for church banners and hangings, &c.

Ground with border in gold and silver embroidery, in the Chinese style, on cord foundation, with couched threads and purl (figs. 303, 304, 305). — This pattern, copied from a very rich Italian embroidery of the 17th century, comprises several kinds of gold embroidery and shews the different effects produced by the various stitches. We have already explained in the foregoing figures how most of the stitches are done; it remains for us to describe briefly the Chinese style of gold embroidery, done without any padding, with double threads. Detail figure 304 shews a pointed leaf embroidered in this manner. To make a good point, begin on one side of the leaf; carry the outside thread to the point, the inside thread to $1/4$ of an inch within it, then bend the two threads and come back. The double threads are laid down side by side and secured by small back-stitches, set at regular distances from one another, more or less far apart according to the size of the threads. For back-stitches use D.M.C Alsa.

Fill in the whole leaf in this way, setting the back-stitches of one row between those of the preceding one. When you have large surfaces to fill, you can vary your effects by setting your back-stitches according to a systematic pattern.

Embroidery with gold purl is rather more complicated to do. The first thing is to fill all the subjects with a thick padding, as described in figure 295, then thread a fine needle with D.M.C

Alsa, bring it out close to the padded motive, then cut little pieces of purl of the required length for the motive to be embroidered, thread a piece on your needle, insert the needle on the opposite side of the motive and bring it out on the near side, as shewn in figure 3o5. If the piece of purl is of the exact length it should just cover the width of the subject. Those unaccustomed

Fig. 3o6. Ground in fancy embroidery with lace braid and leaf-shaped spangles. Materials : D.M.C Embroidery gold thread No. 40 and leaf-shaped spangles according to figure, D.M.C Alsa, in Golden yellow 782.

to this work will find it difficult at first to cut the pieces of purl of the right length, but a little practice is all that is needed.

In the border of the design, fig. 3o3, the volutes are embroidered on a cord foundation, in D.M.C Embroidery gold thread (Or fin à broder) No. 3o: the outside petals in D.M.C Embroidery gold thread (Or fin à broder) No. 3o, in couched threads with a single thread; the inside petal is overlaid with gold purl, the two little drooping leaves, with silver purl. The big leaves or the ground are in D.M.C Embroidery silver thread (Argent fin à broder) No. 20; the volutes, in D.M.C Embroidery gold thread (Or fin à broder) No. 20, in the Chinese manner; the little leaves are embroidered with couched threads in D.M.C Embroidery gold thread (Or fin à broder) No. 30, used single.

The raised ornaments, represented light in the engraving, are covered with silver purl. All the other lines and volutes are ornamented with D.M.C Gold cord (Cordonnet d'or) fastened with invisible stitches in D.M.C Alsa. We advise beginning with the subjects embroidered in the Chinese manner; then going on to the parts done with couched threads and the embroidery on a cord foundation, then sew on the cord and quite at the last do the purl embroidery, which is the most delicate part or the work.

This large handsome design is intended for church embroidery. The little border at the bottom, that finishes it off, can be used alone as a trimming for various objects.

Ground in fancy embroidery with lace braid and leaf-shaped spangles (fig. 306). — Begin with the little roses, composed of spangles, fasten on first the eight long ones which form the outer centre, each with two back-stitches, through two holes at the points of each spangle. In order to place them very regularly fasten the two vertical ones on first, then the two horizontal ones, then the four oblique ones and last of all the small centre ones.

After making all the stars put on the picot braid which divides the ground into lozenges, tacking it first to ensure straight lines, and sewing it on with invisible stitches.

The way this braid is made is described in the chapter on "Pillow Laces", fig. 997: see also, "Needlework Trimmings", fig. 1040.

This pattern, seeing the little difficulty it presents, is useful for ornamenting sofa cushions, chair-backs, the fronts of dresses and other articles of the kind.

Border in appliqué embroidery with braid setting and ornamental stitches.

Appliqué work

Appliqué work is the laying on of pieces of one kind of stuff on to a foundation of a different kind, so as to form a pattern — these pieces of various shapes and sizes, taking the place of solid needle-made embroidery.

This mode of producing works of many colours was already known in the middle ages, before all the various materials for satin stitch embroidery we now have at our disposal were obtainable.

The appliqué pieces are pasted on to the stuff foundation, and finished off round the edges by fine cord sewn on with invisible stitches or by flat stitch or some other embroidery. Gold and silver threads, spangles and purl, used for the ornamental stitches, add to the effect of this kind of work.

We also give a reproduction in this chapter of a specimen of appliqué work done with braids of different widths, in place of the cut out pieces of stuff.

Stuffs. — Appliqué work may be done on silk, velvet, brocade, plush, linen and leather. As the appliqué stuff is to replace needle-made embroidery, it must be such as to stand out in bold relief from the foundation.

To add to the effect, different kinds of stuff may be appliquéd on to the same foundation as may be seen from some of the specimens given here.

Materials. — As has already been said the appliqué pieces are mostly laid down with cord, but may also be outlined with flat stitch embroidery.

For these cords we advise our readers to use the implement illustrated by fig. 1026, by means of which they can make them for themselves of any size they require.

As material use either a rather loosely twisted thread, D.M.C Pearl cotton (Coton perlé) or D.M.C Floss flax (Lin floche) or else D.M.C Embroidery gold and silver threads (Fils d'or et d'argent) and D.M.C Gold chiné (Chiné d'or).

For sewing them on use D.M.C Alsa and for the ornamental stitches take a loose silk, D.M.C Persian silk (Soie de Perse), which is also best for the embroidered outlining in flat stitch.

Fig. 307. Border in appliqué work with cord setting.
Materials : D.M.C Pearl cotton No. 8 or D.M.C Floss flax No. 16, in Cachou brown 437, D.M.C Gold chiné, blue and gold, and D.M.C Alsa, in Golden yellow 782.

Fig. 308. Ground with border in appliqué work with setting of cords and ornamental stitches.
Materials : D.M.C Pearl cotton No. 5 or D.M.C Floss flax No. 8, in Mandarin yellow 746, Black fast dye 310, Paroquet green 906 and Orange yellow 444 ; D.M.C Persian silk, in Orange yellow 1113 and Golden green 1146, and D.M.C Embroidery gold thread No. 20.

Preparatory work. — Most stuffs used for appliqué work have to be backed first with very fine tissue paper.

This is done in the following manner with paste made of wheat starch which dries quicker than any other. Spread the paste on the paper with a brush, carefully removing all the little lumps there may be in it. The paste should only be just liquid enough to make the stuff and the paper adhere together and above all must never penetrate to the right side of the stuff and shew damp spots. When the paper has been evenly spread with the paste, lay your stuff upon it and smooth and press it down with a clean cloth, stroking it out carefully in the line of the thread to prevent any air remaining between it and the paper which would cause it to pucker or get dragged.

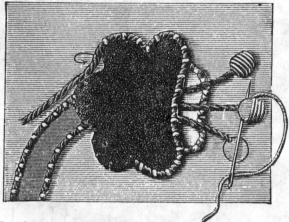

Fig. 309. Detail of figure 308.

You next lay several sheets of paper without a mark or a fold in them on a perfectly smooth flat board and upon these your paper-lined stuff, covered in its turn with several loose sheets of paper, and lastly on these you lay a second board with several stones or heavy weights upon it to keep them all in their place and act as a press.

Leave the stuff under this press until it be perfectly dry.

You will find that any kind of fabric, even the slighter ones, can be rendered available in this manner for appliqué work ; nor are plush or velvet in the least degree injured by the process.

Whilst the stuffs are drying transfer the whole pattern on to the foundation on to which it is to be appliquéd. On the paper lined stuff when dry trace only the parts that are to be appliquéd then cut them out with a very sharp pair of scissors, so as to avoid the threads along the edges being unravelled or frayed.

The foundation stretched on a frame is next to be placed on a board or table, in such a manner that only the stuff rests upon it, whilst the frame projects on the four sides.

Then cover the cut out detached figures with paste again on the wrong side and fit them into their proper places upon the foundation.

This second pasting should be done as quickly as possible, so that a board with weights upon it, to serve as a press, may be laid down on all the pieces at once.

Fig. 310. Border in appliqué work with cord setting and embroidery stitches.
Materials : D.M.C Floss flax No. 8 or D.M.C Pearl cotton No. 5, in Maize yellow 579 and Yellow green 734, D.M.C Persian silk, in Maize yellow 1069, Yellow green 1278, Crimson red 1185 (*) ; D.M.C Embroidery gold thread No. 20.

The board must not be removed until the paste be dry.

Before you begin the framing or outlining of the appliqué

(*) These numbers refer to the colours on the colour cards of the articles stamped with the D.M.C trade mark. These cards can be consulted at all the mercers' and needlework shops.

pieces fasten them down on the foundation with overcasting-stitches which will be hidden later on by the outlining.

The framing or setting. — You either sew on the cord with invisible stitches on the surface, opening it a little at each stitch so as to slip in your needle and thread between the twist (see "Gold Embroidery", fig. 292), or else with visible overcasting stitches in a bright colour.

In either case it must be so laid on so as quite to hide the cut edges and keep them from fraying, for rough edges in

appliqué work mean bad workmanship.

Should you wish to frame the appliqué figures with flat embroidery, you must bring out your needle close to the cut edge and insert it, from above, a fraction of an inch within the edge.

Both cord and flat stitch setting should be of a subdued shade and, if possible, of a colour to match the foundation.

Fig. 311. Detail of figure 310.

Border in appliqué work with cord setting (fig. 307). — Our engraving, fig. 307, represents one of those embroideries, of Spanish origin, in which the foundation and the appliqué stuff are of the same pattern.

The foundation is blue silk, the old gold velvet appliqué, laid down with invisible stitches. Close to be brown cord, to soften the transition to the blue silk. is placed a fine cord in D.M.C Gold chiné (Chiné d'or) blue and gold.

The cords are made with the implement illustrated by figure 1026, of D.M.C Pearl cotton (Coton perlé) No. 8 or D.M.C Floss flax (Lin floche) No. 16 which you use double, twisting the two threads first to the right, then to the left.

The chiné cords are made of three single threads and are similarly twisted.

This pattern is suitable for trimming furniture, carpets, curtains, portières and panels of all sorts.

Ground with border in appliqué work with setting of cords and ornamental stitches (figs. 308 and 309). — The foundation is ivory white satin; in the border the two horizontal stripes and the turned back leaves are cut out in garnet red velvet; the light calyx of the flower in snow white satin, the inside of the flower and the stalk forming a cross, in grey green silk. All the motives are outlined with cords, fastened on with visible

Fig. 313.
Detail of figure 312.

overcasting stitches. The red velvet is edged with black cord; the white satin with white and the green silk with green. As regards the pattern of the ground all the appliqué flowers are in garnet coloured velvet with white satin centres; the stalks, as well as the oval figures, the shape of a shuttle, are in green silk.

After sewing down all the motives with a few stitches on to the silk ground, do the Russian stitch which ornaments the inside of the oval figures and the horizontal band which unites the stalks of the flowers with D.M.C Embroidery gold thread (Or fin à broder) No. 20, then you begin the setting

Fig. 312. Narrow border in applique work with flat stitch setting.

Materials: D M.C Persian silk, in Myrtle green 1140 and Crimson red 1185.

of cords, sewing them down with overcasting stitches in
yellow. Finally you embroider the stalks of the stamens in
green D.M.C Persian silk (Soie de Perse), and the stamens
themselves in yellow silk. (See fig. 3o9.)

Here, as in the border, the motives in garnet red velvet

Fig. 314. Ground in appliqué work with back-stitch setting.
Materials : D.M.C Pearl cotton No. 8, in Beetle green 3347.

are edged with black, the white with white, the green with green.
The cords are made of two single threads of D.M.C Pearl

cotton (Coton perlé) No. 5, twisting the two threads first to the right then to the left.

This pattern can be used for any kind of rug or table-cover; the work may be lessened by using only the border with a centre of plain stuff. The pattern of the ground is suitable for cushion and chair covers.

Border in appliqué work with cord setting and embroidery stitches (figs. 310 and 311). — The appliqué parts, in white, yellow and red satin, stand out well on the black velvet ground. The setting is done with white and old gold cords, sewn down with invisible stitches. The two colours are easily distinguishable in the engraving. The cord outside the figures, is edged with a whole thread of dark red D.M.C Persian silk (Soie de Perse), secured by overcasting stitches, also in dark red, which helps to make the pattern stand out on the velvet ground.

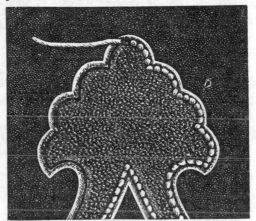

The veins of the wide stalks, in yellow satin, are worked in stem stitch in yellow silk; those of the big red leaves in red silk. The velvet ground is powdered with detached stitches in D.M.C Embroidery gold thread (Or fin à broder) No. 20.

The cords are made with three single threads of D.M.C Floss flax (Lin floche) No. 8; the first twist is given to the right, the second to the left.

Fig. 315. Detail of figure 314.

This border is suitable for trimming altar-cloths, &c., as well as household furniture. When the article in question is of big dimensions, the border should be worked separately and sewn on afterwards.

Narrow border in appliqué work with flat stitch setting (figs. 312 and 313). — This is a specimen of appliqué work set with flat stitch. The ground is red velvet, the appliqué old gold satin. After sewing on all the motives with invisible stitches, outline them with flat stitch, as illustrated in figure 313. You must take great care to make the stitches the same length throughout.

Fig. 316. Table-cover in appliqué work with braid.
Materials: D.M.C Superfine braid Nos. 1 $\frac{1}{2}$, 8, 16 and 28, D.M.C Alsatian thread
No. 150 and D.M.C Pearl cotton No. 3. in écru.

The stalk is worked in green, the leaves in red, with D.M.C Persian silk (Soie de Perse).

Fig. 317. Detail of figure 316. Half the natural size.

When you have finished the outlines embroider the veins of the leaves, which should be slightly padded first.

This border can be turned to many uses, such as the trimming of blotting-books, glove-boxes, newspaper-holders, &c.

Ground in appliqué work with back-stitch setting (figs. 314 and 315). — This is a new variety of appliqué work.

The ground is of emerald green velvet, and the appliqué, of yellow leather, back-stitched on with green brilliant thread.

You transfer the pattern on to yellow leather (Danish leather); cut out the figures, a little distance beyond the outlines, pounce the pattern on the velvet and paste on the leather figures.

The back stitching is done in D.M.C Pearl cotton (Coton perlé) No. 8, Beetle green 3347, and is explained in figure 315.

When the outlining is done the work is finished.

The combination of velvet and leather makes this work specially suitable for chair and footstool covers. Made in Swedish leather it can be used for sachets and blotting-books.

Table-cover in appliqué work with braid (figs. 316 and 317). — This pattern was copied from a saddle-cloth of the 18th century; all the figures are done with D.M.C Superfine braid (Lacets superfins) écru, of four different widths. After tracing the pattern on pink linen, tack the braids over the whole cover — the narrow ones need not be tacked — then back-stitch them on carefully with D.M.C Alsatian thread (Fil d'Alsace) No. 150, as invisibly as possible.

When you come to the rounded parts sew down the outside edge of the braid first, and then the inside, which has to be first gathered. See also "Linen Embroidery", fig. 250.

At the corners make a fold in the braid on the right side, and secure the fold with a few stitches, as explained in the same chapter.

The big spaces in the border are divided into squares by narrow braid and ornamented with little stars in chain stitch. In the sprays which adorn the interior of the cover, the veins of the big leaves are worked in flat stitch, whilst the small leaves and the centres of the flowers are done with knot stitch in D.M.C Pearl cotton (Coton perlé) No. 3, écru.

To give a better idea of the effect of this kind of embroidery, we have given, besides the small engraving representing the whole cover, a part of the border, reduced to half its original size, by which our readers can judge of the work.

Border, iris pattern in tent stitch embroidery.

Tapestry

Tapestry is of very ancient origin and has always been a favorite feminine occupation.

In these days we include under the name every kind of embroidery done on counted threads, and in which the stitches entirely cover the stuff on which the work is done. The varieties of tapestry are many; namely all embroidery on canvas, in cross stitch, tent stitch, gobelin stitch and straight stitch, besides knotted stitch and knitting stitch work, &c.

We will begin this chapter by some directions as to stuffs and materials, then pass on to review the different tapestry stitches, describing how they are worked and end with some simple patterns for grounds, borders and rugs. (*)

Stuffs. — The stuff on which tapestry is done, is called canvas. There are two different sorts of canvas in use for tapestry, called respectively, plain (single thread) canvas and Penelope (double thread) canvas. Both are made in different sizes. Almost all the different kinds of stitches can be done on either the one or the other canvas.

(*) See at the end of the volume the list of the albums of the D.M.C Library containing a large variety of patterns for all kinds of work.

For carpets, properly speaking, a linen foundation is preferable to a canvas one because the soft threads of the linen can be drawn closer together than the canvas threads which are always stiff.

Preparatory work. — Tapestry can either be done in a rame, or in the hand, in the latter case, the ends of the piece of canvas should be weighted with stones or lead to prevent puckering.

Before beginning a piece of work, the stitches should be marked out in tens; directions for this are given in the chapter "Linen Embroidery", fig. 154.

Needles. — The proper tapestry needles are long, strong and blunt, with long eyes, wide enough to be easily threaded. They are to be had, in all needlework and haberdashery shops, under the name of tapestry needles.

Materials. — For a long while, wool and silk were the only materials in use for tapestry, but within the last few years great progress having been made in the manufacture and dyeing of cotton threads, these have begun to play a great part in tapestry work. Silk, unrivalled for rich and handsome embroidery, is not suitable for articles that are to be subject to much use and wear; its delicate and fragile nature offers too little resistance to outside influences of time and weather. Wool though better as regards wear than silk, has the great disadvantage of being subject to the ravages of moths, whereas cotton, is exposed to no such destructive influence and is cheaper than silk; moreover when long use has somewhat spoiled its first freshness, it can be recovered by very simple processes.

Amongst the cottons suitable for tapestry, two we specially recommend have lately been brought into the market, D.M.C Special stranded cotton (Mouliné spécial) and D.M.C Pearl cotton (Coton perlé) (*), both remarkable for their suppleness and brilliancy. The latter article is also to be had in shaded colours.

D.M.C Special stranded cotton (Mouliné spécial) is a loose thread, made in Nos. 14 and 25, which is a very good substitute for wool and silk, where it is a case of filling in big plain surfaces.

(*) See at the end of the last chapter the tables of the sizes and colours of the cotton, flax and silk articles, mark D.M.C. — The French names, in brackets, are those stamped on the labels of the D.M.C articles.

D.M.C Pearl cotton (Coton perlé) Nos. 1, 3, 5 and 8 gives handsome raised stitches and it is used in preference to any other for stitches in which several threads cross each other.

Besides these two kinds of cotton thread which in many cases can very well take the place of silk and wool, we may mention for simpler work, D.M.C Floss flax or flourishing thread (Lin floche) and D.M.C Embroidery cotton (Coton a broder). For rich handsome embroidery, to be done entirely in silk, for a loose material use D.M.C Persian silk (Soie de Perse). In any case take care to select materials which will produce stitches which hide the canvas entirely, the threads of which should never be visible between the rows of stitches.

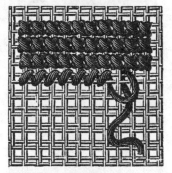

Fig. 318.
Plain cross stitch.

Plain cross stitch (fig. 318). — Plain cross stitch, called also marking stitch, is the foundation of all tapestry stitches. It is worked in two lines, one going and one returning. In the first the thread is carried diagonally from left to right across a square of threads, that is to say, two vertical and two horizontal ones, and then downwards, underneath the two horizontal or transverse threads. In the return journey, the stitches are carried from the right hand lower corner of the square to the upper left hand corner so that the four points of the two stitches form a perfect square.

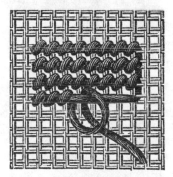

Fig. 319.
Half cross stitch.

Half cross stitch (fig. 319). — If the cotton is too coarse, in proportion to the canvas to make the complete cross stitch, as above described, carry the thread back from right to left along the whole line the stitches are to occupy and make the half stitches across it from left to right; the same in the case of a piece of work with a part of the pattern ready worked.

Straight gobelin stitch (fig. 320). — This is always worked in horizontal rows. Carry the thread vertically over two threads of the stuff and leave each time one thread of stuff between the stitches.

Oblique gobelin stitch (figs. 321 and 322). — The oblique gobelin stitch is worked on plain canvas over one vertical and

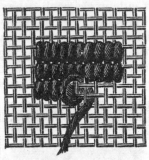

Fig. 320.
Straight gobelin stitch.

two horizontal threads. If your work is mounted in a frame you can do this stitch going to and fro, otherwise, you must turn the work round and bring out your needle behind the last made stitch. For the same stitch on Penelope canvas, you need rather a coarser needle, which will make its way easily between the threads of the canvas and separate them sufficiently for the thread not to fray in being drawn through.

Both these stitches, straight gobelin and oblique lend themselves remarkably well to the reproduction

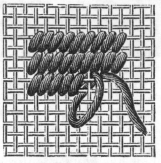

Fig. 321.
Oblique gobelin stitch on plain canvas.

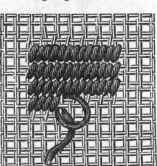

Fig. 322.
Oblique gobelin stitch on Penelope canvas.

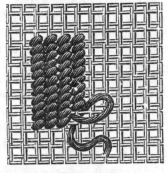

Fig. 323.
Reps stitch on Penelope canvas.

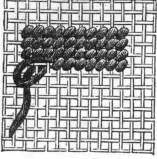

Fig. 324.
Tent stitch.

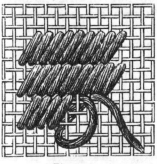

Fig. 325.
Wide gobelin stitch.

of old gobelin patterns; by their means a very good imitation of the old originals is obtainable.

Reps stitch (fig. 323). — This stitch is an imitation of reps. It is worked in vertical lines over one horizontal and two vertical threads.

Tent stitch (fig. 324). — This is simply the first half of a cross or marking stitch worked over a single thread each way. The engraving shews the working of one row, from right to left. To ensure very regular stitches the thread must be carried forward, underneath two vertical threads of the canvas.

This stitch is generally used in conjunction with other kinds of stitches, for the more delicate lines, the little flowers and leaves and in figure designs, for the flesh of the personages, whilst the rest is done in cross stitch or other analogous stitches.

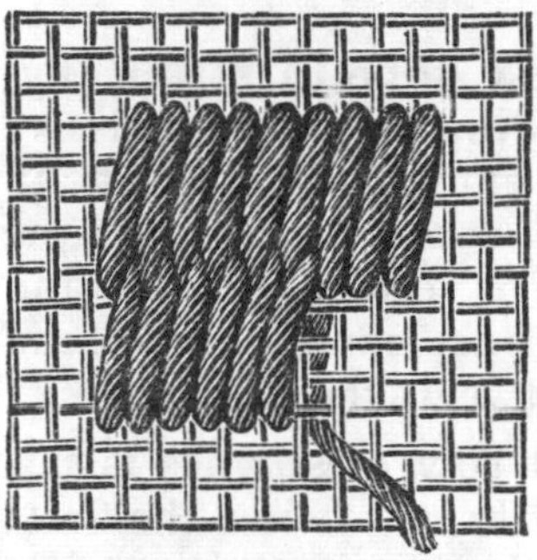

Fig. 326.
Encroaching gobelin stitch.

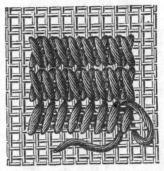

Fig. 327.
Oblong cross stitch.

Fig. 328.
Oblong cross stitch with back-stitch.

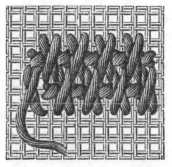

Fig. 329.
Double stitch.

Fig. 330.
Rice stitch.

Fig. 331.
Double stitch set two ways.

Wide gobelin stitch (fig. 325). — This stitch covers two vertical and three horizontal stitches and advances one thread of the canvas at a time.

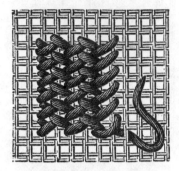

Fig. 332. Plait stitch.

Fig. 333. Fern stitch.

Fig. 334. Stem stitch.

Encroaching gobelin stitch (fig. 326). — For filling large grounds we recommend encroaching gobelin stitch, which consists of oblique stitches over five vertical threads and one horizontal one, leaving one thread of the stuff between the stitches.

The second row of stitches is begun only four threads below the first; the stitches will consequently project above, taking in the last thread of the stuff of the row above, thus forming encroaching stitches.

Oblong cross stitch (fig. 327). — This is a cross stitch over one and two threads, or over two and four threads. It is very useful for fillings, because, covering as it does a double number of threads, it takes half the time of ordinary cross stitch. It may be varied by turning the crosses first one way and then the other.

Oblong cross stitch with back stitch (fig. 328). — After making one cross stitch as described in figure 327, that is over four vertical and two horizontal threads, secure it in the middle by a horizontal back stitch across it, over two threads of the stuff.

Double stitch (fig. 329). — Make an ordinary cross stitch over each second intersection of the threads; then make a second row of stitches between those of the first row, but over one and three double threads, so that one stitch project on both sides beyond the first stitch. In the succeeding rows a square stitch comes beneath a long one and a long stitch beneath a square one.

Rice stitch (fig. 33o). — Begin by filling in the whole ground with big square cross stitches, over four threads each way, then over these the so-called "rice" stitches. These cross the four points of the big cross stitches and meet in the space between where they form another cross. The big cross stitches should be done in rather coarse cotton, the rice stitches in a finer number of a different colour.

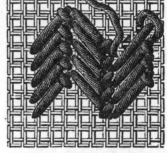

Fig. 335. Fish-bone stitch.

Double stitch set two ways (fig. 331). — This consists of diagonal and upright cross stitches, alternately. Begin by working from left to right; carrying the thread downwards over four vertical threads and between two horizontal ones, as the last row of stitches in the engraving shews. Coming back you cross the first stitches and pass the thread always in a straight line under the two threads of the canvas.

Fig. 336. Diagonal web stitch.

In the second journey going and the second returning, the stitches are set the opposite way to the first stitches. Gold thread is used for this second set of stitches; D.M.C Embroidery gold thread (Or fin à broder) or D.M.C Gold chiné (Chiné d'or) (*) are the best for the purpose.

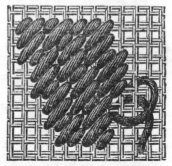

Fig. 337. Cashmere stitch.

Plait stitch fig. 332). — This is a stitch which needs to be done with a certain attention if you wish to work it by going to and fro. The easier way is to take the thread back each time to the starting point. Carry the thread from left to right downwards over four vertical and two horizontal threads, and on the wrong side, from right to left, under two threads as the figure shews.

(*) See at the end of the last chapter the tables of the sizes and colours of the cotton, flax and silk articles, mark D.M.C. — The French names, in brackets, are those stamped on the labels of the D.M.C articles.

Fern stitch (fig. 333). — This stitch is worked in successive rows; the thread passes over two double threads each way and runs horizontally from right to left under the middle pair of threads at the bottom and then upwards slanting over two double threads, to the right, see also print.

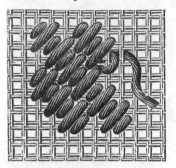

Fig. 338. Florentine stitch.

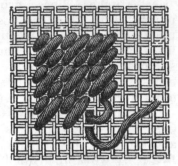

Fig. 339. Mosaic stitch.

Stem stitch (fig. 334). — Make a slanting stitch over two or four vertical and horizontal threads, and bring the thread back under one or two threads above the starting point of the first stitch. The stitches of the second row

Fig. 340. Hungarian stitch.

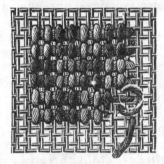

Fig. 341. Renaissance stitch.

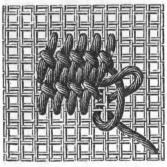

Fig. 342. Knotted stitch.

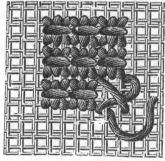

Fig. 343. Smyrna cross or devil stitch.

are set the contrary way: when the rows are all finished make lines of back stitches between them in a different colour.

Fish-bone stitch (fig. 335). — The difference between this stitch and the preceding one is that after passing the working thread over three or six threads each way you secure it by

Fig. 344. Star stitch.

a back stitch over the last intersection of the canvas threads. These fish-bone stitches are worked according to the direction of the long stitch, now from left to right, now from right to left.

Diagonal web stitch (fig. 336). — Stretch diagonal threads across the whole surface your stitches are to cover, and then over these diagonal threads make overcasting-stitches. If you are working this

Fig. 345. French stitch. First stitches to the left.

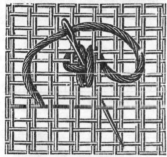

Fig. 346. French stitch. Stitches on the right.

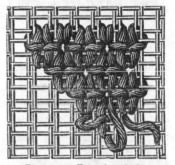

Fig. 347. French stitch. Series of stitches finished.

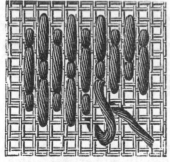

Fig. 348. Parisian stitch.

Fig. 349. Greek stitch.

stitch on Penelope canvas enter and draw out your thread between the pairs of threads of the canvas. In the next rows, the stitches must be set the inverse way, which gives the embroidered surface the appearance of a diagonal or twilled material.

Cashmere stitch (fig. 337). — To imitate this texture in needlework, make first one stitch over one crossing over the canvas threads, and then two stitches over two crossings, lengthways and breadthways.

Florentine stitch (fig. 338). — This is worked in slanting lines, the thread being carried diagonally first over two and

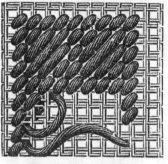

Fig. 350. Scotch stitch.

then over four crossings of the canvas threads.

Mosaic stitch (fig. 339). — The first row of this stitch consists of one short

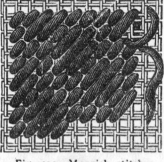

Fig. 351. Moorish stitch.

slanting stitch and one long, alternately; the second row of short stitches only. The third row is like the first.

Hungarian stitch (fig. 340). — To give a clear explanation of this stitch, it is represented in the engraving in two shades, but when it is used for filling in a ground it should be done

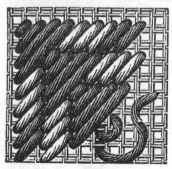

Fig. 352. Oriental stitch.

in one colour only. It is worked in horizontal lines, one encroaching upon the other, so as completely to cover the stuff.

Begin by

Fig. 353. Shell stitch.

a vertical stitch over two threads of the canvas, then make a stitch over four threads, which projects one thread beyond the first stitch, above and below, then end with a vertical stitch over two threads, and after skipping two vertical threads of the canvas, make a second group of stitches, and so on.

The engraving indicates how, in the second row, the long stitches are set exactly in the middle between two groups of stitches, so that all the stitches touch each other.

Renaissance stitch (fig. 341). — This stitch can be recommended for big surfaces. Begin by a horizontal stitch over two double threads, secured on the left and in the middle by a vertical back stitch over a double thread ; then, going down to the next double thread, you make another horizontal stitch with two back stitches across it. This series of stitches corresponds to a square of a drawn pattern (tapestry type). To bring out each group of stitches clearly we have worked them in two quite different shades.

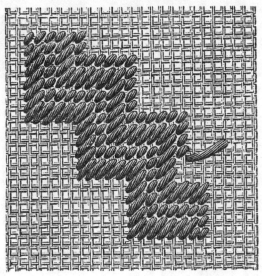

Fig. 354. Jacquard stitch.

Knotted stitch (fig. 342). — Carry the thread over two horizontal and six vertical threads, then bring the needle back vertically, four threads lower down, insert it two threads higher up, behind the stitch just made, therefore over the middle threads, after which take the needle down to the line of the stitches.

In the following rows the stitches extend over four threads downwards and encroach on two threads of the first row, so that the stitches of one row lie between those of the previous one.

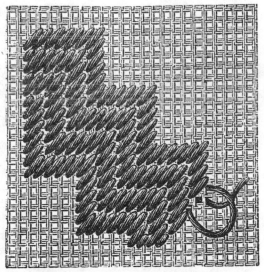

Fig. 355. Byzantine stitch.

Smyrna cross or devil stitch (fig. 343). — Make first a plain cross stitch over four threads each way, then over that another cross stitch, standing upright. The same stitch can be made over six and eight threads; if you work over more than four threads, you must increase the number of stitches in proportion.

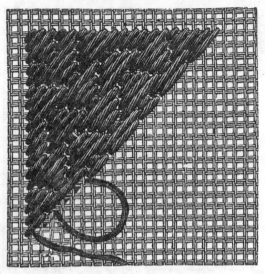

Fig. 356. Milanese stitch.

Star stitch (fig. 344). Each little star is composed of eight stitches which meet in one centre.

Begin by a slanting stitch over a double thread, descending from right to left you ascend vertically under the double thread, then make a vertical stitch on the right side of the work, followed by a slanting stitch, starting from the left corner, and then a horizontal stitch, and so on until the star is complete. To ensure the stars being very regular they should be worked in horizontal rows and each group of stitches should be begun in the same direction.

French stitch (figs. 345, 346, 347). — Introduce the thread from the wrong side out to the right side, then take it upwards over four single or two double threads; stick the needle in to the left under a double

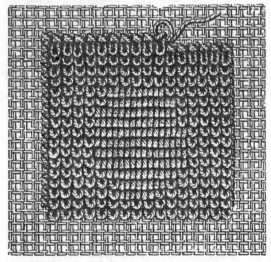

Fig. 357. Velvet stitch, cut and uncut.

thread, fig. 345, then bring it back over the first stitch, insert the needle in the middle of the four threads and conduct it downwards by the side of the first stitch. You then make a stitch to the right similar to the one just made to the left.

When you have finished a stitch take the needle in a slanting line, under one thread, fig. 346, to the next stitch. The whole pattern is worked in diagonal lines.

Parisian stitch (fig. 348). — This stitch, though it is generally worked on silk canvas, can also be worked on the different cotton and linen stuffs.

It makes a very good grounding in cases where the material is not intended to be completely hidden as the illustration shews. The stitches are made over two and six single threads of the canvas, or over one and three double ones. (Alternately a long stitch) and a short one.)

Greek stitch (fig. 349). — This differs from the ordinary cross stitch in the slanting direction given

Fig. 358. Grounding in zig-zag lines in flat stitch.

Fig. 359. Grounding in vertical stripes in flat and plait stitch.

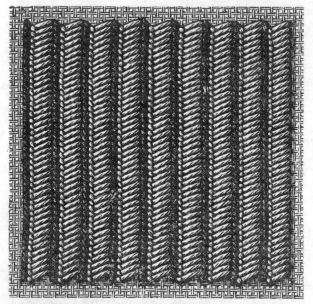

Fig. 360. Grounding in vertical stripes in fish-bone
stitch and gobelin stitch.

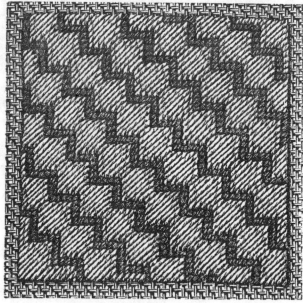

Fig. 361. Grounding in diagonal stripes in flat stitch
and gobelin stitch.

to the threads and the manner in which it is begun. You make the first stitch upwards from below and from right to left over two double threads, bring the needle back horizontally under two double threads, then make a second slanting stitch downwards to complete the cross stitch, from left to right, four double threads beyond the starting point of the first stitch and complete the cross; then bring out the needle, skipping, on the wrong side horizontally two double threads. The next stitch is made like the first.

The rows may be united, either by the short side of the stitch or by the long, but the same course must be adopted throughout. This stitch is much used in Slavonic countries for ornamenting linen

garments and
there the rows
are mostly joined
together, the short
stitches encoun-
tering the long
ones, whereas in
many Greek em-
broideries we find
first the short
stitches joined to
the long and then
in the succeeding
rows, the long
stitches joined to
the long. A coarse
thread that covers
the ground well is
preferable to a
finer one, seeing
that this stitch
has no value
unless it covers the
material entirely.

Scotch stitch
(fig. 350). — Scotch
stitch is formed
of squares com-
posed of slanting
stitches made over
one, two, three,
two and one
double threads
and separated one
square from the
other by a row of
gobelin stitches.

Moorish stitch
(fig. 351). — Here,
instead of as in
the Scotch stitch,
surrounding the
squares on the

Fig. 362.
Grounding in squares in flat stitch.

Fig. 363.
Grounding in vertical stripes in stem
and plait stitch.

four sides with a frame of small stitches, the squares succeed
each other in diagonal lines, so that the stitches form steps.
Half cross stitches, over a double thread separate the rows
of squares.

Oriental stitch (fig. 352). — Here you make four diagonal
stitches, over one, two, three and four crossings of the threads
of the canvas respectively, which four stitches form triangles,
one above the other.

The empty spaces between the rows are filled with gobelin
stitches covering two threads.

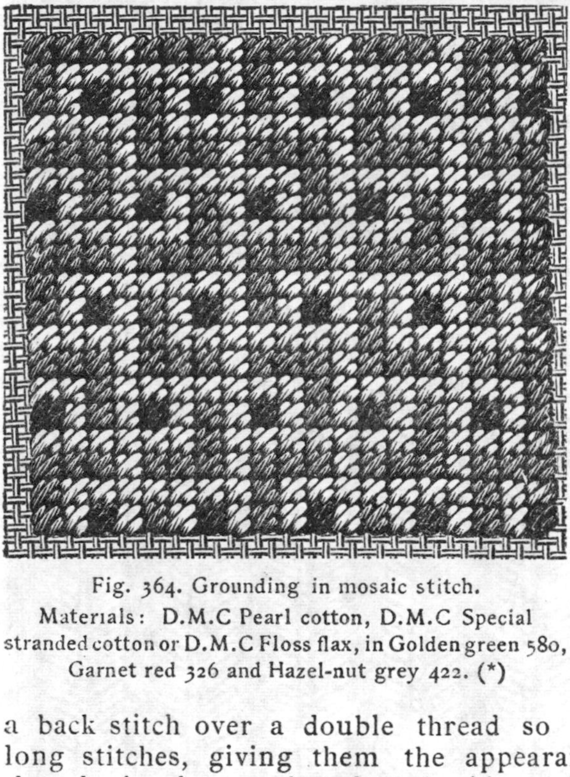

Fig. 364. Grounding in mosaic stitch.
Materials: D.M.C Pearl cotton, D.M.C Special
stranded cotton or D.M.C Floss flax, in Golden green 580,
Garnet red 326 and Hazel-nut grey 422. (*)

Shell stitch (fig. 353). — Carry the thread over six double horizontal threads and then up again over the same number, leaving only one double thread of the canvas between. When you have made the fourth vertical stitch in this manner, you bring the needle down or up again and out behind the third double vertical thread and between the second and third horizontal threads; then make a back stitch over a double thread so as to unite the four long stitches, giving them the appearance of a cluster of threads in drawn thread embroidery. Draw a thread of a different colour twice through these back stitches so as to form small knots like shells over the stitches beneath. Horizontal back stitches over two double threads fill the spaces between the rows of long vertical stitches.

(*) These numbers refer to the colours on the colour cards of the articles
stamped with the D.M.C trade mark. These cards can be consulted at all the
mercers' and needlework shops.

Jacquard stitch (fig. 354). — If you have a large plain surface to cover you should choose a stitch that is itself a pattern. Jacquard stitch, and others we shall describe later on will be found to produce the effect of brocaded stuff.

The first row of stitches is composed of six slanting stitches underneath one another over two double threads, and six

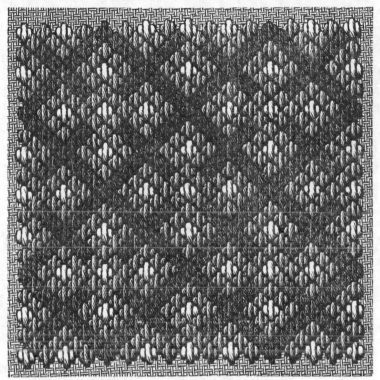

Fig. 365. Grounding in Hungarian stitch.
Materials: D.M.C Pearl cotton, D.M.C Special stranded cotton or D.M.C Floss flax, in Paroquet green 906, Locust-bean brown 356 and Cream yellow 712, or D.M.C Persian silk, in Beetle green 1200, Copper red 1134 and Maize yellow 1069. (*)

beside one another, from left to right, also over two double threads.

The second row consists of the same number of stitches, similarly worked downwards and to the side, only, over one double thread.

_____

(*) See at the end of the last chapter the tables of the sizes and colours of the cotton, flax and silk articles, mark D.M.C.

Byzantine stitch (fig. 355). — Here, you make the same number of stitches as in the preceding figure but with this difference that the two rows of stitches are made either over two double threads, or four single ones.

Milanese stitch (fig. 356). — This pretty ground is produced by small triangles composed of four stitches and opposed the one to the other. In the first diagonal row you make descending,

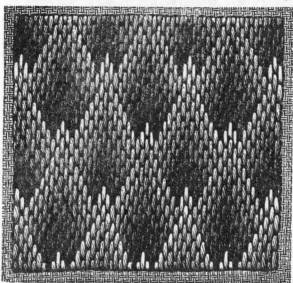

Fig. 366. Grounding in Hungarian stitch.
Materials : D.M.C Special stranded cotton or
D.M.C Floss flax,
in Black fast dye 310, Cream yellow 712, Locust-bean brown 758, 357, 356, 303, 355,
Golden green 580, 581, 582, 583, 584, D.M.C Persian silk,
in Black 1187, Cream white 1220, Copper red 1132,
1227, 1133, 1134, 1135,
Olive green 1434, 1195, 1196, 1197, 1198. (*)

a back stitch alternately over one and over four crossings of the canvas threads, in the second row, ascending, a back stitch over three and two crossings of the canvas threads, in the third row, descending, over three and two crossings, in the fourth row ascending, over one and four crossings. The long stitches of the next row are placed before the little stitch and the little stitch before the long stitch of the last row.

Velvet stitch, cut and uncut (fig. 357). — This stitch by means of which a very good imitation of the Oriental carpets can be produced, and which is also called Astrachan stitch, consists of loops, each secured by a cross stitch. The best way to ensure these loops being even and regular is to make them over an ivory or wooden mesh, or a wide piece of whalebone.

(*) See at the end of the last chapter the tables of the sizes and colours of the cotton, flax and silk articles, mark D.M.C.

The engraving shews clearly how this simple stitch is made. It can be varied, by opening the loops, which gives the embroidery a velvety appearance.

In the engraving only the middle loops are cut, for the cut and the uncut can both be introduced into the same piece of work.

Thus the pattern represented in figures 382 and 383 can be executed in the cut and the uncut stitch, the borders being done in the uncut, the centre parts in the cut.

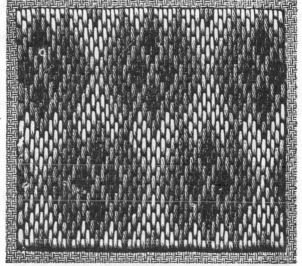

Tapestry groundings.—We now pass to the explanation of the stitches employed in a small series of groundings suitable for large surfaces. In general these groundings are worked in a single colour, or in two shades of one colour, according to the pattern the grounding is intended for.

As materials a loose or a twisted thread can be used; the choice must depend on the stitch.

Fig. 367. Grounding in Hungarian stitch.

Materials: D.M.C Special stranded cotton or D.M.C Floss flax, in Morocco red 3328, Black fast dye 310, Moss green 471, 469 and 936 and Maize yellow 579, D.M.C Persian silk, in Crimson red 1185, Black 1187, Golden green 1385, 1144, 1146 and Cream white 1220.

We again recommend D.M.C Special stranded cotton (Mouliné spécial), D.M.C Floss flax (Lin floche), D.M.C Pearl cotton (Coton perlé), or D.M.C Persian silk (Soie de Perse).

Grounding in zig-zag lines in flat stitch (fig. 358). — The pattern is composed of zig-zag lines. The wide stripes are worked over six threads of the stuff, the narrow ones over two. Each line takes nine flat stitches, set slanting. If the grounding is to be in two colours, take the lighter one for the wide stripes, the darker for the narrow ones.

Grounding in vertical stripes in flat and plait stitch (fig. 359). — The stripes in flat stitch take twelve threads of the stuff. Each stripe is composed of two rows of horizontal stitches, forming a zig-zag line, the shortest stitch of which covers two threads of the stuff, the longest ten, the plait stitch covers three threads in width, two in height.

Grounding in vertical stripes in fish-bone stitch and gobelin stitch (fig. 360). — The light stripes are formed of a half row of fish-bone stitches over four horizontal threads and two vertical. The dark lines, between the stripes of fish-bone stitches, are worked in gobelin stitch over one thread of the stuff.

Fig. 368. Grounding in Hungarian stitch.
Materials: D.M.C Special stranded cotton or D.M.C
Floss flax, in Black fast dye 310,
Blue grey 591, 592, 593, 594, and Cachou
brown 434, 435, 436, 437;
D.M.C Persian silk, in Black 1187, Steel blue 1103,
1104, 1105, 1106,
and Tender brown 1048, 1049, 1050, 1051.

Grounding in diagonal stripes in flat stitch and gobelin stitch (fig. 361). — Begin by the dark zig-zag lines in gobelin stitch over one thread of the stuff. When these are done, fill in the foundation with slanting flat stitches, the smallest one over two threads, the longest over six.

Grounding in squares in flat stitch (fig. 362). — Each square takes nine slanting flat stitches, the smallest one over one thread, the longest — the middle one — over five threads. The engraving shews the arrangement of the colours.

Grounding in vertical stripes in stem and plait stitch (fig. 363). — Stem stitch is worked over eight vertical threads and two horizontal. We recommend the light colour for the wide stripes in stem stitch, the dark for the plait stitch.

Grounding in mosaic stitch (fig. 364). — The simple little grounding is suitable for little articles made by children. It is worked in mosaic stitch, fig. 339; the triangles in bright green, the dark stitches in dark red and the foundation in grey.

Grounding in Hungarian stitch (fig. 365). — This pattern is worked in Hungarian stitch, described by figure 340.

As regards the arrangement of the colours, the interlaced figures are embroidered in green and ivory white, the ground in copper red.

Hungarian stitch. — This kind of embroidery in which each figure of the pattern is worked in a single colour, but in the whole series of shades of that colour, is known by the name of "Hungarian stitch".

The four following designs, distinguished for their rich colouring, are used for cushions of all kinds where they replace the coloured stuffs. (*)

They should be worked in a very loose material, such as D.M.C Persian

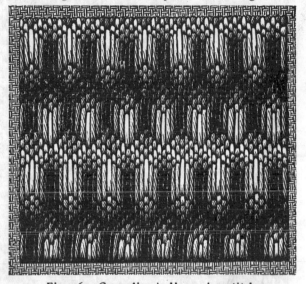

Fig. 369. Grounding in Hungarian stitch.
Materials : D.M.C Special stranded cotton or
D.M.C Floss flax,
in Black fast dye 310, Pistachio green 319, 320, 368, 369
and Raspberry red 3686, 3687, 3688 ;
D.M.C Persian silk, in Black 1187, Myrtle green 1140,
1228, 1138, 1137 and Raspberry
red 1150, 1148, 1437.

silk (Soie de Perse), D.M.C Special stranded cotton (Mouliné spécial) or D.M.C Floss flax (Lin floche).

Grounding in Hungarian stitch (fig. 366). — Begin the pointed figures by the five black stitches, made over 4 horizontal threads. To these five black stitches, add five coloured

---

(*) See at the end of the volume the list of the albums of the D.M.C Library, containing a large variety of patterns for all kinds of work.

rows — one series of red, one of green — in which the number of stitches increases always by two, and finish the figure with three stitches in white at the point.

Fig. 370. Grounding in mediæval embroidery in straight stitches set contrariwise.
Materials : D.M.C Pearl cotton, D.M.C Special stranded cotton
or D.M.C Floss flax, in Mauve violet 316, Old blue 930, Golden green 582, Rust
yellow 365 and Geranium red 350 ;
D.M.C Persian silk, in Scabious violet 1202, Delft blue 1246, Golden green 1145,
Maize yellow 1072 and Old red 1038.

Grounding in Hungarian stitch (fig. 367). — The diagonal lines which traverse the whole of the pattern and which frame the black lozenges, are worked in red; the triangles, which touch the lozenges, are worked in three shades of green, the foundation in ivory white. All the stitches are vertical over four threads of the stuff.

Grounding in Hungarian stitch (fig. 368). — The dark lines, which form the outlines of the figures, are worked in black, in vertical stitches over four threads of the stuff.

The fillings of the figures are worked alternately in four shades of brown and four of blue.

Grounding in Hungarian stitch (fig. 369). — The black horizontal line is made up alternately of one straight stitch over eight threads, and three over two. Above this black line come four rows in shades of green, and below it three rows in shades of pink. In this manner the lightest shades meet.

Grounding in mediæval embroidery in straight stitches set contrariwise (figs. 370 and 371). — The original of this design is a piece of tapestry of the 14th century. The whole composition of the pattern with its simple conventional birds and trees, indicates its age. (*)

The embroidery is executed on plain canvas, in a loose silk, in vertical stitches over four threads of the stuff, worked in horizontal rows as shewn in the explanatory figure 371.

Fig. 371.
Detail of figure 370.

Begin by the little tree between the birds, which is worked in Golden green 582; then come the birds in Mauve violet 316 and the dark flowerets in Old blue 930.

The light octagons are filled in with light yellow (Rust yellow 365, stitches; the rest of the foundation is covered with Geranium red 350.

Grounding in modern tapestry in half cross stitch (fig. 372). — The size of our book did not admit of our giving the present chapter all the importance we could have wished.

(*) See at the end of the volume the list of the albums of the D.M.C Library, containing a large variety of patterns for all kinds of work.

We should have liked to introduce some interesting modern designs to our readers, such as those represented in figure 372.

Fig. 372. Grounding in modern tapestry in half cross stitch.
Materials: D.M.C Pearl cotton or D.M.C Special stranded cotton, in Rust
yellow 365 and Greenish grey 597,
or in Mandarin yellow 745 and Garnet red 358. (*)

(*) See at the end of the last chapter the tables of the sizes and colours of the cotton, flax and silk articles, mark D.M.C.

Conventional flowers and leaves form the basis of designs of this sort, and are specially suited for tapestry work in half cross stitch and tent stitch. (*)

Border in tent stitch or "petit point" (fig. 373). — This border with D.M.C Pearl cotton No. 1 is worked entirely in tent stitch, fig. 324; it presents no difficulties whatever in the working.

The flowers are outlined with dark pink, Raspberry red 3685,

Fig. 373. Border in tent stitch or "petit point".
Materials: D.M.C Pearl cotton, D.M.C Special stranded cotton or D.M.C
Floss flax, in Raspberry red 3685 and 3688, Moss green 469
and Cachou brown 738.

and filled in with light pink, Raspberry red 3688; the calices and stalks are embroidered in green, Moss green 469. For the ground of the border take a faded yellow, Cachou brown 738. This pattern adapts itself specially well to the decoration of panels and doorhangings.

When used for table-covers, the border should be worked

(*) See at the end of the volume the list of the albums of the D.M.C Library, containing a large variety of patterns for all kinds of work.

in cross stitch on a cream coloured stuff, and the ground left un-worked.

Embroideries in imitation of Oriental carpets. Here follow some embroidery stitches by means of which an admirable imitation of Oriental carpets can be achieved.

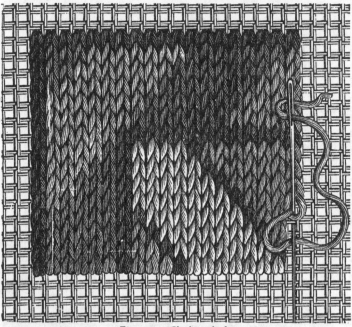

Fig. 374. Chain stitch.

Fig. 375. Knitting-stitch.

Chain stitch and knitting stitch are used for the reproduction of Sumac carpets, whilst single and double knot stitch — also called Smyrna stitch — serve for copying carpets or rugs in knot stitch.

Chain stitch (fig. 374). — Very interesting embroideries are to be met with here and there in museums, in the shape of hangings and panels, worked in chain stitch.

It is the best stitch for patterns in a variety of colours, as they blend together better in it, than in any other. The first stitch is always completed by the next, and its very shape helps to soften the contrast of colours.

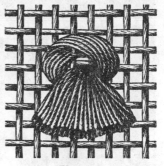

The explanation given on figure 229 will have shewn our readers that chain stitch cannot be worked to and fro like other stitches; the rows must all be begun from the same side and finished in one journey. Nor can you continue and finish a colour, as in cross stitch embroideries; you are obliged to go on with the line begun and change the thread each time you come to another colour.

Fig. 376.
Single knotted stitch.

Knitting-stitch (fig. 375). — This stitch is the reproduction in embroidery of the Sumac rugs and is suitable for designs in many colours. It has a good deal of resemblance, with plaited Spanish stitch, figs. 177 and 178, and is also worked as that is, in two rounds; the stitches are set diagonally over two double vertical threads and half a double horizontal thread.

Fig. 377.
Single knotted stitch.

The second row is worked the opposite way and completes the stitch. In order to copy in knitting-stitch, a pattern printed in square types, count the left part where the two half stitches meet as a stitch.

Fig. 378. Single knotted stitch.

For this stitch it is advisable to provide yourself with a number of needles, one for each colour you are going to use; and the same for the chain stitch described above.

Single knotted stitch (figs. 376, 377, 378). — The
Oriental carpets with their short fleecy knots can be imitated

Fig. 379. Persian border in single knotted stitch.
Materials: D.M.C Floss flax, D.M.C Special stranded cotton or D.M.C
Alsatia, in Cardinal red 347, Geranium red 352, Azure blue 3325, Indigo blue 322,
Golden green 580, Cream yellow 712, Mandarin yellow 741, Scabious
violet 396, Beetle green 3348. (*)

Fig. 380. Double knotted or Smyrna stitch.

_____

(*) See at the end of the last chapter the tables of the sizes and colours of
the cotton, flax and silk articles, mark D.M.C.

by means of single knotted stitch which is very similar to single
Malta stitch, figs. 260 and 261. Here too each stitch is composed

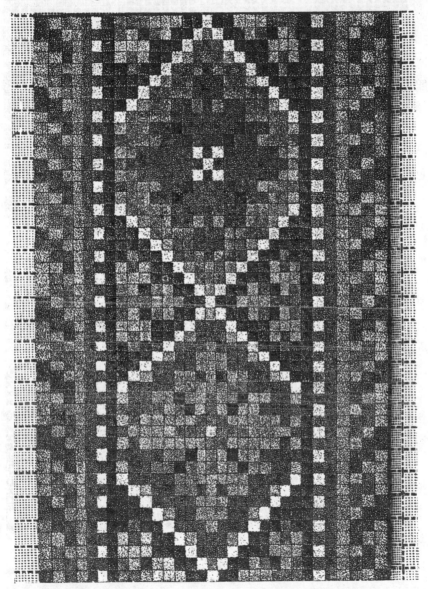

Fig. 381. Border in double knotted or Smyrna stitch.
Materials: D.M.C Special stranded cotton, D.M.C Floss flax or D.M.C Alsatia,
in Rust yellow 308, Blue fast dye 799, Cachou brown 437,
Rust brown 3310, Black fast dye 310.

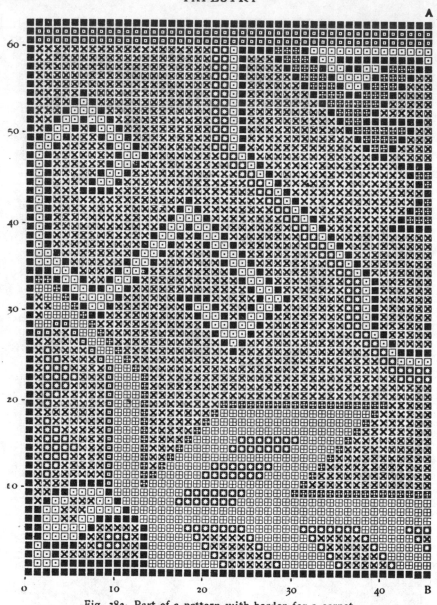

Fig. 382. Part of a pattern with border for a carpet.

Materials: D.M.C Special stranded cotton, D.M.C Pearl cotton, D.M.C Floss flax or D.M.C Persian silk.

Explanation of the colours — Of the cotton and the flax threads: ■ Black fast dye 310, ⊠ Garnet red 358, ⊞ Geranium red 350, ◻ Solid blue 824, ⊞ Solid blue 813, ◻ Beetle green 3347, ⊡ Hazel-nut grey 422.

Of the silk: ■ Black 1187, ⊠ Old pink 1008, ⊞ Copper red 1134, ◻ Indigo blue 1013, ⊞ Indigo blue 1011, ◻ Myrtle green 1139, ⊡ Otter brown 1042.

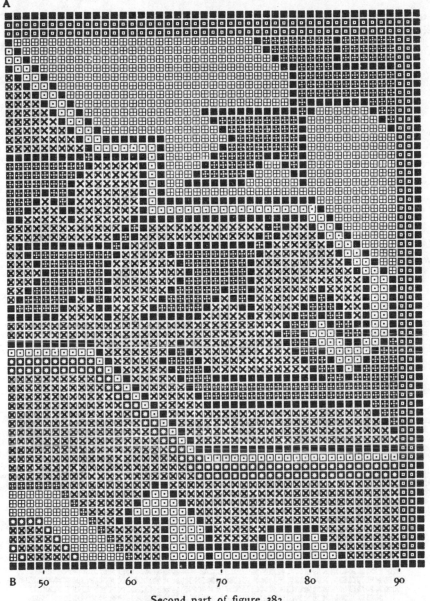

Second part of figure 282.

of two little meshes of thread which are fastened into the stuff by a back stitch.

To economise thread and ensure regularity in the knots or tassels a kind of mesh is used terminating in a small blade

at one end, over which the thread which is to produce the
loops afterwards to be cut is carried.

When you have finished a row of stitches, draw out the

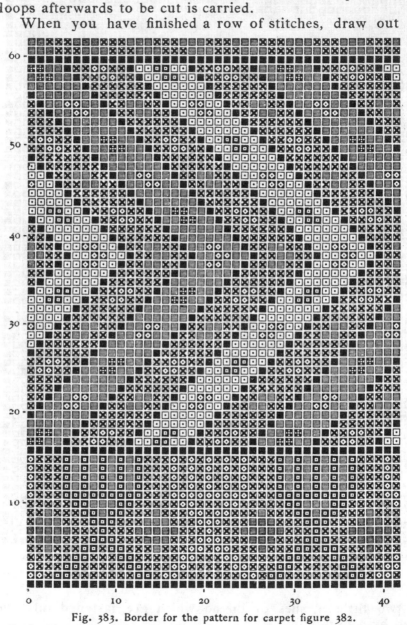

Fig. 383. Border for the pattern for carpet figure 382.
Explanation of the colour signs not given beneath figure 382 : Of the cotton
and flax threads : ◻ Beetle green 3345, ▦ Rust brown 3313.
Of the silk : ◻ Myrtle green 1141, ▦ Rust brown 1156.

mesh so that the blade, if there be one, passing through the loops open them at the top, if there be no blade, you open the loops with scissors.

Figure 376 shews you a single stitch, still open, figure 377 a single stitch, closed, whilst figure 378 shews a few stitches made over a mesh.

As may be seen by these explanations, each stitch occupies a square of stuff, two threads in height by two in width.

Persian border in single knotted stitch (fig. 379). — Our border, copied from a Persian embroidery of the 17th century, was worked in single knotted stitch. The depth of the fleece or nap is rather less than ¼ of an inch.

The material chosen for it was D.M.C Floss flax and the stitches are made with eight whole threads. The principal figures are outlined alternately with red and cream, and filled in with two shades of blue or red, with a yellow centre; the scalloped leaves are worked in two shades of green and light red. The upright columns between the principal figures are outlined with blue and filled in with red and yellow, and the lines connecting them with the principal figures are in dark green. The little borders, top and bottom, are edged inside with green, and outside with yellow and filled in with red and cream; the ground is in light violet.

Double knotted or Smyrna stitch (fig. 380). — With this stitch a good imitation of the oriental rugs and carpets can be produced.

It is not unlike double Malta stitch, figs. 262 to 265. It is worked in horizontal rows, each stitch covering four threads of the stuff in width; and four horizontal threads are left between the rows of stitches.

In figure 380 the course of the work is clearly shewn.

When you have finished a row of stitches cut them carefully to the required height. All irregularities of the nap or fleece must be shorn away with sharp scissors when the whole is finished.

Border in double knotted or Smyrna stitch (fig. 381). This border, suitable for a bedside rug is embroidered in double knotted stitch in five colours. The lightest shade is Rust yellow 308; the next shade darker is Blue fast dye 799; the medium shade, Cachou brown 437; the dark, Rust brown 3310; the darkest, Black fast dye 310. The material, is either D.M.C Special stranded cotton (Mouliné spécial) No. 14, by using three threads together or D.M.C Alsatia

No. 3o by using 10 threads together. The depth of the nap is, in this instance $\frac{5}{8}$ of an inch.

Part of a pattern with border for a carpet (figs. 382 and 383). — Our space does not admit of our reproducing more than a quarter of this pattern given in two pieces ; see the points of junction at A and B. The colours selected should be of the very softest tints. A black line separates the four quarters of the pattern. Of the four, the right top quarter and the bottom left one are filled in with blue, whilst the top left quarter is worked as indicated in figure 382.

After adding on at the bottom the wide stripe, fig. 383, you repeat the little border in red, blue and green. In this latter a very good effect can be produced by varying the ground colour of the different detached subjects of which it consists.

Patterns of needlework. — Besides the different kinds of work described above a great choice of patterns for tapestry will be found in the following publications of the D.M.C Library : *Motifs for Embroideries I and II, Motifs for Coptic Embroidery II and III,* and *Works of various kinds.* (*)

(*) See at the end of the volume the list of the albums of the D.M.C Library.

Insertion. — Plain stitches and overs.

Knitting

Knitting is one of the earliest kinds of needlework and the one that has been brought to the greatest perfection. It would be impossible to invent new stitches or patterns; we have therefore confined ourselves to describing the stitches in general use, and reproducing such patterns as we think likely to be most useful to our readers, who can then make their own selection.

Formerly knitting was practically confined to the making of stockings and yet there are numberless other useful and ornamental articles, such as mufflers, motor scarves, shawls, counterpanes, cradle covers, gloves, laces of all sorts, &c. which can be made with knitting needles.

Besides its useful side, knitting is a pleasant pastime that can be resorted to at odd moments and carried on, whilst talking or even reading.

Knitting consists of loops or stitches, as they are generally called, formed by means of two needles.

In round knitting, four or five needles are necessary for the better handling of the work.

Through the loops thus formed being connected together in unbroken continuity, a very elastic fabric is produced, specially adapted for making warm and close fitting wearing apparel.

Knitting needles. — These whether of steel, wood or bone must always be of a size to suit the thread used.

Materials. — Soft silky threads, slightly twisted, are the best for knitting, but for some articles thread with a stronger twist which shews up the pattern better should be used.

For articles of wearing apparel in which the knitted fabric takes the place of a woven one, we recommend D.M.C Knitting cotton (Coton à tricoter), or D.M.C Knitting cotton, bell mark (Retors pour mercerie), D.M.C Alsatia, D.M.C Pearl cotton (Coton perlé), or D.M.C Floss crochet cotton (Crochet floche). (*) We particularly recommend the two latter articles. Pearl cotton is made up in balls of 5o grammes, in Nos. 3, 5 and 8. The Floss crochet cotton made up in balls of 20 grammes

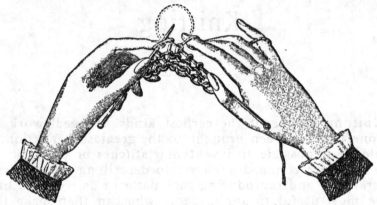

Fig. 384. Position of the hands in knitting.

weight, is a thread of 6 strands slightly twisted. Bed and sofa covers, and coarse lace and insertions may also be made with D.M.C Flax thread for knitting (Lin pour tricoter), D.M.C Crochet cotton (Coton pour crochet), D.M.C Shaded Pearl cotton (Coton perlé ombré) and D.M.C Knotting cotton (Fil à pointer).

For fine lace the pattern shews up better with a strongly twisted thread, such as D.M.C Alsatian thread (Fil d'Alsace), D.M.C Crochet cotton, 6 cord (Cordonnet 6 fils), D.M.C Special crochet cotton (Cordonnet spécial), D.M.C Flax thread for knitting (Lin pour tricoter), D.M.C Flax lace thread (Lin pour dentelles) and D.M.C Alsatia in fine numbers, all highly to be recommended for the purpose.

(*) See at the end of the last chapter the tables of the sizes and colours of the cotton, flax and silk articles, mark D.M.C. — The French names, in brackets, are those stamped on the labels of the D.M.C articles.

Position of the hands in knitting (fig. 384). — Lay the thread over the fifth finger of the right hand and twist it round it, then take it under the middle fingers and over the forefinger which must be kept close to the work. The third finger and the thumb hold the work.

The left hand plays a more or less passive part; having merely by a slight movement of the forefinger, to pass the loops in succession on to the needle in the right hand, which forms the stitches.

The Germans lay the thread over the left hand which enables the hand to move much more quickly. There are some ways of casting on which can only be done in the German fashion.

To prevent irregularity in the stitches, the needles should never protrude more than about ½ an inch from the stitches.

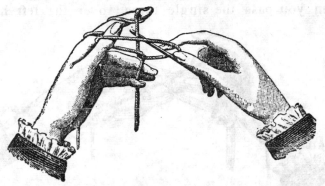

Fig. 385. Crossed casting on with a single thread.

All excessive movement of the arms, which renders knitting very tiring should be avoided.

Casting on. — Casting, or setting on, as it is sometimes called, is the formation of the first row of stitches which is to constitute the foundation of the work.

There are four ways of casting on: (1) crossed casting on, which can be done in four different ways; (2) knitting on; (3) slipping on, which may also be done in two ways; (4) casting on with picots.

(1) a. **Crossed casting on with a single thread** (fig. 385). — Pass the thread under the left hand and make a loop round the thumb, so that the thread runs between the thumb, and the forefinger. An end of thread, long enough to make the number of stitches to be cast on must be left on the side of the thumb. Put the needle in from below, into the loop which

is round the thumb, and pass it from right to left under that part of the thread which lies between the forefinger and the thumb, then bring the thread through the loop on the thumb; draw the thumb out and lay the loop on the needle.

For the next stitches lay the thread over the thumb so that the needle lies outside the thumb. Put in the needle under the thread nearest the point and complete the stitch as before.

This way of casting on is generally done over two needles, one of them being drawn out before the knitting-off is begun, thus producing rather loose stitches for the second row to be made on, and ensuring a loose outer edge.

(1) b. **Crossed casting on with a threefold thread.** — This way is similar to the last, only that the thread is taken threefold and is drawn by the needle through the loop which is formed at the bend of the thread.

Then you pass the single thread over the left hand and

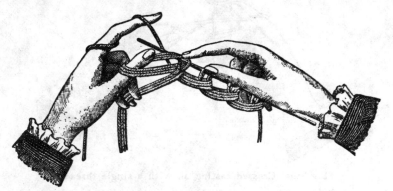

Fig. 386. Double crossed casting on with a threefold thread.

the triple one round the thumb, as in fig. 385, and make the same stitches as in the foregoing casting on.

The triple thread makes a broad chain at the base of the loops.

(1) c. **Double crossed casting on with a threefold thread** (fig. 386). — This can be done with a single or a triple thread. In our engraving it is done with a triple one. The first stitch is made, as we have already described, only that you must keep the loop on the thumb and put the needle into it a second time, lay hold of the thread from behind, cast on a second stitch on to the needle, and then only withdraw your thumb and drop the loop. In this manner two loops are made at once quite close together.

(1) d. **Crossed casting on forming a chain** (fig. 387). —
Begin always by making one such stitch as described in
figure 385 : for the second stitch and for every second subsequent

stitch, bring the
end of the thread
to the inside of the
palm of the hand,
so that it lies be-
tween the thumb
and the forefinger;
the other stitches
are again made in
the manner ex-
plained in figure
385.

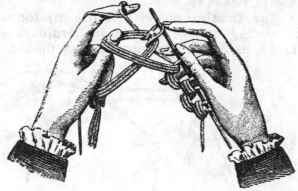

(2) **Knitting on
stitches** (fig. 388).

Fig. 387. Crossed casting on forming a chain.

Begin with a plain crossed stitch, then take the thread and
the needle in the left hand and a second needle in the right
hand, and catch the second needle into the stitch on the left
needle, put the thread on the right needle and draw it through
in the form of a loop through the loop on the left needle.

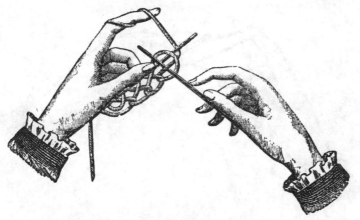

Fig. 288. Knitting on stitches.

Then transfer it as a new stitch on to the left needle on which
you will then have two stitches; catch the needle again into
the last stitch and draw the thread through it, as before to
form a third stitch, and so on.

This way of casting on is used for articles that are to have a double edge, because stitches thus made are easier to pick up than tighter ones, but it should not be used where the stitches so made form the actual edge, as the loops would remain too open.

(3) a. **Casting on with single slip loops** (fig. 389). — Begin by casting on one loop in the ordinary way, next, lay the thread, as in German knitting over the left hand, but twisting

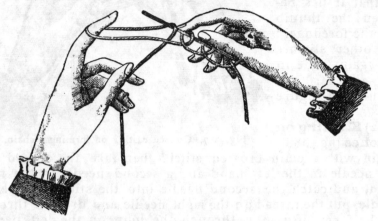

Fig. 389. Casting on with single slip loops.

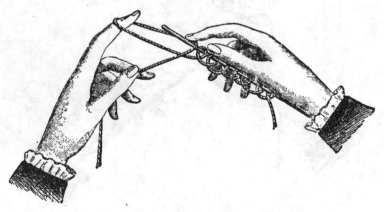

Fig. 390. Casting on with double slip loops.

it once only round the forefinger, then put the needle upwards from below, under the thread that lies on the outside of the forefinger; draw out the finger from the loop on the needle; take the thread on the forefinger again, put the needle into the loop and so on.

(3) b. **Casting on with double slip loops** (fig. 390). —
Begin by casting on a stitch in the ordinary way, then lay
the thread over the forefinger, the reverse way, so that it
crosses between your hand and your body, and not outside
the hand. Pass the needle upwards from below, under the
inside thread, and slip this thread under the form of a loop
on to the needle. Continue to cast on, inserting the needle,
alternately, under the front and back threads. This method is
specially suitable for open patterns, where you have to increase
several times in succession.

(4) **Casting on with picots** (fig. 391). — Cast on two
stitches in the ordinary way and turn the work. Lay the thread
over the needle, put the needle into the first stitch, from right
to left, slip the stitch on to your right needle; knit off the

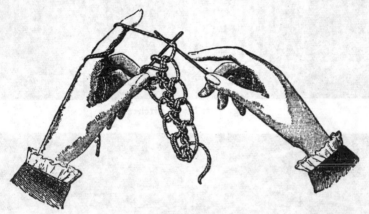

Fig. 391. Casting on with picots.

second stitch plain and draw the first stitch over the second
one. Turn the work and continue to cast on stitches in this
manner to the required length.

Then pick up the picots thus formed with an auxiliary
needle and knit them off like ordinary stitches.

This way of casting on may be varied in the following
manner. After casting on the stitches, as in fig. 391, throw
the thread over the needle and knit two stitches together.

Stitches. — By different ways of interlacing the threads,
different kinds of stitches are produced. The following ones
are in the most frequent use.

Plain stitches (fig. 392). — This is the easiest stitch and
the first one a child is taught. It is executed as follows: Put

the right-hand needle, upwards from below, under the front part of the first stitch on the left-hand needle, lay the thread from right to left under the needle, draw it through the loop and drop the loop off the left needle.

Plain knitting is employed in all cases where a perfectly smooth even surface is required. The wrong side looks quite different from the right side where it presents the appearance of vertical lines, like plaits.

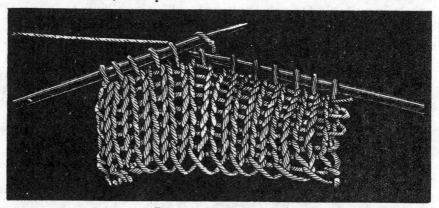

Fig. 392. Plain stitches.

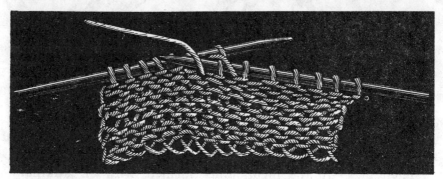

Fig. 393. Back or seam stitch.

Back or seam stitch (fig. 393). — You may also purposely knit the wrong side of plain knitting. This is termed purling and is done in the following way: lay the thread over the left hand needle, and put in the right one, downwards from above behind the thread of the left needle, lay the thread upwards from below round the right needle, draw the thread with the needle through the loop on the left needle and drop the latter loop off the left needle.

This stitch is used in knitting piqué patterns and for marking certain lines in plain knitting, such for example as the seams of stockings.

Plain stitch taken from the back (fig. 394). — Put the needle in from right to left, under the outside part of the stitch; leave the thread behind the needle, then lay it from right to left over the needle and draw it through the stitch.

In plain stitches taken from the back, the two threads of the

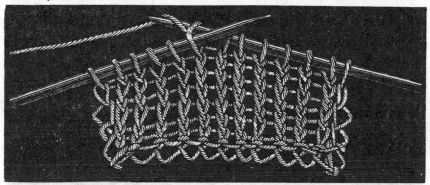

Fig. 394. Plain stitch taken from the back.

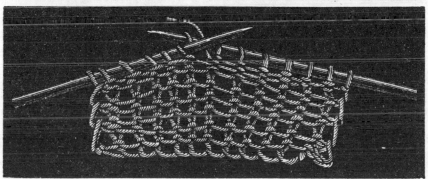

Fig. 395. Back or seam-stitch taken from the back.

loops are crossed, instead of lying side by side as in plain knitting.

Back or seam stitch taken from the back (fig. 395). — Put the needle into the second part of the stitch, upwards from below and knit the stitch like any other back stitch. Back or seam stitch taken from the back is only used for certain openwork patterns.

Overs (fig. 396). — These form holes in plain knitting and are used for openwork pattern and for increasing.

To make an over, lay the thread over the needle, and in the next row knit this loop like any other stitch.

Each over adds a stitch to the preceding number of stitches. In cases, therefore, where the number is to remain the same you have to make as many intakes as overs. Overs can only be made ·in conjunction with other stitches.

Dot stitches (fig. 397). — These form raised spots in plain knitting and are made as follows : knit one plain and leave it on the left hand needle ; replace the loop made with

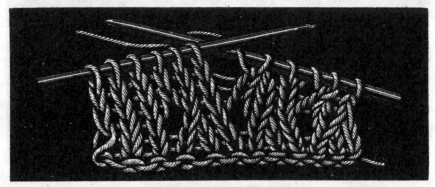

Fig. 396. Overs.

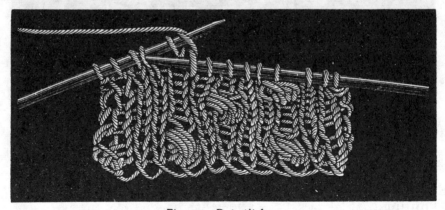

Fig. 397. Dot stitches.

the right needle on the left needle and knit it off as a plain stitch. Repeat the same process four or five times, making all the new stitches issue from the same stitch on the left needle. When you have five loops on the right needle, drop the stitch on the left needle and pull the four first loops over the last one.

Cable or chain stitch. — Chain stitches are used for strengthening and equalising the edges of articles that are made in stripes or bands. They can be made in two ways, either, you knit off all the stitches on one needle; turn the work; put the needle into this last stitch, as if you were going to knit it from the back and slip it on to the needle, without knitting it, the thread to lie behind the needle.

In the second manner of making the chain, you knitt off all the stitches on one needle to the last, lay the thread over the needle, as for a back stitch, pass the stitch on to the right needle, turn the work, and knit one plain stitch to begin with.

Names of the stitches. — Out of the stitches that have already been described, many others are formed, which are frequently referred to in knitting directions and recipes. We give here all the names which will be used in the descriptions that will follow, reverting at the same time to some of the stitches already described.

Single over, or increase, shewn in fig. 396. — Throw the thread once over the right needle.

Double over or two increases. — Throw the thread twice round the right needle.

Plain intake or decrease. — Knit two stitches together plain as if they were one. This is done when the intake is to lie from left to right.

Purled intake or decrease. — Purl two stitches together. This is done when you want the intake to be very visible in a piece of plain knitting; or on the wrong side in the case of a piece of work composed of stripes; when the intake on the wrong side is to incline to the right.

Plain intake or decrease taken from the back. — Take two stitches from the back and knit them together plain. This is done when the intake is to incline to the left.

Purled intake or decrease taken from the back. — Purl two stitches together from behind. This is done when, in articles, made up of stripes, the decrease has to be made on the wrong side, and is to slant to the left on the right side.

Slipping or not knitting a stitch, is passing a stitch from the left needle to the right one without knitting it.

Pulling over. — This means slipping a stitch from the left needle to the right one without knitting it, knitting the next stitch plain, and pulling the slipped stitch over the knitted one. In this manner two or three stitches can be pulled over a knitted one.

Casting off. — To prevent the stitches from unravelling they are finished off, when the work is done, in the following manner. Knit two plain, pull the first over the second, thus dropping it, so that only one remains on the needle. Knit the next stitch plain and pull the following one over it and so on. This chain of stitches, must neither be too tight nor too loose, but just as elastic as the rest of the work.

Materials for stockings. — Stockings may be made of silk, wool, cotton or linen. It is useless to dwell here on the special merits of these different materials, people must decide for themselves which to choose. But we cannot too highly recommend for the purpose D.M.C Knitting cotton (Coton à tricoter), D.M.C Knitting cotton, bell mark (Retors pour mercerie), D.M.C Knitting cotton, bell mark, special quality (Retors spécial pour mercerie), D.M.C Alsatia or D.M.C Flax thread for knitting (Lin pour tricoter) (*); all the more as they are now to be had in a very large number of shades, almost entirely fast colours.

Another material which should always be used for strengthening the heels and toes is D.M.C Felting cotton (Coton à feutrer). This article may, if necessary, be replaced by D.M.C Pearl cotton (Coton perlé) N° 12.

Stocking knitting. — A stocking consists of five parts: (1) the top, (2) the knee, (3) the leg, (4) the heel, (5) the foot.

(1) The top may be either ribbed, or knitted in an open-work stitch of some kind, or with a double toothed edge, see figs. 398 and 399.

(2 and 3) The knee and the calf, that is to say the part of the stocking between the top and the heel, are generally plain knitted; only childrens' stockings are sometimes fancy knitted or ribbed.

(4) The heel is worked as straight knitting, forwards plain and back purled. It is shaped to the foot by the intakes at the end of the heel.

(5) The foot is knitted plain, with intakes from the heel onwards to get rid of the superfluous stitches. Then knit a

---

(*) See at the end of the last chapter the tables of the sizes and colours of the cotton, flax and silk articles, mark D.M.C. — The French names, in brackets, are those stamped on the labels of the D.M.C articles.

plain piece, of the required length, without a seam stitch till you begin to decrease for the toe, which can be worked in several different ways.

To ensure the right proportions between the several parts of a stocking, the following directions should be attended to. The top never counts, in measuring the length of the leg. When the top part is finished, you make the seam, at the beginning of the first needle of the round, of one, or two purled stitches. Sometimes you see a narrow pattern of purled stitches in place of the plain seam. This seam marks the middle of a stocking.

For ordinary short stockings, or rather socks, knit plain from the bottom row of the top part, till the piece forms a square; the same length, that is, as the width of the stocking.

For stockings that are to cover the knee, knit half as much again, that is, one and a half times the width of the stocking; then you begin the intakes to form the calf of the leg. Pull the third stitch after the seam, over the second, and knit together the two last but one before the seam.

You repeat these intakes, first three or four times after every twelve rounds, then, invariably after eight, until the calf is one and a half time the width of the knee in length and only three quarters the width of the knee in width.

For the ankle, knit a plain piece, half the width of the knee in length, without any intakes.

Before beginning the heel divide the stitches on to the four needles, exclusive of the seam stitches and put two stitches more than the quarter of the whole number on to the needles right and left of the seam. For a heel to fit well, it should be as long as it is wide. To strengthen the heels and toes, they are frequently knitted with double thread. D.M.C Felting cotton (Coton à feutrer) made expressly for the purpose, and already referred to, page 252, should be wound round the thread of which the rest of the stocking is made.

For the instep, the part between the heel and toe, you must go on decreasing from the heel, until you have two stitches less on each needle than you had at the ankle.

Then knit the plain part of the foot, which should be as wide as the ankle, after which proceed to decrease for the toe, which should be a quarter the length of the whole foot. In spite of this careful subdivision, it is always well to count the stitches to ensure perfect regularity. The number of stitches cast on, at the outset, or the same sized stockings, must depend upon the size of the material employed.

Scalloped edge (figs. 398 and 399). — The simplest edge for a stocking, and also the strongest, is one that forms little teeth like cats' teeth.

Having cast on the stitches, knit from six to ten rounds plain according to the size of the cotton, then one round of alternate intakes and overs. Repeat the same number of plain rounds, then with a sixth needle take up as many of the cast on stitches, as you have stitches on one needle. Turn this needle inwards and place it against the outside needle and knit off the stitches on the two needles together. See that you knit the corresponding stitches off together, otherwise the cats' teeth will be crooked.

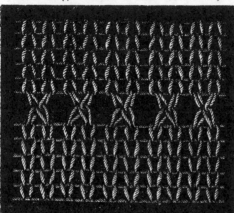

Fig. 398. Scalloped edge. Open.

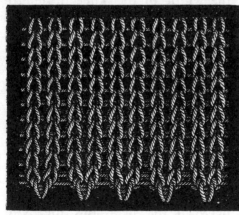

Fig. 399. Scalloped edge. Folded over.

Common heel (fig. 400). This is the simplest and commonest form of heel and may be knitted either with or without an outside seam. After having divided the stitches into four and put two more on to each of the heel needles than on the others, make, according to the size of the material, from fifteen to twenty seams. For the outside seam knit plain, in the purled round, the three first stitches of the right needle and the three last of the left one.

When you have made the required number of seams, finish the right needle and knit only one third of the stitches on the left needle. Supposing that there are twenty-four stitches on one needle, knit off 8, slip the next, knit 1, and pull the slipped stitch over, knit 2 plain, turn the work, slip the first stitch and purl the next 8 stitches of the second needle; purl the 9ᵗʰ and 10ᵗʰ together, purl 2, turn the work to the right side and slip the first stitch on to the right needle. By means of these successive intakes after the 8 stitches, the knitting forms a plait on both sides of the heel.

In all heels made after this pattern, the intakes must begin on the right side and the last one must be made on the wrong side, so that once the heel is finished and the work turned you can go on knitting plain.

When you have decreased all the stitches to the seams, pick up the loops on the sides of the heel with an auxiliary needle and knit them on to the left heel needle, then knit the stitches reserved for the instep, pick up the loops of the right chain and mount them on to the fourth needle.

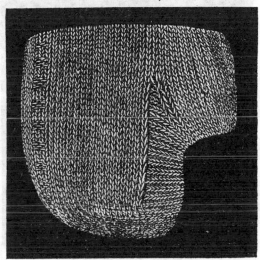

Fig. 400. Common heel.

In the next round, knit all the stitches of the first needle, but the last 4 ; make an intake with the first and second stitches and knit the 2 last plain.

Knit the 2 first stitches of the fourth needle plain, slip the third, knit the fourth and pull the slipped stitch over. Repeat these intakes, with two plain rounds between each until you have an equal number of stitches on all four needles.

Heel in steps (fig. 401). — After dividing the stitches, make from 12 to 14 seams. Knit the right needle, then knit of the left needle as many stitches as you have seams at the side : turn the work and begin the needle with the seam you made first. Knit off as many stitches of the second as you took from the first.

Make the same number of seams as you made in the first part of the heel. When the seams are finished, take up the stitches of the chain on both sides; decrease by knitting together the last stitch of the small part and the first of the big part; knit two; turn the work; slip the first stitch, knit to the second side, and make another intake, as in the first part.

When you have decreased all the stitches, take up the chain of the first seams and begin the intakes for the instep.

A heel made like this is no more trouble than the former one, it fits closely to the foot and consequently wears well.

Plain heel (fig. 402). — Those who do not like purling, will find, in the two following patterns, the way to knit heels altogether plain.

Knit off the stitches of the first needle after the seam, then take two spare needles, and cast on to each 8 more stitches,

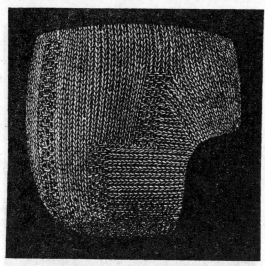

than you have on a heel needle, join the stitches of the third needle to those of the fourth and knit the first round plain.

2nd round — knit together the 1st and 2nd and the 9th and 10th of the first auxiliary needle; one intake with the 10th and 9th last stitches and one intake with the last but one and the last of the second auxiliary needle.

3d, 5th, 7th, 10th, 11th, 13th, 14th, 16th, 17th, 19th and 20th rounds — plain.

Fig. 401. Heel in steps.

4th round — knit together the 1st and 2nd stitches, the 7th and 8th of the first auxiliary needle and the 8th and the 7th last stitch, and the last but one and the last of the second auxiliary needle.

6th round — knit together the 1st and 2nd, and the 5th and 6th of the first auxiliary needle, and the 6th and 5th last stitch, and the last but one and the last of the second auxiliary needle.

8th round — knit together the 1st and 2nd and the 3d and 4th of the first auxiliary needle, the 4th and 3d last stitch and the last but one and the last of the second auxiliary needle.

9th round — after the two last intakes, purl together: the

4th and 3d before the end of the 1st and 3d needles, and the 3d and 4th at the beginning of the 2nd and 4th needles.

12th, 15th and 18th rounds — decrease the same as in the 9th round.

21st round — knit 2 plain at the beginning of each needle; purl together the 2 next stitches, and the 4th and 3d before the end of each needle; knit the last stitches plain.

Continue these intakes, knitting two rounds between plain, until the purled intakes meet. After the two plain rounds make one round with one purled intake over the intakes, then knit four more rows plain, divide the stitches that are left for the sole on two needles and cast off on the wrong side.

Now take up the loops of the auxiliary stitches and, in the following rounds make: 1 intake with the last and the first stitches of the first and second needles, one intake with the last and the first of the 3d and 4th needles.

With the last extra stitches make purled intakes; then knit two rounds plain over each round in which there is an intake.

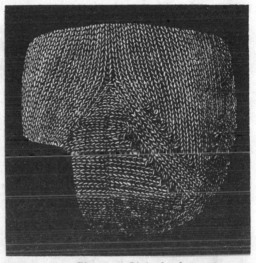

Fig. 402. Plain heel.

Another plain heel (fig. 403). — For this heel again, in order to knit it entirely on the right side, spare needles are required.

Supposing that you have 20 stitches on each needle, cast on 28 on to each spare needle; then make an intake with the 4th and 3d stitches at the end of the 1st and 3d needles, 1 intake with the 3d and 4th of the 2nd and 4th needles, so that 4 plain stitches come between two intakes. Go on decreasing, knitting 2 rounds plain after each intake, until you have only 6 stitches left on each needle. Then make one more intake with the first and last stitches of each needle, knit one round plain over them and finish with a chain on the wrong side of the heel. Then take up the loops of the auxiliary stitches and make the instep.

Italian stocking (fig. 404). — The heel, sole and toe ot a stocking generally wear out long before the instep. The Greeks and Italians have a way of economising time and material and·facilitating the renewal of those parts that wear out soonest by knitting the upper part of the foot in two pieces. After knitting the heel in one or other of the ways already described, lay aside the needles which served to make the heel, knit a straight piece, to and fro with two needles, of the desired length for the upper part of the foot. You must keep a chain along all the edges and a narrow seam of one or two stitches.

In the sole, which you make when you have finished the upper part of the stocking, the intakes must be made directly after ·and before the seam. When you have the same number of rounds in the two pieces, join them and begin the toe.

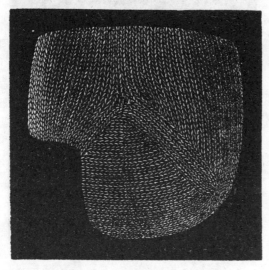

Fig. 403. Another plain heel.

Sew up the slits left open on both sides with a needle and thread taking care to unite the loops that lie exactly opposite to each other.

In this way wheń one or other part of the stocking wears out you unpick these seams at the sides, and put in new pieces as required without any ditficulty.

Toe (fig. 405). — In describing this part of a ŝtocking we will begin as we did in the case of the heel, with the easiest and the commonest form of toe.

Begin by dividing the stitches you have on your needles into four equal parts.

Make a plain intake with the 4th and the 3d last stitches of the first and third needle and knit plain the 2 last stitches; then knit plain the 2 first stitches of the 2nd and 4th needle, slip the 3d, knit the 4th and pull over the 3d.

To begin with, knit 2 rounds plain after every round with intakes; afterwards only one round.

When you have only 4 stitches left on each needle, transfer them to two needles, in the direction of the width of the stocking, and knit them together, two and two, on the wrong side.

Toe (fig. 406). — Divide the stitches by 8, 10 or 12. Supposing them to be divisible by 10, you knit 8 plain; knit the 9th and 10th together, knit 8 plain again, make another intake, and so on through the whole round.

Then knit as many rounds plain as you left stitches between two intakes. In the succeeding rounds with intakes you will have one stitch less between each intake, so that in the second round you will have an interval of 7 stitches and you knit 7 rounds plain, and so on to the 7th intake, when there will remain 2 stitches followed by 2 rounds. When there

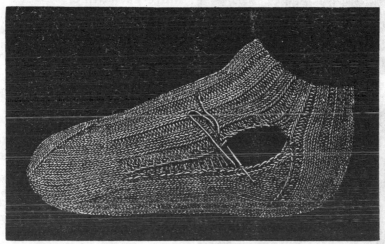

Fig. 404. Italian stocking.

are only 4 stitches left on the needles, turn them in to the wrong side of the stocking and finish them off with a chain.

Toe (fig. 407). — Begin the intakes with the 2 first stitches on each needle by slipping the first stitch and pulling it over the second.

Knit one round plain after each round with intakes. In the 2nd round make the intake with the 3d and 4th stitches, in the 3d round with the 5th and 6th stitches, in the 4th round with the 7th and 8th stitches, so that when finished the intakes form a kind of spiral round the toe. Finish off in the usual way.

Toe (fig. 408). — We add a description of one other kind of toe, quite as shapely and easy to knit as the preceding ones.

1st round — 1 purled intake with the two first stitches on each needle.

2nd and 3d, 5th and 6th, 8th and 9th, 11th and 12th, 14th and 15th, 17th and 18th rounds plain.

Fig. 405. Toe.

4th round — knit 1, 1 purled intake with the 2nd and 3d stitch, and with the two last ones.

7th round — knit 2, 1 purled intake with the 3d and 4th stitch, and with the two last ones.

In the next rounds with intakes, knit one plain stitch more each time.

When the two seams meet pull the last stitch on each needle over the first stitch on the next needle; knit the stitches between the intakes plain. Go on decreasing in this way until the last stitches.

Repairing knitting. — Knitted articles are repaired by reconstructing the stitches or loops with a needle and thread. When the loops are not actually torn, but are nearly so, they can be strengthened, by new ones made over them.

Materials for mending stockings. — The thread used for mending a stocking ought always to be a little finer than that of which it is made. The best for the purpose is either

Fig. 406. Toe.

D.M.C Darning cotton (Coton à repriser) or D.M.C Special stranded cotton (Mouliné spécial) (*), for as they are made of several strands, loosely twisted together, they can easily be subdivided as required.

(*) See at the end of the last chapter the tables of the sizes and colours of the cotton, flax and silk articles, mark D.M.C. — The French names, in brackets, are those stamped on the labels of the D.M.C articles.

Strengthening the stitches (figs. 409 and 410). — This can be done in two ways. In figure 409 bring the needle out between two horizontal bars, then pass it over a vertical bar, put it in beside the same and bring it out between the next horizontal bars. The second row of loops is made coming back, you take up two threads on the left with the needle, pass it downwards over a thread, take up the thread on the needle, and so on.

In fig. 410, when you have brought out the needle carry it over one thread to the right and upwards over two threads, take up the two threads on the left, pass downwards over two horizontal threads and over one thread to the left and insert the needle again at the place where you first brought it out; then take up two threads on the left, pass over one thread on the right and upwards over two horizontal threads, &c.

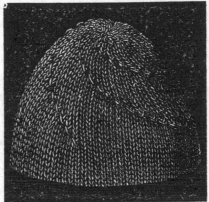

Fig. 407. Toe.

For the next row turn the work so that the finished part comes at the top; then pass downwards over one horizontal thread, bring out the needle between two threads that lie apart from each other, and pass again downwards over two horizontal threads, take up two threads on the left, pass upwards over two threads and over one thread to the right, take up two threads, and so on.

Fig. 408. Toe.

Disengaging the stitches (fig. 411). — When the loops are broken new ones have to be made: the broken ones must all be unravelled and the torn threads cut, so that the horizontal threads are quite freed; on the vertical sides, cut the threads so that the loops form an edge and you have a square hole in the corners of which you disengage from two to four loops, which you turn in to the wrong side of the work and secure with a few stitches.

The darns we describe further on should be done on a ball, as you are sure then not to draw the stitches too tight.

Repairing plain knitting on threads stretched horizontally (figs. 412 and 413). — Run a horizontal thread across on the wrong side, in the place of each broken thread, securing it in the sound part of the stocking, about two loops from the edge of the hole. When you have made this foundation, put your needle in on the right side near the stitch nearest to the sound part on the left. Then, descending, pick up

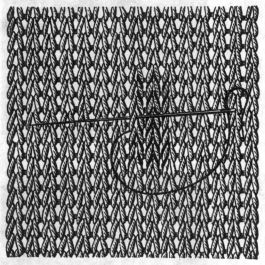

Fig. 409. Strengthening the stitches.
First way.

the nearest horizontal thread, upwards from below, so that the thread you are working with, lies to the left of the needle and in this manner, cover all the horizontal threads you have laid.

When you have taken up the last thread downwards from above, to the left of the nearest stitch, bring it back to the right of the stitch you put it in at.

In reascending to make the second half of the stitch, you must again lay your thread to the left of the needle, fig. 413.

When you have reached the last thread, put the needle into the loop it came out of, and carry your thread to the right to begin the third half journey.

Repairing loops on the right side on threads stretched obliquely across (figs. 414 and 415). — As the illustration shews you have to pick up all the disengaged loops, besides two or three on either side of the hole. The number and length of the threads stretched across must correspond with the number and length of those they are to replace.

Then fasten in, on the right side of the work, a rather finer thread than the one used for the knitting, make a few stitches over the existing ones and in the row which is to be filled in.

Put the needle, upwards from below, into the first dis-engaged loop, under the two threads that issue from the same stitch, and put it in again into the same loop between the two diagonal threads, bringing it out upwards from below, through the next stitch, and so on. The new loop must be exactly the same size as the knitted ones. At the end of the row, as at the beginning, make a few stitches beyond the edge of the hole. Work back in the same way with the difference that you reverse the work.

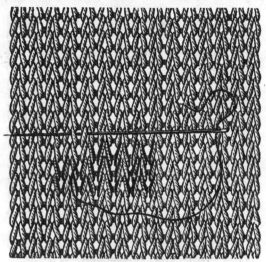

Fig. 410. Strengthening the stitches. Second way.

Repairing stitches by purling over threads stretched obliquely (fig. 416).—Lay the auxiliary threads, and cover them with horizontal stitches, the same as in repairing plain knitting. The stitches which embrace two threads stretched obliquely are made in a double row and those of one row come between those of the preceding one.

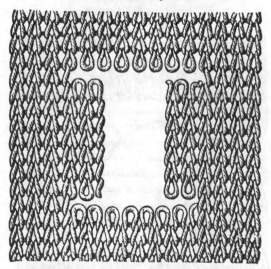

Fig. 411. Disengaging the stitches.

Repairing a ribbed pattern over threads stretched obliquely (fig. 417). — It often happens that knitted articles with a pattern in them have to be repaired; in this case it is desirable to make an invisible darn, so that the pattern may not be interrupted. We give, as an example, a darn made in a piece of ribbed knitting, consisting of two plain and two purled stitches, the most common combination. Here again the darn is made over threads stretched obliquely; the plain and the purl stitches are made in the order indicated in the engraving, according to the directions given for figures 415 and 416. Figure 417 shews the passage from the plain to the purl stitches.

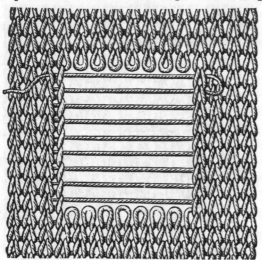

Fig. 412. Repairing plain knitting on threads stretched horizontally.
Stretching the threads.

Repairing plain knitting (fig. 418). — When a torn piece of knitting has to be replaced by a new piece, fasten the new piece to the old with a sewing needle and thread, the same thread the knitting is done with.

For this purpose you must clear the loops and slip them on to knitting needles to prevent their unravelling. The loops that are to be connected must lie exactly opposite to each other. Put in your needle upwards from below, into the first empty upper loop, slip it from the knitting needle, put in the sewing needle downwards from

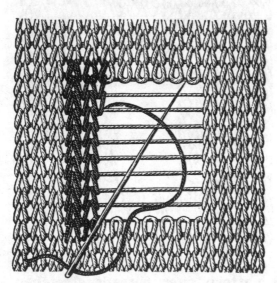

Fig. 413. Repairing plain knitting on threads stretched horizontally.
Covering the threads.

above, into the lower loop exactly opposite the upper one, and upwards from below into the next loop and draw up the thread just enough for the newly made loop to be of the same size as the knitted ones.

You then put the needle into the top part, downwards from above, into the same loop you took up before, bring it out from underneath through the next loop; draw out the thread, to form the new loop and descend again to the next, and so on.

Repairing purled knitting (fig. 419). — To repair ribbed surfaces consisting of alternate rows of plain and purl, proceed as follows: hold the article so that the row of purled stitches comes exactly opposite the upper part.

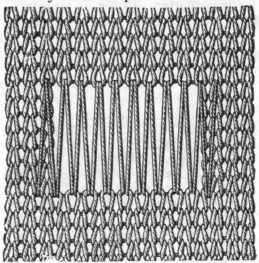

Fig. 414. Repairing loops on the right side on threads stretched obliquely across. Stretching the threads.

Enter your needle downwards from above through the first loop of the top part; join the two lower loops, as in fig. 418, carry the needle upwards again, and insert it upwards from below through the first loop of the top part and the next loop downwards from above. In this manner you get a row of plain stitches between the two stripes of purled stitches.

Piqué pattern (fig. 420). — The following

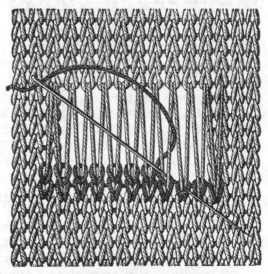

Fig. 415. Repairing loops on the right side on threads stretched obliquely across. Covering the threads.

patterns may be used for all sorts of articles, bed-covers, petticoats, vests and so forth: suiting the material to the object for which it is to serve: either one or other size of D.M.C Knitting cotton (Coton à tricoter), D.M.C Knitting cotton, bell mark (Retors pour mercerie), D.M.C Crochet cotton (Coton pour crochet), D.M.C Alsatia, D.M.C Pearl cotton (Coton perlé), D.M.C Floss crochet cotton (Crochet floche) or D.M.C Flax thread for knitting (Lin pour tricoter).

Cast on a number of stitches divisible by six.

1st to 6th row — 5 purl, knit 1 from behind.

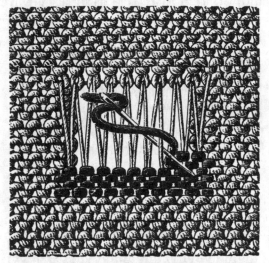

Fig. 416. Repairing stitches by purling over threads stretched obliquely.

7th to 12th row — 2 purl, knit 1 from behind, 3 purl.

Repeat from the 1st row.

Piqué pattern (fig. 421). — Cast on a number of stitches divisible by 14.

1st and 2nd row — purl 7, knit 1, purl 1, knit 1, purl 1, knit 1, purl 1, knit 1.

3d and 4th row — knit 7, purl 1, knit 1, purl 1, knit 1, purl 1, knit 1, purl 1.

Repeat from the first row.

Stripe for counterpanes, piqué pattern (fig. 422). — This pattern worked in stripes of different colours, gives us an opportunity of pointing out to our readers that in choosing two colours for a piece of work, one dark and one light, it is well to take a finer number in the dark colour than in the light. The blue, red and dark brown dyes thicken and swell the thread, whereas the light dyes do not affect the size at all.

Cast on 28 stitches:

First needle — slip 1, knit 2, 1 over, knit 2, purl 1, knit 1, purl 2, knit 5, purl 2, knit 1, purl 1, knit 1, purl 1, knit 1, purl 1, knit 1, purl 1, knit 1, 1 over, knit 3.

2nd needle — slip 1, purl 2, 1 purled intake, purl 1, knit 1, purl 1, knit 1, purl 1, knit 1, purl 1, knit 2, purl 5, knit 2, purl 1, knit 1, purl 1, knit 1, 1 purled intake, purl 3.

3ᵈ needle — slip 1, knit 2, 1 over, knit 2, purl 1, knit 1, purl 1, knit 1, purl 2, knit 5, purl 2, knit 1, purl 1, knit 1, purl 1, knit 1, purl 1, knit 1, 1 over, knit 3.

4ᵗʰ needle — slip 1, purl 2, 1 purled intake, purl 1, knit 1, purl 1, knit 1, purl 1, knit 2, purl 5, knit 2, purl 1, knit 1, purl 1, knit 1, purl 1, knit 1, 1 purled intake, purl 3.

5ᵗʰ needle — slip 1, knit 2, 1 over, knit 2, purl 1, knit 1, purl 1, knit 1, purl 1, knit 1, purl 2, knit 5, purl 2, knit 1, purl 1, knit 1, purl 1, knit 1, 1 over, knit 3.

6ᵗʰ needle — slip 1, purl 2, 1 purled intake, purl 1, knit 1, purl 1, knit 2, purl 5, knit 2, purl 1, knit 1, purl 1, knit 1, purl 1, knit 1, purl 1, knit 1, 1 purled intake, purl 3.

7ᵗʰ needle like the 5ᵗʰ = 8ᵗʰ needle like the 4ᵗʰ = 9ᵗʰ needle like the 3ᵈ = 10ᵗʰ needle like the 2ⁿᵈ.

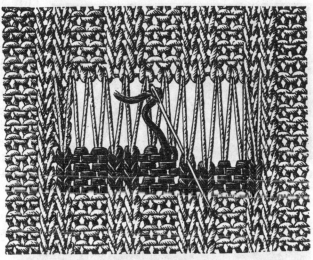

Fig. 417. Repairing a ribbed pattern over threads stretched obliquely.

Repeat from the 1ˢᵗ needle.

Join the stripes by any kind of crochet stitch; several suitable ones will be found in the ensuing chapter.

Knitted square, piqué pattern (fig. 423). — Cast on 2 stitches on to each of the four needles. Repeat all the directions followed by * three times.

1ˢᵗ row — 1 over, knit 1, 1 over, knit 1 *.

2ⁿᵈ row — 1 over, knit 3, 1 over, knit 1 *.

3ᵈ row — 1 over, purl 1, knit 3, purl 1, 1 over, knit 1 *.

4ᵗʰ row — 1 over, purl 2, knit 3, purl 2, 1 over, knit 1 *.

5ᵗʰ row — 1 over, purl 3, knit 3, purl 3, 1 over, knit 1 *.

6ᵗʰ row — 1 over, purl 4, knit 3, purl 4, 1 over, knit 1 *.

7ᵗʰ row — 1 over, purl 5, knit 3, purl 5, 1 over, knit 1 *.

8ᵗʰ row — 1 over, knit 2, purl 4, knit 3, purl 4, knit 2, 1 over, knit 1 *.

9th row — 1 over, knit 4, purl 3, knit 3, purl 3, knit 4, 1 over, knit 1 *.

10th row — 1 over, knit 6, purl 2, knit 3, purl 2, knit 6, 1 over, knit 1 *.

11th row — 1 over, knit 8, purl 1, knit 3, purl 1, knit 8, 1 over, knit 1 *.

12th row — 1 over, knit 1, cross 2 (that is, knit the second stitch first and then the first), knit 5, purl 2, knit 3, purl 2, knit 5, cross 2, knit 1, 1 over, knit 1 *.

13th row — 1 over, purl 1, knit 7, purl 3, knit 3, purl 3, knit 7, purl 1, 1 over, knit 1 *.

14th row — 1 over, purl 2, knit 1, cross 2, knit 3, purl 4, knit 3, purl 4, knit 3, cross 2, knit 1, purl 2, 1 over, knit 1 *.

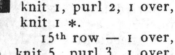

Fig. 418. Repairing plain knitting.

15th row — 1 over, purl 3, knit 5, purl 5, knit 3, purl 5, knit 5, purl 3, 1 over, knit 1 *.

16th row — 1 over, purl 4, knit 1, cross 2, knit 3, purl 4, knit 3, purl 4, knit 3, cross 2, knit 1, purl 4, 1 over, knit 1 *.

17th row — 1 over, purl 5, knit 7, purl 3, knit 3, purl 3, knit 7, purl 5, 1 over, knit 1 *.

18th row — 1 over, knit 2, purl 4, knit 1, cross 2, knit 5, purl 2, knit 3, purl 2, knit 5, cross 2, knit 1, purl 4, knit 2, 1 over, knit 1 *.

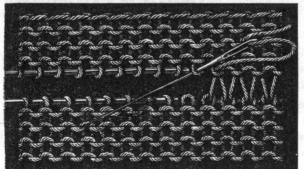

Fig. 419. Repairing purled knitting.

19th row — 1 over, knit 4, purl 3, knit 9, purl 1, knit 3, purl 1, knit 9, purl 3, knit 4, 1 over, knit 1 *.

20th row — 1 over, knit 6, purl 2, knit 1, cross 2, knit 5,

purl 2, knit 3, purl 2, knit 5, cross 2, knit 1, purl 2, knit 6, 1 over, knit 1 *.

21st row — 1 over, knit 8, purl 1, knit 7, purl 3, knit 3, purl 3, knit 7, purl 1, knit 8, 1 over, knit 1 *.

22nd row — 1 over, knit 1, cross 2, knit 5, purl 2, knit 1, cross 2, knit 3, purl 4, knit 3, purl 4, knit 3, cross 2, knit 1, purl 2, knit 5, cross 2, knit 1, 1 over, knit 1 *.

23d row — 1 over, purl 1, knit 7, purl 3, knit 5, purl 5,

Fig. 420. Piqué pattern.

knit 3, purl 5, knit 5, purl 3, knit 7, purl 1, 1 over, knit 1 *.

24th row — 1 over, purl 2, knit 1, cross 2, knit 3, purl 4, knit 1, cross 2, knit 3, purl 4, knit 3, purl 4, knit 3, cross 2, knit 1, purl 4, knit 3, cross 2, knit 1, purl 2, 1 over, knit 1 *.

25th row — 1 over, purl 3, knit 5, purl 5, knit 7, purl 3, knit 3, purl 3, knit 7, purl 5, knit 5, purl 3, 1 over, knit 1 *.

26th row — 1 over, purl 4, knit 1, cross 2, knit 3, purl 4, knit 1, cross 2, knit 5, purl 2, knit 3, purl 2, knit 5, cross 2, knit 1, purl 4, knit 3, cross 2, knit 1, purl 4, 1 over, knit 1 *.

27th row — 1 over, purl 5, knit 7, purl 3, knit 9, purl 1, knit 3, purl 1, knit 9, purl 3, knit 7, purl 5, 1 over, knit 1 *.

Finish the square by 3 rows of purl and a chain.

Plain English knitting or brioche pattern (fig. 424). — This is a very easy and elastic stitch, suitable for all sorts of articles of clothing. — It is used chiefly for mufflers and motor scarves and is done with two needles.

Cast on a number of stitches divisible by 2.

1st needle — 1 over, put the needle into the next stitch, as

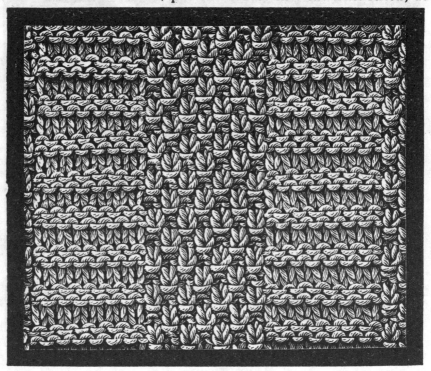

Fig. 421. Piqué pattern.

if for a purl, slip the stitch from the left needle to the right, knit 1, 1 over, and so on.

2nd needle — 1 over, slip 1, knit the over and the slipped stitch together.

Go on repeating the second needle.

In making a circular article you must make alternately one round with plain intakes and one round with purled intakes.

Double English knitting (fig. 425). — This is done with four needles and must be begun on the wrong side of the articles.

Cast on a number of stitches divisible by 2.

1st needle — 1 over, slip 1, as in the preceding pattern, knit 1.

2nd needle — purl 1, slip the over from the left needle to the right one, purl 1.

3d needle — 1 purled intake, 1 over, slip 1.

4th needle — slip the over, purl 2.

5th needle — 1 over, slip 1, 1 purled intake.

Repeat from the 2nd needle.

Tunisian knitting. — These stitches are specially suitable for articles which are to be embroidered, as the stitches form very regular squares which serve as a foundation for the

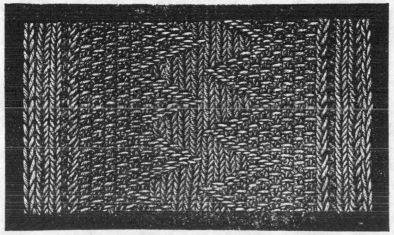

Fig. 422. Stripe for counterpanes, piqué pattern.
Materials : D.M.C Knitting cotton Nos. 6 to 12 or D.M.C Knitting cotton, bell mark, Nos. 6 to 15, in white and Indigo blue 334 or in écru and Morocco red 3328. (*)

embroidery. Both patterns must be begun on the wrong side of the work.

Tunisian knitting with slanting stitches (fig. 426).

1st needle — 1 over, slip 1.

2nd needle — 1 plain intake, taken from the back.

(*) These numbers refer to the colours on the colour cards of the articles stamped with the D.M.C trade mark. These cards can be consulted at all the mercers' and needlework shops.

Tunisian knitting with horizontal stitches (fig. 427).
1st needle — slip 1, 1 over.
2nd needle — 1 plain intake, taken from the back.

Fig. 423. Knitted square, piqué pattern.
Materials : D.M.C Knitting cotton No. 6, 8 or 10, D.M.C Crochet cotton
No. 8, 10 or 12, D.M.C Alsatia No. 15 or 20, or D.M.C Flax thread for knitting
No. 4, 6 or 8, in white or écru. (*)

Piqué pattern with coloured tufts (fig. 428). — The
foundation consists of plain and purled stitches ; certain ones,
worked with a coloured thread form the little tufts or balls.

Cast on a number of stitches divisible by 4.

1st, 3d, 5th and 7th row, with écru thread : knit 1, purl 1,
knit 1, purl 1.

_____

(*) See at the end of the last chapter the tables of the sizes and colours of
the cotton, flax and silk articles, mark D.M.C.

2nd row — with the écru thread: purl 1, — with the coloured thread: knit 1, — with the écru thread: purl 1, knit 1.

4th and 8th row — with the écru thread: purl 1, knit 1, purl 1, knit 1.

6th row — with the écru thread: purl 1, knit 1, purl 1. — with the coloured thread: knit 1.

Repeat from the 1st row.

Plaited stitch (fig. 429). — This stitch is generally worked in stripes joined together with stripes of plain knitting, for bed spreads and cradle covers.

In plaited stitch you have to cross the

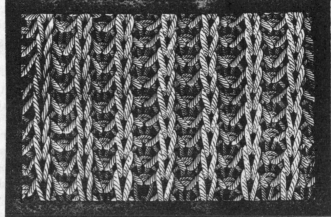

Fig. 424. Plain English knitting or brioche pattern.

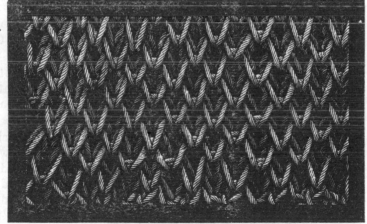

Fig. 425. Double English knitting.

stitches, that is to say, you knit the second stitch first, and then the first on the left needle.

By crossing two or more stitches in some rows, without slipping them, they by degrees form a plait, as shewn in figure 429. Cast on a number of stitches divisible by 6.

1st to the 4th row — purl 2, knit 4.

5th row — purl 2, cast 2 stitches on to a spare needle and leave this needle hanging inside the work; knit 2 other stitches, then the 2 on the auxiliary needle, purl 2, and so on.

6th row — purl 2, knit 4.

Repeat from the 1st row.

You can also make a double plait with 6 stitches; in which case you cross the stitches alternately to the right and left.

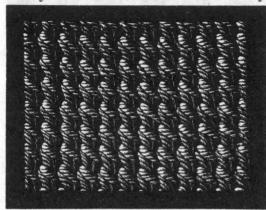

Fig. 426.
Tunisian knitting with slanting stitches.

Turkish stitch (fig. 430). — 1st needle — 1 over, pull over 1 stitch, 1 over, pull over 1 stitch, and so on.

2nd needle — 1 over, pull over 1, 1 over, pull over 1, and so on.

Openwork pattern with two kinds of thread (fig. 431). — A variety of pretty articles, such as openwork stockings, shawls and scarves, and curtains, can be made after this pattern, using two different sizes of thread.

To give it and the following pattern the full effect, coarse needles should be used.

The description of all the following patterns is based on work done in round knitting.

Cast on a number of stitches divisible by 8.

1st and 2nd round — with the coarse thread, purl all the stitches.

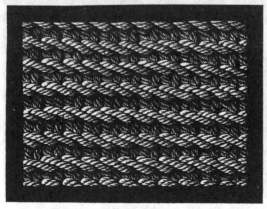

Fig. 427.
Tunisian knitting with horizontal stitches.

3d round — purl 1, a double over, purl 7.

4th round — with the fine thread: slip 1, drop the double over, slip 1, 1 over, 1 plain intake, 1 over, 1 plain intake, 1 over, 1 plain intake.

5th round — slip the 2 slipped stitches (in the coarse thread), knit 6, slip the 2 slipped stitches, knit 6, and so on.

6th round — slip 2, repeat 3 times: 1 over, 1 plain intake.

7th round — like the 5th; 8th round — like the 6th; 9th round — like the 7th.

10th round — knit all; with the coarse thread 11th and 12th rounds — purled.

Arrange so that in the 13th round the double over comes between the stitches formed by the 2 stitches that proceed from the 2nd over and the 2nd plain intake of the 8th round.

Openwork knitting pattern with two kinds of thread (fig. 432). — Cast on a number of stitches divisible by 4.

1st and 2nd round — purl with the coarse thread.

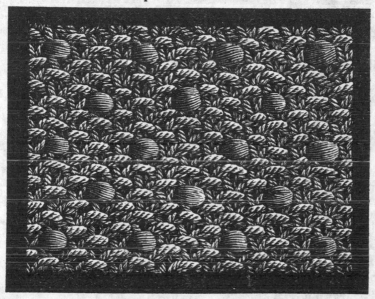

Fig. 428. Piqué pattern with coloured tufts.
Materials : D.M.C Knotting cotton No. 30, écru, and D.M.C Special stranded cotton No. 25, in Turkish red 321. (*)

3d, 5th, 7th, 9th and 14th rounds — with the fine thread, plain.

4th round — 1 over, pull over 1, knit 2.

6th round — knit 1, 1 over, pull over 1, knit 1.

8th round — knit 2, 1 over, pull over 1.

10th and 11th round — with the coarse thread: purl.

12th round — plain.

_____

(*) See at the end of the last chapter the tables of the sizes and colours of the cotton, flax and silk articles, mark D.M.C.

1 3th round — with the fine thread : 1 over, 1 plain intake. Repeat from the 1st round.

Openwork knitting pattern (fig. 433). — Cast on a number of stitches divisible by 9.

1st round — 1 over, slip 1, 1 plain intake, pull over the slipped stitch, 1 over, knit 1, 1 double over, knit 4, 1 double over, knit 1.

2nd round — knit 3, slip the next stitch, drop the double over, knit 4 = turn the work = purl 4 = turn the work = knit 4, drop the double over, slip the next stitch.

Fig. 429. Plaited stitch.

3d round — 1 over, slip 1, 1 plain intake, pull over the slipped stitch, 1 over, drop the slipped stitch, knit first and in front of the other stitches, the stitch that comes after the double over, then the 4 other plain stitches, and lastly, pick up the dropped stitch and knit it on the right side of the work.

4th and 6th rounds — knit plain.

5th round — 1 over, slip 1, 1 plain intake, pull over the slipped stitch, 1 over, knit 6.

Repeat from the 1st round.

Openwork knitting pattern (fig. 434). — Cast on a number of stitches divisible by 14.

1st and 3d round — 1 over, 1 plain intake, knit 9, pull over 1, 1 over, knit 1 taken from behind.

2nd, 4th, 6th, 8th, 10th, 12th and 14th rounds — knit 13, knit 1 taken from behind.

5th round — 1 over, 1 plain intake, knit 2, 1 plain intake, 1 over, knit 1, 1 over, pull over 1, knit 2, pull over 1, 1 over, knit 1 taken from behind.

7th round — 1 over, 1 plain intake, knit 1, 1 plain intake, 1 over, knit 3, 1 over, pull over 1, knit 1, pull over 1, 1 over, knit 1 taken from behind.

9th round — 1 over, 2 plain intakes, 1 over, knit 5, 1 over, then pull over 1 stitch twice, 1 over, knit 1 taken from behind.

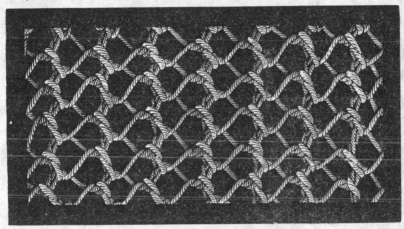

Fig. 430. Turkish stitch.

11th round — 1 over, 1 plain intake, knit 2, 1 over, pull over 1, knit 1, 1 plain intake, 1 over, knit 2, pull over 1, 1 over, knit 1 taken from behind.

13th round — 1 over, 1 plain intake, knit 3, 1 over, slip 1, 1 plain intake, pull over the slipped stitch, 1 over, knit 3, pull over 1 stitch, 1 over, knit 1 taken from behind.

Openwork knitting pattern (fig. 435). — Patterns 435 and 436 are most suitable for scarves, shawls, hoods, &c. According to the size of the cotton, ivory or steel needles should be used; steel are best for any number of D.M.C Knitting cotton (Coton à tricoter) (*), finer than No. 16.

(*) See at the end of the last chapter the tables of the sizes and colours of the cotton, flax and silk articles, mark D.M.C. — The French names, in brackets, are those stamped on the labels of the D.M.C articles.

Cast on a number of stitches divisible by 4.

1st round — 1 over, pull over 1, knit 2.

2nd round — knit 1, 1 over, pull over 1, knit 1.

3d round — knit 2, 1 over, pull over 1.

4th round — knit 3, * 1 over, pull over 1, knit 2, * *; repeat from * to * *, 1 over, pull the last stitch over the 1st of the 3 stitches on the right side of the 1st needle.

5th round — knit 1, 1 plain intake, 1 over, knit 1.

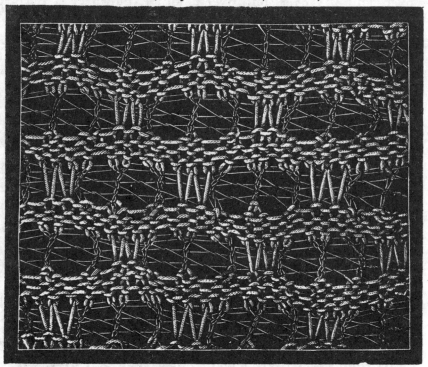

Fig. 431. Openwork pattern with two kinds of thread.
Materials: D.M.C Alsatia No. 15 and D.M.C Crochet cotton 6 cord
No. 60 or 80, in white or écru.

6th round — 1 plain intake, 1 over, knit 2.

7th round — slip 1, * 1 over, knit 2, 1 plain intake, * *; repeat from * to * *, make the last intake with the slipped stitch of the 1st needle.

8th round — 1 over, knit 2, 1 plain intake.

Repeat from the beginning.

Openwork knitting pattern (fig. 436). — Cast on a number of stitches divisible by 3.

1st round — 1 over, slip 1 on to the right needle, knit the 2 next stitches plain, pull the first stitch over them.

2nd round — plain.

3d round — like the first, only note that in this round the stitch which was the third in the first round will be the first in the third.

4th round — plain.

Repeat from the beginning.

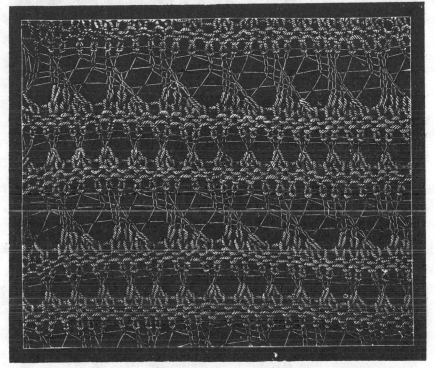

Fig. 432. Openwork knitting pattern with two kinds of thread.
Materials: D.M.C Alsatia No. 15 and D.M.C Crochet cotton 6 cord No. 60 or 80, in white or écru.

Openwork knitting pattern (fig. 437). — Cast on a number of stitches divisible by 14.

1st round — 1 over, knit 1, 1 over, knit 2, purl 3, 1 purled intake with 3 stitches, purl 3, knit 2.

2nd round — knit 5, purl 7, knit 2.

3d round — 1 over, knit 3, 1 over, knit 2, purl 2, 1 purled intake with 3 stitches, purl 2, knit 2.

4th round — knit 7, purl 5, knit 2.

5th round — 1 over, knit 5, 1 over, knit 2, purl 1, 1 purled intake with 3 stitches, purl 1, knit 2.

6th round — knit 9, purl 3, knit 2.

7th round — 1 over, knit 7, 1 over, knit 2, 1 purled intake with 3 stitches, knit 2.

8th round — knit 11, purl 1, knit 2.

Fig. 433. Openwork knitting pattern.

Repeat the whole from the beginning, only the reverse way, so that the purled stitches come on the plain ones and the plain ones on the purled.

Knitted lace (fig. 438). — Knitted lace looks best made of a smooth twisted thread which shews up the pattern clearly on an openwork ground. As a knitted edging makes a pretty finish to almost any kind of knitted article, we give a selection of some of the easiest and yet extremely effective patterns suitable for trimming.

Cast on 9 stitches.

1ˢᵗ needle — slip 1, knit 2, 1 over, 1 plain intake, knit 2, 1 double over, knit 2.

2ⁿᵈ needle — slip 1, knit 2, purl 1, knit 4, 1 over, 1 plain intake, knit 1.

3ᵈ needle — slip 1, knit 2, 1 over, 1 plain intake, knit 6.

4ᵗʰ needle — make a chain of 2 stitches, knit 5, 1 over, 1 plain intake, knit 1.

Repeat from the 1ˢᵗ needle.

Fig. 434. Openwork knitting pattern.

Knitted lace (fig. 439). — Cast on 10 stitches.

1ˢᵗ needle — slip 1, knit 2, 1 over, 1 plain intake, knit 1, 1 double over, 1 plain intake, 1 double over, 1 plain intake.

2ⁿᵈ needle — slip 1, knit 1, purl 1, knit 2, purl 1, knit 3, 1 over, 1 plain intake, knit 1.

3ᵈ needle — slip 1, knit 2, 1 over, 1 plain intake, knit 3, 1 double over, 1 plain intake, 1 double over, 1 plain intake.

4ᵗʰ needle — slip 1, knit 1, purl 1, knit 2, purl 1, knit 5, 1 over, 1 plain intake, knit 1.

5th needle — slip 1, knit 2, 1 over, 1 plain intake, knit 5, 1 double over, 1 plain intake, 1 double over, 1 plain intake.

6th needle — slip 1, knit 1, purl 1, knit 2, purl 1, knit 7, 1 over, 1 plain intake, knit 1.

7th needle — slip 1, knit 2, 1 over, 1 plain intake, knit 11.

8th needle — make a chain of 6 stitches, knit 6, 1 over, 1 plain intake, knit 1.

Repeat from the 1st needle.

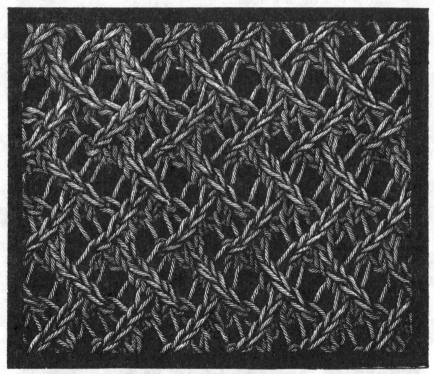

Fig. 435. Openwork knitting pattern.

Knitted lace (fig. 440). — Cast on 13 stitches.

1st needle — slip 1, purl 1, 1 purled intake, 1 over, knit 9.

2nd needle — slip 1, knit 8, 1 over, knit 2, knit 1 taken from behind, knit 1.

3d needle — slip 1, purl 2, 1 over, 1 purled intake, 1 over, knit 9.

4th needle — slip 1, knit 8, 1 over, 1 plain intake, 1 over, knit 2, knit 1 taken from behind, knit 1.

5th needle — slip 1, purl 2, 1 over, 1 purled intake, 1 over, 1 purled intake, 1 over, knit 9.

6^{tb} needle — slip 1, knit 8, 1 over, 1 plain intake, 1 over, 1 plain intake, 1 over, knit 2, knit 1 taken from behind, knit 1.

7th needle — slip 1, purl 2, 1 over, 1 purled intake, 1 over, 1 purled intake, 1 over, 1 purled intake, 1 over, knit 9.

8th needle — slip 1, knit 8, 1 over, 1 plain intake, 1 over, 1 plain intake, 1 over, 1 plain intake, 1 over, knit 2, knit 1 taken from behind, knit 1.

9th needle — slip 1, purl 2, 1 over, 1 purled intake,

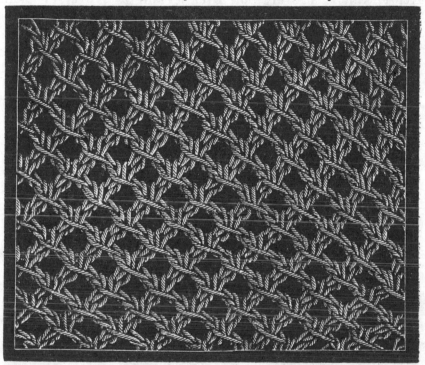

Fig. 436. Openwork knitting pattern.

1 over, 1 purled intake, 1 over, 1 purled intake, 1 over, 1 purled intake, 1 over, knit 9.

10th needle — make a chain of 8 stitches, knit 10, knit 1 taken from behind, knit 1.

Repeat from the first needle.

Knitted insertion (fig. 441). — Cast on 24 stitches.

1st needle — slip 1, knit 2, 1 over, 1 plain intake, knit 1, 1 dot stitch, knit 3, 1 over, pull over 1, 1 plain intake, 1 over, knit 3, 1 dot stitch, knit 3, 1 over, 1 plain intake, knit 1.

2nd, 4th, 8th, 12th and 16th needles — slip 1, knit 2, 1 over, 1 plain intake, purl 14, knit 2, 1 over, 1 plain intake, knit 1.

3d needle — slip 1, knit 2, 1 over, 1 plain intake, knit 3, 1 plain intake, 1 over, knit 4, 1 over, pull over 1, knit 5, 1 over, 1 plain intake, knit 1.

5th needle — slip 1, knit 2, 1 over, 1 plain intake, knit 2, 1 plain intake, 1 over, knit 1, 1 plain intake, 2 overs, pull over 1, knit 1, 1 over, pull over 1, knit 4, 1 over, 1 plain intake, knit 1.

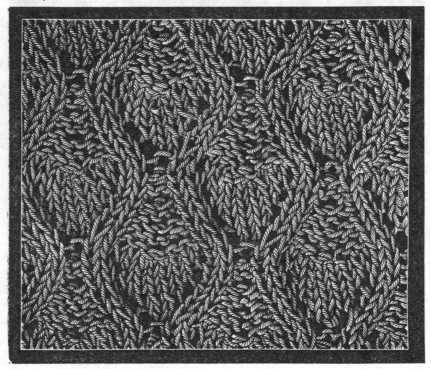

Fig. 437. Openwork knitting pattern.

6th and 14th needles — slip 1, knit 2, 1 over, 1 plain intake, purl 6, knit 1, purl 7, knit 2, 1 over, 1 plain intake, knit 1.

7th needle — slip 1, knit 2, 1 over, 1 plain intake, knit 1, 1 plain intake, 1 over, knit 8, 1 over, pull over 1, knit 3, 1 over, 1 plain intake, knit 1.

9th needle — slip 1, knit 2, 1 over, 2 plain intakes, 1 over, knit 1, 1 plain intake, 2 overs, pull over 1, 1 plain intake, 2 overs, pull over 1, knit 1, 1 over, pull over 1, knit 2, 1 over, 1 plain intake, knit 1.

10th needle — slip 1, knit 2, 1 over, 1 plain intake, purl 4, knit 1, purl 3, knit 1, purl 5, knit 2, 1 over, 1 plain intake, knit 1.

11th needle — slip 1, knit 2, 1 over, 1 plain intake, knit 2, 1 over, pull over 1, knit 6, 1 plain intake, 1 over, knit 4, 1 over, 1 plain intake, knit 1.

13th needle — slip 1, knit 2, 1 over, 1 plain intake, knit 3, 1 over, pull over 1, 1 plain intake, 2 overs, pull over 1, 1 plain intake, 1 over, knit 5, 1 over, 1 plain intake, knit 1.

15th needle — slip 1, knit 2, 1 over, 1 plain intake, knit 4, 1 over, pull over 1, knit 2, 1 plain intake, 1 over, knit 6, 1 over, 1 plain intake, knit 1.

Repeat from the 1st needle.

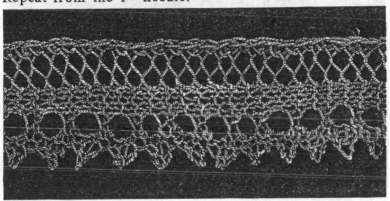

Fig. 438. Knitted lace.
Materials: D.M.C Knitting cotton Nos. 30 to 50, D.M.C Alsatia Nos. 25 to 40, D.M.C Crochet cotton 6 cord Nos. 30 to 50, D.M.C Alsatian thread Nos. 30 to 50, D.M.C Flax lace thread Nos. 25 to 50 or D.M.C Flax thread for knitting Nos. 25 to 50, in white or écru. (*)

Knitted lace with corner (fig. 442). — Cast on 11 stitches. The lace alone without corner requires 16 needles for each scallop.

1st needle — slip 1, knit 1 taken from behind, 1 over, knit 1, 1 over, pull over 1, 1 over, pull over 1, 1 over, pull over 1, knit 2.

2nd, 4th, 6th, 8th, 10th, 12th, 14th and 16th needles — purl.

3^d needle — slip 1, knit 1 taken from behind, 1 over, knit 3, 1 over, pull over 1, 1 over, pull over 1, 1 over, pull over 1, knit 1.

(*) See at the end of the last chapter the tables of the sizes and colours of the cotton, flax and silk articles, mark D.M.C.

5th needle — slip 1, knit 1 taken from behind, 1 over, knit 5, 1 over, pull over 1, 1 over, pull over 1, knit 2.

7th needle — slip 1, knit 1 taken from behind, 1 over, knit 7, 1 over, pull over 1, 1 over, pull over 1, knit 1.

9th needle — pull over 1, knit 1, 1 over, pull over 1, knit 3, 1 plain intake, 1 over, 1 plain intake, 1 over, knit 3.

11th needle — pull over 1, knit 1, 1 over, pull over 1, knit 1, 1 plain intake, 1 over, 1 plain intake, 1 over, 1 plain intake, 1 over, knit 2.

13th needle — pull over 1, knit 1, 1 over, slip 1, 1 plain intake, pull the slipped stitch over, 1 over, 1 plain intake, 1 over, 1 plain intake, 1 over, knit 3.

Fig. 439. Knitted lace.
Materials : D.M.C Knitting cotton Nos. 20 to 40, D.M.C Alsatia Nos. 15 to 25, D.M.C Crochet cotton Nos. 14 to 30, D.M.C Alsatian thread Nos. 30 to 40, D.M.C Flax lace thread Nos. 20 to 40 or D.M.C Flax thread for knitting Nos. 20 to 40, in white or écru.

15th needle — pull over 1, knit 2, 1 plain intake, 1 over, 1 plain intake, 1 over, 1 plain intake, 1 over, knit 2.

Repeat from the first needle.

When you have knitted the required length, begin after the 14th needle to form the corner, which is made in 36 needles.

1st needle — pull over 1, knit 2, 1 plain intake, 1 over, 1 plain intake, 1 over, 1 plain intake, 1 over, knit 1, slip the next stitch on to a spare thread.

2nd, 4th, 6th and 8th needles — slip 1, purl 9.

3d needle — slip 1, knit 1 taken from behind, 1 over, knit 1, 1 over, pull over 1, 1 over, pull over 1, 1 over, pull over 1, slip the next stitch on to the spare thread.

5th needle — slip 1, knit 1 taken from behind, 1 over,

knit 3, 1 over, pull over 1, 1 over, pull over 1, slip the next stitch on to the spare thread.

7th needle — slip 1, knit 1 taken from behind, 1 over, knit 5, 1 over, pull over 1, slip the next stitch on to the spare thread.

9th needle — slip 1, knit 1 taken from behind, 1 over, knit 7, slip the next stitch on to the spare thread.

10th needle — 1 over, purl 10.

11th needle — pull over 1, knit 1, 1 over, pull over 1. knit 3, 1 plain intake, slip the next stitch (1 over) on to the spare thread.

12th needle — 1 over, purl 8.

13th needle — pull over 1, knit 1, 1 over, pull over 1, knit 1,

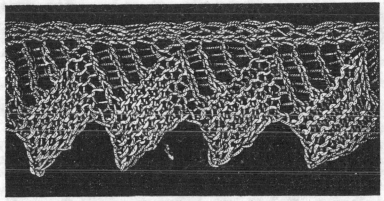

Fig. 440. Knitted lace.

Materials: D.M.C Knitting cotton Nos. 20 to 50, D.M.C Alsatia Nos. 15 to 40, D.M.C Knitting cotton, bell mark, Nos. 15 to 50, D.M.C Alsatian thread Nos. 30 to 60, D.M.C Flax lace thread Nos. 16 to 50 or D.M.C Flax thread for knitting Nos. 16 to 50, in white or écru. (*)

1 plain intake, slip the next stitch (1 over) on to the spare thread.

14th needle — 1 over, purl 6.

15th needle — pull over 1, knit 1, 1 over, slip 1, 1 plain intake, pull the slipped stitch over, slip the next stitch (1 over) on to the spare thread.

16th needle — 1 over, purl 4.

17th needle — pull over 1, knit 2, slip the next stitch (1 over) on to the spare thread.

18th needle — slip 1, purl 2.

(*) See at the end of the last chapter the tables of the sizes and colours of the cotton, flax and silk articles, mark D.M.C.

19th needle — slip 1, knit 1 taken from behind, 1 over, slip 1, take the last stitch you slipped on to the spare thread and knit it taken from behind, pull the slipped stitch over.

20th needle — slip 1, purl 3.

21st needle — slip 1, knit 1 taken from behind, 1 over, knit 2, take the last stitch from the spare thread and knit it taken from behind.

22nd needle — slip 1, purl 5.

23d needle — slip 1, knit 1 taken from behind, 1 over, knit 4, take the last stitch from the spare thread and knit it taken from behind.

24th needle — slip 1, purl 7.

25th needle — slip 1, knit 1 taken from behind, 1 over,

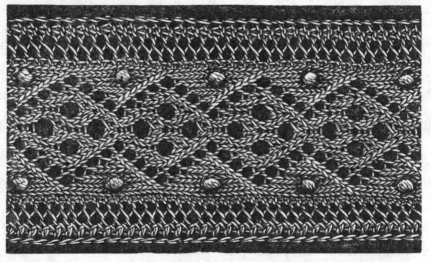

Fig. 441. Knitted insertion.
Materials: D.M.C Knitting cotton Nos. 16 to 50, D.M.C Alsatia Nos. 15 to 40, D.M.C Knitting cotton, bell mark, Nos. 15 to 50, D.M.C Alsatian thread Nos. 30 to 100, D.M.C Flax lace thread Nos. 12 to 50 or D.M.C Flax thread for knitting Nos. 12 to 50, in white or écru.

knit 6, take the last stitch from the spare thread and knit it taken from behind.

26th, 28th, 30th, 32nd and 34th needles — slip 1, purl 9.

27th needle — pull over 1, knit 1, 1 over, pull over 1, knit 3, 1 plain intake, 1 over, take the last stitch from the spare thread and knit it taken from behind.

29th needle — pull over 1, knit 1, 1 over, pull over 1, knit 1, 1 plain intake, 1 over, 1 plain intake, 1 over, take the last stitch from the spare thread and knit it taken from behind.

31st needle — pull over 1, knit 1, 1 over, slip 1, 1 plain intake, pull the slipped stitch over, 1 over, 1 plain intake, 1 over, 1 plain intake, 1 over, take the last stitch from the spare thread and knit it taken from behind.

33d needle — pull over 1, knit 2, 1 plain intake, 1 over, 1 plain intake, 1 over, 1 plain intake, 1 over, take the last stitch from the spare thread and knit it taken from behind.

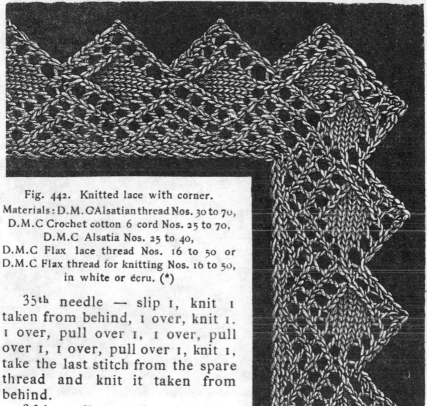

Fig. 442. Knitted lace with corner.
Materials: D.M.C Alsatian thread Nos. 30 to 70,
D.M.C Crochet cotton 6 cord Nos. 25 to 70,
D.M.C Alsatia Nos. 25 to 40,
D.M.C Flax lace thread Nos. 16 to 50 or
D.M.C Flax thread for knitting Nos. 16 to 50,
in white or écru. (*)

35th needle — slip 1, knit 1 taken from behind, 1 over, knit 1. 1 over, pull over 1, 1 over, pull over 1, 1 over, pull over 1, knit 1, take the last stitch from the spare thread and knit it taken from behind.

36th needle — slip 1, purl 11.

Continue to the 3d needle of the description for the lace without corner.

Knitting pattern for bed spread with roses and lace edging (fig. 443). — The knitted roses which form the ground are connected by small hem-stitched squares of linen, and surrounded by a wide lace, gathered at the corners. The roses are made first.

(*) See at the end of the last chapter the tables of the sizes and colours of the cotton, flax and silk articles, mark D.M.C.

Cast on 2 stitches on to each of 4 needles, close the ring.
1st round — 8 times: 1 over, knit 1.

2nd, 4th, 6th, 8th, 10th, 12th, 14th, 16th, 18th, 20th, 22nd and
24th rounds — plain.

Repeat 3 times all the directions followed by *.

Fig. 443. Knitting pattern for bed spread with roses and lace edging.
Materials: D.M.C Flax lace thread No. 25, D.M.C Flax thread for knitting No. 25,
D.M.C Alsatian thread No. 40,
D.M.C Alsatia No. 40 or D.M.C Crochet cotton 6 cord No. 50, in white. (*)

3d round — 1 over, knit 3, 1 over, knit 1 taken from
behind *.

5th round — 1 over, knit 5, 1 over, knit 1 taken from
behind *.

_____

(*) See at the end of the last chapter the tables of the sizes and colours of
the cotton, flax and silk articles, mark D.M.C.

7ᵗʰ round — 1 over, knit 7, 1 over, knit 1 taken from behind *.

Repeat all the directions followed by * 7 times.

9ᵗʰ round — 1 over, pull over 1, 1 plain intake, 1 over, knit 1 *.

11ᵗʰ round — knit 1, 1 over, 1 plain intake, 1 over, knit 2 *.

13ᵗʰ round — knit 2, 1 over, knit 1 from behind, 1 over, knit 3 *.

15ᵗʰ round — knit 3, 1 over, knit 1 from behind, 1 over, knit 4 *.

17ᵗʰ round — knit 4, 1 over, knit 1 from behind, 1 over, knit 5 *.

19ᵗʰ round — knit 5, 1 over, knit 1 from behind, 1 over, knit 6 *.

21ˢᵗ round — knit 6, 1 over, knit 1 from behind, 1 over, knit 7 *.

23ᵈ round — knit 7, 1 over, knit 1 from behind, 1 over, knit 8 *.

25ᵗʰ round — pull over 1, knit 5, 1 over, knit 3, 1 over, knit 5, 1 plain intake, purl 1 *.

26ᵗʰ, 28ᵗʰ, 30ᵗʰ, 32ⁿᵈ, 34ᵗʰ and 36ᵗʰ rounds — knit 17, purl 1 *.

27ᵗʰ round — pull over 1, knit 4, 1 over, knit 5, 1 over, knit 4, 1 plain intake, purl 1 *.

29ᵗʰ round — pull over 1, knit 3, 1 over, knit 1, 1 over, pull over 1, knit 1, 1 plain intake, 1 over, knit 1, 1 over, knit 3, 1 plain intake, purl 1 *.

31ˢᵗ round — pull over 1, knit 2, 1 over, knit 3, 1 over, slip 1, 1 plain intake, pull over the slipped stitch, 1 over, knit 3, 1 over, knit 2, 1 plain intake, purl 1 *.

33ᵈ round — pull over 1, knit 1, 1 over, knit 11, 1 over, knit 1, 1 plain intake, purl 1 *.

35ᵗʰ round — pull over 1, 1 over, knit 1, 1 over, pull over 1, knit 1, 1 plain intake, 1 over, knit 1, 1 over, pull over 1, knit 1, 1 plain intake, 1 over, knit 1, 1 over, 1 plain intake, purl 1 *.

37ᵗʰ round — slip 1, * 1 over, knit 3, 1 over, slip 1, 1 plain intake, pull over the slipped stitch, 1 over, knit 3, 1 over, slip 1, 1 plain intake, pull over the slipped stitch, 1 over, knit 3, 1 over, 1 plain intake, pull over the stitch following the plain intake * *. Repeat from * to * * 7 times, after the 7ᵗʰ time, pull the stitch slipped at the beginning of the round over the plain intake.

38th, 40th and 42nd rounds — plain.

39th round — 1 over, pull over 1, knit 1, 1 plain intake, 1 over, knit 1, 1 over, pull over 1, knit 1, 1 plain intake, 1 over, knit 1, 1 over, pull over 1, knit 1, 1 plain intake, 1 over, knit 1 *.

41st round — knit 1, 1 over, slip 1, 1 plain intake, pull the slipped stitch over, 1 over, knit 3, 1 over, slip 1, 1 plain intake, pull the slipped stitch over, 1 over, knit 3, 1 over, slip 1, 1 plain intake, pull the slipped stitch over, 1 over, knit 2 *.

In conclusion purl 3 rounds, and then make a chain with all the stitches.

When you have knitted the necessary number of roses, hem linen squares, and join them to the roses by overcasting.

For the lace edging cast on 43 stitches.

1st needle — make a chain with 2 stitches, 1 over, knit 1 from behind, 1 over, knit 1 from behind, 1 over, knit 1, 1 over, pull over 1, knit 1, 1 plain intake, 1 over, knit 1, 1 over, pull over 1, knit 1, 1 plain intake, 1 over, knit 1, knit 1 from behind, purl 1, knit 1 from behind, 1 over, knit 1, 1 plain intake, purl 1, pull over 1, knit 1, purl 1, knit 1, 1 plain intake, purl 1, pull over 1, knit 1, 1 over, knit 1 from behind, purl 1, knit 1 from behind, 1 over, 1 plain intake, knit 2.

2nd needle — slip 1, knit 2, purl 1, purl 1 from behind, knit 1, purl 1 from behind, purl 3, knit 1, purl 2, knit 1, purl 2, knit 1, purl 3, purl 1 from behind, knit 1, purl 1 from behind, purl 14, purl 1 from behind, purl 4.

3d needle — make a chain of 2 stitches, 1 over, knit 1 from behind, 1 over, knit 1 from behind, 1 over, knit 3, 1 over, slip 1, 1 plain intake, pull the slipped stitch over, 1 over, knit 3, 1 over, slip 1, 1 plain intake, pull the slipped stitch over, 1 over, 1 plain intake, 1 over, knit 1 from behind, purl 1, knit 1 from behind, 1 over, knit 1, 1 over, 1 plain intake, purl 1, pull over 1, purl 1, 1 plain intake, purl 1, pull over 1, 1 over, knit 1, 1 over, knit 1 from behind, purl 1, knit 1 from behind, 1 over, 1 plain intake, knit 2.

4th needle — slip 1, knit 2, purl 1, purl 1 from behind, knit 1, purl 1 from behind, purl 4, knit 1, purl 1, knit 1, purl 1, knit 1, purl 4, purl 1 from behind, knit 1, purl 1 from behind, purl 15, purl 1 from behind, purl 4.

5ᵗʰ needle — make a chain of 2 stitches, 1 over, knit 1 from behind, 1 over, knit 1 from behind, 1 over, knit 2, 1 over, pull over 1, 1 plain intake, 1 over, knit 2, 1 over, pull over 1, 1 plain intake, 1 over, 1 plain intake, 1 over, knit 1, knit 1 from behind, purl 1, knit 1 from behind, 1 over, knit 3, 1 over, slip 1, 1 plain intake, pull the slipped stitch over, purl 1, slip 1, 1 plain intake, pull the slipped stitch over, 1 over, knit 3, 1 over, knit 1 from behind, purl 1, knit 1 from behind, 1 over, 1 plain intake, knit 2.

6ᵗʰ needle — slip 1, knit 2, purl 1, purl 1 from behind, knit 1, purl 1 from behind, purl 6, knit 1, purl 6, purl 1 from behind, knit 1, purl 1 from behind, purl 16, purl 1 from behind, purl 4.

7ᵗʰ needle — pull over 2 for a chain, 1 over, knit 1 from behind, 1 over, knit 1 from behind, 1 over, knit 1, 1 over, pull over 1, knit 1, 1 plain intake, 1 over, knit 1, 1 over, pull over 1, knit 1, 1 plain intake, 1 over, 1 plain intake, 1 over, 1 plain intake, 1 over, knit 1 from behind, purl 1, knit 1 from behind, 1 over, knit 5, 1 over, slip 1, 1 plain intake, pull the slipped stitch over, 1 over, knit 5, 1 over, knit 1 from behind, purl 1, knit 1 from behind, 1 over, 1 plain intake, knit 2.

8ᵗʰ needle — slip 1, knit 2, purl 1, purl 1 taken from behind, knit 1, purl 1 taken from behind, purl 15, purl 1 taken from behind, knit 1, purl 1 taken from behind, purl 17, purl 1 taken from behind, purl 4.

9ᵗʰ needle — pull over 2 for a chain, 1 over, knit 1 from behind, 1 over, knit 1 from behind, 1 over, knit 3, 1 over, slip 1, 1 plain intake, pull the slipped stitch over, 1 over, knit 3, 1 over, slip 1, 1 plain intake, pull the slipped stitch over, 1 over, 1 plain intake, 1 over, 1 plain intake, 1 over, knit 1, knit 1 from behind, purl 1, knit 1 from behind, 1 over, knit 1, 1 plain intake, purl 1, pull 1 over, knit 1, purl 1, knit 1, 1 plain intake, purl 1, pull 1 over, knit 1, 1 over, knit 1 from behind, purl 1, knit 1 from behind, 1 over, 1 plain intake, knit 2.

10ᵗʰ needle — slip 1, knit 2, purl 1, purl 1 from behind, knit 1, knit 1 from behind, purl 3, knit 1, purl 2, knit 1, purl 2, knit 1, purl 3, purl 1 from behind, knit 1, purl 1 from behind, purl 18, purl 1 from behind, purl 4.

11ᵗʰ needle — pull over 2 for a chain, 1 over, knit 1 from behind, 1 over, knit 1 from behind, 1 over, knit 2, 1 over, pull over 1, 1 plain intake, 1 over, knit 2, 1 over, pull over 1, 1 plain intake, 1 over, 1 plain intake, 1 over, 1 plain intake, 1 over, 1 plain intake, 1 over, knit 1 from behind, purl 1, knit 1 from behind, 1 over, knit 1, 1 over, 1 plain intake, purl 1, pull over 1, purl 1, 1 plain intake, purl 1, pull 1 over, 1 over, knit 1, 1 over, knit 1 from behind, purl 1, knit 1 from behind, 1 over, 1 plain intake, knit 2.

12ᵗʰ needle — slip 1, knit 2, purl 1, purl 1 from behind, knit 1, purl 1 from behind, purl 4, knit 1, purl 1, knit 1, purl 1, knit 1, purl 4, purl 1 from behind, knit 1, purl 1 from behind, purl 19, purl 1 from behind, purl 4.

13ᵗʰ needle — pull over 2 for a chain, 1 over, knit 1 from behind, 1 over, pull over 1, 1 over, pull over 1, knit 1, 1 plain intake, 1 over, knit 1, 1 over, pull over 1, knit 1, 1 plain intake, 1 over, knit 1, 1 over, pull over 1, 1 over, pull over 1, 1 over, pull over 1, knit 1 from behind, purl 1, knit 1 from behind, 1 over, knit 3, 1 over, slip 1, 1 plain intake, pull over the slipped stitch, purl 1, slip 1, 1 plain intake, pull the slipped stitch over, 1 over, knit 3, 1 over, knit 1 from behind, purl 1, knit 1 from behind, 1 over, 1 plain intake, knit 2.

14ᵗʰ needle — slip 1, knit 2, purl 1, purl 1 from behind, knit 1, purl 1 from behind, purl 6, knit 1, purl 6, purl 1 from behind, knit 1, purl 1 from behind, purl 18, purl 1 from behind, purl 4.

15ᵗʰ needle — pull over 2 for a chain, 1 over, knit 1 from behind, 1 over, pull over 1, 1 over, slip 1, 1 plain intake, pull over the slipped stitch, knit 3, 1 over, slip 1, 1 plain intake, pull over the slipped stitch, 1 over, knit 3, 1 over, pull over 1, 1 over, pull over 1, 1 over, 1 plain intake, purl 1, knit 1 from behind, 1 over, knit 5, 1 over, slip 1, 1 plain intake, pull the slipped stitch over, 1 over, knit 5, 1 over, knit 1 from behind, purl 1, knit 1 from behind, 1 over, 1 plain intake, knit 2.

16ᵗʰ needle — same as the 8ᵗʰ.

17ᵗʰ needle — pull over 2 for a chain, 1 over, knit 1 from behind, 1 over, pull over 1, 1 over, pull over 1, 1 purled intake, 1 over, knit 2, 1 over, pull over 1, 1 plain intake, 1 over, knit 2, 1 over, pull over 1, 1 over, pull over 1, knit 1 from behind, purl 1, knit 1 from behind, 1 over, knit 1, 1 plain intake, purl 1, pull over 1, knit 1, purl 1, knit 1, 1 plain intake, purl 1, pull over 1, knit 1, 1 over, knit 1 from behind, purl 1, knit 1 from behind, 1 over, 1 plain intake, knit 2.

18th needle — slip 1, knit 2, purl 1, purl 1 from behind, knit 1, purl 1 from behind, purl 3, knit 1, purl 2, knit 1, purl 2, knit 1, purl 3, purl 1 from behind, knit 1, purl 1 from behind, purl 16, purl 1 from behind, purl 4.

19th needle — pull over 2 for a chain, 1 over, knit 1 from behind, 1 over, pull over 1, 1 over, pull over 1, knit 1, 1 plain intake, 1 over, knit 1, 1 over, pull over 1, knit 1, 1 plain intake, 1 over, knit 1, 1 over, pull over 1, 1 over, 1 plain intake, purl 1, knit 1 from behind, 1 over, knit 1, 1 over, 1 plain intake, purl 1, pull over 1, purl 1, 1 plain intake, purl 1, pull over 1, 1 over, knit 1, 1 over, knit 1 from behind, purl 1, knit 1 from behind, 1 over, 1 plain intake, knit 2.

20th needle — same as the 4th.

21st needle — pull over 2 for a chain, 1 over, knit 1 from behind, 1 over, pull over 1, 1 over, slip 1, 1 plain intake, pull the slipped stitch over, 1 over, knit 3, 1 over, slip 1, 1 plain intake, pull the slipped stitch over, 1 over, knit 3, 1 over, pull 1 over, knit 1 from behind, purl 1, knit 1 from behind, 1 over, knit 3, 1 over, slip 1, 1 plain intake, pull the slipped stitch over, purl 1, slip 1, 1 plain intake, pull the slipped stitch over, 1 over, knit 3, 1 over, knit 1 from behind, purl 1, knit 1 from behind, 1 over, 1 plain intake, knit 2.

22nd needle — slip 1, knit 2, purl 1, purl 1 from behind, knit 1, purl 1 from behind, purl 6, knit 1, purl 6, purl 1 from behind, knit 1, purl 1 from behind, purl 14, purl 1 from behind, purl 4.

23d needle — pull over 2 for a chain, 1 over, knit 1 from behind, 1 over, pull over 1, 1 over, pull over 1, 1 plain intake, 1 over, knit 2, 1 over, pull over 1, 1 plain intake, 1 over, knit 2, 1 over, 1 plain intake, purl 1, 1 plain intake, 1 over, knit 5, 1 over, slip 1, 1 plain intake, pull the slipped stitch over, 1 over, knit 5, 1 over, knit 1 from behind, purl 1, knit 1 from behind, 1 over, 1 plain intake, knit 2.

24th needle — slip 1, knit 2, purl 1, purl 1 from behind, knit 1, purl 1 from behind, purl 15, purl 1 from behind, knit 1, purl 1 from behind, purl 13, purl 1 from behind, knit 4.

Repeat from the 1st needle.

When the lace is finished sew it to the centre of knitted roses, and linen squares; taking care to put plenty of fulness at the corners. See also chapter headed "Needlework Trimmings" the paragraph "Lace trimmings".

Patterns of needlework. — Besides the different kinds of work described above a great choice of knitting patterns will be found in the following publications of the D.M.C Library: *Knitting I and II* and *Works of various kinds.* (*)

(*) See at the end of the volume the list of the albums
of the D.M.C Library.

Crochet lace — Close leaves and bars with picots.

Crochet work

Crochet work which takes its name from the hook, French *croche* or *croc,* with which it is done, is not merely one of the easiest and pleasantest but also one of the most effective kinds of fancywork, considering the time spent upon it.

It is also one of the most useful as it can be applied to domestic requirements of every sort, to dress, underlinen, curtains and furniture, and we feel sure that the patterns contained in this chapter will meet with a favourable reception.

Together with a series of narrow lace edgings for underlinen this chapter contains easy patterns for big bed-covers, chair backs and collars.

Irish guipure, a kind of crochet work, of rather recent invention is in great favour just now. It is too different from ordinary crochet to be dealt with here as it would require lengthy description and very numerous explanatory figures.

We have therefore published a special album dealing exclusively with the subject and containing 100 explanatory figures and 7 plates with various models and 16 patterns on linen.

The crochets, or hooks differ according to the material and the object for which the work is intended; the biggest, generally of tortoiseshell, ivory or box-wood, are used for the heavier kinds of work in wool and cotton, and steel ones generally, for fine work. The so-called "Tunisian" crochet is done with a long straight hook, made all in one piece, of the same thickness throughout.

The hooks should be well polished inside and not too sharp, the backs slightly curved, and the handles, whether of bone, steel or wood light enough not to tire the hand.

Materials. — The varied uses to which crochet work is put calls for a very large choice of materials.

The narrow lace edgings and insertions for trimming under-linen are made with fine round thread, of which there is a large choice, amongst the finer numbers of D.M.C Crochet cotton 6 cord (Cordonnet 6 fils), D.M.C Special crochet cotton (Cordonnet spécial), D.M.C Alsatian thread (Fil d'Alsace), D.M.C Pearl cotton (Coton perlé), D.M.C Alsatia, D.M.C Flax thread for knitting and crochet (Lin pour tricoter et crocheter) and D.M.C Flax lace thread (Lin pour dentelles), in white or écru, with the addition, not unfrequently of a light shade of blue, pink, violet or yellow.

Trimmings for curtains, blinds, table covers and bed spreads are often made of a rather coarse material: such, for instance, as D.M.C Crochet cotton 6 cord (Cordonnet 6 fils) and D.M.C Special crochet cotton (Cordonnet spécial) Nos. 3 to 20, D.M.C Knotting cotton (Fil à pointer) No. 30, D.M.C Alsatia Nos. 15 and 20 or D.M.C Pearl cotton (Coton perlé) Nos. 3 and 5 (*), in white, cream or écru, according to the stuff the article itself is made of.

For big bed spreads, formerly always made of wool, we strongly recommend D.M.C Pearl cotton (Coton perlé) No. 1, a very brilliant and silky material. The same, in Nos. 3, 5, 8 and 12, and D.M.C Alsatia in Nos. 15 to 25 are very suitable for all sorts of fancywork, in place of silk cord.

For mufflers, motor scarves, braces &c., we particularly recommend D.M.C Floss crochet cotton (Crochet floche) a very supple silky thread or D.M.C Pearl cotton (Coton perlé) Nos. 3, 5 and 8.

Explanation of the signs ✱. — In crochet, as in knitting, you often have to repeat a whole series of stitches.

Such repetitions will be indicated by one, two, three, or more asterisks, *, **, *** &c., as the case may be.

Stitches. — In point of fact there is only one, because all crochet work consists of loops made by the little hook or needle, and connected together by being drawn, one through the other.

(*) See at the end of the last chapter the tables of the sizes and colours of the cotton, flax and silk articles, mark D.M.C. — The French names, in brackets, are those stamped on the labels of the D.M.C articles.

It may however, be divided into two kinds, the first, called "German crochet" and the second "Victoria", or "Tunisian" crochet; the latter is also sometimes called "crochet-tricot".

German crochet comprises 7 different kinds of stitches, so called: (1) chain stitch, (2) single stitch, (3) plain stitch, (4) treble stitch, (5) bullion stitch, (6) cluster or pine-apple stitch, (7) double stitch.

The rows are worked, according to the kind of stitch, either to and fro, or all from one end. In the former case you have to turn the work at the end of each row, and make two or three chain stitches at the beginning of the next row, to prevent the contraction of the outside edge.

If on the contrary the rows are all worked one way, the thread must be fastened on fresh each time which you do by

Fig. 444. Position of the hands and explanation of chain stitch.

putting the needle into the first chain stitch of the row before, drawing the thread through so as to form a loop and making the necessary number of chain stitches as in every other row.

At the end of a row you cut the thread and pass it through the last loop: this is always the way to fasten off in crochet work.

Some also make a few extra chain stitches with the ends of the thread at the beginning and end of each row, or fasten them off with a few stitches at the back, or again gather a certain number of threads together and make them into a fringe or tassels as a finish to the work.

(1) **Position of the hands and explanation of chain stitch** (fig. 444). — Take the thread in the left hand between the thumb and forefinger. Hold the needle in the right hand, as you do your pen in writing (held, that is, by the thumb and forefinger and resting on the third finger) and put it into the loop which is held by the forefinger and thumb of your left hand. Take up the thread lying on the forefinger and make

your first stitch as in knitting, tightening the loop just enough to leave an easy passage through it for the needle. The end of

Fig. 445. Single stitch or small close stitch.

the thread must be held by the thumb and forefinger.

The next stitches are made by taking up the thread with the needle and drawing it through the loop. The throwing of the thread over the needle by a jerk of the wrist is called an "over".

(2) **Single stitch or small close stitch** (fig. 445). — Put in the needle, from the right side of the work, under the upper half, either of a chain stitch, or a stitch of the row before, take hold of the thread with the needle and draw it back through the loop of the row below and through the loop which is on the needle, and which proceeds from the last stitch.

Fig. 446. Plain or close stitch.

(3) **Plain or close stitch** (fig. 446). — Put the needle in, as shewn in figure 445, from the right side to the wrong, under the top loop of a preceding row, take the thread with the needle, draw it through the first loop, throw the thread over the needle and draw it through the two loops.

As will be seen by the following illustrations and explanations, the most varied crochet stitches are thus produced.

Rose stitch (fig. 447). This consists of rows of

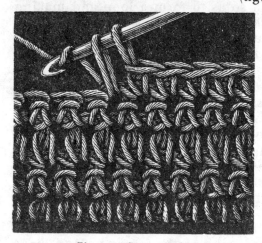

Fig. 447. Rose stitch.

plain stitches, worked to
and fro. Insert the needle
each time under the two
horizontal loops of the
preceding row of stitches.

This straight stitch and
the ribbed stitch, fig. 449,
are generally used for
making braces, mufflers,
shawls, &c.

Russian stitch (fig.
448). — This is worked like
the foregoing, only that all
the rows have to be begun
from the same end, so that
the thread has to be cut
at the end of each row.

Ribbed stitch (fig. 449).
Worked to and fro, the
hook being passed through
the back part only of the
stitches of the preceding
row.

Piqué stitch. — This
stitch also is only worked
on the right side. Put the
needle in under one of the
vertical threads of a stitch
and complete the plain
stitch.

This is a stitch that looks
very well on the wrong
side, as the two threads
of a stitch lie quite close
together. It is particularly
suitable for making warm
garments that are not to be
lined. It requires a large
sized needle, especially if a
very coarse material be used.

Slanting stitch (fig.
450). — Worked entirely
on the right side. Take up

Fig. 448. Russian stitch.

Fig. 449. Ribbed stitch.

Fig. 450. Slanting stitch.

Fig. 451. Russian crossed stitch

Fig. 452. Counterpane stitch.

Fig. 453. Knotted stitch.

the back thread of a stitch of the preceding row, take hold of the crochet thread without throwing it over the needle; then finish the stitch like a plain stitch.

Crossed stitch. — The name given to the preceding stitch when both the threads of the stitches in the foregoing row are taken up, instead of only the back one.

Russian crossed stitch (fig. 451). — To make this stitch which forms diagonal lines, put the needle in between the vertical threads and under the two horizontal threads of the stitches.

Counterpane stitch (fig. 452). — Counterpanes can be made in a less close stitch than those above described. To give more softness and elasticity to the work, throw the thread round the needle, pass it under the two threads of a stitch and catch hold of the thread, bring the needle back under the two threads and under the over, make an over and draw the thread through the two loops on the needle. This stitch is worked to and fro.

Knotted stitch (fig. 453). This stitch which consists of stitches like those described for counterpane stitch figure 452, is worked only on the right side.

Loop stitch (fig. 454). — Worked as follows: Having

put the needle into the loop of a stitch below, carry the thread downwards from above round a slip of cardboard or a flat wooden ruler; then finish the stitch generally by a small close stitch or a Russian stitch.
If you had rather not use the cardboard or the ruler, you can make long loops over your forefinger and hold them with the thumb as you work; but we do not recommend this way to unpractised workers, as it is much more difficult to ensure the loops being quite even and regular.

Each row of long stitches is succeeded by a row of plain. The long loops lie

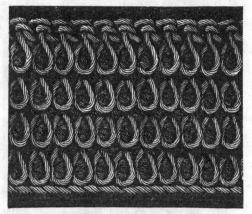

Fig. 454. Loop stitch.

down on the wrong side which becomes afterwards the right side of the work. If you want to make this stitch thicker and fuller, pass the thread two or three times round the ruler or the forefinger and finish off with a plain stitch. If the long loop is threefold, it must be succeeded by a plain stitch. The stitch just described is generally done with a very fleecy material, D.M.C Floss crochet cotton (Crochet floche) and D.M.C Special stranded cotton (Mouliné spécial).

Plain stitches for a chain (fig. 455). — Begin with two chain stitches, put the needle in between the two threads of the first chain stitch, throw the thread over the needle and draw it through in a loop, throw it over again and draw it through the two loops; then put the needle into the left part of the stitch just made, throw the thread over, draw it through, throw it over the needle again, draw it through the two loops, and so on.

Fig. 455.
Plain stitches for a chain.

A chain like this makes a very good substitute for mignardise when that cannot be got of the right size or colour for the required purpose.

(4) **Trebles.** — Trebles are little columns or bars made of loops or stitches. They can be worked, like all other crochet, either to and fro, or all one way.

They are of different kinds; the half or short treble, the plain or ordinary treble, the double treble, called also long stitch, the triple and qua-druple or quintuple treble, called "extra long" stitch, the connected and the crossed treble.

Fig. 456.
Half trebles passed through the whole stitch.

When you work trebles to and fro, you make some chain stitches at the beginning of each row and skip the first treble below, which is replaced by these chain stitches.

Half trebles (fig. 456). Bring the thread from behind round the front of the needle, put the needle in between the stitches of the row before, make an over, bring the needle forward again with the thread, make another over, and draw the thread through all three loops.

Fig. 457.
Plain trebles passed through half a stitch.

Plain trebles (fig. 457). Begin, as for the half treble, by throwing or turning the thread over the needle and putting the needle in under one thread of the stitch beneath, take up the thread on the needle and bring it to the right side, make an over, draw it through two loops, make another over, and draw it through the two remaining loops.

Double trebles (fig. 458). — These are made by making two overs round the needle, then the stitch as for the preceding treble, by drawing the needle with the over through the loops, two by two, until the treble is finished.

Triple and quadruple trebles (fig. 459). — For a triple treble, twist the thread three times round the needle, for a quadruple one, four times, then form the treble or little bar like the others by always uniting two loops. To make a series of trebles of gradually increasing length, bring your needle, at every second treble through the three last loops, so that before making a triple treble, you will have to make columns or bars respectively 1 treble, 1 $\frac{1}{2}$, 2 and 2 $\frac{1}{4}$ trebles, long.

Fig. 458.
Double trebles passed through half a stitch.

This difference in the length of the bars is often necessary, in making flowers, leaves and scalloped edges in crochet work.

Connected trebles (fig. 460). — The trebles, or bars, which are connected together may be worked to and fro and replace the plain stitches. Having made your chain, make a treble of the desired length, make as many loops as you make overs for

Fig. 459.
Triple trebles passed through the whole stitch.

the treble; take up besides the uppermost thread of the stitch nearest the treble, throw the thread over the needle, bring it back to the right side and pass the needle through the loops, two and two.

Crossed trebles (figs. 461 and 462). — This sort of treble produces an open or transparent stitch which is often used for the footing of lace edgings and for insertions.

Fig. 460. Connected trebles.

On a foundation of chain or any other stitch, make as follows: 3 chain (these count as a plain treble), miss 1 stitch of the row beneath, make a plain treble in the 2nd stitch, 4 chain, 1 over, insert the needle between the loops of the treble and the connected chain stitches and finish with a treble and 1 chain stitch.

Next make a double over, put the needle into the 2nd following stitch of the row beneath, make another over, pass the needle through the loop, make another over, and unite the two next

Fig. 461. Crossed trebles one above the other.

loops. There remain 3 loops on the needle. Make an over, put the needle into the 2nd loop of the row beneath, make an over and bring the needle back to the right side.

Unite the five loops on the needle two by two, make 1 chain, 1 over, put the needle into the upper parts of the connected trebles and finish with a plain treble, and so on.

You can also lengthen these trebles if you wish, but in that case, the width of the crossed treble must correspond with its height; they should also always be made with an even number of overs.

Trebles for a chain (fig. 463). — A quicker way of making a wide foot-

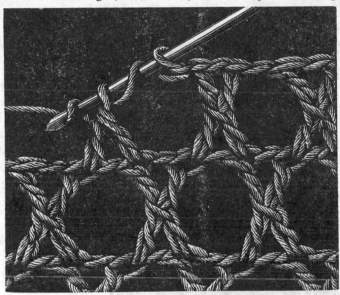

ing for a crochet lace is to make the trebles as follows:

4 chain stitches, 2 overs, put the needle into the first of the 4 chain, 1 over, draw the thread through the stitch, * 1 over, draw the thread through the next 2 loops

Fig. 462.
Crossed trebles set between those of the row beneath.

and repeat twice from * = ** 2 overs, put the needle into the left bottom part of the treble, close the treble as before and repeat from **.

(5) **Bullion stitch** (figs. 464 and 465). — For bullion stitch choose a needle which is a little thicker towards the handle and finer at the other end than you would take for any other crochet stitch.

Begin by a chain of very loose stitches, then wind the thread several times very evenly round the needle and then put the needle into a loop of the chain, make a single over and then draw it with another over through all the other overs.

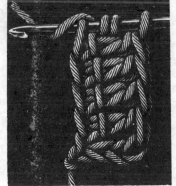

Fig. 463. Trebles for a chain.

The trebles in bullion stitch, fig. 465, are made in the same way as the plain stitch shewn in figure 464: only that you wind the thread at least ten or twelve times round the needle which you then draw through the whole number of overs at once, with the exception of the two last, which you join together by a new over. To facilitate the passage of the needle hold all the overs in their place with the thumb and forefinger of the left hand.

Bullion stitch can only be done with a very loose thread, with D.M.C Floss crochet cotton (Crochet floche) or D.M.C Special stranded cotton (Mouliné spécial) (*), for instance, but trebles in bullion stitch can be worked in any of the D.M.C materials.

Fig. 464. Loops in bullion stitch.

Fig. 465. Trebles in bullion stitch.

(6) **Cluster or pine-apple stitch** (fig. 466). — This stitch generally serves as an insertion between rows of plain crochet.

Make an over, put the needle in under a stitch of the preceding row, make an over, draw it through as a loop, make another over, put in the needle again under the same stitch, bring it back, make a third over, and pass a third time under the same stitch, bring the needle back, make a fourth over, bring back the needle, make another over and draw the needle through the first eight loops upon it, make another over and draw the needle through the two last loops.

Then, after making one chain stitch, begin the same stitch over again and set it in the second stitch of the row beneath.

(7) **Double stitch** (fig. 467). — A rather coarse thick thread, like D.M.C Knitting cotton (Coton à tricoter) Nos. 6 to 12, D.M.C Crochet cotton 6 cord (Cordonnet 6 fils) and D.M.C Special crochet cotton (Cordonnet spécial) Nos. 3 to 10, D.M.C Knotting cotton (Fil à pointer) Nos. 10 to 30, or D.M.C Flax

(*) See at the end of the last chapter the tables of the sizes and colours of the cotton, flax and silk articles, mark D.M.C. — The French names, in brackets, are those stamped on the labels of the D.M.C articles.

thread for knitting and crochet (Lin pour tricoter et crocheter)
Nos. 3 to 12 is better for this stitch than a loose fleecy thread
which is apt to render it indistinct. Take up a loop of thread
to the right and left of a stitch of the row before, so as to
have three loops on the needle, counting that of the last
stitch, make an over and draw it through the three loops.

Then take up a
loop again next to the
one made on the left
and which now lies on
the right, take a loop
in the next stitch,
make an over and
draw it through all
the loops.

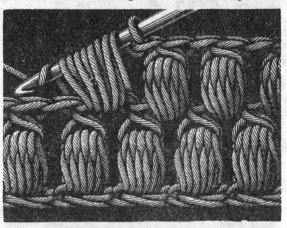

**Raised stitch
with the trebles
in one row set
between those of
the row beneath**
(fig. 468). — All the
stitches of this cate-
gory require a foun-
dation of a few plain
rows for the raised
trebles. In figure 468
you will see that in
the fourth row of
plain stitches the
fourth stitch is a
double treble attached
to a loop of the same
fourth stitch of the
first row.

Fig. 466. Cluster or pine-apple stitch.

Fig. 467. Double stitch.

Skip the stitch of
the preceding row
hidden under the
treble, make 3 plain stitches, one double treble, and so on.

This row finished, turn the work and make a plain row. In
the next row, which is the 6th, make first 1 plain stitch, 1 double
treble which you connect with the 3d row at the 2nd plain
stitch before the 1st treble, 3 plain, 1 double treble, and so on.

In the 8th row of plain stitches the trebles are placed in the same order as in the fourth.

Raised stitch with crossed trebles (fig. 469). — Begin, as in figure 468, by three rows of plain stitches. The fourth row is begun with 2 plain stitches, which are followed by: * 1

Fig. 468. Raised stitch with the trebles in one row set between those of the row beneath.

double treble attached to the upper part of the first stitch of the 1st row; the two last loops of this treble remaining on the needle; make a double over for the next treble, put the needle into the 4th following stitch of the 1st row, throw the thread over the needle, finish the treble up to the three last loops which you crochet together. Skip the stitch behind the treble, make three more plain stitches, and repeat from * placing the next 1st treble in the same loop with the preceding treble and skipping three stitches always at the bottom.

After this row turn the work,

Fig. 469. Raised stitch with crossed trebles.

make a row of plain stitches, and turn the work round again to the right side.

The second row of trebles begins with a double treble, the crossing of the trebles is done as is seen in the engraving.

Raised stitch with dots in pine-apple stitch (fig. 470). — After making three plain rows, begin the 4th row with 3 plain

stitches, draw a little loop of thread out of the next stitch,
then continue with : * 6 trebles in the 4th plain stitch of the
1st row, leave the last loop of each treble on the needle, so
as to have on it eight loops in all; throw the thread over the
needle and draw it through all the loops; skip the loop under
the dot out of which a loop was brought, make 3 plain
stitches and repeat from *.

Make three rows of plain stitches to follow. In the 4th row
the dots are inverted.

Raised stitch with dots with trebles set contrariwise
(fig. 471). — After making three rows of plain stitches, make

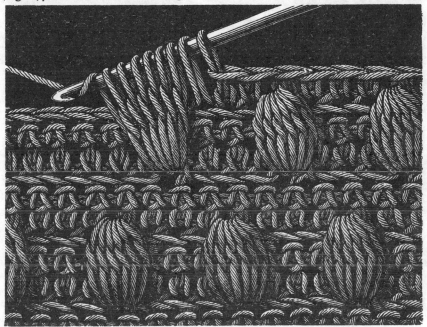

Fig. 470. Raised stitch with dots in pine-apple stitch.

3 more plain stitches at the beginning of the 4th row, then,
in the 4th stitch of the 1st row: * 1 chain, 6 trebles, drop
the last loop of the 6th treble, put the needle into the chain
stitch between the last plain stitch and the first treble, take
up the empty loop of the last treble and draw it through the
one on the needle; skip the stitch under the dot, make 5 plain
stitches and repeat from *. In the next rows, the dots are
placed between the dots of the rows beneath.

**Raised stitch with dots in pine-apple stitch, set in
oblique lines** (fig. 472). — On the foundation rows of plain

stitches, make on beginning the 4th row, as 4th stitch, a quadruple pine-apple stitch, fig. 466, then 4 plain stitches, 1 pine-apple stitch, and so on. The next row plain throughout. In the second row with dots make: 1 plain stitch more and set the pine-apple stitches in the loops on the left of the 2nd of the 3 rows covered by the first dots. Each subsequent raised stitch you make will be one stitch in advance of the last; so that they run in diagonal lines across the surface.

Close shell stitch (fig. 473). — This stitch which can only be worked in rows, all one way and with a very loose thread

Fig. 471. Raised stitch with dots with trebles set contrariwise.

is very suitable for children's garments. It is very easy and has the additional merit of being very quickly done and can be finished off at the end of each row.

On a foundation of chain or any other crochet stitch you choose, 1st row: 1 chain stitch, 7 trebles in the first stitch or the row beneath, * 1 chain, 7 trebles in the 5th stitch and repeat from *.

2nd row — ** 7 trebles in the chain stitch of the last row which separates 7 trebles, 1 plain in the 4th of the 7 trebles of the 1st row and repeat from **.

In the 3d row, set the trebles in the plain stitch of the 2nd row.

Picots. — The last row of most crochet work is ornamented with picots, so-called, small points of various shapes and sizes ; there are close picots, chain picots and lace picots.

Close picots may be subdivided into large and small, pointed and rounded, picots with rounded leaves and picots with pointed leaves.

Small rounded picots. — These may either be made separately and then sewn on, or, made at once, on to a

Fig. 472. Raised stitch with dots in pine-apple stitch, set in oblique lines.

crochet border. In the first case, you make : 1 plain stitch in the edge, * 3 chain, then coming back over these stitches : 1 plain stitch on the 2nd and 1 on the 1st chain stitch, skip 1 or 2 stitches of the row beneath, 1 single ; repeat from *.

Large rounded picots. — 5 chain, skip 3 stitches, 1 treble on the 2nd and 1 on the 1st chain stitch. When you want to attach these picots to a piece of work, fasten them by 1 single stitch missing 3 or 4 stitches, instead of one or two as just directed for the small picots.

Pointed picots. — Cast on 6 chain, then, in returning and skipping the 6th stitch : 1 single, 1 plain, 1 half treble, 1 single treble, 1 double treble.

Picots with leaves. — * 4 chain, 3 plain trebles in the 1st chain, 1 single in the same stitch with the trebles, 2 or 3 chain and repeat from *.

When these picots serve as a finish to a straight edge, make single stitches in the preceding row instead of chain stitches.

Chain picots. — For the small chain picots, make : 5 chain, 1 plain in the 1st of the 5 chain. For the large picots, 5 chain and 1 treble in the 1st.

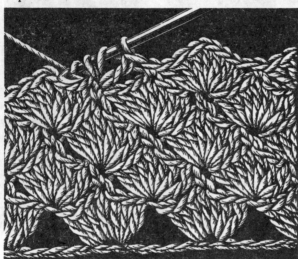

Fig. 473. Close shell stitch.

Picots in bullion stitch or picots in post stitch. — 5 chain, 1 treble in bullion stitch drawn up into a ring and joined to the 5th chain stitch, 5 chain, and so on.

Drooping picots (fig. 474). — 5 chain, drop the loop, put the needle into the 2nd of the 5 chain, take up the dropped loop and draw it through the stitch.

Lace picots (figs. 475 and 476). — Figure 475 represents picots formed of chain stitches, as follows : 2 chain, put the needle into the 1st, 1 over, bring the thread back to the front, 2 chain ; * bring the needle out through the 2 loops, put the needle into the 2nd loop and into the 1st chain at the same time, draw the thread through in a loop, make 2 chain and repeat from *.

In order to make the picots more firm and even it is advisable to make them over a coarse knitting-needle or over a mesh.

Figure 476 represents picots attached by plain stitches to the edge of a finished piece of work, such as a final row or a

chain of chain stitches: this is done as follows: 1 plain, draw
out the loop to the proper length for a picot and slip it on to
a mesh, put the needle into the horizontal parts of the last
stitch, turn the thread round the needle, draw it through in a
loop, make 1 plain stitch in the next stitch, and so on.

Picots with an edging of trebles (fig. 477). — Begin by
7 chain, 1 plain on the 4th chain, 1 triple treble on the 1st of
the 7 chain, * 1 picot of 4 chain closed by 1 plain stitch,
1 triple treble set in the 2nd of the 3 overs of the triple treble
and repeat from *.

How to copy tapestry patterns in crochet work
(figs. 478 and 479). — Printed cross stitch and embroidery

Fig. 474. Drooping picots.

patterns can very well be copied in crochet work, especially
when they are only in two colours, or rather, are drawn in
one colour on a plain ground. To reproduce these patterns in
crochet you make nothing but rows of chain stitches and
trebles, one above the other, thus forming a surface of little
squares. For every square marked on the pattern you count
for the crochet grounding 1 treble and 2 chain stitches; for
the solid squares, 3 trebles.

The squares formed by the chain stitches, should always
begin and end with a treble.

You begin each row with 3 chain stitches — see also p. p. 299
and 304 — and always finish with a treble.

When a solid square comes between open squares, count
4 trebles for the solid square, because the last treble of the
last open square touches the three trebles of the solid or full
square.

Thus, for 2 full squares, side by side: 7 trebles and for 3,
10 trebles.

Embroidery patterns worked in several colours can be reproduced in crochet either by trebles and rows worked one way only, cutting off the thread at the end of each row, or by plain stitches worked in rows to and fro.

When not more than three colours are used you can pass two threads under the stitches; if that number be exceeded, leaves the ones not in use for the moment on the wrong side of the work and only bring them to the right side as they are wanted; leaving the one you have been working with on the wrong side in its turn. Of course the threads not in use can only be disposed of in this way when the work has a right and a wrong side, otherwise they must be carried along under the stitches.

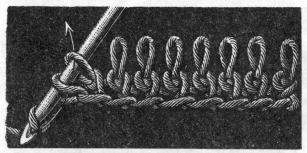

Fig. 475. Lace picots.

Fig. 476. Lace picots.

The colours should alternate in the order prescribed by the pattern; and observe that the last stitch before a change of colour cannot be finished with the same colour it was begun with, the new colour must be drawn through the last loop, which must be drawn up with the new thread.

Bosnian crochet. — In Bosnia a special kind of crochet is made, somewhat resembling woven braids, which owing to its strength and elasticity is particularly well suited for waistbands, collars and cuffs and braiding.

The patterns are composed entirely of single stitches worked in one or more colours. Of the various materials bearing the D.M.C mark, we can specially recommend for crochet in one colour, D.M.C Crochet cotton 6 cord (Cordonnet 6 fils), D.M.C Special crochet cotton (Cordonnet spécial), D.M.C Knotting cotton (Fil à pointer) and D.M.C Flax thread for knitting and crochet (Lin pour tricoter et crocheter); for crochet in several colours, D.M.C Pearl cotton (Coton perlé) and D.M.C Alsatia. (*)

Bosnian crochet braid in one colour (fig. 480). — Begin by a row of chain stitches; by placing alternately the single stitches in the little front loop or the back loop of the rows beneath, you form the pattern.

1st to the 3d row — single stitches in the little back loops.

4th to the 5th — single stitches in the little front loops.

6th to the 7th — single stitches in the little back loops.

8th to the 15th alternate 3 single stitches in the little back loops with 3 in the front ones. Recede one stitch towards the left, in each row of the pattern, so as to form oblique stripes.

16th to the 17th row — single stitches in the little back loops.

18th to the 19th row — single stitches in the little front loops.

20th row — single stitches in the little back loops.

Bosnian crochet braid in colours (fig. 481). — Here the pattern is produced by the change of colours. Work the whole in single stitches set in the back loops. The change of colours is shewn in the model. (See also figs. 478 and 479).

Crochet square (fig. 482). — Begin with 4 chain stitches, close the ring by making 1 single on the 1st chain stitch.

Fig. 477.
Picots with an edging of trebles.

1 chain, 2 plain on the next chain stitch, 3 plain on each of the next 3 chain, 1 plain on the stitch on which the 2 first plain are worked.

Slip the next stitch, that is to say, put the needle in between the horizontal parts of the first plain stitch of the preceding row and draw out the thread without making a stitch.

(*) See at the end of the last chapter the tables of the sizes and colours of the cotton, flax and silk articles, mark D.M.C. — The French names, in brackets, are those stamped on the labels of the D.M.C articles.

Then make 1 chain and 2 plain on the slipped stitch. After which you make 3 plain on the 2nd of the 3 plain which form the corner and 1 plain on all the other stitches of the preceding row.

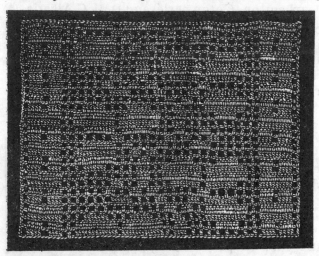

Fig. 478. Openwork crochet after a tapestry pattern.

The beginning and end of each row are worked in the way described above.

Our engraving represents a square executed in consecutive rows.

When you use a stitch that has to be worked to and fro you must turn the work at the end of each row and come back on the stitches you have just made.

Crochet hexagon (fig. 483). Cast on 7 chain, 12 plain on the first 6; finish the row and make the ring in the same

Fig. 479. Close crochet after a tapestry pattern.

way as described for the last figure = turn the work = * 1 plain, 3 plain on the 2nd plain of the preceding row; repeat 5 times from *. Finish the row by 1 single stitch = turn the work = 1 plain, 3 plain on the 2nd of the first

3 plain; 3 plain, and so on. These hexagons can be made of any size; they are generally joined together by means of trebles.

Coloured star worked into a light ground (fig. 484). — Begin by 3 chain stitches, close the ring = 2 plain stitches on each of the 3 chain, then 1 plain with the dark thread and

Fig. 480. Bosnian crochet braid in one colour.
Materials: D.M.C Crochet cotton 6 cord or D.M.C Special crochet cotton Nos. 3 to 20, D.M.C Knotting cotton No. 30,
or D.M.C Flax thread for knitting and crochet Nos. 4 to 12, in white or écru.

Fig. 481. Bosnian crochet braid in colours.
Materials: D.M.C Pearl cotton or D.M.C Alsatia, in Black fast dye 310, Cardinal red 304, Blue fast dye 800, Golden yellow 781 and Beetle green 3346. (*)

1 with light, intended for the foundation on each of the 6 stitches. For the change of colours see p. 315.

In each subsequent row make one dark stitch more; make the increase regularly, that is to say, making 2 stitches on the

(*) These numbers refer to the colours on the colour cards of the articles stamped with the D.M.C trade mark. These cards can be consulted at all the mercers' and needlework shops.

last light stitch that precedes the dark stitches. Proceed in this way until you have 8 dark stitches, then decrease again by one dark stitch each row until there is only one remaining.

These rounds can be used for the bottoms of purses, for the crowns of caps and for lamp mats.

Tunisian crochet. — Tunisian crochet is also called "crochet-knitting", because, as in knitting, you have to cast on all the stitches of a row on to one needle.

As we already said at the beginning of this chapter, Tunisian crochet must be done with a long straight needle, with a knob at one end.

The Tunisian crochet stitches are made on the right side and form a supple and elastic fabric. These stitches are used particularly for mufflers, motor scarves, braces, children's shoes, &c.

It can be close or open ; but there are not so many kinds of stitches as in German crochet.

Fig. 482. Crochet square.

A row of chain stitches forms the foundation of Tunisian crochet; a row of single stitches ends it.

Plain Tunisian crochet (fig. 485). — After casting on a number of chain stitches corresponding with the width you wish your work to be, begin the first row, "the loop row" as it is called.

Put the needle into the second chain stitch, draw a loop through, and so on until you have taken up all the chain stitches ; all the loops remain on the needle. After the last stitch of the "loop row", begin the second row which completes the stitch.

Turn the thread round the needle, pass it the first time

through 1 loop, then turn the thread round the needle and draw it through 2 loops, turn it again round the needle and draw it again through 2 loops, and so on until you have reached the last stitch. In the next row you take up the vertical loops formed by the stitches of the row beneath.

Straight plaited Tunisian stitch (fig. 486). — Begin by a row of plain Tunisian stitches, then in the next row skip the first loop pick up the second and return to the first, so

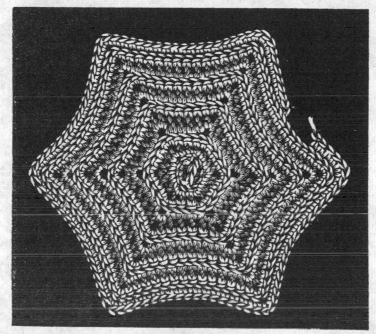

Fig. 483. Crochet hexagon.

that the two loops are crossed. Finish the row as indicated for the preceding model.

Diagonal plaited Tunisian stitch (fig. 487). — Begin the stitch the same as the last one, making first a plain row then a plaited one, taking up first the second loop and then the first, and finishing with the second row as usual.

In the third row, pick up the first loop as usual and draw the third loop through the second, thus producing diagonal lines across the surface of the work.

Open Tunisian stitch. — Open stitches in Tunisian crochet are very easy to make. The first row of loops is made as in plain Tunisian crochet. In the returning row, you alternately join 2 and 3 or 3 and 4 loops of the last row and replace them by the same number of chain stitches.

In the subsequent rows, to make the row of loops you draw the needle through the chain stitches.

Decreasing and increasing in Tunisian crochet (fig. 488). Our illustration shews you how to decrease on both sides and

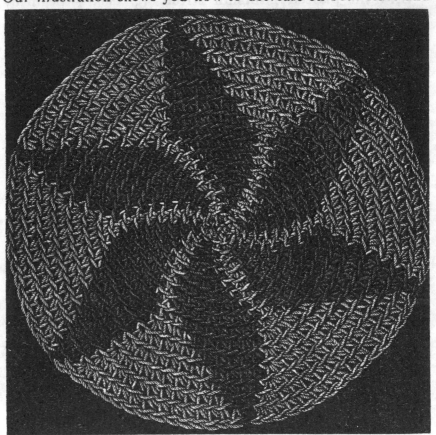

Fig. 484. Star on plain ground.

by that means form scallops. You decrease by one stitch each row on the right and on the left. On the right you crochet the two first stitches together and the two last on the left at the end of the row; returning on one stitch, and so on to the last row.

You increase in the same order, on the right and on the left. To make an increase you pick up one horizontal loop of the stitch in question.

Square with coloured tufts (fig. 489). — Our engraving represents a single square — a number of such squares joined together form a handsome counterpane. Four or six colours may be introduced into a square or all the tufts made in the same colour with equally good effect.

Cast on 13 chain and close the ring.

1st row — 1 plain on the 1st of the 13 chain, 5 chain, 1 plain on the 4th chain, 5 chain, 1 plain on the 7th chain, 5 chain, 1 plain on the 10th chain, 5 chain, 1 plain on the 13th chain.

2nd row — * 1 plain on the 1st plain of the 1st row, 1 plain on the 1st of the 5 chain; 5 chain, 1 plain on the 5th chain. Repeat 3 times from *.

3d row — 5 plain on the 3 chain beneath and on the chain stitch which precedes and the one that come after these plain stitches; 5 plain, and so on.

Fig. 485. Plain Tunisian crochet.

4th row — continue to increase as in the 3d row and here make the first tuft, see fig. 466, after the 3d plain stitch in each triangle of the square. In the subsequent rows, increase the number of tufts until

Fig. 486. Straight plaited Tunisian stitch.

the square reaches the desired width. The tuft stitches are made in every second row with 3 plain stitches between. For the arrangement of the tufts see figure 489.

The coloured thread is only introduced at the tufts and must be cut off each time a group of tufts is finished. The ends of the coloured threads must be worked in under the stitches of the next row.

The square may be of any size; it is bordered by small

picot scallops, by means of which the different squares may
be joined together.

Pattern of a counterpane worked in stripes (fig. 490).
This is intended for a child's coverlet and is worked in pale
blue and white; the stripes and the lace border in white; the
setting and the intersecting lines partly in white, partly in blue.

The material recommended is D.M.C Pearl cotton (Coton
perlé) No. 1.

For the first stripe cast on 29 chain = then coming back:
miss 3 chain, pass the needle through the 4th and 5th stitch,
draw up the 3 loops all together = 2 chain, pass the needle
again through 2 chain stitches, and draw up the three loops
together, 2 chain, and so on.

Begin each row with 3 chain stitches, which will afterwards
form picots at the edge of the stripe. Returning, make the
1st loop over the 3 chain
stitches, the 2nd over
the chain stitch which
comes after the collected
loops of the row beneath
(which are always to be
skipped afterwards) and
continue taking up only
the chain stitches.

When the stripes are
finished, take a thread
of a different colour
from the foundation and
make in each of these
picots, 1 plain stitch

Fig. 487. Diagonal plaited Tunisian stitch.

and 3 chain stitches. This row is followed by another in cluster
stitch, worked in white, see fig. 466, with 2 chain stitches
between the groups of stitches = then another coloured row,
consisting of 2 chain stitches and 1 plain on each loop of
the chain stitches of the preceding row. These rows are only
made along the long sides of the stripes which are joined
together later on; on the exterior sides, these rows are only
made when the coverlet is finished; the stitches then follow
each other all round the four sides. The second stripe of the
same width as the first is done in Tunisian stitch; one row
of plain stitches in colour, then a row of 1 plain and 3 chain
border it, besides one row of cluster stitches in white, then a
row of 2 chain and 1 plain in colour.

The stripes are joined together with single stitches worked on the wrong side in colour, taking up 1 loop of the stitch on the right and 1 on the left alternately.

When you have joined the stripes make the outside border consisting of 7 straight rows and a scalloped lace edging.

1st row — in colour: 1 plain in each picot, 3 chain, 1 plain, and so on along the long sides of the stripes = along the short sides, the side of the chain stitches cast on, or of the last row: 1 plain, 3 chain, miss 2, 1 plain.

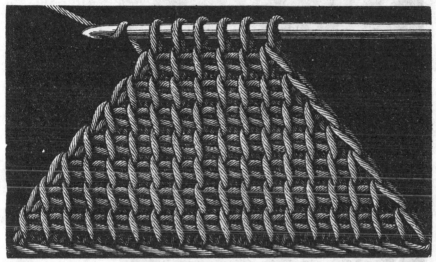

Fig. 488. Decreasing in Tunisian crochet.

2nd row — in white or écru : 1 cluster stitch, fig. 466, on each picot formed by the 3 chain stitches of the 1st row with 2 chain stitches between ; at the corners you must make 3 cluster stitches in the picot.

3d, 4th and 5th rows — in colour: like the 1st. Increase at the corners by making 1 plain, 3 chain, 1 plain in the same chain stitches.

6th row — in white, the same as the 2nd.

7th row — in colour: 1 treble on each stitch of the preceding row, 3 trebles on the corner stitch.

The scallops extend over 13 stitches of the preceding row with 3 stitches between them : that is why it is best to make the corner scallops first, to count the stitches both ways and divide those that there are over and above between the different scallops.

To make the corner scallop, fasten on the thread on the wrong side on to the stitch before the 3 stitches that were added to turn the corner: 6 chain, 1 single on the 4th treble to the right, 1 single on the next treble = turn the work to the right side = * 1 chain, 1 treble on the 6 chain;. repeat 7 times from *; therefore 8 trebles in all = after the 8th treble: 1 chain, miss 1·treble of the row beneath, 1 single on the 2 next trebles = turn the work = 2 chain, 1 cluster stitch between each treble, 9 cluster stitches in all, then 2 chain, miss 2 trebles of the row beneath, 1 single on the next 2 trebles = turn the work = 2 chain and 1 cluster stitch over the 1st, the 2nd, the 3^{d} and 4th pairs of chain stitches of the preceding row; over 5th, 6th and 7th chain stitches, 2 cluster stitches with 2 chain; over the other chain stitches, again:

Fig. 489. Square with coloured tufts.
Materials: D.M.C Pearl cotton Nos. 3, 5 or 8, or D.M.C
Alsatia Nos. 20 or 25,
in Ash grey 415 and Garnet red 335 or Mahogany brown 301
and Blue fast dye 820. (*)

1 cluster stitch; then 2 chain, miss 1 treble, join on to the 2nd treble = fasten off.

For the scallops on the right side, divide the stitches between the corner scallops equally. Count on the wrong side of the left corner 11 stitches to the right, fasten the thread on to the 11th stitch, * 5 chain, miss 2 trebles of the row beneath, 1 single on the 3^{d}, 1 single on the next stitch, 1 treble on the 5 chain, repeat 5 times and finish with 1 chain,

(*) See at the end of the last chapter the tables of the sizes and colours of the cotton, flax and silk articles, mark D.M.C.

1 single on the 2nd treble of the row beneath, 1 single on the next treble = turn the work = 2 chain and 1 cluster stitch between each treble of the preceding row, 2 cluster stitches between the 3d and 4th treble = after the 8th stitch : 2 chain, miss 1 treble, 1 plain on each of the 2 next trebles = turn the work = 2 chain, 1 cluster stitch to be repeated 3 times over 2 chain stitches of the preceding row, on the 4th, 5th and 6th chain stitches : 2 cluster stitches and 2 chain ; on the last 3 chain the same stitches as on the first, then 2 chain, miss 1 treble of the row beneath, 1 single over the next 11 stitches and repeat from *.

The last row consists of open picots, consisting of 5 chain and 1 single between each cluster stitch ; after the last of these stitches and in the indent of the scallops, on the straight line make only 2 chain and 1 plain on the 2nd stitch missed between the scallops, 2 chain ; the last scallop but one and the last and the first and the second are to be joined together by the 3d of the 5 chain stitches.

Hairpin crochet (fig. 491). — This is done on a kind of large steel hairpin or two-pronged fork.

Very pretty lace, fringe, gimp headings, in fact a number of other little articles, forming an agreeable variety to the kinds of work we have described thus far, can be made by the help of this little implement. Here we shall only give our readers a few specimens such as will best teach them how the work is done.

Materials. — For washing lace to trim underlinen with D.M.C Crochet cotton 6 cord (Cordonnet 6 fils) and D.M.C Flax lace thread (Lin pour dentelles) are the best ; for furniture fringes, D.M.C Alsatia or D.M.C Pearl cotton (Coton perlé) and in order to produce the effect of loose soft silk D.M.C Special stranded cotton (Mouliné spécial), D.M.C Floss crochet cotton (Crochet floche) or D.M.C Floss flax (Lin floche).

Stitches. — Begin as usual with a very loose chain stitch, then withdraw the needle from the loop and insert the left prong of the fork upwards from below and take hold of it with the thumb and middle finger of the left hand. The thread you work with should always be turned towards you.

Then put the thread over the right prong from the front, put the needle into the loop which is on the left prong, catch hold of the thread, draw it through the loop, throw the thread over the needle, draw it through the loop which is on the

Fig. 490. Pattern of a counterpane worked in stripes.
Materials: D.M.C Pearl cotton No. 1 or 3, in écru and Azure blue 3325, or
in Geranium red 352 and Garnet red 358, or in Solid blue 813
and Raspberry red 3685.

needle, then throw the thread from behind round the left prong, turn the prong to the right (the thread then surrounds the right prong); put the needle upwards from below into the loop which is on the left prong; throw the thread on to the needle, bring it back again, close the loops, and so on. Once the prong is covered with loops, slip them off, re-insert the two prongs of the fork into the 4 or 5 last loops and continue the work.

These stitches can be doubled, or you can make several trebles in each loop, or arrange the plain stitches in different ways.

Hairpin insertion (fig. 492). — Make first three stripes with the fork, covering each thread with 2 plain stitches. Then you join the stripes by the loops, by skipping a left loop over a right one, then a right one over the next left one.

At the end of the stripe, you fasten off the last loops by a few stitches. To strengthen the edges join 2 loops together by 1 plain, 2 chain, 1 plain, and so on.

Hairpin lace (fig. 493). — After having made 2 sufficiently long stripes of hairpin crochet with 2 trebles in each loop, join the loops, 2 and 2, with a thread of a colour to contrast with the rest of the work.

1 plain stitch joining 2 loops on the right, 2 chain, 1 plain joining 2 loops on the left, 2 chain, return to the right, and so on until you have taken up all the loops. This forms the zig-zag line in the middle. The scalloped edge of the lace is made in 2 rows.

1st row — join 3 loops by: 1 plain and 5 chain.

2nd row — on the 5 chain stitches: 1 plain, 1 half-treble, 3 trebles, 1 picot with 5 chain, 3 trebles, 1 half-treble, 1 plain.

The footing of this lace is made like the one in figure 492.

Hairpin lace (fig. 494). — This pattern worked in D.M.C Pearl cotton (Coton perlé) No. 5 (*), is suitable as a border for small rugs and table-covers and curtain headings. Begin with the two stripes of hairpin crochet made with 1 plain stitch in each loop. The loops of thread are collected together

---

(*) See at the end of the last chapter the tables of the sizes and colours of the cotton, flax and silk articles, mark D.M.C. — The French names, in brackets, are those stamped on the labels of the D.M.C articles.

by a few rows of crochet in a different colour; unite 4 loops by 1 plain stitch, * 3 chain, unite 2 loops by 1 plain, 3 chain, unite 2 loops by 1 chain, then 5 times 3 chain and 1 plain in the next loop, 3 chain, unite 2 loops, 3 chain, unite 2 loops, 3 chain, unite 8 loops, and repeat from *.

The same row is repeated on the 2nd side of the stripe of hairpin crochet; only you must begin with 3 separate loops, and you must set the separate loops exactly on the half ring formed by the 8 loops united by 1 plain.

The two stripes are connected by the 2nd of the chain stitches of the two little scallops at the top of the big scallop.

When the two stripes are joined together, fill the empty square spaces between with little stars made in two rounds in light thread.

1st row — * 1 treble on the second loop of the 3 chain, which comes after the united loops, 3 chain, 1 treble on the next chain stitches, 3 chain, 2 trebles joined by the last overs on the next 2 loops, 3 chain, 1 treble on the next chain stitches, 3 chain, 1 treble on the next chain stitches, 3 chain, 1 treble on the last chain stitches of the first stripe and 1 treble on the first chain stitches of the second stripe, at the same time draw up the last overs, 3 chain and repeat once from *, finish with 1 single on the 1st treble and the 2 next chain stitches.

2nd row — 3 chain, 1 treble over each chain stitch loop of the first row, 1 single on the 3d chain stitch; fasten off.

Footing of the lace. — 1st row, with a light colour — 1 quintuple treble on the first 3 chain stitches, 1 quadruple treble on the next chain stitches, 1 triple treble on the next chain stitches, at the same time drawing up the last overs of these 3 trebles, * 5 chain, 1 treble on the next chain stitches, 3 chain, 1 plain on the next chain stitches, 3 chain, 1 plain on the next chain stitches, 3 chain, 1 treble on the next chain stitches, 5 chain, on the next 6 loops make:

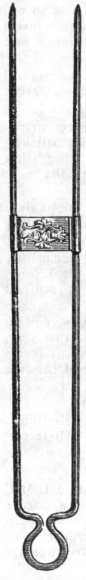

Fig. 491.
Steel hairpin for crochet.

1 triple treble, 1 quadruple treble, 2 quintuple trebles, 1 quadruple treble and 1 triple treble joined together by the last overs, then repeat from *.

2nd row — 1 plain on each stitch of the last row.

The edge of the lace, worked in coloured thread, is formed by a row of loops of 4 chain stitches, 1 plain on each loop beneath ; in the indent between two big scallops, skip the 4 chain stitches between the plain stitches.

Lace made on English point lace braid (fig. 495). — On the lace braid work a row of trebles, with 1 chain stitch between each, and on this row of trebles make two other rows for the lace, as follows :

1st row — 1 treble on one of the trebles of the row before,

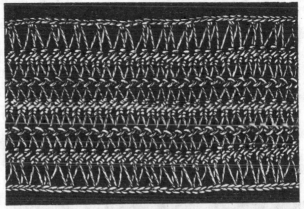

* 5 chain, 1 treble on the stitch in which the 1st treble is placed, 5 chain, skip 3 trebles of the row beneath, 1 treble on the 4th treble of the row beneath, and repeat as often as necessary from *.

2nd row — ** 1 treble on the 3d of the chain stitches between the two trebles placed in one stitch of the first row ; 3 chain, 1 treble in the

Fig. 492. Hairpin insertion.

Materials : D.M.C Knotting cotton No. 30, D.M.C Crochet cotton 6 cord or D.M.C Special crochet cotton No. 15, D.M.C Pearl cotton No. 8 or D.M.C Flax thread for knitting and crochet No. 16, in white or écru. (*)

same stitch, 3 chain, 1 treble in the same stitch, 3 chain, 1 plain in the 3d of the next 5 chain stitches, 3 chain and repeat from **.

Crochet lace on braid (fig. 496). — 1st row — 3 plain very close together in the braid, 13 chain, come back and join to the 1st plain. * In each of the first 6 chain : 1 plain = in the 7th chain : 3 plain, then on the other chain stitches : 6 plain.

(*) See at the end of the last chapter the tables of the sizes and colours of the cotton, flax and silk articles, mark D.M.C.

In the braid : 7 plain, 13 chain, connect them to the right with 3ᵈ plain and repeat from *.

2ⁿᵈ row — * skip 2 plain stitches of the scallop, 5 plain to arrive at the 2ⁿᵈ increased stitch of the first row, 3 plain on the 2ⁿᵈ increased stitch, 5 plain in the next stitches. Repeat from *.

To make an insertion of this lace, let go the thread after the 2ⁿᵈ of the 3 stitches which have to come at the point of the scallop, then put the needle into the stitch of the finished stripe, take up the thread again, draw it through the 2ⁿᵈ stitch and continue along the second side of the scallop in the same way as on the first.

Crochet lace on English point lace braid (fig. 497). — To make the little rings: — 1 plain stitch in the braid, 10 chain, then coming back, 1 single stitch in the 4ᵗʰ chain.

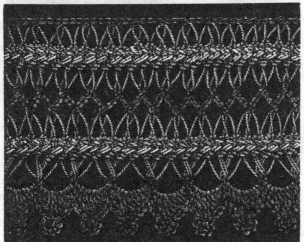

Fig. 493. Hairpin lace.
Materials : D.M.C Crochet cotton 6 cord No. 20, D.M.C Pearl cotton No. 8 or 12, or D.M.C Alsatia No. 20, Cachou brown 434 and Beetle green 3346, or Rust brown 3314 and Scabious violet 327. (*)

In this first ring you make: 1 plain, 1 half treble, 12 trebles, 1 half treble, 1 plain, 1 single in the 4ᵗʰ chain stitch; 3 chain, 1 plain in the braid far enough from the 1ˢᵗ chain stitch to prevent the rings from overlapping each other. Then 10 chain, 1 single in the 4ᵗʰ chain, 1 plain, 1 half treble, 2 trebles, drop the loop, put the needle into the 10ᵗʰ treble of the first ring, pick up the dropped loop, bring it forward to the right side, make 10 trebles, and so on.

For the footing : 1 treble, 1 chain, skip a few threads of the braid, 1 treble.

(*) See at the end of the last chapter the tables of the sizes and colours of the cotton, flax and silk articles, mark D.M.C.

Crochet guipure lace on English point lace braid
(fig. 498). — This charming little lace edging makes a very
good substitute for real guipure lace. It can be made on a
row of trebles just as well as on a lace braid or on a
mignardise the picots of which have been first raised by plain
and chain stitches. It is even advisable to edge the point lace

Fig. 494. Hairpin lace.
Materials: D.M.C Pearl cotton Nos. 3 to 12 or D.M.C Alsatia Nos. 20 and 25,
in Rust yellow 308 and Turkish red 321, or Blue fast dye 797
and Smoke grey 644.

braid with a row of plain stitches: as it is easier then to
make the scallops of the lace regular.

In the braid:

* 6 plain, 11 chain, skip a space equal to 6 bars of
the braid used for our pattern (or six plain stitches);
in the braid: 6 plain stitches very close together, 8 chain,
1 single in the 9th of the 11 chain, 12 chain, 1 single in

the 3ᵈ of the 11 chain, 8 chain, 1 single close to the 1ˢᵗ ot the first 6 plain.

1ˢᵗ scallop — 7 plain, 5 chain, join them coming back to the 4ᵗʰ plain; in the 5 chain: 6 plain; in the 8 chain: 3 plain.

2ⁿᵈ scallop — in the 12 chain: 5 plain, 5 chain, join them coming back to the 3ᵈ plain = in the 5 chain: 6 plain = in the 12 chain: 5 plain, 5 chain, join them coming back to the 3ᵈ plain = in the 5 chain: 6 plain = 5 plain in the 12 chain stitches beneath, 5 chain, join them coming back to the 3ᵈ plain = in the 5 chain: 6 plain = 2 plain in the 12 chain underneath.

3ᵈ scallop — like the first, then repeat from *.

Crochet lace made with medallion braid (fig. 499). — For the vertical leaves you must prepare separate medallions. Begin by 1 treble on the stalk between 2 medallions, 2 chain, 1 plain in the medallion : * 2 chain, 1 picot in bullion stitch made with 5 rounds of the thread, 2 chain, 1 plain in the medallion. Repeat once from *; 2 chain; take a detached medallion ; ** 1 plain, 2 chain, 1 picot, 2 chain ; repeat 6 times from **, the 4ᵗʰ picot must come on the point of the medallion, then make 1 more single on the 1ˢᵗ plain, then continue with 1 treble on the stalk between the 2 lower medallions, 2 chain, 1 plain in the next medallion, *** 2 chain, 1 picot, 2 chain, 1 plain. Repeat once from ***, 2 chain, and repeat from the beginning of the lace.

Footing of the lace. — 1ˢᵗ row — 1 double treble quite close to the stalk of the medallion, * 4 chain, 1 treble distant from the stalk of the medallion about a third of the width of the selvedge, 4 chain, 1 treble, 4 chain, 2 double trebles, one in the medallion on the right, the other in the medallion on the left ; draw up the last loops of the 2 trebles together and repeat from *.

2ⁿᵈ row — In each of the loops formed by the 4 chain ot the preceding row : 1 plain, 3 chain, 1 picot in bullion stitch, 7 chain, 1 picot, 3 chain, 1 plain on the next chain stitches and so on.

3ᵈ row — 1 plain on the 4ᵗʰ of the 7 chain stitches, 5 chain, 1 plain, and so on.

4ᵗʰ row — 1 plain on each stitch of the row before.

Crochet lace made with medallion braid (fig. 500). — Begin with the outside edge and make for the 1ˢᵗ row —

1 treble towards the end of the 1st medallion, * 6 chain, 1 picot, 6 chain, 1 treble at the beginning of the 2nd medallion, 6 chain, 1 picot, 6 chain, 1 treble towards the end of the medallion, 7 chain, 1 picot, 7 chain, 1 treble at the beginning of the 3d medallion, 6 chain, 1 picot, 6 chain, 1 treble towards the end of the 3d medallion, 6 chain, 1 picot, 6 chain, 1 treble on the 4th medallion, 2 double trebles which unite the 4th to the 1st medallion of the next scallop; 1 treble at the end of the 1st medallion; join and at the same time draw together the last loops of these 4 trebles. Repeat from *.

2nd row — Between each treble and each picot beginning from the 1st picot: ** 1 plain, 3 chain, 1 picot, 7 chain, 1 picot, 3 chain. Repeat 6 times from **, add 1 plain, then make between 2 scallops = 3 chain, 1 picot, 3 chain.

3d row — repeat 6 times: 1 treble on the 4th of the 7 chain stitches, 8 chain = in the indent join 2 trebles.

4th row — 15 plain over each loop of 8 chain.

Fig. 495. Lace made on English point lace braid. Materials: D.M.C Flax lace thread Nos. 25 to 70, D.M.C Alsatian thread Nos. 50 to 70 or D.M.C Crochet cotton 6 cord Nos. 80 to 100, white. (*)

Inside junction — Begin between 2 medallions, fasten on the thread and make 1 plain on the bar between the medallions of two scallops, 6 chain, 1 picot, now make all the drooping picots, 7 chain, 1 double treble

Fig. 496. Crochet lace on braid. Materials: D.M.C Superfine braid and D.M.C Alsatian thread Nos. 30 to 70 or D.M.C Special crochet cotton Nos. 40 to 100. (*)

at the beginning of the 1st medallion, 5 chain, 1 triple treble at the end of the medallion, 1 triple treble at the beginning of the 2nd medallion, draw up at the same time the last loops of the 2 trebles; 5 chain, 2 triple trebles united in the medallions right and left; 5 chain, 2 triple trebles joined together, one at the end, the other at the

---

(*) See at the end of the last chapter the tables of the sizes and colours of the cotton, flax and silk articles, mark D.M.C.

beginning of the 3^d and 4th medallion; 2 chain, 1 picot, in bullion stitch 2 chain, 1 single in the last loop of the first triple trebles, 10 chain, 1 plain in the last loop of the last trebles; 5 chain, 1 double treble at the end of the 4th medallion, 5 chain, 1 plain in the 10 chain above the picot, 5 chain, 1 plain in the 1st double treble; 12 chain, 1 single in the loop of the last double treble, 7 chain, 1 picot, 6 chain, 1 plain on the stalk between the 2 medallions, and so on.

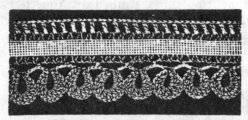

Fig. 497. Crochet lace on English point lace braid.

Materials: D.M.C Alsatian thread Nos. 30 to 50, D.M.C Crochet cotton 6 cord or D.M.C Special crochet cotton Nos. 80 to 100, in white.

2nd row — * 1 treble on the 6 chain stitches before the 1st picot, 6 chain, 1 treble on the 7 chain after the 1st picot, 6 chain **, 1 treble on the 12 chain stitches in the middle, repeat from ** to *, 6 chain and continue from the beginning

3^d row — 1 plain in the braid which serves as footing, 2 chain, 1 plain in the last loop of chain stitch, 2 chain, 1 plain in the braid. Continue in this manner going to and fro to join the crochet work to the braid.

Crochet lace with mignardise (fig. 501). This lace makes a very useful, serviceable trimming for underlinen of all kinds.

Begin by picking up all the picots along two rows of mignardise, by making 1 plain and 1 chain.

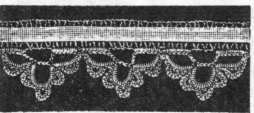

Fig. 498. Crochet guipure lace on English point lace braid.

Materials: D.M.C Alsatian thread Nos. 70 to 90, D.M.C Crochet cotton 6 cord or D.M.C Special crochet cotton Nos. 80 to 150, in white.

The rows of crochet in between consist of: 1 treble on 1 chain, 3 chain, skip 2 picots of the mignardise, 1 treble between the 3^d and 4th picot, and so on. On the second side, make the same stitches passing the thread, after the 2nd chain stitch, and from the wrong side to the right through the 2nd chain stitch of the first stripe.

The edge, which forms very strong scallops, is worked in two rows.

1st row — 1 treble between 2 picots, 3 chain, skip 2 picots, 1 treble, 3 chain, and so on.

2nd row — 1 treble on 3 chain, * 3 chain, 1 treble on the next 3 chain, 3 chain, 3 trebles, 7 chain, turn back, join them to the 1st of the 3 trebles close together, 2 chain, join them to the 2nd isolated treble, 12 trebles on the 7 chain; leave the last loops of the last treble on the needle and join them to those of the next isolated treble; repeat from *.

Crochet ground (*) (fig. 502). — This ground, as well as the next is intended for making purses, reticules and tobacco pouches, &c.

The pattern itself is worked in a single row, with a row of chain stitches to finish.

It is begun on a number of chain stitches divisible by 8.

1st row — * 4 plain on the first 4 chain stitches, 1 picot, 4 plain on the next 4 chain, 9 chain, join them to the 1st plain, on the 9 chain : 7 plain, 3 picots joined by 1 single and 7 plain; repeat from *.

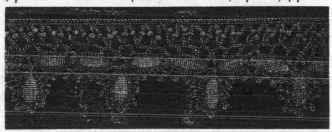

Fig. 499. Crochet lace made with medallion braid.
Materials : D.M.C Alsatian thread Nos. 50 to 100, D.M.C Crochet cotton 6 cord or D.M.C Special crochet cotton Nos. 40 to 80, in white.

2nd row — 1 plain stitch in each of the middle picots with 8 chain stitches between.

In the following rows the scallops are to be interverted.

Crochet ground (fig. 503). — This ground requires as a foundation a number of chain stitches divisible by 13.

1st row — 4 trebles on the first chain, * skip 4 chain, 4 trebles on the 5th chain, skip 3 chain, 1 plain, 5 chain, skip 3 chain, 4 trebles on the 4th stitch; repeat from *.

2nd row — 4 trebles on the 1st treble of the row before, ** 4 trebles on the 8th treble, 3 chain, 1 single on the 3d chain of the 2 scallops of 5 chain, 3 chain, 4 trebles on the 1st treble of the next figure; repeat from **.

(*) See at the end of the volume the list of the albums of the D.M.C Library, containing a large variety of patterns for all kinds of work.

3¹ row — 4 trebles on the 1st treble of the 2nd row, ✱ ✱ ✱
4 trebles on the 8th treble, 5 chain, 1 single on the 2nd single
of the row beneath, 3 chain, join them to the 3d of the
5 chain, 3 chain, 4 trebles on the 1st treble following; repeat
from ✱ ✱ ✱.

In the next 3 rows the figures are inverted, so that the
clusters of trebles come above groups of spiders.

Ground composed of crochet stars (fig. 504). — Grounds
like this are most often used for cushion-covers and chair backs
of all kinds: for the latter purpose they are sometimes edged

Fig. 500. Crochet lace made with medallion braid.
Materials: D.M.C Crochet cotton 6 cord or D.M.C Special crochet cotton Nos. 40
to 80, or D.M.C Alsatian thread Nos. 50 to 80, in white: (✱)

with a narrow band of velvet or plush trimmed with a narrow
crochet lace.

Star — 1st row — 20 chain, join them to the 1st chain;
3 chain which count as a first treble, 4 trebles on the next
4 chain, 6 trebles on the next 3 chain, 1 picot of 5 chain
stitches, 1 picot of 7 chain, 1 picot of 5 chain, 1 single on the
1st chain stitch of the first picot, 6 trebles on the next 3 chain,
5 trebles on the next 5 chain, 4 chain, 1 picot of 5 chain,
1 picot of 7 chain, 1 picot of 5 chain, 1 single on the 1st chain

---

(✱) See at the end of the last chapter the tables of the sizes and colours of
the cotton, flax and silk articles, mark D.M.C.

stitch of the 1st picot, * 27 chain, join them to the 7th chain stitch, 2 single on the chain stitches towards the picots, finish the scallop like the former one, 4 chain, 3 picots joined together by 1 single, repeat twice from *; 4 chain, join them to the first scallop.

2nd row — to be worked inwards — ** 5 chain, 1 plain on the chain stitch before the scallop, 5 chain, 3 double trebles joined by the last overs on the chain stitches within the scallop, 5 chain, 1 plain on the chain stitch after the scallop, repeat 3 times from **.

3d row — 1 plain on each chain stitch and on the double trebles, skip the plain stitches; fasten off the thread.

4th row — 1 treble before and after the double trebles and over the plain stitches, 3 chain, 1 treble before and after the next double trebles, 3 chain, 2 trebles, 3 chain, 2 trebles, 3 chain, join them to the 1st treble.

5th row — 2 single, 1 plain on the 2nd of the 3 chain, 1 chain, 1 plain on the 2nd chain, 1 chain, 1 plain on the 2nd chain, 1 chain, 1 plain on the 2nd chain, 1 chain, join it to the 1st plain; fasten off the thread.

The detached stars are to be joined together by the middle and corner picots.

Lace with two rows of leaves (fig. 5o5). — This is one of the pleasantest crochet patterns to work we know.

The leaves are made separately, and fastened into a foundation resembling net made with thread at least two numbers finer than that used for the leaves.

Leaf with 5 petals: 8 chain, make a ring = 2 plain on the ring = 1st petal: 11 chain, skip 3 chain, 1 half-treble on the 8th chain stitch, 1 chain, skip the 7th, 1 treble on the 6th chain, 1 chain, 1 treble on the 4th chain, 1 chain, 1 treble on the 2nd chain, 1 chain, 2 plain on the ring.

2nd petal: 15 chain, skip 3, 1 half-treble, * 1 chain, skip 1, 1 treble. Repeat 4 times from *; add: 1 chain, 2 plain on the ring.

3d petal: 21 chain, skip 3, 1 half-treble, ** 1 chain, skip 1, 1 treble. Repeat 7 times from **; add: 1 chain, skip 1, 2 plain on the ring.

The 4th petal like the 2nd; the 5th like the 1st.

When the 5 petals are finished, make 2 single stitches on the 2 first plain stitches of the ring; then along the chain stitches of the 1st petal : 2 plain, 7 trebles, 2 trebles on the 10th; then descending: 7 trebles, 2 plain and 2 single on the 2 plain stitches of the ring.

On the 2nd petal make : 3 plain, 10 trebles, 2 trebles on the 14th chain stitch, 10 trebles, 3 plain, 2 single on the 2 plain stitches of the ring.

On the 3d petal: 2 single, 3 plain, 14 trebles, 2 trebles on the 20th chain stitch, 14 trebles, 3 plain, 2 single and then 2 more single on the 2 plain-stitches of the ring.

The 4th petal is worked like the 2nd, the 5th like the 1st.

For the stalk : 14 chain, skip 1, 9 plain on the next 9 chain ; 6 chain, skip 1, 5 plain on the 5 chain, 4 plain on the stitches that remain free, 2 single on the ring, fasten off the thread with a few stitches.

Fig. 501. Crochet lace with mignardise.
Materials — According to the mignardise selected: D.M.C Alsatian thread Nos. 30 to 70 or D.M.C Crochet cotton 6 cord Nos. 30 to 80, in white. (*)

When you have leaves enough ready, join them to-gether by a row of picots, working from left to right, as follows: * take the 2nd petal on the right side of a leaf, put the thread in at the 14th treble: make 2 plain, 1 picot, 1 plain on the stitch the picot is on = in all the leaves the 3d plain stitch before the picot and the 1st after it, meet in the same stitch beneath = 2 plain, 1 picot, 3 plain, 2 chain = on the 8th treble of the 3d petal: 1 plain, then 2 more plain on the next stitches, ** 1 picot, 3 plain. Repeat 6 times from ** and

(*) See at the end of the last chapter the tables of the sizes and colours of the cotton, flax and silk articles, mark D.M.C.

finish with 2 chain. On the 7th treble of the 4th petal: 1 plain, 2 plain on the next 2 stitches, *** 1 picot, 3 plain. Repeat 4 times from ***.

On the 5th treble of the 5th petal: 1 plain, then on the next 4 chain, 4 plain ****.

Now repeat round each leaf from * to * *, then, instead of the 1st picot on the 3^d petal, make 4 chain, then put your

Fig. 502. Crochet ground.
Materials : D.M.C Crochet cotton 6 cord or D.M.C Special crochet cotton Nos. 20 to 60, D.M.C Alsatian thread Nos. 30 to 70, D.M.C Alsatia Nos. 20 to 40 or D.M.C Pearl cotton Nos. 5 to 12, in white or écru.

needle into the 2nd plain stitch to the right, between the 1st and 2nd picot of the leaf before, 4 chain, close the picot. From this point, the preceding series of stitches replaces the picot which comes immediately after the * *; continue to ****.

Foundation for the footing of the lace, with a single row

of leaves. — When all the leaves are joined together, take the finer number of thread and fasten it on to the end of the little stalk; then make: ✳ 2 chain, 1 plain on the 9th stitch of the 1st petal; 6 chain, skip 2, 1 plain on the 3d stitch; 6 chain, 1 plain on the 3d, 1 chain, 1 plain on the 7th stitch of the 2nd leaf; 6 chain, 1 plain on the 3d; 2 chain, 1 plain on the 7th stitch counted from below, of the 5th

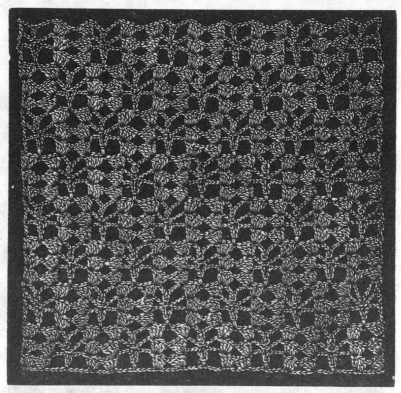

Fig. 503. Crochet ground.

Materials: D.M.C Crochet cotton 6 cord or D.M.C Special crochet cotton Nos. 15 to 50, D.M.C Alsatian thread Nos. 30 to 50, D.M.C Alsatia Nos. 20 to 40 or D.M.C Pearl cotton Nos. 5 to 12, in white or écru. (*)

petal of the next leaf, 3 chain, 1 single on the last stitch of the long stalk; 3 chain, then returning, draw the thread through the 3d of the last 6 chain of the 1st leaf, 3 chain, returning draw the thread through the 3d of the second set

(*) See at the end of the last chapter the tables of the sizes and colours· of the cotton, flax and silk articles, mark D.M.C.

oi 6 chain stitches of the 1st petal; 6 chain, 1 plain on the 2nd of the last 3 chain, 6 chain, 1 plain on the 1st stitch of the stalk; 6 chain, 1 plain on the chain stitch between the 2 stalks, 7 chain, 1 plain at the top of the little stalk, then repeat from *.

The network of the next rows, which may be of any width you like, consists of: 6 chain, 1 plain in the loop of the row before.

For the last row of the network but one, make 4 chain,

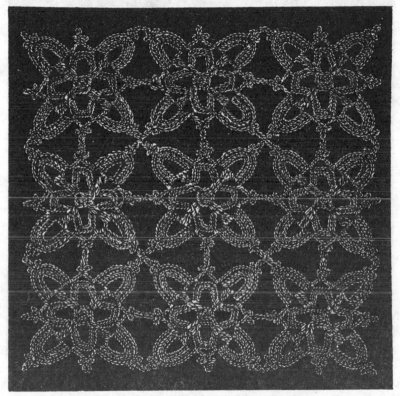

Fig. 504. Ground composed of crochet stars.
Materials : D.M.C Alsatian thread Nos. 30 to 50, D.M.C Alsatia Nos. 15 to 25
or D.M.C Pearl cotton Nos. 5 to 12, in white or écru.

1 plain above each loop, then finish the lace with a row of plain stitches.

The following is the way to join two rows of leaves together that have been already edged with picots.

Fasten the thread, on to the little stalk, * 3 chain, 1 plain on the 8th stitch of the 1st petal, 2 chain, draw the thread

through the 4th picot of the middle of the 3d petal of the top
leaf, 2 chain, 3 plain on the 1st petal of the row beneath,
1 picot, 3 chain, 1 picot, 3 chain. In the 2nd petal of the bottom
leaf, from the 7th stitch onwards : 3 plain, 1 picot, 3 plain.

In the fifth petal of the next leaf below begin at the 8th
free stitch, counted from left to right : 3 plain, 4 chain,

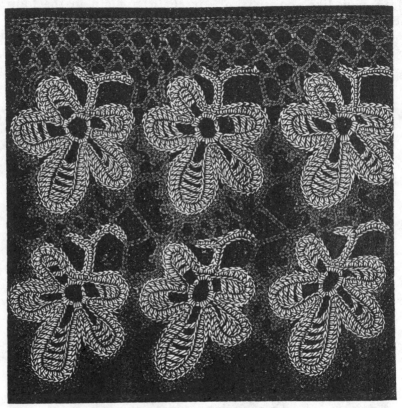

Fig. 505. Lace with two rows of leaves.
Materials: D.M.C Pearl cotton Nos. 5 and 8 or D.M.C Alsatia Nos. 20 and 25,
in Golden green 580 and Indigo blue 334, or in Scabious violet 395
and Rust brown 3314. (*)

1 single on the long stalk, 5 chain, 1 single on the 2nd picot
to the right of the preceding bottom leaf, 5 chain, 1 single on
the 4th picot to the right of the 4th petal of the leaf above,
4 chain, 1 plain on the 4th plain stitch of the stalk; 3 chain,

(*) See at the end of the last chapter the tables of the sizes and colours of
the cotton, flax and silk articles, mark D.M.C.

1 single on the 1st picot to the left of the 3d petal of the upper leaf, 3 chain, skip 2 stitches of the stalk, 1 plain on the stalk, 3 chain, 1 single on the next picot of the upper leaf, 3 chain. 1 plain on the 2d stitch of the little stalk, 3 chain, 1 single on the next picot of the upper leaf, 3 chain, 1 plain at the end of the little stalk. Repeat from *.

In this way you can join 3 and even 4 rows of leaves together and make a beautiful lace which will form an extremely handsome trimming for church linen.

If you want the leaves to stand out from the network ground, you can use two shades of thread, the lighter for the leaves, the darker for the ground.

Crochet lace with squares (fig. 506). — This is always a favorite and effective pattern, in any sized thread. We cannot pretend that the design itself is new; it is even very likely that many of our readers are familiar with it in pillow lace. But we thought that those who are not fond of making pillow lace will welcome this reproduction of it in crochet as it makes such a good durable trimming both for wearing apparel and furniture. For the latter purpose it should be made in one or other of the strong unbleached materials, mentioned at the foot of the engraving: for the former in one or other of the finer threads specially indicated as suitable for the purpose. (*)

The squares which are begun in the centre are worked in continuous rows and always on the right side.

Cast on 5 chain and close the ring.

1st row — * 5 chain, 1 plain on the ring. Repeat 3 times from *.

2nd row — 1 chain on the first 5 chain stitches : * 1 plain, 5 chain, 1 plain = 2 chain. Repeat 3 times from *.

3d row — on the first 5 chain stitches of the 2nd row : * 1 plain, 4 chain, 1 plain, 2 chain, 1 plain on the next 2 chain stitches, 2 chain. Repeat 3 times from *.

On the 4th and to the 11th row — continue to increase as in the 3d row, until on the 4 sides you have 11 chain stitches between the 4 chain stitches in the corners.

12th row — 1 plain, * 5 chain, 1 plain; ** 1 picot consisting of 4 chain, 1 plain between the 1st and 2nd plain stitches of the preceding row, 2 chain, 1 plain between the

(*) See at the end of the volume the list of the albums of the D.M.C Library, containing a large variety of patterns for all kinds of work.

next 2 plain. Repeat from ** until you have 6 picots, then repeat 3 times from *; fasten off the thread.

Join the next squares together as you finish them. After the last 12th plain stitch make: 2 chain, drop the loop, put

Fig. 500. Crochet lace with squares

Materials: D.M.C Crochet cotton 6 cord or D.M.C Special crochet cotton Nos. 15 to 100, D.M.C Knotting cotton No. 30, D.M.C Pearl cotton Nos. 5 to 12, or D.M.C Flax thread for knitting and crochet Nos. 20 to 45, in white or écru.

the needle into the 3d of the 5 chain stitches which form one of the corners of a finished square; draw the dropped loop through; make 2 chain, finish the square with 1 single stitch.

For the star that connects the squares, begin by making 10 chain, close the ring.

On this ring make : * 4 chain, 1 picot, 4 chain, connect the 2 picots right and left of the joined squares by a treble ; 4 chain, 1 picot, 3 chain, drop the loop, put the needle into the first of the first 4 chain stitches, draw the thread through, 2 chain on the ring, 8 chain, 1 treble on the 3^d picot and 1 on the 4^{tb} picot of the square = coming back : 8 single on the 8 chain ; 2 plain on the ring and repeat 3 times from *, fasten off the thread.

For the half star that fills the space beneath the footing of the lace : 9 chain, close the ring = 9 chain, 1 treble on the 1st picot of the square ; 4 chain, 1 picot, 3 chain ; draw the thread through the 1st of the 9 chain stitches ; 2 plain on the ring = 8 chain ; connect the 3^d and 4th picots of the square by 1 treble on each picot, 8 single stitches on the 8 chain, 2 plain on the ring = 4 chain, 1 picot, 4 chain, 1 treble on the first and last picot of the 2 opposite squares, 4 chain, 1 picot, 3 chain, drop the loop, draw it through the 1st of the 4 chain stitches, 2 plain on the ring = 8 chain, connect the 3^d and 4th picots by 2 trebles ; 8 single, 2 plain on the ring = 4 chain, 1 picot, 4 chain, 1 treble on the last of the picots, 8 chain, draw the thread through the 1st of the 4 chain, fasten off.

The footing is made as follows : * 1 plain on the point of the square ; 17 chain stitches up to the ring ; 3 plain on the ring ; 17 chain and repeat from *. A row of plain stitches or trebles completes the footing.

The outer edge of the scallops is worked in two rows.

1st row — * 1 treble on the 1st picot ; 4 chain and repeat 5 times from *. On the 5 chain stitches on the point of the square : 1 double treble, 4 chair 1 triple treble, 4 chain, 1 double treble ; then finish the second side of the square like the first. Make no chain stitches at the point where 2 scallops join.

2nd row — 2 plain, 1 picot, 2 plain over 4 chain, at the point add 1 picot on the triple treble. On the last and first 4 chain stitches where 2 scallops join, only 4 plain.

Lace with stars (fig. 507). — Before proceeding to describe this lace we would point out to our readers that to obtain a good result the chain stitches that encircle the stars and those that form the trebles must be made with the greatest regularity. Some hands make loose stitches, some tight, it would therefore be well to make a trial row first so as to ascertain whether the number of stitches we have found to be right corresponds in length to the same number worked by another hand; then it will be seen whether it is necessary to increase or diminish the number indicated.

You begin with the middle stars, cast on 18 chain, close the ring, mount it on a mould, wind a soft thread such as D.M.C Darning cotton (Coton à repriser) No. 25 (*), seven or eight times round the mould and cover this ring with 30 plain stitches joining the last to the first by one single stitch.

Fig. 507. Lace with stars.
Materials : D.M.C Alsatian thread Nos. 30 to 70, D.M.C Knotting cotton No. 30, or D.M.C Flax thread for knitting and crochet Nos. 20 to 45, in white, écru or Cream yellow 712.

1st row — * 13 chain; return, skip the first chain stitch, and on the other 12 make : 1 single, 2 plain, 2 half trebles, 2 trebles, 2 double trebles, 3 triple trebles, skip 4 stitches of the preceding row, 1 single on the 5th stitch, and repeat 5 times from *.

2nd row — 5 single on the stitches of the first pyramid, * 3 chain, pass them to the wrong side of the work, 1 single

---

(*) See at the end of the last chapter the tables of the sizes and colours of the cotton, flax and silk articles, mark D.M.C. — The French names, in brackets, are those stamped on the labels of the D.M.C articles.

on the 5th stitch of the same pyramid, 17 chain, 1 single on the 5th stitch of the next pyramid, repeat 5 times from *. After the 5th time make single stitches up to the point of the 1st pyramid.

3d row — * 1 plain on the chain stitch above, which was skipped in the 1st row; 9 chain, 1 plain on the 9th of the 17 chain stitches, 9 chain. Repeat 5 times from *.

4th row — 1 plain on each stitch of the preceding row.

5th row — * 6 plain, 3 chain, skip 2 stitches of the last row. Repeat 14 times from *.

6th row — 1 plain on each of the bottom stitches of the last row. After every 7 plain, 1 picot. In the whole circumference there will be 19 picots separated from each other by 7 plain stitches; in order just to get round, you must twice skip plain stitch under a picot.

In joining the rings, be careful to arrange them so that 9 picots are turned towards the edge and 8 towards the footing.

The 10th and the 19th picot serve to connect the stars.

Outside edge — 1st row — 1 treble between the 19th and the 1st picot, * 7 chain, 1 treble between the 2 next picots. Repeat 8 times from *. After the 10th treble, make no more chain stitches; it is followed by another treble placed between the 19th and the 1st picot of the next star.

2nd row — On the first 7 stitches of the preceding row: 4 plain, 3 half trebles; on the next stitches: 3 trebles, 1 picot, 3 trebles, 1 picot, and so on; so that you will always have to make 18 picots and 19 times 3 trebles in the semicircle = on the last 7 chain stitches: 3 half trebles, 4 plain stitches.

The big scallops are connected by little ones, for which starting from the indent of the scallop you make first 4 plain, 3 half trebles, 3 trebles, 1 picot, 2 trebles, 7 chain, drop the loop, put the needle into the same treble of the preceding scallop; draw the loop through and make on the 7 chain: 1 plain, 1 half treble, 3 trebles, 1 picot, 3 trebles, 1 half treble, 1 plain and continue the big scallop as described above.

The ground and the footing are composed of rings and trebles. Begin by making a ring similar to the one in the centre of the star, as follows: 16 chain which you cover with 28 plain = 3 plain, 10 chain, skip 1 plain, 3 plain = 10 chain, skip 1 plain, 3 plain = 5 chain, 1 single on the 12th picot of the 1st star; 5 chain, skip 1, 3 plain = 5 chain,

1 single on the 11ᵗʰ picot of the star; 5 chain, skip 1, 3 plain = 5 chain, 1 single on the 18ᵗʰ picot of the 2ⁿᵈ star; 5 chain, skip 1, 3 plain = 5 chain, 1 single on the 17ᵗʰ picot, 5 chain, skip 1, 3 plain = 10 chain, 1 single on the 1ˢᵗ plain stitch of the ring, fasten off and cut the thread.

The row of trebles to follow is worked from right to left — * 1 septuble treble between the 12ᵗʰ and the 13ᵗʰ picot, 7 chain, 1 sextuple treble on the same stitch the 1ˢᵗ treble is on, 1 quintuple treble between the 13ᵗʰ and the 14ᵗʰ picot; 7 chain, 1 quadruple treble on the same stitch as the preceding treble, 1 triple treble between the 14ᵗʰ and the 15ᵗʰ picot ** , 7 chain, repeat from ** to * between the next picots. The three long loops of the ring made of chain stitches are to be picked up by a treble, the middle loop by 1 plain stitch followed by 7 chain.

A row of plain stitches forms the last row of this lace.

Guipure lace (fig. 508). — For this charming lace which seems at first sight to present some difficulties but which will disappear in the course of working, we advise our readers to take by preference D.M.C Cotton lace thread (Fil à dentelle) No. 50 (*), D.M.C Crochet cotton 6 cord (Cordonnet 6 fils) or D.M.C Special crochet cotton (Cordonnet spécial) No. 50, in écru.

Begin with the lozenge shaped figures in the centre, by making a ring formed of 5 chain stitches.

1ˢᵗ row — 5 chain, 1 picot, 2 chain, 1 treble on the ring; 5 chain, 1 treble on the ring, 2 chain, 1 picot, 2 chain, 1 treble on the ring; 5 chain, draw the thread through the 3ᵈ of the first 5 chain stitches.

2ⁿᵈ row — 12 chain, * 1 treble on the 1ˢᵗ treble of the 1ˢᵗ row = 4 chain, 1 treble on the 3ᵈ of the next 5 chain = 5 chain, 1 treble on the same stitch the last treble is on = 4 chain ** , 1 treble on the second treble of the 1ˢᵗ row; 9 chain. Repeat from * to ** and join the 4 last chain stitches to the 3ᵈ of the first 12.

3ᵈ row — 1 chain, 4 plain on the 4 lower stitches; 3 plain on the 5ᵗʰ of the 9 remaining stitches of the 12 chain of the preceding row = 12 plain, then 5 plain on the 3ᵈ of the 5 chain stitches between the 2 trebles = 12 plain, 3 plain on

---

(*) See at the end of the last chapter the tables of the sizes and colours of the cotton, flax and silk articles, mark D.M.C. — The French names, in brackets, are those stamped on the labels of the D.M.C articles.

the 5th of the second 9 chain stitches; 12 plain, 5 plain on the 3d of the 5 chain, 7 plain; close the ring with 1 single stitch.

4th row — 3 chain; 1 treble on each of the next 5 plain; 3 trebles on the 6th plain, 1 treble on each of the next 15 stitches; 5 trebles on the 16th; 15 trebles more on the 2nd side; again 3 trebles on the 16th stitch; 15 trebles on the

Fig. 508. Guipure lace.

Materials : D.M.C Alsatian thread Nos. 30 to 100, D.M.C Crochet cotton 6 cord Nos. 25 to 100, D.M.C Cotton lace thread Nos. 30 to 100, D.M.C Flax lace thread Nos. 20 to 70 or D.M.C Pearl cotton Nos. 5 to 12, in écru or Cream yellow 711 and 712. (*)

3d side; 5 trebles on the 16th; 9 trebles and join the stitch to the 3d of the 3 chain.

5th row — 1 chain, 6 plain, 3 plain on the 7th plain, * 18

(*) See at the end of the last chapter the tables of the sizes and colours of the cotton, flax and silk articles, mark D.M.C.

plain; 3 plain on the 19th stitch. Repeat twice from *, 11 plain, close the ring with 1 single stitch.

6th row — 1 chain, 1 picot, 3 plain, 1 picot, 3 plain, and so on, make on the middle stitch at the point: 2 plain, 1 picot, 2 plain, so that there will. be 7 picots on each side of the lozenge before and after the picot at the point; fasten off the thread.

The oblong squares that connect the lozenges require 6 rows of plain stitches = make a chain of 14 = turn the work = 13 plain; add 5 more rows of the same number of stitches. On the short side and along the edge of the square: 1 picot, 3 plain, * 9 chain; returning, miss 1 chain; 1 plain, 1 half treble, 3 trebles, 1 half treble, 2 plain = on the second half of the short side: 3 plain, 1 picot on the corner = along the long side of the square : 3 plain **, 1 picot, 3 plain ***. Repeat twice from * to *** and only once from * to **.

The row of trebles that frame the little leaves begins with 2 plain on the first picot, then come: * 3 chain, 1 picot, 3 chain, 1 treble on the 9th chain stitch of the little leaf on the short side = 1 chain, 1 picot, 1 chain, 1 triple treble on the 9th chain stitch of the leaf, join this figure to the lozenge which ends with 1 single stitch; 1 chain, 1 picot, 1 chain, 1 treble on the little leaf = 3 chain, 1 picot, 3 chain, 1 plain on the picot which forms the corner of the oblong square = 3 chain, 1 picot, 3 chain, 1 treble on the point of the leaf on the long side of the square, 3 chain, 1 treble on the same stitch the 1st treble is on, 3 chain, 1 treble on the stitch on which the 2 first trebles are = 3 chain, 1 picot, 3 chain, 1 plain on the corner picot. Repeat once more from * and fasten off the thread.

The openwork ground that surrounds the lozenges and the squares is the same above and below. It is composed of squares and leaves rather bigger than those round the squares, already described above.

6 chain, 1 sextuple treble on the 2nd picot of the lozenge after the corner picot counting upwards from below; 6 chain, 1 triple treble on the 4th picot of the lozenge. Coming back over the 2 trebles of 6 chain, and in 3 journeys to and fro, make: 13 plain. After the 2nd row of plain stitches: 1 quintuple treble on the sixth picot of the lozenge, then finish the 4 other rows of plain stitches.

After finishing the 6th row, pass at once to the leaves above the lozenge, ** 15 chain, 1 plain on the stitch that forms the point of the lozenge or of the small square = turn the work to the wrong side = on the chain stitches: *** 3 plain, 1 half treble, 4 trebles, 1 half treble, 3 plain = turn the work to the right side = in coming back and starting from the point of the leaf: 1 chain, 1 plain on each of the lower stitches ****.

For the second leaf opposite the first, 13 chain = turn the work = repeat as in the first leaf from *** to ****.

This second leaf being finished like the first, you will have reached the point of the leaf from which you pass to the 2nd little square for which make, 6 chain, 1 quintuple treble on the 2nd picot that follows the leaves, 3 chain, 1 triple treble on the 4th picot, counting from the leaf, 6 chain, 1 sextuple treble on the 6th picot of the lozenge; retain the 2 last lo ps of the treble on your needle; 1 sextuple treble on the picot between the 3 chain stitches of the little square with leaves; draw up the last loops of this treble with those of the preceding treble = 6 chain, 1 triple treble on the picot on the long side of the square; coming back make 2 rows of 13 plain on the 2 trebles of 6 chain stitches.

Here you draw 1 of the chain stitches, which are between the 2 long trebles and the 3 last of the 6 chain stitches, through the last of the 13 plain. After the 2nd row of plain: 1 sextuple treble on the stitch of the 1st treble set on the little leaf above the square facing the lozenge = 4 rows of plain to complete the square and repeat from **.

The preceding directions apply equally to the part beneath the footing, only it has to be worked from right to left.

The big scallops that form the edge of the lace are worked each separately.

In the corner to the right of the small square, make: 1 double treble on the 1st plain stitch, 2 chain, 1 double treble on the 5th plain; 2 chain, 1 double treble on the 9th, 2 chain, 1 double treble on the stitch that forms the corner of the square = 2 chain, 1 plain at the extremity of the 1st long leaf, 9 chain = 1 quadruple treble on the stitch between the 2 leaves, 2 chain, 1 quadruple treble on the same stitch the 1st quadruple treble is on, 2 chain, 1 more quadruple treble on the same stitch = 9 chain, 1 plain at the extremity of the 2nd long leaf = turn the work = 1 chain, 1 plain on each of the stitches, 27 plain in all = turn the work = 1 chain, 1 plain, * 2 chain, skip 1 plain, 1 plain on the second plain stitch. Repeat 12 times from *. Turn the work and continue placing the plain stitches on the 2 chain of the inside row. Decrease by one stitch each row and from each side and fasten off the thread at the last.

Fasten on the thread at the foot, not at the point of the scallop, and make plain stitches all round it; up to the point there should be 20, in all therefore 40.

The openwork edge of the scallops is made entirely of double trebles. — When the 40th stitch is made: 2 chain, 1 double treble on the 1st plain stitch of the little square = turn the work = * 2 chain, 1 double treble, on the 2nd of the plain stitches which form the edge of the scallop **. Repeat 8 times from * to **. After the 8th repeat 2 chain, 1 double treble on the next plain stitch, 2 chain, 1 double treble on the next plain stitch, 2 chain, 1 double treble on the next stitch: in all make 5 double trebles and 4 times 2 chain without missing any stitches, then repeat 9 times from * to ** = *** 2 chain, 1 single on the 4th treble of the square = 2 chain, 1 single on the 3d treble = turn the work = make on the right side: **** 2 chain, 1 double treble on the treble of the row beneath; continue in this manner to the 8th treble, after the 8th treble: ***** 10 chain, come back to the 7th treble, draw the loop of the 10 chain through it = on the 10 chain: 16 plain = after the 16th, draw the loop through the upper parts of the 8th treble ******.

2 chain, 1 double treble, 2 chain, 1 double treble, 10 chain, come back and fasten the chain stitches to the last treble but one = on the 10 chain: 6 plain, 1 picot, 2 chain, 1 picot, 2 plain, 1 picot, 6 plain and join as for the preceding scallop *******; 2 chain, 1 double treble, 2 chain, 1 double treble, repeat once from ***** to *******, repeat a second time from ***** only to ******; then from **** to ***** as on the first side, but make 1 treble less, then 1 double treble on the 4th plain stitch of the little square = 2 chain, skip 3 plain of the square, 1 double treble on the 4th, 2 chain, skip 3, 1 double treble on the stitch forming the angle of the little square = 2 chain, 1 plain on the stitch at the extremity of the leaf; 9 chain and begin again as for the first scallop.

Having come to the second scallop, on the second row of trebles at the sign **** make: 2 chain, 1 treble to the left on the scallop you just finished = retain the last loops of the treble on the needle, 1 double treble on the scallop to the right and join it to the second treble; draw the 4 loops together at the same time = 2 chain, 1 double treble on the left, 1 double treble on the right = 7 chain, drop the loop, bring it to the right side through the 4th treble of the scallop on the right = on these 7 chain stitches: 1 single, 1 plain, 1 half treble, 2 trebles, 1 half treble, 1 plain, 1 single, 1 double treble on the edge to the left = 2 chain, 1 double treble, 2 chain, 1 double treble, 10 chain; join them to the 6th treble of the right scallop = coming back on the 10 chain: 4 plain, 1 picot, 4 plain, 1 picot, 4 plain, 1 picot, 4 plain = join by the double treble, 2 chain, 1 double treble, 2 chain, 1 double treble, 2 chain, 1 double treble.

Repeat twice from ***** to *******, and a 3d time from ***** to ******.

The footing of the lace is worked in 5 rows from right to left.

1st row — * 3 chain, 1 double treble on the 6th plain stitch of the square = 1 chain, 1 double treble on the 8th plain of the square = 3 chain, 1 drooping picot = 3 chain, 1 plain on the stitch at the extremity of the long leaf = 3 chain, 1 drooping picot = 3 chain, 2 quadruple trebles between the two leaves, 3 chain, 1 drooping picot, 3 chain, 1 plain on the last stitch of the second leaf, 3 chain, 1 picot. Repeat from *.

2nd row — 1 plain on every stitch of the preceding row.

3d row — 1 treble, * skip 1 stitch, 1 treble, skip 1 stitch, 1 treble, skip 1, 1 treble = turn the work = 1 plain on each of the 4 trebles = turn the work = come back and make 4 plain on the first 4 stitches; 5 chain, skip 2 stitches of the last row, 1 treble on the 3d plain and continue from *.

4th row — 1 treble on each of the 4 plain, 1 chain between each treble; 2 chain after 4 trebles.

5th row — 1 plain on every stitch of the 4th row.

Crochet lace with metal threads. Imitation of filigree lace (fig. 509). — Begin with green and gold chiné and by a number of chain stitches divisible by 38.

1st and 2nd rows — with green and gold chiné — 1 plain on every stitch.

3d row — with D.M.C Embroidery gold thread (Or fin) No. 40 — 1 treble, 1 chain, skip 1, 1 treble, 1 chain, and so on.

4th and 5th rows — with black and gold chiné — 1 plain on every stitch of the preceding row.

6th row — with écru and gold chiné — * 14 single, 8 chain, skip 1, 1 crossed quadruple treble separated below by

1 plain stitch, above by 3 chain, 8 chain, skip 1, 8 single, 8 chain, skip 1, 1 crossed quadruple treble separated below by 1 plain, above by 3 chain, 8 chain, skip 1, 6 single; repeat from *.

Small semicircles in red and gold chiné — 1 plain on the 11th and on the 12th single stitches, ** 1 plain on the last single but one and 1 plain on the 1st chain, draw together the last loops of these two stitches, continue along the whole semicircle with 19 plain, 2 plain joined together by the last loops on the last chain stitch and on the 2nd single ***, 4 plain; repeat once from ** to ***; 2 plain — turn the work — skip 2 plain, 19 plain, 2 plain joined together by the last loops on the 1st and 3d stitches of the row beneath,

Fig. 509. Crochet lace with metal threads imitation of filigree lace.
Materials: D.M.C Embroidery gold thread No. 40, D.M.C Gold chiné, in black and gold, green and gold, blue and gold, red and gold and écru and gold. (*)

continue with 2 plain, then 2 plain joined together by the last loops on the 1st and 3d of the next stitches, 19 plain, fasten off the thread.

The semicircles of the next scallop are worked with green and gold chiné.

Small pyramid — begin it on the wrong side of the work with D.M.C Embroidery gold thread (Or fin) No. 40 — 1 single on the 12th plain of the 1st semicircle, 3 chain, 1 crossed quadruple treble separated above by 2 chain stitches, set below in the corners formed by the semicircles, 3 chain, 1 single on the 8th stitch of the 2nd semicircle = turn the work without fastening off the gold thread = continue with blue and gold chiné: skip the 1st single, 10 plain on the chain stitches and on the crossed treble = turn the work = skip 1 stitch, 9 plain = turn the work = skip 1, 8 plain = turn the work = skip 1, 7 plain = turn the work = skip 1, 6 plain = turn the work = skip 1, 5 plain = turn the work = skip 1, 4 plain = turn the work = skip 1, 3 plain = turn the work = skip 1, 2 plain = turn the work = skip 1, 1 plain ; fasten off; continue with the gold thread, on the right side of the work with 1 picot (4 chain and 1 plain) and 1 plain on the pyramid, make 4 picots on each side of the pyramid and 1 picot on the point, then fasten off the thread. In the next scallop the pyramid is worked with red and gold chiné.

Big semicircle in green and gold chiné — 1 single on the 11th stitch of the first lower semicircle, 19 chain, 1 plain on the picot at the point of the pyramid, 19 chain, 2 single on the first empty plain stitches of the second lower semicircle = turn the work = 19 plain on the chain stitches, 1 plain on the middle plain stitch, 19 plain on the chain stitches, 1 single on the 1st empty plain stitch of the lower semicircle; fasten off the thread. Afterwards every second big semicircle is to be worked with blue and gold chiné.

7th row — with écru and gold chiné — 9 plain on the single stitches of the 6th row, 2 plain joined together by the last loops, on 10th single stitch and the 1st plain of the 1st semicircle, then continue with 8 plain and 39 plain on the big semicircle, 8 plain over the second small lower semicircle, 2 plain joined by the last loops on the last plain stitch of the small semicircle and on the 1st single stitch, 2 plain on the next single stitch and repeat from the beginning of the row.

Openwork row — with D.M.C Embroidery gold thread (Or fin) No. 40 — 1 single on the 8th plain stitch, 2 chain, 1 treble on the 2nd plain that comes after the 2 connected loops, **** 2 chain, 1 treble on the 2nd plain; repeat 25 times from ****, 2 chain, fasten them to the 2nd plain stitch after the 2 connected stitches; fasten off.

8th row — with green and gold chiné — 7 single on the single, 2 plain over the chain stitches and 1 plain over the treble and repeat from the beginning.

9th row — with D.M.C Embroidery gold thread (Or fin) No. 40, miss 2 single, 3 single on the single stitches beneath,

miss 2 single, 2 plain on the plain stitches of the semicircle,
* * * * * 1 picot of 4 chain and 1 plain, 4 plain, repeat 18
times from * * * * *, 1 picot, 1 plain.

The next scallops have to be joined to the foregoing ones
by the 3 first picots at the foot of the scallops.

Crochet lace with corner. Imitation of Reticella (fig. 510).
1st row — On a string of chain stitches or on a row of
trebles, alternate: 1 treble, 1 chain = in the corner, or at the
place reserved for the corner: 1 treble, 2 chain, 1 double
treble, 2 chain, 1 treble, so that 3 trebles and twice 2 chain
stitches come to be united on one stitch.

2nd row — 1 plain on every stitch of the 1st row: 3 plain
on the 2nd of the 3 trebles at the corner.

3d row — count, starting from the 2nd of the 3 stitches at
the corner and not counting the 2nd stitch, towards the right,
make 1 plain on the 52nd, the 51st, the 50th and 49th plain
= 8 chain, miss 1 chain, 1 plain on every 7 chain stitches =
1 plain on the second side and on each of the 7 chain =
3 plain on the 8th; 1 plain on each of the first 7 plain.

On every one of the next 11 stitches of the 2nd row: 1 plain
= 4 chain, skip 4, 1 triple treble on the 5th stitch of the 2nd
row, 4 chain, 1 triple treble on the same stitch, 4 chain,
1 triple treble on the same, 4 chain, skip 4, 1 plain on the
5th stitch = turn the work = on each loop of 4 chain stitches:
7 plain; 28 in all = 1 single on the 10th of the 11 plain =
turn the work = miss the 28th plain and crochet over the
27 others: 3 plain, 1 picot, 3 plain, 11 chain; miss the 11th,
10 plain on the other stitches = on the second side of the
chain of chain stitches: 4 plain, 8 chain, join them to the 6th
of the 11 first plain stitches of this row.

On the 8 chain: 5 plain, 3 chain, join them to the 5th plain
stitch of the 1st leaf made in this row = on the 3 chain:
3 plain = on the remaining stitches of the 8 chain : 6 plain.

Along the leaf: 3 plain, 1 picot, 3 plain = on the stitch at
the point of the leaf: 3 plain; then descending on the second
side: 3 plain, 1 picot, 7 plain.

On the rest of the 28 plain stitches: 3 plain, 1 picot,
4 plain, * 11 chain, skip the 11th, 10 plain = on the second
side of the chain: 4 plain, 6 chain, join them to the 4th of the
last 7 plain stitches of the preceding leaf = on the 6 chain:
9 plain. Continue on this 3d leaf of the row: 3 plain, 1 picot,
3 lain and 3 plain on the stitch at the point = 1 plain on

each of the next 3 stitches, then 1 picot, 7 plain ** == on the 28 stitches: 4 plain, 1 picot, 3 plain. Repeat from * to **, 3 plain, 1 picot, 3 plain, skip the last of the 28 plain. On the preceding row: *** 5 plain, 8 chain, join to the 4th of the last 7 plain of the last leaf; 11 plain on the 8 chain.

On the preceding row: * 5 plain, 8 chain, skip 1 chain, 1 plain on each chain stitch == on the second side: 4 plain,

Fig. 510.
Crochet lace with corner.
Imitation of Reticella.

Materials: D.M.C Alsatian thread No. 30, D.M.C Knotting cotton No. 30, D.M.C Crochet cotton 6 cord Nos. 15 to 30, or D.M.C Special cotton lace thread Nos. 15 to 30, in white or écru. (*)

3 chain, join them to the 6th of the last 11 plain, 3 plain on the 3 chain, 3 plain on the leaf, 3 plain on the stitch at the point, 7 plain on the leaf. Repeat from * and fasten the little horizontal bar to the leaf on the right.

Continue on the second row and to make the corner: 9 plain, **** 4 chain, 1 triple treble on the 2nd of the

(*) See at the end of the last chapter the tables of the sizes and colours of the cotton, flax and silk articles, mark D.M.C.

3 stitches at the corner and repeat 4 times from ✳✳✳✳ = 4 chain, skip 3 of the second row, 1 plain on the 4th = turn the work = on each treble of 4 chain, 6 plain, 36 in all; join the last to the 8th of he 9 plain = turn the work = returning on the 36 stitches: 3 plain, 1 picot, 3 plain, 11 chain, skip the 11th, 1 plain on each of the 10. On the second side of the chain: 4 plain, 8 chain, join them to the 4th of the 9 plain = on the 8 chain: 5 plain, 3 chain, join them to the 4th plain of the last little leaf: 3 plain = on the remaining stitches of the 8 chain: 6 plain.

Continue on the leaf: 3 plain, 1 picot, 3 plain, 3 plain on the stitch at the point, 3 plain, 1 picot and 7 plain.

Continue on the 36 stitches: ✳✳✳✳✳ 3 plain, 1 picot, 3 plain = 11 chain, skip the 11th, 10 plain, on the second side of the chain: 4 plain, 6 chain, join them to the 4th of the last 7 plain stitches of the last leaf, 9 plain on the chain stitches.

On the leaf: 3 plain, 1 picot, 3 plain, 3 plain on the stitch at the point, 3 plain, 1 picot, 7 plain ✳✳✳✳✳✳. Repeat 3 times from ✳✳✳✳✳ to ✳✳✳✳✳✳ and add: 3 plain, 1 picot, 3 plain.

Continue on the 2nd row: 4 plain, 8 chain, join to the 4th of the last 7 plain = on the 8 chain: 11 plain = on the 2nd row, 4 plain, 8 chain = returning, skip the 8th stitch; 7 plain on the other stitches. On the second side of the chain, 4 plain, 3 chain, join them to the 6th of the last 11 plain = on the 3 chain: 3 plain, 3 plain on the stitch at the point, 7 plain.

Begin again with 4 plain, join the next leaf to the last leaf ending with 3 chain and 3 plain.

4th row — 1 plain on the 1st little leaf made in the 3d row, ✳ 7 chain, 1 plain on the 2nd leaf = 7 chain, 1 triple treble on the 5th of the 9 plain between 2 leaves = 7 chain, 1 plain on the 3d leaf = 7 chain, 1 triple treble = 7 chain, 1 plain on the 4th leaf = 7 chain, 1 plain on the 5th leaf = 5 chain, 1 plain on the 1st leaf of the corner scallop. Repeat from ✳ with this difference that you must make 4 triple trebles on the corner scallop.

5th row — on the first 7 chain of the 4th row: 12 plain = ✳ on the next chain stitches: 12 plain = turn the work = make, working to and fro and decreasing by one stitch each row, rows of plain stitches until but one stitch remains = along the side of the pyramid: 10 single. Repeat 3 times from ✳,

12 plain on the next 7 chain, 6 plain on the 5 chain, 12 plain on the first 7 chain at the corner.

On the corner scallop, there must be 7 pyramids.

This is how these 7 are fitted in at the corner: * 1st pyramid on 12 plain stitches on the first chain stitches = 2nd pyramid on 10 plain on the second chain stitches and on 2 plain stitches on the 3d chain stitches = 3d pyramid on 7 plain on the 3d chain stitches and on 5 plain on the 4th chain stitches ** = 4th pyramid on 6 plain on the 4th chain stitches and 6 plain on the 5th chain stitches = repeat from ** to *; then 12 plain on the next 7 chain stitches and 6 plain on the 5 chain.

6th row — * 1 plain on the 1st pyramid, 5 chain, 1 crossed quadruple treble, the branches of which are connected by 5 chain; 5 chain, repeat twice from * = 1 plain on the 4th pyramid, 4 chain, 1 plain on the 1st pyramid of the corner scallop = 5 chain, 1 crossed quadruple treble the branches of which are connected by 5 chain, 5 chain, join them to the next pyramid = 5 chain, and so on.

7th row — 6 plain on the first 5 chain of the 6th row; 6 plain on the next chain = 8 chain; bring the chain back to the right, join it on between the 6th and the 7th of the plain stitches.

On the 8 chain: 4 plain, then 8 chain; take it back and join it to the 1st plain = on the 8 chain: 12 plain.

Continue on the small scallop: 3 plain, 1 picot, 8 plain = on the next 5 chain: 6 plain, 8 chain, join them again to the 4th of the 8 plain stitches on the scallop = on the 8 chain: 3 plain, 1 picot, 8 plain = on the 2 next bars of 5 chain stitches: 12 plain = 8 chain, join them between the 6th and 7th of the last 12 plain stitches = on the 8 chain: 5 plain, 8 chain, join them to the 1st plain stitch of the 3d finished scallop = on the 8 chain: 5 plain, 3 chain, join them to the 4th plain stitch of the 3d finished scallop = on the 3 chain: 2 plain, 1 picot, 2 plain = on the next scallop: 3 plain, 1 picot, 3 plain, and 6 more plain on the next scallop = 8 chain, join them to the first of the last 6 plain = on the 8 chain: 5 plain, 1 picot, 3 plain, 1 picot, 3 plain, 1 picot, 5 plain = on the lower scallop: 5 plain = on the lower row: 6 plain, 8 chain, join them to the first of the last 5 chain stitches of the last scallop = on the 8 chain: 3 plain, 1 picot, 8 plain.

On the 2 sets of 5 chain that come after the 12 plain = 8 chain, join them to the 6th and 7th of the 12 plain; on the

8 chain 5 plain = 8 chain, join them to the 1st of the 12 plain; on the 8 chain 5 plain = 3 chain, join them to the 4th of the 8 plain stitches of the last finished scallop, on the 3 chain, 2 plain, 1 picot, 2 plain = on the next chain stitches 3 plain, 1 picot, 3 plain = on the next chain stitches 3 plain, 1 picot, 8 plain, on the chain stitches of the lower row 6 plain = 8 chain, join them to the 4th of the 8 plain; on the 8 chain 12 plain, 6 plain on the chain stitches that connect 2 scallops.

Carry on the little scallops all round, the middle one is repeated 4 times at the corner; to join 2 scallops you have to make, starting from the 2nd little scallop on the right, after the 12 plain stitches, of the 1st little scallop, 8 chain stitches, join them to the 1st plain stitch of the last little scallop of the preceding big scallop = on the 8 chain 3 plain, 1 picot, 3 plain, 1 picot, 3 plain, 1 picot, 3 plain.

Crochet lace. Imitation of "guipure" lace (fig. 511). — This kind of lace and insertion is mostly used for trimming curtains and blinds. It somewhat resembles embroidery on a net ground, called "filet-guipure."

Begin by a row of 40 chain stitches.

1st row returning on the chain stitches — skip 4, 6 trebles, 3 chain, skip 2 chain, 1 plain, 3 chain, skip 2, 1 treble, 3 chain, skip 2, 1 plain, 3 chain, skip 2, 13 trebles, 3 chain, skip 2, 1 plain, 3 chain, skip 2, 1 treble.

2nd row — turn the work — 8 chain, 13 trebles on 13 lower trebles, 5 chain, 1 treble on the next treble, 5 chain, 7 trebles on the last 7 stitches.

3d row — turn the work — 9 chain, skip 4 chain, 6 trebles, 3 chain, skip 2 trebles, 1 plain, 3 chain, skip 2 trebles, 7 trebles, 3 chain, skip 2 chain, 1 plain, 3 chain, skip 2 chain, 1 treble, 3 chain, skip 2 trebles, 1 plain, 3 chain, skip 2 trebles, 1 treble, 3 chain, skip 2 trebles, 1 plain, 3 chain, skip 2 trebles, 1 treble, 3 chain, skip 2 chain, 1 plain, 3 chain, skip 2 chain, 1 treble.

4th row — turn the work — 8 chain, 1 treble on the next treble, 5 chain, 1 treble on the next treble, 5 chain, 1 treble on the next treble, 5 chain, 7 trebles on the 7 trebles beneath, 5 chain, 7 trebles on the last 7 stitches.

5th row — turn the work — 9 chain, skip 4 stitches, 6 trebles, 3 chain, skip 2 trebles, 1 plain, 3 chain, skip 2 trebles, 1 treble, 3 chain, skip 2 chain, 1 plain, 3 chain, skip 2 chain, 1 treble on the 1st treble, 3 chain, 1 plain on the 4th treble, 3 chain, skip 2 trebles, 7 trebles, 3 chain, skip 2 chain,

1 plain, 3 chain, 1 treble on the treble below, 3 chain, skip 2 chain, 1 plain, 1 treble on the treble below, 3 chain, skip 2 chain, 1 plain, 3 chain, skip 2 chain, 1 treble.

6th row — turn the work — 8 chain, 1 treble on the next lower treble, 5 chain, 1 treble on the next treble, 5 chain, 7 trebles on the 7 lower trebles, 5 chain, 1 treble on the next treble, 5 chain, 1 treble on the next treble, 5 chain, 7 trebles on the last 7 stitches.

7th row — turn the work — 9 chain, skip 4 stitches, 6 trebles, 3 chain, skip 2 trebles, 1 plain, 3 chain, skip 2 trebles, 1 treble, 3 chain, skip 2 chain, 1 plain, 3 chain, skip 2 chain, 13 trebles, 3 chain, skip 2 trebles, 1 plain, 3 chain, skip 2 trebles, 7 trebles, 3 chain, skip 2 chain, 1 plain, 3 chain, 1 treble on the treble beneath, 3 chain, skip 2 chain, 1 plain, 3 chain, skip 2 chain, 1 treble.

8th row — turn the work — 8 chain, 1 treble on the next treble beneath, 5 chain, 7 trebles on the 7 lower

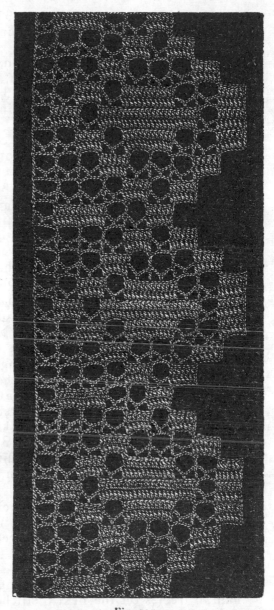

Fig. 511.
Crochet lace. Imitation of "guipure" lace.
Materials: D.M.C Knotting cotton No. 30, D.M.C Crochet cotton 6 cord Nos. 5 to 25, D.M.C Flax thread for knitting and crochet Nos. 16 to 40, or D.M.C Alsatia Nos. 15 to 40, in white or écru.

trebles, 5 chain, 13 trebles on the 13 lower trebles, 5 chain, 1 treble on the treble beneath, 5 chain, 7 trebles on the last 7 stitches.

9th row — turn the work — 3 chain, skip 1 treble, 6 trebles, 3 chain, skip 2 chain, 1 plain, 3 chain, skip 2 chain, 25 trebles, 3 chain, skip 2 trebles, 1 plain, 3 chain, skip 2 trebles, 7 trebles, 3 chain, skip 2 chain, 1 plain, 3 chain, skip 2 chain, 1 treble.

10th row — turn the work — 8 chain, 7 trebles on the 7 trebles beneath, 5 chain, 25 trebles on the 25 trebles beneath, 5 chain, 7 trebles on the last 7 stitches.

11th row — turn the work — 3 chain, skip 1 treble, 6 trebles, 3 chain, skip 2 chain, 1 plain, 3 chain, 1 treble on the lower treble, 3 chain, skip 2 trebles, 1 plain, 3 chain, skip 2 trebles, 13 trebles, 3 chain, skip 2 trebles, 1 plain, 3 chain, skip 2 trebles, 7 trebles, 3 chain, skip 2 trebles, 1 plain, 3 chain, skip 2 trebles, 1 treble, 3 chain, skip 2 chain, 1 plain, 3 chain, skip 2 chain, 1 treble.

12th row — turn the work — 8 chain, 1 treble on the next treble beneath, 5 chain, 7 trebles on the 7 trebles below, 5 chain, 13 trebles on the 13 trebles beneath, 5 chain, 1 treble on the next treble, 5 chain, 7 trebles on the last 7 stitches.

13th row — turn the work — 7 single on the first 7 trebles, 3 chain, 6 trebles on the next 6 stitches, 3 chain, skip 2 chain, 1 plain, 3 chain, 1 treble on the next treble, 3 chain, skip 2 trebles, 1 plain, 3 chain, skip 2 trebles, 1 treble, 3 chain, skip 2 trebles, 1 plain, 3 chain, skip 2 trebles, 7 trebles, 3 chain, skip 2 trebles, 1 plain, 3 chain, skip 2 trebles, 1 treble, 3 chain, skip 2 chain, 1 plain, 3 chain, 1 treble on the next treble, 3 chain, skip 2 chain, 1 plain, 3 chain, skip 2 chain, 1 treble.

14th row — turn the work — 8 chain, 1 treble on the 1st treble, 5 chain, 1 treble on the next treble, 5 chain, 7 trebles on the 7 trebles below, 5 chain, 1 treble on the next treble, 5 chain, 1 treble on the next treble, 5 chain, 7 trebles on the last 7 stitches.

15th row — turn the work — 7 single on the first 7 trebles, 3 chain, 6 trebles on the next 6 stitches, 3 chain, skip 2 chain, 1 plain, 3 chain, skip 2 chain, 7 trebles, 3 chain, skip 2 trebles, 1 plain, 3 chain, skip 2 trebles, 1 treble, 3 chain, skip 2 chain, 1 plain, 3 chain, 1 treble on the treble below, 3 chain, skip 2 chain, 1 plain, 3 chain, 1 treble on the treble below, 3 chain, skip 2 chain, 1 plain, 3 chain, skip 2 chain, 1 treble.

16th row — turn the work — 8 chain, 1 treble on the next treble below, 5 chain. 1 treble on the next treble, 5 chain, 1 treble on the next treble, 5 chain, 7 trebles on the 7 trebles below, 5 chain, 7 trebles on the 7 trebles below.

17th row — turn the work — 7 single on the first 7 trebles, 3 chain, 6 trebles on the next 6 stitches, 3 chain, skip 2 trebles, 1 plain, 3 chain, skip 2 trebles, 1 treble, 3 chain, skip 2 chain, 1 plain, 3 chain, skip 2 chain, 13 trebles, 3 chain, skip 2 chain, 1 plain, 3 chain, skip 2 chain, 1 treble.

Repeat from the 2nd row.

Crochet insertion. Imitation of filet-guipure (fig. 512). — Begin by a row of 64 chain stitches.

1st row — returning over the chain stitches — skip 3 chain, make 12 trebles on the next chain stitches, * 11 chain, skip 5 chain, 1 treble, 2 chain, skip 2 chain, 1 treble, 2 chain, skip 2 chain, 1 treble, repeat twice from *, 11 chain, skip 5 chain, 13 trebles.

2nd row — turn the work — 3 chain, skip the 1st treble, 11 trebles on the 2nd and the 10 following trebles beneath to the 12th, skip the 13th treble and the next 2 chain stitches, ** 7 single on the 3d to the 9th chain stitch, 2 chain, 1 treble on the 2nd of the 3 trebles of the row beneath, 2 chain, ***; repeat twice from ** to ***, 7 single on the 3d and 9th or the next 11 chain stitches, skip the 1st treble, 12 trebles on the last stitches of the preceding row.

3d row — turn the work — 3 chain, 6 trebles on the 2nd and 5 following trebles to the 7th, **** 11 chain, 1 treble on the 1st single, 2 chain, 1 treble on the 4th single, 3 chain, 1 treble on the 7th single *****; repeat once from **** to *****, 6 trebles on the next stitches, 2 chain, skip 2, 1 treble, 2 chain, skip 2, 1 treble, repeat once from **** to *****, 11 chain, skip 5 trebles, 7 trebles on the last stitches.

4th row — turn the work — 3 chain, skip 1 treble, 5 trebles, repeat twice from ** to ***, 7 trebles on the trebles beneath, 2 chain, 1 treble on the treble beneath, 2 chain, repeat once from ** to ***, 7 single on the 3d and 6 next of the 11 chain, skip 1 treble, 6 trebles.

5th row — turn the work — 3 chain; repeat twice from **** to *****, 18 trebles on the next 18 stitches, 2 chain, skip 2, 1 treble, 2 chain, skip 2, 1 treble. Repeat once from **** to *****, 1 triple treble, on the last stitch of the row beneath.

Fig. 512. Crochet insertion. Imitation
of filet-guipure.
Materials: D.M.C Crochet cotton 6 cord or
D.M.C Special crochet cotton Nos. 10 to 50,
D.M.C Alsatia Nos. 15 to 40, or D.M.C Flax thread
for knitting and crochet Nos. 20 to 45,
in white or écru.

6th row — turn the work — 1 single on the triple treble, 6 single on the next chain stitches, 2 chain, 1 treble on the treble beneath, 2 chain, repeat once from ** to ***, 19 trebles on the trebles beneath, 2 chain; 1 treble on the treble beneath, 2 chain; repeat once from ** to ***, 7 single on the 3d and 6 next of the chain stitches, up to the 9th.

7th row — turn the work — 5 chain, 1 treble on the 4th single, 2 chain, 1 treble on the 7th single; repeat once from **** to *****; 11 chain, 19 trebles on the 19 trebles beneath; repeat twice from **** to *****.

8th row — turn the work — 5 chain, 1 treble on the treble beneath, 2 chain; repeat once from ** to ***, 7 single on the 3d and 6 following chain stitches, up to the 9th, skip 1 treble, 17 trebles; repeat twice from ** to ***, 1 treble on the 3d of the 5 chain stitches below.

9th row — turn the work — 3 chain; repeat once from **** to *****, 12 trebles on the next 12 stitches, 11 chain, skip 5 trebles,

7 trebles, 11 chain, skip 5 trebles, 13 trebles, 2 chain, skip 2 stitches, 1 treble, 2 chain, skip 2 stitches, 1 treble, 8 chain, 1 triple treble on the last stitch of the preceding row.

10th row — turn the work — 1 single on the triple treble, 6 single on the next chain stitches, 2 chain, 1 treble on the treble beneath, 2 chain, 12 trebles on the first 12 trebles, skip the 13th treble, 7 single on the 3^d and the next 6 chain stitches, up to the 9th, skip 1 treble, 5 trebles, skip 1 treble, 7 single on the 3^d and next 6 chain, up to the 9th, skip 1 treble, 12 trebles, 2 chain, 1 treble on the treble below, 2 chain, 7 single on the 3^d and next 6 chain, up to the 9th.

11th row — turn the work — 5 chain, 1 treble on the 4th single, 2 chain, 1 treble on the 7th single, 24 trebles on the next stitches, 11 chain, skip 5 trebles, 25 trebles, 2 chain, skip 2 single, 1 treble, 2 chain, skip 2 single, 1 treble on the last stitch of the row.

12th row — turn the work — 5 chain, 1 treble on the treble below, 2 chain, 24 trebles, skip 1 treble, 7 single on the 3^d and 6 next chain, up to the 9th, skip 1 treble, 24 trebles, 2 chain, 1 treble on the treble below, 2 chain, 1 treble on the 3^d of the 5 chain.

13th row — turn the work — 3 chain, ****** 11 chain, 1 treble on the 1st treble below, 2 chain, 1 treble on the 4th treble below, 2 chain, 1 treble on the 7th treble below *******, 12 trebles, 11 chain, 7 trebles on the 7 single, 11 chain, skip 5 trebles, 13 trebles, 2 chain, skip 2 trebles, 1 treble, 2 chain, skip 2 trebles, 1 treble, 8 chain, 1 triple treble on the last stitch.

14th row — turn the work — 1 single on the triple treble, 6 single on the chain stitches, 2 chain, 1 treble on the treble beneath, 2 chain, 12 trebles on the 12 trebles beneath, skip the 13th treble, 7 single on the 3^d and the 6 following chain stitches, up to the 9th, skip 1 treble, 5 trebles, skip 1 treble, 7 single on the 3^d and 6 following chain stitches, up to the 9th, skip 1 treble, 12 trebles, 2 chain, 1 treble on the treble beneath, 2 chain, 7 single on the 3^d and 6 following chain stitches, up to the 9th.

15th row — turn the work — 5 chain, 1 treble on the 4th single, 2 chain, 1 treble on the 7th single; repeat once from ****** to *******, 11 chain, skip 5 trebles, 19 trebles on the next stitches, 11 chain, 1 treble on the 6th treble, 2 chain, skip 2 stitches, 1 treble, 2 chain, skip 2 stitches, 1 treble; repeat once from **** to *****.

16th row — turn the work — 5 chain, 1 treble on the treble beneath, 2 chain; repeat once from ** to ***, 7 single on the 3^d and 6 following chain stitches, up to the 9th, skip 1 treble, 17 trebles, skip 1 treble; repeat twice from ** to ***, 1 treble on the last stitch.

17th row — turn the work — 3 chain; repeat twice from **** to *****, 18 trebles on the trebles, 2 chain, 1 treble on the 4th single, 2 chain, 1 treble on the 7th single; repeat once from **** to *****, 8 chain, 1 triple treble on the last stitch.

18th row — turn the work — 1 single on the triple treble, 6 single on the chain stitches, 2 chain, 1 treble on the treble beneath, 2 chain; repeat once from ** to ***, 19 trebles on the 19 trebles, 2 chain, 1 treble on the treble beneath, 2 chain; repeat once from ** to ***, 7 single on the 3^d and 6 following chain stitches, up to the 9th.

19th row — turn the work — 3 chain, 6 trebles, on the 2nd and 5 following single stitches, up to the 7th, repeat once from **** to ***** and once from ****** to *******, 6 trebles on the trebles beneath, 2 chain, skip 2 trebles, 1 treble, 2 chain, skip 2 trebles, 1 treble; repeat once from **** to *****, 11 chain, 7 trebles on the 7 single.

20th row — turn the work — 3 chain, skip 1 treble, 5 trebles; repeat twice from ** to ***, 7 trebles on the trebles beneath, 2 chain, 1 treble on the treble beneath, 2 chain; repeat once from ** to ***, 7 single on the 3^d and 6 following stitches, up to the 9th, skip 1 treble, 6 trebles.

21st row — turn the work — 3 chain, skip 1 treble, 12 trebles on the next stitches; repeat once from **** to *****, once from ****** to *******, and once from **** to *****, 11 chain, 13 trebles on the last stitches.

Repeat from the 2nd row.

Crochet chair back (fig. 513). — This, should be worked in D.M.C Knotting cotton (Fil à pointer) No. 30, D.M.C Crochet cotton 6 cord (Cordonnet 6 fils) or D.M.C Special crochet cotton (Cordonnet spécial) Nos. 5 to 20. In the fine numbers of D.M.C Crochet cotton 6 cord (Cordonnet 6 fils) (*), it works out much smaller, so that it would need

---

(*) See at the end of the last chapter the tables of the sizes and colours of the cotton, flax and silk articles, mark D.M.C. — The French names, in brackets, are those stamped on the labels of the D.M.C articles.

four joined together to make a chair back of reasonable size. The four pyramids, meeting in the centre of the square thus formed, should be connected by trebles.

In the same manner a number joined together could be made into cradle coverlids, table covers and curtains, &c.

Fig. 513. Crochet chair back.
Materials: D.M.C Knotting cotton No. 30, D.M.C Crochet cotton 6 cord or D.M.C Special crochet cotton Nos. 5 to 20, D.M.C Flax lace thread Nos. 16 to 30, in white, écru or Maize yellow 579.

Begin by 5 chain, close the ring with 1 single stitch.

1st row — 5 chain, * 1 treble on the ring, 2 chain, repeat 6 times from *, 1 single on the 3d of the first 5 chain stitches.

2nd row — *, on the 2 chain of the last row 4 plain; repeat 7 times from *.

3d and 4th rows — 1 plain on each stitch of the last row.

5th row — 10 chain, * skip 1 stitch of the last row, 1 double treble on the next stitch, 4 chain; repeat 14 times from *, 1 single on the 6th of the 10 chain.

6th row — * 4 plain on the 4 chain, 1 plain on the treble; repeat 15 times from *.

7th row — 2 plain, * 1 picot, 5 plain; repeat 14 times from *, 1 picot, 3 plain; the 3d of the 5 plain should be above the double treble.

8th row — 12 chain, 1 treble on the 3d of the plain stitches after the 1st picot, * 9 chain, 1 treble on the 3d of the next 5 plain stitches, repeat 15 times from *, 9 chain, 1 single on the 3d of the 12 chain stitches.

9th row — * on the first 9 chain 13 plain, on the next 9 chain 6 plain; 9 chain, join them to the 7th of the previous 13 plain; on the 9 chain 15 plain, on the chain stitches beneath 7 plain; repeat 7 times from *.

10th row — 12 single along the first scallop, 1 plain on the 7th, 8th and 9th of the 15 plain on the row before; 5 chain, 1 drooping picot, 5 chain, 1 drooping picot, 5 chain, 1 plain on the 7th, 8th and 9th of the next 15 plain stitches; repeat 6 times from *, 5 chain, 1 drooping picot, 5 chain, 1 drooping picot, 5 chain.

11th row — 1 plain on every stitch and picot of the row before, 160 stitches in all.

12th row — 4 chain, skip 1 plain of the last row, 1 treble on the next stitch, * 1 chain, skip 1 stitch of the row before, 1 treble on the next stitch; repeat 77 times from *, 1 chain, 1 single on the 3d of the 4 chain stitches.

13th row — 1 single on the next chain stitch, * 5 chain, skip 1 stitch, 1 plain, 1 treble, 2 double trebles, skip 3 stitches of the last row, 1 single on the 4th stitch; repeat 39 times from *.

14th row — 4 single along the first pyramid, 1 plain on the chain stitch at the point which was missed over in the last row; * 5 chain, 1 plain on the point of the next pyramid; repeat 38 times from *, 5 chain, 1 single on the point of the first pyramid.

15th row — 4 chain, skip 1 stitch of the preceding row, 1 treble on the next stitch, * 1 chain, skip 1, 1 treble on the next stitch; repeat 117 times from *, 1 chain, 1 single on the 3d of the 4 chain stitches.

16th row — 15 plain on the 15 stitches of the last row.
* 15 chain, join to the 7th chain stitch, counted from right
to left: 2 plain on the ring = 10 chain, 1 single on the 4th
plain stitch to the right, skip the 1st chain stitch, 1 single on
the 9th, 8th, 7th of the 10 chain, 6 chain, skip 1, 1 single.
1 plain, 1 treble, 3 chain, skip 2 chain, 1 treble on the 3d of
the chain stitches that come before the 3 single, 1 plain,
1 single, 1 chain, 2 plain on the ring = ** 6 chain, join them
to the 2nd of the last 3 chain stitches, 7 chain, skip 1, 1 single,
1 plain, 2 trebles, 3 chain, skip the 6th and 5th of the first
6 chain stitches, 1 treble, 1 plain, 1 single, 1 chain, 2 plain
on the ring *** = repeat 4 times from ** to *** =
6 chain, join them to the 2nd of the last 3 chain stitches,
6 chain, skip 1, 1 single, 1 plain, 1 treble, 3 chain, skip the
6th and the 5th of the last 6 chain, 1 treble, 1 plain, 1 single,
1 chain, 2 plain on the ring = 6 single on the remaining
6 chain stitches, 4 plain of the stitches of the row beneath,
3 chain, join them to the 2nd of the last 3 chain stitches,
3 single on the chain stitches, 11 plain on the stitches of the
row beneath; repeat 15 times from *; join the 1st and the
2nd scallop to the last and last but one scallop of the leaf
before by 1 single stitch; when you have reached the 6th
scallop of the 16th leaf, join this latter by 1 single stitch to
the 2nd scallop of the 1st leaf, and the 7th scallop of the 16th
to the 1st of the 1st leaf, fasten off the thread.

17th row — Join the thread to the point of the 2nd scallop
on the right of the leaf that forms the corner; 13 single,
1 picot of 3 chain stitches on the point of the 3d scallop,
14 single, * 1 picot of 3 chain on the point of the 4th scallop,
14 single, 1 picot of 3 chain on the point of the 5th scallop,
27 single, 2 chain on the point of the 3d scallop of the 2nd
leaf = turn the work = 1 triple treble placed on the picot of
the 5th scallop of the first leaf = turn the work = finish the
picot, 14 single, 2 chain, 1 quadruple treble placed on the
point of the preceding scallop, finish the picot, 14 single,
1 picot of 3 chain on the point of the 5th scallop of the 2nd
leaf, 27 single, 2 chain on the point of the 3d scallop of the
3d leaf, 1 triple treble on the picot of the 5th scallop of the
2nd leaf, finish the picot, 14 single, 1 picot of 3 chain on the
point of the 4th scallop, 14 single, 1 picot of 3 chain on the
point of the 5th scallop, 27 single, 2 chain on the point of the
3d scallop of the 4th leaf, 1 triple treble on the point of the
5th scallop of the 3d leaf, finish the picot, 14 single, 1 picot

of 3 chain on the point of the 4th scallop of the 4th leaf,
14 single, 2 chain, 1 quadruple treble on the picot of the 4th
scallop of the 4th leaf ✳✳, finish the picot, 27 single, 2 chain,
1 triple treble on the picot of the 5th scallop of the 4th leaf,
finish the picot, 14 single ✳✳✳; repeat twice from ✳ to ✳✳✳
and once from ✳ to ✳✳, join the 5th scallop of the 16th leaf
to the 3d scallop of the 1st leaf by 1 triple treble, and end
with 13 single, fasten off the thread.

To make the little leaves in the corners, fasten the thread
to the 4th scallop of a leaf placed in the direction of the
corner; 15 chain, join them on the right to the 7th chain
stitch, 2 plain on the ring = 9 chain, join them to the 3d
scallop of the leaf beneath; on the 9 chain 3 single, 7 chain,
skip 1 stitch, 1 single, 1 plain, 2 trebles, 3 chain, skip the 6th
and the 5th of the 9 first chain stitches, 1 treble, 1 plain,
1 single, 1 chain, 2 plain on the ring = ✳ 6 chain, join them
to the 2nd of the last 3 chain stitches, 7 chain, skip 1, 1 single,
1 plain, 2 trebles, 3 chain, skip the 6th and the 5th of the 6
last chain stitches, 1 treble, 1 single, 1 chain, 2 plain on the
ring ✳✳ = repeat 4 times from ✳ to ✳✳ = 6 chain, join them
to the 2nd of the last 3 chain stitches, 7 chain, skip 1, 1 single,
1 plain, 2 trebles, 5 chain, join them to the 5th scallop of
the leaf beneath; on the 5 chain 3 single, 1 chain, skip the
6th and the 5th of the last 6 chain stitches, 1 treble, 1 plain,
1 single, 1 chain, 2 plain on the ring = on the rest of the
first 13 chain stitches 6 single, fasten off the thread.

Fasten the thread on the 3d scallop on the same stitch
as the single stitch that follows the 9 first chain stitches,
10 single, 2 chain, 1 triple treble on the picot of the 16th leaf,
finish the picot, 14 single, 1 picot of 3 chain on the point of
the 2nd scallop, 14 single, 1 picot of 3 chain on the point of
the 3d scallop, 14 single, 1 picot of 3 chain on the point of
the 4th scallop, 14 single, 1 picot of 3 chain on the point of
the 5th scallop, 14 single, 1 picot of 3 chain on the point of
the 6th scallop, 14 single, 2 chain, 1 triple treble on the picot
of the 3d scallop of the 2nd leaf, finish the picot, 10 single,
fasten off the thread.

Repeat the same figure in the three other corners.

18th row — ✳ 1 plain on the picot of the 4th scallop of the
3d leaf, 4 chain, 1 triple treble on the picot of the 5th scallop
of the 3d leaf, 5 chain, 1 double treble on the same picot,
3 chain, 1 triple treble on the picot of the 3d scallop of the

4th leaf, 5 chain, 1 triple treble on the picot of the 4th scallop of the 4th leaf, 8 chain, 1 double treble on the same picot, 3 chain, 1 quadruple treble on the picot of the 1st scallop of the isolated leaf in the corner, 6 chain, 1 triple treble on the same picot, 1 chain, 1 double treble on the picot of the 2nd scallop of the corner leaf; 6 chain, 1 double treble on the same picot, 5 chain, 1 plain on the picot of the 3^d scallop of the corner leaf, 3 chain, 1 triple treble on the picot of the 4th scallop, 7 chain, 1 triple treble on the same picot, 7 chain, 1 triple treble on the same picot, 3 chain, 1 plain on the picot of the 5th scallop of the corner leaf, 5 chain, 1 double treble on the picot of the 6th scallop of the corner leaf, 6 chain, 1 double treble on the same picot, 1 chain, 1 triple treble on the picot of the 7th scallop of the corner leaf, 6 chain, 1 quadruple treble on the same picot, 3 chain, 1 double treble on the picot of the 4th scallop of the 6th leaf, 8 chain, 1 triple treble on the same picot, 5 chain, 1 triple treble on the picot of the 5th scallop of the 6th leaf, 3 chain, 1 double treble on the picot of the 3^d scallop of the 7th leaf, 5 chain, 1 triple treble on the same picot, 4 chain. Repeat 3 times from *.

19th row — 1 plain on every stitch of the row below, 3 plain on the corner stitch.

20th row — 2 single on the 2 first plain of the row beneath, 4 chain, * skip 1 stitch of the preceding row, 1 treble, 1 chain; repeat from *. Make 68 trebles on each side, on the corner stitch 1 treble, 2 chain, 1 double treble, 2 chain, 1 treble, fasten off the thread.

21st row — * 1 plain on the chain stitches that come before the double treble, 6 chain, skip 1 chain, 1 plain, 2 trebles, 2 double trebles, 1 plain on the 2 chain stitches after the double treble, 6 chain, skip 1, 1 plain, 2 trebles, 2 double trebles, skip 2 lower trebles, 1 plain on the next chain stitch, ** 6 chain, skip 1, 1 plain, 2 trebles, 2 double trebles, skip 3 of the trebles beneath, 1 plain ***.

Repeat 21 times from ** to ***, 6 chain, skip 1, 1 plain, 2 trebles, 2 double trebles, skip 2 of the trebles beneath, 1 plain ****; repeat again 3 times from * to ****.

22nd row — 6 single along the pyramid, 1 picot of 3 chain on the point, 6 single along the second side; work round all the other small pyramids in the same manner.

Crochet chair back made up of squares (fig. 514). — This is one of the prettiest patterns for cut work taken from an old collection by Sibmacher and adapted by us here to crochet.

We have worked this pattern ourselves both in D.M.C Crochet cotton 6 cord (Cordonnet 6 fils) No. 15 and D.M.C Alsatian thread (Fil d'Alsace) No. 120 and can assure our readers from personal experience that in both the result was equally handsome, and in any number of these two materials indicated here is open to choice.

Fig. 514. Crochet chair back made up of squares.
Materials : D.M.C Alsatian thread Nos. 30 to 100, D.M.C Crochet cotton 6 cord or D.M.C Special crochet cotton Nos. 25 to 50, or D.M.C Flax lace thread Nos. 25 to 50, in white or écru. (*)

1st row — 4 chain, close the ring.

2nd row — 2 plain on each chain, 8 in all; draw the loop of the last stitch through the first.

3d row — 6 chain, * 1 treble, 3 chain, repeat 6 times

(*) See at the end of the last chapter the tables of the sizes and colours of the cotton, flax and silk articles, mark D.M.C.

from *, join to the 3ᵈ of the 8 chain. In all with the 3 chain: 8 trebles.

4ᵗʰ row — 5 plain over the loops of 3 chain, 1 plain on the treble.

5ᵗʰ row — 6 chain, 1 plain on the 3ᵈ of the plain stitches beneath, * 3 chain, 1 treble on the treble beneath; 3 chain, 1 plain on the 3ᵈ stitch of the row beneath. Repeat 6 times from *, then add 3 chain, 1 single on the 3ᵈ of the 6 chain.

6ᵗʰ row — 8 chain, * 1 plain on the treble of the last row, 7 chain; repeat 6 times from *, 1 plain on the 1ˢᵗ of the 8 chain.

7ᵗʰ row — 3 chain, 1 treble on the same stitch beneath; 1 treble on each chain stitch, 2 trebles on each plain stitch of the row beneath; in all, including the 3 chain, 72 trebles, join to the 3ᵈ chain.

8ᵗʰ row — * 8 chain, 1 plain between the 2 added trebles, therefore between the 8ᵗʰ and the 9ᵗʰ = turn the work = on the wrong side 12 plain — turn the work back to the right side = take up 1 loop of each of the 12 stitches for the Tunisian stitch that is made in 10 rows and decreasing by one stitch in each row, alternately on the right and left, draw up the 3 last overs together, 1 chain, and make descending on the left side, 1 single on each row of the pyramid you just made, finish with 1 single stitch on the plain stitch that comes after the 8 chain. Repeat 7 times from *.

9ᵗʰ row — all along the pyramid: 3 plain, 1 picot, 3 plain, 1 picot, 3 plain, 1 picot, 1 plain, 3 plain on the stitch at the point. Repeat the same number of stitches on the second side and on all the pyramids = after the 9ᵗʰ row, fasten off the thread.

10ᵗʰ row — fasten the thread on to a stitch at the point of the pyramid, * 7 chain, 5 overs, draw the loop through the 2ⁿᵈ picot on the side of the pyramid on which you are working, draw the needle back through 2 overs, make 2 overs more and put the needle into the middle picot opposite and on the same level and draw together successively twice 2 overs and a 3ᵈ time 3 and the last times 2 and 2 = 7 chain, 1 double treble, join it to the 3ᵈ over of the 3 trebles just made, 7 chain, 1 plain on the point of the next pyramid = 7 chain, 7 overs, put the needle into the loop of the 2ⁿᵈ succeeding picot, draw together 3 times 2 overs, 1 triple treble on the picot opposite and on the same level, draw the overs together 2 by 2, and by 3 on reaching the 4th over, and 2 by 2 those that remain = 7 chain, 1 quadruple treble, join it to the 4th over, 7 chain, 1 triple treble, join that also to the 4th over, 7 chain, 1 plain on the next pyramid. Repeat 3 times from *.

11th row — 1 plain on each of the stitches of the last row and 3 plain on those that form the corner.

12th row — 1 single on the first plain, 5 chain, 1 treble on the 3^d plain, 2 chain, 1 treble on the 3^d plain, and so on to the corner till you have 14 trebles, including the first chain stitches = on the corner stitch: 3 times 2 chain stitches with 2 trebles besides, then continue the same as on the first side.

Between the trebles of one corner and the other there should be 20 trebles and 21 times 2 chain and the same number on the 4 sides, 1 single on the 3^d of the 5 chain.

13th row — 1 plain on every stitch of the last row, 62 in all, on each side, exclusive of the 3 chain at the corner.

14th row — 14 single on the foregoing stitches, * 1 chain, 24 plain = 4 plain of the preceding row, not counting the 3 added stitches which must remain empty = after the 24th stitch, turn the work, 1 chain, skip 2, 22 plain, passing the needle under the 2 loops of the stitch beneath = turn the work = 1 chain, 21 plain = turn the work = 1 chain, 20 plain = continue to decrease in the same proportion until you have 3 stitches left and fasten off the thread.

In all the intakes skip the last stitch but one coming back and the 1st going and always begin on the right side with 1 chain.

For the second half of these triangular figures which must be worked from right to left, fasten the thread on to the 5th stitch after the 3 increases and make 23 plain stitches = 7 plain stitches must remain between the two triangular figures made of plain stitches = turn the work = 1 chain, 22 plain, skip the last stitch but one = turn the work = 1 chain, skip 1, 21 plain, 1 chain, 3 overs, put the needle into the 4th of the 7 stitches between the two figures, draw it back once through 2 overs, make 1 more over, put the needle into the last stitch of the 3^d row opposite, draw it back once through 2 overs, then through 3, then twice through 2 = turn the work = 20 plain, and so on, until you have made 10 transverse trebles = fasten off the thread and then repeat the same series of rows on the other sides.

15th row — do not cut off the thread on the 4th side, 5 chain, * 1 treble on the stitch from which the 5 chain stitches started which count as the 1st treble, 2 chain, 1 treble on the last plain stitch of the first half of the triangular figures: 2 chain, 1 treble in the middle of the 10th transverse treble; 2 chain, 1 treble on the first plain stitch of the 2nd triangular figure, 2 chain, 1 treble on the 3d and last top stitch of the triangular figure; 2 chain, 1 treble on the same stitch the last treble is on.

Then, along the edge: 10 trebles connected by 2 chain stitches, 1 of which trebles must always be placed on a row of plain stitches = after the 10th treble: 5 chain, 1 plain stitch on the 6th plain of the 13th row; 5 chain, again 11 trebles connected by 2 chain = after the 11th treble: 2 chain and repeat 3 times from *, on the last side make only 10 trebles and join them after the 2 chain stitches to the 3d of the 5 chain.

16th row — on all the pairs of chain stitches: 3 plain and 6 plain on the 5 chain.

17th row — Repeat 8 times: 7 chain, 1 plain on the 6th chain of the last row = * for the 9th and the 10th scallop only 5 chain. The plain stitch that comes after the 9th scallop must always come exactly above the corner stitch of the 13th row = after the 10th scallop: 1 plain; then 13 scallops with 7 chain, 1 plain on the 6th stitch. Repeat twice from * = after the 13th scallop, 2 small scallops, up to the end of the row 5 scallops more of 7 chain stitches.

18th row — make 7 plain stitches over 7 chain, 5 chain, drop the treble, returning put the needle into the 4th plain and draw the loop through = on the 5 chain: 3 plain, 1 picot, 3 plain = on the 7 chain beneath 3 more plain = on the 9th scallop formed of 5 chain, only 5 plain = on the 10th scallop only 3 plain = then 5 chain, bring them back and join them to the 3d plain stitch of the 9th scallop and finish the picot.

When such squares are made use of in any number and have to be joined together, connect 13 picots, the 14th, the corner one is left free.

The 4 free picots are joined by a little star.

Crochet collar (fig. 515). — We have as far as possible avoided describing articles in this book that are subject to the changes of fashion, and if we have made an exception in the case of this collar composed of squares, stars, lozenges and lace edging it is because the shape is one that will never be out of date. Fine and delicate work like this can only be executed in a very fine material and the best effect will be obtained by the use of écru thread.

Their soft tone and gloss imitate old work better than a white material. D.M.C Special cotton lace thread (Fil à dentelle, qualité spéciale) (*) or D.M.C Flax lace thread (Lin pour

Fig. 515. Crochet collar.
Materials: D.M.C Alsatian thread No. 100, D.M.C Special crochet cotton No. 100 or D.M.C Special cotton lace thread No. 100, in écru, or D.M.C Flax lace thread No. 50, in white.

(*) See at the end of the last chapter the tables of the sizes and colours of the cotton, flax and silk articles, mark D.M.C. — The French names, in brackets, are those stamped on the labels of the D.M.C articles.

dentelles) is the best material for the collar in question. Begin with the straight edged figures, and then make the connecting pieces between. The four squares with half stars at the two ends of the collar and on the right and left of the centre figure are equal on all sides, whereas the three in the outside scallops are rather narrower on the outer than on the inner side where they join the foundation.

Inner squares: 1st row — 5 chain, close the ring; 5 chain, * 1 treble on the ring, 2 chain; repeat 6 times from * and join to the 3d chain stitch.

2nd row — 3 plain over 2 chain; 1 plain on each treble.

3d row — 9 chain, * 1 treble on the treble of the 1st row, 6 chain. Repeat 6 times from * = join to the 3d of the 9 chain = 8 trebles in all counting the first chain stitches.

4th row — small leaf = * 10 chain; returning, skip the 1st chain: 1 plain, 1 half treble, 4 trebles, 1 half treble, 1 plain, 1 single = on the 6 chain of the 3d row: ** 1 plain, 1 half-treble, 1 treble, 3 double treble, 1 treble, 1 half treble, 1 plain ***. Repeat once more from ** to *** and 3 times from * to *** = then along the 1st leaf to the 10th stitch: 10 single.

5th row — starting from the point: * 7 chain, 1 triple treble on the 5th stitch of the little scallop of the 4th row, 7 chain, 1 triple treble on the next scallop, 7 chain, 1 plain on the point of the 2nd leaf. Repeat 3 times from *.

6th row — * 3 plain on the stitch that forms the point, 1 plain on each chain stitch and on every treble of the last row = 15 stitches in all up to the 2nd treble = turn the work = returning: 1 chain, 1 double treble on the 4th plain, 1 chain, 1 double treble, 1 chain, 1 double treble, 1 chain, 1 double treble, 1 chain, 1 double treble, 1 chain, join them to the 4th plain = turn the work = make over each chain stitch: 2 plain and on each treble 1 plain and 1 picot over the 1st, 2nd, 4th and 5th treble; 8 plain. Repeat 3 times from *.

7th row — 1 single, 1 plain on the 2nd of the 3 stitches at the point, * 9 chain, 1 double treble between the two first picots of the half circle formed in the last row; 8 chain, 1 triple treble on the 3d treble of the half circle, 8 chain, 1 double treble between the 3d and 4th picots of the half circle, 9 chain, 1 plain on the corner-stitch. Repeat 3 times from *.

8th row — 19 plain on the chain stitches of the 7th row, 3 plain on the corner stitch, 23 plain on the chain stitches and the trebles = turn the work = returning: 2 chain, 1 double treble on the 19th stitch; add on the same stitch: 2 double trebles with 2 chain between = to finish 2 chain, join them to the 5th plain = turn the work = on the chain: * 1 plain, 1 picot, 1 plain and 1 plain on the treble. Repeat 3 times from *.

Add further: 4 plain on the chain stitches of the 7th row = turn the work = 5 chain, 1 double treble on the 1st treble of the small half circle; then 3 times more: 5 chain, and twice: 1 double treble on each of the trebles beneath = after the last 5 chain: join to the 4th plain = turn the work.

In this row the points are made with: 8 chain, skip 1 = returning: 1 single, 1 plain, 1 half treble, 1 treble, 1 treble 1 ½ treble long, 2 double trebles, 1 plain on the 5 chain. The 2nd point must be placed half in front, half behind the treble; make 7 points in all = after the 7th point: 8 plain on the chain stitches of the 7th row = turn the work = * 7 chain, 1 plain on the stitch at the top of the point and repeat 6 times from * = 7 chain: 1 plain on the 9th plain = turn the work = draw the thread through the 1st plain stitch = 1 plain treble on each chain stitch, 1 picot at the top of the point, add 4 more trebles and 12 chain, join them to the 4th treble before the 1st picot. On the 12 chain: 5 plain, 1 picot, 4 plain, 1 picot, 4 plain, 1 picot, 5 plain, 4 trebles up to the next picot, 1 picot, 4 trebles; 12 chain, join them to the treble nearest the 1st scallop, and so on = make 7 scallops in all; after the 7th add 4 trebles more on the 2 last chain = to the 4th treble join 2 plain which are followed by the 3 plain stitches at the corner = at the next scallop you join the 1st picot of the 1st scallop to the 3d picot of the last scallop by 1 single stitch. Having finished the figure described above on the 4 sides, fasten off the thread.

The edging of these top squares should be begun on the inner and narrower side and at the 3d little scallop: * 1 plain on the middle picot of the 3d scallop, 5 chain, 1 double treble on the 1st picot of the 4th scallop; 5 chain, 1 triple treble on the 2nd picot of the same scallop, 5 chain, 1 double treble on the 3d picot of again the same scallop, 5 chain, 1 plain on the picot in the middle of the 5th scallop; 10 chain, 1 plain on the picot in the middle of the 6th scallop, 9 chain **, 1 double treble on the picot in the middle of the 7th and 1 double treble on the picot in the middle of the following 1st scallop and at the same time draw the last overs of the 2 trebles together. Repeat once from ** to *, therefore the reverse way. The trebles must be carried all round the star on the picots we have just indicated. Continue with: ∗∗∗ 10 chain, 1 treble on the 6th scallop, 11 chain, 2 quadruple trebles joined by the last overs to the picots of the 7th and 1st scallops, 11 chain, 1 treble on the 2nd scallop, 11 chain, 1 treble on the 3^d scallop, 8 chain, 1 treble 2 ½ trebles long, 8 chain, 1 treble 3 ½ long, 8 chain, 1 double treble, 8 chain, 1 plain, 12 chain, 1 treble, 14 chain ∗∗∗∗, 2 triple trebles united by the last overs, repeat from ∗∗∗∗ to ∗∗∗, therefore the reverse way. Finish with a row of plain stitches, make 1 stitch on every stitch of the last row, 3 plain on the stitches that form the corner. On the narrow edge you should have 65 stitches, on the wide edge 91 and on the two sides 75, not counting the 3 corner stitches.

To make the same figure forming a part of the large outside scallops, repeat the same rows as you have in the inner square up to the 7th row and make half this one again exactly according to the first description. In the second half, make 1 chain stitch less in the intervening trebles, than in the first half.

8th row — make the first half of this row like the 8th row of the inner square = in the second half, a quarter of which is 4 chain stitches narrower, the little wheels number likewise: 4 picots. The number of chain stitches and the trebles of the setting is also the same, only instead of 7 points you only make 5.

Make the setting towards the top in exactly the same way as in the wide part of the upper square, that is, as you did starting from the 3^d scallop of the 1st semicircle to the 5th scallop of the 2nd semicircle. From this point the series of stitches changes so as to obtain a rounded edge: ∗∗ 10 chain, 1 treble on the 6th scallop; 17 chain, 2 triple trebles joined by the last overs to the 7th and 1st scallops; 17 chain, 1 treble on the 2nd of the 5 scallops; 17 chain, 1 treble on the 3^d scallop; 17 chain, 1 treble on the 4th scallop, 18 chain ∗∗, 2 triple trebles joined by the last overs to the 5th and 1st scallops. Repeat once more from ∗∗ to ∗ = add a row of plain stitches on every stitch of the row before; 3 plain on the top corner stitches. You will thus have 3 figures with rounded edges on one side.

The second kind of square consists of 8 leaves inside and you begin by making a ring of 5 chain stitches.

1st row — 5 chain, ∗ 1 treble, 2 chain. Repeat 6 times from ∗ and join to the 3^d of the 5 chain.

2nd row — 3 plain over 2 chain, 1 plain on each treble.

3d row — 3 chain, * 7 chain, miss 1 coming back; 1 single, 1 plain, 1 half treble, 1 treble, 1 double treble, 1 triple treble, 1 treble over the treble of the 2nd row; 7 chain. Repeat 7 times from * = make no treble at the last repeat, but after finishing the 8th point, join to the 3d of the 3 chain and make 7 single stitches along the 1st point.

4th row — * 1 plain on the stitch you skipped at the point, 5 chain, 1 triple treble on the treble of the 3d row, 5 chain. Repeat 7 times from *.

5th row — 3 chain, 1 treble on every stitch of the 4th row; join to the 3d of the 3 chain, 96 trebles in all, including the 3 chain.

6th row — * 10 chain, 1 plain on the treble above the triple treble of the 4th row: 10 chain, 1 plain on the treble above the little point. Repeat 7 times from *.

7th row — * 15 plain on the 10 chain = on the 2nd scallop make only: 7 plain, 10 chain, join them to the 8th plain of the 1st scallop, 15 plain = on the lower scallop: 8 plain and repeat 7 times from *.

Fasten off the thread and fasten it on to the middle of one of the 8 scallops.

8th row — * 19 chain, skip 1, 1 plain, 1 half treble, 1 treble, 1 treble 1 $\frac{1}{2}$ treble long, 1 double treble, 1 treble 2 $\frac{1}{2}$ trebles long, 1 triple treble, 1 treble 3 $\frac{1}{2}$ trebles long, 1 quadruple treble, 1 quintuple treble, 1 sextuple treble, after passing through the 3d over make 1 quadruple treble between the 2 plain scallops, then finish the sextuple treble, 7 chain, 1 plain on the next scallop and repeat 7 times from *.

9th row — * 7 plain on the 7 chain; 1 plain on each stitch of the pyramid, 3 plain on the stitch at the point, 1 plain on each stitch of the pyramid; 4 plain on the next 7 chain = turn the work = skip 4 stitches, 1 treble, 1 chain, skip 1 plain, 1 treble on the 2nd stitch after the 6th treble, skip no more stitches between the trebles; place the 8th, 9th and 10th trebles on the 2nd of the increased stitches. Repeat on the opposite side the reversed way and join to the 4th of the plain stitches = make in all 17 trebles = turn the work = 1 plain on each chain stitch, 1 plain on each treble and 1 picot after every 3d plain stitch = on the stitch at the point make 2 plain separated by 1 picot; 11 picots in all = to finish: 3 more plain on the 7 chain and repeat the whole 7 times from *; fasten off the thread.

The little wheel on the right at the top of the square begins with 9 chain to form the ring = 16 plain on the ring, 4 chain, * 1 treble, 1 chain = repeat 14 times from *, 1 single on the 3ᵈ of the 4 chain; 16 trebles in all, including the chain stitches = then on every treble and every chain stitch: 1 plain = after 3 plain: 1 picot = fasten the 1ˢᵗ picot of the little wheel to one of the scallops of the big wheel on the 3ᵈ picot counted from below; finish the picot of the little wheel and make 3 plain, 1 picot, 3 plain, 1 picot, 3 plain, 2 chain, fasten these 2 chain stitches to the 3ᵈ picot of the 2ⁿᵈ scallop, finish the picot, * 3 plain, 1 picot; repeat again 6 times from *, make 11 picots in all. The left wheel is made and fastened on in the same manner as the right one.

The wheels at the bottom of the square require for the foundation ring: 13 chain, on which make 21 plain = 4 chain, * 1 treble, 1 chain = repeat 19 times from *, 1 single on the 3ᵈ of the 4 chain, 21 trebles in all, including the chain stitches = 3 plain, 1 picot, 3 plain, 1 picot, 3 plain, 1 picot, 3 plain, 2 chain, join them to the 4ᵗʰ picot of the 8ᵗʰ scallop; finish the picot, 3 plain, 1 picot, 3 plain, 2 chain, join them to the 2ⁿᵈ picot of the 8ᵗʰ scallop, finish the picot, 3 plain, 1 picot, 3 plain, 2 chain, join them to the 10ᵗʰ picot of the 7ᵗʰ scallop, finish the picot, 3 plain, 1 picot, 3 plain, 2 chain, join them to the 8ᵗʰ picot of the 7ᵗʰ scallop, finish the picot, 3 single, 1 picot, and so on until there are 14 picots round the wheel.

Make a similar wheel on the second side.

The edging of this second kind of square is also slightly different; for the bottom figures, fasten the thread to the 6ᵗʰ picot of the 1ˢᵗ scallop in front of the little wheel, then, working from right to left, count: * 12 chain, 1 plain on the 2ⁿᵈ empty picot of the wheel; 9 chain, 1 triple treble on the 4ᵗʰ picot of the wheel = upwards: 9 chain, 1 double treble on the 6ᵗʰ picot of the wheel, 9 chain, 1 plain on the 6ᵗʰ picot of the 2ⁿᵈ scallop, 12 chain **, 1 quadruple treble on the 9ᵗʰ picot of the 2ⁿᵈ scallop, keep 2 overs of the treble on the needle, make 2 more overs, fasten the treble to the 3ᵈ picot of the 3ᵈ scallop, finish the treble, repeat once from ** to *, therefore the reverse way, 1 plain on the 6ᵗʰ picot of the 4ᵗʰ scallop, *** 14 chain, 1 sextuple treble on the 9ᵗʰ picot of the 4ᵗʰ scallop, keep 2 overs of the treble on the needle, make 4 more overs, fasten the treble to the 3ᵈ picot of the 5ᵗʰ scallop, finish the treble, 14 chain, 1 plain on the 6ᵗʰ picot of the 5ᵗʰ scallop, 12 chain, 1 double treble on the 2ⁿᵈ picot of the big wheel, 9 chain, 1 triple treble on the 4th picot of the wheel, 13 chain, 1 double treble on the 6th picot of the wheel, 14 chain, 1 plain on the 6th picot of the 6th scallop, 16 chain ****, 1 septuple treble on the 9th picot of the 6th scallop; keep 3 overs of the treble on your needle, make 4 more overs, fasten the treble to the 3^{d} picot of the 7th scallop, and repeat once from **** to ***, the reverse way therefore and finish with 1 single.

A row of plain stitches completes the square; at each corner 3 plain on the same stitch, on the short top edge make 65 stitches, on the two sides 75 and on the outer edge 91, exclusive of the three stitches at the corners. Make 3 of these squares for the collar.

The same star with rounded edges after finishing the star as described above, add two big wheels with 14 picots to the upper edge.

Begin the outline between the two wheels = 1 plain on the 6th picot of the 1st scallop; 16 chain, 2 quintuple trebles, of which only the last overs are connected, on the 9th and 3^{d} picots of the 1st and 2nd scallop = 16 chain, 1 plain on the 6th picot of the 2nd scallop; * 16 chain, 1 plain on the 2nd empty picot of the wheel; 11 chain, 1 quadruple picot on the 4th picot, 10 chain, 1 treble on the 6th picot of the wheel; 16 chain, 1 plain on the 6th picot of the 3^{d} scallop; 17 chain, 2 sextuple trebles united on the 10th and 2nd picots of the 3^{d} and 4th scallops; 17 chain, 1 plain on the 6th picot of the 4th scallop; 17 chain, 2 sextuple trebles joined on the 10th and 2nd picots of the 4th and 5th scallops; 17 chain, 1 plain on the 6th picot of the 5th scallop; 19 chain **, 2 sextuple trebles on the 10th and 2nd picots of the 5th and 6th scallops. Repeat from ** to *, and make 4 figures with rounded edges.

A row of plain stitches completes the square.

When all the figures for the ground are finished join them together by trebles of a suitable length. Introduce the thread at the stitch that forms the point of the 8 pointed square and on the enlarged side: 1 plain, 6 chain, skip 3 stitches, 3 plain on the next 3 plain; 4 chain, skip 2; 3 plain on the next 3 plain.

Make 10 loops, in this way, of 4 chain and 3 plain stitches, make 2 loops of 3 chain and 2 plain = then on the next square at the edge of the collar, miss as many stitches as were left empty on the first square; 2 plain and draw the over each time through the 2 last stitches of the opposite square

= 1 chain, 1 single on the chain stitches of the opposite side; 1 chain, 2 plain on the edge of the second square, 1 chain, 1 single on the chain stitches of the opposite square; 1 chain, skip 2 stitches of the 2nd square, 3 plain, 1 chain, 1 single on the opposite chain stitches, 1 chain, skip 2, 3 plain. From this point onwards fasten all the bars of chain stitches to the loops produced by the same stitches on the 2nd square. Make the 1st bar with 5 chain, over which make 4 plain, 1 chain, skip 2, 3 plain = for the 2nd bar 7 chain, over which make 6 plain, then add 1 chain, skip 2 plain, 3 plain = the 3^{d} bar requires 9 chain, 8 plain, 1 chain, skip 2, 3 plain = the 4th bar: 11 chain, 5 plain, 1 picot, 5 plain, 1 chain, skip 2, 3 plain = the 5th bar: 13 chain, 4 plain, 1 picot, 4 plain, 1 picot, 4 plain, 1 chain, skip 2, 3 plain = on the 6th bar: 16 chain, 5 plain, 1 picot, 5 plain, 1 picot, 5 plain, 1 chain, skip 2, 3 plain = the 7th bar: 19 chain, 5 plain, 1 picot, 4 plain, 1 picot, 4 plain, 1 picot, 5 plain, 1 chain, skip 2, 3 plain = the 8th bar: 21 chain, 5 plain, 1 picot, 5 plain, 1 picot, 5 plain, 1 picot, 5 plain, 1 chain, skip 2, 3 plain, = the 9th bar: 26 chain, 5 plain, 1 picot, 5 plain, 1 picot, 5 plain, 1 picot, 5 plain, 1 picot, 5 plain, 1 chain, skip 2, 3 plain = the 10th and last bar: 28 chain, 32 plain, 2 chain, 1 plain, fasten off the thread.

Once the 7 top figures are finished and joined together add on the 7 bottom ones, each separately by a row of plain stitches, made on the wrong side of the work.

Below the first square with the semicircles comes the 8 pointed star, below the next square, the one with the semi-circles.

A narrow edging forms the outside border of the big scallops. Fasten the thread on to the corner stitch of the 1st square, then: * 5 plain, 1 picot, 5 plain, 14 chain, join them to the first of the first 5 plain, on the 14 chain: 5 plain, 1 picot, 11 plain, 1 picot, 5 plain = on the stitches along the square: 5 plain, 1 picot, 5 plain; then 14 chain, join them to the 1st plain stitch = 5 plain, 1 picot, 5 plain, 14 chain, join them coming back to the 6th of the 11 plain stitches of the 1st scallop; on the 11 chain 4 times 5 plain stitches and 3 times 1 picot = on the half finished scallop: 5 plain, 1 picot, 5 plain ** = on the plain stitches of the edge: 4 plain, 1 picot, 4 plain, 12 chain, return, fasten them to the 1st of the 4 plain = on the 12 chain: 4 plain, 1 picot, 4 plain, 1 picot, 4 plain,

1 picot, 4 plain * * * = repeat once from * to * * * and make here the little scallop with 10 plain, then repeat from * to * *.

The scallops vary a little on the rounded sides.

There the stitches should number 122, counting from the corner to the treble that marks the middle at the bottom. The single or detached scallops of the border are all to be made over 8 stitches; the triple scallops are made over 20 stitches, make no little scallop between the 4th, 5th and 6th triple scallops; all round the first figure there are 9 triple scallops and 8 single ones. After the 8th single scallop, make 3 plain stitches on the 2 connecting chain stitches and 4 plain on the bar of 32 plain stitches. On the 32 plain stitches of the last bar: 4 plain, 1 picot, 4 plain, 12 chain, carry them back and fasten them to the 1st of the 4 plain stitches = on the 12 chain: 5 plain, 2 chain, draw the over through the picot in the middle of the last single scallop, 2 chain, close the picot, 9 plain, 1 picot, 5 plain = on the bar: 4 plain, 1 picot, 4 plain, 12 chain, carry them back and fasten them to the 1st plain stitch; 5 plain, 1 picot, 4 plain, 12 chain, join them to the 5th plain or the 1st scallop; 5 plain, 1 picot, 9 plain, 1 picot, 5 plain = on the half finished scallop: 5 plain, 1 picot, 5 plain = on the bar: 4 plain, 1 picot, 4 plain, 12 chain = bring them back and join them to the 1st plain, 5 plain, 1 picot, 4 plain, 12 chain, join them quite close to the scallop above = 5 plain, 1 picot, 4 plain, 12 chain, bring them back and join them to the 5th plain stitch of the scallop above = 5 plain, 1 picot, 5 plain, 1 picot, 5 plain, 1 picot, 5 plain, on each of the 2 half finished scallops: 5 plain, 1 picot, 5 plain = finish with 4 plain, 2 plain on the 2 chain and repeat the same series of scallops round all the rounded parts.

The lozenges that fill the empty spaces between the large figures are made in 7 rows on a little ring formed of 5 chain stitches.

1st row — 5 chain, 1 treble on the ring, 2 chain, 8 trebles in all including the bar of chain stitches.

2nd row — 3 plain over 2 chain, 1 plain on each treble.

3d row — 7 chain, 1 treble over the treble beneath, 5 chain, 1 treble, 8 trebles in all.

4th row — * on 5 chain, 1 plain, 1 half treble, 1 treble, 3 double trebles, 1 treble, 1 half treble, 1 plain * *; 7 chain, skip 1, 1 plain, 1 treble, 2 double trebles, 1 treble, 1 plain * * *. Repeat once from * to * *. Then, repeat the whole series again 3 times and make 5 single stitches along the scallop.

5th row — 9 chain, * 1 plain on the top stitch of one of the small leaves, 7 chain, 1 treble on the middle stitch of the scallop, 7 chain, 1 treble on the next scallop; 9 chain, 1 plain on the next leaf, 9 chain, 1 treble on the scallop, 7 chain **, 1 treble on the scallop, 7 chain, repeat once from * to ***, 1 single on the 3d chain.

6th row — 1 plain on every stitch of the last row, 3 plain on the points.

7th row — to begin after the 3 corner stitches, * 4 plain, 1 picot, 4 plain, 10 chain, fasten them to the 1st of the first 4 plain stitches, on the 10 chain: 4 plain, 1 picot, 3 plain, 1 picot, 3 plain, 1 picot, 4 plain **; repeat twice from * to **, 1 plain and 3 plain on the point, 8 chain, fasten them to the first of the 4 plain, on the 8 chain: 4 plain, 1 picot, 3 plain, 1 picot, 3 plain, 1 picot, 4 plain; repeat 3 times from * to **; 4 plain, 8 chain, fasten them to the first of the 4 plain, on the 8 chain make: 4 plain, 1 picot, 3 plain, fasten them to the middle picot of the 2nd triple scallop of the 2nd square; then, starting from the 2nd picot of the 3d scallop of the lozenge, make 6 chain, join them to the middle picot of the 1st triple scallop; coming back, on the 6 chain: 5 plain, 1 picot, 5 plain and finish the scallop of the lozenge; 4 plain, 8 chain, fasten them to the first of the 4 plain; on these 8 chain make: 4 plain, 1 picot, 3 plain, 2 chain, fasten them to the middle picot of the scallop underneath the connecting bar, finish the picot, 3 plain, 1 picot, 4 plain; repeat 3 times from * to ** and fasten the lozenge by the first little scallop to the 9th triple scallop by a bar of 6 chain stitches as on the opposite side: 4 plain, 8 chain, fasten them to the first of the 4 plain, on these 8 chain make: 4 plain, 1 picot, 3 plain, 2 chain, fasten them to the middle picot of the 8th triple scallop of the 1st square, 3 plain, 1 picot, 4 plain, fasten off the thread.

The lace that finishes off the top of the collar must be made to stand up; for which purpose make a row of double trebles on the plain stitches. Decrease by 3 or 4 stitches in each square.

When this row of trebles is finished, fasten off, and begin again on the right and at the foot of the 1st treble along which make 4 plain, upon these, follow: * 21 plain on the row of trebles, put the needle in under the 2 loops of the trebles = turn the work = 2 chain, skip 4 plain, 1 double treble on the 5th stitch, 2 chain, 1 double treble, 2 chain, 1 double treble, 2 chain, skip 4 plain, 1 single on the 5th stitch = turn the work = ** 1 plain, 1 picot, 1 plain, 1 plain on the treble; repeat 3 times again from ** and add 4 plain on the trebles = turn the work = 6 chain, 1 double treble on the treble beneath; again 3 times 6 chain and 2 double trebles; join the 4th set of 6 chain stitches to the 4th plain stitch = turn the work = 1 plain on the 6 chain; 8 chain, skip the 1st chain and on the next chain stitches make: 1 plain, 1 half treble, 2 trebles, 1 treble 1 $\frac{1}{2}$ treble long; 2 double trebles, 1 plain on the 6 chain.

The next point comes above a treble; make 7 points in all. After the 7th: 5 plain on the trebles beneath = turn the work = then 7 chain as an interval, 1 plain on each point. The 8th set of 7 chain stitches are joined to the 5th plain stitch of the border = turn the work = add: 2 chain, draw the loop from the wrong side to the right through the 2nd plain stitch; 8 trebles, 1 picot, 4 trebles, 12 chain, bring them back over the picot, join them to the 3d treble; 5 plain, 1 picot, 4 plain, 1 picot, 4 plain, 1 picot, 5 plain, 5 trebles on the chain stitches = on each point: 1 picot and over the picot 1 scallop like the one made in the square. On the 7th point only one picot = after the last picot, 8 trebles on the last chain stitches: skip 2 of the trebles beneath; then continue the plain stitches to the number of 27 and repeat from *.

In the semicircles that follow, make only 5 little scallops; and join the first and last of them by the first and last picot: the last semicircle, like the first must have 6 little scallops.

Patterns of needlework. — Besides the different kinds of work described above a great choice of crochet patterns will be found in the following publications of the D.M.C Library: *Crochet work, Ist, IInd and IIIrd Series, Irish crochet Lace* and *Works of various kinds.* (*)

(*) See at the end of the volume the list of the albums of the D.M.C Library.

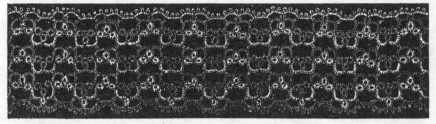

Tatting insertion. — Double knots, single picots and Josephine picots.

Tatting

A chapter on this kind of work, somewhat resembling crochet in its construction, seems to follow naturally on our last and also serves as a preparation for the next on macramé.

The English term "Tatting" is said to be derived from the word "tatters" and to denote the fragile disjointed nature of the fabric. The term "Frivolité" is essentially French and has been adopted in most European countries.

By the Italians it was formerly called "occhi" whilst in the East it still bears the name of "makouk" from the shuttle used in making it.

Tatting ought rather to be classed as braid work than as lace.

Worked in one colour, in a brilliant thread of a certain fineness, it is used as a trimming for dresses and cloaks; whilst in several colours in a coarser thread, tatted braids or gimps serve as trimmings for upholstered furniture, curtains and hangings of all kinds and cushions.

For children's clothes, aprons, collars and cuffs of all sorts it should be worked in light colours and in moderately fine materials.

For trimming bed- or underlinen a fine thread should always be used.

Shuttles. — The tatting shuttle is made of two oval blades, of either bone, ivory, mother-of-pearl or tortoiseshell, pointed at both ends and joined together in the middle. The shape is important, for a good shuttle contributes materially to the quick and perfect execution of the work. In the 18th century when tatting was in great vogue much longer shuttles than the present ones were used because they had much more voluminous materials, such as silk cord, to carry.

The shuttle ought not to be more than 2 ¾ in. long and ¾ in. wide: the two ends should be sufficiently close together to prevent the thread from escaping too freely; this is more especially important in tatting with two shuttles.

The centre piece that joins the two oval blades together should have a hole large enough in it for the thread, that is to be wound upon the shuttle to be fastened into it. In filling the shuttle be careful not to wind on too much thread at once, or the blades will gape apart at the ends and get soiled and frayed by constant contact with the hands.

Materials. — Considering the various uses to which tatting may be applied a large variety of materials lies open to choice, provided a sufficiently twisted one be selected.

For trimming childrens' clothes and underlinen, we recommend more especially D.M.C Alsatian thread (Fil d'Alsace) in balls, D.M.C Crochet cotton, 6 cord (Cordonnet 6 fils), D.M.C Special crochet cotton (Cordonnet spécial) and D.M.C Knotting cotton (Fil à pointer); for bed-linen D.M.C Flax lace thread (Lin pour dentelles) and D.M.C Flax thread for knitting (Lin pour tricoter) (*) are the best.

Used as braid, either for dresses or cloaks, or for upholstery, D.M.C Pearl cotton (Coton perlé) or D.M.C Alsatia is the most suitable material.

Tatted work is often finished off or joined together by a few rows of crochet; in that case the crochet should be worked in the same material as the tatting, only in a coarser number.

Knots or double stitches. First position of the hands (fig. 516). — The construction of the knots or stitches seems at first to present great difficulties; but our readers will soon master them if they let themselves be guided in their first

_____

(*) See at the end of the last chapter the tables of the sizes and colours of the cotton, flax and silk articles, mark D.M.C. — The French names, in brackets, are those stamped on the labels of the D.M.C articles.

attempts by our directions. One thing to be constantly attended
to from the outset is that the right hand as soon as it has
passed the shuttle through the loop, must stop with a sudden
jerk and remaining immovable hold the thread tightly stretched,
until the left hand has closed the knot.

After filling the shuttle with the proper quantity of thread,
take hold of the end of the thread with the thumb and forefinger of the left hand, take the shuttle in the right hand, lay
the thread over the third and fourth fingers of the left hand,

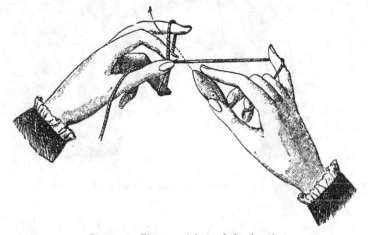

Fig. 516. First position of the hands.

bring it back towards the thumb and cross the two threads
under the fingers, as shewn in figure 516.

Pass the thread issuing from the shuttle round the little
finger of the right hand, and give the shuttle the direction
shewn in the engraving.

Second and third position of the hands (figs. 517 and
518). — Pass the shuttle between the first and third fingers in
the direction indicated by the arrow in figure 517 and bring
it out behind the loop.

Here the first difficulties for beginners arise, and until they
have sufficiently mastered the movements of both hands not
to confuse those of the left hand with those of the right we
advise them to pay careful heed to the following instructions.

In the first place the end of the thread between the shuttle
and the left hand must not be more than 8 to 10 inches long.
As soon as the shuttle has passed through the loop, put the
right hand on the table and stretch out the thread tightly,
keeping the left hand meanwhile, perfectly motionless.

When the right hand has assumed its passive position, the third and fourth fingers of the left hand lift up the loop and close it, whilst they separate enough to give tension to the thread. By this movement a knot is formed, the first half of the "double knot", which is the most common one in tatting.

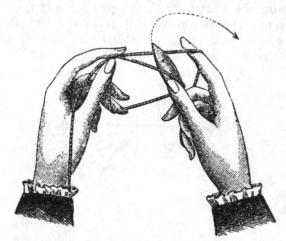

Fig. 517. Second position of the hands.

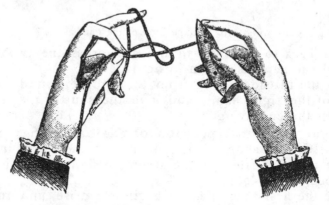

Fig. 518. Third position of the hands.

Take care therefore not to forget that the thread in the right hand must never move whilst the left hand is active; and that it is only that part of the thread which is laid over the left hand that forms the knot.

The right hand or shuttle thread must always be free to run through the knots; it would be impossible to continue to

move it if it were to form a knot itself, for it would no longer
have the free play necessary for loosening or tightening the
loop on the left hand.

Fourth position of the hands (fig. 519). — The second
part of a stitch or knot is made by the following movements:
pass the shuttle, as shewn in figure 519, from left to right,

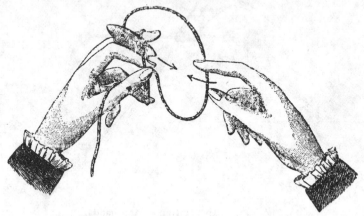

Fig. 519. Fourth position of the hands.

between the first and third fingers, under the extended loop;
the right hand seizes the shuttle in front of the empty loop
and extends the thread; the left hand closes this second knot
like the first.

Two knots joined together then form a double knot.

Single knots or Josephine picots (figs. 520 and 521). —
Sometimes too a series of single knots consisting merely of

Fig. 520. Single or half knots.
Small Josephine picot.

Fig. 521. Single or half knots.
Big Josephine picot.

the first knot is made; such a series is called: Picot Josephine.
These picots can be made of 4 or 5 knots only, as shewn in
figure 520, or of 10 or 12 knots, as in figure 521.

Fifth position of the hands (fig. 522). — When the second
knot, forming the double knot, is finished, the hands resume

the position shewn in figure 516. Figure 522 reproduces this position and at the same time shews a few double knots completed.

Position of the hands for making a picot (fig. 523). — Picots are introduced in tatting patterns, as in knitting and macramé.

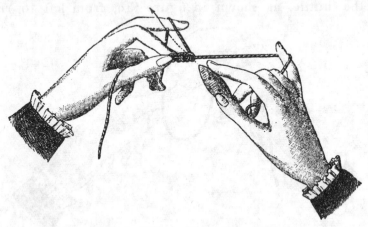

Fig. 522. Fifth position of the hands.

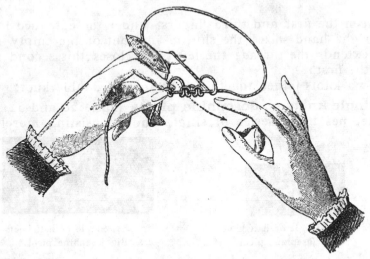

Fig. 523. Position of the hands for making a picot.

These picots serve to connect the different parts of the work and with their help a great variety of pretty combinations can be made.

Figure 523 shews how the picots are made.

Open and close picots (figs. 524 and 525). — These are formed of single knots, by leaving a loop on the extended thread, as shewn in figure 524, and a short distance between the last knot and the one to follow; you then finish the second half knot, and after having tightened it, join it to the preceding knots.

The picot represented in figure 525 then forms itself quite naturally.

In all descriptions of tatting the knot that follows the picot is independent of the loop.

Thus, if the directions prescribe: 2 stitches or knots, 1 picot, 3 knots, 1 picot, 2 knots, &c., you must always count the knot that served to form the loop, and not make 2 knots, 1 picot, 4 knots, &c.

Fig. 524. Open picot.

How to join the rings by means of picots. — To join the various rings, ovals, &c., by means of picots, take up the thread that runs over the left hand with a crochet needle inserting it into the picot downwards from above and drawing the thread through; pass the shuttle through this loop that issues from the picot and tighten it like any other knot.

Fig. 525. Close picot.

Tatting with two shuttles (fig. 526). — Two shuttles are used in tatting when the little rings are not to be connected at their base by a thread, or when you want to hide the passage of the thread to another group of knots, or when you use threads of different colours.

When you work with two shuttles, tie the ends of the two threads together. Put one thread over the third finger of the left hand, wind it twice round the fourth finger, and leave the shuttle hanging down. Take the second shuttle in the right hand and make the same movements with it as you do in working with one shuttle only.

Detached scallops (fig. 527). — Make 12 double knots with one shuttle, then tighten the thread so as to draw them together into a half ring; the first knot of the next scallop must be so close to the last knot of the preceding scallop as to touch it.

Scallops joined together at the top (fig. 528). — With one shuttle make 4 double knots, 1 picot, * 8 double knots, 1 picot, 4 doubles, close the half ring, 4 doubles, pass the thread through the 2ⁿᵈ picot of the preceding scallop and repeat from *.

Scallops with picots (fig. 529). — Make with one shuttle: 4 doubles, 1 picot, * 3 doubles, 1 picot, 2 doubles, 1 picot, 2 doubles, 1 picot, 3 doubles, 1 picot, 4 doubles; close the ring.

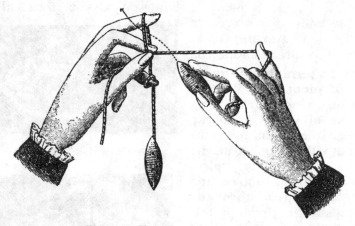

Fig. 526. Tatting with two shuttles.

Leave sufficient length of thread before beginning the next ring for the rings not to overlap each other = make 4 doubles, draw the left hand thread through the 5ᵗʰ picot of the last ring and repeat from *.

Tatted insertion (fig. 530). — Make with one shuttle a ring like the ones in figure 529, turn the work = then, leaving not more than ¼ of an inch of thread, make a second ring = turn the work = leave the same length of thread free again, begin a 3ᵈ ring and connect in after the 4ᵗʰ double with the 5ᵗʰ picot of the 1ˢᵗ ring = turn the work each time after a ring is finished, so that all the top rings appear worked on the right and all the bottom ones on the wrong side of the work.

When this insertion is used for underlinen, the picots should be strengthened by a little crochet heading: several kinds are shewn in the subsequent figures.

Tatted insertion (fig. 531). — To be made with two shuttles. Tie the two ends of thread together and begin with one thread and one shuttle and make a ring, as in figures 529 and 530 = turn the work =

Fig. 527. Detached scallops.
Materials : D.M.C Alsatian thread Nos. 30 to 70, D.M.C Knotting cotton Nos. 20 to 30, or D.M.C Flax lace thread Nos. 16 to 70, white or écru. (*)

with the second shuttle make a similar ring quite close to the first; then pass the thread you have been working

Fig. 528. Scallops joined together at the top.
Materials : D.M.C Alsatian thread Nos. 30 to 70, D.M.C Crochet cotton 6 cord or D.M.C Special crochet cotton Nos. 20 to 60, or D.M.C Flax lace thread Nos. 16 to 70, white or écru. (*)

with over the left hand, take the shuttle which remained free in the right hand and make 6 doubles on the 2nd thread = turn the work = after which again make a ring above and one below with a single shuttle, taking care to connect the rings by the picots, as shewn in figures 529 and 530.

Fig. 529. Scallops with picots.
Materials : D.M.C Alsatian thread Nos. 30 to 70, D.M.C Crochet cotton 6 cord Nos. 25 to 60, or D.M.C Flax lace thread Nos. 16 to 70, white or écru. (*)

Edging of tatting and crochet (fig. 532). — Make with one shuttle : 1 double, 1 picot, 2 doubles, 1 picot, 2 doubles, 1 picot, 2 doubles, 1 picot twice the

Fig. 530. Tatted insertion.
Materials : D.M.C Alsatian thread Nos. 30 to 70, or D.M.C Flax thread for knitting Nos. 12 to 45, white or écru. (*)

(*) See at the end of the last chapter the tables of the sizes and colours of the cotton, flax and silk articles, mark D.M.C.

length of the others, 2 doubles, 1 picot, 2 doubles, 1 picot, 2 doubles, 1 picot, 2 doubles, 1 long picot, 1 double = close the ring = fasten off the two ends of thread by a few stitches at the back.

Continue as explained above, but before making the last double connect the begun ring with the preceding one by a long picot, then make the last double knot and fasten off the threads.

When you have made a sufficient number of rings, pick up the picots with crochet trebles, 3 chain stitches apart. On this first row crochet a second one consisting of: 1 plain stitch on the treble of the 1st row, 2 chain, 1 picot, 2 chain.

Fig. 531. Tatted insertion.
Materials: D.M.C Alsatian thread Nos. 30 to 70, or D.M.C Special crochet cotton Nos. 30 to 80, white or écru. (*)

To finish the bottom part of the work, make 1 plain stitch on the 1st picot, 3 chain, 1 plain on the 2nd picot, 3 chain, 1 plain on the 3d picot, 3 chain, 1 plain on the 1st picot of the next ring. A row of plain stitches forms a footing to the edging.

Fig. 532. Edging of tatting and crochet.
Materials — For the tatting: D.M.C Alsatian thread or D.M.C Crochet cotton 6 cord No. 50. — For the crochet: D.M.C Alsatian thread or D.M.C Crochet cotton 6 cord No. 80, white or écru. (*)

Tatted edging The first row is made with one only, as in figure 528.

(fig. 533). — To be made with two shuttles.

The 2nd and the 3d row with two shuttles.

Fasten the thread of the right hand shuttle on to the first picot; then on this thread with the left hand thread, make the same number of double knots and picots as in the 1st row, and connect each half ring with the picot of the preceding row. In the 3d row, place 3 picots between the 8 double knots above.

Edging of tatting and crochet (fig. 534). — To be made with two shuttles in two colours. After making a string of rings with the light thread, like the ones in figure 532, fasten the ends of thread of the shuttle with the dark thread and the shuttle with the light thread to the first picot that comes after the long one. Holding the light thread in the right hand with the dark one laid across the left, make : * 3 doubles, 1 picot, 3 doubles, put the right hand thread through the next picot = 3 doubles, 1 picot, 3 doubles, put the right hand thread separately through the two picots of the rings and continue from *.

The next row is also made with two shuttles — the light thread again in the right hand; the dark thread in the left hand is to be fastened to the first dark picot, then make : ** 4 doubles, 1 picot, 2 doubles, 1 picot, 2 doubles = turn the work = with the right hand shuttle make : 6 doubles, put the thread through the little picot, formed above the middle picot of the 2nd row, 6 doubles, close the ring = turn the work = make

Fig. 533. Tatted edging.
Materials : D.M.C Alsatian thread Nos. 30 to 70, or D.M.C Knotting cotton Nos. 20 to 30, white or écru.

with two shuttles : 2 doubles, 1 picot, 2 doubles, 1 picot, 4 doubles, put the light thread through the 2 dark picots and repeat from * *.

The footing is made in two rows.

1st row — * 1 treble on the first picot, 3 chain, 1 plain on the 2nd picot, 3 chain, 1 treble on the last picot of the ring, 1 chain, repeat from *.

2nd row — 1 treble, 1 chain, skip 1, 1 treble, 1 chain, and so on.

Edging in tatting and crochet (fig. 535). — Worked with two shuttles in two colours. With the shuttle with the light colour on it = 2 doubles, 1 short picot, 2 doubles, 1 long picot, ∗ 2 doubles, 1 picot of the ordinary size, 2 doubles, 1 picot, 2 doubles, 1 picot, 2 doubles, 1 picot, 2 doubles, 1 picot, 2 doubles, 1 long picot, 2 doubles, 1 short picot, 2 doubles, close the ring = turn the work = with 2 shuttles, the dark thread over the left hand, the light one in the right: 3 doubles, 1 short picot, 3 doubles, 1 long picot, 2 doubles = turn the work = with the light thread: 4 doubles, put the thread through the 9th picot of the 1st ring, make 4 doubles, 1 picot, 4 doubles, close the ring = turn the work = with 2 shuttles, the dark thread over the left hand, the light one in the right: 2 doubles, 1 long picot, 3 doubles, 1 short picot,

Fig. 534. Edging of tatting and crochet.

Materials — For the tatting: D.M.C Alsatian thread No. 30, D.M.C Alsatia No. 20, D.M.C Flax thread for knitting No. 12 or D.M.C Pearl cotton No. 5, in Cream yellow 711 and Solid blue 813, or in Maize yellow 579 and Garnet red 335. — For the crochet: D.M.C Alsatian thread No. 50, D.M.C Alsatia No. 30, D.M.C Flax thread for knitting No. 25 or D.M.C Pearl cotton No. 8, in Cream yellow 711 or Maize yellow 579. (∗)

3 doubles = turn the work = with the light thread: 2 doubles, put the thread through the empty picot of the little ring, make 2 doubles, put the thread through the long picot of the big ring, then repeat from ∗. The dark semicircles are to be connected by the little picot.

The outside edge, in crochet, is worked in two rows.

1st row = ∗ 1 plain stitch on the 1st of the 5 picots of the big ring, 4 chain, 1 plain on the 2nd picot, 4 chain, 1 plain on the 3d picot, 4 chain, 1 plain on the 4th picot, 4 chain, 1 plain on the 5th picot and repeat from ∗.

2nd row — 2 plain on the first chain stitches = over the 2nd and 3d loop of chain stitches: 1 plain, 1 half treble, 2 trebles, 1 half treble, 1 plain; on the last 4 chain stitches: 2 plain.

For the footing make: 1 plain on the long picot, 5 chain,

(∗) These numbers refer to the colours on the colour cards of the articles stamped with the D.M.C trade mark. These cards can be consulted at all the mercers' and needlework shops.

ı plain on the next picot, 3 chain, ı double treble on the little picot, leave the 2 last overs of the treble on the needle = 2 trebles on the first lower loop of the double treble, keep the last overs of these 2 trebles also on the needle, after the 3ᵈ treble draw the needle through all the loops, 3 chain, and so on.

The last row consists of: * ı treble over 5 chain, 3 chain, ı treble, ı chain, ı treble, 3 chain, repeat from *.

Edging in tatting and crochet (fig. 536). — Made with two shuttles in two colours. Begin with the light colour: 6 doubles, ı picot, 6 doubles, close the ring = turn the work =

Fig. 535. Edging in tatting and crochet.

Materials — For the tatting: D.M.C Alsatian thread No. 30, D.M.C Alsatia No. 20, D.M.C Flax thread for knitting No. 25 or D.M.C Pearl cotton No. 5, in Golden green 582 and Scabious violet 397, or in Rust brown 3314 and Cardinal red 346. For the crochet: D.M.C Alsatian thread No. 50, D.M.C Alsatia No. 30, D.M.C Flax thread for knitting No. 35 or D.M.C Pearl cotton No. 8, in Golden green 582 or in Rust brown 3314. (*)

make a second ring like the first = turn the work. With two shuttles, the dark thread on the left hand, the light one in the right: 6 doubles, ı picot, 6 doubles = turn the work = with one shuttle and the light thread: 6 doubles, fasten the thread to the picot of the opposite ring, 6 doubles, close the ring = turn the work = make a second ring like the first ones = turn the work = with both shuttles: 6 doubles, ı picot, 6 doubles, and so on.

Make three rows of half rings connected by rings. In the second and third row pass the thread from the ring through

___

(*) See at the end of the last chapter the tables of the sizes and colours of the cotton, flax and silk articles, mark D.M.C.

the picot to which the 2nd ring in the first row was fastened, and connect the half rings likewise by picots.

For the outside scallops, make with the light thread: * 5 doubles, put the thread through the picot that connects 2 rings, 5 doubles, close the ring = turn the work = with two shuttles, the dark thread on the left hand, the light one in the right:

Fig. 536. Edging in tatting and crochet.

Materials — For the tatting: D.M.C Alsatia No. 20, D.M.C Flax thread for knitting No. 25 or D.M.C Pearl cotton No. 8, in Cachou brown 437 and Blue fast dye 799, or in Ash grey 415 and Geranium red 352.

For the crochet: D.M.C Alsatia No. 30, D.M.C Flax thread for knitting No. 35 or D.M.C Pearl cotton No. 12, in Cachou brown 437 or Ash grey 415. (*)

4 doubles = turn the work = with the light thread: 2 doubles, 1 picot, 2 doubles, 1 picot, 2 doubles, put the thread through the picot of the half ring of the 3^d row, 2 doubles; then 8 more picots with 2 doubles between each of them, close the ring = turn the work = with two shuttles: the dark thread over

_____

(*) See at the end of the last chapter the tables of the sizes and colours of the cotton, flax and silk articles, mark D.M.C.

the left hand, the light one in the right: 4 doubles, 1 long
picot, 2 doubles, 1 picot, 2 doubles, 1 picot, 2 doubles = turn
the work = with the light thread: 4 doubles, put the thread
through the 3ᵈ picot of the big ring, 4 doubles, close the ring
= turn the work = with two shuttles: the dark thread over
the left hand, the light one in the right: 2 doubles, 6 picots
with 2 doubles after each = turn the work = with the light
thread: 4 doubles, put the thread through the 3ᵈ picot of the
big ring, 4 doubles, close the ring = turn the work = with

Fig. 537. Insertion in tatting and crochet.

Materials — For the tatting: D.M.C Special crochet cotton No. 30,
D.M.C Alsatia No. 20, D.M.C Flax thread for knitting No. 25 or D.M.C Pearl
cotton No. 5, in Golden yellow 781 and Scabious violet 395, or in
Tender pink 776 and Cachou brown 434.
For the crochet: D.M.C Special crochet cotton No. 50, D.M.C Alsatia No. 30,
D.M.C Flax thread for knitting No. 35 or D.M.C Pearl cotton No. 8,
in Golden yellow 781 or in Tender pink 776.

two shuttles, the dark thread over the left hand, the light one
in the right: 2 doubles, 1 picot, 2 doubles, 1 picot, 2 doubles,
1 long picot, 4 doubles, put the thread through the 6ᵗʰ picot
of the big ring, 4 doubles = turn the work = repeat from *.
The isolated scallops must be connected in working by long
picots.

The footing is done in crochet.

1ˢᵗ row — 1 treble on the picot that connects 2 little rings,

9 chain, 1 plain on the picot of the half ring, 9 chain, and so on.

2nd row — 1 treble on every stitch.

To make an insertion to go with this edging, make two rows of half rings with the crochet footing above described, top and bottom.

Insertion in tatting and crochet (fig. 537). — Fill two shuttles, one with the light, the other with the dark thread. Begin with the dark colour and make: * 4 doubles, 1 picot, 8 doubles, 1 picot, 4 doubles, close the ring = turn the work.

Fig. 538. Insertion in tatting and crochet.
Materials — For the tatting : D.M.C Special crochet cotton No. 40,
D.M.C Alsatia No. 20, D.M.C Flax thread for knitting No. 12 or D.M.C Pearl
cotton No. 5, in Maize yellow 579 or in Cream yellow 711.
For the crochet : D.M.C Special crochet cotton No. 60, D.M.C Alsatia No. 30.
D.M.C Flax thread for knitting No. 25 or D.M.C Pearl cotton No. 8,
in Maize yellow 579 or in Cream yellow 711. (*)

With two shuttles, take the light thread in the left hand and the dark thread in the right: 4 doubles, 1 picot, 2 doubles, 1 picot, 2 doubles, 1 picot, 4 doubles, put the right hand thread through the picot of the first ring, then add : 4 doubles, 1 picot, 2 doubles, 1 picot, 2 doubles, 1 picot, 4 doubles = turn the work.

(*) See at the end of the last chapter the tables of the sizes and colours of the cotton, flax and silk articles, mark D.M.C.

With one shuttle and with dark thread: 4 doubles, put the thread through the picot of the first ring, 8 doubles, 1 picot, 4 doubles, close the ring; then leaving a short length of thread between, make: 6 doubles, put the thread through the picot of the preceding ring, 8 doubles, 1 picot, 6 doubles, close the ring * *. Repeat from * to * * and join first the ring on the side to the middle ring by the side picot.

When you have thus made two equal lengths, join them together with crochet, using a thread finer than the tatting thread and make:

1st row: 1 plain in the 1st picot, 5 chain, 1 plain in the middle picot, 5 chain, 1 plain on the 3d and 1st picot, and so on.

2nd row: Over the 5 chain: 1 sextuple cluster stitch (fig. 466) and 5 chain.

In the 2nd row on the opposite side of the tatting, take out the crochet needle at the 3d chain stitch and put it in from beneath into the corresponding stitch of the opposite row; in this manner join the two insertions together so as to complete the pattern.

Insertion in tatting and crochet (figs. 538 and 539). — Made with one shuttle. — Begin with two strings of half rings

Fig. 539. Working detail of figure 538.

consisting of: 16 doubles with 4 short and 3 long picots between them. Leave a length of thread between, equal to the diameter of the ring.

When the two strings of half rings are finished, crochet with the fine thread: 1st row — 6 plain on each length of thread between and beneath the scallops.

In the 2nd row: 5 chain, 1 plain on the 3 plain of the 1st row.

In the row that connects the two strings of tatting. put the 3d chain stitch into the corresponding stitch of the opposite row.

For the outside edge make: 1st row — 1 plain on the 1st short picot, 8 chain, * 1 treble on the 2nd short picot, 7 chain, 1 treble on the 3d short picot, 8 chain, 1 plain on the 4th short picot, 1 plain on the short picot opposite, 3 chain, pass the thread through the 4th of the 8 chain, 4 chain, then repeat from *.

For the 2nd row make: 1 plain on each of the 3 last of the 8 chain, * * 1 picot of 5 chain on the treble, 4 plain on the next 4 chain, 1 picot, 1 plain on the same stitch the 4th plain before the picot is on, 3 plain, 1 picot, 3 plain, skip the 1st and last stitches, then make 3 plain on the next scallop and repeat from * *.

Medallion in tatting (fig. 540). — Take two colours and fill two shuttles with the light and two with the dark thread.

With one of the shuttles filled with the light thread, make 24 doubles and 12 picots, 6 very short and 6 long; close the ring and fasten off the ends on the wrong side by a few stitches.

For the next 4 rows take 2 shuttles.

1st row — with the light threads = fasten the ends on to a short picot and make: * 3 doubles, 1 short picot, 2 doubles, 1 long picot, 2 doubles, 1 long picot, 2 doubles, 1 long picot, 2 doubles, 1 short picot, 3 doubles; put the right hand thread into a short picot of the first ring, repeat the series five times from * and connect the half rings by the short stitch. When you come to the 6th half ring instead of making the second short picot, put the left hand thread into the little picot of the first half ring, then finish the last 3 doubles, cut the

Fig. 540. Medallion in tatting.
Materials: D.M.C Knotting cotton No. 30,
D.M.C Alsatia No. 30, D.M.C Flax thread for knitting No. 25 or D.M.C Pearl cotton No. 8, in white and Tender pink 776, or in Indigo blue 311 and Rust brown 3314. (*)

threads, put them through the picot of the ring and fasten them off at the back.

2nd row — with two shuttles and with two light threads = fasten the ends to a big picot, then make: * 4 doubles, 1 short picot, 4 doubles, put the right hand thread through the picot of the first row and repeat the series 17 times from *.

(*) See at the end of the last chapter the tables of the sizes and colours of the cotton, flax and silk articles, mark D.M.C.

3ᵈ row — with two shuttles and with two dark threads =
fasten one end to one of the picots of the last row and make:
4 doubles, put the right hand thread through the picot of
the 2ⁿᵈ row, make 1 big picot, 4 doubles, and so on all round
the medallion, so that you have 18 scallops.

4ᵗʰ row — With two shuttles filled with the dark thread =
fasten one end to one of the picots of the 2ⁿᵈ row and make:
* 2 doubles, 1 picot, 2 doubles, 1 picot, 2 doubles, 1 picot,
2 doubles, pass the right hand thread through the next picot
from the 2ⁿᵈ row and begin again from *.

Medallion in tatting (fig. 541). — This pretty star can
be used for pincushion covers, sachets, lamp mats, &c. and
may be worked in two colours and with two shuttles.

1ˢᵗ row — with one shuttle filled with light thread: 12
doubles and 6 picots, close the ring.

2ⁿᵈ row — with two shuttles, the dark thread across the left
hand, the light thread in the right hand. Fasten the end of
one thread to a picot of the ring: 2 doubles, 1 long picot,
2 doubles, 1 long picot, pass the right hand thread through
the next picot of the ring, 2 doubles, 1 picot, 2 doubles, and
so on. After the 12ᵗʰ picot fasten off the threads.

3ᵈ row — with one shuttle filled with the light thread:
* 3 doubles, put the thread through one picot of the 2ⁿᵈ row,
make 3 doubles, close the ring = turn the work = leave ¼ in.
of thread = 4 doubles, 1 picot, 4 doubles, close the ring =
turn the work = leave ¼ in. of thread again and repeat
11 times from *.

4ᵗʰ row — with two shuttles, the dark thread over the left
hand, the light one in the right = fasten one end of thread
to one of the picots of one of the 12 rings of the 3ᵈ row,
* 3 doubles, 1 picot, 3 doubles = with one shuttle filled with
dark thread: 3 doubles, put the thread through the dark
picot, 3 doubles, 1 picot, 3 doubles, 1 picot, 3 doubles, close
the ring = 3 doubles, fasten the thread to the 2ⁿᵈ picot of the
1ˢᵗ ring, 3 doubles, 1 picot, 3 doubles, close the ring =
3 doubles, fasten the thread to the picot of the 2ⁿᵈ ring,
3 doubles, 1 picot, 3 doubles, 1 picot, 3 doubles, close the
ring = continue with two shuttles: 3 doubles, put the thread
through the second picot of the 3ᵈ ring, 3 doubles, fasten
the right hand thread to the picot of the ring of the 3ᵈ row
and repeat 11 times from * and connect the rings by empty
picots.

5th row — with two shuttles and the light thread over the left hand, the dark in the right: fasten one thread to a picot between two little rings: 6 doubles and 2 picots over each of the lower rings and 10 doubles and 4 picots over the upper rings.

Fig. 541. Medallion in tatting.
Materials: D.M.C Knotting cotton No. 30, D.M.C Alsatia No. 20, D.M.C Flax thread for knitting No. 12 or D.M.C Pearl cotton No. 5, in Golden yellow 781 and Scabious violet 395, or in Geranium red 352 and Cachou brown 434. (*)

Pattern for bed spread in tatting and crochet (fig. 542.) — This pattern which resembles old lace is composed of big

(*) See at the end of the last chapter the tables of the sizes and colours of the cotton, flax and silk articles, mark D.M.C.

stars with raised centres in tatting, connected by little ones in crochet. The border is joined on to the foundation by a crochet braid edged with two rows of little tatted rings forming raised edges.

Octagon star — Small rings to be made with one shuttle and in the coarse thread: 1 double, 1 picot, 2 doubles, 1 picot, 2 doubles, 1 picot, 2 doubles, 1 picot, 2 doubles, 1 picot, 2 doubles, 1 picot, 2 doubles, 1 picot, 2 doubles, 1 picot, 1 double, close the ring and fasten off the threads.

Begin by making the 16 little inside rings of the star, then outside these 8 times 3 rings, to form the eight points. For the order in which these rings are to be connected, see the engraving.

For the centre of the star which is worked in relief, make 11 little rings as follows. With one shuttle: * 3 doubles, 1 picot, 3 doubles, 1 picot, 3 doubles, 1 picot, 3 doubles, close the ring; repeat 10 times from * and leave $\frac{1}{8}$ in. of thread between the rings.

Crochet bars made with the coarse thread — on the empty length of thread before the first ring: 1 plain, 1 plain on the thread between the 1st and 2nd rings, 1 plain between the 2nd and 3d, 1 plain between the 3d and 4th, 1 plain between the 4th and 5th and 1 between the 5th and 6th, these 2 plain stitches are to be set on the plain stitch that precedes the 1st ring; 1 plain between the 6th and 7th and 1 between the 7th and 8th, these 2 plain stitches are to be set on the plain stitch between the 1st and 2nd rings; 1 plain between the 8th and 9th and 1 between the 9th and 10th, these 2 plain stitches are to be set on the plain stitch between the 2nd and 3d rings; 1 plain between the 10th and 11th rings and 1 plain on the thread that follows the 11th ring, these 2 plain stitches are to be set on the plain stitch between the 3d and 4th rings, 1 single on the next stitch, 10 chain, fasten them to the empty picot of a little ring between two points, skip the first chain stitch, 9 single, 1 plain on the next plain, * * 10 chain, fasten them to the empty picot of the 2nd ring following, skip the first chain stitch, 9 single, 1 plain on the next plain stitch; repeat 6 times from * *, finish with 1 single. Fasten off the thread. The isolated stars are connected by picots as shewn in the engraving.

Little stars in crochet in the fine thread — 5 chain, close the ring.

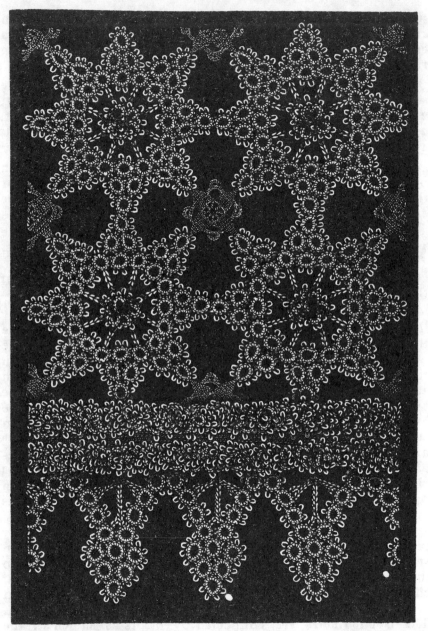

Fig. 542. Pattern for bed spread in tatting and crochet.

Materials — For the tatting: D.M.C Knotting cotton, D.M.C Crochet cotton 6 cord,
D.M.C Flax thread for knitting or D.M.C Pearl cotton. — For the crochet:
D.M.C Knotting cotton and D.M.C Alsatian thread, D.M.C Crochet cotton 6 cord,
D.M.C Flax thread for knitting or D.M.C Pearl cotton, in white or écru.

1st row — 5 chain, * * * 1 treble on the ring, 2 chain; repeat 6 times from * * *, 1 single on the 3d of the 5 chain.

2nd row — 1 chain, 2 plain on the same stitch the single stitch is on, 3 plain on the 2 chain, 1 plain on the treble, 5 plain on the 2 chain, * * * * 3 plain on the treble, 3 plain on the 2 chain, 1 plain on the treble, 3 plain on the 2 chain; repeat twice from * * * *, 1 single on the chain stitch and 1 single on the first plain.

3d row — 9 plain = turn the work = skip 1, 8 plain = turn the work = skip 1, 7 plain = turn the work = skip 1, 6 plain = turn the work = skip 1, 5 plain = turn the work = skip 1, 4 plain = turn the work = skip 1, 3 plain = turn the work = skip 1, 2 plain = turn the work = skip 1, 1 plain, join this little pyramid to an empty point of the big star between the middle picots and fasten off the thread.

Work the other three little pyramids in the same way; the bars that connect them are to be begun after the second row of plain stitches, therefore, after the 8 plain, make 7 chain, join them to the finished pyramid, on the 7 chain: 8 plain, 6 chain, join them on the right to the 4th plain, on the 6 chain: 8 plain and 4 plain on the 7 chain, then finish the pyramid like the first.

The edging is also formed of little rings in tatting; each point requires fourteen which are connected by the picots in the order shewn in the engraving.

The crochet bars, worked in the coarse thread are begun on the wrong side of the work: * * * * * 1 plain on the 3d empty picot of the first ring of the point counting from left to right, 3 chain, 1 plain on the next picot, 20 chain = turn the work = join them to the first picot of the next ring, 1 single on the 2nd chain, 2 chain, join them to the next picot, 1 single on the 2nd chain, 5 single, 13 chain, join them to the empty picot of the second ring following, 1 single on the 2nd chain, 2 chain, join them to the empty picot of the next ring, 1 single on the 2nd chain, 11 single, 7 chain, join them to the first empty picot of the second ring following, 1 single on the 2nd chain, 2 chain, join them to the next picot, 1 single on the 2nd chain, 5 single, then 4 more single, 9 chain = turn the work = 1 plain on the 2nd empty picot of the next ring, 3 chain, 1 plain on the next picot, 2 chain and repeat from * * * * *.

The braid that connects the edging with the foundation is worked separately in the coarse thread.

Begin with 8 rows ot plain stitches to which you add the raised border. This consists of little tatted rings, like those inside the big stars, which we described above; add them to the 8 rows of plain stitches by a ninth and tenth row in which you take 1 tatted ring in each plain stitch. A row of trebles divided by 2 chain stitches completes the braid on both sides. The foundation and the edging are sewn on to the braid by overcast stitches.

We refer those who wish to simplify the work to figure 443, which represents a pattern for a bed spread in which the stars are joined together by squares of linen which in the pattern just described might take the place of the crochet squares.

Patterns of needlework. — Besides the different kinds of work described above a choice of patterns for tatting will be found in the publication: *Works of various kinds*, of the D.M.C Library. (*)

(*) See at the end of the volume the list of the albums of the D.M.C Library.

Macramé stripe — Pattern composed of bars, flat knots and shell knots.

Macramé

Macramé is an Arabic word signifying an ornamental fringe or trimming which has been adopted as the term for a certain kind of hand work, produced by the knotting, plaiting and tying together of threads; it is also known by the name of knotted fringe.

We have given the preference to the Arabic term, because it has a more comprehensive meaning, seeing that not only fringes and scallops but stripes, gimps, squares and wheels can be made in macramé.

Until its revival about twenty years ago, save here and there in convents, it was an almost forgotten art which accounts for its having been first regarded as a new invention The variety of uses to which it can be applied, its great durability and strength, make it well worthy of notice in the present work. The difficulties likely to repel many at first sight are soon overcome if the instructions given in the following pages are carefully observed and a little practice will soon enable a worker to copy the charming designs that accompany them and produce results, some of them recalling the wooden lattices in the windows of Eastern dwellings familiar to many no doubt under the name of "moucharabieh".

Cushions and other requisites for macramé (figs. 543 and 544). — The only really important requisite for macramé is a plain well stuffed cushion, mounted on wood. (See fig. 543).

It should be made so that it can be screwed to a table like the Swiss tambour frames.

There are other kinds of macramé cushions, but we have

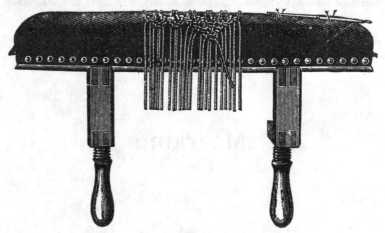

Fig. 543. Macramé cushion.

not found them very practical; some make the constant friction of the fingers against the little board that replaces the cushion, unavoidable; others are not heavy enough to withstand the rapid movements necessarily made as soon as a certain skill

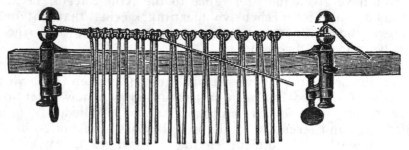

Fig. 544. Clamps for macramé.

has been acquired. The cushion shewn in figure 543 will serve for every kind of macramé work and patterns that require a heading or a border of picots cannot be worked on any other.

The pegs with rounded heads at the ends of the cushion are for fixing and winding the long threads upon which carry the knots and which we shall call "cords" in future.

For pieces of work of any considerable size, for long lengths of fringe, for example, the cushion is far less practical than the metal clamps with round headed pegs attached to them top and bottom, represented in figure 544, which admit of any number of loops being knotted on to the cords at a time because they can be moved nearer or further apart as desired.

Fig. 545.
Knotting threads on to a cord.

Besides the cushion and the clamps you must have some big glass headed pins, made expressly for the purpose of fixing

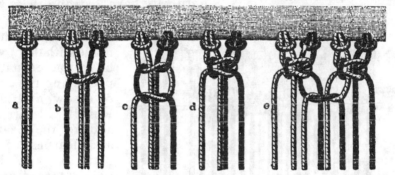

Fig. 546. Knotting on threads on to a stuff edge and formation of a flat knot.

the loops and picots; a crochet needle for pulling the threads through the stuff when they have to be knotted on to an edge, scissors and a French metre or yard measure, to measure the threads with. To all these accessories may further be added a metal comb and ruler for equalising and pressing the ends of the fringe.

The length of the threads must depend on their substance and thickness; for a knot will

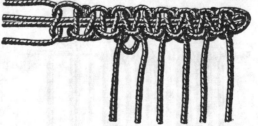

Fig. 547. Knotting threads on to a knotted heading.

use up more of a coarse stiff thread than of a fine soft one, on which account the right length, kind, number of threads to be used are given with each pattern. If for any reason the

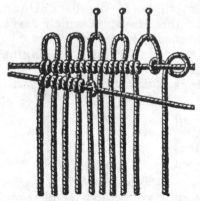

Fig. 548. Knotting on threads with plain picots.

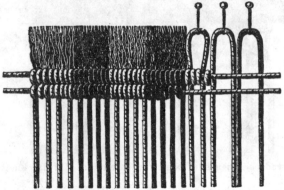

Fig. 549. Knotting on threads with a fringe heading.

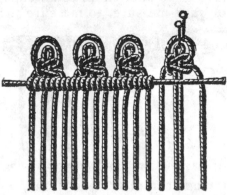

Fig. 550. Knotting on threads with picots and flat knots.

materials indicated should not be taken, the worker must bear in mind that the coarser and stiffer the thread the more must be allowed for the knots, and vice versâ.

This will prevent the necessity of a preliminary trial which generally means lost time, before definitely beginning the work.

Materials. — Macramé consisting almost entirely of knots, requires very stout tough threads, which will not break in the working. Such threads will naturally have a strong twist and consequently be very round; the knots made with them will be very accentuated, producing the effect of a row of beads, which will greatly add to the beauty and clearness of the patterns. A less twisted thread, being softer and looser would fray in the handling and the work when finished would present an unsatisfactory fluffy appearance.

For fringes and braids in several colours for trimming upholstery, curtains, &c. the best cotton material to select is D.M.C Knotting cotton (Fil à pointer). A good substitute for silk is D.M.C Pearl cotton (Coton perlé), made in more than 3oo shades, in Nos. 1, 3, 5, 8 and 12, or D.M.C Alsatia. For trimming table and household linen, the thread should always match the stuff; if the article be embroidered, a little colour may be introduced in the macramé; but we should advise as little colour as possible. As to the kind of thread, we recommend D.M.C

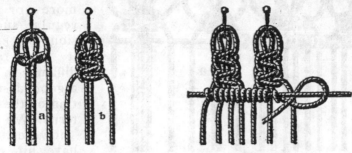

Fig. 551.   Fig. 552.
Knotting on threads with picots and two flat knots.

Flax thread for knitting (Lin pour tricoter), D.M.C Crochet cotton 6 cord (Cordonnet 6 fils) and D.M.C Special crochet cotton (Cordonnet spécial), in the coarse numbers. (*)

Formation of the knots. — Beginners should be careful in macramé as in tatting to keep the threads, which according

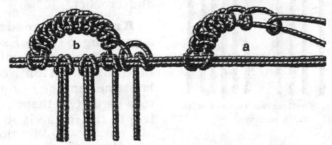

Fig. 553. Knotting on threads with scallops.

to our description, carry the knots, perfectly motionless. These threads, as has already been said, will in future always be called cords, whilst the thread with which the knots are made will be called the "knotting thread".

These two threads often change places; now the "knotting thread" becomes the "cord", now the cord becomes the "knotting thread". The interlacing of the thread which forms the knot is a kind of loop which is drawn tightly over a thread.

(*) See at the end of the last chapter the tables of the sizes and colours of the cotton, flax and silk articles, mark D.M.C. — The French names, in brackets, are those stamped on the labels of the D.M.C articles.

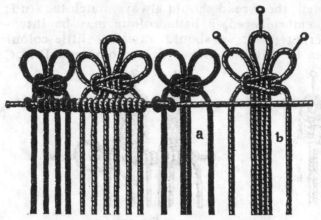

Fig. 554. Knotting on threads with loops.

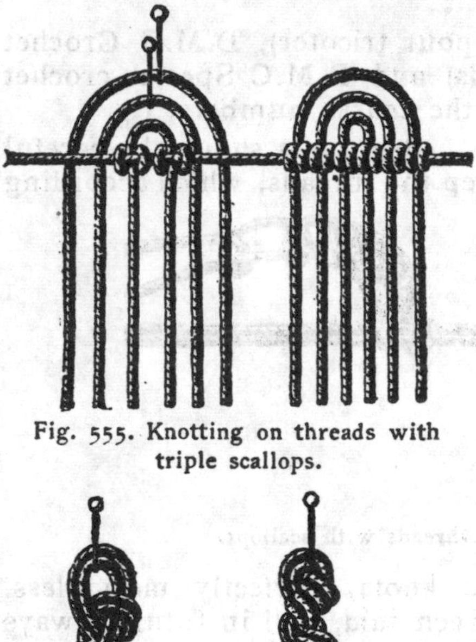

Explanation of the pattern. As macramé consists of a more or less regular succession of knots, it was rather difficult to give a good description of the patterns. We hope however, to have hit on a good way of explaining the course to follow for the crossings of the threads and the changing of the colours by proceeding by "series of knots" instead of by rows as for knitting and crochet.

Fig. 555. Knotting on threads with triple scallops.

Knotting threads on to a cord (fig. 545). — Excepting when you work with the ravellings of a stuff, you must knot the lengths of thread on to a cord. Cut them twice the length the fringe is to be and fold them in half; the loop thus produced serves to fasten them round the "cord" which forms the heading of the fringe. Put the loop over the cord from behind, downwards from above, put the ends through

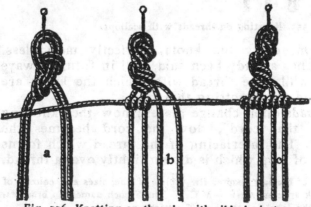

Fig. 556. Knotting on threads with ribbed picots.

the loop and draw the knot tight, as shewn in the engraving where the first detail, letter *a*, shews the loop open, the second detail, letter *b*, the loop shut.

Knotting on threads on to an edge of stuff and formation of a flat knot (fig. 546). — Push your crochet needle out through the edge of the stuff from beneath, catch hold of the loop produced by folding the thread in half, draw it to the wrong side of the edge and put the ends through the loop, *a;* place, in this manner two threads folded in half rather near one another and make the first interlacing of the threads for

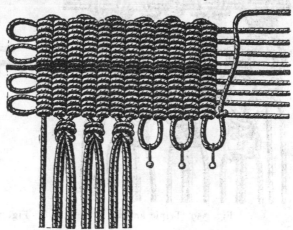

Fig. 557. Knotting on threads to form a gimp heading.

the flat knot. Then take the two outer threads of the four hanging down and pass the right thread under and the left one over the two middle threads. Whilst making this movement to cross the outer threads, hold the two inner threads tightly extended with the 3ᵈ and 4ᵗʰ fingers of the left hand, letter *b*. The return of the two crossed threads is accomplished as shewn in the 3ᵈ detail, *c;* then tighten the thread and the flat knot is made as shewn in the 4ᵗʰ detail, *d.* In the 5ᵗʰ detail, *e*, two flat knots are shewn, finished; this detail shews too how you pass to a third knot for which you connect two right threads with two left ones.

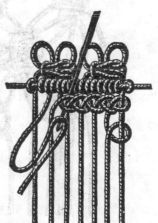

Fig. 558. Plaited knot.

Knotting threads on to a knotted heading (fig. 547). — Make a string of flat knots, fig. 546, detail *d,* on a double cord and knot on your threads on to the loops of the double knots putting the loop through from the right side so that it lies at the wrong side.

It is best in this case to knot on double threads so that the braid beneath the heading may not be too open.

Knotting on threads with plain picots (fig. 548). — Fasten the lengths of thread on to the cushion with pins

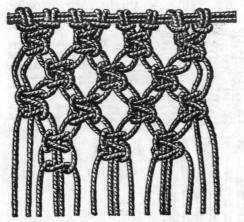

Fig. 559. Triple knots.

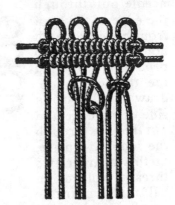

Fig. 560. Small collecting knot.

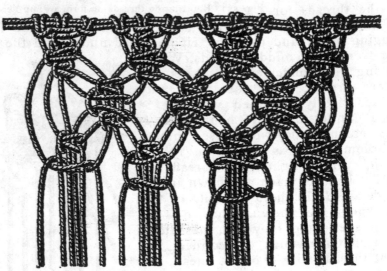

Fig. 561. Big collecting knot.

about ¼ in., or at most ½, apart: fix the cord to one of the pegs on the left and hold it tightly stretched with the right hand in a horizontal line. Make the knots with the left hand, take each end of the threads held by the pins, singly

and pass it twice, upwards from below, over the cord. The
first time the thread stops on the left, the second time it
passes likewise from right to left, so that when the second
passage is accomplished, the thread is held between two loops
or knots which form again the "double knot". (See fig. 548
this double interlacing.)

One series of knots forms a bar. The second bar is like
the first. Hold the cord as close to the first bar as possible so
that the vertical threads may not be visible between; the two
bars may be horizontal, vertical or oblique as will be
subsequently seen.

Knotting on threads with a fringe heading (fig. 549). —
After knotting on the threads with a picot heading according

to the foregoing
directions, cut the
loops and unravel
and comb out the
ends. The stronger
the twist of the
thread the richer
and fuller will be
the fringe.

**Knotting on
threads with
picots and flat
knots** (fig. 550). —
Pin two threads on
as before very close
together, make a
flat knot, fig. 546,
tying the outside

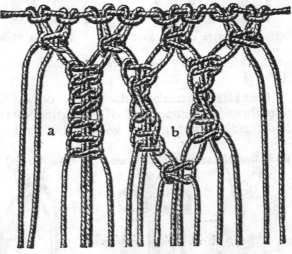

Fig. 562. Plaited and waved knots.

threads over the inside ones, and loop the ends over a cord
to make a bar of knots.

Knotting on threads with picots and two flat knots
(figs. 551 and 552). — Pin the two threads on as above, make
first one flat knot and then another. Note figure 551; the detail
letter *a* shews the beginning of the knot, detail *b* the picot
with two knots beneath. Figure 552 shews the picots secured
by a horizontal bar of knots beneath them.

Knotting on threads with scallops (fig. 553). — For
scallops the threads must be cut much longer than those that
are to be knotted on in the middle of the scallops. The knots

ot the scallops must turn outwards, and 12 knots are made
with the left hand thread over the right one, letter *a*, then
knot on two double threads under the scallop and, finally,

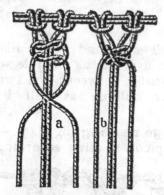

Fig. 563. Single crossed knot.

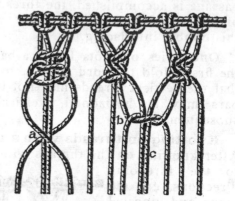

Fig. 564. Double crossed knot.

make knots with the threads that come from the scallops,
detail *b*.

Knotting on threads with loops (fig. 554). — Pin on
two threads, folded in half, a little distance apart, detail *a*,
and bind them together with a flat knot. Pin on three more

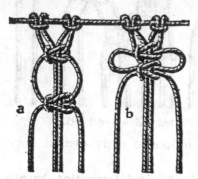

Fig. 565. Looped picot.

Fig. 566. Knotted picot.

threads quite close to them and unite them by a big "collecting
knot", fig. 561, made over 4 threads. A big "collecting knot"
is a flat knot, made over more than two threads. The rest ot
the knotting on is done in the usual way.

Knotting on threads with triple scallops (fig. 555). —
Knot on three single threads in succession: first the middle
one; then the second one with the knot to the right and left

and the loop long enough to form the scallop, then the third in the same way.

Knotting on threads with ribbed picots (fig. 556). — Take a double thread and make two bars of knots, as in

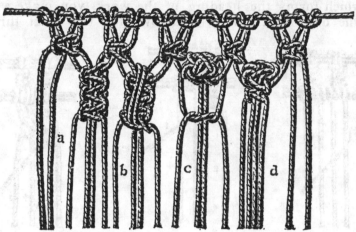

Fig. 567. Knot with beads or small shell knots.

detail *a*, then finish and secure the picots by a horizontal bar, as shewn in *b* and *c*.

Knotting on threads to form a gimp heading (fig. 557). — This way of knotting on makes a broad gimp, consisting entirely of vertical bars made over a single cord.

Along one edge of the gimp this cord forms picots which are fixed with pins. When the gimp is finished meshes of thread can be knotted on to these picots for making either a fringe or a macramé grounding.

Plaited knot (fig. 558). — This knot occurs chiefly in Italian and Slavonic work where it replaces the horizontal bars of knots. As figure 558 shews, the row of knots is begun with the second thread on the right with which a loop is formed on the first thread. The third

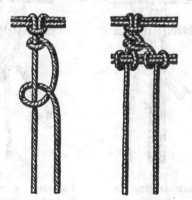

Fig. 568.
Button-holeloop
to the right.

Fig. 569.
Fastening the threads
to the cord.

thread is then crossed in front of the second and drawn out with a crochet needle behind the first loop that was tightened.

Triple knots (fig. 559). — These are flat knots followed by a third half knot, in other words, the first half of a flat knot.

Small collecting knot (fig. 560). — This is a knot which connects several threads together. Having finished the double bar which forms the heading of the work, you make a knot with the first right hand thread over the two next threads.

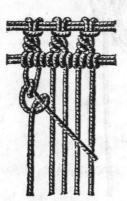
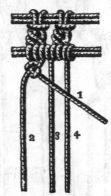
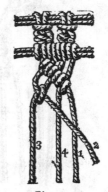

Fig. 570.
Bar slanting to
the right.
First knot open.

Fig. 571.
Bar slanting to the right.
Thread 2 knotted
over thread 1.

Fig. 572.
Bar slanting to the right.
Threads 3, 4 and 1 to be
knotted over thread 2.

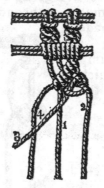
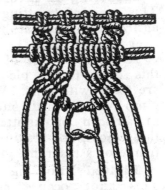

Fig. 573.
Bar slanting to
the left.
First knot open.

Fig. 574.
Bar slanting to the left.
Threads 2, 1 and 4 to be
knotted over thread 3.

Fig. 575.
Bars connected
by a
flat knot.

For this purpose you make a loop with the right hand thread, cross it over two threads, then under these same threads into the loop and draw it up carrying the knot behind so as only to have a single thread in front.

Big collecting knot (fig. 561). — As was already said in the description relating to figure 554, flat knots which unite more than two threads are called big collecting knots. The engraving shews, first, the flat knot made over two threads, finished, and the first crossing of the threads for the collecting knot: the next detail shews the second crossing of the threads; the third, how the collecting knots may be continued, as desired, over 4 threads, and the fourth how the big collecting knot is generally made to finish with a flat knot.

Plaited and waved knots (fig. 562). — Plaited knots are formed by an unbroken continuance of the first intercrossing of the threads of the flat knot, detail *a,* waved knots by a slight twist of the knots from left to right, detail *b.*

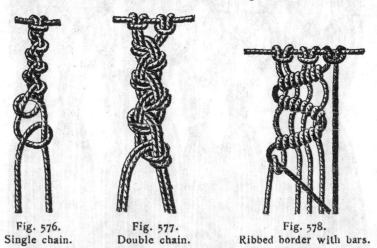

Fig. 576.
Single chain.

Fig. 577.
Double chain.

Fig. 578.
Ribbed border with bars.

The plaits of these waved knots are fixed by joining the threads of opposite clusters together, two and two, by a flat knot.

Single crossed and double crossed knots (figs. 563 and 564). — Two plain crossings of the threads, letter *a,* to begin with, after which you rapidly turn the knot to the wrong side, whilst, at the same time, drawing it up tightly, thus the first knot is formed, which detail *b* shews completed.

The second knot, fig. 564, is formed by 3 plain crossings, letter *a,* after which you rapidly reverse the threads to form the knots, letter *b.* To make a series of these knots you must always reverse the order of the threads after each completed knot, as the third detail, letter *c,* shews.

Looped picot (fig. 565). — Looped picots are made along a plait of flat knots placed a little distance apart, so that the thread between the knots forms a picot when they are pushed close together. Figure 565, letter *a*, shews a picot begun, letter *b*, one finished.

Knotted picot (fig. 566). — Knotted picots are formed after one or more flat knots. The picot is produced by a knot

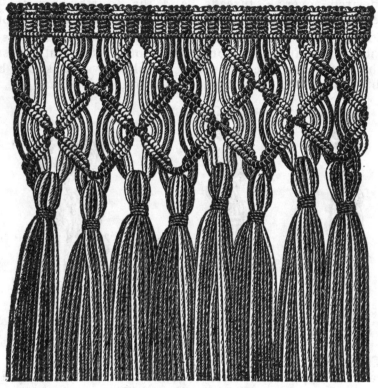

Fig. 579. Macramé fringe.
Materials: D.M.C Knotting cotton Nos. 10 to 30, D.M.C Crochet cotton 6 cord Nos. 1 to 30, D.M.C Alsatia Nos. 20 and 25, D.M.C Pearl cotton Nos. 1 to 8, D.M.C Flax thread for knitting Nos. 3 to 20, in Indigo blue 311, Turkish red 321 and white. (*)

made with the outside thread; this knot is placed quite close to the flat knot. In order to get it as near as possible to the latter, stick a big pin into the loop and with that push it into

(*) These numbers refer to the colours on the colour cards of the articles stamped with the D.M.C trade mark. These cards can be consulted at all the mercers' and needlework shops.

its place and leave the pin there until the knot is made. These picots are always made along both sides and can be repeated several times along a string of knots. Letter *a* shews the crossing of the threads for the picots, letter *b* the picots finished and followed by a flat knot.

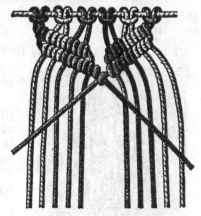

Knot with beads or small shell knots (fig. 567). — These are made by turning the threads back over a series of flat knots already completed. Detail *a* shews 3 flat knots finished, detail *b*, how to turn the inside threads back over the knots and between the threads; detail *c* shews that the threads which served to make the knots are brought between the two threads coming from

Fig. 580. Detail of figure 579.

the left and right and form the first interlacing of a flat knot; detail *d* shews the bead knot finished and followed by a flat knot.

Bars of knots to the right and left (figs. 568, 569, 570, 571, 572, 573, 574, 575). — After knotting on a sufficient number of threads on to a double cord, make a 2 button-hole loops with the right hand thread round the left one, fig. 568.

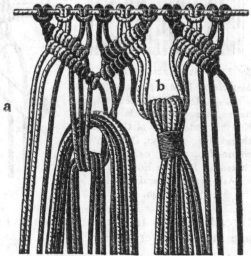

It is advisable to finish a series of knots throughout the whole length required, before passing to another; the work becomes more regular because the hand

Fig. 581. Detail of figure 579.

gets accustomed to the kind of jerk required for making the knot, and by continued practise greater quickness is attained.

Then make a straight bar by knotting each thread twice over the cord, fig. 569; these knots should be as close together as possible.

When this bar is finished, begin the oblique bars, slanting from left to right with 4 threads, fig. 570.

The first thread on the left, marked by 1 in figure 571, serves as cord for threads 2, 3, 4, which you loop successively over thread 1.

Figure 572 represents threads 2, 3, 4 knotted over thread 1

and shews, besides how in the second row of the bar, thread 2 becomes a cord and replaces thread 1, and how threads 3, 4, 1, are thrown and knotted twice over thread 2, which must be held tightly stretched in the right hand. The knots are made with the left hand.

In figure 573 representing a bar, inclined from right to left, the threads 3, 2, 1 are knotted over

Fig. 582. Macramé fringe.

Materials : D.M.C Knotting cotton No. 30, D.M.C Crochet cotton 6 cord, Nos. 1 to 10, D.M.C Alsatia Nos. 20 and 25, D.M.C Alsatian thread Nos. 30 to 50, D.M.C Pearl cotton Nos. 3 to 8, or D.M.C Flax thread for knitting Nos. 3 to 16, in Ash grey 415 and Cardinal red 346.

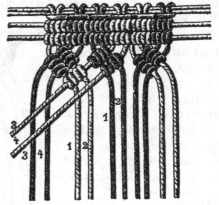

Fig. 583. Detail of figure 582.

thread 4; then in the second row, fig. 574, the threads 2, 1, 4 are knotted over thread 3.

Here it is the left hand that holds the thread extended from right to left and the right hand that makes the knots. Figure 575 explains how the double bars are joined together by a flat knot.

Single chain (fig. 576). — In macramé the single chain, made with two single threads, is produced by constantly reversing the position of the threads and by the direction given them whilst the knots are being made, in other words, by knotting them alternately over each other, that is, each in turn serving as cord for the other.

Double chain (fig. 577). — The double chain is made in the same way as the single, only with two and sometimes even with three threads. These two kinds of chains are generally used in macramé gimps and braids and are a means of passing from one colour to another or of conducting the threads from one part of the work to another, to carry on the pattern, which could not be done in any other way.

Ribbed border with bars (fig. 578). — Here contrary to the way the bars of knots, described in figures 570 to 575, are made, the same cord runs to and fro under the 4 knotting threads.

In order to distinguish the knotting threads from the cord more easily, the latter is represented in the figure in a darker shade.

Macramé fringe (figs. 579, 580, 581). — Entire

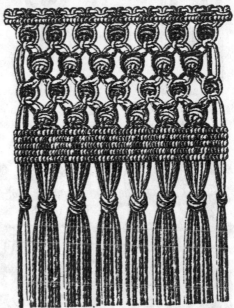

Fig. 584.
Fringe with mosaic border and shell knots.

Materials: D.M.C Knotting cotton No. 30, D.M.C Crochet cotton 6 cord or D.M.C Special crochet cotton Nos. 10 to 30, D.M.C Alsatia No. 20 or D.M.C Pearl cotton Nos. 1 to 8, in Mahogany brown 401, Cardinal red 347 and écru. (*)

length of the threads for No. 3 of D.M.C Pearl cotton (Coton perlé): 32 in.

1st series — knot the threads on, as shewn in figure 545, and in the following order: 1 double blue thread, 1 double white, 1 double red, and so on.

2nd series — make a horizontal bar of knots, figs. 548, 549, 550, over a second cord.

(*) See at the end of the last chapter the tables of the sizes and colours of the cotton, flax and silk articles, mark D.M.C.

Fig. 585. Knot open.
Detail of figure 584.

Fig. 586. Knot closed.
Detail of figure 584.

3ᵈ series — 3 button-hole knots, fig. 568, executed each with two threads.

4ᵗʰ series — the same as the 2ⁿᵈ.

5ᵗʰ series — make slanting bars of double knots to the right and left, counting 6 threads for each bar, therefore 12 threads in all. The 1ˢᵗ and 12ᵗʰ thread are covered with knots with the 10 threads that separate them. In the 2ⁿᵈ series of knots which forms the double bar make another double knot over the cord with the thread that served as cord in the preceding row.

When the slanting bars are finished, bring them as close together as possible, tighten the last thread on the right and make another double knot with the left thread; the position of all the threads is clearly described in figure 580. Then continue the bars in the opposite direction, so that the cord on the left is stretched over the right hand group of threads, and the cord on the right over the left hand group.

Fig. 587. Macramé fringe.
Materials : D.M.C Special crochet cotton Nos. 3 to 15,
D.M.C Knotting cotton No. 30
or D.M.C Alsatia No. 15, in Geranium red 352,
Golden yellow 781 or Scabious violet 396.

Make 3 rows of double bars and then take always 3 threads of a left hand group and 3 of a right hand one, tie them loosely together in a plain knot, put in, above the knot, a bunch of 8 threads, 6 in. long, fig. 581, detail *a*, draw up the

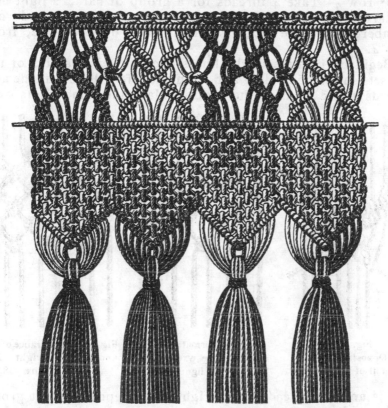

Fig. 588. Fringe with foundation, worked on the wrong side.
Materials: D.M.C Knotting cotton No. 30, D.M.C Crochet cotton 6 cord Nos. 5 to 25, D.M.C Pearl cotton Nos. 1 to 8 or D.M.C Alsatian thread Nos. 30 to 50, in Indigo blue 312 and Azure blue 3325. (*)

knot close to the bars and wind thread of a different colour several times round it, detail *b*, to form the tassel.

Macramé fringe (figs. 582 and 583). — Entire length of the threads for No. 30 of D.M.C Knotting cotton (Fil à pointer) 26 in., including the fringe.

(*) See at the end of the last chapter the tables of the sizes and colours of the cotton, flax and silk articles, mark D.M.C.

1st row — knot on the threads as in figure 545, 1 light thread, 2 dark, 2 light, 2 dark, and so on, finish with 1 light thread.

2nd row — 1 double horizontal bar of knots, over double cords.

3[d] row — Take 4 threads for a group of bars; 2 light and 2 dark ones on each side; the two sets of threads are numbered in figure 583, a working detail of figure 582, from 1 to 4.

Begin by making all the knots over threads 1 and 2 of the left set, so that threads 3 and 4 on the left will be outside and threads 1 and 2 inside the group. Make the same knots over

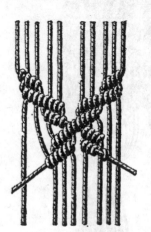 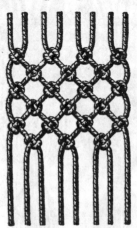 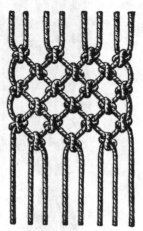

Fig. 589.	Fig 590. Formation of the	Fig. 591. Appearance of the
Opposing bars.	knots on the wrong side.	knots on the right side.
Detail of figure 588.	Detail of figure 588.	Detail of figure 588.

the 3[d] and 4th thread on the right, then repeat the left group again, and so on.

Repeat from the beginning, and make 2 double knots over thread 3 on the right, fig. 583, with threads 1 and 2 on the left, then again 2 knots over thread 4 on the right. These are again followed by a row of dark bars, and so on; make in all 6 rows of dark and 5 rows of light bars, the lower end is finished by a double horizontal bar of knots.

If you wish to use this pattern as a gimp, fasten off the threads by means of knots of which an explanation is given in figure 609.

Fringe with mosaic border and shell knots (figs. 584, 585, 586). — Entire length of threads for No. 30 of D.M.C Knotting cotton (Fil à pointer): 36 in.

1st series — knot on an écru and a brown thread, as in figure 545, beginning and ending with a single écru thread, followed by a single bar of double knots.

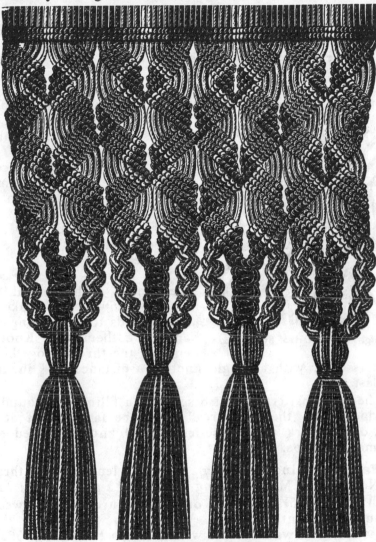

Fig. 592. Macramé fringe.
Materials: D.M.C Crochet cotton 6 cord Nos. 3 to 25,
D.M.C Pearl cotton Nos. 3 to 5 or D.M.C Knotting cotton No. 30, in Locust-bean brown 357 and 355 and Blue fast dye 796. (*)

(*) See at the end of the last chapter the tables of the sizes and colours of the cotton, flax and silk articles, mark D.M.C.

2nd to the 5th series — 4 rows of knots, such as are shewn on an enlarged scale in the making, in figure 585, and in figure 586, closed, and preceded and followed by a flat knot.

The colours alternate in the shell knots; in the 2nd and 4th series, the shell knots are framed by the light thread, in the 3^d and 5th by the dark.

6th series — 1 horizontal bar of double knots on a fresh cord.

7th series — add another cord, make another horizontal bar of knots and between every two double light knots loop on

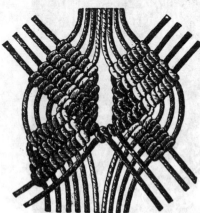

Fig. 593. Detail of figure 592.

one red thread, the loop that fastens it to the cord, taking the place of the knot.

8th series — add a 3^d cord, and with the red threads make 2 double knots between the écru knots.

9th series — add a 4th cord, make a half-knot with every red thread.

10th series — add a 5th cord, then make 1 horizontal bar, as in the 6th series; take the red threads to the wrong side and leave them out. Knot the ends of the threads together in clusters of 6, with a single knot at a distance of $\frac{5}{8}$ in. from the last bar.

The same pattern can also serve as a filling or grounding, in which case, the red thread, must be fastened off at the back of the work and the series of shell knots repeated after the mosaic stripe.

Macramé fringe (fig. 587). — Entire length of the threads for No. 3o of D.M.C Knotting cotton (Fil à pointer) (*): 32 in.

1st series — first knotting on, as in figure 556, followed by a double horizontal bar.

2nd series — waved knots with 4 single twists, fig. 562.

3^d series — double horizontal bar.

4th series — with 6 threads: 1 double oblique bar from

(*) See at the end of the last chapter the tables of the sizes and colours of the cotton, flax and silk articles, mark D.M.C. — The French names, in brackets, are those stamped on the labels of the D.M.C articles.

left to right, 1 bar from right to left and connect them
together by the last threads.

5th series — with the 4 threads coming from the groups of
bars; 1 single chain, fig. 576, with 4 crossings of the threads,

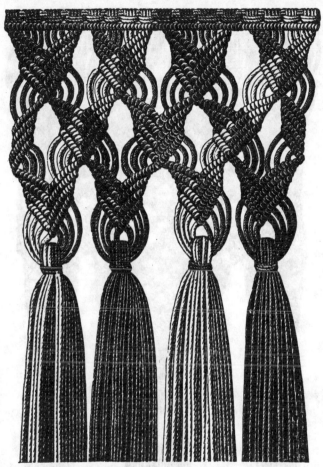

Fig. 594. Macramé fringe.
Materials: D.M.C Knotting cotton No. 30, D.M.C Alsatia No. 20 or D.M.C Pearl
cotton Nos. 3 to 5, in Cream yellow 711, Rust yellow 308 and
Rust brown 3314 and 3311. (*)

quite close to the point where the groups meet and 1 single
chain with 7 crossings, made with the 2 outside threads.

(*) See at the end of the last chapter the tables of the sizes and colours of
the cotton, flax and silk articles, mark D.M.C.

6th series — similar groups of bars to those of the 4th series, but set the reverse way and terminating with a single horizontal bar. For the tassels, add a thick bunch of threads to each group of 6 threads issuing from the work.

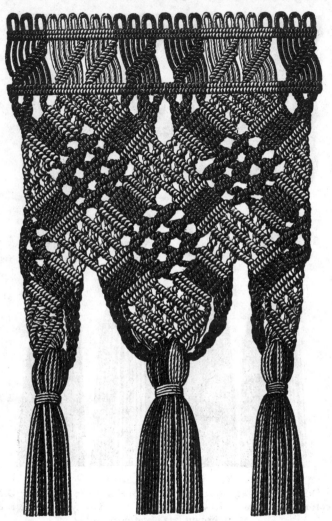

Fig. 595. Macramé fringe.
Materials : D.M.C Knotting cotton No. 30, D.M.C Alsatia No. 20, D.M.C Pearl cotton Nos. 3 to 5 or D.M.C Flax thread for knitting Nos. 3 to 12, in Cream yellow 711 and Beetle green 3346. (*)

(*) See at the end of the last chapter the tables of the sizes and colours of the cotton, flax and silk articles, mark D.M.C.

Fringe with foundation, worked on the wrong side (*)
(figs. 588, 589, 590, 591). — Entire length of threads for No. 30
of D.M.C Knotting cotton (Fil à pointer): 40 in.

Begin by knotting on in the ordinary way with 5 light
blue threads and 5 dark blue and then make, after the
horizontal bar, and from left to right: on the 1st thread a
double knot with the 2nd, and a double knot with the 3d thread.

Then, over the 2nd thread which has become the 1st, make
double knots with the four next threads; then missing 2 of
the threads on the left, make 2 double knots over the 3 with
the 2 following threads.

Make a similar group from right to left, and downwards,
only at the centre of the figure, at the 3d change of thread
make 5 double knots instead of 2 and let the last knots
count for the new bottom
group of bars, set contrariwise, see fig. 589.

Between two of these
groups of contrary bars make
a flat knot with 2 right hand
and 2 left hand threads.

When the second hori-
zontal bar is finished, turn
the work and continue
working on the wrong side,
making then only plain
double knots, inclining
alternately one row from
right to left, the next from
left to right, as shewn in
figure 590.

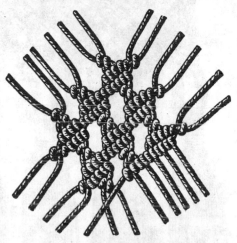

Fig. 596. Detail of figure 595.

When 10 such rows are finished, divide the knots into
groups and make one knot less on each side of a group, to
form the pointed scallops; then turn the work round again
to the right side, where the knots made on the wrong side,
present the appearance shewn in figure 591; finally finish off
the scallops with a plain bar all round, and make the tassels
with the ends of thread hanging from each scallop.

Macramé fringe (figs. 592 and 593). — Entire length of
the double threads for D.M.C Knotting cotton (Fil à pointer)
No. 30: 60 in.; length of the single threads: 30 in.

(*) See, at the end of the volume, the list of the albums of the D.M.C Library,
containing a large variety of patterns for all kinds of work.

1st series — knot on, as in figure 549, in the following order: 2 double blue threads, 3 single dark brown threads, 1 double light brown thread, 3 single dark brown threads, then 4 double blue, and so on; ending with 2 double blue.

2nd series — divide the threads into groups, leaving the brown threads in the middle and 4 blue ones on either side. Begin on the left = cover the 4th blue thread, which is the nearest to the first brown one with double knots made with the 1st, 2nd and 3d dark brown thread and the 1st light brown one = cover the 3d blue thread with the 4 brown ones and the 4th blue one which was the cord in the 1st row of knots = cover the 2nd blue thread with the 4 brown and the 4th and 3d blue threads = cover the 1st blue thread with the 4 brown and the 4th, 3d and 2nd blue.

In detail 593 the blue threads are

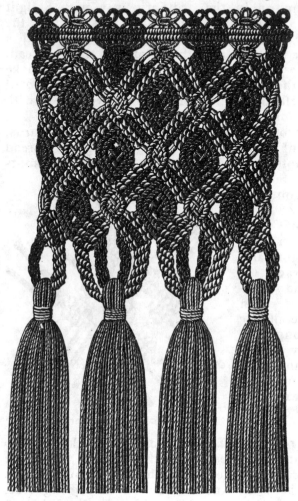

Fig. 597. Macramé fringe.
Materials: D.M.C Knotting cotton No. 30, D.M.C Alsatia No. 20, or D.M.C Pearl cotton No. 3, in Rust yellow 308 and Solid blue 813.

represented by the darkest shade, the brown ones by the medium and light.

When the quadruple bar, slanting from left to right is finished, make a similar bar from right to left, then join them together by a double knot and pass the 1st left hand blue thread under the right hand group and the 1st right hand blue thread under the left group.

2nd series — make similar groups the reverse way, so that the brown knots come next to the last blue ones, and the blue knots again terminate the groups of bars; the brown threads will be stretched between the preceding group and the following one.

3d and 5th series — like the 1st.

4th series — like the 2nd.

After the 5th series of groups, take the 4 brown threads on either side of the blue knots and make them into a double chain, fig. 577, consisting of 12 knots, and make 4 flat knots with the blue threads.

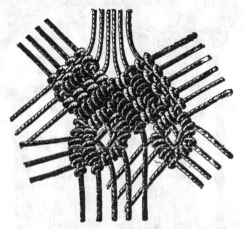

Lastly, unite all the threads of a group of bars and make them into a handsome tassel by the addition of supplementary threads.

Macramé fringe (fig. 594). — Entire length of the threads for No. 30 of D.M.C Knotting cotton (Fil à pointer) (*): 40 in. The knotting on is done with threads taken double,

Fig. 598. Detail of figure 597.

beginning with the darkest shade and ending with the lightest.

The pattern is so easy that we need only refer our readers to figure 575 and 593 for the change and crossing of the threads, merely observing that the bars should be made alternately from right to left and from left to right and that, moreover, the cord coming from the left is only to be covered by 3 threads, whilst the one from the right must always be covered by 4.

Macramé fringe (figs. 595 and 596). — Entire length of the threads for No. 30 of D.M.C Knotting cotton (Fil à pointer): 56 in.

(*) See at the end of the last chapter the tables of the sizes and colours of the cotton, flax and silk articles, mark D.M.C. — The French names, in brackets, are those stamped on the labels of the D.M.C articles.

1ˢᵗ series — knot the threads on with picots with a double horizontal bar, fig. 548, with 6 light and 6 dark threads, begin and end with 3 dark threads.

2ⁿᵈ series — double oblique bars with 6 single threads — followed by a double horizontal bar.

3ᵈ series — begin with the light threads and make bars as in figure 618, but from left to right, therefore reversed, and

Fig. 599. Macramé fringe.

Materials: D.M.C Knotting cotton No. 30, D.M.C Alsatia No. 25, D.M.C Pearl cotton Nos. 3 to 5 or D.M.C Flax thread for knitting Nos. 3 to 12, in Geranium red 352, Cardinal red 346 and écru.

finish them at the sides by 2 long bars of light thread, followed by 6 short bars of dark.

For the lozenges consisting of nine little leaves, see fig. 596.

The light figures in the ends of the scallops are bordered
by the dark threads; and all the threads are collected at the
bottom and with the addition of a supplementary bunch,
made into a tassel.

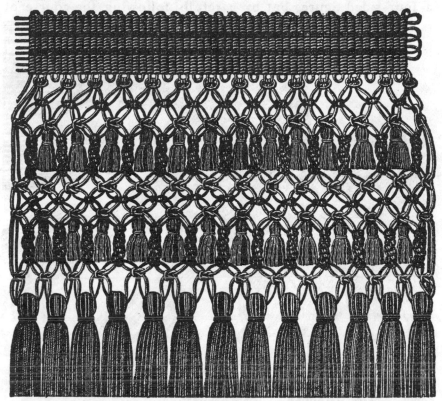

Fig. 600. Fringe with three rows of tassels.
Materials : D.M.C Pearl cotton Nos. 1 to 5, D.M.C Special crochet cotton Nos. 3 to 30,
D.M.C Alsatia No. 20, D.M.C Flax thread for knitting Nos. 3 to 12 or D.M.C
Knotting cotton No. 30, in Indigo blue 312 and écru. (*)

Macramé fringe (figs. 597 and 598). — Entire length or
the threads for No. 30 of D.M.C Knotting cotton (Fil à
pointer) : 68 in.

This effective pattern is not difficult, save in appearance,
so that it is not necessary to describe it in detail. For the
knotting on, see fig. 554, for the plain bars, figs. 570 to 575,
and the collecting knots, fig. 561, are all the indications that

(*) See at the end of the last chapter the tables of the sizes and colours of
the cotton, flax and silk articles, mark D.M.C.

should be required by those who have followed the explanations given in the course of this chapter.

The only point that might present any difficulty is that where the threads cross each other inside the bars and form a four-sided figure, but by carefully following the course of

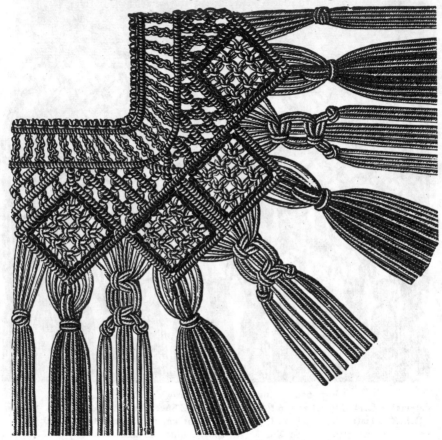

Fig. 601. Macramé fringe with corner.
Materials: D.M.C Knotting cotton No. 30, D.M.C Alsatia No. 20, D.M.C Pearl cotton Nos. 3 to 5 or D.M.C Flax thread for knitting Nos. 3 to 12, in Maize yellow 579 and Garnet red 309. (*)

the knots, illustrated in figure 598, the difficulty will soon be solved.

Tassels made with the two shades of thread finish off the fringe at the bottom.

(*) See at the end of the last chapter the tables of the sizes and colours of the cotton, flax and silk articles, mark D.M.C.

Macramé fringe (fig. 599). — Entire length of the threads for No. 3 of D.M.C Pearl cotton (Coton perlé): 32 in.

1st series — knot on as in figure 545, but in the reverse way, with threads taken double, to count as single in the working directions = * 1 dark red thread, 3 écru, 1 dark red, 1 light red, 3 écru, 1 light red and repeat from *, then make a plain horizontal bar.

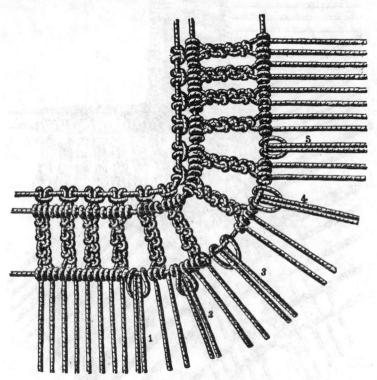

Fig. 602. Addition of the first supplementary threads.
Detail of figure 601.

2nd series — make 1 double chain with 5 twistings of the thread.

3d series — 1 plain horizontal bar.

4th series — make big collecting knots, fig. 561, with the écru threads over the 4 double red threads and flat knots over the écru threads.

5th series — make flat knots over the écru threads with 2 red threads and 1 écru.

6th series — make flat knots with and over the écru threads that are in the middle of the group of knots.

7th series — like the 5th. Then take the red threads from right to left, roll them between the thumb and forefinger from

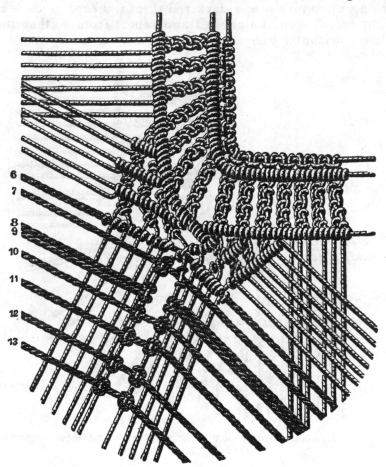

Fig. 603. Addition of the second supplementary threads.
Detail of figure 601.

left to right, tacking each cluster separately, as in making a cord.

When you have twisted them several times, join the 2 clusters together and then twist them from right to left.

Fasten off the cord thus made with a knot, below which the ends of thread form a little tassel.

Collect all the écru threads together and make them into a thick tassel by the addition of supplementary threads.

Fringe with three rows of tassels (fig. 600). — As a fringe of this kind is chiefly used for trimming rugs, curtains and furniture the coarsest numbers of the materials named at the foot of the engraving should be chosen. Length of the

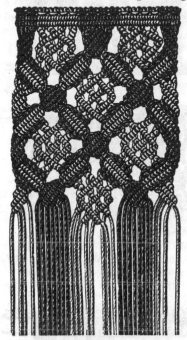

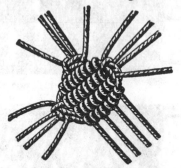

Fig. 605. Shell knot.
Detail of figure 604.

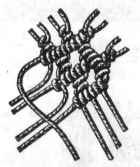

Fig. 604. Macramé ground.
Materials : D.M.C Crochet cotton 6 cord
Nos. 15 to 30,
D.M.C Knotting cotton No. 30,
D.M.C Alsatian thread Nos. 30 to 50,
or D.M.C Alsatia No. 25,
in Cream yellow 711 and Indigo
blue 322. (*)

Fig. 606. Openwork motive.
Detail of figure 604.

double threads for No. 1 of D.M.C Pearl cotton (Coton perlé): 56 in.

The interlacings and crossings of the threads are so simple that we need only refer our readers to figure 557 for the knotting on of the threads and to figure 562 for the waved plait. The little tassels between the knots are made separately and fastened on to the knots by the thread from which they hang.

(*) See at the end of the last chapter the tables of the sizes and colours of the cotton, flax and silk articles, mark D.M.C.

Macramé fringe with corner (*) (figs. 601, 602, 603). —
Length of the threads for No. 3o of D.M.C Knotting cotton
(Fil à pointer): 46 in.

Fig. 607. Macrame border.

Fig. 608. Macramé border.
Materials : D.M.C Knotting cotton No. 30, D.M.C Pearl cotton Nos. 3 to 8, D.M.C
Alsatia No. 20, D.M.C Alsatian thread Nos. 30 to 70 or D.M.C Flax thread for
knitting Nos. 3 to 20, in Rust brown 3310, Cardinal red 346, Indigo
blue 322 or Golden yellow 781.

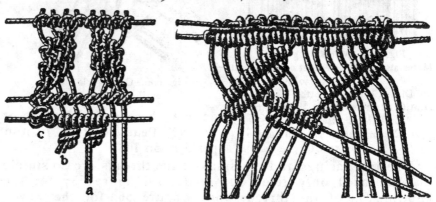

Fig. 609. Detail of figures 607 and 608.   Fig. 610. Detail of figure 608.

Macramé fringes, cannot, from their nature, be gathered
round a corner, like lace, crochet and netted edgings.

_____

(*) See, at the end of the volume, the list of the albums of the D.M.C Library,
containing a large variety of patterns for all kinds of work.

The close knots make it impossible to draw up the cord on which they are knotted, enough to give the fringe the necessary length of outside edge.

The number of threads must therefore be increased at the corner in order to turn it properly.

In the detail of figure 602, 5 supplementary threads are added to the 4th series of knots, as shewn in figure 602.

A group of intercrossed bars takes 16 threads, answering to 4 groups of little squares placed between the lozenges.

Then, the bars having been prepared beforehand, as shewn in figure 603, a supplementary thread, thread 6, is passed

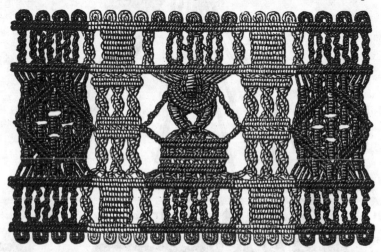

Fig. 611. Macramé border.

Materials: D.M.C Crochet cotton 6 cord or D.M.C Special crochet cotton Nos. 10 to 20, D.M.C Knotting cotton No. 30, D.M.C Alsatia No. 20, D.M.C Pearl cotton Nos. 3 to 5 or D.M.C Flax thread for knitting Nos. 3 to 12, in écru, Turkish red 321 and Indigo blue 312.

through the double knot which unites the bars in the middle. (In the engraving the supplementary threads are distinguished by a darker shade). It is on thread 6 that the bar that goes from right to left is made.

You next knot 7 more threads on to the threads between which the supplementary thread passes. Thread 7 is knotted on single, threads 8 and 9 are knotted on double, threads 10, 11, 12, 13 are knotted on single, so that threads 7, 10, 11, 12 and 13 connect the cords, whilst only threads 8 and 9 are knotted on separately on each side.

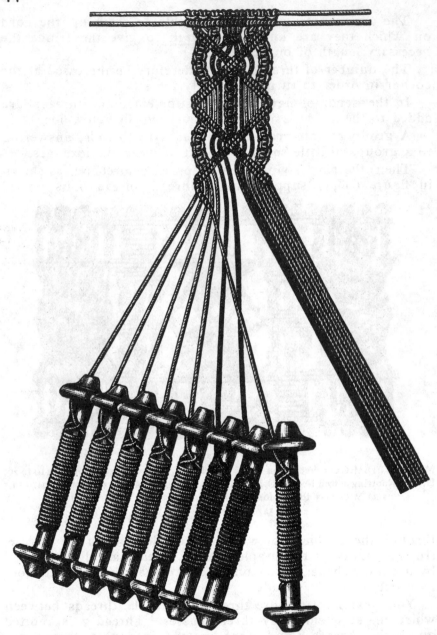

Fig. 612. Gimp made with macramé shuttles.
Materials : D.M.C Crochet cotton 6 cord Nos. 1 to 10, D.M.C Knotting cotton No. 30,
D.M.C Alsatian thread Nos. 30 to 50, D.M.C Alsatia No. 25 or D.M.C Flax
thread for knitting Nos. 3 to 20, in Solid blue 827 and Rust brown 3313.

The bars formed by the knots of the supplementary threads must be quite close together like every other double bar.

We have purposely set the cords some distance apart in order to enable our readers to distinguish the added threads from the existing ones.

At the point of junction of the bars, fasten a very long

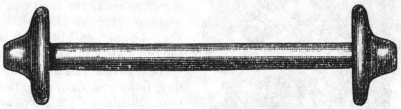

Fig. 613. Macramé shuttle. Natural size.

red thread, with which to make the knots over the 14 threads inside the lozenge.

Bend the 7th thread to the right and the 1st to the left and make a double knot over each of the two threads with the coloured thread.

The middle of the lozenge is filled in with 9 flat knots; when they are made, continue knotting the red thread along both sides; a plain bar in white thread borders the lozenge outside.

Knotted tassels and tassels with fancy knots on them, which take 10 threads, complete this fringe.

Macramé ground (figs. 604, 605, 606). — Length of the threads, according to the size of the ground, to be wound on macramé shuttles.

1st series — knot on the threads, as in figure 545, begin with 2 blue threads, then 4 cream and 4 blue alternately, end with 2 blue followed by a double horizontal bar.

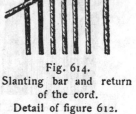

Fig. 614.
Slanting bar and return of the cord.
Detail of figure 612.

2nd series — begin in the middle, with 2 flat knots made with 4 blue threads; with the 4 blue threads on the left make a quadruple bar over the 4 blue threads on the right. These quadruple bars called "shell knots" are shewn in detail, fig. 605.

Unite the blue threads at the sides by flat knots.

The beginning and the continuation of the openwork motives are explained in figure 606.

The threads that proceed from the last group of knots serve for making the bar of knots, the two inside rows of which are light and the two outside ones, dark.

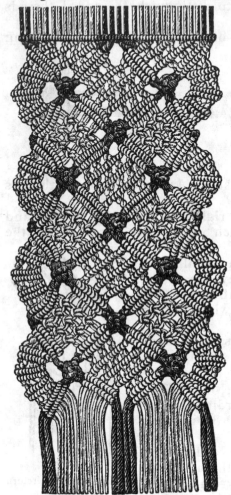

Fig. 615. Gimp with big shell knots.
Materials: D.M.C Crochet cotton 6 cord Nos. 5 to 20, D.M.C Knotting cotton No. 30, D.M.C Alsatia No. 20 or D.M.C Pearl cotton Nos. 3 to 5, in Golden green 582 and Cardinal red 347. (*)

When this two-coloured shell bar is finished all the cream threads are again collected to make the next openwork motive, so that all the shell knots are blue and all the openwork motives cream.

Macramé borders (figs. 607, 608, 609, 610). — These two borders are worked width ways; so that 20 in. will suffice for the length of the threads of D.M.C Knotting cotton (Fil à pointer) No. 30.

Knot the threads on for both these borders, as in figure 545, followed by a single horizontal bar. For figure 607, make triple oblique bars of knots, with 4 threads, one slanting from right to left, the other from left to right; then make a single horizontal bar and add another series of triple bars slanting the opposite way: complete the pattern by a horizontal bar, turn the work, fix another cord and make a second horizontal bar upon it, but on the wrong side of the work and finish by tying the threads together, two and two, as shewn in figure 609, letter a, cut them, letter b, and press the knot hard on the wrong side, letter c.

(*) See at the end of the last chapter the tables of the sizes and colours of the cotton, flax and silk articles, mark D.M.C.

For figure 608 you must count 8 single threads for each repetition of the subject.

Make all the double oblique bars, slanting from right to left, first, fig. 610, then counting from left to right, take the 5th thread as the first cord, see again figure 610, and begin the 2nd series of bars of knots, slanting from left to right.

Fasten off the threads after this series of knots as seen in detail figure 609.

Macramé border (fig. 611). Entire length of the threads for No. 30 of D.M.C Knotting cotton (Fil à pointer): 60 in.

1st series — knot on the threads with round double picots, followed by a double horizontal bar. The colours succeed each other as follows: * 4 blue scallops, 4 écru, 5 red, 4 écru, repeat from *.

Fig. 616. Big shell knot begun. Detail of figure 615.

Fig. 617. Big shell knot completed. Detail of figure 615.

2nd series — begin by a little chain with 2 single threads, fig. 576, and with 7 changes of the threads = * with the 12 following threads: 3 flat knots; then under these 3 knots 6 little chains with 6 changes of the threads; after the 3d, connect the 2nd chain with the 3d, the 4th with the 5th. Finish every 2 chains with a flat knot.

Over the last blue threads make: 1 waved plait, fig. 562, b = on the 14th écru thread: 1 bar of double knots with 4 goings and 3 returns = on the 2 first red threads: 1 waved plait and repeat from *.

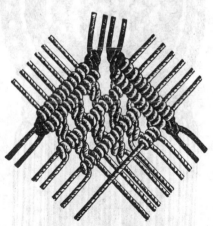

Fig. 618. Insertion of the threads. Detail of figure 615.

3d series — add 2 more cords to make a double horizontal bar.

4th series — with the blue threads: 5 big shell knots, figs. 616 and 617, 1 triple bar of double knots to the left and right = between the bars 9 big shell knots = 1 triple bar of double knots to the right and left and finish above with 5 big shell knots.

With the écru threads: 3 flat knots, 1 double horizontal bar over the last écru thread; 3 waved plaits with 12 changes of the threads, 1 more double bar, join the cord to the outside thread of the 3^d blue bar.

With the red threads: 1 big shell knot, figs. 616 and 617, over 12 threads; at the bottom in the shape of a semicircle: 1 double bar; on both sides of the big shell knot with the 2 outside threads, 1 little chain, made with 7 changes of the threads; join the red thread on the left to the light thread that comes from the double bar.

Later on, to connect the different figures, the light thread on the left of the next figure is passed through the red chain, and so on = 4 collecting knots over 6 red threads right and left, 1 collecting knot over all the red threads and 1 on either side over 6 red threads.

After connecting the threads on both sides, continue the little chain with 3 changes of the threads = over the first red thread of the left chain, make 1 double horizontal bar with all the loose threads = under the bar, 4 flat knots = 1 single horizontal bar = 10 double knots over a single thread = 1 double bar of knots.

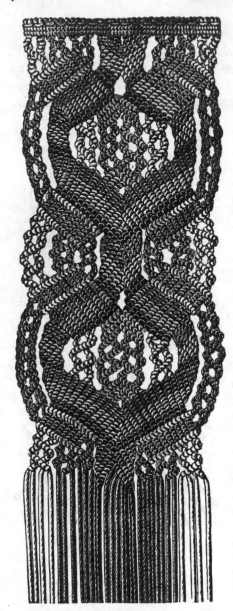

Fig. 619. Macramé gimp with crossed bars. Materials: D.M.C Crochet cotton 6 cord, D.M.C Knotting cotton, D.M.C Alsatia or D.M.C Pearl cotton, in Black 310, Beetle green 3346 and 3348, Cachou brown 435 and 437, Indigo blue 334.

From this point procéed with the écru threads: 1 row of double knots, 1 double horizontal bar and 3 waved plaits, then join: 2 blue threads with 2 écru and 2 écru with 2 red to form flat knots.

The bottom border is made like the top one; then to finish off the bottom one, fold the threads back so as to form picots and sew them to the horizontal bar.

Gimp made with macramé shuttles (figs. 612, 613, 614). Prepare 8 double threads of the length required for the gimp. So as not to have to add to the thread in the middle of a piece of work and to avoid having long ends of thread hanging down in your way, we advise a macramé shuttle being used as a kind of spool somewhat like those used in making pillow lace.

Fig. 620.
Bar crossed from left to right.
Detail of figure 619.

These simplify the work and being made hollow they can be mounted on the spindle of any sewing-machine.

For fastening off the thread see "Pillow Laces" fig. 966.

Knot on the threads, as in figure 545, 3 blue, 2 brown and 3 blue; followed by a single bar of knots; then leave 2 threads on the right and 2 on the left, and with every 4 threads between make 3 flat knots. Make double knots over the 16th thread on the right, with the 15th, 14th, 13th, 12th, 11th, 10th and 9th threads; then make knots with the same threads over the 15th thread.

Make a similar bar on the left over the 1st thread with the 2nd, 3d, 4th, 5th, 6th, 7th and 8th thread and with same threads over the 2nd. To connect the two bars make double knots with the cords of the left bar on the cords of the right bar.

Fig. 621.
Bar crossed from right to left.
Detail of figure 619.

On the two sides and with the 4 outside blue threads: 4 flat knots, fig. 546, *d;* 2 more bars on the right and left, but in the opposite direction, and knotting up to the last thread, fig. 614. Take the 4 middle threads and make 7 flat knots, and then bring the bars of knots back to the middle.

The return of the thread is also shewn in figure 614.

Gimp with big shell knots (figs. 615, 616, 617, 618). —
Fill the macramé shuttles with the requisite length of thread,
for the length of gimp required.

1st series — knot the threads on, as in figure 549, in the
following order: 1 dark coloured double thread, 6 light double
ones, 2 dark double ones, 6 light double ones, 1 dark double
one, followed by a
single bar.

2nd series — from
left to right and on
the dark thread: one
double knot with
the 2nd thread; on
the light thread:
1 double knot with
the 2nd; from right
to left double knots
with the 3d, 2nd and
1st light threads on
the 4th light thread
= from left to right:
1 double knot with

Fig. 622.
Macramé gimp with corner.
Materials: D.M.C Knotting
cotton No. 30; D.M.C Alsatia
No. 25 or D.M.C Pearl cotton
No. 3, in Ash grey 318 and
Cardinal red 347 or in Golden
green 580 and Scabious
violet 395.

the 6th light thread on the 5th thread and
with the 4th thread on the 3d = from right
to left: 5 double knots on the 8th light
thread = from left to right: 1 double knot
over the 9th thread, 1 double knot over the
7th, 1 over the 5th = from right to left: 7
double knots over the 12th thread = from
left to right: 3 detached double knots.

Then from left to right and from right
to left = with 6 light threads: 2 double
bars slanting over the 2 dark threads (see
also the top of figure 618); join the 4 dark
threads in the middle and make a big shell knot with them,
fig. 616, which consists of 6 flat knots, fig. 617, take 2
threads on the right and 2 on the left, turn them down
to the left and right and then from the wrong side to
the right over the threads that come from the bars and close
with a flat knot.

On the sides make a scallop of 3 double bars and between
each bar 1 little chain with two changes of threads. Fill the
empty space under the big outside shell knot with 9 flat knots;

under the middle knot, make bars of intercrossed knots, like those described in figure 618.

Macramé gimp with crossed bars (figs. 619, 620, 621). Wind the threads on macramé shuttles and knot them on as in figure 545, in the following order: 2 light blue double threads, 2 light green double threads, 2 dark green double threads, 1 double dark brown, 1 single black, 2 double light brown, 1 single black, 1 double dark brown, 2 double dark green, 2 double light green, 2 double light blue.

Begin on both sides with the openwork groups of crossed bars, figs. 620 and 621, with 4 blue threads, with 4 changes outwards and 3 inwards = of the bars with 4 light green threads with 3 changes outwards and 2 inwards = of the crossed bars with 4 dark green threads with 2 changes outwards and 3 inwards. On the 1st dark green thread, 1 double knot, the 4 light green threads and the 4 blue.

Fig. 623.
Detail of braid,
figure 622.

The other 2 dark green threads are knotted from right to left, then from left to right, the 4 light green threads and the 4 blue which together form 8 bars across the first bar = then knot the 8 first threads again over the last dark green thread = add 1 crossed bar with 14 changes of the threads outwards and 12 inwards. As shewn in figures 620 and 621.

Middle group, left side: 1 double knot with the first dark brown thread over the second thread; for the first bar 3 double knots with the black thread and with the 2 dark brown threads over the 1st light brown one.

In the 2nd bar, knot the 1st light brown thread; in the 3d bar, knot the 2 light brown threads over the black one.

On the right a similar group slanting from right to left.

On the left — over the 1st light brown thread on the right, 1 double knot with 2 dark brown threads, 2 light brown threads and 1 black one, all coming from the left.

On the right — over the 1st dark brown coming from the left: 1 double knot with 1 dark brown thread, 2 light brown threads, 1 black one.

On the left — over the dark brown thread coming from the right: 1 double knot with 1 dark brown thread, 2 light brown threads and 1 black.

On the right — over the dark brown thread, 1 knot with
2 light brown threads and 1 black.

On the left — a similar group to the one on the right.

On the right — over the first dark brown thread, 1 knot
with 1 brown thread and 1 black.

On the left — the same as on the right.

Fig. 624. Macramé rosette.

Materials: D.M C Knotting cotton No. 30, D.M.C Alsatia No. 20 or D.M.C Pearl
cotton No. 3, in écru, Tender pink 3326 and Garnet red 335 and 309, or in Cream
yellow 711, Azure blue 3325 and Indigo blue 334 and 312. (*)

On the right — over the last light brown thread, 1 knot
with the black thread.

On the left — over the 4 light green threads, then over
4 blue; 1 knot with each of the 2 dark brown and the 2 light
brown and with the black one, that is to say 8 cross bars =

(*) See at the end of the last chapter the tables of the sizes and colours of
the cotton, flax and silk articles, mark D.M.C.

1 double knot with the first dark brown thread over the 2nd of the same colour = 2 double knots with the 2 dark brown threads over the 1st light brown one = 3 double knots with 2 dark brown threads and 1 light brown thread over the 2nd light brown one = 4 double knots with 2 dark brown threads and 2 light brown ones over the black thread = after which make 5 other bars taking the last thread turned inwards for the cord.

Make similar groups, slanting from right to left, then, beginning again on the left in the middle make the knots with the 4 light green threads over the first thread of the same colour running from right to left.

On the right — knot 3 light green threads over the 1st thread coming from the left and repeat the same group again twice on both sides. The third bar forms at the same time the first scallop of a triple crossed bar; which you have also to make on the right.

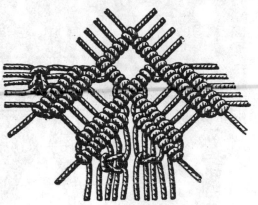

Fig. 625. Detail of figure 624.

The two crossed bars end with a triple group of bars; the last bar on the right counts only one double knot.

There remain to be made on both sides crossed bars in light blue, which number 3 whole scallops inside and 1 whole one outside and one half one top and bottom.

Knot all the other threads over the 4 blue threads and the 4 light green ones = in the middle, knot the right and the left threads alternately, until the black ones meet at the bottom.

Turn the group of green and blue bars again inwards from outside and finish it off by a crossed bar with 3 scallops on the inner side.

Macramé gimp with corner (figs. 622 and 623). — For this, you have to fix the threads folded at the middle of their length on the macramé cushion and wind them on both sides on to macramé shuttles.

Work the gimp both ways and on the right side where the two ends meet, fasten the threads invisibly on the wrong side of the work.

The gimp, fig. 622, requires 8 light and 8 dark threads; fasten them on so that the 8 light threads are in the middle with 4 dark ones on either side, and begin the work by the oblique bars worked with the light threads over the dark ones. You then make the two bars turned outwards at the corner and the one turned inwards; these figures being finished,

Fig. 626. Macramé border with scallops.
Materials : D.M.C Knotting cotton No. 30, D.M.C Crochet cotton 6 cord Nos. 5 to 20, D.M.C Alsatia No. 15, D.M.C Pearl cotton Nos. 3 to 8 or D.M.C Flax thread for knitting Nos. 3 to 12, in white or écru.

count 6 dark threads in the middle of the gimp which serve to make the dark quadruple bar turned towards the corner. With the 4 outer light threads knot the little chains which encircle the corner in the form of a scallop, and then continue with three oblique light bars and the corner is finished. You now have 8 light threads in the middle and 4 dark ones on either side; the dark threads serve to make the little outside

dark leaves; the light threads are connected in the middle by
a waved knot, fig. 562 *a*, with 2 changes of the threads.

Continue the pattern by making the light oblique bars;
figure 623 shews clearly how the dark figure with 4
little leaves is made.

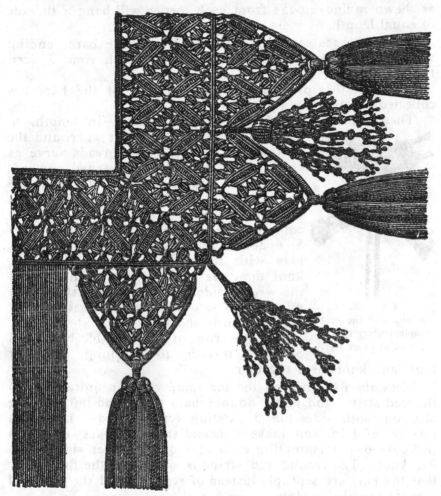

Fig. 627. Fringe with pointed scallops and large tassels.
Materials: D.M.C Knotting cotton No. 30, D.M.C Crochet cotton 6 cord Nos. 10 to 50,
D.M.C Alsatia Nos. 15 to 25, D.M.C Pearl cotton Nos. 3 to 8
or D.M.C Alsatian thread Nos. 30 to 50. (*)

(*) See at the end of the last chapter the tables of the sizes and colours of
the cotton, flax and silk articles, mark D.M.C.

Macramé rosette (figs. 624 and 625). — Entire length ot the écru threads: long threads 40 in. and short threads 20 in.; length of the coloured threads: 80 in. and 160 in.

Begin in the middle, take 8 écru threads, 40 in. long and knot the inside square with them, the bars set contrariwise, as shewn in figure 625; from each corner will hang 4 threads of equal length.

These threads serve as cords for the double bars, ending with a double knot, for which you add each time 4 écru threads.

The four threads hanging on each side of the bars are collected together by a flat knot.

Then take the 6 coloured threads, 80 in. in length, to make the sextuple bars that surround the centre figure. The écru threads serve as cords. The dark threads turned towards the middle are knotted first, then the medium light ones and lastly the light ones. The little triple chain, which has to come between the groups of bars, counts 5, 6 and 7 knots. After finishing the 8 bars with the little intermediate chains, knot the ends of the coloured threads on the wrong side of the work, fasten them off with a few overcasting stitches and cut them off quite short.

Fig. 628.
Addition of the first supplementary thread. Detail of figure 627.

For the row of light double bars, add 32 écru threads 40 in. long, four by four, and knot them together.

Place the flat knot on the macramé cushion quite close to the red stripe and make double bars right and left, adding also on both sides the 3 existing écru threads. Leave an interval of ¼ in. and make a second series of bars, as shewn in figure 624, terminating each time on the outer side with a flat knot. The second red stripe is made like the first, only that the bars are septuple instead of sextuple and the coloured threads are 160 in. long.

To make the scallops which surround the rosette, add 48 écru threads, 20 in. long. Join them together 3 by 3 at their middle by a flat knot, fastened on the cushion, close to the red stripe, and go on making double bars. At every second group add one écru thread, until you have eight for every group of knots. Leave an interval of ¼ in. and make

the second row of bars; in the third row the bars are placed
so as to form scallops; inside the lozenges collect the threads
together by a flat knot.

When the work is finished fasten off all the threads by
making 6 plain picots with them round each scallop.

This kind of rosette is very strong and serviceable for a
lamp mat or pincushion cover.

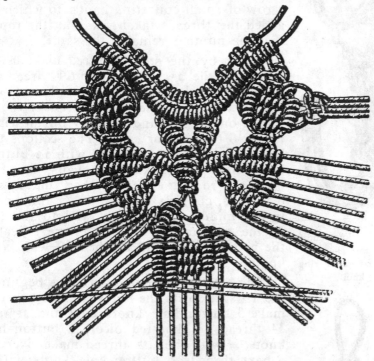

Fig. 629. Addition of other supplementary threads. Detail of figure 627.

Macramé border with scallops (fig. 626). — Entire
length of the threads for No. 3o of D.M.C Knotting cotton
(Fil à pointer) (*): 70 in.

Knot on the threads with round single picots, as in
figure 548 with a double horizontal bar followed by a row of
small collecting knots, see figure 56o, and a second double
horizontal bar.

In the actual border, the pattern consists of two different

(*) See at the end of the last chapter the tables of the sizes and colours of
the cotton, flax and silk articles, mark D.M.C. — The French names, in brackets,
are those stamped on the labels of the D.M.C articles.

figures, the smaller of which requires 12 threads in the width; the big figures take 22 threads, 10 threads intended for knotting, the 2 middle ones are fastened off on the wrong

side of the work. Between every two figures skip 2 threads, which are fastened off at the back, and when the whole border is done, finish off the pattern by two double bars and a row of small collecting knots, to which are added the threads taken away at the top so that the number remains the same.

Begin by the small figure, make a flat knot with the 3d, 4th, 5th and 6th thread and a flat knot with the 7th, 8th, 9th and 10th thread, then knot the triple bars over the 1st thread on the left and the 12th on the right, taking 6 threads for each. The scallops that border the figures are made with 12 button-hole knots and 2 knotted picots, fig. 566, over 2 cords; the vertical bar, made with 6 threads, consists of 4 flat knots and 1 picot in the middle to the right and to the left. At the bottom the triple bars are repeated, the reverse way, and finished off with 2 flat knots.

Fig. 630.
Chinese knot and double chain prepared for a ring knot.

The big figure of the border is begun by the 1st scallop on the left with the 1st thread, make 3 button-hole knots over the 2nd and 3d threads, 1 knotted picot, 4 button-hole knots = with the 4th thread make over the 3 next threads 6 button-hole knots with a picot on them = with the 10th thread, make 3 button-hole knots over the 8th and 9th threads, 1 picot, 3 button-hole knots, then continue on the left with the threads that come from the second scallop with 4 double knots over the 2 cords, to which add 1 more picot and 2 button-hole knots, after which unite these threads with those that come from the first scallop by a flat knot. Divide

Fig. 631.
Ring knot formed by a small chain.

the 6 united threads in two and make a scallop to the left with 12 button-hole knots and 2 picots and to the right a scallop with 9 button-hole knots and 2 picots, which you again unite below by a flat knot.

Repeat the same series of knots on the right side of the figure, only reversed.

You will have 8 threads in the middle which will serve to make the central figure, composed of 4 triple bars, finished off at the bottom, to the right and left by scallops, as at the top.

Scallops — each scallop takes 39 threads. Between the scallops make 1 little picot with 2 threads and 2 double knots and fasten off the threads on the wrong side.

The 39 threads for each scallop are divided into 9 parts; the 1st, 5th and 9th counting 5 threads each, the other six only 4.

Begin with the 1st group of threads on the left, and make 2 flat knots over 3 threads, followed by 2 little chains right and left, that is with the 1st and 2nd and with the 4th and 5th threads which number 8 single knots and which are united at the bottom by 2 flat knots.

With the 2 next sets of threads 2 flat knots followed by a shell of knots, see fig. 605; with the threads that hang down on the left, make 4 flat knots, take 5 threads of the 1st set on the left and make 1 flat knot over 7 threads, bring out 2 threads on the wrong side of the work, make a flat knot over 5 threads, bring out 2 threads, make a flat knot over 3 threads, followed by a figure with little chain, described above. With the 4 threads that come out on the right from the shell knot, make a scallop and with the first thread on the left make over the 3 next threads 9 button-hole knots, 1 picot, 9 button-hole knots. With the 4th set of threads, make a scallop consisting of 7 button-hole knots, 1 picot and 7 button-hole knots, and with the 5th set of threads, make a similar figure as with the 1st, but always finish with one flat knot.

The right part of the scallop is made in the same manner only the reverse way, then make 3 flat knots over the 3 middle sets of threads, that is, over 11 threads, leave out 3 threads, take the threads of the big scallops right and left, 3 flat knots over 16 threads; divide the threads so as to have 5 threads right and left and 8 threads in the middle.

Make right and left the figure with the little chains, unite them to the outer figures by 3 flat knots, draw out 5 threads and repeat the same figure once more.

With the 8 middle threads, make a bar with 14 waved knots, then divide the 8 threads in two to make the bars with 4 flat knots with picots right and left, join these bars to the outside figures by a flat knot, draw out 4 threads, then make a scallop with 5 button-hole knots, 1 picot and 5 button-hole knots.

The 5 threads coming from the left scallop are knotted over the 5 threads coming from the right scallop, then on each side make a picot knotted with 5 threads, secured afterwards invisibly at the back.

Fringe with pointed scallops and large tassels (figs. 627, 628, 629, 630, 631, 632, 633, 634). — Entire length of the threads for No. 30 of D.M.C Knotting cotton (Fil à pointer): 104 in.

The present pattern with which this chapter concludes is not only one of the prettiest but also one requiring the greatest care and accuracy, more especially with regard to the right direction of the cords. The groups of double knots and the bars must be made as close as possible so as to make the pattern very distinct and give each figure its proper value.

For each repetition of the subject 16 double threads are wanted.

You begin the half stars, on each side of the lozenges, with the 15th and 16th double thread of the first figure and make 3 button-hole knots with the 4th thread over the 3 threads, fig. 628.

Over 2 cords on the left and 1 on the right, that is, over 3 threads: 5 button-

Fig. 634.
Big pendant of
the tassel
in figure 627.

hole knots with the 4th thread, and with the disengaged threads, 1 flat knot over each of the 4 threads.

This forms a small shell knot, on either side of which, make 3 button-hole knots over 3 threads.

For the groups of bars on either side of the shell knot: take the 11th, 12th, 13th and 14th double thread on the left, the 3^d, 4th, 5th and 6th thread on the right. These groups are joined by button hole knots.

Knot the 4 threads of the left group over the 1st cord on the right; knot over these 4 the 2 next threads on the right; knot the 4 threads on the left over the 4th thread on the right; make 2 button-hole knots with the 4th thread over the 3 threads at the bottom and on the side.

Over the 4 threads that come from the left and right: two quadruple bars; cross the upper threads after the second row of bars, make with the next thread 2 button-hole knots over the 4th thread, then finish the 3^d and 4th bar of knots.

To make the olive-shaped groups of knots on both sides, take as cord the threads that come from the big shell knot.

Figure 628 shews the adding on of the first supplementary thread, fig. 629, the addition of 13 more threads, which, knotted on to the first form with it the group of bars on the diagonal corner line.

For the big shell knot that follows, take 2 more additional threads and 1 thread from the preceding figure.

Add on 2 more supplementary threads to the disengaged threads left and right. These 4 threads will serve again as cords for the groups of bars left and right.

The 4th group of bars which forms the corner of the fringe is knotted on the 4 threads that come from the big shell knot on to which the 4th set of 12 supplementary threads is knotted. The shell knot at the bottom requires 4 more supplementary threads. The pattern ends at the bottom with a half star and a double bar separates the grounding from the big scallops which begin likewise with 2 half stars and 5 big shell knots. Beneath the half stars come 4 groups of bars, one whole star, 2 big shell knots right and left, and lastly 2 fresh groups of bars joined by a big shell knot which comes at the point of the scallop.

All the threads that come from the groups are then collected together at the top of the scallops and covered with close overcasting stitches so as to form a kind of thick round cord round the scallop widening towards the point, where the

threads are so disposed as to form a very voluminous tassel.
The fringe is further ornamented by 6 or 8 other tassels,
made separately, hung on to the twisted part.

Between the scallops come rich pendants for which a large
knotted berry has first to be made, called also "fraise", with
21 cords as shewn in figure 632.

Collect the 21 threads all together to begin with; then
make 2 rows of knots on 12 threads, 1 row of knots over 15
threads, 3 rows on 21 threads, 1 row on 15, and 2 on 12;
then cut the ends all equal and turn them inwards to fill up
the hollow space inside the berry, stuffing it besides if necessary
with wadding to make it perfectly firm and hard, and closing
it up with a few stitches at the ends. To this you attach 5 big
and 6 little pendants.

The little ones, fig. 633, are begun with the Chinese knot,
fig. 630, which terminates in a double chain, formed into a
ring knot.

You cut 3 threads of the chain when you have a double
chain, 1 thread when you have a single chain, turn the threads
inwards and fasten them off by a few stitches (see the top of
figure 633).

The remaining thread is made into a little loop on which
you hang 3 small ring knots, made of a single chain, fig. 631,
with a loop, top and bottom formed of the ends of the thread.

The large pendant, fig. 634, begins by a single chain which
is made into a tassel, in the loop of which hang: 2 Chinese
knots ending with a tassel and a loop, then 3 small pendants,
composed of tassels and loops, made of a single chain, as
shewn in figure 631.

The "fraise" is ornamented at the top by a crochet or knotted
braid, an explanation of which will be found in the chapter on
"Needlework Trimmings", figs. 1032 to 1039, and to which
the tassels between the scallops of the fringe are hung.

Patterns of needlework. — Besides the different kinds of
work described above a great choice of patterns for macramé
will be found in the following publications of the D.M.C
Library: *Macramé* and *Works of various kinds*. (*)

(*) See at the end of the volume the list of the albums
of the D.M.C Library.

Insertion in embroidered netting with fillings and outlines in darning stitch.

Netting

Netting is a handicraft so ancient that it would be difficult to say where or when it was first practised. All the primitive races of man used nets for catching fish and game and were consequently familiar with the art of netting.

Consisting, in its simplest form, of loops secured and rendered independent of one another by knots it has gone through many transformations and developments until it has attained such perfection as to have become a favorite and attractive occupation. In conjunction with embroidery to which it is made to serve as a foundation the most charming effects are produced and places are still to be found where a large part of the population is engaged in this industry, in one form or other executed in every variety of material.

In Persia, for instance, we meet with the finest silk netting embroidered with gold and silver; in Italy with a kind resembling in the style of its embroidery the "Punto tagliato"; in France with the so-called "Filet-Richelieu" (*). Netting may be classed under two headings: netting proper and embroidered or artistic netting.

As a substitute for hand or machine-made netting a fabric called "lacis" or "canevas-filet" is often used.

(*) See at the end of the volume the list of the albums of the D.M.C Library, containing a large variety of patterns for all kinds of work.

The implements required for plain netting (figs. 635, 636, 637). — Netting as we have already said consists of loops, called stitches, secured by knots. These stitches are made by means of needles and meshes or spools. The needles are made of steel, wood or bone, for fine work steel must be used, the ends resemble pincers with a hole bored through them below the fork in which the thread is secured, fig. 635, before it is wound on lengthways between the forks; the middle of the needle is like an ordinary knitting needle.

Wooden and bone needles are only used for twine and coarse materials; the forks at the ends are bigger and the shaft is not pierced as shewn in figure 636.

The quantity of thread wound on to the needle must depend on the size of the mesh or spool employed, so that it may slip through the loops or stitches without difficulty.

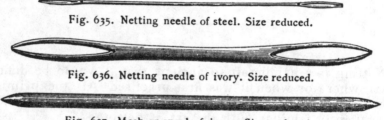

Fig. 635. Netting needle of steel. Size reduced.

Fig. 636. Netting needle of ivory. Size reduced.

Fig. 637. Mesh or spool of ivory. Size reduced.

The mesh or spool, fig. 637, whether of ivory, bone, steel or wood should be smooth and round and of the same thickness throughout, so that the loops made upon it may all be of one size and easily slipped off. For making fringes a flat ruler takes the place of the mesh.

Needle and mesh must correspond in size with the stitches and the thread employed.

Besides these two implements a heavy cushion is necessary on which to pin the foundation loop of coarse thread, which holds the netting whilst it is being made.

Materials. — The choice of the thread depends absolutely on the purpose of the work. Cotton, linen thread and silk can all be used : netted articles of one colour are generally made in cotton or linen thread; those in several colours in silk or in a thread which imitates silk.

Of the D.M.C articles we recommend for netting, D.M.C Flax thread for knitting (Lin pour tricoter), D.M.C Flax lace thread (Lin pour dentelles), D.M.C Alsatia, D.M.C Crochet cotton 6 cord (Cordonnet 6 fils), D.M.C Special crochet cotton (Cordonnet spécial), D.M.C Alsatian thread (Fil d'Alsace) and D.M.C Pearl cotton (Coton perlé). (*)

All these materials have an equal uniform twist and do not knot in the working.

Netting stitches. — The shape of the loops or stitches in netting is always square or oblong. Patterns are produced in plain netting by the use of different sized meshes. By different ways of passing the thread over the mesh and connecting the loops together, different stitches are produced, of which the following are the most important: 1° plain loop, 2° double loop, 3° oblong loop and 4° slipped loop.

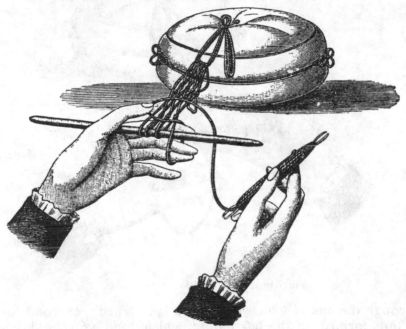

Fig. 638. Plain loop. First position of the hands.

1° **Plain loop. First position of the hands** (fig. 638). — Every kind of netting must be begun on a foundation loop of strong thread, from 4 to 8 in. long, fastened to the heavy cushion with a pin. Fasten the shuttle thread to the foundation loop. Take the mesh in the left hand, holding it between the

(*) See at the end of the last chapter the tables of the sizes and colours of the cotton, flax and silk articles, mark D.M.C. — The French names, in brackets, are those stamped on the labels of the D.M.C articles.

thumb and the forefinger, stiffening the other fingers extended beneath. Take the netting needle filled with thread in the right hand and pass the thread downwards over the mesh and inside over the 2nd, 3d and 4th fingers, carry it upwards behind these 3 fingers and lay it to the left under the thumb by which it has to be held fast.

Second and third positions of the hands (figs. 639 and 640). — Carry the thread downwards again behind the 4 fingers and put the needle upwards from below through the loop on the fingers and through the loop at the back of the mesh, or

Fig. 639. Second position of the hands.

through the one to which the thread is fastened; a second loop is thus formed on the left hand; which loop you hold back with the little finger of the left hand. Then gradually tightening the thread, disengage your fingers from the loop held by the thumb and then tighten the loop that is round the 2nd, 3d and 4th fingers. Keep the last loop on the little finger until the first is quite closed. Then only draw your little finger out of the loop; tighten the knot thus completing a stitch.

The next stitches are made in the same way, whether they are to serve for casting on, or for a netted foundation.

When you have cast on a sufficient number of loops, draw out the mesh, turn the work and for beginning a new row hold the mesh beneath the finished row of stitches. You then pass the shuttle through the last stitch of the preceding row and make as many knots as there are loops.

These loops form a plain or diagonal net for which you have to turn the work at the end of each row, as you work to and fro.

2º **Double loops.** — To make a double loop, twist the thread two or three times round the mesh that makes the loops two or three times longer than the others.

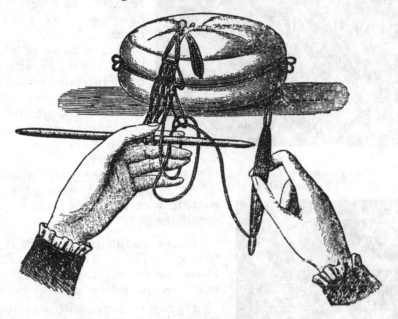

Fig. 640. Third position of the hands.

3º **Oblong loops.** — For oblong loops, the knots must be made a little distance from the mesh.

4º **Slipped loops.** — Carry the thread over the mesh and the fingers the same as for a plain loop, pass the shuttle the same as for every other loop, but draw out the mesh before tightening the knot.

Patterns produced in netting by the use of meshes of different widths. — Plain netting can be varied by making one or two rows over a narrow mesh and the same number of rows over a wider one, using first one mesh and then the other, at regular intervals.

Pattern produced in netting by increases and intakes (fig. 641). — A great variety of patterns can be made by uniting

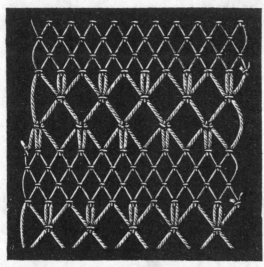

several loops together with a knot in one row and adding the same number in the next.

You may increase and decrease like this in the same row or at regular intervals. In figure 641 two sizes of thread are used.

Three rows of plain loops are made with the fine thread, one row with the coarser on a mesh proportionately wider, one row in which you net every two loops together.

Fig. 641.
Pattern produced in netting by increases and intakes.

These are followed by three rows of plain netting with the fine thread on the small mesh.

Loose loops in clusters (figs. 642 and 643). — These clusters of loose loops in the netting are made in the following way:

1st row — begin with one loop, the knot of which must be a little distance from the mesh, put the thread over the mesh and the needle through the loop where the knot is; repeat this three or four times, taking care to make all the loops of the same length. Then unite all the loops with one knot, carrying the needle from right to left round the loops instead of putting it through the loop of the previous row.

Fig. 642.
Loose loops in clusters.

2nd row — make one loop on each loop of the first row, but not on the loops that form the cluster.

In this manner many different patterns can be produced on a foundation of plain netting.

Netting composed of plain, double and oblong loops (fig. 644). — Netting composed of large and small loops is the kind generally used as a foundation for embroidery. Further on we give two pretty embroidered grounds, see figs. 709 and 710. In figure 644 the netted loops are square, but the embroidery can also be done on a diagonal ground.

1st row — consists entirely of a double and a plain loop alternately.

2nd row — entirely of oblong loops, made by passing the thread only once over the mesh.

The knot that closes the double loop must come as close to the mesh as possible, the one that closes the plain loop must be made at the head of this loop, so that when the row is finished, the top of all the loops should be in a line.

In the 3d row which is like the first, the plain loops must come between the small holes and the double loops between the large ones.

In the same way nets may be made by alternating four, nine or sixteen small loops with one big loop and the corresponding number of oblong loops.

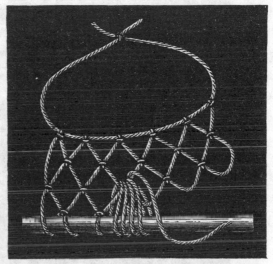

Fig. 643.
Formation of the loose loops.

Circular netting composed of long and short loops (fig. 645). — Make 30 or 31 loops over a rather big mesh with a coarse double thread, then draw up the thread on which the loops are strung, as tightly as possible, so as to form quite a small ring in the centre and fasten off.

For the next row, also made in coarse double thread, fasten the thread on to a long loop and make loops on each loop of the preceding row, over a fine mesh. Use the same mesh for

all the subsequent rows which should be worked in a fine
thread taken single.

If you want to avoid fastening on the thread afresh for
each row, you must make a slipped loop, see p. 471.

Circular netting formed by increases (fig. 646). — Make
12 loops on the foundation loop, close the ring, then go on
making a row with one knot in the first loop and two knots

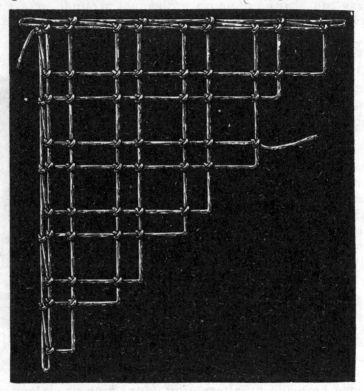

Fig. 644. Netting composed of plain, double and oblong loops.

in the second until the net is the right circumference; in the
subsequent rows, increase by one loop, that is to say, make
two knots in each of the preceding increases.

Square of netting with closed loops (figs. 647 and 648).
To make squares of netting and to get regular squares begin
by making two loops or three knots. Make two knots in each
of the following rows so that each row is increased by one
loop. Continue to increase until you have one loop more than
the square should number.

Following this row, with the extra loop, make a row without either increase or intake and begin the intakes in the next row, joining the two last loops of each row together by a knot.

Slip the two last loops.

Square of netting with empty loops (figs. 649 and 650). — Instead of beginning a square from the corner as just described it may be begun from the middle. Cast on the required number of loops, make an intake in each

Fig 645. Circular netting composed of long and short loops.

row, by skipping the last loop of the row. In coming back your first knot will therefore be made on the last loop but one of 'the preceding row, fig. 649. To complete the square fasten the thread on again, to the end of the thread of the last row, then make the same rows as at the beginning, see fig. 650.

Stripes of straight netting edged with empty and with closed loops (figs. 651 and 652). These stripes can be

Fig. 646. Circular netting formed by increases.

begun and finished in two different ways. The simplest way, especially when they are to be embroidered afterwards, is to cast on the needful number of loops, to decrease on one side by dropping a loop, fig. 651, or by joining two loops together with a knot, fig. 652, and to increase on the other side by making two knots on one loop.

Fig 647. Square of netting with closed loops, begun.

Great care must be taken not to change the order of the intakes and the increases as any mistake of this kind would interrupt the lines of squares and interfere with the subsequent embroidery, unless there should be more loops in the stripe than there are stitches in the pattern, in which case the superfluous loops might be cut away when the embroidery is finished. See that the loops do not become too short on the side of the increases, as very often happens because the double knot that comes from the increase takes more room than the intake, in which two loops are united by one knot.

Fig. 648. Square of netting with closed loops, finished.

Straight netting with a closed footing and a scalloped edge with empty loops (fig. 653). — To make stripes of straight netting begin by a square. After making two loops on the foundation loop, make rows with increases to the number of twelve. Then make an increase regularly in every row to the left and in the rows to the right leave the 3 outside loops empty.

Continuing the increases on the left net 4 rows without

increasing or decreasing on the right, then, in the next rows leave the outside loop empty.

Square frame of netting (fig. 654). — Handkerchief, counterpane and chair-back borders can be netted in one piece leaving an empty square inside. After casting on the loops as for an ordinary square of netting, letter *a*, increase them to the number of 8, letter *c*, then make 4 loops, skip the last 4 of the preceding row, turn, make 5 loops, increase at the last loop, turn, make 4 loops and decrease at the last loop, turn, make 5 loops, increase at the last, turn, make 4 loops, decrease at the last, then increase at the last, turn, make 4 loops, and decrease at the last, turn, make 5 loops, increase at the last, turn, make 4 loops, decrease at the last, turn, make 5 loops, increase at the last, cut the thread.

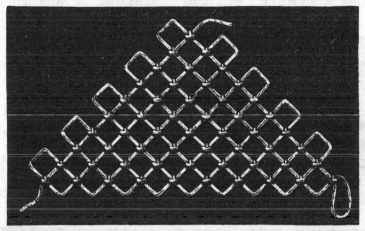

Fig. 649. Square of netting with empty loops, begun from the middle.

Fasten the thread on to the outside edge at *c* where the 4 empty loops are, make 4 loops, turn, make 5 loops, increase at the last, turn, make 4 loops, decrease at the last, turn, make 5 loops, increase at the last, turn, make 4 loops, decrease at the last and increase at the same, turn, make 4 loops, decrease at the last, turn, make 5 loops, increase at the last, turn, make 4 loops, decrease at the last, turn, make 5 loops, increase at the last, then cut the thread which is to be fastened afterwards to the outside edge.

Slip the 1st loop, make 6 loops and join the two separate stripes by a knot between the 3d and 4th loops, the last loop of the stripe on the left with the first of the stripe on the

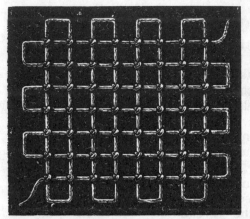

Fig. 650. Square of netting with empty loops, finished.

right, decrease at the last of the 6 loops, turn, make 6 loops, turn, make 5 loops, turn, make 4 loops, turn, make 3 loops, turn, make 2 loops, turn, slip the 2 last loops.

Embroidered netting Embroidered or artistic netting still known under the names of Filet Guipure, Cluny Guipure and Richelieu Guipure, &c. is a netted ground on which patterns of one kind or another are worked in a variety of stitches, producing the most charming effects.

Implements. — Besides scissors, needles and thread, a light steel frame is the only thing

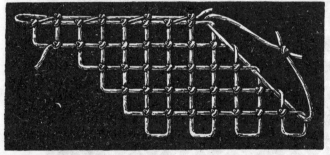

Fig. 651. Stripe of straight netting terminating with empty loops.

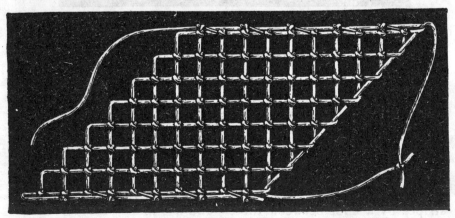

Fig 652. Stripe of straight netting terminating with closed loops.

required for embroidered netting and this makes it a very favorite form of fancywork.

Steel frame for embroidered netting (fig. 655). The frame on which the netting is mounted should be made of wire strong enough not to bend in the using. In shape it may be square or oblong, according to the work that ·is to be stretched upon it. This frame must be covered first with wadding or tow, fig. 655, and then with thin ribbon, wound tightly round it, especially at the corners, so that it may be quite firm and not twist about when the netting is sewn in. The ends of the ribbon should be secured by a few stitches.

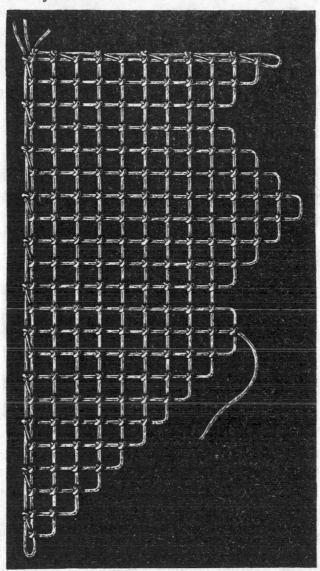

Fig. 653. Straight netting with a closed footing and a scalloped edge with empty loops.

Mounting the netting on the frame (fig. 656). — When the netting is exactly the size of the inside of the frame, it need only be fastened in with overcasting stitches, set very close together at the corners.

Mounting the netting on the frame with an auxiliary tape (fig. 657). — If on the contrary the netting is smaller than the frame, the space between it and the frame must be filled up all round with a linen tape sewn on all round the netting.

The tape must be eased on in the sewing so as to form little gathers all round. By this means the netting can be tightly

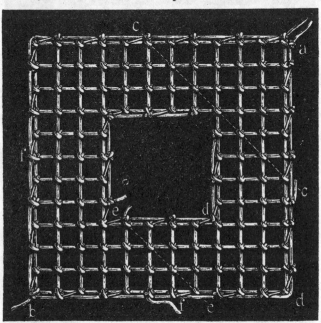

stretched without out tearing the threads of the outside loops.

Figure 657 shews how to sew on the tape, to fold it at the corners and to fix the netting into the frame.

Needles. — Special needles are used for this work, long and blunt and called needles for filet-guipure.

Materials. For embroidering on netting the same kind

Fig. 654. Square frame of netting.

of materials should be used as for the netted foundation; twisted threads for the different lace stitches and linen stitch, soft loose threads for darning stitch and for the outlines.

The best twisted threads to use are D.M.C Flax lace thread (Lin pour dentelles), (*) D.M.C Flax thread for knitting (Lin pour tricoter), D.M.C Alsatia or D.M.C Pearl cotton (Coton perlé; and for darning and outlining, either, D.M.C Special stranded cotton (Mouliné spécial), D.M.C Floss flax or flourishing thread (Lin floche) or D.M.C Persian silk (Soie de Perse).

(*) See at the end of the last chapter the tables of the sizes and colours of the cotton, flax and silk articles, mark D.M.C. — The French names, in brackets, are those stamped on the labels of the D.M.C articles.

Stitches. — The little squares of the netting serve as a foundation for a number of different stitches which lend themselves to so many combinations that we are sure that amongst those we are going to describe, not a few are unknown to our readers. We can safely affirm that a good number of them have never been described or illustrated in any work that has come to our notice hitherto.

Embroideries made on net by machine. — The various embroidery stitches on net can also be worked with the machine. Embroidery on coarse net should be done with D.M.C Alsa and on fine net with D.M.C Alsatian twist (Retors d'Alsace), using the same quality of thread for the bobbin and the shuttle.

Darning stitch (fig. 658). — The simplest stitch for covering a netted ground is the ordinary darning stitch. It is made over the number of squares prescribed by the patterns, by drawing the thread in and out and backwards and forwards as many

Fig. 655.
Steel frame for embroidered netting.

Fig. 656. Mounting the netting on the frame.

times as is necessary to fill them up. This is the stitch mostly used for reproducing a cross stitch pattern on a netted

ground and is specially recommended for covering large
surfaces, curtains, counterpanes and such like as it is quickly
done and shews up the pattern to advantage.

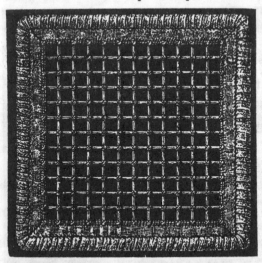

Fig. 657. Mounting the netting on the frame
with an auxiliary tape.

Linen stitch (figs.
659, 660, 661). — This
is the stitch most often
met with in old embroi-
deries ; the solid parts
of the flowers and leaves
and the borders being
generally worked in it.

After fastening the
thread on to a knot of
the netting, run it twice
to and fro over and
under the threads of
the netting, so that every
second thread passes at
the end of the rows
under the thread of the
netting and over the
thread as it is brought
back upwards again.

This forms the foun-
dation of the linen
stitch which is completed
by the second series of
stitches made by alter-
nately taking up a thread
and missing one as in
linen darning (fig. 55).
The thread may also be
carried both ways over
the threads of the
squares in which case
you should draw an
uneven number of
threads through the
squares, as with an even
number the crossing of

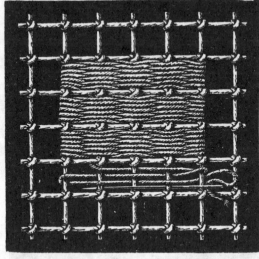

Fig. 658. Darning stitch.

the threads will never be regular at the last square.

When linen stitch is used for the border of a pattern and
a corner has to be formed, you begin by carrying the threads

over a given number of squares. In this first layer the threads must be left very slack and to ensure their being all the same length, lay a fine mesh or a thick knitting needle on the last square and stretch the threads over it. After carrying your second layer of threads thus over a few squares remove the mesh or needle.

The threads of the first layer become gradually shorter from being constantly taken up and dropped by the passing of the second threads in and out of them and end by being just long enough to prevent the last embroidered squares from being too tightly stretched.

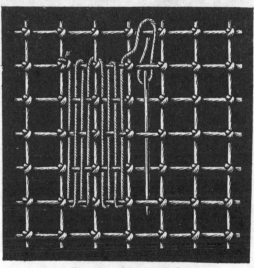

Fig. 659. Linen stitch.
Placing the first stitches.

On reaching the corner, you cross the threads of the next row, as shewn in figure 661. The first threads of the second side form the linen foundation in the corner square; from the second corner square you pass to the third; from the third to the fourth, passing under and over the threads that were stretched across for the first corner.

Loop stitch (point d'esprit) (figs. 662 and 663). — This is a light open stitch chiefly used

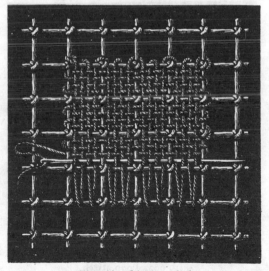

Fig. 660. Linen stitch.
Placing the second stitches.

for making a less transparent foundation than plain netting.
Fasten the thread to the middle of a vertical bar of the

netting, then make a loose loop to the middle of the next horizontal bar, fig. 662. These loops are always made from left to right; the thread is placed on the right, the needle passes downwards from above under the bar and in front of the working thread. The size of the loop must equal half the height of a bar of the netting.

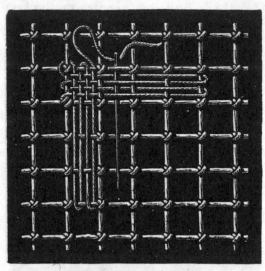

Fig. 661. Linen stitch.
Formation of the corners.

For the second row back, turn the work, make one stitch over the vertical bar of the net, pass the thread under the bar of the net as in the first row, then over the loop and under the bar which is below the loop.

Figure 663 shews how to connect the rows of "point d'esprit" and how to pass the needle through the stitches of the preceding row.

Star composed of long loose stitches thrown across several squares (figs. 664, 665, 666). — This star covers 16 squares of netting. Fasten the thread to the middle knot of the 16 squares, then carry it in a diagonal line, from left to right, under one knot of the netting and bringing it back to the

Fig. 662. Loop stitch.
First and second course of the thread.

other extremity of the square formed by the 16 squares of the netting, run the needle under the knot and lay the threads three times in the same way. In this manner the bottom rays of the star are formed, see fig. 664.

For the stitches that complete the figure, you start from the middle, and following the direction indicated by the arrow, cover the netting with 3 threads in a vertical line and 3 in a horizontal line, fig. 665.

When these are laid, slip the needle 4 or 5 times round in a circle under the diagonal and over the straight threads — not under the threads of the netting — then fasten off at the back.

Figure 666 shews a star, completed.

Leaves in darning stitch (figs. 667 and 668). This is a kind of stitch specially used for the fine delicate leaves in embroidered netting.

Starting from the middle carry the needle first to the right and then to the left under the threads of the foundation and push the stitches, as you make them close together with the point of the needle. This you will do best by holding the work so as to make the stitches towards you. Stretch the threads across first,

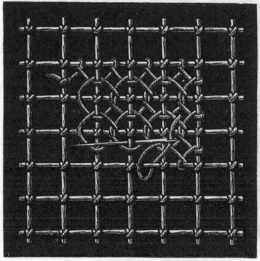

Fig. 663. Loop stitch.
Completed rows.

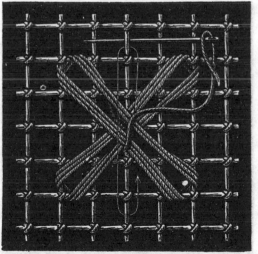

Fig. 664. Star composed of long loose stitches
thrown across several squares.
Laying the underneath threads.

as seen in the engraving, to the number of 2 or 3. then make the leaf with one, often even with several veins.

For a leaf with only one division or vein like the left one in figure 668, run the needle through in the middle of the threads, whereas for a leaf with two or three veins you must divide the threads into 3 or 4 clusters as the case may be.

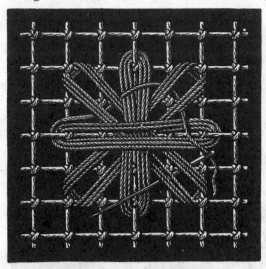

Fig. 665. Star composed of long loose stitches thrown across several squares. Laying the top threads.

In embroidering leaves of this kind in darning stitch you must draw the stitches at the top and bottom rather tighter than in the middle so as to give them the proper shape. If you wish them to be very slender at the bottom you can finish them off with a few overcasting stitches. Figure 668 shews you two leaves completed; one with one vein, the other with two.

Pointed scallops in darning stitch (fig. 669). — Besides the stitches with which the loops of netting are filled and the leaves worked upon them, pointed scallops like triangles can be made in darning stitch across each square loop of netting. The simplest way to work these scallops, is to carry your thread, as shewn in the illustration, to and fro over the square from

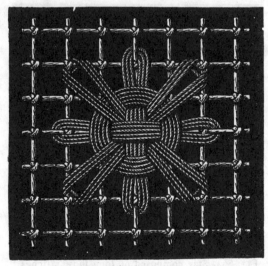

Fig. 666. Star composed of long loose stitches thrown across several squares. Star completed.

the knot in one corner to the middle of the bar above and

downwards to the opposite knot, round which the thread is
then carried and taken upwards again to the middle. As the
darning stitch must always be begun from the top you will

have two foundation
threads on one side and
three on the other.
Here also you must
push the darning
stitches together as
closely as possible with
the needle as you make
them.

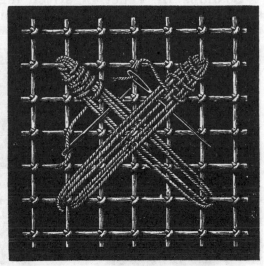

Fig. 667. Leaves in darning stitch.
Begun.

**Scallops in button-
hole stitch** (fig. 670).
Another quite as pretty
and easy way of work-
ing scallops on a netted
foundation is by making
two button-hole stitches
before crossing to the
opposite side.

Veined scallops (fig.
671). — A third way of
making scallops is by
first stretching a thread
to and fro in the middle
of the square, after
which you slip the
needle from left to right
under the middle thread
and underneath the left
bar from above. Then
carry the needle from
right to left over the
foundation thread and
under the right bar, and
so on.

The one thread must
be drawn tightly round
the other so that the

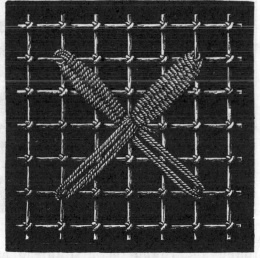

Fig. 668. Leaves in darning stitch.
Completed.

stitches produce a round and even vein like a small cord on
the back of the scallop. You must make enough stitches

to cover the thread completely and fill the bottom part of the square.

Scallops in Venetian stitch (fig. 672). — The prettiest scallops of all and those most in character with embroidered netting are those worked in Venetian stitch. You begin by making 8 or 10 button-hole stitches over the bar of the netting, then you continue the same stitch, to and fro, making one stitch less each row until there is only one left to make, by which you fasten the point of the scallop to the bar above. The thread must then be carried back on the wrong side to the next figure.

Fig. 669. Pointed scallops in darning stitch.

Wheels embroidered in darning stitch (figs. 673 and 674). — To make wheels or spiders as they are also called, you have first to fasten your thread to the middle knot of four squares, thence carry it diagonally to the right and left (fig. 673, right detail) across the empty squares of netting and the knot and bring it back to the middle, winding it

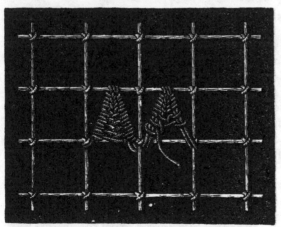

Fig. 670. Scallops in button-hole stitch.

round and round the first thread as you do so. You must make enough overcasting stitches round them to give these diagonal threads the appearance of a closely twisted cord.

Having returned to the centre carry the working thread round and round, under and over the corded threads and under the bars of the netting until the wheel thus formed covers half the bars of the netting.

Figure 674 shews, on the right, the finished wheel, as just described, whereas on the left is shewn how to make a wheel by dropping and picking up threads as in a darn. The last drawing also shews, that when the thread that forms the foundation of the wheel starts from a corner, it remains single in the first square until the wheel is finished; then when the wheel has attained the necessary circumference the needle is slipped back along the little spoke, opposite to the single thread and through the wheel and the single thread is overcast like the others.

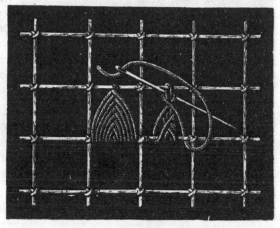

Fig 671. Veined scallops.

Ribbed wheels (fig. 675). — Prepare a foundation as for the wheels above described, then make a back stitch over a bar of the netting, slip the needle under the next bar and continue the back stitches until they cover the threads of the netting.

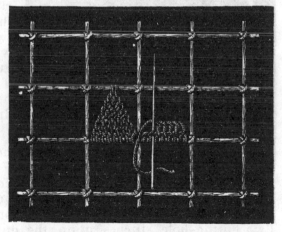

Fig. 672. Scallops in Venetian stitch.

Ribbed squares or lozenges (fig. 676). — These do not require foundation threads to be laid; the back stitches are made directly upon the netting. Both sides of the wheels and lozenges can be used, as may be seen from the engraving where the right and the wrong side meet together.

Wheels framed with button-hole stitches (fig. 677). —
When a wheel does not fill up a big square of netting sufficiently it may be encircled with loops or half button-hole
stitches to fill up the space left empty round it.

The left part of our illustration shews how the thread
having been passed
under the wheel and
twisted once round the
thread of the netting is
carried round the square
forming 8 loops.

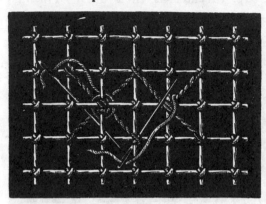

Fig. 673. Laying the first threads for a wheel
and the wheel begun.

The arrow indicates
the way in which the
loops are picked up and
how the first ring of
stitches round the wheel
is finished.

The second detail of
the same figure explains
the course the thread
that forms a second
ring, has to take through
the first loops and be-
tween the bars. The
white line serves as a
guide for the stitches.
The third detail re-
presents a wheel quite
finished.

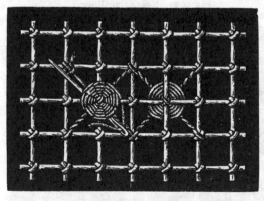

Fig. 674. Wheels worked in darning stitches
set in two ways.

**Star with button-
hole stitches** (fig. 678).
Few figures in embroi-
dered netting are so
quickly executed as the
one here represented.

Two button-hole stitches upon the outside bar of a square
and a single crossing of the thread at the bottom produce
elongated triangles which should always be begun from the
knot.

Two triangles face each other in each of the four squares
round one centre square, which is ornamented with a small
wheel.

Rounded corners with button-hole stitches (fig. 679). —
Darning stitches made over a thread carried diagonally across
one square and over four bars of the netting produce this
pretty subject. The detail on the left shews the work begun.

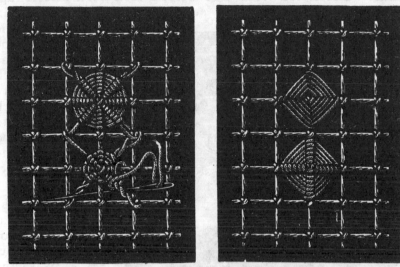

Fig. 675. Ribbed wheels.   Fig. 676. Ribbed lozenges.

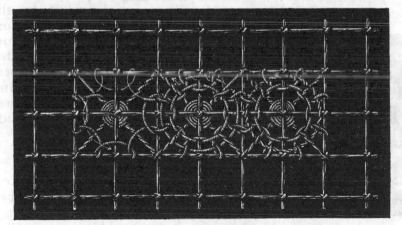

Fig. 677. Wheels framed with button-hole stitches.

Linen stitch framed with darning stitch (fig. 680). —
There are some patterns it would be almost impossible to
transfer on to netting unless the outlines could be softened
by darning stitches as shewn in the foregoing figure. When
linen stitch is bordered by darning stitches these should not

be as numerous as in figure 679; you may also, instead of stopping the stitches at each corner, carry them round a square as shewn in the left detail of the figure.

Linen stitch set with bar stitch and cord stitch (fig. 681). — Linen stitch is often set with bar or cord stitch in which case the setting can be done with the thread with which the squares were filled, or a much coarser thread may also be used which greatly enhances the effect of the setting.

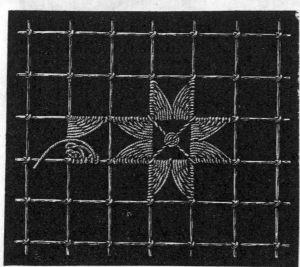

Fig. 678. Star with button-hole stitches.

Flower in post stitch on a foundation of linen stitch (fig. 682). — With the help of post stitch, described in the chapter on "Embroidery upon White Stuff" and illustrated in figure 79, a great variety of details and supplementary ornaments can be made on a foundation of linen stitch.

Bordering in button-hole stitch (fig. 683). — Scalloped edges in netting

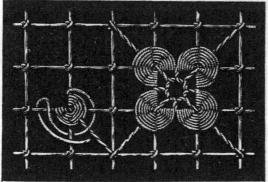

Fig. 679. Rounded corners with button-hole stitches. should be button-holed always from right to left; two or three padding threads should be laid on first over the bars of the netting and the button-holing done over these.

The bars of the netting must not be cut away until the edge is finished.

Cut work in embroidered netting (fig. 684). — Here cut work means half covering the bars of the netting with button-hole stitches and cutting away the other half with scissors. The inner bars are often or- namented with a double button-hole edging, fig. 684, and knotted picots. You se- parate the stitches of the first row of button – holing slightly so as to be able to introduce the stitches of the second row be- tween them. (See the chapter on "Needle- made Laces", figures 869 and 872.)

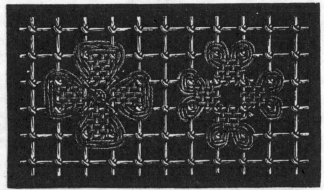

Fig. 680. Linen stitch framed with darning stitch.

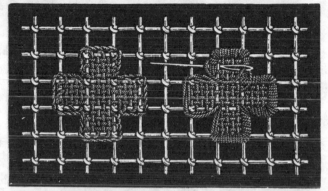

Fig. 681. Linen stitch set with bar stitch and cord stitch.

Ground worked in double loop stitch (fig. 685). — In the 1ˢᵗ row carry your thread, over one bar and slip it behind a knot; in returning follow the same course so that 4 threads cross each other in each square.

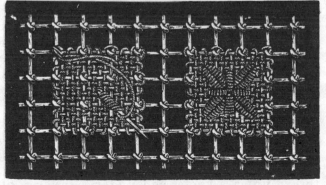

Fig. 682. Flower in post stitch on a foundation of linen stitch.

In the 3ᵈ row turn your needle downwards, as in the 1ˢᵗ and 2ⁿᵈ row, but above under 3 threads; in the 4ᵗʰ row put the thread into the double loop already completed.

Ground in waved stitch (fig. 686). — To make this stitch pass the thread in each row of the netting over two squares and behind a knot.

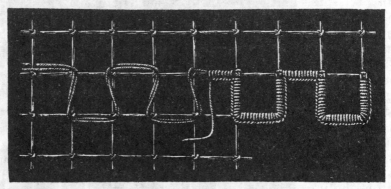

Fig. 683. Bordering in button-hole stitch.

Ground in intersecting loop stitch (fig. 687). — Begin by covering the whole surface to be embroidered with plain loop stitches, then stretch threads diagonally across the squares of the netting and the loop stitches; one set of threads running over the stitches and under the knots of the netting, the other under the first and second threads of the loop stitches and over the first crossed threads and the knots.

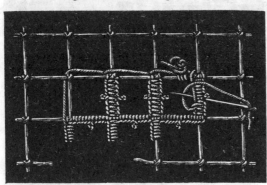

Fig. 684. Cut work in embroidered netting.

The laying and stretching of these threads must, it is hardly necessary to say, be systematically and regularly done.

Ground worked in horizontal lines (fig. 688). — Make half cross stitches over 4 squares of netting, then pass the thread unter 3 knots, and under 2 squares of the netting. In the second row, cross the threads over those of the first row, as is shewn in our engraving.

Ground formed of intersected loop stitches (fig. 689). —
Cover one whole row of squares with cross stitches and skip
3 rows of squares. When you have covered the necessary
number of rows with cross stitches, take a long needleful of

thread and pass your
needle upwards from
below and from right
to left under the two
bars of the third upper
square; then descend to
the first square of the
3 rows beneath and pass
from right to left under
the bars, so as to keep
an interval of 3 squares
between the fresh
stitches. The next row
of stitches is made in
the same way, so that
the stitches are not only
set contrariwise but
cover each other reci-
procally.

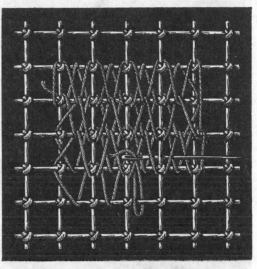

Fig. 685. Ground worked in double loop stitch.

Latticed ground
(fig. 690). — Begin by
running the thread to
and fro under 2 vertical
bars and over 3 hori-
zontal ones. When the
ground is entirely cover-
ed, carry your thread
from right to left under
the bars over which the
threads of the first rows
cross each other; then
take it over the oblong
crosses, that extend over
5 squares of netting and
pass it in the same
line under the bars of
the netting.

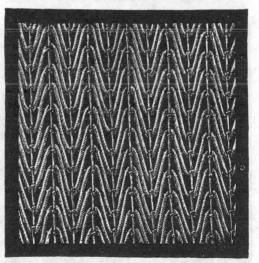

Fig. 686. Ground in waved stitch.

Coming back the long stitches cross each other over the
stitches of the first rows.

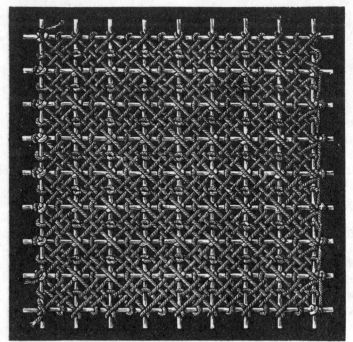

Fig. 687. Ground in intersecting loop stitch.

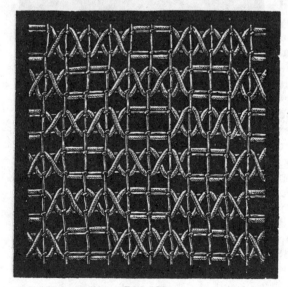

Fig. 688.
Ground worked in horizontal lines.

Ground worked in Russian stitch (fig. 691). — Begin at the top, pass the thread, from right to left, under one bar of the netting, carry it downwards over 4 squares and pass it again, from right to left, under the second vertical bar; then upwards again over 4 squares of the netting, and so on.

The stitches of the next row are made in the same way; only you must see that the loops formed by the stitches all come on the same line of knots of the netting.

Ground worked with two sizes of thread. — Herewith begins the series of stitches referred to at the beginning of the chapter, copied in part from one of the oldest and most curious pieces of embroidered netting that exists. In grounds worked with two sizes of thread all the stitches that are to be made in the coarser size should be made first.

Ground worked in darning stitch and loop stitch (point d'esprit) (fig. 692). — The coarser thread was used for the darning stitches which have to be made first, and for the almond shaped stitches that connect them; the finer thread for the loop stitches in the intermediate squares.

Fig. 689. Ground formed of intersected loop stitches.

Ground with little wheels and loop stitch (fig. 693). — Take a coarse thread and finish all the wheels first, each over 4 bars of the netting; then, with a finer thread make loop stitches in rows between them, as in figure 663.

Ground in squares of darning stitch with loop stitch between (fig. 694). — Darning stitches worked horizontally with the coarse thread, over 4 squares of the netting alternate with

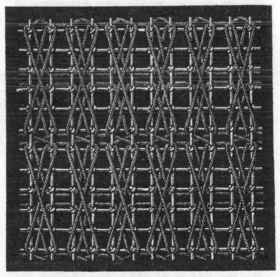

Fig. 690. Latticed ground.

loop stitches made in fine thread covering the same number of squares.

Diagonal ground (fig. 695). — Carry the needle with the coarse thread under the first knot, from right to left, then

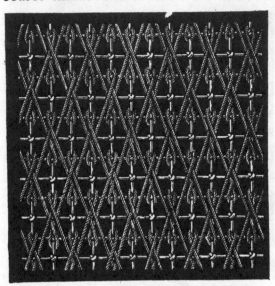

Fig. 691. Ground worked in Russian stitch.

under the next knot, from left to right. Repeat these same stitches twice, to and fro, so that the squares of the netting are edged diagonally with a double layer of threads. When you have made these first stitches over the whole ground take the fine thread and make loop stitches in the intermediate squares, passing your needle regularly over the double stitch. Lastly, intersect the loop stitches with diagonal threads and pass the needle each time through the knot of the netting.

Diagonal ground with cross stitches (fig. 696). — To make this pattern, which is very like the preceding one, work 3 diagonal stitches to and fro across the corners of the squares of the netting, then in a fourth and fifth row, make cross stitches with fine thread over the first stitches.

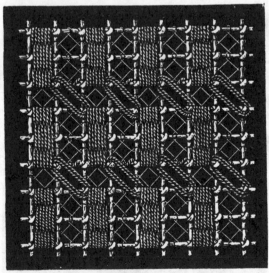

Fig. 692. Ground worked in darning stitch and loop stitch (point d'esprit).

Ground worked with darning and overcast stitches (fig. 697). — Patterns worked chiefly in darning stitches always present a closer and heavier appearance than those we have just been describing; they should therefore only be used where a very well covered shaded surface is required.

Fill a diagonal line of squares with darning stitches, fig. 658, set them as closely as you can, but an equal number in each square, then carry a thread diagonally across the intermediate empty squares and double it, coming back by overcasting stitches.

Ground with squares of darning stitches, and little wheels (fig. 698). — In figure 698 fill the squares with the same darning stitches as in figure 697, and instead of the long corded diagonal threads across the intermediate squares make a wheel in each.

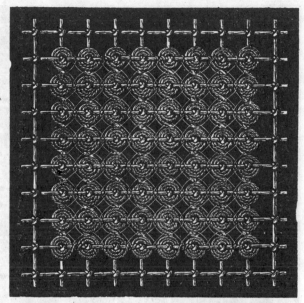

Fig. 693. Ground with little wheels and loop stitch.

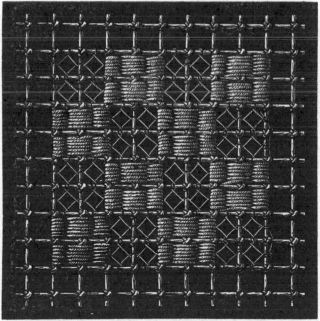

Fig. 694. Ground in squares of darning stitch with loop stitch between.

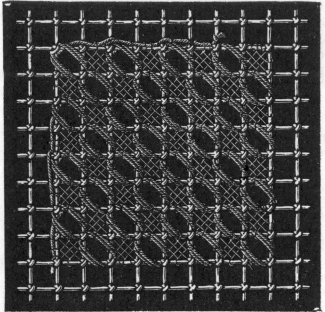

Fig. 695. Diagonal ground.

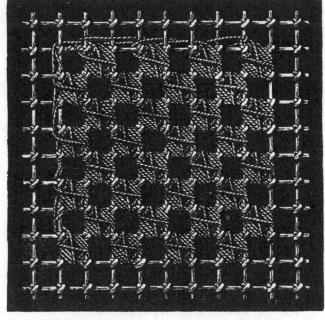

Fig. 696. Diagonal ground with cross stitches.

Ground with squares of darning stitches and big wheels (fig. 699). — In figure 699 the darning stitches as well as the wheels cover 4 loops of the netting.

Ground with big wheels (fig. 700). — Big surfaces may be entirely covered with big wheels made in one or other of the ways described in figures 673 to 675.

Ground worked in darning stitch and cross stitch (fig. 701). — Begin, as before with the darning stitches and then proceed to the cross stitches. To give them the correct shape, finish all the rows of stitches one way first;

in the next rows that cross the first introduce the thread between the stitches that were crossed first.

Ground of geometrical figures (fig. 7o2). — This pattern, quite different from all the preceding ones, consists of simple geometrical lines.

Fasten the thread to a knot of the netting, then carry it, always diagonally under 3 other knots of the netting and repeat this 3 times; after which carry it once round the fourth knot of the netting to fasten it and come back to the knot already encircled, and repeat the 4 rounds as in the first instance. By always bringing back the

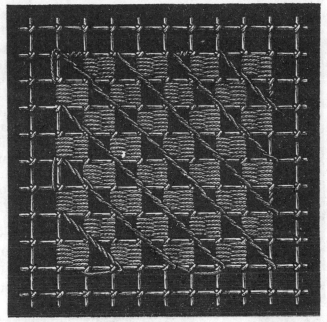

Fig. 697. Ground worked with darning and overcast stitches.

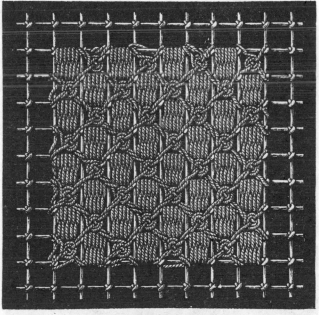

Fig. 698.
Ground with squares of darning stitches, and little wheels.

thread to the knot whence the new square is to begin, you
will have 4 threads on two of the sides and 5 on the other two.

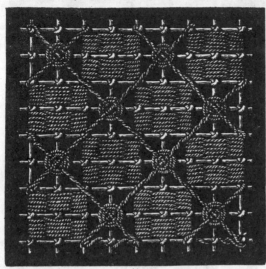

Fig. 699. Ground with squares of darning stitches
and big wheels.

**Netted insertion
embroidered in darn-
ing stitch** (fig. 703). —
This insertion will be
welcome to those of
our readers who lack
the patience necessary
for work of a more
elaborate nature, as a
means of making with-
out any great expendi-
ture of time or labour
charming trimmings
for curtains, bed or
table-linen.

Straight netting has
already been fully des-
cribed in figures 648,
652 and 654, and darn-
ing stitch, in
figure 658. We
recommend
those who do
not care to
take the
trouble   of
making   the
netted ground
themselves to
use canvas net
(Filet canevas)
a pretty ma-
terial, which
is   an   exact
imitation   of
hand-made
netting,   and
very durable.
The wide bor-
der is worked
in horizontal

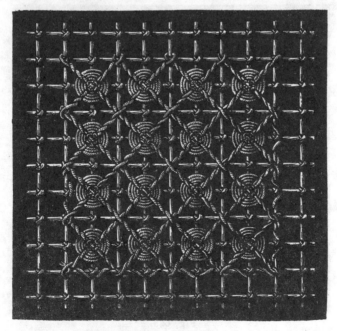

Fig. 700. Ground with big wheels.

rows, the little scalloped edge, in vertical stitches.

Square in Richelieu netting (*) (figs. 704 and 7o5). — Richelieu netting differs from every other kind of embroidered netting in simplicity of execution and originality of design.

Worked on a very fine netted ground we find flower and leaf subjects, forming little sprays, sometimes grouped round an elegantly shaped vase.

Fig. 7o1. Ground worked in darning stitch and cross stitch.

The principal figures are worked in linen stitch; their outlines set round with coarse thread stand out clear and strong on the netted ground. This same coarse thread is also used for the little twigs, stalks, and sprays.

For the netted ground and the linen stitch use D.M.C Flax lace thread (Lin pour dentelles) or D.M.C Alsatia, in the

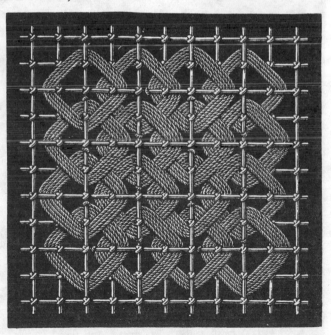

Fig. 7o2. Ground of geometrical figures.

(*) See at the end of the volume the list of the albums of the D.M.C Library. containing a large variety of patterns for all kinds of work.

Fig. 703. Netted insertion embroidered in darning stitch.
Materials — For the netting : D.M.C Flax thread for knitting or D.M.C Alsatia.
For the embroidery: D.M.C Floss flax or D.M.C Special stranded cotton,
in white or écru.

fine numbers. For the outlines take the coarse numbers of
D.M.C Flax lace thread (Lin pour dentelles) or D.M.C Pearl
cotton (Coton perlé).

The linen stitch here is done in two rows instead of four,
as described in figures 659 to 661.

Fig. 704. Square in Richelieu netting.
Materials: D.M.C Flax lace thread Nos. 6 and 40, in white, or D.M.C Alsatia
No. 30 and D.M.C Pearl cotton No. 3, in écru. (*)

After fastening the thread to a knot of the netting carry
the needle, to and fro, under and over the loops of the netting
so as to take up every alternate thread; coming back you take
up the threads previously skipped.

(*) See at the end of the last chapter the tables of the sizes and colours of
the cotton, flax and silk articles, mark D.M.C.

In the second row of stitches, which completes the linen stitch, you repeat the same stitch, just as in linen darning, that is taking up one thread and skipping the next.

The outlining with the coarse thread, as well as the way to do the little stalks and sprays are clearly illustrated by the engraving and require no further explanation.

Ground of netting, embroidered with different stitches (fig. 706). — We have already had occasion in the foregoing explanations to point out the great advantage of embroidering with two sizes of thread but it is only in a larger and more important piece of work that it is possible really to judge of the excellent effect produced by the use of two quite different sizes of thread. (*)

Fig. 7o5. Working detail of figure 7o4.
Flower in linen stitch.

The principal lines of the pattern, fig. 706, in darning stitch are worked with D.M.C Knotting cotton (Fil à pointer), an extremely coarse and twisted material, whilst the loop stitches as well as the wheels within them are in D.M.C Crochet cotton 6 cord (Cordonnet 6 fils).

The actual piece of work, reproduced here, was worked in écru thread, but there is no reason why several colours should not be introduced, for instance Mahogany brown 771 for the ground, Cardinal red 347 for the darning stitches, and D.M.C Gold chiné (blue and gold) for the other ornamental stitches.

Ground of netting embroidered in many colours (fig. 707). — The particular charm of this otherwise unpretending pattern, is due to the variety of the materials and colours introduced.

The netting in D.M.C Pearl cotton (Coton perlé) No. 8, Cachou brown 434, is covered over first with loop stitches,

---

(*) See at the end of the last chapter the tables of the sizes and colours of the cotton, flax and silk articles, mark D.M.C.

sparsely scattered ; these stitches in Ash grey 415 are connected by darning stitches in D.M.C Pearl cotton (Coton perlé) No. 8, Lime-tree grey 392.

D.M.C Special stranded cotton (Mouliné spécial) (*) in Geranium red 350, is used for the little centre squares as well

Fig. 706. Ground of netting, embroidered with different stitches.
Materials: D.M.C Knotting cotton No. 30 and D.M.C Crochet cotton 6 cord No. 15,
in white and écru, or D.M.C Pearl cotton Nos. 5 and 8, in Mahogany brown 771,
Cardinal red 347 and D.M.C Gold chiné, blue and gold.

as for the stitches in Old gold 680 that encircle the red stitches.

Border with embroidered netted ground, in the Persian style (fig. 708). — The plain loops of the netting

(*) See at the end of the last chapter the tables of the sizes and colours of the cotton, flax and silk articles, mark D.M.C. — The French names, in brackets, are those stamped on the labels of the D.M.C articles.

are in D.M.C Alsatia No. 3o ; the embroidery in D.M.C Gold
and silver embroidery thread No. 40, used threefold, which
gives more relief to the stitches and takes less time to work.

The outside stitches of the scalloped lines of the little
border are worked in gold and the inner ones in silver, and

Fig. 7o7. Ground of netting embroidered in many colours.
Materials — For the netting : D.M.C Pearl cotton No. 8, in Cachou brown 434.
For the embroidery : D.M.C Pearl cotton No. 8, in Ash grey 415 and Lime-tree
grey 392, and D.M.C Special stranded cotton No. 25, in Geranium
red 350 and Old gold 680. (*)

both require double rows worked to and fro. In the first row,
you take the thread, horizontally under two vertical loops,
then slanting upwards, through a knot of the netting, again
under two vertical loops ; then slanting downwards over a
knot of the netting, under the two next vertical loops, and so

(*) These numbers refer to the colours on the colour cards of the articles
stamped with the D.M.C trade mark. These cards can be consulted at all the
mercers' and needlework shops.

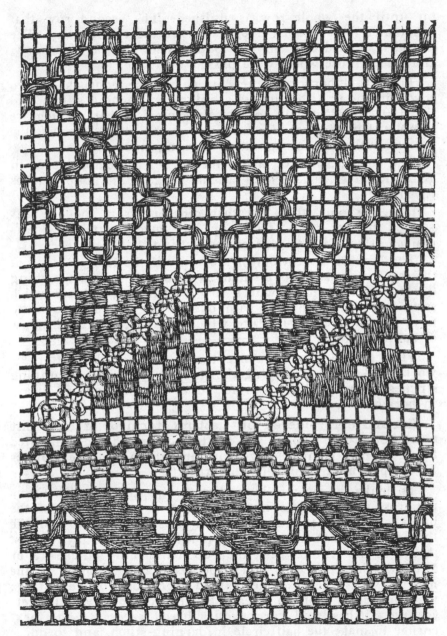

Fig. 708. Border with embroidered netted ground, in the Persian style.
Materials: D.M.C Alsatia No. 30, in Garnet red 309 and D.M.C Embroidery
gold and silver thread No. 40.

on until the whole row is finished. The second row that terminates the scalloped line, is worked the reverse way. The thread is carried over all the loops raised in the first row, and under those which were passed over.

The actual border, worked in gold, also consists of two rows; in the first the figures are done in darning stitch, and the first thread is lain for the intermediate bars, which are completed in the second return row at the same time that the bottom outline of the figures in darning stitch is done.

The detached figures, above the border are embroidered in gold and silver, the darning stitches in gold, the loop stitches in silver.

Here the loop stitch is rather different from the one described further back. The loops are made round the knots instead of round the loops of the netting.

The loop at the bottom of the vein of the leaf is made at the same time as the loop stitch, as follows : after surrounding the loop of the netting with a row of running stitches which serve as padding, cover it with overcasting stitches, so as to form a corded eyelet-hole, to which you further add a row of running stitches.

The checked ground above that completes the pattern is worked in gold, by carrying the thread, by means of running stitches in broken lines over four loops of the netting, always in horizontal rows.

Ground embroidered on netting formed of different sized loops (fig. 709). — The netting, described and illustrated by figure 644, composed of plain, oblong and double loops is here reproduced richly embroidered. (*)

To make the isolated loop stitches the thread which forms the cross in the middle must be taken to the middle of the bar, the loops that form the stitch must be finished and the thread taken back to its starting point. There you lay the first thread of the centre wheel, then do the darning stitches, 4 or 5 of which cross each other between 2 bars only of the netting, whilst the next ones extend over 4 bars of the netting; then you cover half the thread stretched diagonally with overcasting stitches, and carry your thread across to the next corner to make the half circle in darning stitch, and so on.

(*) See at the end of the volume the list of the albums of the D.M.C Library, containing a large variety of patterns for all kinds of work.

Ground embroidered on netting formed of different sized loops (fig. 710). — Here the netting is formed of one big loop and a square consisting of nine small loops, with oblong loops between; on this ground the two kinds of stars represented in the engraving are embroidered.

The bigger stars are worked in darning stitches in the shape of pyramids, surrounding a little star formed of threads stretched across the square, and overcast.

The little stars consist of triangles in darning stitch worked

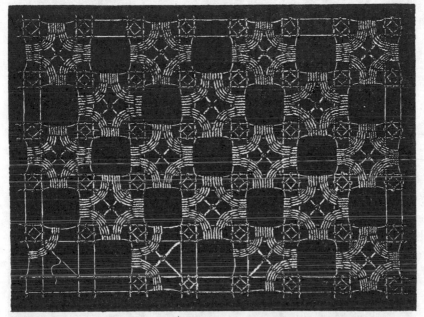

Fig. 709. Ground embroidered on netting formed of different-sized loops.
Materials: D.M.C Flax thread for knitting or D.M.C Alsatian thread, in white or écru. (*)

round a thread stretched across in a diagonal line forming a little spider in the centre.

Two squares in embroidered netting (figs. 711 and 712). These two squares worked on a plain netted ground, make very nice chair-backs, combined with plain squares of linen; or joined together by an insertion of lace.

One of the following edgings should be selected to trim

(*) See at the end of the last chapter the tables of the sizes and colours of the cotton, flax and silk articles, mark D.M.C.

these squares outside. For all these patterns use D.M.C Flax
lace thread (Lin pour dentelles), the same number for the
embroidery as for the netting.

When the netting is fixed in the frame begin the embroidery with the parts worked in linen stitch, figs. 659 to 661,
and then do the exterior parts in loop stitch, figs. 662 and 663.

Then proceed to the little raised leaves in darning stitch

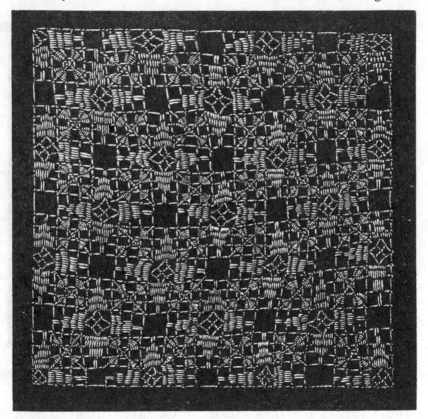

Fig. 710. Ground embroidered on netting formed of different sized loops.
Materials: D.M.C Flax lace thread or D.M.C Alsatian thread, in white or écru.

with two veins, figs. 667 and 668, then the stalks and the
spider in the centre and the ring in linen stitch and darning
stitch, which surrounds the stalks of the leaves; and last of
all make the loop stitch inside the circle.

In the second square you proceed in the same manner.
After doing the parts worked in linen stitch and darning stitch
embroider the outlines of the leaves which require 6 rows of

darning stitches, then make the stalks, and last of all the
inner circle consisting of six rows of darning stitches.

Two edgings in embroidered netting (figs. 713 and 714).
For these two edgings, you may make the netting either in
straight stripes or scalloped, with loops left empty, as described at the beginning of this chapter.

Fig. 711. Square in embroidered netting.
Materials: D.M.C Flax thread for knitting, D.M.C Flax lace thread or
D.M.C Alsatian thread, in white or écru. (*)

After finishing the embroidery, button-hole the edge, and
if the embroidery is worked on a straight stripe, cut out the
superfluous loops.

(*) See at the end of the last chapter the tables of the sizes and colours of
the cotton, flax and silk articles, mark D.M.C.

33

In figure 713 the ground is filled in with loop stitches; the stars, in button-hole stitch are made as in figure 678; they are ornamented inside with a little spider and surrounded by a ring made of four rows of darning stitches, which throws up the pattern to better advantage.

In figure 714 the ground is also filled in with loop stitches;

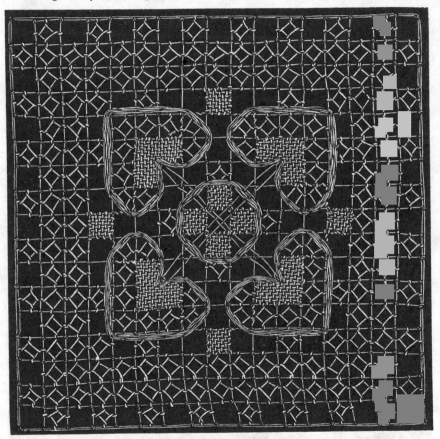

Fig. 712. Square in embroidered netting.
Materials : D.M.C Flax thread for knitting, D.M.C Flax lace thread or
D.M.C Alsatian thread, in white or écru.

the footing consists of detached squares of darning stitches, whilst the chief figure represents a square with a little ribbed wheel in the middle and triangles in button-hole stitch in the four corners.

Insertion in embroidered netting (fig. 715). — This insertion is composed of two different subjects, separated by bars in linen stitch. Each subject is surrounded by loop stitches and triangles in button-hole stitch.

The subjects themselves are made up of triangles in button-hole stitch, differently disposed and surrounded by four rows of darning stitches; a lozenge in darning stitch surrounds the spider in the centre.

Fig. 713. Lace edging in embroidered netting.
Materials: D.M.C Flax thread for knitting or D.M.C Alsatian thread, in white or écru. (*)

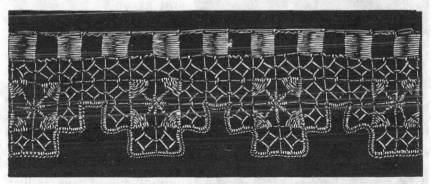

Fig. 714. Lace edging in embroidered netting.
Materials: D.M.C Flax thread for knitting or D.M.C Alsatian thread, in white or écru. (*)

Square in cut netting (fig. 716). — There are few patterns that admit of the use of all the stitches described hitherto, in such a satisfactory manner as this square. On a ground of very fine netting, first, with a coarser number of thread, you do the linen stitch, then the ground of the lace, and the

___

(*) See at the end of the last chapter the tables of the sizes and colours of the cotton, flax and silk articles, mark D.M.C.

ribbed wheels, fig. 675, the cut out bars, fig. 684, in the middle, wheels set very close together, fig. 700, and bars in darning stitch, fig. 668.

Edging in cut netting (fig. 717). — In this edging several shades are again introduced; thus the netting is done in snow white and the lace stitches, in cream; the wheels of the border, which fill the squares almost entirely are also embroidered in the same shade; for the raised wheels and the star, we used Scabious violet 397; for the long bars in darning stitch, Golden green 582, for the crosses in linen stitch, alternately, violet and green.

Embroideries on "lacis" or net canvas. — A fabric was devised already a long while ago to replace hand-made netting especially the very fine kind which is slow and tedious to do. This fabric, called "lacis" or "canvas net", an excellent imitation of the hand-made netting, is now made, in écru, in white and in colours, with loops of different sizes, and the work done upon it is in no way inferior to the finest done upon knotted netting.

The most interesting embroideries on this fabric are those done on the large kind with the big loops and in coarse thread, they

Fig. 715. Insertion in embroidered netting.
Materials: D.M.C Flax thread for knitting or D.M.C Alsatian thread, in white or écru.

are not to be distinguished from those in cut stitch, the
net ground presenting the effect of a linen ground of drawn
threads. There are also charming embroideries in straight
stitch, worked in coloured silk on coloured "lacis" with very
small meshes. The first embroideries on canvas net, known
under the name of Sicilian embroideries came to us from

Fig. 716. Square in cut netting.
Materials: D.M.C Flax lace thread or D.M.C Alsatian thread, in white or écru. (*)

Italy and Spain where this kind of work was always specially
cultivated.

The patterns on a large scale are worked in darning stitch
for all the solid parts and the outlines are embroidered.

Stuffs. — The modern stuffs are made with meshes of
different sizes, in white, cream and in colours.

(*) See at the end of the last chapter the tables of the sizes and colours of
the cotton, flax and silk articles, mark D.M.C.

Materials. — As lacis is a very supple stuff it is advisable to use a soft material for embroidering upon it, and we recommend either D.M.C Special stranded cotton (Mouliné spécial), D.M.C Pearl cotton (Coton perlé), D.M.C Floss flax (Lin floche) or D.M.C Persian silk (Soie de Perse).

For the outlines a more twisted thread may exceptionally be taken, such as D.M.C Flax lace thread (Lin pour dentelles), D.M.C Knotting cotton (Fil à pointer), or even a metal thread : D.M.C Fine gold or silver thread (Or ou Argent fin), D.M.C Turkish gold cord (Ganse turque) and D.M.C Gold chiné (Chiné d'or).

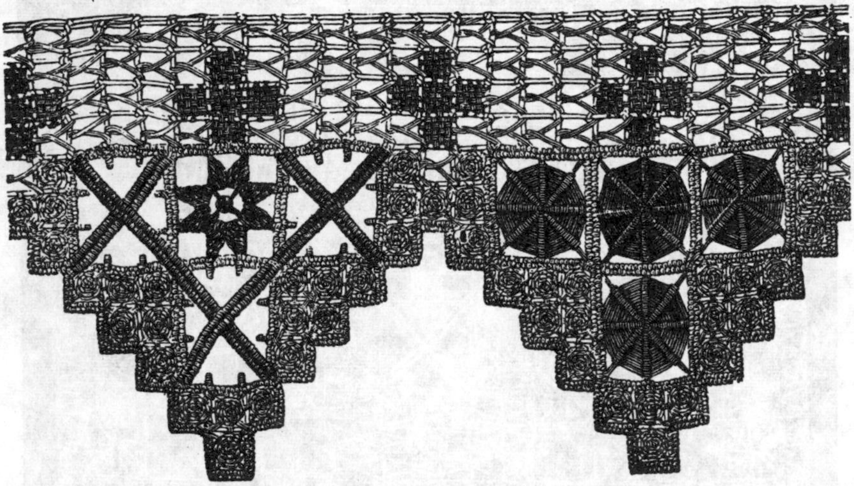

Fig. 717. Lace edging in cut netting.

Materials — For the netting and embroidery : D.M.C Pearl cotton No. 8 or D.M.C Alsatia No. 20, in Snow-white, Maize yellow 579, Scabious violet 397 and Golden green 582. (*)

Embroideries made on lacis by machine. — Like the embroideries on net the patterns of embroidery on lacis can also be worked with the machine.

For filling in the figures in darning stitch use D.M.C Alsatian twist (Retors d'Alsace) for both the upper and the underneath threads, and D.M.C Alsa for the outlines.

To imitate a ground of overcast bars, use D.M.C Alsatian twist (Retors d'Alsace) for the upper thread and D.M.C Machine thread (Fil pour machines) No. 150 for the underneath thread.

(*) See at the end of the last chapter the tables of the sizes and colours of the cotton, flax and silk articles, mark D.M.C.

Insertion in embroidery on lacis. Imitation of Richelieu net (fig. 718). — For the ground take cream canvas net with big meshes, woven of fine thread; the embroidery is the same as in the square, fig. 704.

To give greater richness to the embroidery D.M.C Gold chiné (Chiné d'or), écru and gold, was used for the linen stitch, and D.M.C Turkish gold cord (Ganse turque) No. 12 for the outlining.

Bordor in embroidery on lacis. Imitation of cut work (figs. 719 and 720). — This pattern is particularly interesting owing to its being easy and pleasant to work, and the solid look of the embroidery reminds one of the Italian cut stitch work.

A very coarse canvas-net serves as a foundation. The pattern in darning stitch and the ground of overcast bars are made exactly after the directions given in the chapter on "Openwork

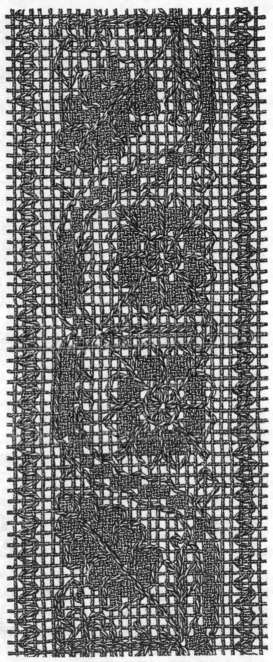

Fig. 718. Insertion in embroidery on "lacis". Imitation of Richelieu net.

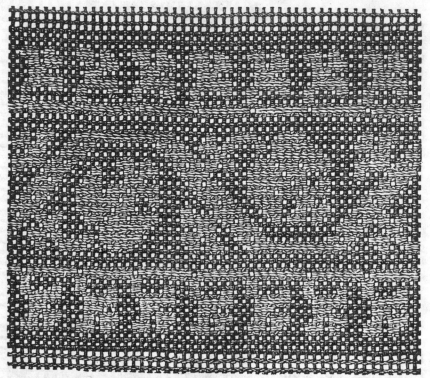

Fig. 719. Border in embroidery on "lacis". Imitation of cut work.
Materials: D.M.C Pearl cotton or D.M C Floss flax, in Maize yellow 579 and
Rust brown 3313.

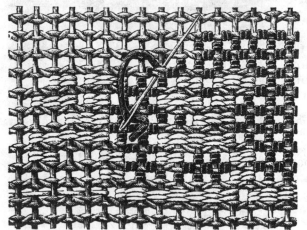

Fig. 720. Working of the figures in darning stitch and
the ground in overcast bars.

on Linen". Figure 720 shews part of the work in progress, the darning stitch is worked to and fro, in two rows, the overcast bars, made in diagonal rows take two overcast stitches each.

The materials that should be used are D.M.C Pearl cotton (Coton

Fig. 721. Border in embroidery on "lacis". Sicilian style.
Materials: D.M.C Persian silk, in Cream white 1220, Rust brown 1156, Old
gold 1259, Old lilac 1076 and 1078, Indigo blue 1012, Beetle green 1223
and Old pink 1003 and 1006.

Fig. 722. Border in embroidery on "lacis" in darning stitch
with corded outlines.

perlé) in dark brown for the bars, and in cream for the darning stitches.

Border in embroidery on lacis, Sicilian style (fig. 721). Worked on a bronze coloured canvas ground, this handsome border, rich in colour, is one of the most charming patterns in our book, not only on account of its being so simple to work, in flat stitch and stroke stitch, but also because of the number of colours that can be introduced into it.

Many patterns in cross stitch can be embroidered in the same manner and almost all the conventional flower designs, can, with very slight changes, be worked in flat stitch on canvas-net. (*)

The embroidery itself is done on counted threads, without

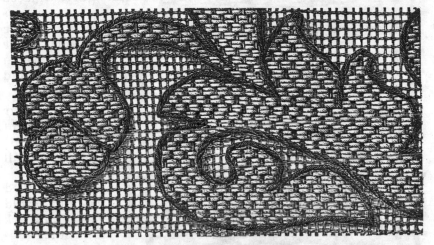

Fig. 723. Detail of figure 722.

tracing. This mode of working has the advantage of facilitating the change of colours, as the ends of two coloured threads have only to be joined by a weaver's knot.

As most embroideries on lacis are not lined, the different threads must be knotted together when you change colours, so as not to have long irregular stitches in all directions on the wrong side which might shew through and spoil the effect.

You make the weaver's knot so that once tightened it lies at about the middle of the stitch.

(*) See at the end of the volume the list of the albums of the D.M.C Library, containing a large variety of patterns for all kinds of work.

To work with several colours you must of course have a separate needle for each colour.

Our border is embroidered entirely in D.M.C Persian silk (Soie de Perse). In the centre of the big figures are two small yellow lozenges and two green ones in a red frame which is surrounded by four detached figures embroidered in dark blue. The flowers are worked in lilac or light pink, with stalk and calyx in bright green; the little figures placed in the angles of the blue subjects are rust brown outside and white inside.

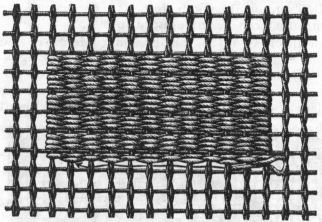

Fig. 724. Darning stitch in fine thread.

At the four extremities of the central figure are small rectangular figures worked in old gold yellow and dark pink; the framing, in the form of a lozenge, is in dark green, dark pink, dark lilac and dark blue.

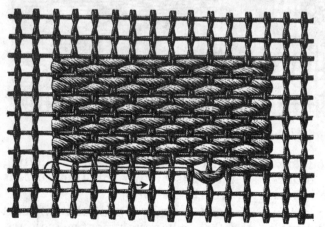

Fig. 725. Darning stitch in coarse thread.

The repetitions of the principal figure are worked in the same colours but so that four light lilac flowers are turned towards the interior of the border, and one whole pink flower and two halves towards the outside edge.

The broken line in stroke stitch is in dark pink and old gold yellow; in the little flowers that finish the border outside, all the colours used in the actual border are alternately introduced.

Border in embroidery on lacis in darning stitch with corded outlines (figs. 722 and 723). — Just as in embroidery on linen, embroidery on canvas-net can be done on a tracing. In this case the subjects of the patterns are covered with

darning stitches to be subsequently outlined

Figure 722 represents one of these patterns, the working of which is explained by figure 723.

As may be seen, the darn-ing stitch is done in one row, going and coming once through the series of loops and taking up every second thread of the stuff.

The outlining is done in two rows of running stitch-es which must join, and being set quite close to the darning

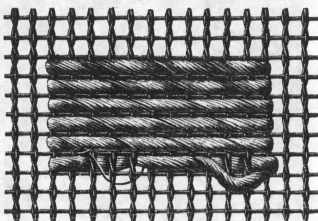

Fig. 726. Inverted darning stitch.

Fig. 727. Single darning stitch in oblique lines.

stitches border all the different parts of the pattern like a cord.

Dark blue canvas was used for the foundation; the darning stitch requires a loose material, such as D.M.C Persian silk (Soie de Perse), in Otter brown 1209; for the

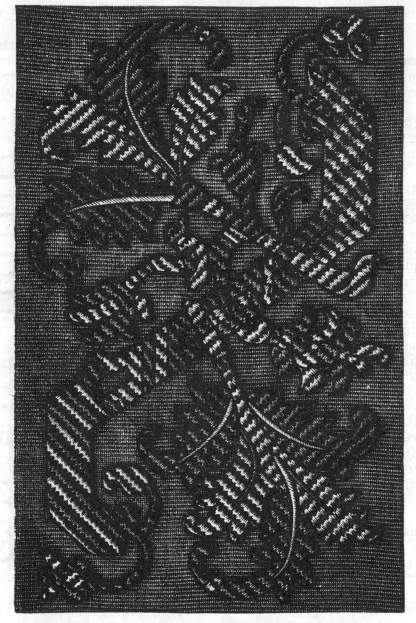

Fig. 728. Cushion-cover in embroidery on lacis with filling stitches and corded outlines.

Materials : D.M.C Persian silk, in Maize yellow 1069 and Rust brown 1229 and D.M.C Pearl cotton No. 5 or D.M.C Floss flax No 8, in Solid blue 825.

outlines use D.M.C Pearl cotton (Coton perlé) No. 5 or
D.M.C Floss flax (Lin floche) No. 8, in Geranium red 817.

Fig. 729. Detail of cushion figure 728.

The silk may, if desired, be replaced by D.M.C Special
stranded cotton (Mouliné spécial).

Darning stitches of different kinds (figs. 724, 725, 726,
727). — We add here a few kinds of darning stitches which

may also be used as fillings for the stripe, fig. 722. In figure 724 the darning stitch worked with a fine thread is explained which necessitates passing five or six times through each series of loops of the stuff. When it is done with a coarse thread you only have to pass through the loops twice. (See fig. 725.)

Instead of regularly picking up every other thread you may make the stitches over several loops skipping the same number between the stitches; coming back you cover the skipped loops, reversing the stitches at the same time, fig. 726.

Lastly, figure 727 shews a stitch worked in a single journey. The stitches are made over two loops; the third is picked up. By regularly setting each stitch one thread of the canvas behind the other, you get a ground of oblique lines.

Cushion cover in embroidery on lacis with filling stitches and corded outlines (figs. 728 and 729). — This embroidery shews more variety then the last one, in point of execution. The fillings are different and worked in two colours. The outline here also consists of two rows of running stitches touching each other and forming a little cord. (See fig. 729.) The veins of the leaves and the stalks are worked in slanting flat stitch, the direction of which changes according to the figure you are embroidering.

For the ground take dark red canvas-net; for the fillings, two shades of yellow and bright blue for the outlines. For lining the work when it is finished, it is best to take a stuff of the same blue, as it will shew through the meshes of the canvas the work will present a quieter appearance.

Patterns of needlework. — Besides the different kinds of work described above a great choice of patterns for netting will be found in the following publications of the D.M.C Library: *Embroidery on net, French net-work, Net-work Embroidery I and II, Drawn thread work II* and *Works o various kinds.* (*)

(*) See at the end of the volume the list of the albums of the D.M.C Library.

Insertion with rows of openwork and embroidered stars.

Openwork on Linen

Openwork is the term applied to every kind of needle-work to which the drawing out of the warp or woof threads, of a material is the necessary preliminary.

By grouping together and sewing over the threads that remain in different ways, the most varied combinations and the richest patterns can be produced, which can either be used as the sole ornament or as an adjunct to cross stitch or other embroidery in a piece of needlework.

Openwork on linen is of two kinds: for the one the drawing out of one layer of either the warp or the woof threads is the first step, for the other the drawing out of both warp and woof. The former is the Italian "Punto tirato", or as it is now commonly called, single openwork, the other the Italian "Punto tagliato", or cut openwork.

Materials. — Coarse stuffs made to imitate those on which the embroideries of mediæval times were done, require for the openwork a thread of the same thickness as that of the stuff on which the embroidery is done. The choice lies between D.M.C Flax lace thread (Lin pour dentelles), D.M.C Flax thread for knitting (Lin pour tricoter) Nos. 3, 4, 6, 8, 10 and 12,

D.M.C Crochet cotton 6 cord (Cordonnet 6 fils), D.M.C Special crochet cotton (Cordonnet spécial) Nos. 5, 10, 15 and 20, D.M.C Alsatia Nos. 15, 20, 25, 30 and 40 and D.M.C Knotting cotton (Fil à pointer) Nc. 20 or 30. (*)

For finer stuffs, the best materials are D.M.C Flax lace thread (Lin pour dentelles) or D.M.C Flax thread for knitting (Lin pour tricoter) Nos. 12, 16, 20 and 25, D.M.C Floss flax or flourishing thread (Lin floche) Nos. 16 to 100, D.M.C Crochet cotton 6 cord (Cordonnet 6 fils) Nos. 30 to 100, D.M.C Alsatian thread (Fil d'Alsace) Nos. 30 to 100 and D.M.C Alsa No. 40.

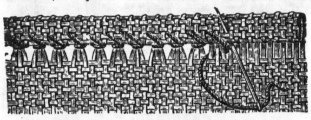

Fig. 730. Single hem stitch.

Fig. 731. Second hem stitch.

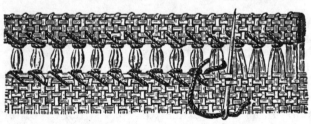

Fig. 732. Ladder hem stitch.

If the embroidery be in colours, the openwork can be done with coloured thread; in this case we recommend D.M.C Embroidery cotton (Coton à broder), D.M.C Pearl cotton (Coton perlé), D.M.C Alsatia, D.M.C Special stranded cotton (Mouliné spécial) and D.M.C Floss flax (Lin floche).

Single openwork (punto tirato). — This, in its simplest form, is the ornamental latticed hem, produced, as we have just said by drawing out some of the warp or the woof threads of the stuff. Openworked hems are the foundation of this kind of work.

(*) See at the end of the last chapter the tables of the sizes and colours of the cotton, flax and silk articles, mark D.M.C. — The French names, in brackets, are those stamped on the labels of the D.M.C articles.

Such hems take the place of the ordinary hem (fig. 8), when something more decorative is required for the object in view.

To render the copying of our patterns easier, we give in each case the number of threads that have to be drawn out.

Openwork insertions worked by machine. — Openwork insertions can be more quickly worked by machine than by hand.

Narrow ones can be worked without their being mounted on a tambour frame, but in that case the shuttle thread should be very tightly stretched.

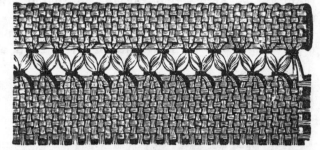

Fig. 733. Serpentine hem stitch.

For the shuttle thread always take D.M.C Machine thread (Fil pour machines) No. 150, D.M.C Alsatian twist (Retors d'Alsace) for the top thread and D.M.C Alsa No. 40 for the coloured insertions.

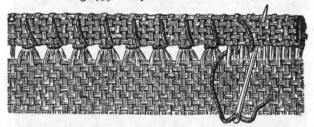

Fig. 734. Antique hem stitch.
Wrong side.

Single hem stitch (fig. 730). Draw out, according to the quality of your

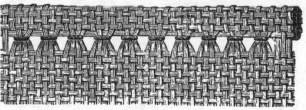

Fig 735. Antique hem stitch.
Right side.

stuff, two to four threads, below the edge of the turning and tack your hem down to two threads above the isolated threads. Fasten in your thread on the left and slip your needle in from right to left under four or five isolated threads, draw it out and put it upwards from below under one or two threads of the folded edge.

The same stitch is used for preventing the fringes of table-cloths and napkins from unravelling. (See the chapter "Needlework Trimmings", figs. 1041 to 1044.)

Second hem stitch (fig. 731). — You prepare this as you did the preceding one and work, likewise from left to right, only with this difference, that after passing your needle under the three vertical threads, you stick it into the hem downwards from above, above two threads so that it comes out exactly at the sharp edge of the fold.

These stitches which can also be made on the right side of a piece of work form a kind of little cord at the bottom of the hem.

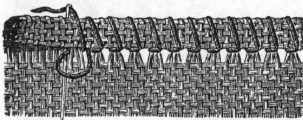

Fig. 736. Another antique hem stitch.
Wrong side.

Ladder hem stitch (fig. 732). Having finished the hem as shewn in figure 730, draw out a few more threads of the stuff, 5 to 7 at the outside.

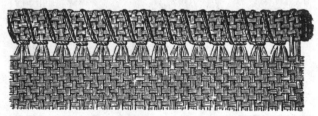

Fig. 737. Another antique hem stitch.
Right side.

Then turn the work round and make a second row of stitches, similar to the first; grouping the same threads together as before, forming thus little perpendicular bars, like the rungs of a ladder, hence the name, ladder stitch.

Serpentine hem stitch (fig. 733). — Here again you begin as in figure 730, taking up always an equal number of threads. In your second row of stitches, pick up half the threads of one cluster and half of the next together, so as to divide the bars, thereby making the clustered threads, slant first one way and then the other, forming a serpentine line.

Antique hem stitch (figs. 734 and 735). — In the handsome old linen embroideries, dating from the days of the Renaissance one often sees two ways of making a hem, rarely to be found described in modern manuals of needlework. Figs. 734 to 737 illustrate these two openwork hems on a magnified scale.

Draw out a thread sufficiently far from the edge to leave room for an ordinary hem (in transparent or very fine stuffs no threads should be drawn out), then roll this edge, (it must not be folded), fasten in your thread on the left and make your stitches, from right to left, as follows: slip the needle from right to left, under 4 vertical threads of the rolled hem, draw it out and pass it under the hem bringing it out again in the middle of the threads which are to form the next cluster. The result is that when a cluster consists of 4 threads, you bring out the needle in the middle of the 4, and one thread below the top edge of the rolled hem. Figure 735 shews this hem on the right side.

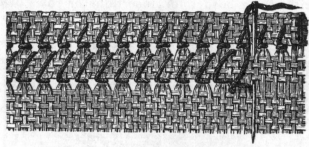

Fig. 738. Double-rowed openwork hem.
Wrong side.

Another antique hem stitch (figs. 736 and 737). — You make the roll the same as in figures 734 and 735 ; but the stitches are made from right to left. Instead of drawing the working thread

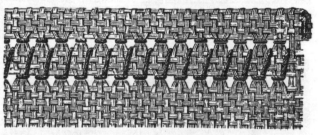

Fig. 739. Double-rowed openwork hem.
Right side.

through the stuff, twist it round the roll, thus the stitch is visible on the wrong and the right side of the hem.

Double-rowed openwork hem (figs. 738 and 739). After making any one of the hems already described, draw out one more thread of the stuff, leaving between the first and second thread you drew out one thread more than there are in the cluster of the first row. Then collect together the same vertical threads that were collected together in the first row. The way to work these stitches is shewn in figure 738; the right side with the vertical stitches is shewn in figure 739.

Four-sided openwork stitch. — Before going on to the rows of openwork, we will describe the four-sided openwork stitch which occurs in the different kinds of linen embroidery. Although generally done without the removal of any of the threads of the stuff, it may be classed in the same category with openwork on linen as it has an open appearance, and is used in the same kind of work as openwork, properly so-called.

A pattern is never worked entirely in this stitch; it is used either as a border for insertions or rows of openwork, or to form a separation between lozenges or squares in a pattern with large sized stroke stitches.

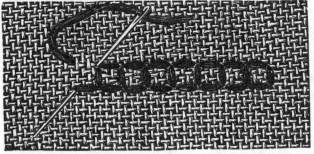

Fig. 740.
Four-sided openwork stitch, worked horizontally.
Right side.

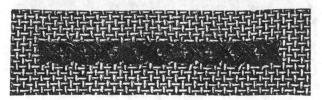

Fig. 741.
Four-sided openwork stitch, worked horizontally.
Wrong side.

It is met with in old Italian and German linen embroideries, as well as in Hungarian and Slav work. It is worked sometimes in straight sometimes in slanting rows; in the former case it is done in one journey, in the latter in two. The stitches are made over 3 or 4 threads of the stuff; by pulling the thread very tight, some of the threads of the stuff are drawn close together, which produces the open appearance, mentioned above.

Four-sided openwork stitch, worked horizontally (figs. 740 and 741). — This stitch is worked from right to left. Begin with a vertical stitch made upwards over 4 threads, then take the needle to the back of the work descending 4 threads towards the left, make one horizontal stitch to the right, which at the bottom touches the vertical stitch, reascend on the wrong side 4 threads to the left, then make a second

horizontal stitch to the right, which touches the vertical stitch
at the top, and finally draw out the needle below to the left of
the horizontal stitch. Continue with a vertical stitch, and so on.

**Four-sided openwork stitch worked in slanting and
serpentine lines** (figs. 742 and 743). — This is also begun
from the right side by a horizontal stitch over 4 threads, you
then descend in a slanting direction under 4 threads, towards
the left, make on the right side a vertical stitch upwards to
meet the horizontal stitch, make again on the wrong side a
slanting stitch, descending to the left to make a horizontal
stitch to the right, and so on. Finish with a vertical stitch.

The second
row which
completes the
stitch is made
in the same
way, only that
you begin it
with a vertical
stitch so as to
form the
squares. On
the wrong side
of the work
you get two
single lines
and one
double one of
slanting
stroke stitches.

The wrong
side of this
four-sided
stitch is often

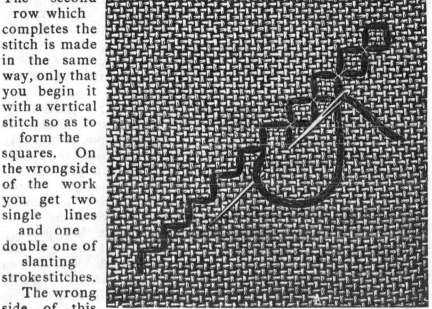

Fig. 742. Four-sided openwork stitch, worked
in slanting lines.

used as the right side. In this case, the slanting stitches are made
on the right side of the work and the square ones on the wrong.

Figure 743 shews this stitch used in serpentine lines as a
small insertion. On the right side where the direction of the
lines is changed, the slanting stitches form cross stitches.

Single three-rowed openwork (fig. 744). — This pattern
and the following ones can be used beneath as ornaments to
a hem and also as insertions between stripes of embroidery
or woven stuff.

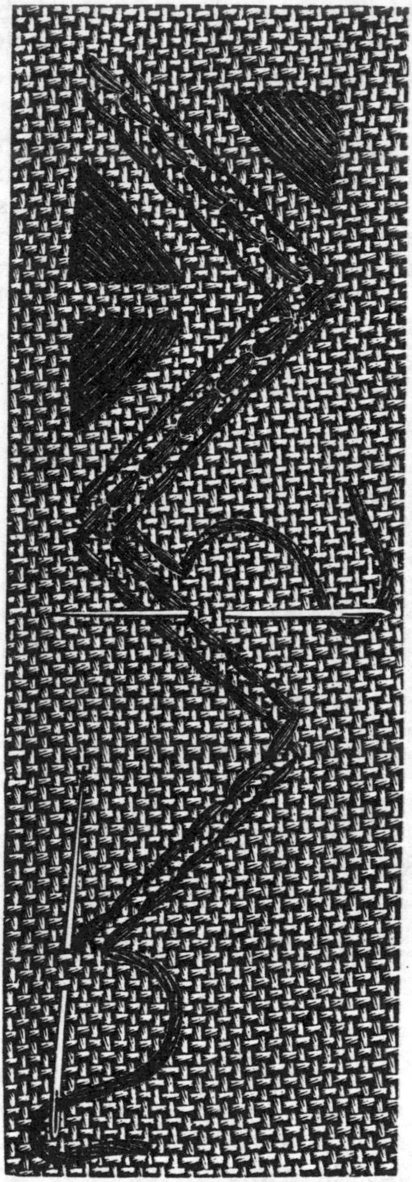

Figure 744 is so easy to work that it will be found most useful in cases where the object is to produce a good deal of effect at the expense of the smallest possible amount of labour.

Make six rows of hem stitching, as in fig. 730; the first and the sixth rows to serve as a finish top and bottom, the second and fifth after drawing out 6 threads of the stuff, the third and fourth, after drawing out 8 threads. All the clusters must consist of an equal number of threads. The first and third row must be worked after figure 733, the middle one after figure 732. Divide the threads of the vertical clusters of the middle row, equally in two, then insert the needle from right to left under half the threads of the second cluster, whilst, by another movement you bring the eye of the needle back from right to left, pick up the second half of the first cluster of threads, which then passes under and in front of the threads of the first cluster. You must be careful not to pull the thread too tight.

Openwork with two threads across (fig. 745). — By drawing out 12 threads of the stuff and after having bordered the edges with the stitch, described in figure 730, made over 3 disengaged threads, you can make two series of stitches, drawing the clusters in opposite directions.

Fig. 743. Four-sided openwork stitch, worked in serpentine lines.

Openwork with three cross threads (fig. 746). — Draw out 25 threads of the stuff; overcast both edges with slanting stitches over 6 threads. Draw the clusters together in the middle, crossing one half over the other, as shewn in figure 744; then draw in other threads above and below the middle

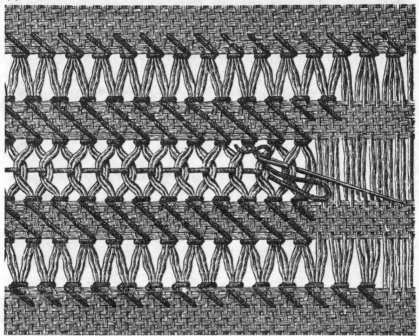

Fig 744. Single three-rowed openwork.

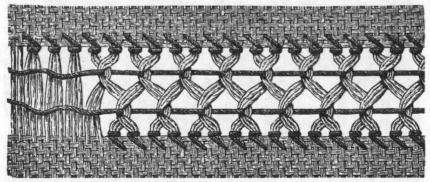

Fig. 745. Openwork with two threads across.

one, taking the same course through the clusters. Then with a second thread overcast the clusters, enclosing them in this way between the two threads.

Double-rowed cluster openwork (fig. 747). — Draw out twice 12 threads of the stuff leaving an interval of 4 threads between, and secure the edges as shewn in figure 730, with stitches over 2 threads. After fastening in the thread make

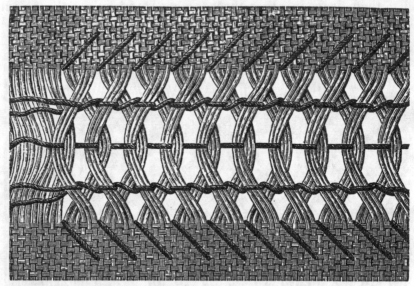

Fig. 746. Openwork with three cross threads.

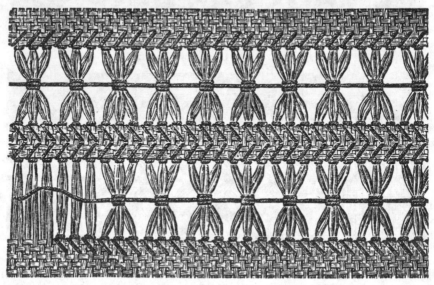

Fig. 747. Double-rowed cluster openwork.

three back stitches round every three clusters. At the third stitch slip the needle under the two first to fasten the thread.

The thread should be given a little play in its course from one group of clusters to another.

Openwork with darning stitch (fig. 748). — Draw out 14 threads. Insert your needle and thread between two clusters and pass it as if you were darning, to and fro in and out of them, until they are encased half way down with stitches.

In so doing, work with the eye of the needle forward and the point turned to your thimble. To pass to the second

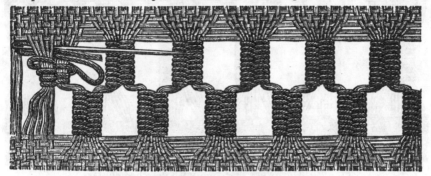

Fig. 748. Openwork with darning stitch.

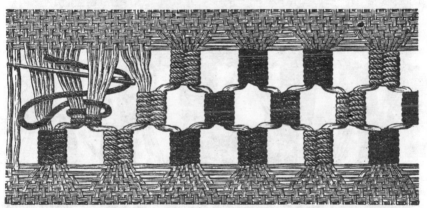

Fig. 749. Openwork with darning stitch.

cluster of stitches, take a back stitch under the isolated threads and begin the second cluster by dividing the threads as shewn in the figure. The darning stitch is also described in the chapter on "Netting" (see figs. 667 and 668).

Openwork with darning stitch (fig. 749). — After drawing out 18 threads of the stuff, group the threads together and make the same stitch, as in figure 748. The clusters or bars, worked likewise over 10 threads may be made in different colours. Our pattern is worked in three, one for every three clusters forming diagonal lines from left to right, upwards from below.

Openwork insertion with detached clusters (fig. 750). Draw out 20 threads. The stitches that bind the edges are made

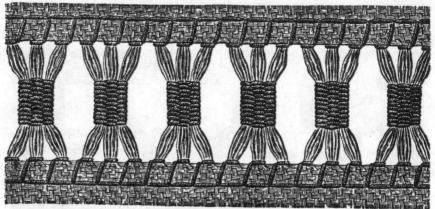

Fig. 750. Openwork insertion with detached clusters.

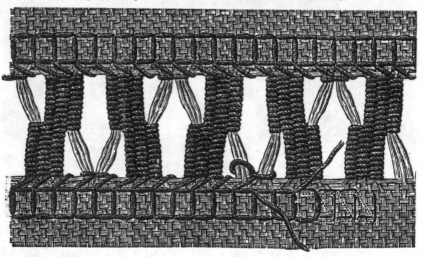

Fig. 751. Openwork insertion with darning and overcasting stitches.

over 4 threads, as in figure 740. The clusters grouped together and secured on both sides are bound three and three together in the middle, by 10 or 12 darning stitches. The thread must be fastened and cut off after each group is finished.

Openwork insertion with darning and overcasting stitches (fig. 751). — Before drawing out the 15 threads, make on both sides the two-sided stitch in the following way: pass the thread vertically over 4 horizontal threads, bring the needle out on the right, 3 threads from the vertical stitch, to make a back stitch to the left, then come back obliquely on the wrong side and bring the needle out on the right, 3 threads from the starting point of the vertical stitch, to make a second back stitch to the left, then go on with the first vertical stitch. The course of the stitches is shewn, on the wrong side, by a dotted line, on the right by black lines.

Then make the darning stitches over 9 threads or 3 clusters to half their length, when you leave out, first a cluster on the

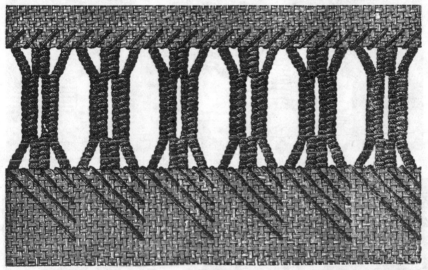

Fig. 752. Openwork insertion with darning and overcasting stitches.

right, then one on the left, to take of the next one what is necessary. The result is that two bars of threads and two bars of darning stitches, alternately face each other. Oblique overcasting stitches over the threads that remain between the border of two-sided stitches and the bars of darning stitches, finish the insertion.

Openwork insertion with darning and overcasting stitches (fig. 752). — Draw out 20 threads, overcast both edges with stitches over 3 vertical and 3 horizontal threads. Then make slanting stitches, proceeding out from these, over 3, 6 and 9 threads respectively, all three terminating in perpendicular line, one below the other.

For the openwork twist your thread six times quite

tightly round the first cluster of three threads, then take it up to the edge. Then pass to the second and third cluster which you cover with 6 darning stitches, succeeded by 12

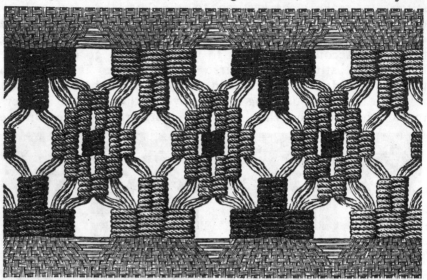

Fig. 753. Openwork insertion in darning stitch.

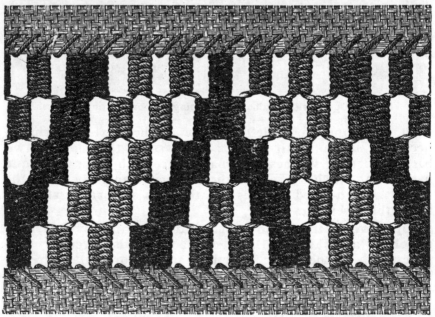

Fig 754. Persian openwork insertion with single and double columns.

stitches on the first and second cluster until there is only
enough space left uncovered for the 6 overcasting stitches.
The second part is finished the reverse way from the first.

Openwork insertion in darning stitch (fig. 753). —
Draw out 28 threads. The pyramids are made over 6 clusters
of 3 threads each, in a medium and dark shade of the same
colour. The centre figure, in a third shade lighter than the

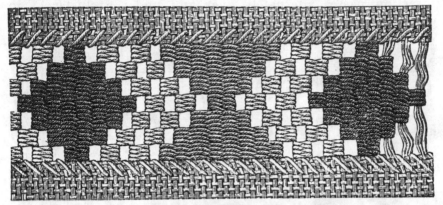

Fig. 755. Persian openwork insertion with squares.

Fig. 756. Openwork insertion with wheels.

two first, groups 3 clusters of the left and 3 of the right ones
together. The little dark point in the middle is in dark red
or black as a contrast to the other shades.

**Persian openwork insertion with single and double
columns** (fig. 754). — Draw out 30 threads. One figure of
this insertion takes 20 clusters of 3 threads. The pattern is
worked entirely in darning stitch in two colours.

Persian openwork insertion with squares (fig. 755).
Figure 755 for which 20 threads must be drawn out can also
be worked in three different colours or three different shades.
Each figure of this insertion takes 18 clusters of 3 threads.

Openwork insertion with wheels (fig. 756). — The
edges are bound with cross stitches, fig. 45. A wheel connects
4 clusters. The thread fastened on in the middle of the
insertion passes alternately over and under a cluster as in
darning. You make several rows, stopping where the thread

Fig. 757. Three-rowed openwork insertion with wheels.

went in to make the wheel, and pass under the wheel to reach
the next 4 clusters. For the wheels, see the chapter on
"Netting", figs. 673 and 674.

Three-rowed openwork insertion with wheels (fig.
757). — Draw out 5 threads for the narrow stripes top and
bottom and 22 for the large central part and collect the
threads of the stuff into clusters of 4. The narrow stripes are
bordered with cross stitches, which may be made on the
wrong or the right side; the dotted line marks the crossing

of the working thread, on the wrong side. The middle clusters
are united on both sides by a knotted back stitch, represented

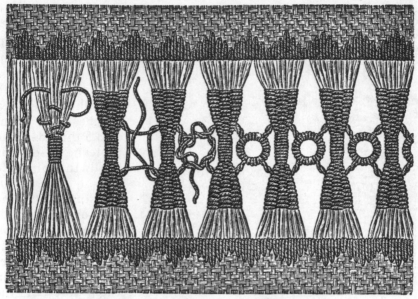

Fig 758. Openwork insertion with eyelets.

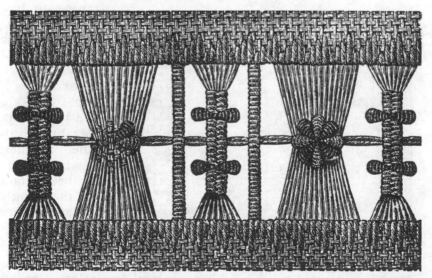

Fig. 759. Openwork insertion with rosettes and picots in post stitch.

in the engraving, then they are collected together in the
middle by 3 overcasting stitches, after which you pass the

thread to the intersection of the threads of the two first rows of stitches, to make a wheel over 5 threads, before passing to the next bars.

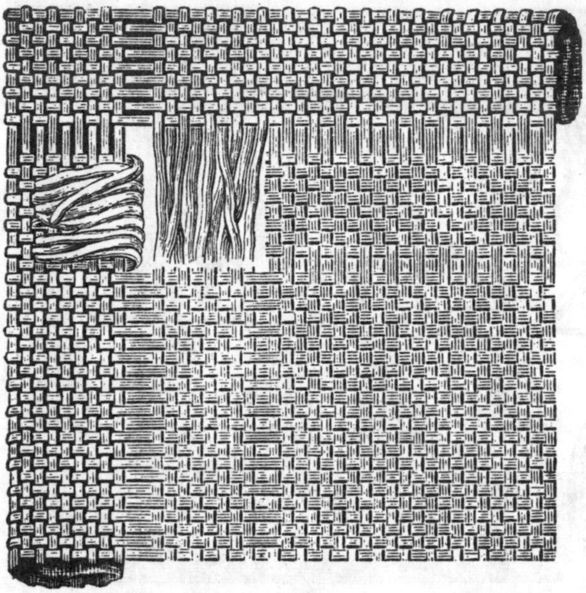

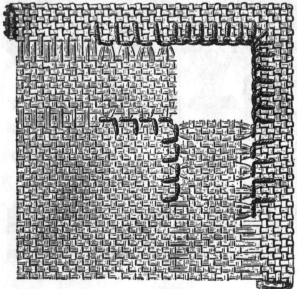

Fig. 760. How to cut and isolate the threads at the corners.

Openwork insertion with eyelets (fig. 758). Draw out 28 threads. Bind the edges with straight two-sided stitches over from 2 to 5 threads. The pattern itself is begun in the middle over 9 threads of the stuff with 8 or 9 overcasting stitches, then you divide the threads into three equal parts and add, on each side of the first stitches, 12 to 14 darning stitches, leaving, at most only $\frac{2}{3}$ of an inch in width of isolated threads uncovered. When two bars of darning stitches are finished join them together by 4 button-hole stitches, then wind your thread three times round the single thread and cover the ring with close corded stitches.

Openwork insertion with rosettes and picots in post stitch (fig. 759). —

Fig. 761. Securing the threads in the corner with button-hole stitches.

Draw out 24 threads. The edges are bound with two-sided stitches over 2, 3, 4 and 5 threads respectively. For the middle threads count 4 isolated threads for the clusters round which the working thread must be tightly wound, 8 threads for the bar of darning stitches, ornamented with picots in post stitch (see "Embroidery upon White Stuff", fig. 79), and 16 threads for the rosette.

Connect the threads of the stuff by a wheel which you cover entirely with post or winding stitch. The loop that connects one bar with another is made as you go along. Having reached the desired point, you take the thread to the first bar and come back to finish it. As may be seen by the engraving, the pattern is worked in two shades.

Arrangement of the corners in openwork insertions (figs. 760, 761, 762, 763). —

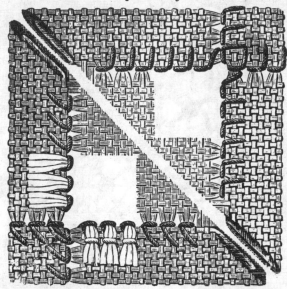

Fig. 762. Turning over and securing the threads on the wrong side of a piece of work.

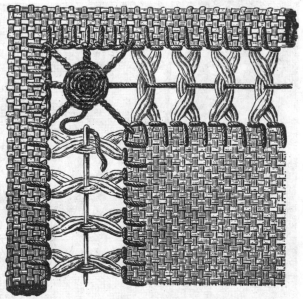

Fig. 763. Filling in the corner of openwork with a wheel.

When a square of work is bordered by an openwork insertion,

Fig. 764. Formation of the corner of the openwork, fig. 757.

you must cut and loosen the threads on both sides, about ⅜ of an inch from the edge of the hem, as seen in fig. 760. You push the loose threads into the turning of the hem and fasten them in by button–hole stitches, fig. 761, or else, if there is to be no break in the hem-stitching, turn them in on to the wrong side and fasten them down with a few stitches, fig. 762.

Figure 763 represents an openwork insertion in which the empty corner is filled by a wheel.

You take the thread of the openwork to the opposite edge, insert it in the hem, then bring it back to the centre of the wheel you are going to make, lay the other spokes, make the wheel over

Fig. 765. Formation of the corner of the openwork, fig. 747.

7

threads, fasten the thread of the opposite side to the second

line of open-
work, pass it
under the
wheel and
make the
eighth spoke
by taking the
thread over
to the second
line of open-
work.

**Forming
the corners
of open-
work in-
sertions
consisting
of several
rows** (figs.
764 and 765).
In such cases
the corners
may be made
in two diffe-
rent ways;
you either
cut them at
once in each
stripe of
stuff, or you
draw out all
the threads
to the hem.
We give a
specimen of
each way.

Figure 764
shews the
corner of the
openwork,
fig. 757, for
which the

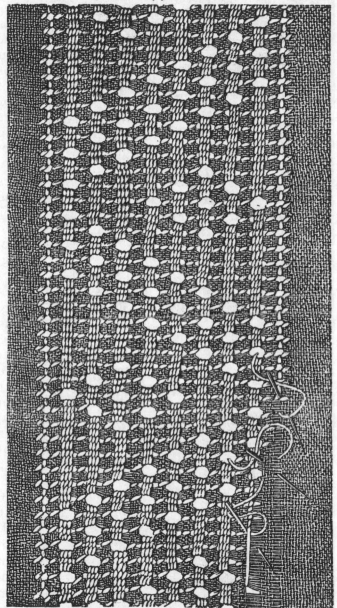

Fig. 766. "Myreschka" border. Russian openwork.
Materials: D.M.C Flax thread for knitting, D.M.C Alsatia,
D.M.C Alsatian thread or D.M.C Crochet cotton 6 cord,
in white or écru.

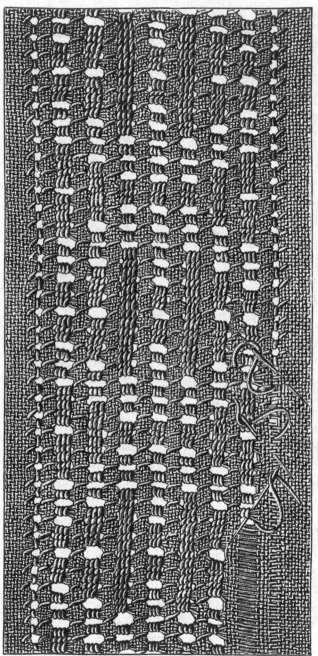

Fig. 767. "Prutik" border. Russian openwork.

threads have been cut to the very edge of each stripe of stuff. The little corners are filled with a single spider with four branches, the big corner by a double spider with twelve branches. (For the way these spiders are made see the chapter on "Netting" figures 673 and 674).

The corner fig. 765, of the insertion fig. 747, is more troublesome. Here all the threads near the hem have been cut; the loose threads that come from the middle stripes of stuff are transformed into bars covered with darning stitches, see figs. 667 and 668, and the four empty corners are filled in with spiders with eight branches.

Russian openwork stitches "Myreschka" and "Prutik".
A kind of openwork long practised in Southern Russia, is distinguished from others, by its peculiar mode of execution. The threads are only cut in a horizontal direction and the loose vertical threads are overcast at the same time as the horizontal stripes of stuff.

Russian openwork is divided into two different kinds, called "Myreschka" and "Prutik". In the former, the pattern is formed solely by darning stitches, in the latter the darning stitch alternates with overcast bars. It is advisable only to cut the threads as you work, that is, one row at a time, not the whole length of the border at once.

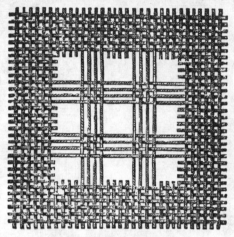

Fig. 768.
Cutting out threads in the stuff.

"Myreschka" border. Russian openwork (fig. 766). — The stitch which terminates the border, top and bottom, and for which you draw out 2 threads of the stuff, is identically the same as the stitch, fig. 730, and is worked over 5 vertical threads. For the pattern itself draw out 5 threads and leave 4.

All the rows are worked from right to left excepting those of the top border, which are worked from left to right.

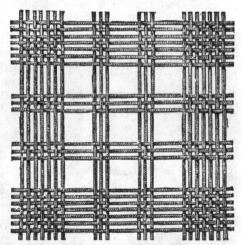

Fig. 769. Drawing out threads throughout the whole surface of the stuff.

The stripe of stuff, 4 threads in height, is covered with vertical stitches — 5 threads apart, like the stitches of the first row of the border — which lead at the same time from one group of darning stitches to the other. Beginning on the right, you make as many vertical stitches as the pattern requires, to reach the left of the figure worked in darning stitch; here you carry a thread over all the clusters to be covered with darning

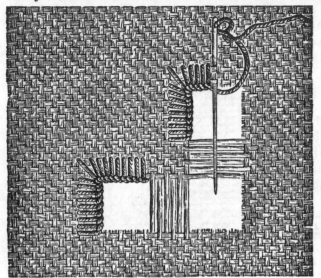

stitch, then on returning, you take the thread under each cluster, and between every two clusters make a vertical overcasting stitch over the thread previously laid. The way to lay this thread and overcast it is shewn in the engraving.

Fig. 770. Button-holed edge for cut stitch embroidery.

In every stripe of the stuff consisting of 4 threads, you repeat this process of laying and overcasting three times, after which you go on with the vertical stitches over the stripe of stuff, to reach the next figure.

The subsequent rows are done in the same way after a drawn or an embroidered pattern. The last row, in the same stitch as the first, is worked from right to left, like the other rows of the border.

Fig. 771. Overcasting the edge for embroidery in cut stitch.

"Prutik" border. Russian

openwork (fig. 767). — This is very much like the "Myreschka" openwork, excepting that it presents a rather more transparent effect, due to the overcast bars that form the ground, on which the figures worked in darning stitch stand out clear.

Cut stitch (Punto tagliato). — For embroidery done in cut stitch, the threads of the stuff have to be drawn out in the length and the width; the number of course depends not only on the pattern but on the stuff. The threads that remain between serve as foundation for the embroidery stitches.

Stuffs, the warp and woof threads of which are of the same size, should be selected so that the empty spaces left after cutting out threads should be perfectly square.

Cut stitch done by machine. — Like the drawn-thread patterns the cut stitch ones can also be done by machine. For directions as to the working see page 531.

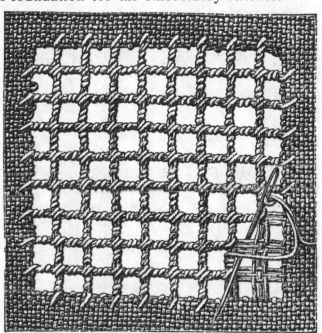

Fig. 772. First openwork ground. With horizontal and vertical bars.

Cutting out threads in the stuff (fig. 768). — Many embroideries in cut stitch are bordered by another kind of embroidery. In such cases the threads should be cut to a fraction of an inch within the work and only then isolated, so as to keep a clean edge in the stuff. An equal number of threads must be drawn out both ways. For most patterns the number of threads left equals the number removed. Figure 768 shews 4 threads drawn out and 4 left.

Drawing out threads throughout the whole surface of the stuff (fig. 769). — In figure 769 where the threads are "framed" to the edge, you will notice 4 threads removed and 3 kept. This difference is admissible when you want to make the work more transparent than it would be if the same number of threads were drawn out and embroidered over.

Button-holed edge for cut stitch embroidery (fig. 770). In some very close linens you can cut the threads without its affecting the finish of the work, but in the case of coarser stuffs and when the open spaces end in steps, the cut edges should be button-holed, figs. 36, 37 and 69.

Overcasting the edge for embroidery in cut stitch (fig. 771). — Overcasting or cording the raw edges is quite as good a way of strengthening them as button-holing them, especially in the case of patterns finely indented. Calculate, before cutting into the stuff, how many threads have to be drawn or cut out, run in a tacking thread to mark the pattern you are going to work and then cut away, two threads within the line marked by the tacking

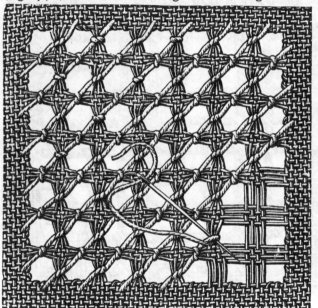

Fig. 773. Second openwork ground. With clusters joined together in oblique lines.

thread, the stuff that has to be removed, and at once overcast the rough edge over two padding threads.

Openwork grounds. — In the eight following figures we present our readers with a series of grounds which can be used independently as ornamental designs for various kinds of small articles; they can also be arranged in stripes or used as fillings in big patterns.

First openwork ground, with horizontal and vertical bars (fig. 772). — In height and width: cut 3 threads leaving 3 threads between. Drawing out the cut threads gives you a net like ground. The isolated threads are overcast in diagonal rows so as to form round bars, each crossing of the threads is covered with an oblique stitch; the bars, according to their direction, with two or three vertical or horizontal stitches, as the engraving indicates.

Second openwork ground. With clusters joined together in oblique lines (fig. 773). — In height and width: cut 4 threads leaving 4 threads between. Here the ground is likewise worked in diagonal rows; the pattern is formed by a coarse thread that connects the clusters by a single knot, made, as can be seen from the engraving.

Third openwork ground, with loop stitches set opposite ways (fig. 774). — In height and width: cut 4 threads leaving 4 threads between.

Here the pattern is produced by

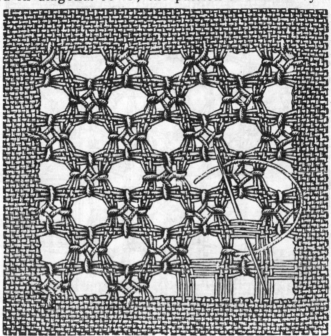

Fig. 774. Third openwork ground. With loop stitches set opposite ways.

detached loop stitches, see fig. 662 in the chapter on "Netting", placed in every alternate empty space and surrounding the 4 disengaged threads of the web.

As can be seen from the engraving, these stitches are worked in diagonal lines and the passage of the thread from one stitch to the other is hidden under the little square of stuff.

Fourth openwork ground. With lines of loop stitches (fig. 775). — In height and width: cut 6 threads leaving 6 threads between.

This ground looks more covered than the former one, each empty space is filled with a loop stitch, looped over three disengaged threads of the network and worked in vertical lines. By the clusters being divided in this manner you get oval eyelet holes between the squares of stuff.

Fifth openwork ground. With diagonal network (fig. 776). — In height and width: cut 4 threads, leaving 4 threads between.

Begin by making the diagonal network, of threads stretched across and covered with overcasting stitches, set a good distance apart.

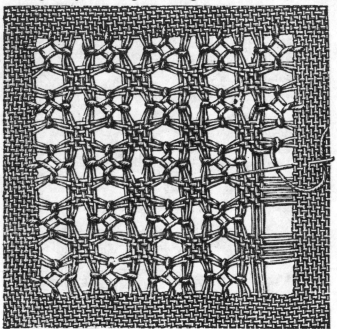

In the engraving all the threads running from right to left are stretched and overcast, as well as part of those running from left to right and crossing the former ones; it also shews how the threads are stretched

Fig. 775. Fourth openwork ground. With lines of loop stitches.

across and overcast. When the network is finished, you frame each square of stuff — which appears covered by a thread stretched diagonally across — with square stitches which are worked in horizontal rows.

Sixth openwork ground. With knotted clusters and spiders between (fig. 777). — In height and width: cut 9 threads, leaving 9 threads between.

With the disengaged threads you make clusters, knotted together horizontally and vertically with a knot described in figure 773.

When all the clusters are finished, lay the oblique threads that complete the spiders. Here the thread passes — always in a slanting direction — over the 1st, 2nd and 3d, under the 4th, 5th and 6th and over the 7th, 8th and 9th of the nine threads of the squares of stuff, which gives greater firmness to the openwork. You begin by stretching the threads across from left to right, then when this first layer is finished, you lay the threads across in the opposite direction, taking care to unite them in the middle by a knot, and put a spider with

eight branches in each empty space.

Seventh ground with vertical and horizontal clusters, single spiders and wheels in darning stitch (fig. 778). — In height and width : cut 12 threads, leaving 12 threads between. The disengaged threads, divided into 3

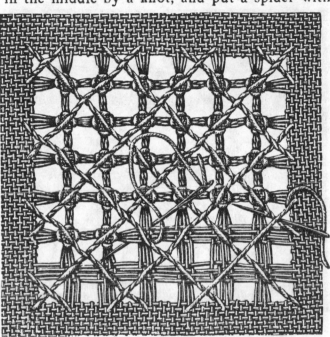

Fig. 776. Fifth openwork ground.
With diagonal network.

equal clusters are divided and crossed in horizontal and vertical lines. When all the clusters are crossed, you lay the diagonal threads, which should pass over the 1st, 2nd, 3d and 4th, under the 5th, 6th, 7th and 8th, and over the 9th, 10th, 11th and 12th threads of the squares of stuff. At the points of intersection connect the isolated threads by a plain knot, thus forming spiders.

Finally the squares of stuff are ornamented by a small wheel in darning stitch, made by passing the thread four times under the diagonal threads.

Eighth openwork ground. With connected clusters, spiders in loop stitch and lozenges in flat stitch (fig. 779). In height and width: cut 12 threads leaving 12 between.

Divide the disengaged threads into two equal groups, connected in the middle by a single knot set vertically. The empty spaces are filled with a loop stitch set in the corners of the squares of stuff and connected each time with the cross threads by a single knot. Lastly you ornament the squares of stuff with lozenges in straight stitch, worked alternately vertically and horizontally.

Border in cut stitch and straight stitch (fig. 780). — To join lace edgings and insertions or stripes of coloured embroidery a little simple band of cut stitch and straight stitch work is often used, such as the one represented in figure 780.

Fig. 777. Sixth openwork ground. With knotted clusters and spiders between.

The pattern is finished off, top and bottom, by a row of square openwork stitches, figs. 740 and 741, worked over 3 threads of the stuff; the same stitch, worked in diagonal lines, fig. 742, divides the interior of the band into squares and triangles. You begin by filling the triangles with horizontal straight stitches, then you cut out the threads in the inside of the square for the openwork figure and overcast the edges. (See fig. 771.)

The clusters of threads are overcast so as to form bars, then you ornament the squares inside with four little crosses, composed of two intercrossed overcast bars.

As regards the materials, take D.M.C Flax lace thread (Lin pour dentelles), for the cut stitch work; D.M.C Special stranded cotton (Mouliné spécial), for the straight stitch. We specially recommend white thread, and écru or cream linen being used for this pattern.

Border. Norwegian work "Hardanger" (figs. 781 and 782). — This border is a specimen of Norwegian openwork, known under the name of "Hardanger". The ground is coarse écru linen, the embroidery is in straight stitch worked

with D.M.C Pearl cotton (Coton perlé) No. 5, white; the bars in darning stitch, and the loop stitches are worked in D.M.C Flax lace thread (Lin pour dentelles) No. 25. (*)

You begin by embroidering the outlines in flat stitch with ornamental stitches over 4 threads of the stuff; then with a sharp

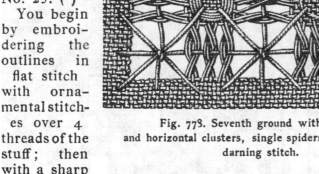

Fig. 778. Seventh ground with vertical and horizontal clusters, single spiders and wheels in darning stitch.

pair of scissors, carefully cut out the threads for the openwork parts of the pattern.

Figure 782 shews the way to do the bars in darning stitch and the fillings in loop stitch.

(*) See at the end of the last chapter the tables of the sizes and colours of the cotton, flax and silk articles, mark D.M.C. — The French names, in brackets, are those stamped on the labels of the D.M.C articles.

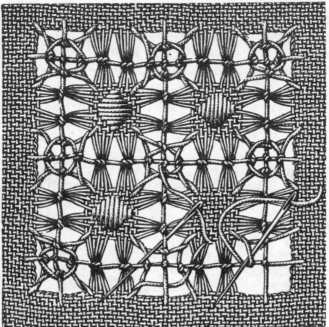

Fig. 779. Eighth openwork ground. With connected clusters, spiders in loop stitch and lozenges in flat stitch.

If intended as a border for towels, or for a sideboard cover, this border may be finished off with an openworked hem, and a little fringe or edging of pillow‑lace; in any case with only a small trimming, not to detract from the effect of the actual border.

Border in cut stitch

Fig. 780. Border in cut stitch and straight stitch.
Materials: D.M.C Flax lace thread and D.M.C Special stranded cotton, in white.

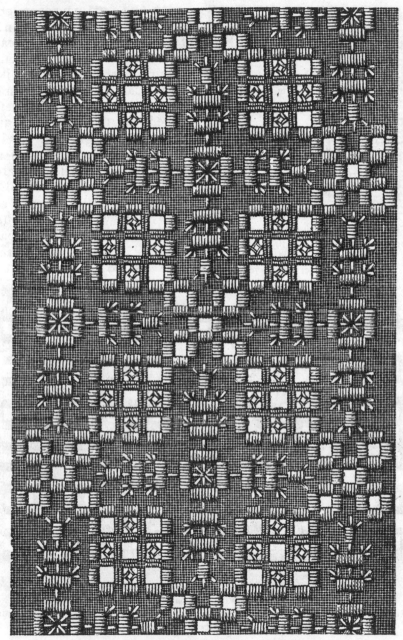

Fig. 781. Border in Norwegian work "Hardanger".
Materials: D.M.C Pearl cotton No. 5 and D.M.C Flax lace thread No. 25, in white.

Fig. 782. Overcasting the edges and working the bars in darning stitch and spiders in loop stitch.
Detail of border figure 781.

with the pattern reserved in linen stitch (figs. 783 and 784). — There are a great many embroideries in cut stitch where the pattern is, what is called "reserved". This means the pattern being left naked, in the midst of an embroidered ground. It is very difficult, especially when the pattern is at all elaborate and made up of small details, to cut away the threads of the linen without injuring the linen foundation. What is done in these cases therefore is to withdraw the

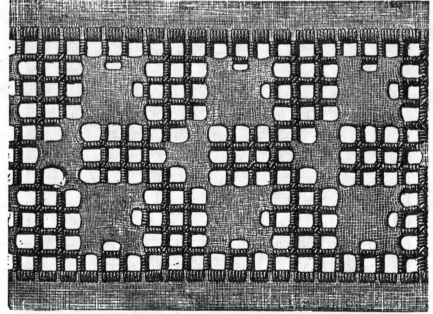

Fig. 783. Border in cut stitch with the pattern reserved in linen stitch.
Materials : D.M.C Floss flax or flourishing thread, in Indigo blue 334 (*) and white or écru.

(*) This number indicates a colour on the colour cards of the articles stamped with the D.M.C trade mark. These cards can be consulted at all the mercers' and needlework shops.

threads throughout the whole surface indicated by the
pattern, and after finishing all the bars draw in with the
needle new threads to form the reserved pattern. The way
to remake the linen ground is shewn in figure 784, where,
more clearly to explain how the threads intersect each other,
the threads of the stuff are printed light, and those that are
run in for the linen stitch, dark.

This border can be worked on almost any stuff, the
threads of which can be counted, and is very suitable for

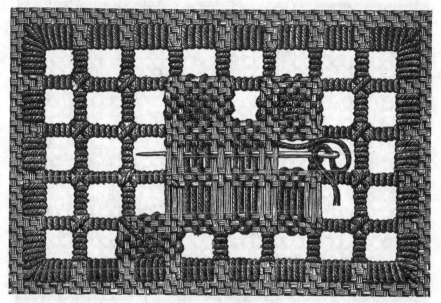

Fig. 784. Working the linen stitch for reserving a pattern in the cut stitch.
Detail of figure 783.

trimming table-cloths, napkins, towels, aprons and other
articles of the kind, more than we can enumerate here.

If combined with cross stitch embroidery the little bars
should be of the same colour as the embroidery. The actual
pattern, in linen stitch may be worked in white or écru
according to the ground on which you are working.

Border in cut stitch with pattern in darning stitch
(figs. 785 and 786). — The stitch shewn in figure 786 is
easier and pleasanter to work than the preceding one.
It is done in the same way as the darning stitch in net

guipure, fig. 658, that is by taking up the bars of the stuff as many times as you drop them. Take a loose thread for this filling and a twisted thread in a coarser number for the bars.

The details of figure 786 make fuller explanations unnecessary. The choice of stuff for this border must depend on the object it is intended for, as it may be used as a trimming alike for curtains, table-cloths, napkins, &c.

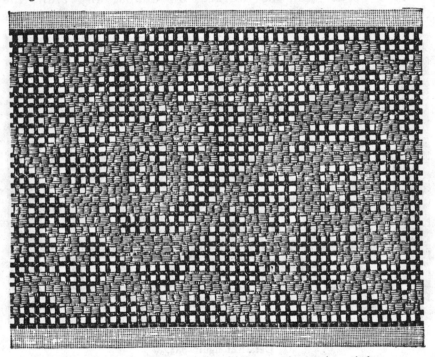

Fig. 785. Border in cut stitch with pattern in darning stitch.

Materials: D.M.C Pearl cotton No. 5, in Rust brown 3314 and D.M.C Special stranded cotton No. 25, in Blue grey 593. (*)

If worked on a white ground and with a view to being joined to white stuff or embroidery of any kind, a very refined and charming effect will result from the use of cream thread for the bars and snow-white thread for filling in the pattern which should stand out in strong relief from the ground.

_____

(*) See at the end of the last chapter the tables of the sizes and colours of the cotton, flax and silk articles, mark D.M.C.

Border in cut stitch. Italian style (figs. 787 and 788). The variety of stitches employed in this pattern reminds one a little of the Reticella lace. It may be worked in any width and makes an extremely rich and appropriate decoration for ecclesiastical linen and furniture.

The course of the work is explained by figure 788. You draw out 10 threads of the stuff each way, leaving 6 to serve as foundation for the bars.

The threads of the cut edges are thickly covered with close

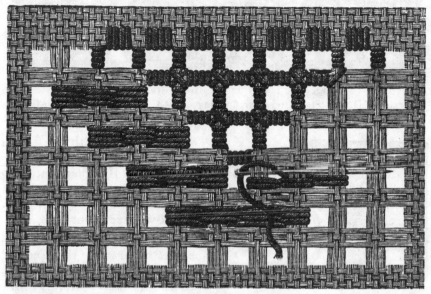

Fig. 786. Working of the darning stitch for reserving a pattern
in the cut stitch. Detail of figure 785.

overcasting stitches, the outside hem is done as explained in figures 736 and 737.

The rings in button-hole stitch are made on 3 threads stretched, when the bars are finished, from the middle of one bar to the other. The wheels or spiders are begun in the corner of a square, and finish, as the arrow indicates, at the same point.

Border in cut stitch. Greek style (fig. 789). — After all the foregoing explanations, this classical design, of Greek origin will not be found difficult to copy. The original, in very fine linen, shews 48 threads drawn out for the big

squares and 6 left for the bars. For the narrow border
we counted 21 threads drawn out each way. The cut edges

Fig. 787. Border in cut stitch. Italian style.
Materials: D.M.C Flax thread for knitting, D.M.C Alsatia or D.M.C Alsatian
thread, in white or cream.

Fig. 788. Working detail of the
border, fig. 787.

are bordered with the stitch
illustrated in figures 736
and 737. Between the two
rows of stitches, 4 threads of
linen remain, forming a
narrow insertion.

The long bars that cross
each other in the second
square are made with double
rows of button-holing, ornamented with picots, de-
scribed in the chapter on
"Needle-made Laces", figs.
869 and 872.

**Small cloth. Mexican
openwork** (figs. 790 and
791). — Our engraving, fig.
790, illustrates a particular
kind of openwork on linen
which is very popular in
S.America, principally in
those countries which were
once inhabited by Spaniards.
It is commonly known as

Mexican openwork. The following directions will serve to describe the working of our pattern.

After binding the inside edges with button-hole stitches, see fig. 770, draw out, in the height and width, 7 times 20 threads of the stuff leaving 6 spaces between of 12 threads each, so as to get a net-work of large empty squares.

Fig. 789. Border in cut stitch. Greek style.
Materials: D.M.C Flax thread for knitting, D.M.C Alsatia or D.M.C Alsatian thread, in white or cream. (*)

Then begin the embroidery, at the bottom in the left-hand corner, with a long diagonal stitch extending to the middle of the first square of stuff, and coming back to the point whence it started with a second similar stitch; at the third diagonal stitch unite the two threads just laid top and bottom

---

(*) See at the end of the last chapter the tables of the sizes and colours of the cotton, flax and silk articles, mark D.M.C.

by a button-hole stitch. All the empty squares are filled in succession in this way by 3 long diagonal stitches extending from left to right.

The second row is begun at the bottom in the right-hand corner. It is worked almost the same way as the first; the sole difference being that you connect the threads wherever they intersect each other. (See the explanatory detail, fig. 791.)

When the entire ground is covered in this way with

Fig. 790. Small cloth. Mexican openwork.
Materials: D.M.C Floss flax No. 30, D.M.C Alsatia No. 30 or D.M.C Alsatian thread No. 30, in white. (*)

(*) See at the end of the last chapter the tables of the sizes and colours of the cotton, flax and silk articles, mark D.M.C.

diagonal threads, you work the little leaves in darning stitch, see also figs. 667 and 668, concealing the thread on the wrong side behind the squares of stuff. Lastly you add the rings, carrying your thread from point to point in a circle and securing it at each point by a single knot. Those that touch the little leaves in darning stitch are

Fig. 791. Working the open ground of the small cloth figure 790.

single rings; the others that surround the plain squares of stuff are double.

As an outside trimming you leave a band of stuff about 2 in. wide, hem stitched, then after edging the outer border of the linen band with the stitch, illustrated in fig. 730, you unravel the vertical threads to the length of 1 ⅝ in. to form the fringe.

Small table-cloth. Danish openwork "Hedebo" (figs. 792 and 793). — The name "Hedebo" is already known to our readers, as an example of this Danish work accompanied the embroidered insertion, fig. 152. Here we give a specimen of

Fig. 792. Small table-cloth. Danish openwork "Hedebo".
Materials : D.M.C Flax thread for knitting No. 30, D.M.C Alsatia No. 40, in white. (*)

openwork on linen of the same kind, a little table-cover with richly embroidered openwork corners, edged with needle made lace.

For the triangles, cut out 12 times 28 threads of the stuff

(*) See at the end of the last chapter the tables of the sizes and colours of the cotton, flax and silk articles, mark D.M.C.

leaving 11 intervals of 12 threads between and then button-
hole the edges.

The network of threads is made into bars in darning stitch
and the pattern itself is worked as you finish the bars. The
model shews three big stars, or rather squares; the two side ones
consist of 8 triangles in darning stitch, worked over a thread

Fig. 793. Quarter of the small table-cloth figure 792.
Reduced to a third.

stretched diagonally round a centre composed of four spiders;
the third square, the one in the corner, is made up of four
little pyramids and semicircles in button-hole stitch ornamented
with picots. The other empty spaces contain little rosettes,
pyramids and rings in button-hole stitch, besides divers
spiders formed of overcast bars.

For the little band of openwork, draw out 15 threads of the stuff; connect the liberated threads with overcasting stitches, as shewn in figure 793.

In the chapter on "Needle-made Laces", figs. 958 and 959, clear directions for making the lace edging are given; for an explanation of the various stitches employed in the openwork triangles we refer our readers to the same chapter.

Patterns of needlework. — Besides the different kinds of work described above a great choice of patterns for openwork on linen will be found in the following publications of the D.M.C Library: *Drawn thread work I* and *II* and *Hardanger Embroideries.* (*)

(*) See at the end of the volume the list of the albums of the D.M.C Library.

Stripe of embroidery on tulle. Imitation of Bruges lace.

Embroidered Laces

As a natural sequel to the chapter on openwork on linen we have here collected, under the title of "Embroidered Laces", different kinds of embroideries which, though often worked on a stuff foundation, resemble actual lace in their open and transparent appearance.

We shall begin by presenting our readers with some patterns in imitation of the Dresden laces which used to be exclusively worked on a cambric ground.

Adapted to modern taste and executed on a foundation of canvas or a loose make of linen, this kind of embroidery is called "Colbert Embroidery".

In the second part of the chapter we shall speak of embroideries on tulle giving some simple designs in darning stitch, followed by handsomer ones worked with different kinds of fillings and specimens of appliqué work on tulle.

The last part of the chapter will deal with the so-called Spanish laces, worked in coloured silks, and gold and silver thread, upon or without a linen foundation.

Dresden lace. — In the 18th century, in Germany, scarves, collars and even head-dresses of fine cambric, trimmed with a very handsome kind of openwork embroidery, were made, called "Dresden lace".

The design of these embroideries was always composed of conventional flowers with ornaments in the rococo style.

The different kinds of Dresden lace are distinguished by their mode of execution. In the first kind, the figures of the pattern are outlined with a running, sewing, or overcasting stitch; the ground is openworked throughout and some parts of the figures are filled in with damask stitches.

In the second kind, the outlines of the large figures, which have to be well spaced out, and the smaller figures, with narrow surfaces, are embroidered on the wrong side with a very close cross stitch, which gives them a certain relief; the ground is left plain and the inside of the figures is covered with stitches of various kinds. To avoid the troublesome work of the fine cross stitching at the back, button-holing or herring-boning may be substituted for it.

In a very handsome piece of lace the ground is openworked throughout and the figures of the design are embroidered with different kinds of stitches. For the larger exterior portions of a figure damask stitches are chosen, for the insides, less important ones and for the openwork ground a very quiet pattern.

Stuffs. — Work of this kind is immensely simplified and facilitated by the use of stuffs imitating an openwork ground. By using rather a coarse stuff you can increase the scale of the pattern, but the proportions must be carefully preserved so that the general effect may not be spoiled.

Worked on moderately coarse stuffs, this kind of lace is used for trimming curtains and blinds; pincushion covers and little squares for all sorts of purposes, are also made of it; worked on finer stuffs it is used for trimming collars, cuffs and other articles of dress; also for ecclesiastical dress and furniture such as albs, rochets and altar-cloths; for the latter the embroidery must be done on the cloth itself.

In Colbert embroidery, which is done on a foundation of coarse canvas or stiff linen, the character of the embroidery is also somewhat modified. For the outlines a cord is substituted for the sewing stitch; whilst the embroidery instead of being in white or cream is in several colours, with the addition, as the case demands, of gold or silver thread. The figures of the design are covered with damask stitches and the ground is openworked.

These embroideries are highly decorative and are used for cushions, panels, chair-backs, &c.

Materials. — For embroidering on a cambric ground take the finer numbers of D.M.C Flax lace thread (Lin pour dentelles) and D.M.C Floss flax or flourishing thread (Lin floche), in white; for embroidering on canvas, D.M.C Pearl cotton (Coton perlé), D.M.C Crochet cotton 6 cord (Cordonnet 6 fils), D.M.C Special crochet cotton (Cordonnet spécial), and for certain straight stitches, D.M.C Special stranded cotton (Coton mouliné spécial), in white or écru. (*)

For Colbert embroidery we recommend as twisted thread D.M.C Pearl cotton (Coton perlé) and as loose thread D.M.C Special stranded cotton (Mouliné spécial) or D.M.C Persian silk (Soie de Perse); for the outlines, take D.M.C Turkish gold cord (Ganse turque); D.M.C Gold chiné (Chiné d'or) and D.M.C Gold

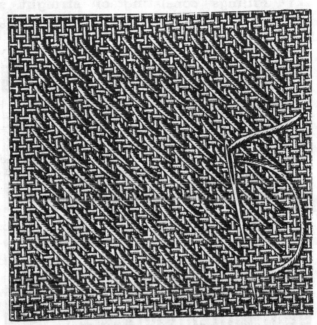

Fig. 794. First damask stitch.

and silver embroidery threads (Or et argent fins) may also be used to heighten the effect of certain damask stitches worked in a floss material.

Stitches for fillings. — The beauty and general effect of these embroideries greatly depend on the choice of the fillings. We shall class them in three principal groups.

1° Fillings consisting of straight stitches, called "damask stitches".

(*) See at the end of the last chapter the tables of the sizes and colours of the cotton, flax and silk articles, mark D.M.C. — The French names, in brackets, are those stamped on the labels of the D.M.C articles.

2• Openwork fillings, produced by drawing together the threads of the stuff, called "openwork grounds" and

3• Fillings consisting of openwork grounds and damask stitches.

To facilitate to our readers the reproduction of the various stitches we are going to describe, we give the number of threads each figure requires.

1• **Fillings consisting of straight stitches, called "Damask stitches"**. — The patterns of these grounds are composed of vertical, horizontal or oblique straight stitches; they sometimes imitate figured stuffs. In that case they cover the ground almost entirely, forming small figures with hardly any stuff visible between.

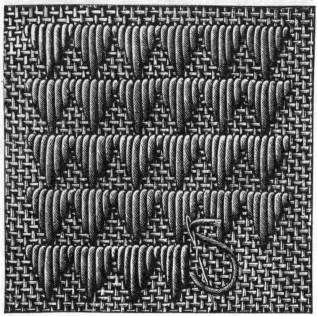

Fig. 795. Second damask stitch.

The use of these stitches for the different parts of flowers, leaves or ornaments has already been mentioned in connection with "Piqué" embroidery, fig. 153, in the chapter on "Embroidery upon White Stuff".

First damask stitch (fig. 794). — Each group takes 4 threads in height and 4 in width.

The close pattern is composed of oblique encroaching straight stitches, worked in oblique rows. Bring out your thread on the right side of the work, carry the needle upwards from right to left over 4 threads of the stuff, and bring it back on the right side under 6 horizontal and 2 vertical threads. Then make another oblique stitch from right to left over 4 threads, and so on. The second row of stitches is

worked in the same way; the stitches are set between those
of the former row into which they encroach over two threads
of the stuff.

Second damask stitch (fig. 795). — Each group takes
8 threads in height and 6 in width.

Our pattern is composed of rows placed one above the
other, of small scallops pointing downwards, consisting of
vertical straight stitches.

Begin with a straight stitch upwards over 2 threads of the
stuff, then bring the needle out on the right under 4 horizontal
threads and 1 vertical, to make the second vertical stitch
upwards over
4 threads; in
the same way,
make a third
stitch over 6
threads and a
fourth upwards
over 8 threads,
and then again
gradually de-
crease the
height of the
stitches; the
last stitch —
which may be
regarded as the
first stitch of
the next scallop
— numbers 2
threads in
height. The
whole row of

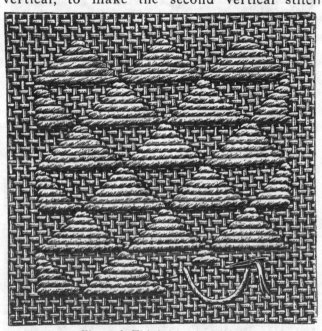

Fig. 796. Third damask stitch.

scallops is worked like this. The straight edge of one row
touches the points of the row above.

Third damask stitch (fig. 796). — Each group takes
6 threads in height and 12 in width. The pattern is formed of
oblique rows of inverted triangles, composed of horizontal
stitches.

You begin at the top with the shortest stitch, made from
left to right over 2 threads of the stuff; this is followed by
5 horizontal stitches, gradually increasing in width, to the
left and right, by one thread of the stuff, so that the longest

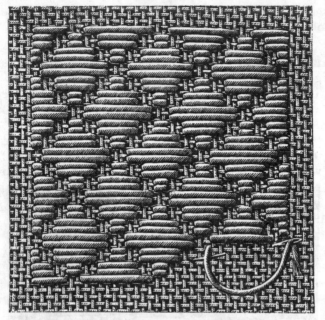

Fig. 797. Fourth damask stitch.

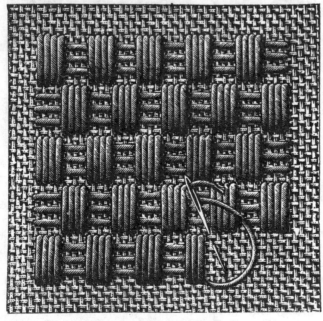

Fig. 798. Fifth damask stitch.

stitch covers 12 threads. You then pass to the next triangle on the left, and in this way the inversion of the triangles follows naturally.

Fourth damask stitch (fig. 797). — Each group takes 12 threads in height and the same in width.

In this pattern the stuff of the ground is almost entirely covered by the lozenges, each consisting of 10 horizontal straight stitches. These lozenges are set in oblique rows, as follows: after bringing out the thread at the desired place, you make a horizontal stitch from left to right over two threads of the stuff; repeat this stitch underneath, leaving one thread between, then descending always one thread at a time, make 2 stitches, over 6 vertical threads, increasing by 2 threads right and left; 2 horizontal stitches over 10 threads form the middle of the lozenge. For the next stitches, decrease again by 2 threads in the same manner as you increased, so that the last stitches, like the two first will be over 2 threads.

Fifth damask stitch (fig. 798). — Every group takes 8 threads in height and in width. Begin by 4 vertical stitches over 8 horizontal threads; then take the needle downwards from above under 2 horizontal threads and one vertical, see also figure 798, and make the 3 horizontal stitches from left to right, leaving 2 threads between them. When the third horizontal stitch is made, descend to the right again under 2 horizontal threads and 1 vertical, to proceed with the 4 vertical stitches. The second row of the pattern is worked

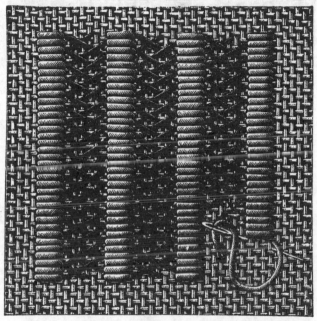

Fig. 799. Sixth damask stitch.

just like the first, only the figures must be inverted, so that the horizontal stitches come under the vertical ones and the vertical ones under the horizontal.

Sixth damask stitch (fig. 799). — Each subject takes 2 threads in height and 10 in width.

Vertical lines of horizontal stitches alternate with lines of Russian stitch. Begin by the lines of horizontal straight stitches, which are 4 threads wide; 6 threads are left between these lines: over which threads make the crossed stitching-stitch, see fig. 75. After bringing the needle out between the

4th and 5th of the 6 intermediate threads, make an oblique stitch downwards from right to left over 4 vertical threads and 2 horizontal ones; bring the needle out 2 threads higher up, to make a second oblique stitch downwards to the right over 6 vertical and 3 horizontal threads, which will cross the first stitch; pass the needle vertically under 2 horizontal threads, make one oblique stitch to the left, and so on.

This ground is greatly improved by being worked in two kinds of thread; a coarse thread should be chosen for the straight stitches and a fine one for the crossed stitching.

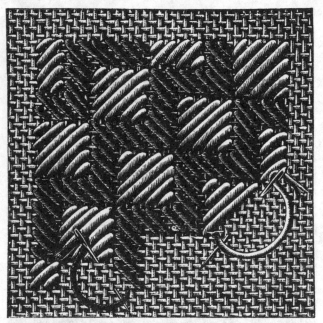

Fig. 800. Seventh damask stitch.

Seventh damask stitch (fig. 800). — Each subject takes 12 threads both ways. Squares of oblique straight stitches, separated by zigzag lines form a ground that entirely covers the stuff.

You begin by the zig-zag lines which require 5 oblique stitches each way, over 4 threads of the stuff, with 2 threads between. These lines are so placed as to enclose squares of stuff, 8 threads wide, within them. These squares are then covered with straight stitches set the opposite way from the stitches of the zig-zag lines. The first and the seventh stitch of the squares are made over 2 threads of the stuff, the second and sixth over 4, the third and fifth over 6 and the fourth over 8.

Eighth damask stitch (fig. 801). — Each subject takes 8 threads in height and 6 in width. The vertical lines of the pattern are made as follows: after bringing the needle out, make a horizontal stitch from right to left over 2 threads,

then descending to the right, under 2 threads each way, make
a second horizontal stitch, and so on. The intervals between
the rows numbers 4 threads; in these you work the little
squares consisting of 3 straight stitches over 4 horizontal
threads, skipping 4 threads of the stuff between each square.
In the next row of intervening spaces, the little squares are
inverted, that is to say, set between the squares of the row
before.

2º **Openwork grounds.** — By drawing the thread of a
stuff tightly together in groups of various sizes by means of
stitches, open-
work grounds
can be pro-
duced that are
very like the
openwork
grounds on
linen described
in the foregoing
chapter.

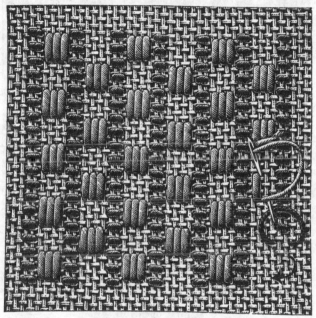

These open-
work grounds
are done with-
out drawing out
any threads,
and contrary to
the openwork
on linen which
requires a close
fabric, can only
be done on a
loosely woven

Fig. 801. Eighth damask stitch.

one. They are used as fillings and are of two kinds.

1º The openwork stitches done with a very fine thread
and where the pattern is formed solely by the different grouping of the threads of the stuff, see figs. 802 to 806.

2º The stitches worked in a coarse thread producing a
raised effect on the stuff foundation. In these the pattern is
not formed solely by the threads of the stuff, but by the
embroidery thread as well, which produces raised stitches, see
figs. 807 to 811.

First openwork ground (fig. 802). — Each subject takes
5 threads both ways.

This ground is worked in oblique rows. You begin by a vertical stitch upwards over 4 threads, then carry the needle downwards from right to left under 4 threads of the stuff, make a horizontal stitch over 4 threads from left to right, come back on the wrong side, downwards from right to left, under 4 threads of the stuff, to begin again with the vertical stitch upwards which meets the preceding horizontal stitch. Continue the row as described above. When you come to the second row of stitches, skip one thread of the stuff in a slanting direction and continue the work as before.

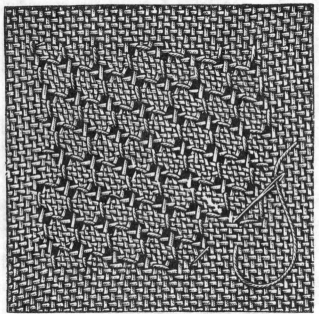

In this way, by drawing the threads of the stuff together, you will get a cross formed by the threads that were skipped between the two rows of stitches.

To produce the openwork pattern, the thread that unites the threads of the stuff must be very tightly drawn.

Fig. 802. First openwork ground.

Second openwork ground (fig. 803). — Each subject takes 6 threads both ways.

This ground is worked in two directions, in horizontal and vertical rows; finish all those in one direction first, before you begin those that go the opposite way, and which cross the first.

Begin with the horizontal rows, taking the needle upwards from below, vertically over 4 threads of the stuff, and return in a slanting direction under 4 horizontal and 4 vertical threads and make a second vertical stitch upwards. Between the third and fourth stitches skip only 2 vertical threads on the wrong side, then continue with the vertical stitch. In this manner the interval between the vertical stitches numbers alternately 4 and 2 threads of the stuff. The vertical rows that cross the horizontal ones consist of horizontal stitches made in the same way.

The pattern when finished consists of little squares framed with square stitches with little openwork crosses between, formed by the two threads of the stuff that were left between the squares.

Third openwork ground (fig. 804). — Each subject takes 6 threads both ways. Here the threads of the stuff are drawn together by loop stitches. (See the chapter on "Netting", figures 662 and 663.)

As the engraving shews, the loop stitches are worked in slanting rows.

After bringing out the needle, skip, upwards from below to the right, 5 threads of the stuff, and

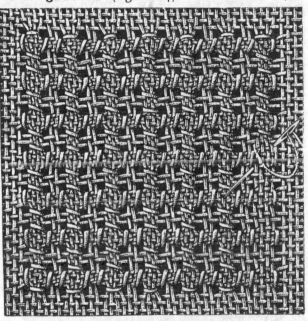

Fig. 803. Second openwork ground.

make a loop stitch over 3 horizontal threads, then make a similar stitch to the right over 3 threads and a third one downwards over 3 threads; to complete the fourth stitch, pass the needle over the first stitch and, skipping, on the wrong side to the left, downwards from above, 3 horizontal and 6 vertical threads, proceed to make the second loop stitch.

Fourth openwork ground (figs. 805 and 806). — Each subject takes 8 threads both ways. This ground, which is rather more complicated than the former ones, is worked in

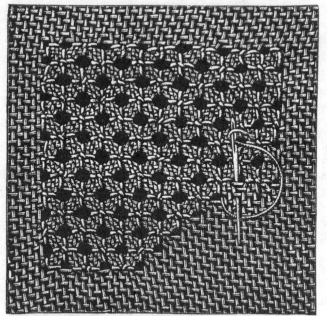

Fig. 804. Third openwork ground.

Fig. 805. Fourth openwork ground.
First and second row.

3 rows. First you do the zig-zag rows that form the checked pattern of the ground. These take 5 horizontal stitches worked from left to right over 4 threads of the stuff, with one thread between, then you take your needle on the wrong side downwards from right to left, under 4 threads to make 5 vertical stitches upwards from below, after which you skip on the wrong side, obliquely downwards, 4 threads of the stuff, to proceed with the 5 horizontal stitches.

By at once adding these zig-zag rows, you get little squares of stuff, consisting of 4 threads each way, which are then covered by

a cross stitch, framed by a **square** stitch, made in two rows.
Begin in the top right hand corner of the square, carry the
thread obliquely **under** the 4 disengaged threads, make a
vertical stitch upwards, take the needle horizontally from left
to right under 4 threads, returning, make a horizontal stitch
over these 4 threads, take the needle back vertically under
the first vertical stitch, and make an oblique stitch upwards
from left to right over 4 threads. To pass to the next stitch,
make a long oblique stitch on the wrong side of the work,
bringing the needle out at the bottom of the left hand corner
of the next
little square.

Here you fill
the square in
the same
manner   by
beginning with
the   vertical
stitch upwards
from   below.
When you have
finished   these
rows over the
whole surface
of   the   em-
broidery   you
proceed to the
third   row,
which   com-
pletes   the
ground. These
rows must be
worked the op-

Fig. 806. Fourth openwork ground.
Third row.

posite way to the preceding ones but the stitch is the same.

When the ground is finished you have squares with
little crosses within them and if you hold it up to
the light, you will see the long oblique stitches at
the back, forming with the framed crosses on the right
side, little stars.

Fifth openwork ground (fig. 807). — Each subject takes
4 threads both ways.

This ground, rather like coarse tulle, is worked in horizontal
rows and to produce the proper effect, the threads of the stuff

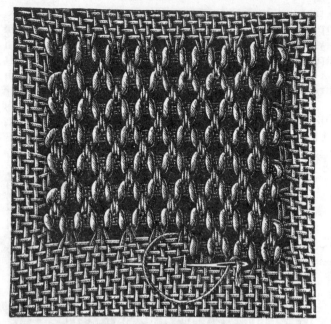

Fig. 807. Fifth openwork ground.

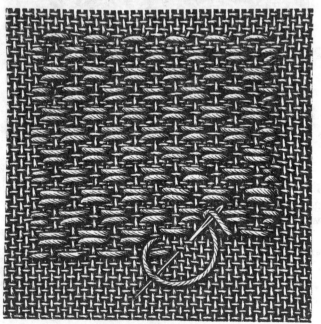

Fig. 808. Sixth openwork ground.

have to be drawn very tightly together. You begin by an oblique stitch upwards from left to right, over 2 vertical and 4 horizontal threads, then take your needle horizontally to the right under 4 threads, to make an oblique stitch downwards to the right over 2 vertical and 4 . horizontal threads, skip, on the wrong side to the left, 4 vertical threads, to begin again with the first oblique stitch, and so on.

The next rows are inverted in such a manner as always to give you 4 oblique stitches in the same hole of the stuff.

Sixth openwork ground (fig. 808). —

Each subject takes 6 threads both ways. This ground is done in 2 horizontal rows and is very easy to work.

The first horizontal stitch is made from left to right over 5 threads, you then take your needle slanting downwards from left to right under 2 threads of the stuff, to make a second horizontal stitch to the right over 5 threads, then on the wrong side, going upwards obliquely to the left, skip 2 threads of the stuff, to proceed with the first horizontal stitch. The next rows are worked in the same way, leaving one thread between each and inverting the stitches so as always to have 2 parallel horizontal stitches. In this manner you will have little open-work crosses between the embroidered stitches, consisting of the threads of the stuff which were left between the horizontal stitches.

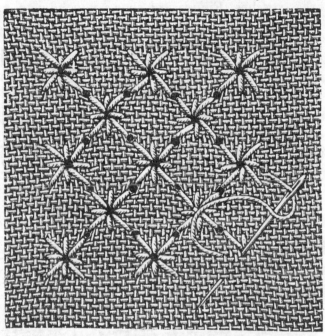

Fig. 809. Seventh openwork ground.

Seventh openwork ground (fig. 809). — Each subject takes 16 threads both ways.

This ground is composed of inverted stars that divide the stuff into lozenges. The star stitch is described in the chapter on "Tapestry", by fig. 344. By drawing the thread tightly as you work, you will get little holes in the centres of the stars.

We shall meet with this stitch several times again as a small detached figure for ornamenting squares or lozenges in subsequent grounds.

Eighth openwork ground (figs. 810 and 811). — Each subject takes 8 threads both ways.

Consisting of two rows of oblong cross stitches, crossed
obliquely the one over the other this ground produces a
charming effect worked with a rather coarse thread.

Figure 810 shews the first rows of cross stitches made upwards from left to right. You begin by an oblique stitch over
6 vertical and 3 horizontal threads, then you skip, on the
wrong side of the work, upwards to the left and in a slanting
direction, 2 threads of the stuff, to continue on the right side
with a long oblique stitch; returning, you finish the row of
cross stitches. Figure 811 shews you how to make the second
rows of cross
stitches across
the first ones.

Between the
raised crosses,
the drawing
together of the
stuff, produces
little open-
work crosses.

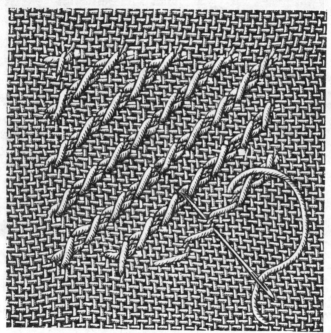

3° **Open-
work
grounds
with figures
made with
straight
stitches.** —
These grounds
composed of
openwork
stitches and
little figures
worked in
straight or in

Fig. 810. Eighth openwork ground.
First row of cross stitches.

some fancy stitch, represent the richest kind of all these
fillings. We give eight of them in this chapter, but our
readers will find no difficulty in inventing others, as the combinations that can be made are infinite. With regard to
materials, a twisted thread should be taken for the openwork
stitches and a loose one for the little figures in straight stitch.
See our article on materials, page 575.

First openwork ground with bars in straight stitch
(fig. 812). — Each subject takes 12 threads both ways. Oblique

bars worked
in horizontal
rows divide
the ground
into lozenges.

Begin the
bars by an
oblique stitch
descending 2
threads from
right to left,
then come up
on the wrong
side under 2
vertical
threads and
1 horizontal
one, to make
an oblique
stitch down-
wards over 1
thread, then
come up again
under 2 ver-
tical threads
and 1 hori-
zontal one, to
make a second
oblique stitch
downwards
over 2 threads
of the stuff,
and so on.
Each bar num-
bers 9 oblique
stitches, 5 long
and 4 short
stitches. After
the 5th long
stitch, you
bring the
needle out at
the same place

Fig. 811. Eighth openwork ground.
Second rows of cross stitches.

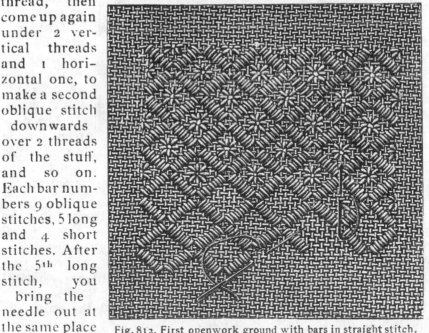

Fig. 812. First openwork ground with bars in straight stitch.

it came out of at the last stitch, and make a second bar like the first in the opposite direction. The next rows of bars must be inverted to form the lozenges of stuff which are to be adorned with a star stitch.

To work this stitch, bring the needle out in the middle of the lower bar on the right, make an oblique stitch from right to left, upwards over 2 threads of the stuff, followed by a two-sided horizontal stitch to the right, then an oblique stitch downwards from above to the left, a vertical stitch upwards, and in this way make 8 stitches which meet in the middle of the lozenge and form an eyelet-hole.

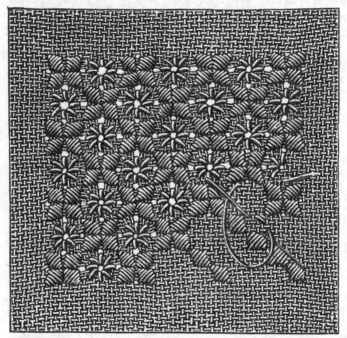

Fig. 813. Second openwork ground with lozenges in straight stitch.

Second openwork ground with lozenges in straight stitch (fig. 813). — Each subject takes 16 threads both ways. The pattern is made up of little figures composed of 4 lozenges in straight stitches set slanting, alternating with star stitches.

The little lozenges each number 7 stitches, the 1st and the 7th are made diagonally over 1 thread of the stuff, the 2nd and 6th over 2 threads, the 3d and 5th over 3 and the 4th over 4. As the engraving shews, the little lozenges are made in two oblique rows that cross each other. The star stitches, that fill the empty squares, number 8 stitches that meet in the centre; the oblique stitches are made over 3 threads of the stuff, the horizontal and the vertical stitches over 4.

Third openwork ground with lines in straight stitch (fig. 814). — Each subject takes 13 threads in height and 4 in width.

Two rows of inverted square stitches form the waved openwork line that also figures in the chapter "Openwork on Linen", see figs. 740 and 741. Between these double rows of square stitches worked over 4 threads of the stuff, 5 threads of the stuff are left empty, to be afterwards traversed by straight vertical stitches, placed just under the vertical stitches of the square stitch above.

Fourth openwork ground with lines of cross stitch (fig. 815). — Each subject takes 3 threads in height and 15 threads in width.

This ground in diagonal lines consists of double rows of cross stitches and rows of the openwork stitch explained in the chapter "Openwork on Linen", by fig. 743.

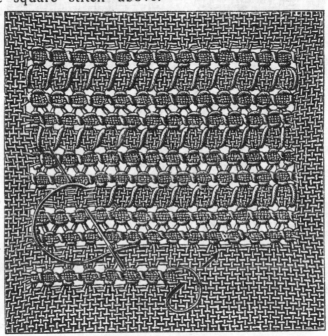

Fig. 814. Third openwork ground with lines in straight stitch.

Begin by the rows of cross stitches, worked to and fro in horizontal lines.

Between the double rows of cross stitches there is an interval of 9 threads, to be filled with openwork stitches as soon as the cross stitch work is finished. The first stitch must be made upwards from below, over 3 threads of the stuff, then you come back vertically under 3 threads for a second oblique stitch upwards to the left, after which, on the wrong side and to the right, you skip 3 threads in a horizontal direction, to continue with an oblique stitch upwards to the left, and so on.

The second row which finishes the openwork stitch is made in the same manner, but downwards from above. The empty spaces where the two oblique stitches meet form the openwork.

Fifth openwork ground with cross and star stitch figures (fig. 816). — Each subject takes 12 threads in height and 3o threads in width.

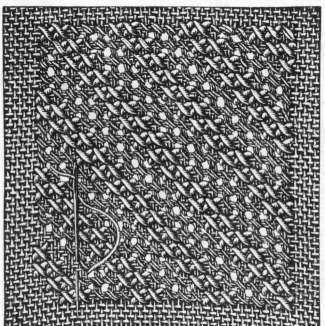

Fig. 815. Fourth openwork ground with lines of cross stitch.

This ground, on a bigger scale than the others, is used for covering large surfaces. The division of the ground is formed by two rows of square stitches worked over 3 threads of the stuff. Two parallel serpentine lines traverse the stripes of stuff between the rows of open square stitch. These serpentine lines are formed by straight cross stitches worked over 6 vertical and 6 horizontal stitches; the empty spaces between the two rows of cross stitch are embroidered with star stitches, and detached knot stitches are placed between the teeth of the serpentine lines.

Sixth openwork ground with figures in button-hole stitch and squares in cross stitch (fig. 817). — Each subject takes 24 threads both ways.

Like the preceding pattern, this one is particularly suitable for covering large surfaces. Before beginning the actual pattern the whole ground must be openworked, see fig. 743. This is done in diagonal lines, as follows: you make an oblique stitch to the left over 3 threads, you descend 3 threads on the wrong side, make a second oblique stitch upwards to the left, then pass the needle horizontally to the right under 3 threads, and make a third oblique stitch to the left.

The next row is worked the reverse way, that is, downwards from above. By pulling the working thread very tight you get a very transparent ground on which to embroider the pattern. The diagonal lines that divide the whole ground into lozenges are composed of straight cross stitches, made, each of them, over 2 groups of threads. Beginning at the top you take your thread downwards, vertically over 2 groups of threads, jump

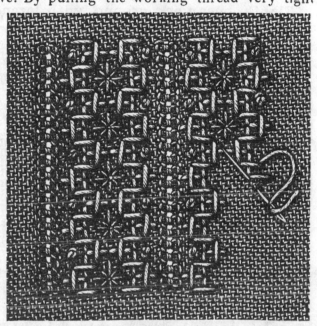

Fig. 816. Fifth openwork ground with cross and star stitch figures.

on the wrong side from right to left obliquely upwards over one group of threads, and then make the next vertical stitch downwards. In the second row, returning, you complete the crosses by horizontal stitches. When all the rows of cross stitches are finished you surround the hole in the centre of the lozenges with button-hole stitches thus forming a raised border round it.

Seventh openwork ground with squares of straight stitches (fig. 818). — Each subject takes 24 threads both ways.

The checked ground is composed of double rows of square stitch, fig. 740; the squares of stuff are filled, each with

4 little squares of straight stitches, set slanting. The square stitch, which must be made first, is worked over 3 horizontal and 3 vertical threads.

For the empty parts of the stuff, you leave an interval of 18 threads, on which you embroider the big squares in straight stitch, formed of four small squares, each consisting of 15 oblique stitches, the shortest of them made over 1 thread and the longest over 8; the long ones to meet in the middle.

Eighth openwork ground with lozenges in straight stitch and crossed stitching (fig. 819). — Each subject takes 28 horizontal and 26 vertical threads.

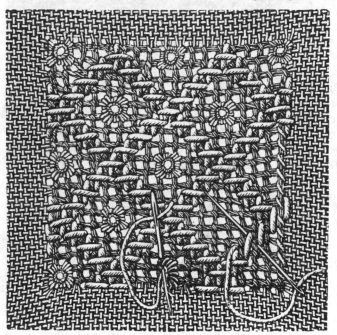

Lozenges with wide frames in straight stitch and openwork centres alternate with quadruple squares in crossed stitching.

The framing of the lozenges is begun at the left point, with a vertical stitch downwards over 2 threads

Fig. 817. Sixth openwork ground with figures in button-hole stitch and squares in cross stitch.

of the stuff, passing upwards to the right on the wrong side of the work; with 1 oblique stitch over 3 horizontal threads and 1 vertical, you make on the right side a second stitch over 4 horizontal threads. Continuing thus, make vertical stitches over 6, 8 and 10 threads, respectively, and bring the needle out at the top again, after which you make 9 more vertical straight stitches over 6 threads, ascending 1 thread at each stitch. The 9th stitch forms the point of the lozenge;

then make 8 stitches descending on the right, and begin again
with the long stitch over 10 threads, followed by 4 stitches,
each, one thread shorter top and bottom than the one before,
so that the last — at the right corner of the lozenge, only
covers 2 threads. At the bottom you end the lozenge by 17
vertical stitches over 6 horizontal threads. In the middle you
embroider a little figure composed of 4 groups of 3 horizontal
straight stitches over 4 threads of the stuff; this figure is
framed by a serpentine line of double overcasting stitches
over 2 threads
of the stuff.

The squares
of crossed stitch-
ing are worked
in oblique rows.

**Dresden lace
on a cambric
ground** (figs.
820, 821, 822). —
This fine delicate
pattern is com-
paratively easy
to work, though,
embroidered as
it is on fine
cambric, it re-
quires a great
deal of patience.

After tracing
the design and
mounting the
stuff in a frame,

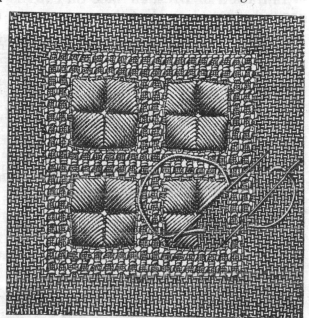

Fig. 818. Seventh openwork ground with squares
in straight stitch.

begin by filling the inside of the figures with the stitches,
figs. 805, 806, 814, 819, then you embroider the outlines and
the delicate little subjects of the pattern, with crossed back
stitching, which will give a raised effect and more substance
to these parts, so that they will shew up better on the transparent ground. An explanation of this crossed back stitching
has been given in the chapter on "Embroidery upon White
Stuff", figs. 74 and 75, but is illustrated here again by figs.
821 and 822. Figure 821 gives the right side of the work; it
shews how the needle makes first one back stitch on the
right and one on the left of the leaf; figure 822 shews the

back of the work, which forms a very regular crossed seam. When the grounds and the outlines are finished you take the work out of the frame to make the button-hole edges; after every fourth stitch you add, outside, a button-holed picot (see the chapter on "Needle-made Laces", fig. 869).

For all the crossed back-stitching we recommend D.M.C Floss flax or flourishing thread (Lin floche) No. 3o, and Nos. 6o and 100 of the same for the fillings and button-holing.

Imitation of Dresden lace on canvas with openwork ground (fig. 823). — For those who prefer less elaborate and minute work, we give here a lace embroidered on tammy cloth, which is an imitation, in a coarser style, of Dresden lace. After tracing the design, begin by openworking the ground with the stitch figure 804. The inside of the flowers is filled with stitch, fig. 812, the leaves with stitch, fig. 813; you may substitute for these any one of the other stitches described in this chapter.

Fig. 819. Eighth openwork ground
with lozenges in straight stitch and crossed stitching.
Right side.

When the ground and the fillings are done, embroider the outlines with stem stitch so as to make them stand out in relief upon the ground and distinctly define the non-embroidered parts, where the canvas remains empty.

The lace is finished off at the bottom by a row of plain button-hole stitches, worked over a padding of 2 rows of running stitches.

For the fillings take D.M.C Floss flax (Lin floche) No. 25, and No. 16 for the outlines in stem stitch.

Cushion in Colbert embroidery (figs. 824 and 825). Big patterns worked on coarse transparent stuffs with various fillings and corded outlines are known under the name of Colbert embroideries. We give a specimen of the same in the cushion figure 824.

The explanatory engraving, fig. 825, is big enough to enable a worker to copy the fillings, which are moreover described in the present chapter ; we merely observe that the Hungarian stitch, see the chapter on "Tapestry", fig. 340, has been used for filling the volutes.

The stuff used for the foundation is tammy cloth, the fillings are worked with D.M.C Persian silk (Soie de Perse), Maize yellow 1069 and Rust brown 1154, with D.M.C Gold

Fig. 820. Dresden lace on a cambric ground.
Materials : D.M.C Floss flax Nos. 30. 60 and 100, in white. (*)

(*) See at the end of the last chapter the tables of the sizes and colours of the cotton, flax and silk articles, mark D.M.C.

embroidery thread (Or fin à broder) No. 3o (*) introduced here and there.

The little leaves, the calices and stalks are worked in encroaching flat stitch, and in two colours. When all the fillings are done, you openwork the ground by means of stitch, fig. 808. The material to use for this is D.M.C Special crochet cotton (Cordonnet spécial) No. 20.

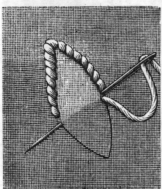

Fig. 821. Leaf worked with crossed back stitch. Right side.

When the ground is finished outline the different figures with D.M.C Turkish gold cord (Ganse turque) No. 6 for the bigger and more important parts and cord No. 12 for the smaller ones. A row of stem stitches in brown silk, outside the Turkish gold cord, completes the embroidery.

Net lace. — In net lace, the pattern is generally worked in darning stitch, whether it be the entire figures, or merely the outlines. In the latter case the subjects should be filled in with other stitches. Sometimes the figures, generally in cambric, are appliqué on to the net, in which case they are outlined with buttonhole stitches and the net takes the place of an openwork ground.

Fig. 822. Leaf worked with crossed back stitch. Wrong side.

The simplest patterns are done with a single outline in darning stitch, either with counted stitches, or on a traced line. In patterns with fillings, the latter are done with counted stitches; the outlines are always done on a tracing, done with a single thread, and then covered with a cord or with a stitch of one kind or another.

This is an imitation of Brussels or Brabant lace; the net foundation replaces the needle-made ground; whilst the

---

(*) See at the end of the last chapter the tables of the sizes and colours of the cotton, flax and silk articles, mark D.M.C. — The French names, in brackets, are those stamped on the labels of the D.M.C articles.

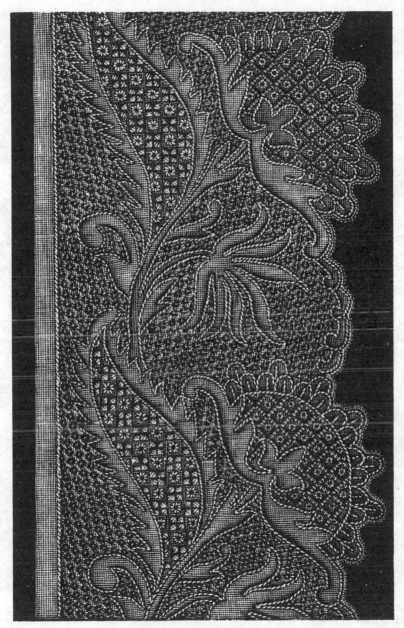

Fig. 823. Imitation of Dresden lace on canvas with
openwork ground.

Materials: D.M.C Floss flax Nos. 16 and 25 or D.M.C Pearl cotton Nos. 5 and 8,
in white or Cream yellow 712.

Fig. 824 Cushion in Colbert embroidery.
Materials : D.M.C Persian silk, in Maize yellow 1069 and Rust brown 1154,
D.M.C Special crochet cotton No. 20, in Maize yellow 579, D.M.C Turkish gold
cord Nos. 6 and 12, D.M.C Embroidery gold thread No. 30. (*)

(*) These numbers refer to the colours on the colour cards of the articles
stamped with the D.M.C trade mark. These cards can be consulted at all the
mercers' and needlework shops.

Fig. 825. Part of the cushion, fig. 824. Half its natural size.

fillings take the place of the different fancy grounds made
with bobbins, and are finished off with a thick outline, like
real lace.

Materials. — For embroidering on net, use one or more strands of a loose silky material; for fine white or cream net, D.M.C Special stranded cotton (Mouliné spécial) No. 25, D.M.C Pearl cotton (Coton perlé) Nos. 8 and 12 or D.M.C Persian silk (Soie de Perse); for black net, only silk is used. Coarse net, often used for the modern kinds of work, requires a coarser material, such as D.M.C Special stranded cotton (Mouliné spécial) No. 14, D.M.C Pearl cotton (Coton perlé) Nos. 3 and 5, and D.M.C Floss flax (Lin floche).

Appliqué work on net requires two kinds of thread: one pliable one, moderately twisted, D.M.C Embroidery cotton

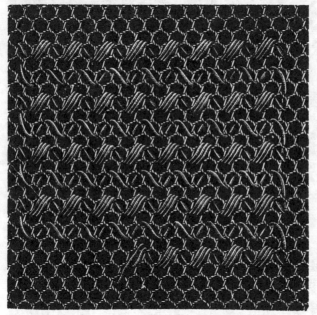

(Coton à broder), for the button-hole stitches; and a very round thread, with a strong twist, D.M.C Alsatian thread (Fil d'Alsace), for the bars and spiders in the cut out parts.

Preparatory work. — For embroidering on net you begin by tracing the pattern on linen-paper or waxed cloth, then stretch the net very smoothly over the tracing, so as to avoid

Fig. 826. First openwork pattern on net.

dragging or puckering it as you work, which spoils the look of the whole when it is finished. In patterns with fillings you trace the outlines first with running stitches following the lines of the tracing beneath, using for this a fine thread, then you proceed to the actual embroidery.

Embroideries on tulle done by machine. — Patterns worked in darning stitch and applications on tulle can easily be done by machine.

For the darning stitch take D.M.C Alsatian twist (Retors d'Alsace) in Nos. 20 to 100 for the top and underneath threads.

The applications on tulle should be embroidered in corded stitch over a padding thread.

For the corded stitch take D.M.C Embroidery cotton (Coton à broder) on reels, in Nos. 80 to 120, for the padding thread D.M.C Special crochet cotton (Cordonnet spécial) Nos. 5 to 30 and for the underneath thread D.M.C Machine thread (Fil pour machines) No. 150. (*)

Openwork patterns on net. — We shall begin by presenting our readers with a series of small grounds, powderings and insertions, very easy to work, for subsequent use in the lace patterns that follow.

First openwork pattern on net (fig. 826). This stitch has to be worked in one journey to and fro; first plain overcasting stitches going from left to right; returning, you make 3 stitches in one mesh, slanting the contrary way to the first stitches.

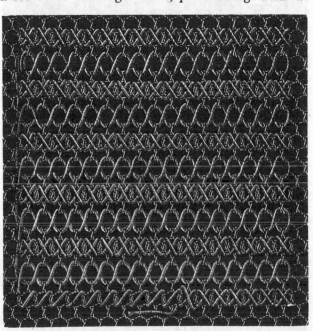

Fig. 827. Second openwork pattern on net.

Second openwork pattern on net (fig. 827). — After a double row of stitches, forming eyelet-holes, make a row of cross stitches, for which you pass the thread under one bar and over one mesh of the net, going, and cover the first stitches in the same manner, coming back.

Third openwork pattern on net (fig. 828). — After one row of cross stitches like those of the last figure, make a second, passing the thread under the bar that is between the

(*) See at the end of the last chapter the tables of the sizes and colours of the cotton, flax and silk articles, mark D.M.C. — The French names, in brackets, are those stamped on the labels of the D.M.C articles.

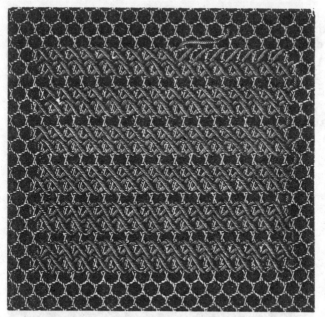

Fig. 828. Third openwork pattern on net.

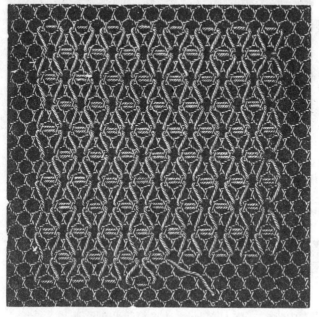

Fig. 829. Fourth openwork pattern on net.

first stitches, so that the two rows of stitches only cover 3 threads of net.

Fourth openwork pattern on net (fig. 829). — Here the thread passes horizontally under two bars and one mesh of net; then descending obliquely over two bars and one mesh, it again passes obliquely under two bars, to ascend obliquely, and so on. In the second rows you make the same stitches, so that four stitches meet in one mesh, and two threads pass under one mesh.

Fifth openwork pattern on net (fig. 830). This is worked in the same manner as figure 829, only that on one side you make three horizontal stitches over the meshes of net, and one oblique stitch under.

Sixth openwork pattern on net (fig. 831). Run the thread to and fro twice, in and out of a row of meshes, as if you were darning. In the next row you make clusters of four stitches each, over two bars and one mesh. After the fourth stitch you slip the needle under the net to the next cluster.

Fig. 830. Fifth openwork pattern on net.

Seventh openwork pattern on net (fig. 832). — Make three slanting stitches over three bars and two meshes of net, then coming back to the mesh whence the first stitches start, make three others in the opposite direction. In the second row the stitches meet in the mesh through

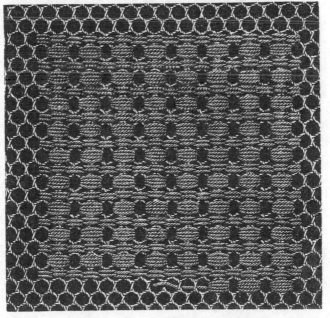

Fig. 831. Sixth openwork pattern on net.

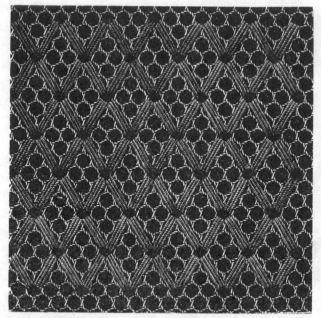

Fig. 832. Seventh openwork pattern on net.

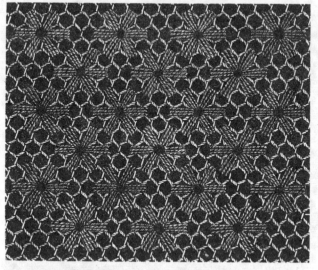

Fig. 833. Eighth openwork pattern on net.

which those of the first row passed.

Eighth openwork pattern on net (fig. 833). — The little stars with six rays, each ray made of three stitches over one mesh, are strewn over the surface, leaving open spaces between The pattern can be made more visible by increasing the number of stitches in each ray.

Ninth openwork pattern on net (fig. 834). Like the stars in the last pattern, the little diamonds here can be set more or less apart. For the centre dots you must see that the passage of the thread to and fro be as little visible as possible. Two or three rows of these figures one above another, produce a very good effect. Used as fillings in other patterns and variously distributed they embellish the plainest ground.

Tenth openwork pattern on net (fig. 835). — The long straight stitches of these diamond-shaped figures are made over three bars and two meshes; the others descend and ascend in the line of the meshes.

Eleventh openwork pattern on net (fig. 836). — This checked pattern again is worked in darning stitch. The threads are drawn through every second oblique row of meshes, over the whole surface that is to be covered, and when the first rows are all finished the second rows are worked across them in the same way. The rows may be set wider apart and the intervening spaces filled in with little stars or flowers.

Twelfth openwork pattern on net (fig. 837). — These big dia-

Fig. 834. Ninth openwork pattern on net.

Fig. 835. Tenth openwork pattern on net.

monds either set separately or connected in rows make a very effective ground, simple and easy as they are to work. A flat loose thread is better than a twisted one for this pattern and the stars inside the diamonds may be embroidered in D.M.C Gold embroidery thread (Or fin à broder).

Thirteenth, fourteenth and fifteenth openwork patterns on net (figs. 838, 839, 840). — These three patterns worked like the following ones in darning stitch, can take the place of crochet, pillow lace or embroidered insertion for trimmnig neck-ties, &c. They are so easy to copy that no further explanation is necessary.

Fig. 836. Eleventh openwork pattern on net.

We only recommend using rather coarse thread to shew up the pattern : D.M.C Pearl cotton (Coton perlé), for instance, or, D.M.C Special stranded cotton (Mouliné spécial) or D.M.C Floss flax (Lin floche) : D.M.C Superfine braid (Lacet superfin) (*), may also be used.

Sixteenth openwork pattern on net (fig. 841). — Carry the thread round one mesh first, before passing to the triangle which is worked in darning stitch over five, four, three, two

(*) See at the end of the last chapter the tables of the sizes and colours of the cotton, flax and silk articles, mark D.M.C. — The French names, in brackets, are those stamped on the labels of the D.M.C articles.

Fig. 837. Twelfth openwork pattern on net.

and one mesh of the net. In the second row opposed to the first, you carry the thread again round the mesh below, before going on to the second triangle.

Seventeenth openwork pattern on net (fig. 842). — This is worked in darning and straight stitch. The thread passes to and fro through four, three, two and one mesh of net;

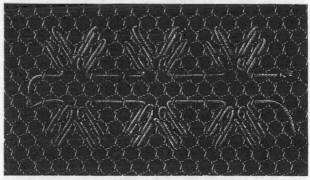

Fig. 838. Thirteenth openwork pattern on net.

the little running pattern between is worked in stitch, fig. 829.

When this pattern is repeated, the points opposed to those of the first row should lean the contrary way. Little stars like

39

those of figure 833, may be substituted for the running pattern between the two rows of scallops.

Insertion made with braid on net (fig. 843). — In order to bring out the pattern and the colours on coarse net, use D.M.C

Fig. 839. Fourteenth openwork pattern on net.

Superfine braid (Lacet superfin) instead of cotton thread. Working with braid needs greater care than with a thread, because it is so apt to get twisted; you can remed this by slipping a coarse needle under the last stitch and laying the braid flat.

Net darning (figs. 844, 845, 846). — To know how to darn and replace the torn meshes of net is an art by means of which very valuable and interesting work may be preserved. Coarse and fine net are both darned in the same way, the only thing is to see that the darning material and the thread of the net match exactly. Tack the torn piece, a little

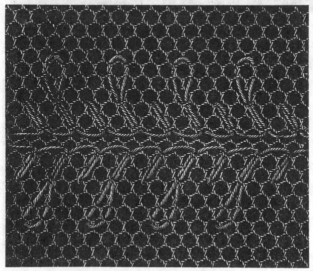

Fig. 840. Fifteenth openwork pattern on net.

outside the tear, on to a piece of coloured paper or waxed cloth; then cut the edges straight to the line of the thread.

It takes three rows of stitches to replace the meshes of net. The first consists of threads laid horizontally from one edge to the other, carried, as in all darning, a little beyond the edges of the hole, and so as to surround each mesh with a slanting stitch.

Begin by making the second stitches in the left corner of the empty space, then surround in a slanting line, the threads first laid, one after the other. These overcasting stitches should be continued a little beyond or outside the rent, so as to attach the new meshes securely to the original ones.

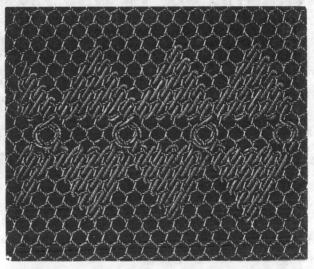

Fig. 841. Sixteenth openwork pattern on net.

In the third row threads are carried across the second and first layers. They must start far enough from the edge for the second layer to be overcast at the same time, so that there may be no slack threads left on the wrong side.

In this third journey, every

Fig. 842. Seventeenth openwork pattern on net.

diagonal thread of the foundation is to be encircled with a stitch, made upwards from below, the cut edges being strength-

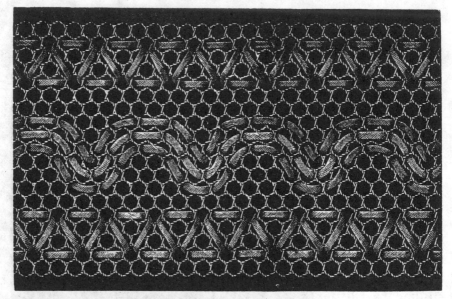

Fig. 843. Insertion made with braid on net.
Materials: D.M.C Superfine braid.

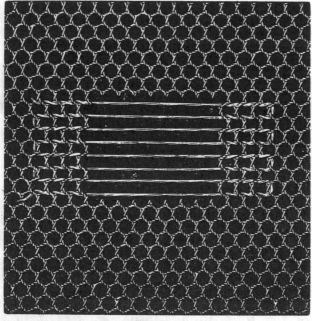

Fig. 844.
Darning on net. Laying the first thread.

ened in the same way.

Then to form the little cross in the fabric, the thread must be conducted by means of a second stitch, under the single horizontal thread, outwards to the next diagonal thread. In place where the net is worn it can be strengthened in the same way, the stitches being made to follow the direction of the threads.

Lace on net worked in darning stitch with button-hole edging (fig. 847). — When you have traced the pattern on linen-paper tack the net upon it and darn over all the lines with D.M.C Floss flax (Lin floche) No. 25. The little flowers and leaves are entirely filled up with a second row of darning stitches made within the outlines. The scalloped edge is made with button-hole stitches over a padding of two rows of running stitches.

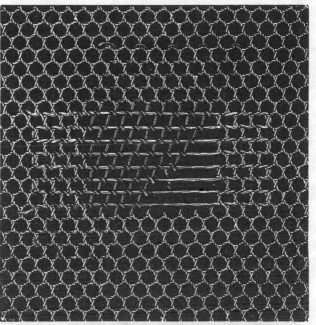

Fig. 845. Darning on net. Laying the second thread.

Handkerchief corner. Lace embroidered in darning stitch on net. Outlines and edge button-holed (fig. 848). — The floral designs, resembling those in real lace, lend themselves

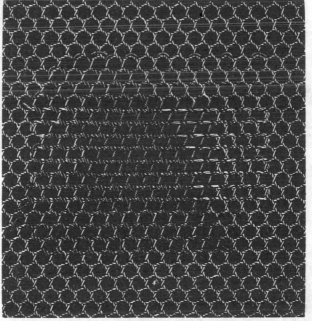

Fig. 846. Darning on net. Laying the third thread.

particularly well to this kind of lace. Tack the net on to linen paper, on which the pattern has been traced, and run over the outlines with very fine D.M.C Floss flax (Lin floche) No. 70, then fill in all the subjects with darning stitch, picking up every second bar of net. Take D.M.C Floss flax (Lin floche) No. 50, for the fillings, and No. 25 of the same for the thick outlines in running stitch.

The outside border of rose scallops is worked over a double tracing.

Wide lace on net with fillings and outlines of crochet braid (figs. 849 and 850). — This wide lace, on large meshed

Fig. 847. Lace on net worked in darning stitch with button-hole edging.
Materials : D.M.C Floss flax or flourishing thread No. 25 or D.M.C Special stranded cotton, in white or Maize yellow 579.

net, is intended for trimming curtains, blinds and altar-cloths.

For want of space this pattern is given in two pieces; see the points of junction at A and B.

Begin by tracing the outlines with D.M.C Special stranded cotton (Mouliné spécial) No. 25, then do the fillings with No. 14 of the same. Use the small stitches illustrated in figures 826 to 832 for the fillings of the leaves and stalks, and those in figures 834, 835 or 837 for the big spaces within the other

Fig. 848. Handkerchief corner. Lace embroidered in darning stitch on net.
Outlines and edge button-holed.
Materials : D.M.C Floss flax or flourishing thread Nos. 25, 50 and 70, in white. (*)

(*) See at the end of the last chapter the tables of the sizes and colours of
the cotton, flax and silk articles, mark D.M.C.

Fig. 849. Wide lace on net with fillings and outlines of crochet braid.
First part.

A B

Fig. 850. Wide lace on net with fillings and outlines of crochet braid.
Second part.

subjects. When you have finished all the stitches, edge the leaves and flowers with a row of chain stitches, the rings with a row of crochet bars made with D.M.C Special stranded cotton (Mouliné spécial) No. 25 ; in the centres of the flowers and the leaves make a little spider in darning stitch. The footing of the lace is composed of a row of Russian stitches edged with chain stitch, followed by a row of openwork bars and a row of close ones.

The border of the lace is ornamented with a row of crochet picots. The crochet is made separately and sewn on to the net with D.M.C Alsatian thread (Fil d'Alsace) No. 5o.

Fig. 851. Lace on net. Imitation of modern needle-point.
Materials : D.M.C Floss flax Nos. 60 and 100, in white. (*)

Lace on net. Imitation of modern needle-point (figs. 851 and 852). — Our engraving shews an imitation of needle-point lace on a net foundation with button-holed outlines. After tracing all the outlines, the opaque parts of the pattern are filled in with the lace stitch to be explained later on in the chapter on needle made lace, in fig. 908. Pick up each time, with the little loops of thread, a mesh of net (see the explanatory engraving fig. 852).

The more transparent parts are filled with simpler open-

(*) See at the end of the last chapter the tables of the sizes and colours of the cotton, flax and silk articles, mark D.M.C.

work stitches, chosen amongst those illustrated in figures 826 to 836. When the openwork stitches are finished, button-hole the outlines over a fourfold auxiliary run thread, then cut away the net inside the rings and flowers and ornament them with a little spider. Then inside the big scallops make a little four-leaved flower in post stitch. If you wish to enrich the lace with a border in cambric or linen, fix it on to the last

Fig. 852. Detail of lace figure 851.

row of button-holing; the edges of stuff that project must be carefully cut off with scissors.

The materials to use for this pattern are D.M.C Floss flax (Lin floche) No. 60, for the button-holed outlines, and No. 100 of the same, for the lace stitches.

Handkerchief corner in appliqué embroidery on net (fig. 853). — The handkerchief corner here represented differs

entirely from the patterns of lace on net hitherto described.
Here the figures are formed of cambric appliqué on the net.
The pattern is traced on the cambric itself; this is then laid,
straight to the thread, on fine net and fastened along the
edges with running stitches. This double layer of stuff is then

Fig. 853. Handkerchiет corner in appliqué embroidery on net.
Materials : D.M.C Embroidery cotton or D.M.C Floss embroidery cotton No. 50
and D.M.C Alsatian thread No. 70, in white. (*)

mounted on waxed cloth, and the outlines first traced with
short stitches, and then button-holed; you must take care
to make the stitches through both the cambric and the net.
When the outlines are finished cut out the cambric round the

(*) See at the end of the last chapter the tables of the sizes and colours of
the cotton, flax and silk articles, mark D.M.C.

figures, so that only the net ground is left. The openwork parts, where the net too is cut away, are filled in with bars and spiders. The right materials for this pattern are D.M.C Embroidery cotton (Coton à broder) No. 50, for the button-holing, and D.M.C Alsatian thread (Fil d'Alsace) No. 70, in white, for the bars and spiders.

Spanish laces. Embroideries done with metal and silk or cotton threads. — The richest embroidered laces are the Spanish or Italian, made with gold and silver thread and

Fig. 854. Insertion in Spanish embroidery.
Materials: D.M.C Embroidery gold thread No. 20, and D.M.C Alsa No. 40,
in Golden green 582 and Golden yellow 782.

brilliant threads, with or without a linen foundation. We give three characteristic examples of this kind of work; the first is an insertion, easy to make, embroidered on écru cambric with gold thread and green cotton thread; the second is a square of Moorish embroidery, rich in colour, with gold fillings and bordering; lastly a specimen of filigree lace in gold and silver and coloured cotton threads.

Materials. — For the three above mentioned patterns we recommend metal threads with a strong twist. The outlines

should be done with the D.M.C Gold and silver threads
button-holed over with a rather soft brilliant thread as
D.M.C Alsa. For the fillings in encroaching flat stitch, in
the Moorish embroidery, we recommend D.M.C Persian
silk (Soie de Perse). For the invisible stitches with which
the gold and silver thread and the spangles are fastened
down, D.M.C Alsa in Golden yellow 782 or in Ash grey 762
should be taken.

Insertion in Spanish embroidery (Figs. 854 and 855). —
In Spanish embroidery all the outlines of the pattern, traced

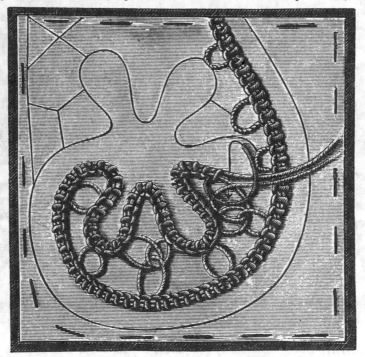

Fig. 855. How to work the outlines with picots of the
insertion figure 854.

on a linen or cambric foundation, are covered with double
gold or silver thread button-holed over with coloured thread.
The fillings are done with gold or silver thread. When the
embroidery is finished the stuff between is cut away, and the
different parts of the pattern are connected by picots made
with the same metal thread as the outlines. Begin with the
outlining, placing two gold threads side by side and fastening
them down with button-hole stitches. Where the pattern

requires it, you make a little loop — a picot — which you likewise secure with a button-hole stitch. Figure 855 shews how to intertwine the picots so as to connect the different figures in the empty spaces between. With regard to the figures, spiders with six rays are embroidered in the insides of the leaves and two threads of gold forming a row of little rings fill all the other parts of the pattern.

Fig. 856. Square in Moorish embroidery.
Materials: D.M.C Embroidery gold thread No. 30 and D.M.C Alsa No. 40.
in Golden yellow 782; D.M.C Persian silk, in Indigo blue 1009, 1010, 1011, 1012 and 1013, Bronze green 1092, 1093, 1094, 1095, 1096 and 1097,
Golden green 1142, 1385, 1143, 1144, 1145 and 1146, Copper red 1132, 1227, 1133, 1134 and 1135. (*)

(*) See at the end of the last chapter the tables of the sizes and colours of the cotton, flax and silk articles, mark D.M.C.

For the foundation take écru cambric, for the button-hole stitches, D.M.C Alsa, in Golden green 582, for sewing down the gold threads in the row of rings, D.M.C Alsa, in Golden yellow 782.

When the embroidery is guite finished cut away the cambric under the picots, close to the outlines of button-hole stitches.

Square of Moorish embroidery (figs. 856 and 857). — This kind ot embroidered lace requires the same preparatory

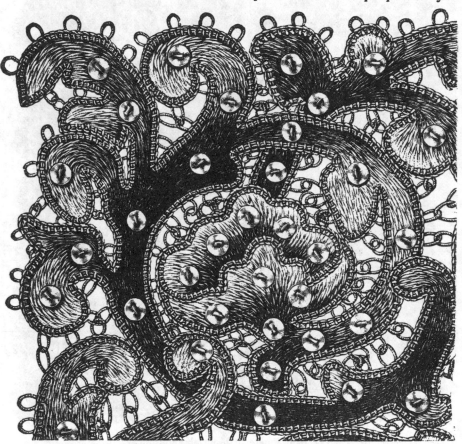

Fig. 857. Quarter of the square figure 856. Natural size.

work as the Spanish, namely the outlining of the figures with a double metal thread. The gold and silver ornamental stitches in the insides of the figures are replaced by a filling in encroaching flat stitch, done with coloured silk on which gold or silver spangles are afterwards sewn.

In figure 857 we give a quarter of the square 856, in the original size. This handsome piece of work may serve for a pincushion cover or sachet.

The materials to use for it are D.M.C Embroidery gold thread (Or fin à broder) No. 30, and D.M.C Alsa, in Golden yellow 782, split and used in single threads, for the outlines; D.M.C Persian silk (Soie de Perse), in Indigo blue and Copper red for the big flowers and the sprays; Bronze green and Golden green for the other ornaments.

Filigree lace (figs. 858, 859, 860, 861). — Filigree lace is the finest of all the Spanish laces; we give a specimen of it

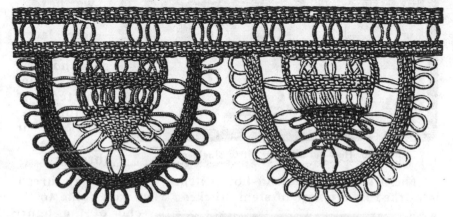

Fig. 858. Filigree lace.
Materials : D.M.C Embroidery gold thread and D.M.C Embroidery silver thread No. 20, D.M.C Alsa No. 40, in Blue fast dye 799,
Smoke grey 642, Cardinal red 346, Golden green 582 and Cream yellow 711. (*)

in our engraving, fig. 858. The original forms the trimming to a silk table-cover of the 17th century, of Spanish origin. It is a more difficult kind of work than the preceding ones and requires a very skilful hand.

The different parts of the design are made of metal threads connected by button-hole stitches in brilliant thread and carried out on a tracing made on linen paper without a stuff foundation.

When you have traced the pattern on the unglazed side of the linen paper, tack the latter on dark waxed cloth, the glazed side of the paper uppermost. The preparatory work

(*) See at the end of the last chapter the tables of the sizes and colours of the cotton, flax and silk articles, mark D.M.C.

consists in embroidering a line in stem stitch, fig. 72, along the top of all those parts of the pattern drawing, the parts on which the first line of button-hole stitches will afterwards have to be made. The stem stitches must go through both

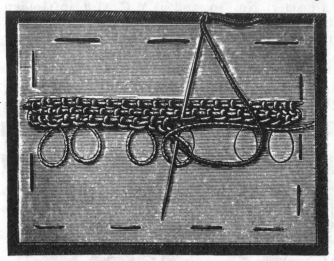

Fig. 859. How to make the little single picots.

linen paper and waxed cloth. This done you proceed to make the actual lace. As we have already said, these laces are made of gold and silver threads, connected by button-hole stitches in coloured thread.

The first row of button-hole stitches, over a metal thread. is worked in the row of stem stitches; when you come to the

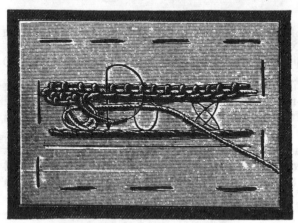

Fig. 860. How to make the interlaced picots.

end of the figure you bend the metal thread round and make a second row of button-hole stitches the opposite way, placing the stitches in the little loops formed by the preceding row. In this manner you add one row of stitches to the other until the whole figure is filled in. In the last row

of button-hole stitches, you make, with the metal threads. picots which serve either as a connecting link between the figures, or as an ornament to the outside border.

When the picots are to connect the different figures, they must be joined by a button-hole stitch to the first row of the part next to be embroidered.

When the thread has to be renewed, a few button-hole stitches should be made over the beginning of the new thread and the end of the old one, and both ends then cut off short.

We recommend beginning figure 858, at the footing of the lace with the row of single picots — two of these being

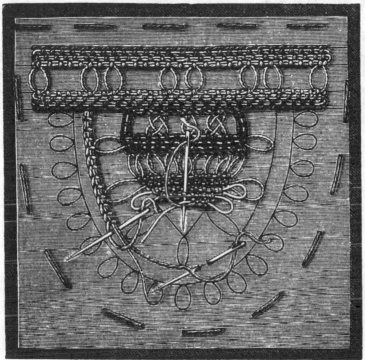

Fig. 861. Working detail of one scallop of the lace figure 858.

always drawn closer than the others — with gold thread and D.M.C Alsa in blue.

A straight red and a green line follow next; at the top of the footing one row of stitches in blue is added to connect the row of picots, then a row in red and a row in green.

You begin the scallops by making the inside horizontal bars with picots interlaced, as shewn in figure 860; the course of the work is shewn in figure 861. The arrangement of the colours varies for every three scallops; blue and green serve for the button-hole stitches over the gold threads, grey and

red over the silver thread. The first scallop begins at the top
in blue; next comes one little pyramid in grey and in red;
the outside semicircle is left green. The second scallop begins
with cream, then comes one little pyramid in green and in
blue, finishing with a semicircle in red. In the third scallop
the green bars are followed by one pyramid in red and in
cream with the semicircle in blue.

When the lace is finished, cut the rows of stem stitches on
the wrong side of the work, stitch by stitch, and the lace will
come away of itself from the foundation. Pick out carefully
any little ends of thread that may remain sticking in the lace.

Patterns of needlework. — Besides the different kinds
of work described above a great choice of patterns for embroidered laces will be found in the following publications
of the D.M.C Library : *Embroidery on Tulle I* and *Works of
various kinds*. (*)

(*) See at the end of the volume the list of the albums
of the D.M.C Library.

Needle-made lace. Venice point of the 16th century.

Needle-made Laces

The kind of work known as needle-made lace is closely related to open work on linen, of which it may be considered the outcome.

It consists of different combinations of button-hole stitches made with a single thread, a needle being the only implement required.

Reticella lace is the most ancient of the needle-made laces and in design it closely resembles open work on linen.

Raised lace with irregular bars, known as Venetian and French point dates from the 17th century.

In the 18th century, laces on a net foundation, such as Alençon and Argentan point, &c. were more in favour. A century later, the very fine needle-made laces of Belgium, Saxony and Bohemia were greatly in vogue but these require such an infinite amount of time and labour that they cannot be numbered amongst the feminine accomplishments suitable for leisure hours in the family circle: their importance is entirely commercial and therefore we do not deal with them more fully in the present work.

The kind of lace most frequently to be met with in the hands of amateurs is Irish lace, (*) which is composed of braids or

(*) See at the end of the volume the list of the albums of the D.M.C Library, containing a large variety of patterns for all kinds of work.

tapes, formed into figures on a traced pattern, joined together by needle-made, corded, or button-hole bars and fillings of different kinds, or by bars alone.

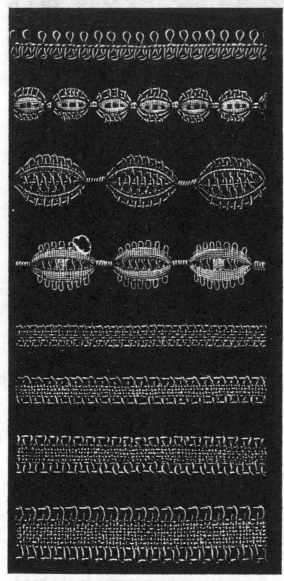

Fig. 862. English braids of different kinds for Irish lace.

Beside the Irish lace, Venetian point worked with rather coarse thread is very much in vogue at present. In addition to these classical laces we shall introduce our readers to several kinds or oriental laces in knot stitch generally worked in silk; then the coarse thread laces of Denmark and Sweden, called "Hedebo", and lastly the fine Spanish and Brazilian laces, known by the name of "Sols", and the handsome old laces of Italian origin.

Braids. — The braids used for making Irish lace are an English speciality. They are manufactured in various shades, generally in écru, white, straw-coloured and black; and there are wide and narrow ones, coarse and fine, with or without openwork edges, with or without picots and medallions of different sizes.

Figure 862 represents the kinds in most general use, in

their original size, together with a specimen picot of purl for the outside edge, also to be had ready made for those who whish to be saved the trouble of making them with the needle.

Materials. — For the bars and the lace stitches in all kinds of laces, we recommend, D.M.C Flax lace thread (Lin pour dentelles) or, D.M.C Flax thread for knitting and crochet (Lin pour tricoter et crocheter), D.M.C Alsatia, D.M.C Special crochet cotton (Cordonnet spécial), D.M.C Alsatian thread (Fil d'Alsace); these all have the brilliancy and suppleness, required for this kind of work, are besides pleasant to work with and can be had to match the braid in shade.

For the oriental laces in knotted stitch, which are generally made in several shades, take D.M.C Knotting cotton (Fil à pointer) or D.M.C Pearl cotton (Coton perlé). (*)

Copying designs for Irish lace. — This is generally done on white transparent English waxed linen with a watery ink free from greasy matter. This tracing linen is glazed on one side only and the tracing is done on the unglazed side as it takes the ink better.

As it is quite transparent, the pattern can be copied directly on to it without recourse to any other tracing process.

Patterns ready traced on this linen are to be had at all embroidery shops for those who do not care for the trouble of tracing them themselves.

It will be found less trying for the eyes to lay a piece of transparent coloured paper or thin stuff under the pattern before beginning to copy it. The Irish lace patterns are all drawn with double parallel lines, between which the braid is tacked on with small running stitches.

How to tack on and gather the braids (fig. 863). — The running stitches must be very regular, and longer on the right side of the work than at the back. At the curves of the lines the sewing must be done on the outside edge of the braid, so that the inside edge is slightly gathered.

When the braid is tacked on over the whole pattern, take a very fine threat and gather all the fulness inside the curves, by making little overcasting, stitches over the selvedge of the braid so that it fits exactly to the pattern.

(*) See at the end of the last chapter the tables of the sizes and colours of the cotton, flax and silk articles, mark D.M.C. — The French names, in brackets, are those stamped on the labels of the D.M.C articles.

The stitches made for the bars and fillings must never be drawn so tightly as to drag out the edges of the braid and thus spoil the lines of the pattern. Nor should the stitches pierce through the tracing linen but merely rest upon it.

When the work is finished turn it round to the wrong side, cut every second or third tacking stitch and pull out carefully all the ends of thread, when the lace will detach itself quite naturally from the foundation.

Fig. 863. How to tack on and gather the braids.

It does not matter which you make first, the bars or [the fillings; we, however, incline towards finishing the bars to begin with, especially when they are made in button-hole stitch, for once the bars are made, there is less risk of puckering or dragging the edges in makings the fillings. When the whole is finished, it is ironed and dressed. (See the chapter "Miscellaneous directions".)

Needles. — There are no needles specially made for lace work; we recommend long ordinary sewing ones of a size to suit the thread selected.

The stitches. — We shall now proceed to give a series of different kinds of pretty stitches, suitable at the same time for other fine laces to be described later on, including Venetian and gauze lace. We cannot claim to have exhausted the list of all the open work lace stitches that exist, but we have collected a sufficient number to meet the taste and capacity of every one.

With regard to the names, we have often found such different

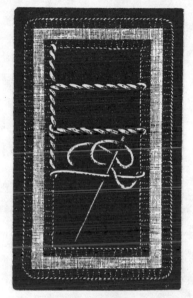

Fig. 864.
Bars in overcasting stitch.

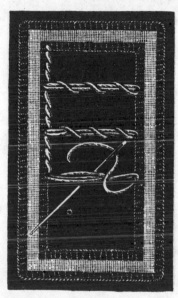

Fig. 865.
Double bars in overcasting stitch.

ones applied to one and the same stitch that we have not attemped to give them special names, excepting in the case of those that have a universally accepted one. We shall distinguish them simply in order by numbers.

Bars in overcasting stitch (fig. 864). — Fasten the thread to the braid and take it across from one selvedge to the other, put the needle in downwards from above and overcast the first thread as often as is necessary to give the two threads the appearance of a cord. If the overcasting stitches are not clos enough, the bars will look loose and untidy and spoil the general effect of the work.

When the bar is finished, continue the overcasting stitches beyond the edge of the braid to the place of the next bar.

Double bars in overcasting stitch (fig. 865). — For these, carry 3 threads across the empty space and overcast them with stitches, but not so closely as the bars of figure 864.

Bars in plain button-hole stitch (fig. 866). — First stretch three threads across, then cover them, from right to left, with button-hole stitches. You will observe in the engraving that the needle is passed eye foremost under the threads;

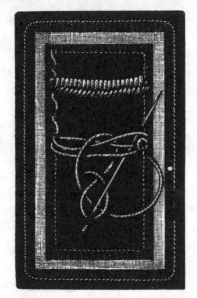
Fig. 866.
Bars in plain button-hole stitch.

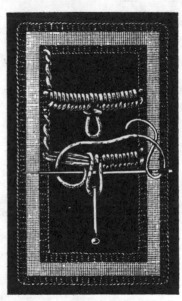
Fig. 867.
Bars with pinned picots.

this may seem strange but it is easier in this way to avoid splitting the threads. The thread with which the button-hole stitches are made must come out from the braid one or two threads distant from the threads laid for the bar, to prevent the bars becoming unequal in length or getting twisted at the beginning.

Bars with pinned picots (figs. 867 and 868). — After covering half or a third of the bar with button-hole stitches, pass the thread without making any loops under the foundation threads, stop the little loop of the thread with a pin which you pass under the work, slip the needle from right to left under the three threads, fig. 867, and tighten the stitch so as to bring it as near the button-hole stitch of the bar as possible.

In figure 868 the picot is made in the same way only with two button-hole stitches between the loop and the button-hole bar.

Bars with Venetian picots (fig. 869). — When you have laid the threads for the button-holing, you make a loop, as in figures 867 and 868, for the picot, then bring the thread back to the middle of the loop, stick in the pin, draw up the threads,

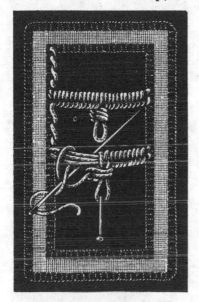

Fig. 868.
Bars with pinned picots.

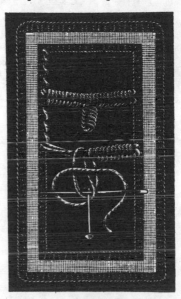

Fig. 869.
Bars with Venetian picots.

pass the needle behind the pin and begin the button-hole stitches quite close to and under the pin, thus covering the threads behind which it is planted.

The pin should be planted at a distance equal to the width of 6 stitches from the bar, and the threads of the filling must be completely hidden under them.

Bars with picots in post stitch (fig. 870). — Stick the needle in to half its length into the last button-hole stitch, twist the thread from left to right ten to twelve times round it, push the needle through the twists, pull up the thread so that the spiral forms a semicircle, and continue the button-hole bar (see also for the post stitch, figs. 79 and 682).

Bars with button-hole picots (fig. 871). — Cover rather more than half the bar with button-hole stitches, then bring the thread back three times, fastening it at about the seventh or eighth button-hole stitch; button-hole over the three threads hung over the bar and finish the bar the same as any other. Picots like this are generally used for edging lace.

Bars with double button-hole stitches (fig. 872). — Over two foundation threads make double button-hole stitches far

Fig. 870. Bars with picots in post stitch.

Fig. 871. Bars with button-hole picots.

enough apart to leave room between for the stitches that come on the other side of the bar.

These double button-hole stitches consist of an ordinary button-hole stitch first and a second one, reversed, made, that is, by passing the needle underneath the foundation threads and then sticking it in downwards under the loop the result being that the thread will come behind the stitch and not in front of it, as in ordinary button-holing.

Branched bars (fig. 873). — Where you want to cover a surface of any size with bars, you are generally obliged to make them with branches springing out of them as shewn in

our engraving. For this purpose you lay the foundation
threads as for any other bar and cover them halfway with
button-hole stitches; from thence you lay a second set of
foundation threads for a second
bar, branching out from the first,
cover these with button-hole
stitches up to the stippling, stretch
a third set of foundation threads,
button-hole these, then the uncovered half of the second set of foundation threads, and lastly the second
half of the first bar.

Plain Russian stitch (fig. 874).
Besides bars such as we have been
describing, all kinds of other stitches
are used for connecting the braids
and filling the spaces between. These
stitches which do duty as an insertion are some of them of a very
elementary nature whilst some demand great skill and patience in the
execution.

Fig. 872. Bars with double
button-hole stitches.

The simplest of all these stitches
is the Russian stitch which resem-
bles cross stitch illustrated by figure 45 and the crossed back
stitch, fig. 75.

Stick your needle downwards under the edge of the braid,
and then upwards
under the opposite
edge, taking care
always to keep the
thread in front of
the needle. You
must be carefut to
leave the same num-
ber of picots of the
braid between the
stitches, and to set
the bottom stitches
exactly in the middle

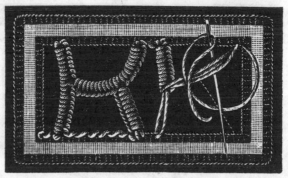

Fig. 873. Branched bars.

between the stitches in the top edge of the braid.

Twisted Russian stitch (fig. 875). — Instead of passing
the needle behind the thread, pass it in front and round it,

so that it should always come out again under the thread which is then twice twisted.

Column stitch (fig. 876). — At the bottom you make plain Russian stitch and at the top the stitch described above fig. 875, with the difference that you twist the second thread three times round the first.

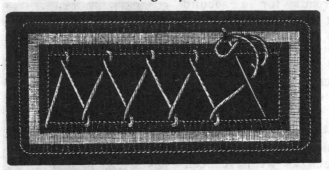

Fig. 874. Plain Russian stitch.

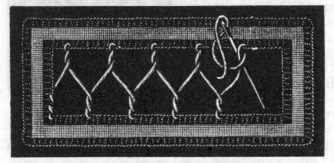

Fig. 875. Twisted Russian stitch.

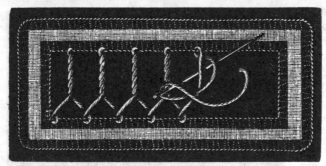

Fig. 876. Column stitch.

Insertion of loops (figs. 877 and 878). Along both edges of the braid make very loose button-hole stitches, all of the same size and at equal distance from each other. This done you pick up each loop with stitches like those of figures 874 and 875.

In figure 878 you see two Russian stitches made in each loop; three or four may be made, according to the degree of non-transparency desired for the insertion.

Insertion with bead stitches (fig. 879). — Join the opposite rows of loops together by four stitches. The threads of these stitches must lie quite flat side by side, and not override each other. After the fourth stitch twist the thread round the bottom loop, then carry it to the next in the same way and make the next four stitches.

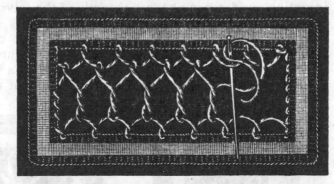

Fig. 877. Insertion of single loops.

Cluster insertion (fig. 880). — Begin by making two bars like those of figure 864, only a little distance apart, and then make a third only overcast half way with the second thread. When you reach the middle of the bars, connect them by five or six button-hole stitches and then overcast the remaining half of the third bar.

For the first bar of the next cluster, bring the needle out close to the third bar of the last one.

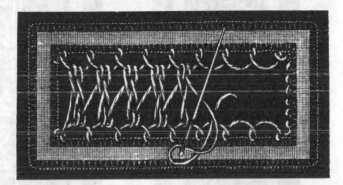

Fig. 878. Insertion of double loops.

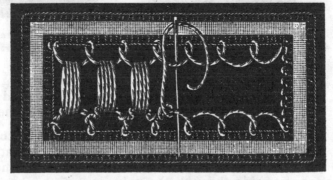

Fig. 879. Insertion with bead stitches.

Insertion with branches (figs. 881 and 882). — Stretch the thread across the middle of the space between the two edges of braid, and from one edge to the other lengthways; pass the needle to the middle of the braid placed across the insertion, under two or three threads of the selvedge, according to the thickness of the braid; then coming back, pass the thread through the selvedges of the long sides, first on the left upwards from below, then on the right, downwards from above, and form the 3 loops, which you connect by a knot, as shewn in figure 881; of course after that you do not make the stitch turned upwards, after that.

Fig. 880.
Cluster insertion.

Fig. 881. Insertion with
single branches.

Figure 882 represents the same beginning and the same interlacing of the threads, but with the added ornament of a big wheel made after the knot that connect the loops.

Insertion with leaves in darning stitch (fig. 883). — Fasten on your thread at the place where, according to the pattern, the first leaf in the insertion is to come, pass it to the opposite side through the selvedge of the braid and bring it back to the starting point, lay threads on both sides, as in figures 881 and 882, unite them by a knot, like the one in figure 881, take the thread up along the middle leaf, draw it through the braid from underneath, and make a little leaf in darning stitch, as described in the chapter on "Netting" by figures 667 and 668.

Insertion with small wheels (fig. 884). — Here you have to make two rows of Russian stitches opposite each other, then take the thread to the level of the point of junction of these stitches; make a wheel over five threads, and slip the needle under the finished wheel to the next intersection of the stitches.

Insertion with big wheels (fig. 885). — Fasten the thread on in the middle of one of the short sides of the insertion, take

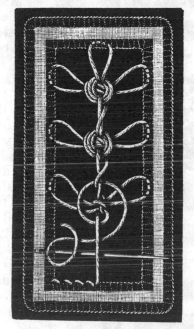

Fig. 882.
Insertion with branches and wheels.

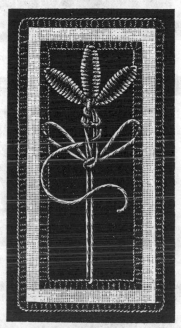

Fig. 883.
Insertion with leaves in darning stitch.

it across the empty space, fix it at the opposite side and then bring it by means of overcasting stitches to the corner of the insertion. From there make a loose loop to the opposite corner, slip the needle under 6 or 8 threads of the edge of the braid, then take it under the thread first laid, and behind the loop, and fasten the stitch on to the opposite edge of the braid.

Take the thread across the empty space again and over the first thread, bring the needle back to the middle, make a big wheel over four threads, slipping the needle always under the same threads, then overcast the single thread, come back to the selvedge and make the second loop, bringing the thread out at the same place as the two other stitches.

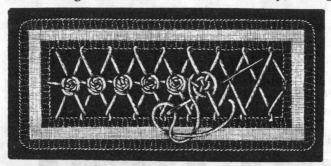

Fig. 884. Insertion with small wheels.

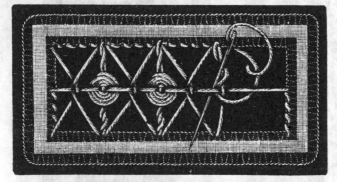

Fig. 885. Insertion with big wheels.

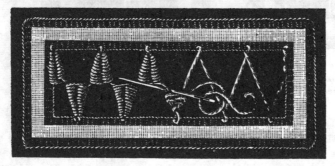

Fig. 886. Insertion with cones.

Insertion with cones (figs. 886 and 887). — Make very wide-apart Russian stitches between two edges of braid, then take the thread to the point of one of these stitches, there fore to the selvedge of the braid; cover half the Russian stitch with darning stitches, thus producing the little cone-shaped scallops. (See also fig. 669). To reach the next scallop, overcast the thread of the Russian stitch.

You can also as in figure 887 double the Russian stitch and make the darning stitches so that the points of the cones meet, and their base rests on the braid.

Insertion with squares (fig. 888). — After making a row of loose button-hole stitches all along the edge of both braids, as in figures 877, 878, 879, draw a thread through the loops to serve as a basis for the Russian stitches with which you connect the two edges. The empty squares between the Russian stitches are filled with button-hole stitches, worked like those in figure 672 in the chapter on "Netting".

Insertion with half-bars (fig. 889). — Fasten the thread on at one of the corners of the braid, then take it to the middle of the width of the braid, draw it through the selvedge on the right and make button-hole stitches over it to the middle of the empty space. Then pass to the right, draw the thread through the opposite selvedge, a little lower down than to the half-bar on the right, and

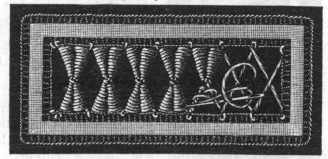

Fig. 887. Insertion with cones.

Fig. 888. Insertion with squares.

cover the thread with the same number of stitches made on the first side.

You can also put more stitches on one side than on the other which makes a pretty variety.

Lace stitches. — In making lace stitches you must be careful to make the same number of stitches in all the empty spaces that are of the same size, and also when you begin a row with a whole stitch to begin the return row with a half one, and so on in regular rotation. The number of stitches should vary with the width of the pattern, and the decreasing

and increasing should always be done at the edge. The stitches must cover as many threads of the braid in length as they do in width.

First lace stitch. Single net stitch (fig. 890). — Make rows of button-hole stitches to and fro, loose enough to form loops for the stitches of the next rows to be made on.

Second lace stitch. Double net stitch (fig. 891). — Leave the same distance between the stitches here as in the last figure, but in each of the loops of the first row make two button-hole stitches close together. It is as well to round the loop a little less than is ordinarily done in single net stitch.

Third lace stitch (fig. 892). — Here you make three button-hole stitches close together, connected by a loop of the thread, just long enough to hold the three button-hole stitches of the next row.

Fig. 889. Insertion with half-bars.

Fourth lace stitch (fig. 893). — Working from left to right make two button-hole stitches rather close together then one double the length.

In the return row, worked from right do left, make one stitch in the loop that is between the two stitches that are close together, and three in the long loop.

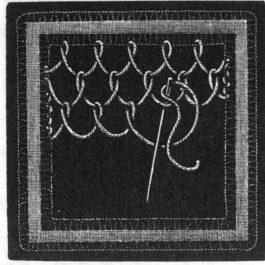

Fig. 890. First lace stitch. Single net stitch.

Fifth lace stitch (fig. 894). — As in figure 893, begin this stitch, working from left to right, but setting three stitches, instead of two, close together, then an intermediate loop as long as the tree together.

Coming back, make one button-hole stitch on each of the loops between the three stitches, and six or eight on the long intermediate loop.

Sixth lace stitch (fig. 895). — Net stitches, at least six or eight bars of the braid apart, and stretched rather tightly, worked from left to right going, are covered, coming back with button-hole stitches enough to hide the thread entirely.

In the third row of stitches draw the thread through the little loop between two sets of button-hole stitches, so that the groups of close stitches form vertical lines on the surface to be covered.

Seventh lace stitch (fig. 896). — Begin, working from right to left by making a row of pairs of button-hole stitches with rather less

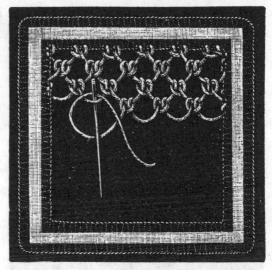

Fig. 891. Second lace stitch.
Double net stitch.

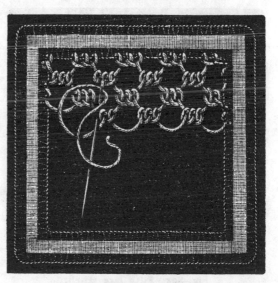

Fig. 892. Third net stitch.

space between them than the space between each pair. Coming back, skip the longest loop and make only one stitch between each pair, and in the third row, two button-hole stitches in each loop.

Eighth lace stitch (fig. 897). — This stitch is commonly called the "pea stitch" on account of the round holes caused by the distribution of the stitches.

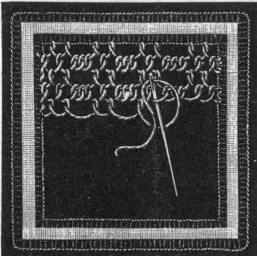

Fig. 893. Fourth lace stitch.

The first row consists of stitches rather close together and all the same distance apart.

In the second row you make one button-hole stitch in the last stitch of the first row, then skipping two loops and three button-hole stitches, make two stitches again in the next loops, and so on. In the third row you again make three stitches in the big loop, and one in the stitch between the stitches of the second row. In the fourth the position of the holes or "peas" is reversed.

Ninth and tenth lace stitches (figs. 898 and 899). — The stitches shewn in these two engravings are known by the name of pyramid or Venetian stitches.

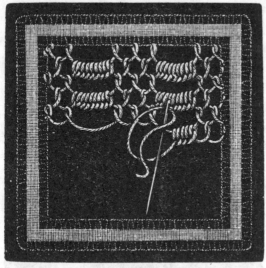

Fig. 894. Fifth lace stitch.

Both begin with a row of very close button-hole stitches. In the stitch, fig. 898, worked in three rows, you skip two stitches in the second row, and make two stitches in the next loops; in the third row you also skip the loops that come under the skipped ones, and make here only one stitch. In the next row you make the same number of stitches again as in the first row.

Figure 899 takes five rows of stitches; the first very close; in the second you make four stitches and miss two of the first row; in the third you make three stitches; in the fourth two, in the fifth only one. The threads that separate the groups of stitches, especially the one between the stitches of the fifth row, must be equally and rather tightly stretched, so that the long loop that necessarily forms itself may be well covered by the stitches of the first row of the next pyramid.

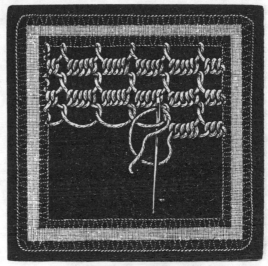

Fig. 895. Sixth lace stitch.

Eleventh lace stitch (fig. 900). — The first row consists solely of single net stitches, the second the same, only with three button-hole stitches in the middle loop; in the third row there are three button-hole stitches in the whole loops on the right and to the left of the three button-hole stitches of the second row, and one stitch in the half loops that immediately precede and follow; the fourth row is the same as the second.

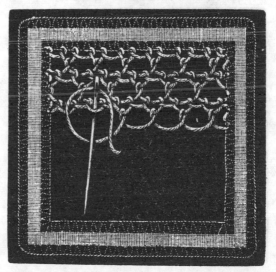

Fig. 896. Seventh lace stitch.

In the fifth row the order of the close stitches is reversed;

they are made in the fourth loop, including the half-bars before and behind the three stitches of the fourth row, so that between two groups of three stitches there will be six isolated button-hole stitches and seven loops.

Twelfth lace stitch (fig. 901). — Fasten on the thread $\frac{1}{4}$ of an inch from the corner on the left side of the selvedge, then take it by overcasting the selvedge to the top edge, and make three very close button-hole stitches; leave a long enough loop or thread for it to be on the level of the first stitch and make three other stitches.

In the second row cover the loops with three button-hole stitches, but tighten the thread between.

The third row is like the first, with the difference that you pass the needle between the threads of the button-hole stitch instead of through the loops.

Thirteenth lace stitch (fig. 902). — The stitch represented below, as well as the two next ones are looped, from left to right and then from right do left.

Fig. 897. Eighth lace stitch.

Fig. 898. Ninth lace stitch.

right and then from right do left.

As this way of working is more unusual than the reverse way from left to right, the proper position of the needle and the course of the thread are indicated in the engraving. Figure 902 requires in the first place two very close button-hole stitches in the edge of the braid, then a third one that terminates the two first at the bottom, made as close to them as possible; the thread that connects the stitches must be drawn very tight, so that the rows of stitches form lines not scallops.

Fourteenth lace stitch (fig. 903). — Begin by a row of button-hole stitches a little distant apart, then make two button-hole stitches in each loop, and under these, instead of one stitch as in figure 902, two button-hole stitches, which gives you an open-work ground with vertical bars.

Fig. 899. Tenth lace stitch.

Fifteenth lace stitch (fig. 904). — This again resembles the two last stitches, and consists of three button-hole stitches made over the edge of the braid or the intermediate bars; these stitches are then connected by a transverse stitch.

Sixteenth lace stitch (fig. 905). —

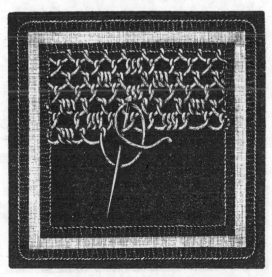

Fig. 900. Eleventh lace stitch.

Begin by a row of net stitches set from right to left, or, as is the case in the engraving, by a row of stitches, called "seed stitches".

The second row worked from left to right consists of short bars set slanting, in the shape of a seed, made like the picot, figure 869. The first stitch passes through the loop of the upper row, the second is made over the two threads, and distant from the loop the space which the three stitches made on the second stitch will occupy.

The first of the four button-hole stitches of the next group must always come quite close to the last of the four stitches of the preceding group.

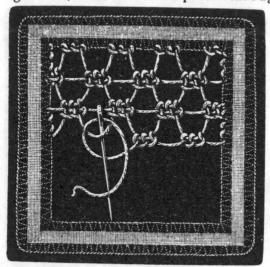

Fig. 901. Twelfth lace stitch.

Seventeenth lace stitch (fig. 906). — This engraving represents the seed stitch worked to and fro, and at the same time shews the direction of the needle for the stitches that go from right do left.

Eighteenth lace stitch (fig. 907). — This figure and the following ones represent a series of lace stitches that often occur in old Venetian lace and may therefore rightly be called Venetian.

They are less open and transparent than those hitherto described, the rows being closer and more com-

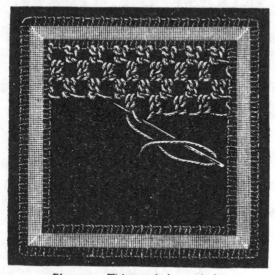

Fig. 902. Thirteenth lace stitch.

pact. You begin with a row of very close loops, then stretch a thread on the same level with them, and coming back slip the needle through each loop and over the stretched thread.

Nineteenth lace stitch (fig. 908). — In the old models we often find stitches like those of figure 907, set very close together which gives the foundation the appearance of a plaited fabric, as represented in figure 908.

Twentieth lace stitch (fig. 909). — Gaps may be left in the rows of close stitches by skipping a few loops coming back, and in the next row, making as many stitches on the bar consisting of three threads as were skipped in the last row but one.

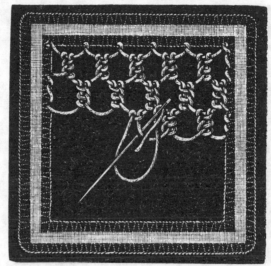

Fig. 903. Fourteenth lace stitch.

These gaps may be arranged in regular order according to a plan traced beforehand, or after your own fancy, there being many different ways of making Irish lace.

Twenty-first lace stitch (fig. 910). — There are other ways of varying Venetian openwork stitches by embroidering the needle-made grounds.

In figure 910 dots are embroidered on the close ground of button-hole stitches, in a less twisted thread than the ground.

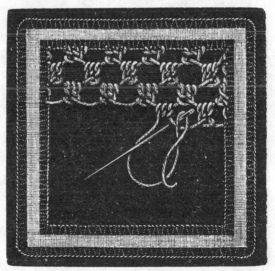

Fig. 904. Fifteenth lace stitch.

Besides the dots, little rings of button-holing or stars in post stitch, or other fancy stitches can be strewn over the ground.

Twenty-second lace stitch (fig. 911). — After fastening your thread on to the left selvedge, hold it fast with the left thumb, stick the needle into the braid at the top and into the

Fig. 905. Sixteenth lace stitch.

loop of the thread, as indicated in the engraving.

When the thread is mounted on the needle pass it through the loop and pull out sufficient thread to make vertical bars of uniform length. In the next row these bars are made the reverse way.

Twenty-third lace stitch (fig. 912). Begin by making the same stitches as in figure 911, from left to right. Then pick up each loop between the vertical bars with an overcasting stitch. Draw up each stitch at once to the required degree, as you cannot pick up more than one loop at a time; and tightening the thread afterwards disarranges the bars which ought to remain quite vertical and even.

Twenty-fourth lace stitch (fig. 913). This is often called Sorrento stitch. It consists of three bars rather close together,

Fig. 906. Seventeenth lace stitch.

separated from the next three by a loop as long as the two short loops between the bars. The thread which you bring back over all the bars, passes once over the little loops and several times over the long ones. In each subsequent row make the first bar between the first and the second of the preceding row, and the third in the long loop, so that the pattern presents diagonal lines of steps.

Twenty-fifth and twenty-sixth lace stitches (figs. 914 and 915). — These two figures shew how the order and arrangement of the bars can be reversed and the position of the groups one above the other varied.

The bars are made as in figure 912. The thread that connects the groups of bars must be tightly stretched so that the rows should all be in straight lines.

Twenty-seventh lace stitch (fig. 916). Between every three bars set close together, leave a space equal to the space they occupy, then come back stretching the thread beneath the bars without passing through them as shewn in figures 907, 908, 910; in the second row make three bars in the empty space, two between the three bars of the first row and three again in the empty space, eighth bars in all. The third row of stitches is like the first.

Fig. 907. Eighteenth lace stitch.

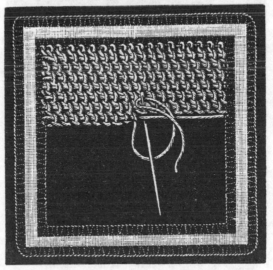

Fig. 908. Nineteenth lace stitch.

Twenty-eighth lace stitch (fig. 917). — Begin by making two rows of net stitch, fig. 890, then two close rows, like figure 908, and one row like figure 912.

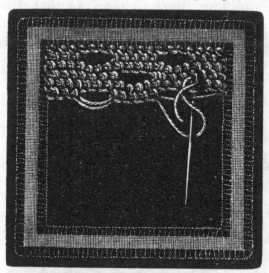

Fig. 909. Twentieth lace stitch.

If you want to lengthen the bars twist the thread once or twice more round the needle.

Twenty-ninth lace stitch (fig. 918). — This stitch, an imitation of Greek net with large meshes, and known as Greek stitch is more suitable for a ground than for fillings; it is also used in place of a ground consisting of bars, figs. 928 and 929.

Make bars, from left to right, a little distance apart, as in figure 911, leaving the loops between rather slack, so that when they have been twice overcast by the returning thread they form a row of slightly rounded scallops. In the next row make the bar in the middle of the loop and raise it sufficiently with the needle for the threads to take the shape of a hexagon, like the meshes of net.

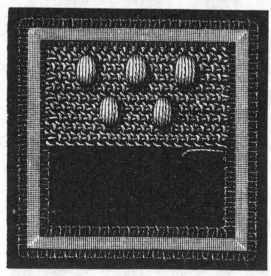

Fig. 910. Twenty-first lace stitch.

When you have a large surface to fill in, begin the stitch in one corner and increase or decrease the number of stitches as the pattern requires.

Thirtieth lace stitch (fig. 919). — After making a row of pairs of button-hole stitches, with long loops between as long as the space between the pairs of stitches, bring the thread

back on a level with the loops, carry it across the empty space, fasten it to the braid and make pairs of button-hole stitches similar to those in the first row.

Thee loops must be perfectly regular; to facilitate this, guide lines may be traced across the pattern and pins stuck in as shewn in the figure, round which to twist the thread.

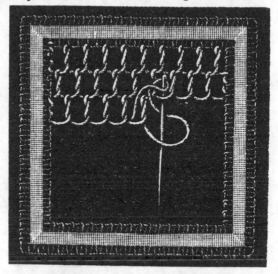

Fig. 911. Twenty-second lace stitch.

Thirty-first lace stitch (fig. 920). — At first sight this stitch looks very like the preceding one but as regards the way the threads are knotted it is quite different

You pass the needle under the loop and under the laid thread, then you stick in the pin at the right height for making the long loop, take the thread round behind the pin, make a loop round the point of the needle, as shewn in the engraving and pull up the knot.

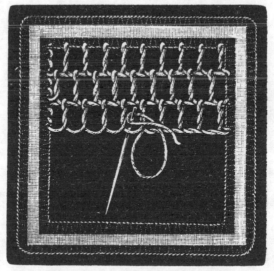

Fig. 912. Twenty-third lace stitch.

Thirty-second lace stitch (fig. 921). — To introduce a greaty variety into lace stitches, netting can also be imitated with the needle. You make a first loop in the corner of a square and continue them in diagonal lines. The loops are secured by means of a knot similar to the one in figure 920, and their regularity and equal length ensured by making them round a pin stuck in at the right place.

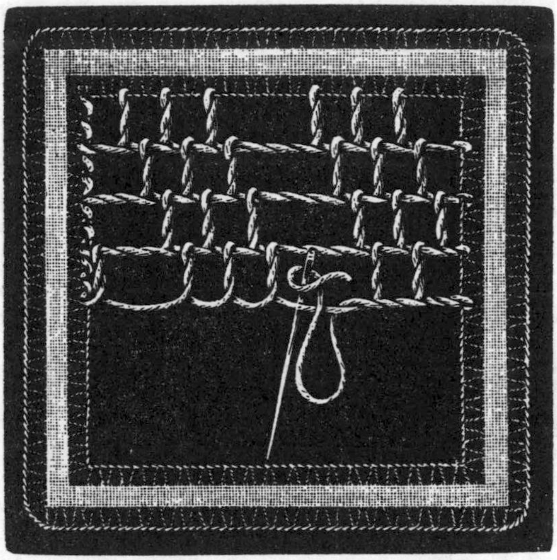

The little squares or meshes must be made with the greatest care and accuracy; that being the case most of the stitches described in the chapter on "Netting" can be worked upon them and the smallest spaces can be filled with pretty openwork stitches, now seldom made excepting in guipure net.

Thirty-third lace stitch (fig. 922). — We have often come across this stitch in very old Irish lace, now very rarely to be had. It looks at first sight merely like a close net stitch, the stitches are so near together. On a nearer examination we saw that it was quite a new stitch.

The loop formed by a singe tulle stitch, is joined at a little distance from the fold by means of a buttonhole stitch.

The stitches are made as close as possible with barely any space between. The first stitch is made like a plain net stitch, the second consists of a knot that ties up the loop of the first stitch.

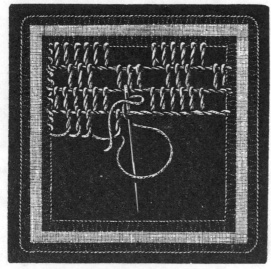

Fig. 913. Twenty-fourth lace stitch.

Fig. 914. Twenty-fifth lace stitch.

Thirty-fourth lace stitch (fig. 923). — To fill in a ground with this stitch, known as the spider or wheel stitch, begin by laying threads diagonally across to and fro at equal distances apart, so that they lie quite flat side by side and do not overlap or get twisted. When the whole surface is covered with these double threads lay similar ones across them, the opposite way. By passing the return thread two or three times under the double threads and over the single thread first laid, pretty little wheels are formed, like those described in the chapter on "Netting", figs. 673 and 674.

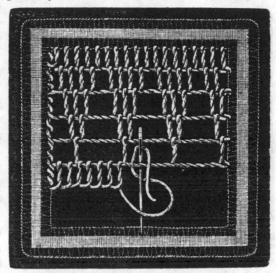

Fig. 915. Twenty-sixth lace stitch.

Thirty-fifth lace stitch (fig. 924). — Begin by making a very regular net foundation, but without knots at the intersection of the threads. Then make a third layer of diagonal threads over the two first so that they all intersect each other at the same point, thus forming six rays diverging from one centre.

With the fourth and last thread which makes the 7th and 8th ray,

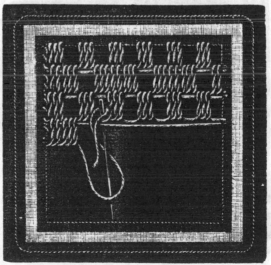

Fig. 916. Twenty-seventh lace stitch.

you make the wheel over seven threads, then slip the needle under the wheel just made, and carry it on to the place for the next stitch.

Thirty-sixth lace stitch (fig. 925). — After covering all the surface that is to be embroidered with threads stretched in horizontal lines cover them with loops going from thread to thread, those of each row joined to those of the row before. The needle will thus have to pass under two threads.

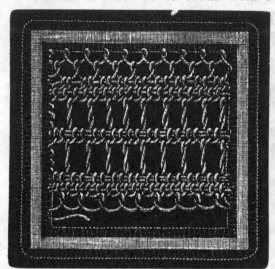

Fig. 917. Twenty-eighth lace stitch.

When this canvas-like ground is made cover it with cones consisting of very close darning stitches, beginning at the top, as shewn in figures 886 and 887.

Thirty-seventh lace stitch (fig. 926). For this stitch you begin by imitating, by means of the first threads laid the Penelope canvas used for tapestry work, covering the surface both ways with two threads rather close together, which cross each other at the points of intersection like the threads of the canvas.

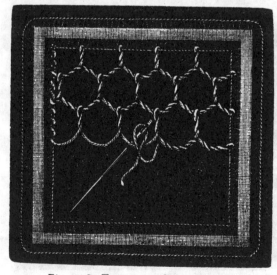

Fig. 918. Twenty-ninth lace stitch.

Then wind the thread several times round the little square spaces between the inter-crossed threads of the ground, and cover it with buttonhole stitches. The closer and thicker the padding under the button-holing, the better the effect will be.

Each of these little button-holed rings should be begun and finished off independently of each other.

Thirty-eighth lace stitch (fig. 927). — Plain net stitch being quicker done than any other, one is tempted to use it more frequently.

But as it produces rather a monotonous effect, it is as well to embroider some ornamental stitch upon it, to enliven it. Buttonholed eyelet holes disposed at regular intervals over it, as shewn in the engraving, will be found to be a great improvement.

Here, as in the preceding figure, each eyelet-hole must be made independently of the others.

Thirty-ninth lace stitch (fig. 928). — Corded bars branching out in different directions, made in overcasting stitch, also make a very effective lace ground. You lay five or six threads, as the course of the bars requires, overcast the ramifications to the point where they join the main line; from there you lay other foundation threads for another branch, so that, arrived at a given point and coming back to finish the overcasting of the threads left bare at first, you will have to overcast from six to eight branches of padding threads.

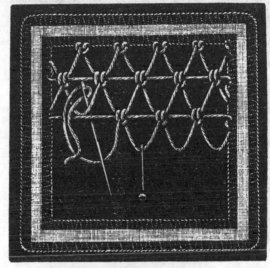

Fig. 919. Thirtieth lace stitch.

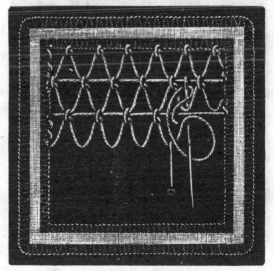

Fig. 920. Thirty-first lace stitch.

Overcasting stitches are always made from right to left so that the work will often have to be turned about different ways.

Fortieth lace stitch (fig. 929). — Of all the different open-work stitches described, we regard this last one of the series as the one that requires most patience.

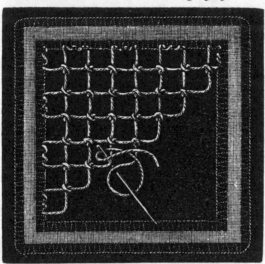

Fig. 921. Thirty-second lace stitch.

It was copied from a piece of very old Brabant lace of which it formed the entire ground.

Although not always included amongst those used in making Irish lace, there is no reason why it should not be so.

Our engraving is the reproduction of the original stitch on a magnified scale, as the original was worked with a thread so fine as to be almost invisible.

In the first row of stitches when the 3 padding threads are laid, make about 8 or 10 button-hole stitches downwards from right to left, to the point whence the next branch issues, for which you again lay 3 foundation threads.

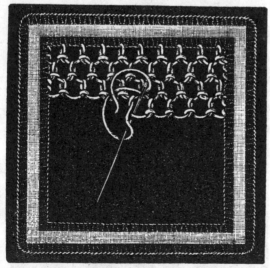

Fig. 922. Thirty-third lace stitch.

Then, when you have come to the end of the row, you fasten the thread on to the braid on the right, and returning, button-hole the second part of the bar, working from right to left. Lay padding threads again and button-hole them and those which were only partly covered before.

A picot, like the one described in figure 869, marks the point of junction of the bars. Any number of these picots can be introduced according to the taste of the worker.

Wheels composed of button-hole bars (figs. 930, 931, 932, 933). — As we have already more than once described how wheels are to be made, not only in the present chapter but also in the one on guipure net we need not refer again at any length to the kind of stitches to use, we shall confine ourselves to giving certain necessary directions as to how to make a wheel composed of button-hole bars in a square opening.

Figure 930 explains the placing of the eight first loops which form the skeleton of the wheel.

In figure 931 you see that a thread has been drawn through the loops, by means of which they are drawn up so as to form a

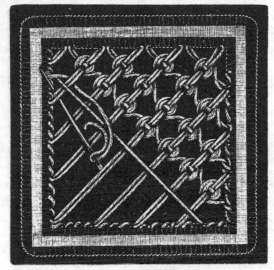

Fig. 923. Thirty-fourth lace stitch.

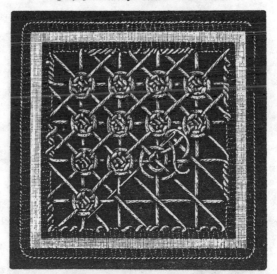

Fig. 924. Thirty-fifth lace stitch.

circle; further that two threads added to the loop serve as padding for the button-hole stitches. These latter should always be begun from the edge of the braid.

Figure 932 shews you the bar, begun in figure 931, in its finished state, with the passage of the thread to the next bar, and figure 933 the button-hole ring with all the bars finished.

Fig. 925.   Thirty-sixth lace stitch.

How to fill circular spaces (figs. 934, 935, 936). — The open-work stitches best suited for this purpose are those which can be worked row upon row decreasing with the inner circumference of the space to be filled, and admit of their number being reduced as required by skipping in one row some of the stitches of a previous row, so as to form a series of concentric rings growing smaller and smaller to the middle.

In tacking braids on to a round pattern as we pointed out at the beginning of this chapter the inside edges must be gathered in by overcasting stitches in very fine thread.

Figure 934 explains how to fill a round space with three rows of net stitches.

It will be seen that the thread of the last loop of the first row is wound round the first loop and then passes to the second ring of loops. The same in the third row, after which you pick up all the loops and fasten off the thread by

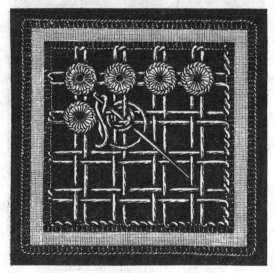

Fig. 926.   Thirty-seventh lace stitch.

working back to the edge of the braid through all the rows
of loops, following the course indicated by the dotted line.

Figure 935 shews how to finish a row of loops with wheels
mounted on three
threads only. In the
first row you make a
wheel over each bar;
in the second the
wheels are only made
over every second bar;
a third row of bars
which you pick up
with a thread com-
pletes the inside of
the circle, then you
work along the bars
with overcasting stitch-
es, fig. 936, to get
back to the edge of
the braid where you
fasten off.

Fig. 927. Thirty-eighth lace stitch.

Needle made picots
(figs. 937, 938, 939). —
The edges and outlines
of Irish lace are gene-
rally bordered with
picots which can be
had ready made, see
fig. 862, as has already
been said. They are
not however very
strong and we do not
advise their being used
for lace that has been
made with care and
patience by hand.

In figure 937 the way
to make picots joined
together is described.

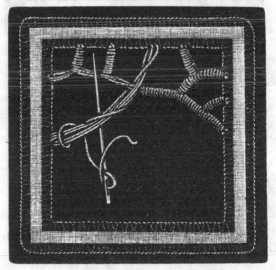

Fig. 928. Thirty-ninth lace stitch.

You begin, as in
figure 921, by making a knot over which the thread is twisted
as the engraving indicates.

It seems needless to repeat that all the loops should be knotted together in a straight line, all be of the same length and the same distance apart.

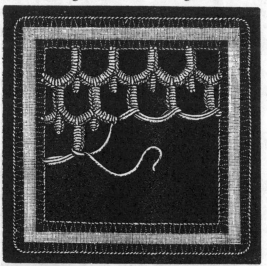

Fig. 929. Fortieth lace stitch.

Figure 938 shews you the kind of needle made picots which are most like the machine made ones, and figure 939 the use of little scallops surmounted by picots made in bullion stitch.

One or even two rows of the lace stitch, fig. 906, the scallops figure 871, or the first rows of figures 919, 920, 921, may be used as picots.

Irish lace with a foundation of bars (fig. 940). — The simplest kinds of Irish lace are those where the figures formed by braids of different kinds are connected by over-cast bars and spiders and fillings in Russian stitch. We give a specimen in figure 940, made with a plain braid and a medallion braid. The overcast bars are worked as described in figure 864; the Russian stitch as in figure 874, and the darning stitch as in

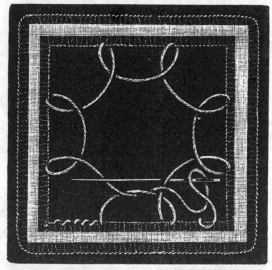

Fig. 930. Wheel of button-hole bars.
Setting and picking up the loops.

figures 673 and 674, in the chapter on "Netting".

A picot braid sewn on with overcasting stitches orms the bottom edge of the lace.

Irish lace with a net ground (fig. 941). — This lace takes more time and care than the preceding one. After having tacked on and gathered the braids, fill in the ground with the stitch, fig. 918. To make this ground very regular we recommend some auxiliary lines being traced on the linen paper, as a guide for the different rows of stitches.

When the whole ground is finsihed proceed to the fillings of the figures, for which select the stitches, figs. 892, 905 and 907. The edge of the lace is trimmed with little scallops ornamented with picots in bullion stitch, fig. 939. A fine flax thread should be used for gathering the braids and a stronger one for the lace stitches.

Venetian laces (figs. 942, 943, 944, 945, 946, 947, 948). — The term "Venetian point" is generally understood to mean needle made lace, the outlines of which are bordered with rich scallops in high relief. The lacemaker calls these reliefs "broiders".

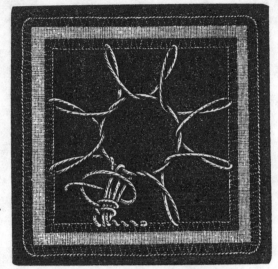

Fig. 931. Wheel of button-hole bars.
Loops picked up and bars begun.

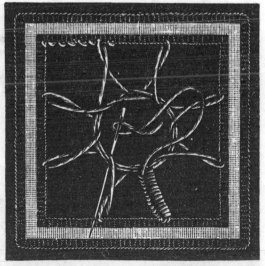

Fig. 932. Wheel of button-hole bars.
First bar finished and passage to the next.

Here as in most cases the first thing to be done is to prepare the design: you begin by lining the paper on which it is traced (a special paper is made for the purpose) with unglazed black paper, then you prick clear round holes along all the lines of the drawing, all exactly the same distance apart, then you remove the tracing and tack the black paper on to rather coarse linen. This done you take from three to five lengths of the thread the lace is to be made with, lay them on the lines marked by the pricked holes and fasten them down at each hole by a stitch made across them.

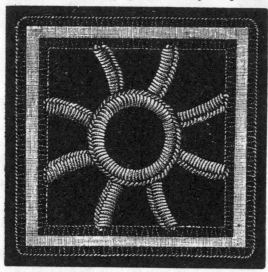

Fig. 933.
Wheel of button-hole bars. Finished.

Figure 942 as well as the others of the same series shews the distance there should be between the holes, and the beginning of the tracing, whilst figure 943 shews the tracing finished even to the eyelet holes, to be afterwards made in the fillings.

The tracing must be quite finished before the openwork, or more correctly speaking, the stitches, can be made. This part of the work must be done with great care so that the

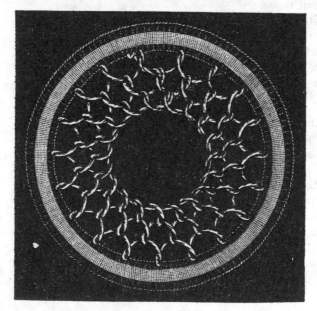

Fig. 934.
Circular space filled with net stitches.

thread should not be soiled. To that end all the parts you are not engaged upon should be covered with blue paper leaving only just the bit you are going to do at once, uncovered.

Besides this take a piece of paper rather bigger than the uncovered part, cut a small hole in it about ¾ in. in diameter and place the hole on the part you are going to begin to work at. In this little uncovered space make the fillings, moving the paper about as you proceed, fig. 944.

The stitches whatever they may be must always end at the traced line without making it too heavy.

We again remind our readers that in doing fine lace work the needle should always be held with the eye, not the

Fig. 935. Circular space filled with bars and wheels. First ring of wheels.

Fig. 936. Circular space filled with bars and wheels. Two rings of wheels finished.

point, turned towards the worker. The stitches will always be more regular and accurate if this advice be followed.

All the parts of the figures are then successively filled with close or openwork stitches, distributed according to the pattern. (See figs. 945 and 946).

This done, all the outlines are covered with close button-hole stitches.

The real old Venetian lace is ornamented with button-holing in very high relief, on a thick padding of threads, as described in figure 150.

Fig. 937. Needle-made picots joined together.

Fig. 938. Detached needle-made picots.

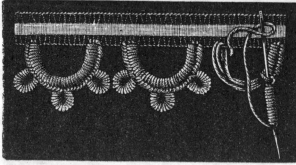

Fig. 939.
Button-hole picots and little picots in bullion stitch.

Modern needle point lace (fig. 949). — In detached figures like the seven last, the outlines are button-holed as soon as the fillings are done but in laces where the different parts are connected by bars or by net work, the button-holing of the outlines is done last. Thus in the lace, figure 949, all the fillings of the flowers and scrolls are finished first, then the net work ground or réseau is done, for which you may substitute if preferred, bars with picots, and last of all come the padded outlines.

This kind of lace requires the same preparatory work as the Venetian only the lace stitches used offer less variety.

The ones most often met with are figures 908 and 890.

Reticella lace (figs. 950 and 951). — The Reticella laces
are generally made on a tracing of thread like those described
for all the above laces. But as the manner of working has
been modified in the lace represented here, we thought it well
to adopt the same method of simplification of which there
are frequent examples to be found in the beautiful pieces of
old needlework, and which consists in substituting a woven
braid for the needle made bars.

You begin by laying and fastening down the braid, D.M.C
Superfine braid (Lacet superfin d'Alsace) (*), upon the lines
of the pattern with very small running stitches: this done
you proceed to make the centre bars, covered with single
button-hole stitches with a row of stitches like those in

Fig. 940. Irish lace with a foundation or bars.
Materials: D.M.C Flax lace thread No. 50, D.M.C floss flax No. 50 or
D.M.C Alsatia No. 40, in white.

figure 922, mounted upon them, then these are succeeded
by another bar, to make which you pick up the loop of the
stitches of the preceding row and a new row similar to the
second finished off with picots like the ones in figure 870.

The pyramids rest with their bases on bars button-holed
on two sides and ornamented inside with picots. The stitches
of the first row must not be set too near together so that

(*) See at the end of the last chapter the tables of the sizes and colours of
the cotton, flax and silk articles, mark D.M.C. — The French names, in brackets,
are those stamped on the labels of the D.M.C articles.

Fig. 941. Irish lace with a net ground.
Materials — For gathering the braids: D.M.C Flax lace thread
No. 70, white; for the lace stitches: D.M.C Flax lace
thread No. 45, white.

there may be room for those of the second row between, as was explained in connection with figure 684 in the chapter on "Netting".

The inside of the pyramids is worked in the stitch illustrated by figure 672 in the chapter on "Netting".

The corners are furnished with semicircular bars.

The lace, as represented in its natural size in figure 950, was worked with D.M.C Alsatian thread (Fil d'Alsace) No. 100, whilst the second engraving, representing the same subject, shews that it can perfectly well be worked with No. 30, a coarser number of the same material. D.M.C Alsatia No. 40 (*) can also be used.

Insertion in knotted stitch (figs. 952 and 953). — Lace worked in knotted stitch such as is represented in these two

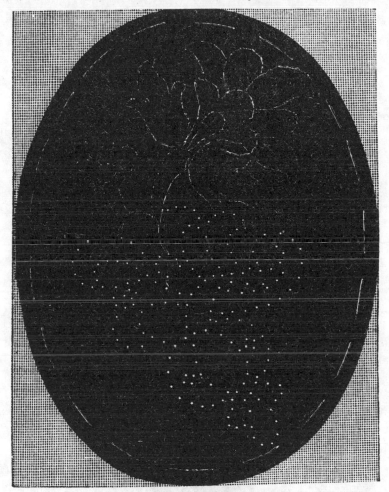

Fig. 942. Venetian lace.

engravings is reputed to be of Italian origin but we find just as perfect specimens of it in Persia and Asia Minor and adhere to the denomination "lace in knotted stitch". No difficulty

_____

(*) See at the end of the last chapter the tables of the sizes and colours of the cotton, flax and silk articles, mark D.M.C.

will be found in making out the construction of the stitch or in following the course of the different rows. It is best to begin with the two rows of stitches that form the perpendicular bars: these are succeeded by the stitches of the little con-

Fig. 943. Venetian lace.

necting bars between. For the picots at the ends of the bars, see fig. 870.

Lace in knotted stitch (figs. 954 and 955). — The charming little lace represented here was copied from a piece of Italian ecclesiastical work.

The stitches, which should be made in the order indicated
in the enlarged engraving, are overcast at the last with a loose
thread, such as D.M.C Floss flax or flourishing thread (Lin

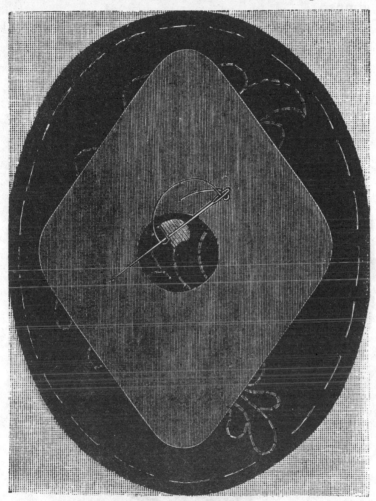

Fig. 944. Venetian lace.

floche) (*), in pale pink. You overcast the oblique bars and
pass over the stitches that connect the two picots.

(*) See at the end of the last chapter the tables of the sizes and colours of
the cotton, flax and silk articles, mark D.M.C. — The French names, in brackets,
are those stamped on the labels of the D.M.C articles.

Smyrna lace (figs. 956 and 957). — The garments of the Turkish women are often ornamented with little flowers and leaves made with the needle, which take the place of fringes and gimps.

These trimmings are not always in the best taste, but the

Fig. 945. Venetian lace.

work is sufficiently interesting for us to give a specimen of it here, to show how the stitches are made. It is of a kind to serve as a trimming for articles embroidered on linen or made of silk and plush.

Very different materials can be used for the purpose but

those quoted at the foot of the engraving will be found most effective.

The thread is first drawn into the edge of the stuff, you then conduct it from right to left and determine the length you wish the squares to be. Then, working from left to right

Fig. 946. Venetian lace.

you cover the first thread with as many knots as there is room for.

Figure 957 shews the formation of the knot, the manner in which the thread passing from left to right forms a loop, and how the needle is passed under the straight stretched thread and through the loop.

A space of rather less than $\frac{1}{8}$ of an inch is left between the stitches, according to the thickness of the thread used.

Fig. 947. Venetian lace.

After covering the first thread with knots conduct the thread to the left edge and make the next row, passing the needle under the stretched thread and under the loops of the upper row.

Be careful not to diminish the number of knots and to see that the four sides of the squares are equal.

After making the necessary number of squares, edge them with picots.

In figure 956 two colours were used. The squares were worked alternately in écru and Rust brown, the picots in brown.

Fig. 948. Venetian lace.
Materials — For the lace stitches: D.M.C Flax lace thread No. 70. For the tracing and padding: D.M.C Floss flax No. 100. (*)

(*) See at the end of the last chapter the tables of the sizes and colours of the cotton, flax and silk articles, mark D.M.C.

Fig. 949. Modern needle point lace.
Materials: D.M.C Flax lace thread No. 70 and
D.M.C Floss flax No. 100, in white. (*)

Danish lace "Hede-bo" (figs. 958 and 959). This lace — already introduced to our readers in the engraving figure 792, where it forms the trimming of the little openwork cloth — is here attached to a linen border but it may also be worked independently and finished off with a row of button-hole stitches worked over traced lines. The engraving figure 959, gives a clear explanation of how the rosettes are made.

After tracing the pattern on linen paper, fix it on waxed cloth; then trace the rings on which you sew two threads secured by overcasting stitches. When you have come round to the starting point, cover the ring with button-hole stitches, beneath which you once more conduct the two tracing threads. Before quite finishing the ring make the little pyramids in button-hole stitch over the button-hole stitches of the ring, throwing the thread each time on coming back over the finished row of stitches so as to begin each row

(*) See at the end of the last chapter the tables of the sizes and colours of the cotton, flax and silk articles, mark D.M.C.

Fig. 950. Reticella lace.
Materials — For the lace stitches : D.M.C Alsatian thread No. 30 or 100, in écru.
or D.M.C Alsatia No. 40, in white.
For the bars : D.M.C Superfine braid, in écru or in white.

from the same side. The stretched thread is overcast each time by the button-hole stitches of the next row.

By making one stitch less each row, a point is formed whence you take the thread back to the ring by little over-casting stitches along the side of the pyramid. You then make a second pyramid opposite the first, finish the ring and fasten

Fig. 951. Detail of figure 950.

off the threads. There where the rings touch they are joined together by a few stitches.

The little centre ring that connects the eight pyramids is ornamented inside by a row of overcast bars, far enough apart to form an openwork ring.

The rosettes are connected at the top by a stripe of linen, ornamented with a row of openwork; the spaces between the rosettes and the border are filled with a little pyramid.

Brazilian lace "Sols" (figs. 960, 961, 962). — This is a specimen of Brazilian lace, known by the name of "Sols", particularly distinguished for the fineness of the work and the design, consisting of rosettes and threads stretched across from them to the edges. Notwithstanding the simplicity of design the work needs a certain skill, as it must be done with a free hand and once a part is finished it is very difficult to undo or alter.

You begin by tracing the design, consisting of rounds and half rounds, on linen paper; each round is divided into as many parts as there are rays in it — in this case into 48 equal parts — marked by lines meeting in the middle. For the arcs between the rosettes, trace nine intervals and eight rays of the same size.

When you have finished the tracing fasten it on waxed cloth, then trace the outlines with running stitches, one

Fig. 952. Insertion in knotted stitch.

stitch to each interval; skipping every other interval. These
stitches are the only foundation for the rest of the work.

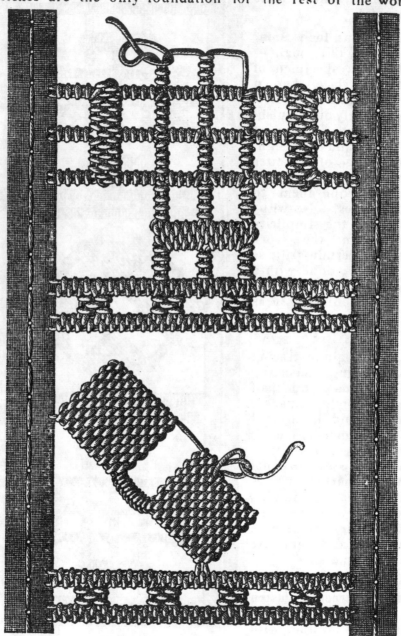

Fig. 953. Detail of figure 952.

Fill a small netting shuttle with thread, fasten it to one of the running stitches by a knot, and cross-ing the ring pass the shuttle through the opposite stitch of the tracing, come back through the nearest stitch, cross the round, to take up the opposite stitch and so on. (See the explanatory engrav-ing, fig. 961.) The thread is passed twice through each running stitch; in this manner you continue to fill the ring with rays; at

Fig. 954. Lace in knotted stitch.

Materials: D.M.C Flax lace thread No. 20, in white, and D.M.C Floss Flax No. 25, in Morocco red 3329. (*)

Fig. 955. Detail of figure 954.

the last ray, you connect all the cross threads by a knot and do not return to the outer circle.

The threads should not be too tightly drawn. You have

Fig. 956. Smyrna lace.
Materials: D.M.C Alsatia No. 20 or D.M.C Pearl cotton No. 3 or 5, in écru and Rust brown 3310. (*)

(*) These numbers refer to the colours on the colour cards of the articles stamped with the D.M.C trade mark. These cards can be consulted at all the mercers' and needlework shops.

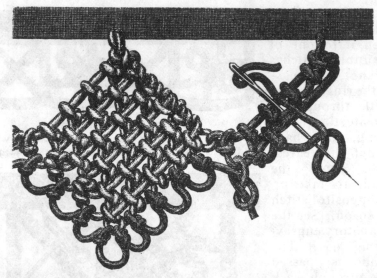

Fig. 957. Detail of figure 956.

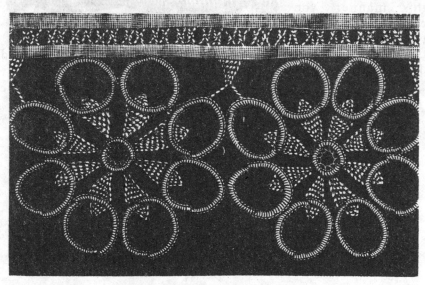

Fig. 958. Danish lace "Hedebo"
Materials: D.M.C Flax lace thread No. 40, D.M.C Alsatia No. 40,
or D.M.C Alsatian thread No. 50, white or écru. (*)

(*) See at the end of the last chapter the tables of the sizes and colours of
the cotton, flax and silk articles, mark D.M.C.

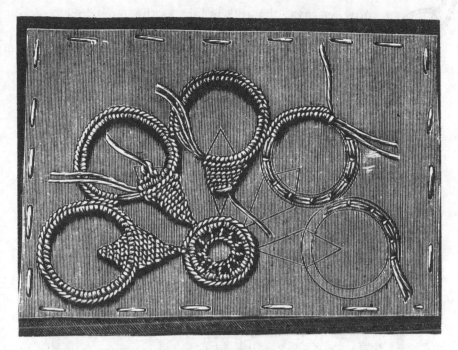

Fig. 959. Detail of figure 958.

Fig. 960. Brazilian lace "Sols".
Materials: D.M.C Flax lace thread No. 50, D.M.C Alsatian thread No. 70
or D.M.C Alsatia No. 40, white.

now 47 rays; the 48^{tb} is laid as the work progresses
from the centre to the inside and this thread serves
as the passage from one row of stitches to the
other.

The pattern itself is worked in two different
stitches: one a knotted stitch like the one used
in openwork on linen for connecting the
clusters of threads, see fig. 773, and the
darning stitch described in the chapter on
"Netting" for making the leaves for the
other, see figs. 667 and 668, and in the
present chapter by figs. 883, 886
and 887.

In the centre of the rosette you

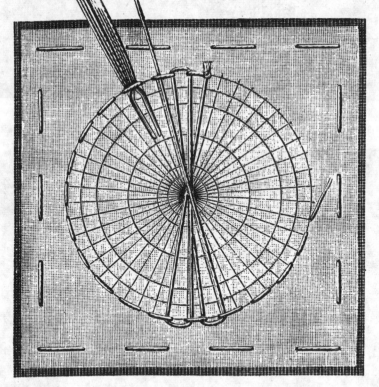

Fig. 961. How to fill the rings for the lace figure 960.

make a wheel with a few rounds of darning stitches, then in
the next row you join six of the cross threads by a knot; in

the second row you divide the 6 threads and join 3 and 3 of each cluster together.

Thus far the two kinds of wheels are made alike.

For one rosette you make 8 little pyramids in darning stitch, the point turned towards the centre, and which must always be begun at the point.

At the beginning of every round the thread must be left free; it is then knotted to the nearest ray. At the end of the

Fig. 962. How to fill the rings for the lace figure 960.

row, knot the thread to the first little loop of the same thread, so that there should be no break in the pattern, and in this way the 48th ray is made.

Outside, the pyramids are connected together by threads stretched in the shape of rounded scallops and of two rings of stretched threads that complete the rosette; you take the thread to the edge where you fasten it off, and then you pass to the next rosette in the middle of which you make the wheel in darning stitch and the two rounds of clusters reversed, and then finish the 48th ray.

The pattern is also worked in darning stitch and with stretched threads beginning always from the centre.

When the rosettes are finished fill the intermediate figures as shewn in figure 960, and with the stitches indicated.

All this being done take a cluster of 3 or 4 threads, lay them near the outlines and make button-hole stitches over them and the tracing stitches all round, then loosen the lace from the linen backing by cutting all the running stitches at the back.

Patterns of needlework. — Besides the different kinds of work described above a great choice of patterns for needle-made laces will be found in the following publications of the D.M.C Library: *Needle-made Laces I, Point Lace, Teneriffe Lace work* and *Works o various kinds.* (*)

Pillow lace in the Flemish style of the 17th century.

Pillow Laces.

Pillow lace may be regarded as an invention of the 16th century. Made in the first instance in Genoa, it spread rapidly throughout Italy, Spain, the Netherlands, Germany and Sweden, and later on to Slavonic countries and S. America. In Eastern countries it is to this day unknown.

Differing from needle made lace, which requires one thread and one needle only to produce all the different stitches contained in the most elaborate of patterns, pillow lace requires an unlimited number of threads and shuttles besides a variety of other implements and accessories.

As it would not be possible in our limited space to describe all the different kinds of pillow lace that exist we shall confine ourselves to the explanation and illustration of a few of those which seem to present the least difficulty of execution.

Implements. — These are various: in the first place a cushion or pillow, whence the name; then bobbins, a winder, patterns, pins, and a pricker with a holder.

The pillow (fig. 963). — In shape and kind this varies with the country and the kind of lace to be made upon it.

Figure 963 represents the one generally used in Saxony where pillow lace is one of the chief industries of the inhabitans

44

of certain districts of the kingdom. In shape it resembles a muff and can be made by any one with a piece of stuff 20 in. wide by 24 long.

Sew the long sides firmly together, hem the short ones and run a cord through to draw them up. Put a round piece of stiff cardboard in, after gathering up one end; stuff the case as full with bran, horsehair or sawdust as possible, lay another round of cardboard in upon the top, and draw up the other end.

These pillows of a most primitive kind and quite easy to make are put into cardboard boxes or baskets with rather high sides and heavily weighted with lead, to keep them steady.

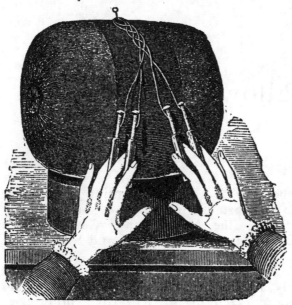

Fig. 963. The pillow.

There are others of a more complicated kind which are mounted on feet or can stand on the table, and as the cylinder is movable you can go on working without interruption.

The whole apparatus consists in a board or stand, 20 in. long and 16 in. wide, resting upon two transverse pieces of wood, 1 ⅜ in. high at the back and ⅝ in. in front. The board is first either quilted or covered with very thick flannel or felt, and then covered with dark green cloth. Two small supports are fixed on to the outside edge of the board, on which the cylinder consisting of two discs that revolve on a rod about 8 ¾ in. long, is mounted.

The rod is covered first with a thick layer of tow, and then with flannel or cloth.

On the left side of the cylinder is a cog-wheel which acted upon by a metal spring attached to the board, allows the cylinder to turn one way only.

In Normandy and in the Vosges a kind of square box quilted outside is used instead of a pillow. The board is 1 ¼ in. higher at the back than in front and has a deep groove in which a padded cylinder revolves on its axis.

This cylinder instead of being above the board, scarcely projects beyond the groove. The part of the box which receives the lace as it is worked off the cylinder fits into a second groove made at the back of the board.

A somewhat different kind of pillow is used for Valenciennes lace.

Lace bobbins (fig. 964). — These are little wooden spools with handles; there are different kinds but only the one we consider best for the use of beginners is shewn here.

It is very important to see that the size of the bobbins is suited to the thread of which the lace is to be made.

The winder (fig. 965). — We advise those who mean to take the work seriously to provide themselves with a winder like the one illustrated here. The winder has to be firmly screwed to a table, then the leather thong is passed round the bobbin, between the spool and the thick part of the handle, and the bobbin is placed in the notch made in the support. The open skein is put on the winder, rolling the thread up from left to right on the bobbin, whilst turning the wooden disk from right to left with the handle in the direction indicated by the arrow.

Stoppage of the thread at the end of the bobbin (fig. 966). — After cutting the thread fasten it at the top of the bobbin by a loop (explained by fig. 966) which whilst it prevents the thread from unwinding too easily is loose enough to allow of its being lengthened or shortened as required.

The pattern. — The pattern, one of the most important accessories in lace making, consists of a design transferred to a card, certain parts of which are pricked out. The lines and their distribution must be clear and correct; as thereupon the perfection of the lace will in great measure depend. To facilitate the making of the

Fig. 964.
Lace
bobbins.

pattern, we repeat the subject several times for each model, and the worker will then trace the whole design from the engraving.

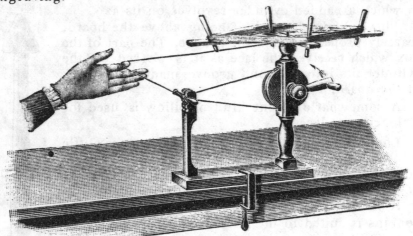

Fig. 965. The winder.

This drawing must then be transferred to thick paper or cardboard which should be lined with very thin stuff, muslin for instance, to prevent its tearing.

The length of the drawing should be made to correspond

Fig. 966. Stoppage of the thread at the end of the bobbin.

with the circumference of the cylinder; as there must be no break in the continuity of the pattern.

If the drawing be too long to fit the circumference of the cylinder the latter can be increased by wrapping several layers of cloth or flannel round it.

The next step is the pricking of the holes which is done as follows: lay the drawing on cloth and perforate all the dots marked with numbers.

The pricker (fig. 967). — Holders like the one represented in the engraving are to be had at every stationer's shop. All that is wanted to complete it is a coarse sewing needle screwed in.

The little holes pricked in the card mark the places for the pins which you stick in as you go along to stop the threads and hold the passings, and round which you twist the threads to make the picots.

The pins. — The pins for this kind of work must be of white metal not steel, on account of the rust; they must be long and round headed, and coarse or fine according to the size of the thread used for the lace.

Materials. — For pillow lace likely to be often washed a medium twisted flax or cotton thread is used, such as D.M.C Flax lace thread (Lin pour dentelles (*), D.M.C Flax thread for knitting and crochet (Lin pour tricoter et crocheter), D.M.C Alsatia and D.M.C Pearl cotton (Coton perlé), in white or écru. Coloured laces are generally made in silk, but as a good substitute for silk we recommend and D.M.C Alsatian twist (Retors d'Alsace), D.M.C Floss flax (Lin floche), D.M.C Pearl cotton (Coton perlé), which is to be had in a great many shades. With D.M.C Shaded Pearl cotton (Coton perlé ombré) laces of a very nice effect may be obtained. D.M.C Embroidery gold thread (Or fin à broder), D.M.C Embroidery silver thread (Argent fin à broder), D.M.C Gold chiné (Chiné d'or), as well as D.M.C Gold cord (Cordonnet d'or), and D.M.C Turkish gold cord (Ganse turque) are used for metallic laces.

Position and movements of the hands (fig. 968). — Pillow lace is almost always made with four bobbins used together; two in each hand, and the passings are formed by the different ways in which you twist and cross the threads.

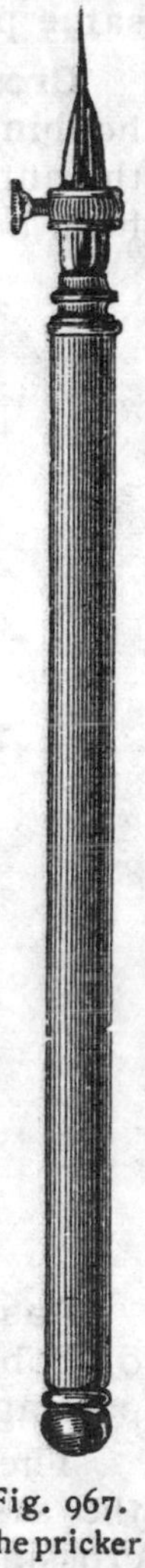

Fig. 967. The pricker

All the patterns require a number of bobbins. But as you only work with two pairs at a time you should fix the others to the side of the pillow with pins, as

(*) See at the end of the last chapter the tables of the sizes and colours of the cotton, flax and silk articles, mark D.M.C. — The French names, in brackets, are those stamped on the labels of the D.M.C articles.

shewn in fig. 968, with never more than 5 inches of thread unwound upon them, that they may not get entangled together.

Twisting (fig. 969). — Twisting means here passing the right bobbin of each pair of bobbins over the left one of the same pair. This movement is always made with one hand.

Crossing (fig. 970). — This signifies passing the inside bobbin of the left pair over the inside one of the right pair; the outside bobbins remaining passive; this movement requires both hands and both pairs of bobbins.

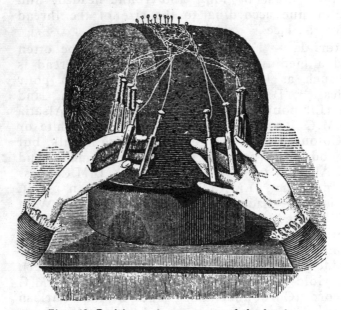

Fig. 968. Position and movements of the hands.

Passings. — When you have twisted and crossed two pairs of bobbins, you have made a "half-passing" and two half-passings make a "double-passing".

The first half-passing varies in form, the second is always the same; it is made by twisting the two pairs once, and crossing the inside bobbins. In the description that follow we call this second half-passing simply a "passing" for the sake of shortness.

The threads are held whilst you are working, by means of pins, at certain parts of the pattern. These pins are generally planted just between the pairs of bobbins you are working with. When the pins have to be stuck to the right or left of the pairs of bobbins you will find a note to that effect in the description of the work.

Grounds. — In pillow lace the principal parts of the pattern are worked with close passings like the net or lattice ground, fig. 972, or the linen ground, fig. 974, sometimes ornamented with little figures in spot stitch, figs. 989 and 991. For the ground and for connecting the figures together open-work stitches are preferable, see figs. 976, 978, 979, 980, 981, 983, or dots, like those in figure 987.

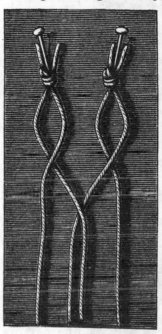

Fig. 969.
Two pairs of bobbins
twisted once.

Fig. 970.
Two pairs of bobbins twisted
once and crossed.

We give a little series of plaits and grounds to be met with in the best known lace patterns which will be good practice for those who are yet new to the work.

A detailed description accompanies each pattern.

The numbering of the pairs of bobbins is from left to right; the first pair on the left of the pattern counts as the first in the description, the first pair on the right has the highest number and counts as the last in the description.

Single plait (fig. 971). — This plait is made with two pairs of bobbins: you twist each pair once, then cross the inside threads. A repetition of this process produces the plait represented in figure 971.

Net or lattice ground (figs. 972 and 973). — Hang on 1 pair of bobbins at points *a, b, c, d, e,* in the pattern figure 973.

Twist the 1st and 2nd pair once, cross = * twist the 2nd and 3d pair once, cross = twist the 3d and 4th pair once, cross = twist the 4th and 5th pair once, cross, stick a pin in at point 1, twist the 4th pair once, twist the 5th pair twice, cross = twist the 3d and 4th pair once, cross = twist the 2nd and 3d pair once, cross = twist the 1st and 2nd pair once, cross, stick a pin in at point 2, twist the 1st pair twice, twist the 2nd pair once, cross; repeat from *.

Linen ground (figs. 974 and 975). — Hang on 2 pairs of bobbins at points *a, b, c,* in the pattern fig. 975.

Cross the 1st and 2nd pair, one passing = * cross the 2nd and 3d pair, one passing = cross the 3d and 4th pair, one passing = cross the 4th and 5th pair, one passing = cross the 5th and 6th pair, one passing, stick a pin in at point 1, do not twist the 5th pair, twist the 6th pair once, cross, one passing = cross the 4th and 5th pair, one passing = cross the 3d and 4th pair, one passing = cross the 2nd and 3d pair, one passing = cross the 1st and 2nd pair, one passing, stick a pin in at point 2, twist the 1st pair once, do not twist the 2nd pair, cross, one passing; repeat from *.

Réseau or torchon ground (figs. 976 and 977). — Hang on 2 pairs of bobbins at points *a, b, c, d, e,* in the pattern fig. 977.

Fig. 971.
Single plait.

Twist the 2nd and 3d pair once, cross, stick a pin in at point 1, one passing = twist the 1st and 2nd pair once, cross, stick a pin in at point 2, one passing = twist the 4th and 5th pair once, cross, stick a pin in at point 3, one passing = twist the 3d and 4th pair once, cross, stick a pin in at point 4, one passing = twist the 2nd and 3d pair once, cross, stick a pin in at point 5, one passing = twist the 1st and 2nd pair once, cross, stick a pin in at point 6, one passing = twist the 6th and 7th pair once, cross, stick a pin in at point 7, one passing = twist the 5th and 6th pair once, cross, stick a pin in at point 8, one passing = twist the 4th and 5th pair once, cross, stick a pin in at point 9, one passing = twist the 3^d and 4th pair once, cross, stick a pin in at point 10, one passing = twist the 2nd and 3^d pair once, cross, stick a pin in at point 11, one passing = twist the 1st and 2nd pair once, cross, stick a pin in at point 12, one passing = twist the 8th and 9th pair once, cross, stick a pin in at point 13, one passing = twist the 7th and 8th pair once, cross, stick a pin in at point 14, one passing = twist the 6th and 7th pair once, cross, stick a pin in at point 15, one passing = twist the 5th and 6th pair once, cross, stick a pin in at point 16, one passing = twist the 4th and 5th pair once, cross, stick a pin in at point 17, one passing = twist the 3^d and 4th pair once, cross, stick a pin in at point 18, one passing = twist the 2nd and 3^d pair once, cross, stick a pin in at point 19, one passing = twist the 1st and 2nd pair once, cross, stick a pin in at point 20, one passing = * twist the 9th and 10th pair once, cross, stick a pin in at point 21, one passing = twist the 8th and 9th pair once, cross, stick a pin in at point 22, one passing = twist the 7th and 8th pair once, cross, stick a pin in at point 23, one passing = twist the 6th and 7th pair once, cross,

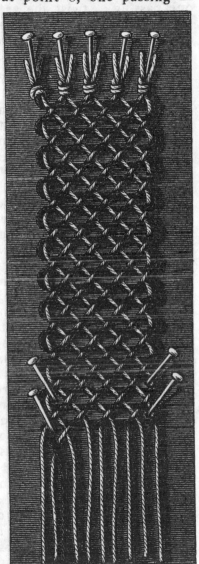

Fig. 972.
Net or lattice ground.

stick a pin in at point 24, one passing = twist the 5th and 6th pair once, cross, stick a pin in at point 25, one passing = twist the 4th and 5th pair once, cross, stick a pin in at point 26, one passing = twist the 3d and 4th pair once, cross, stick a pin in at point 27, one passing = twist the 2nd and 3d pair once, cross, stick a pin in at point 28, one passing = twist the 1st and 2nd pair once, cross, stick a pin in at point 29, one passing; repeat from *.

Dieppe ground (figs. 978 and 977). — Hang on 2 pairs of bobbins at points *a, b, c, d, e,* in the pattern fig. 977.

Twist the 2nd and 3d pair twice, cross, stick a pin in at point 1, one passing = twist the 1st and 2nd pair twice, cross, stick a pin in at point 2, one passing = twist the 4th and 5th pair twice, stick a pin in at point 3, one passing = twist the 3d and 4th pair twice, cross, stick in a pin at point 4, one passing = twist the 2nd and 3d pair twice, cross, stick in a pin at point 5, one passing = twist the 1st and 2nd pair twice, cross, stick in a pin at point 6, one passing = twist the 6th and 7th pair twice, cross, stick in a pin at point 7, one passing = twist the 5th and 6th pair twice, cross, stick a pin in at point 8, one passing = twist the 4th and 5th pair twice, cross, stick in a pin at point 9, one passing = twist the 3d and 4th pair twice, cross, stick in a pin at point 10, one passing = twist the 2nd and 3d pair twice, cross, stick a pin in at point 11, one passing = twist the

Fig. 973.
Pattern of the net or lattice ground figure 972.

1st and 2nd pair twice, cross, stick a pin in at point 12, one passing = twist the 8th and 9th pair twice, cross, stick a pin in at point 13, one passing = twist the 7th and 8th pair twice, cross, stick in a pin at point 14, one passing = twist the 6th and 7th pair twice, cross, stick a pin in at point 15, one passing = twist the 5th and 6th pair twice, cross, stick in a pin at point 16, one passing = twist the 4th and 5th pair twice, cross, stick a pin in at point 17, one passing = twist the 3d and 4th pair twice, cross, stick a pin in at point 18, one passing = twist the 2nd and 3d pair twice, cross, stick a pin in at point 19, one passing = twist the 1st and 2nd pair twice, cross, stick a pin in at point 20, one passing = * twist the 9th and 10th pair twice, cross, stick a pin in at point 21, one passing = twist the 8th and 9th pair twice, cross, stick in a pin at point 22, one passing = twist the 7th and 8th pair twice, cross, stick a pin in at point 23, one passing = twist the 6th and 7th pair twice, cross stick a pin in at point 24, one passing = twist the 5th and 6th pair twice, cross, stick a pin in at point 25, one passing = twist the 4th and 5th pair twice, cross, stick a pin in at point 26, one passing = twist the 3d and 4th pair twice, cross, stick a pin in at point 27, one passing = twist the 2nd and 3d pair twice, cross, stick a pin in at point 28, one passing = twist the 1st and 2nd pair twice, cross, stick a pin in at point 29, one passing; repeat from *.

Tulle ground (figs. 979 and 977). — Hang on 2 pairs of bobbins at points a, b, c, d, e, in the pattern fig. 977.

Twist the 2nd and 3d pair three times, cross, stick a pin in at point 1 = twist the 1st and 2nd pair three times, cross, stick a pin in at point 2 = twist the 4th and 5th pair three times, cross, stick a pin in at point 3 = twist the 3d and 4th pair three times, cross, stick a pin in at point 4 = twist the 2nd and 3d pair three times, cross, stick a pin in at point 5 = twist the 1st and 2nd pair three times, cross, stick a pin in at point 6

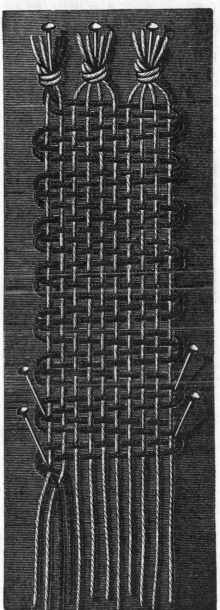

Fig. 974. Linen ground.

= twist the 6th and 7th pair three times, cross, stick a pin in at point 7 = twist the 5th and 6th pair three times, cross, stick a pin in at point 8 = twist the 4th and 5th pair three times, cross, stick a pin in at point 9 = twist the 3^d and 4th pair three times, cross, stick a pin in at point 10 = twist the 2nd and 3^d pair three times, cross, stick a pin in at point 11 = twist the 1st and 2nd pair three times, cross, stick a pin in at point 12 = twist the 8th and 9th pair three times, cross, stick a pin in at point 13 = twist the 7th and 8th pair three times, cross, stick a pin in at point 14 = twist the 6th and 7th pair three times, cross, stick a pin in at point 15 = twist the 5th and 6th pair three times, cross, stick a pin in at point 16 = twist the

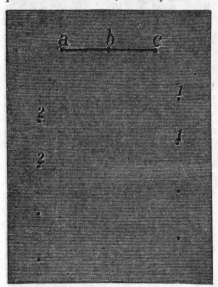

4th and 5th pair three times, cross, stick a pin in at point 17 = twist the 3^d and 4th pair three times, cross, stick a pin in at point 18 = twist the 2nd and 3^d pair three times, cross, stick a pin in at point 19 = twist the 1st and 2nd pair three times, cross, stick a pin in at point 20 = * twist the 9th and 10th pair three times, cross, stick a pin in at point 21 = twist the 8th and 9th pair three times, cross, stick a pin in at point 22 = twist the 7th and 8th pair three times, cross, stick a pin in at point 23 = twist the 6th and 7th pair three times, cross, stick a pin in at point 24 = twist the 5th and 6th pair three times, cross,

Fig. 975.
Pattern of the linen ground figure 974.

stick a pin in at point 25 = twist the 4th and 5th pair three times, cross, stick a pin in at point 26 = twist the 3^d and 4th pair three times, cross, stick a pin in at point 27 = twist the 2nd and 3^d pair three times, cross, stick a pin in at point 28 = twist the 1st and 2nd pair three times, cross, stick a pin in at point 29; repeat from *.

Brussels ground (figs. 980 and 977). — Hang on 2 pairs of bobbins at points *a, b, c, d, e,* in the pattern fig. 677.

Twist the 2nd and 3^d pair twice, cross one passing, stick a pin in at point 1, two passings = twist the 1st and 2nd pair twice, cross, one passing, stick a pin in at point 2, two passings = twist the 4th and 5th pair twice, cross, one passing, stick a pin in at point 3, two passings = twist the 3d and 4th

pair twice, cross, one passing, stick a pin in at point 4, two passings = twist the 2nd and 3d pair twice, cross, one passing, stick a pin in at point 5, two passings = twist the 1st and 2nd pair twice, cross, one passing, stick a pin in at point 6, two passings = twist the 6th and 7th pair twice, cross, one passing, stick a pin in at point 7, two passings = twist the 5th and 6th pair twice, cross, one passing, stick a pin in at point 8, two passings = twist the 4th and 5th pair twice, cross, one passing, stick a pin in at point 9, two passings = twist the 3d and 4th pair twice, cross, one passing,

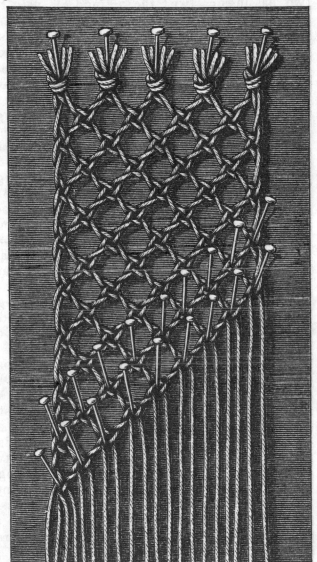

Fig. 976. Réseau stitch.

stick a pin in at point 10, two passings = twist the 2nd and 3d pair twice, cross, one passing, stick a pin in at point 11, two

passings = twist the 1st and 2nd pair twice, cross, one passing.
stick a pin in at point 12, two passings = twist the 8th and
9th pair twice, cross, one passing, stick a pin in at point 13,
two passings = twist the 7th and 8th pair twice, cross, one
passing, stick a pin in at point 14, two passings = twist the
6th and 7th pair twice, cross, one passing, stick a pin in at
point 15, two passings = twist the 5th and 6th pair twice,
cross, one passing, stick a pin in at point 16, two passings =
twist the 4th and 5th pair twice, cross, one passing, stick a

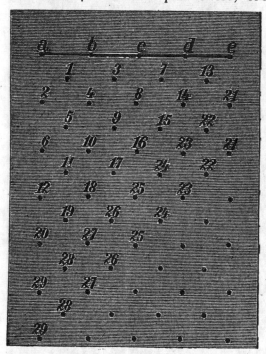

pin in at point 17, two
passings = twist the 3d
and 4th pair twice, cross,
one passing stick a pin
in at point 18, two
passings = twist the 2nd
and 3d pair twice, cross,
one passing, stick a pin
in at point 19, two pass-
ings = twist the 1st and
2nd pair twice, cross,
one passing, stick a pin
in at point 20, two
passings = * twist the
9th and 10th pair twice,
cross, one passing, stick
a pin in at point 21,
two passings = twist
the 8th and 9th pair
twice, cross, one pass-
ing, stick a pin in at
point 22, two passings
= twist the 7th and 8th

Fig. 977.

Pattern of the réseau stitch figure 976, of the
Dieppe stitch figure 978, of the net stitch figure 979
and of the Brussels stitch figure 980.

pair twice, cross, one
passing, stick a pin in
at point 23, two passings
= twist the 6th and 7th
pair twice, cross, one passing, stick a pin in at point 24, two
passings = twist the 5th and 6th pair twice, cross, one passing,
stick a pin in at point 25, two passings = twist the 4th and
5th pair twice, cross, one passing, stick a pin in at point 26, two
passings = twist the 3d and 4th pair twice, cross, one passing,
stick a pin in at point 27, two passings = twist the 2nd and
3d pair twice, cross, one passing, stick a pin in at point 28,

two passings = twist the 1st and 2nd pair twice, cross, one passing, stick a pin in at point 29, two passings; repeat from *.

Virgin ground (figs. 981 and 982). — Hang on 2 pairs of bobbins at points *a, b, c, d, e, f,* in the pattern fig. 982.

Twist the 2nd and 3d pair once, cross, stick a pin in at point 1, one passing = twist the 1st and 2nd pair once, cross, stick a pin in at point 2, one passing = twist the 3d and 4th pair once, cross, stick a pin in at point 3, one passing = twist the 2nd and 3d pair once, cross, stick a pin in at point 4, one passing = twist the 1st and 2nd pair once, cross, stick a pin in at point 5, one passing = twist the 6th and 7th pair once, cross, stick a pin in at point 6, one passing = twist the 5th and 6th pair once, cross, stick a pin in at point 7,

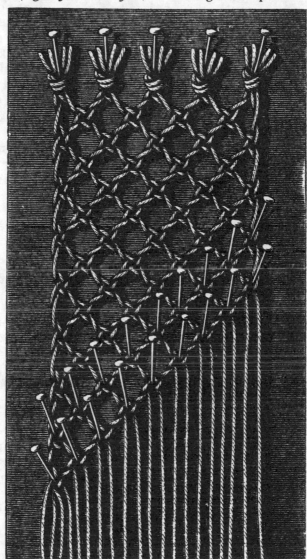

Fig. 978. Dieppe ground.

one passing = twist the 7th and 8th pair once, cross, stick a pin in at point 8, one passing = twist the 6th and 7th pair once, cross, stick a pin in at point 9, one passing = twist the 5th and 6th pair once, cross = twist the 3d and 4th pair once, cross = twist the 4th and 5th pair once, cross, stick a pin in at point 10, one passing = twist the 3d and 4th pair once, cross, stick a pin in at point 11, one passing = twist the 5th and 6th pair once, cross, stick a pin in at point 12, one passing = twist the 4th and 5th pair once, cross, stick a pin in at point 13, one passing = twist the 3d and 4th pair once, cross = twist the 2nd and 3d pair once, cross, stick a pin in at point 14, one passing = twist the 1st and 2nd pair once, cross, stick a pin in at point 15, one passing = twist the 3d and 4th pair once, cross, stick a pin in at point 16, one passing = twist the 2nd and 3d pair once, cross, stick a pin in at point 17, one passing = twist the 1st and the 2nd pair once, cross, stick a pin in at point 18, one passing = * twist the 10th and 11th pair once, cross, stick a

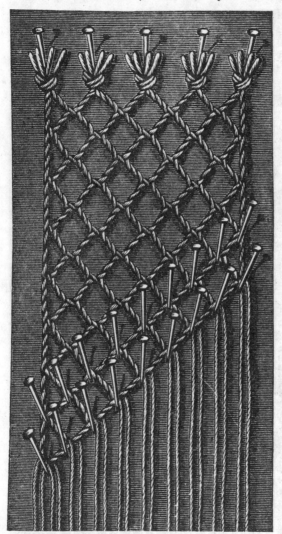

Fig. 979. Tulle ground.

pin in at point 19, one passing = twist the 9th and 10th pair once, cross, stick a pin in at point 20, one passing = twist the 11th and 12th pair once, cross, stick a pin in at point 21, one passing = twist the 10th and 11th pair once, cross, stick a pin in at point 22, one passing = twist the 9th and 10th pair once, cross = twist the 7th and 8th pair once, cross = twist the 8th and 9th pair once, cross, stick a pin in at point 23, one passing = twist the 7th and 8th pair once, cross, stick a pin in at point 24, one passing = twist the 9th and 10th pair once, cross stick a pin in at point 25, one passing = twist the 8th and 9th pair once, cross, stick a pin in at point 26, one passing = twist the 7th and 8th pair once, cross = twist the 5th and 6th pair once, cross = twist the 6th and 7th pair once, cross, stick a pin in at point 27, one passing = twist the 5th and 6th pair once, cross, stick a pin in at point 28, one passing = twist the 7th and 8th pair once, cross, stick a pin in at point 29, one passing = twist the 6th and 7th pair once, cross, stick a pin in at point 30, one passing = twist the 5th and 6th pair once, cross = twist the 3d and 4th pair once, cross = twist

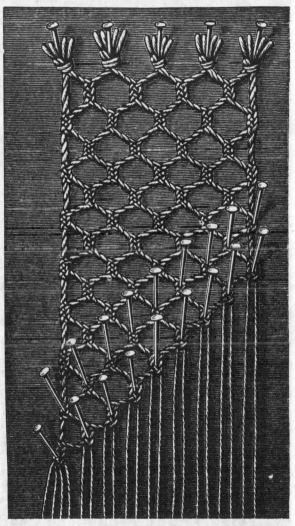

Fig. 980. Brussels ground.

the 4th and 5th pair once, cross, stick a pin in at point 31, one passing = twist the 3d and 4th pair once, cross, stick a pin in at point 32, one passing = twist the 5th and 6th pair once, cross, stick a pin in at point 33, one passing =

45

twist the 4th and 5th pair once, cross, stick a pin in at point 34, one passing = twist the 3^d and 4th pair once, cross=twist the 2nd and 3^d pair once, cross, stick a pin in at point 35, one passing = twist the 1st and 2nd pair once, cross, stick a pin in at point 36, one passing = twist the 3^d and 4th pair once, cross, stick a pin in at point 37, one passing = twist the 2nd and 3^d pair once, cross, stick a pin in at point 38, one passing = twist the 1st and 2nd pair once, cross, stick a pin in at point 39, one passing = twist the 11th and 12th pair once, cross, stick a pin in at point 40,

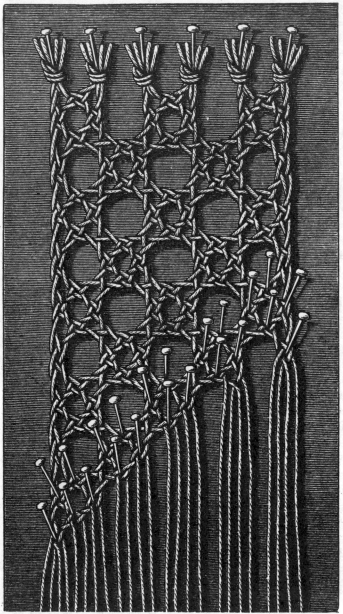

Fig. 981.   Virgin ground.

one passing = twist the 9th and 10th pair once, cross; repeat from *.

Rose ground (figs. 983 and 984). — Hang on 2 pairs of bobbins at points *a, c, d, f,* and 1 pair at points *b* and *e* in the pattern fig. 984.

Twist the 2nd and 3[d] pair twice, cross, stick a pin in at point 1, twist twice cross = twist the 5th and 6th pair twice, cross, stick a pin in at point 2, twist twice, cross = twist the 4th and 5th pair twice, cross, stick a pin in at point 3, twist twice, cross = twist the 3[d] and 4th pair twice, cross, stick a pin in at point 4, twist twice, cross = twist the 2nd and 3[d] pair twice, cross, stick a pin in at point 5, twist twice, cross = twist the 1st and 2nd pair twice, cross, stick a pin in at point 6, twist twice, cross = twist the 2nd and 3[d] pair twice, cross, stick a pin in at point 7, twist twice, cross = twist the 4th and 5th pair

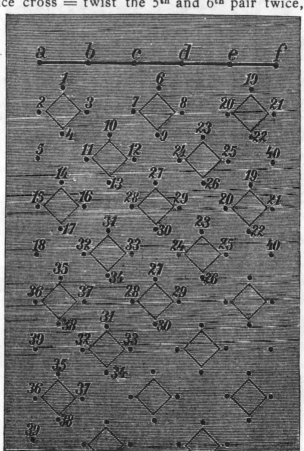

Fig. 982. Pattern of ornamental ground figure 981.

twice, cross, stick a pin in at point 8, twist twice, cross = twist the 6th and 7th pair twice, cross, stick a pin in at point 9, twist twice, cross = * twist the 8th and 9th pair twice, cross, stick a pin in at point 10, twist twice, cross = twist the 7th and 8th pair twice, cross, stick a pin in at point 11, twist twice, cross = twist the 6th and 7th pair twice, cross, stick a pin in at point 12.

twist twice, cross = twist the 5th and 6th pair twice, cross, stick a pin in at point 13, twist twice, cross = twist the 4th and 5th pair twice, cross, stick a pin in at point 14, twist twice, cross = twist the 3d and 4th pair twice, cross, stick a pin in at point 15, twist twice, cross = twist the 2nd and 3d pair twice, cross, stick a pin in at point 16, twist twice, cross = twist the 1st and 2nd pair twice, cross, stick a pin in at point 17, twist twice, cross = twist the 2nd and 3d pair twice, cross, stick a pin in at point 18, twist twice, cross = twist the 4th and 5th pair twice, cross, stick a pin in at point 19, twist twice, cross = twist the 6th and 7th pair twice, cross, stick a pin in at point 20, twist twice, cross = twist the 8th and 9th pair twice, cross, stick a pin in at point 21,

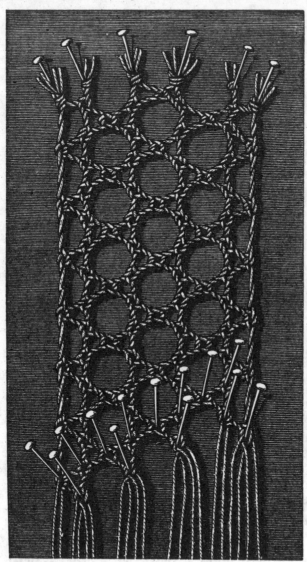

Fig. 983. Rose ground.

twist twice, cross = twist the 9th and 10th pair twice, cross, stick a pin in at point 22, twist twice, cross; repeat from *.

Valenciennes ground (figs. 985 and 986). — This consists of little plaits which require 2 pairs of bobbins each. Hang on 2 pairs of bobbins at point *a* and 4 pairs at points *b* and *c* in the pattern fig. 986.

Twist the 1st and 2nd pair once, cross, five passings = twist the 3d and 4th pair once, cross, five passings = twist the 2nd and 3d pair once, cross, stick a pin in at point 1, one passing = twist the 1st and 2nd pair once, cross, five passings, stick a pin in at point 2, twist once, cross, five passings = twist the 3d and 4th pair once, cross, five passings = twist the 5th and 6th pair once, cross, five passings = twist the 7th and

8th pair once, cross, five passings = twist the 6th and 7th pair once, cross, stick a pin in at point 3, one passing = twist the 5th and 6th pair once, cross, five passings = twist the 4th and 5th pair once, cross, stick a pin in at point 4, one passing = twist the 3d and 4th pair once, cross, five passings = twist the 2nd and 3d pair once, cross, stick a pin in at point 5, one passing = twist the 1st and 2nd pair once, cross, five passings, stick a pin in at point 6, twist once, cross, five passings =

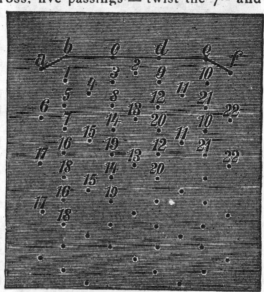

Fig. 984.
Pattern of rose ground figure 983.

twist the 3d and 4th pair once, cross, five passings = twist the 5th and 6th pair once, cross, five passings = twist the 7th and 8th pair once, cross, five passings = * twist the 9th and 10th pair once, cross, five passings, stick a pin in at point 7, twist once, cross, five passings = twist the 8th and 9th pair once, cross, stick a pin in at point 8, one passing = twist the 7th and 8th pair once, cross, five passings = twist the 6th and 7th pair once, cross, stick a pin in at point 9, one passing = twist the 5th and 6th pair once, cross, five passings = twist the 4th and 5th pair once, cross, stick a pin in at point 10, one passing = twist the 3d and 4th pair once, cross, five passings = twist the 2nd and 3d pair once, cross, stick a pin in at point 11, one passing = twist the 1st and 2nd pair once, cross, five passings, stick a pin in at point 12, twist once, cross, five passings = twist the 3d and 4th pair once, cross, five passings = twist the 5th and the 6th pair once, cross, five passings = twist the 7th and 8th pair once, cross, five passings; repeat from *.

Dieppe ground with little spiders (figs. 987 and 988). — Hang on 2 pairs of bobbins at points *a, b, c, d, e*, in the pattern fig. 988.

Twist the 2nd and 3d pair twice, cross, stick a pin in at point 1, one passing = twist the 1st and 2nd pair twice, cross, stick a pin in at point 2, one passing=twist the 4th and 5th pair twice, cross, stick a pin in at point 3, one passing = twist the 3d and 4th pair twice, cross, stick a pin in at point 4, one passing = twist the 2nd and 3d pair twice, cross, stick a pin in at point 5, one passing = twist the 1st and 2nd pair twice, cross, stick a pin in at point 6, one passing = twist the 8th and 9th pair twice, cross,

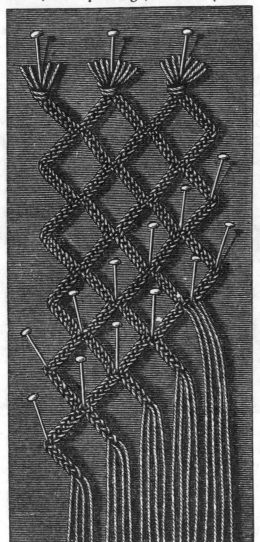

Fig. 985. Valenciennes ground.

stick a pin in at point 7, one passing = twist the 9th and 10th pair twice, cross, stick a pin in at point 8, one passing = twist the 6th and 7th pair twice, cross,. stick a pin in at point 9, one passing = twist the 7th and 8th pair twice, cross, stick a pin in at point 10, one passing = twist the 8th and 9th pair twice, cross, stick a pin in at point 11, one passing = twist the 9th and 10th pair twice, cross, stick a pin in at point 12, one passing = * twist the 5th and 6th pair twice, cross, stick a pin in at point 13, one passing = twist the 4th and 5th pair twice, stick a pin in at point 14, one passing = twist the 3d and 4th pair twice, cross, stick a pin in at point 15, one passing = twist the 2nd and 3d pair twice, cross, stick a pin in at point 16, one passing = twist the 1st and 2nd pair twice,

cross, stick a pin in at point 17, one passing = twist the 6th and 7th pair twice, cross, stick a pin in at point 18, one passing = twist the 7th and 8th pair twice, cross, stick a pin in at point 19, one passing = twist the 8th and 9th pair twice, cross, stick a pin in at point 20, one passing = twist the 9th and 10th pair twice, cross, stick a pin in at point 21, one passing = twist the 5th and 6th pair three times, cross, one passing = twist the 4th pair three times, do not twist the 5th pair, cross, one passing = do not twist the 6th pair, twist the 7th pair three times, cross, one passing = cross the 5th and 6th pair, one passing, stick a pin in at point 22, cross,

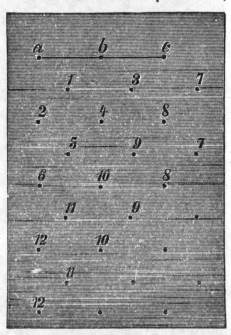

Fig. 986.
Pattern of Valenciennes ground figure 985.

one passing = cross the 4th and 5th pair, one passing = twist the 3d pair twice, twist the 4th pair three times, cross, stick a pin at point 23, one passing = twist the 2nd and 3d pair twice, cross, stick a pin in at point 24, one passing = twist the 1st and 2nd pair twice, cross, stick a pin in at point 25, one passing = cross the 6th and 7th pair, one passing = twist the 7th pair three times, twist the 8th pair twice, cross, stick a pin in at point 26, one passing = twist the 8th and 9th pair twice, cross, stick a pin in at point 27, one passing = twist the 9th and 10th pair twice, cross, stick a pin in at point 28, one passing = cross the 5th and 6th pair, one passing = twist the 4th pair twice, twist the 5th pair three times, cross, stick a pin in at point 29, one passing = twist the 3d and 4th pair twice, cross, stick a pin in at point 30, one passing = twist the 2nd and 3d pair twice, cross, stick a pin in at point 31, one passing = twist the 1st and 2nd pair twice, cross, stick a pin in at point 32, one passing = twist the 6th pair three times, twist the 7th pair twice, cross, stick a pin in at point 33, one passing = twist the 7th and 8th pair twice, cross, stick a pin in at point 34, one passing = twist the 8th and 9th pair twice, cross, stick a pin in at point 35, one passing = twist the 9th and 10th pair twice, cross, stick a pin in at point 36, one

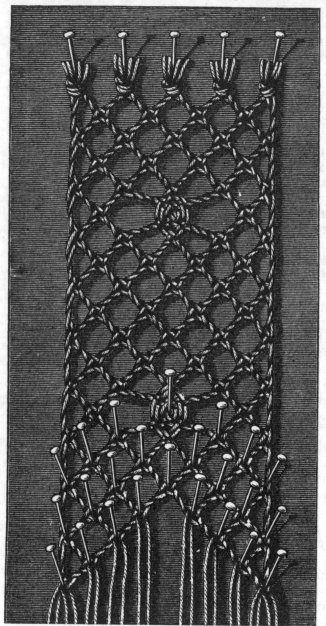

Fig. 987. Dieppe ground with little spiders.

passing = twist the 5th and 6th pair twice, cross, stick a pin in at point 37, one passing = twist the 4th and 5th pair twice, cross, stick a pin in at point 38, one passing = twist the 3d

and 4th pair twice, cross, stick a pin in at point 39, one passing = twist the 2nd and 3d pair twice, cross, stick a pin in at point 40, one passing = twist the 1st and 2nd pair twice, cross, stick a pin in at point 41, one passing = twist the 6th and 7th pair twice, cross, stick a pin in at point 42, one passing = twist the 7th and 8th pair twice, cross, stick a pin in at point 43, one passing = twist the 8th and 9th pair twice, cross, stick a pin in at point 44, one passing = twist the 9th and 10th pair twice, cross, stick a pin in at point 45, one passing; repeat from *.

Réseau ground with squares in spot stitch (figs. 989 and 990). — Hang on 2 pairs of bobbins, at points a, b, c, d, in the pattern fig. 990.

Twist the 2nd and 3d pair once, cross, stick a pin in at point 1, one passing = twist

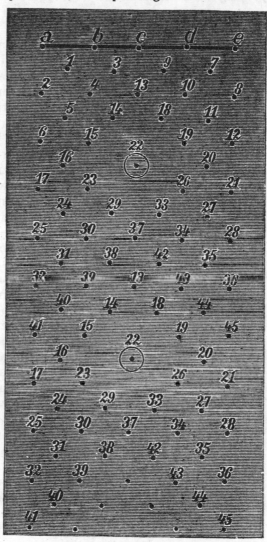

Fig. 988.
Pattern of Dieppe ground figure 987.

the 1st and 2nd pair once, cross, stick a pin in at point 2, one passing = twist the 6th and 7th pair once, cross, stick a pin in at point 3, one passing = twist the 7th and 8th pair once, cross, stick a pin in at point 4, one passing = * twist the 4th and 5th pair once, cross, stick a pin in at point 5, one passing = twist the 3d and 4th pair once, cross, stick a pin in at point 6, one passing = twist the 2nd and 3d pair once, cross, stick a pin in at point 7, one passing = twist the 1st and 2nd pair once, cross, stick a pin in at point 8, one passing = twist the 5th and 6th pair once, cross, stick a pin in at point 9, one passing = twist the 6th and 7th pair once, cross, stick a pin in at point 10, one passing = twist the 7th and 8th pair once, cross, stick a pin in at point 11, one passing = twist the 4th and 5th pair twice, cross, for the square in spot stitch repeat six times: twist the 4th pair twice, do not twist the 5th pair, cross, and to not twist the 4th pair, twist the 5th pair twice, cross (tighten all the passings equally to give the square a good shape), stick a pin in at point 12 = twist the 3d pair once, twist the 4th pair twice, cross, stick a pin in at point 13, one passing = twist the 2nd and 3d pair once, cross, stick a pin in at point 14,

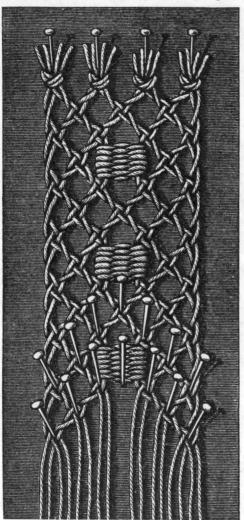

Fig. 989. Reseau ground with squares in spot stitch.

one passing = twist the 1st and 2nd pair once, cross, stick a pin in at point 15, one passing = twist the 5th pair twice, twist the 6th pair once, cross, stick a pin in at point 16, one passing = twist the 6th and 7th pair once, cross, stick a pin in at point 17, one passing = twist the 7th and 8th pair once, cross, stick a pin in at point 18, one passing; repeat from *.

Réseau ground with leaves in spot stitch (figs. 991 and 992). — Hang on 2 pairs of bobbins at points *a, b, c, d,* in the pattern fig. 992.

Twist the 2nd and 3^d pair once, cross, stick a pin in at point 1, one passing = twist the 1st and 2nd pair once, cross, stick a pin in at point 2, one passing = twist the 6th and 7th pair once, cross, stick a pin in at point 3, one passing = twist the 7th and 8th pair once, cross, stick a pin in at point 4, one passing = * twist the 4th and 5th pair once, cross, stick a pin in at point 5, one passing = twist the 3^d and 4th pair once, cross, stick a pin in at point 6, one passing = twist the 2nd and 3^d pair once, cross, stick a pin in at point 7, one passing = twist the 1st and 2nd pair once, cross, stick a pin in at point 8, one passing = twist the 5th and 6th pair once, cross, stick a pin in at point 9, one passing = twist the 6th and 7th pair once, cross, stick a pin in at point 10, one passing = twist the 7th and 8th pair once, cross, stick a pin in at point 11, one passing = twist the 4th and 5th pair

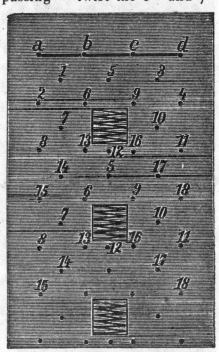

Fig. 990.
Pattern of réseau ground figure 989.

twice, cross, stick a pin in at point 12, for the leaf in spot stitch repeat ten times: twist the 4th pair twice, do not twist the 5th pair, cross, and do not twist the 4th pair, twist the 5th pair twice, cross (draw the 1st and 10th passings tight and leave the intermediate passings looser to give the leaf a good shape) stick a pin in at point 13 = twist the 2nd and 3^d pair once, cross, stick a pin in at point 14, one passing = twist the 1st and 2nd pair once, cross, stick a pin in at point 15, one passing = twist the 6th and 7th pair once, cross, stick a pin in at point 16, one passing = twist the 7th and 8th pair once, cross, stick a pin in at point 17, one passing = twist the 3^d pair once, twist the 4th pair twice, cross, stick a pin in at point 18, one passing = twist the 2nd and 3^d pair once, cross, stick a pin in at point 19, one passing = twist the 1st and 2nd pair once, cross, stick a pin in at point 20, one passing = twist the 5th pair twice, twist the 6th pair once, cross, stick a pin in at point 21, one passing = twist the 6th and 7th pair once, cross, stick a pin in at point 22, one passing = twist the 7th and 8th pair once, cross, stick a pin in at point 23, one passing; repeat from *.

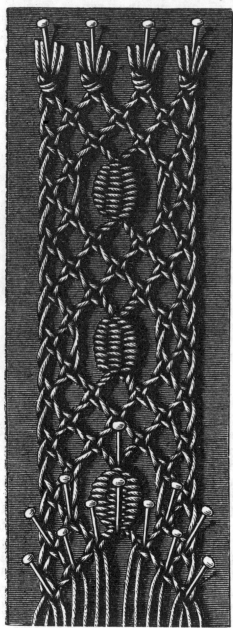

Fig. 991. Réseau ground with leaves in spot stitch.

Eternelle lace in two rows (figs. 993 and 994). — Here follows a series of laces, beginning with the easiest kind, the so-called "Eternelle" and passing on to more complicated and difficult ones. "Eternelle" lace has no pronounced pattern; insertions and lace with scallops, of any width, according to the number of rows can be made of "Eternelle".

For a lace with only one row of holes you must have 5 pairs of bobbins; for two rows, 7 pairs; for three, 9 pairs, that is two pairs more for every additional row.

Insertions take one more pair of bobbins for the second vertical edge.

The engraving in which the éternelle is begun with 7 pairs of bobbins shews how the pattern is prepared. Hang on 3 pairs of bobbins at point *a* and 2 at points *b* and *c* in pattern fig. 994.

* Twist the 2nd and 3d pair once, cross, one passing = twist the 3d and 4th pair once, cross, stick a pin in at point 1, one passing = twist the 4th and 5th pair once, cross, one passing = twist the 5th and 6th pair once, cross, stick a pin in at point 2, one passing = twist the 6th and 7th pair once, cross, one passing, stick a pin in at point 3, twist the 6th pair once, twist the 7th pair twice, cross, one passing = twist the 4th and 5th pair once, cross, one passing = twist the 2nd and 3d pair once, cross, one passing = twist the 1st pair three times, twist the 2nd pair once, cross, one passing, stick a pin in at point 4 (on the right of the 2nd pair); repeat from *.

Torchon lace (figs. 995 and 996). — Hang on 3 pairs of bobbins at points *a* and *b* and 2 pairs of bobbins at points *c* and *d*, in pattern fig. 996.

Twist the 3d and 4th pair once, cross, stick a pin in at point 1, one passing = twist the 4th and 5th pair once, cross = twist the 5th and 6th pair once, cross = twist the 6th and 7th pair once, cross = twist the 7th and 8th pair once, cross = twist the 8th and 9th pair once, cross = twist the 9th and 10th pair once, cross, stick a pin in at point 2, one passing = twist the 8th and 9th pair once, cross = twist the 7th and 8th pair once, cross = twist the 6th and 7th pair once, cross = twist the 5th and 6th pair once, cross = twist the 4th and 5th pair once, cross, stick a pin in

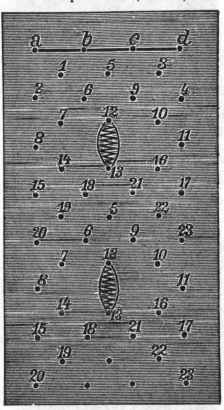

Fig. 992.
Pattern of réseau ground figure 991.

at point 3, one passing = twist the 5th and 6th pair once, cross = twist the 6th and 7th pair once, cross = twist the 7th and 8th pair once, cross = twist the 8th and 9th pair once, cross = twist the 9th and 10th pair once, cross, stick a pin in at point 4, one passing = twist the 8th and 9th pair once, cross = twist the 7th and 8th pair once, cross = twist the 6th

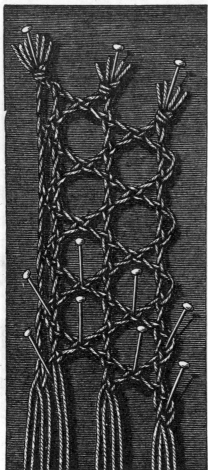

Fig. 993. Eternelle lace in two rows.
Materials: D.M.C Flax lace thread No. 16,
D.M.C Alsatia No. 25, or D.M.C Floss
flax No. 16, in white or écru.

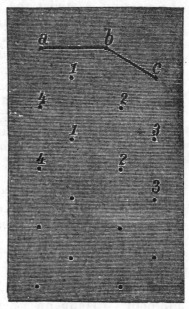

Fig. 994.
Pattern of Eternelle figure 993.

and 7th pair once, cross = twist the 5th and 6th pair once, cross, stick a pin in at point 5, one passing = twist the 6th and 7th pair once, cross = twist the 7th and 8th pair once, cross = twist the 8th and 9th pair once, cross = twist the 9th and 10th pair once, cross, stick a pin in at point 6, one passing = twist the 8th and 9th pair once, cross = twist the 7th and 8th pair once, cross = twist the 6th and 7th pair once, cross, stick a pin in at point 7, one passing = twist the 7th and 8th pair once, cross = twist the 8th and 9th pair once, cross = twist the 9th and 10th pair once, cross, stick a pin in at paint 8, one passing = twist the 8th and 9th pair once, cross = twist the 7th and 8th pair once, cross = twist the 6th and 7th pair once, cross = twist the 2nd and 3d pair once, cross, one passing = twist the 1st pair twice. twist the 2nd pair once, cross, one passing, stick a pin in at point 9 (on the right of the 2nd pair) = twist the 2nd and 3d pair once, cross, one passing = twist the 3d and 4th pair once, cross, stick a pin in at point 10, one passing = twist the 2nd and 3d pair once, cross, one passing = twist the 1st pair twice, twist the 2nd pair once, cross, one passing, stick a pin in at point 11, (on the right of the 2nd pair) = twist the 2nd and 3d pair once, cross, one passing = twist the 4th and 5th pair once, cross, stick a pin in at point 12, one passing = twist the 3d and 4th pair once, cross, stick a pin in at point 13, one passing = twist the 2nd and 3d pair once, cross, one passing = twist the 1st pair twice, twist the 2nd pair once, cross, one passing, stick a pin in at point 14 (on the right of the 2nd pair) = twist the 2nd and 3d pair once, cross, one passing = twist the 5th

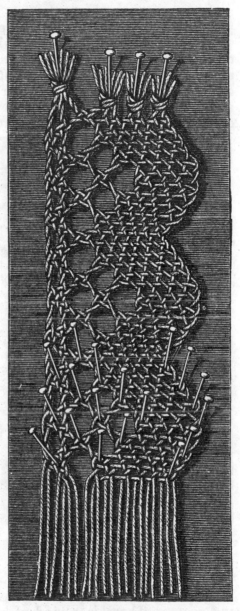

Fig. 995. Torchon lace.

Materials: D.M.C Flax lace thread No. 16, D.M.C Crochet cotton 6 cord No. 20, D.M.C Alsatia No. 25, or D.M.C Pearl cotton No. 8, in white or Maize yellow 579.

and 6th pair once, cross, stick a pin in at point 15, one passing = twist the 6th and 7th pair once, cross = twist the 7th and 8th pair once, cross = twist the 8th and 9th pair once, cross = twist the 9th and 10th pair once, cross, stick a pin in at point 16, one passing = twist the 8th and 9th pair once, cross = twist the 7th and 8th pair once, cross = twist the 6th and 7th pair once, cross = twist the 5th and 6th pair once, cross = twist the 4th and 5th pair once, cross, stick a pin in at point 17, one passing = twist the 5th and 6th pair once, cross = twist the 6th and 7th pair once, cross = twist the 7th and 8th pair once, cross = twist the 8th and 9th pair once, cross = twist the 9th and 10th pair once, cross, stick a pin in at point 18, one passing = twist the 8th and 9th pair once, cross = twist the 7th and 8th pair once, cross = twist the 6th and 7th pair once, cross = twist the 5th and 6th pair once, cross = twist the 4th and 5th pair once, cross. Repeat from the beginning.

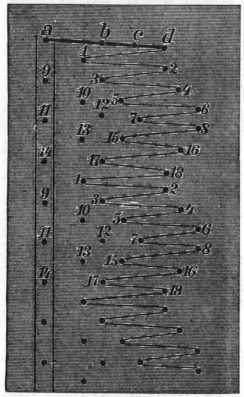

Fig. 996.
Pattern of torchon lace figure 995.

Picots (fig. 997). — For decorating the plain edges of a lace, make, with one of the outside threads, picots formed with the help of a pin stuck into the pattern at a given place. These picots are often met with on plaited bands, as shewn in the engraving fig. 997. (See also figs. 1000 and 1004.)

Crossing with three and four pairs of bobbins (figs. 998 and 999). — There is a kind of lace in which the pattern is principally formed by plaited and twisted bars of threads. In the making of lace of this kind the passings where the bars cross each other, are made with three or four pairs of bobbins. The pairs then count as if they were single threads, and you turn and cross them in the same manner. The pins that hold these crossings are stuck in exactly in the middle of the crossed threads as the engravings indicate.

Figure 998 shews a crossing with three pairs of bobbins, and fig. 999, one done with 4 pairs. These crossings are used in making the laces illustrated in figures 1000 and 1004.

Plaited lace (figs. 1000 and 1001). — Hang on 4 pairs of bobbins at point *a* and 1 pair at point *b*, in the pattern fig. 1001.

Twist the 1st and 2nd pair once, cross, six passings = twist the 3d and 4th pair once, cross, three passings = do not twist the 3d and 4th pair, twist the 5th pair three times, a crossing as in figure 998, stick a pin in at point 1 = twist the 4th and 5th pair once, cross, three passings, one picot to the right at point 2, three passings, one picot to the right at point 3, three passings, one picot to the right at point 4, three passings = twist the 3d pair three times, do not twist the 4th and 5th pair, a crossing as in fig. 998, stick in a pin at point 5 = twist the 3d and 4th pair once, cross, three passings = a crossing as in fig. 999 with the 1st and 2nd and with the 3d and 4th pair, stick a pin in at point 6. Repeat from the beginning.

Insertion with squares in spot stitch (figs. 1002 and 1003). — Hang on 3 pairs of bobbins at points *a* and *f*, 2 pairs at points *b* and *e* and 1 pair at points *c* and *d*, in pattern fig. 1003.

Fig. 997.
Plait with picots.

Twist the 5th and 6th pair once, cross, one passing, stick a pin in at point 1, two passings = twist the 4th and 5th pair once, cross, one passing = do not twist the 3d pair, twist the 4th pair once, cross, one passing, stick a pin in at point 2 = cross the 2nd and 3d pair, one passing = cross the 3d and 4th pair, one passing = twist the 2nd and 3d pair once, cross, four passings, stick a pin in at point 3 = twist the 1st pair three times, do not twist the 2nd pair, cross, one passing = do not twist the 2nd pair, twist the 3d pair once, cross, four passings = twist the 4th and 5th pair once, cross, one passing = twist the 5th and 6th pair once, cross, stick a pin in at point 4, one passing =

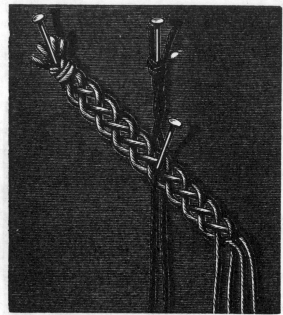

Fig. 998.
Crossing with there pairs of bobbins.

Fig. 999.
Crossing with four pairs of bobbins.

twist the 7th and 8th pair once, cross, one passing, stick a pin in at point 5, two passings = twist the 8th and 9th pair once, cross, one passing = twist the 9th pair once, do not twist the 10th pair, cross, one passing, stick a pin in at point 6 = cross the 10th and 11th pair, one passing = cross the 9th and 10th pair, one passing = twist the 10th and 11th pair once, cross, four passings, stick a pin in at point 7 = do not twist the 11th pair, twist the 12th pair three times, cross, one passing = twist the 10th pair once, do not twist the 11th pair, cross, four passings = twist the 8th and 9th pair once, cross, one passing = twist the 7th and 8th pair once, cross, stick a pin in at point 8, one passing = twist the 6th and 7th pair once, cross, spot stitch six times, see fig. 989 = twist the 5th and 6th pair once, cross, stick a pin in at point 9, one passing = twist the 4th and 5th pair once, cross, one passing, stick a pin in at point 10, two passings = twist the 7th and 8th pair once, cross, stick a pin in at point 11, one

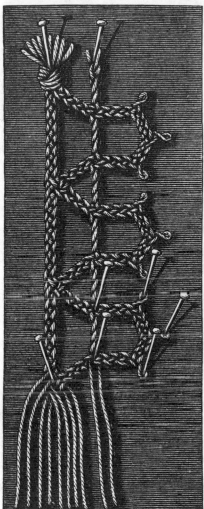

Fig. 1000. Plaited lace.
Materials: D.M.C Flax lace thread
No. 16, in white. (*)

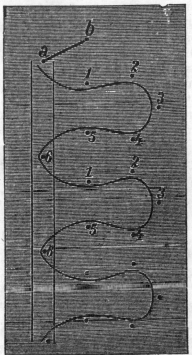

Fig 1001.
Pattern of plaited lace figure 1000.

passing = twist the 8th and 9th pair once, cross, one passing, stick a pin in at point 12, two passings. Repeat from the beginning.

Plaited lace (figs. 1004 and 1005). — Hang on 2 pairs of bobbins at points *a* and *d*, 4 pairs at point *b* and 3 pairs at point *c*.

Cross the 8th and 9th pair, one passing = cross the 7th and 8th pair, one passing = cross the 6th and 7th pair, one passing = cross the 5th and 6th pair,

(*) See at the end of the last chapter the tables of the sizes and colours of the cotton, flax and silk articles, mark D.M.C.

one passing = cross the 4th and 5th pair, one passing = cross the 3d and 4th pair, one passing = twist the 2nd and 3d pair once, cross, one passing = twist the 1st and 2nd pair once, cross, one passing, stick a pin in at point 1, twist the 1st pair twice, twist the 2nd pair once, cross, one passing = twist the 2nd and 3d pair once, cross, one passing = twist the 3d pair once, do not twist the 4th pair, cross, one passing = cross the 4th and 5th pair, one passing = cross the 5th and 6th pair, one passing = cross the 6th and 7th pair, one passing, stick a pin in at point 2, cross, one passing = cross the 5th and 6th pair, one passing = cross the 4th and 5th pair, one

Fig. 1002. Insertion with squares in spot stitch.
Materials: D.M.C Pearl cotton No. 5 or 8, D.M.C Floss flax No. 8 or 16, in white or Maize yellow 579. (*)

passing = cross the 3d and 4th pair, one passing = twist the 2nd and 3d pair once, cross, one passing = twist the 1st and 2nd pair once, cross, one passing, stick a pin in at point 3, twist the 1st pair twice, twist the 2nd pair once, cross, one passing = twist the 2nd and 3d pair once, cross, one passing = twist the 3d and 4th pair once, cross, one passing, stick a pin in at point 4, two passings = twist the 2nd and 3d pair once, cross, one passing = twist the 1st and 2nd pair once, cross, one passing, stick a pin in at point 5, twist the 1st pair twice, twist the 2nd pair once, cross, one passing = twist the

(*) These numbers refer to the colours on the colour cards of the articles stamped with the D.M.C trade mark. These cards can be consulted at all the mercers' and needlework shops.

2nd and 3^d pair once, cross, one passing = twist the 3^d and
4th pair once, cross, one passing = twist the 8th and 9th pair
once, cross, one passing = twist the 10th and 11th pair once,
cross, two passings = crossing as described in figure 999 with
8th, 9th, 10th and 11th pair, stick a pin in at point 6 = twist
the 10th and 11th pair once, cross, two passings = twist the
11th pair once, a picot at point 7, twist the 10th and 11th pair
once, cross, two passings = twist the 8th and 9th pair once,
cross, two passings = cross the 6th and 7th pair, two passings
= crossing with the 6th, 7th, 8th and 9th pair, stick a pin in

at point 8 = twist
the 6th and 7th pair
once, cross, three
passings, stick a pin
in at point 9 = twist
the 5th pair three
times, do not twist
the 6th pair, cross, one
passing = cross the
6th and 7th pair, one
passing = twist the
8th and 9th pair once,
cross, two passings,
twist the 9th pair once,
a picot at point 10,
twist the 8th and 9th
pair once, cross, one
passing, stick a pin in
at point 11 = twist
the 7th pair three
times, do not twist
the 8th pair, cross, one
passing = cross the
8th and 9th pair, one

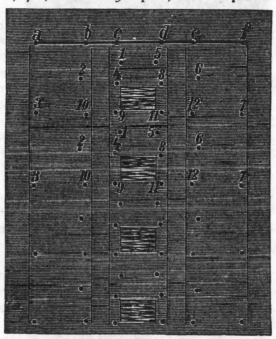

Fig. 1003.
Pattern of insertion with squares figure 1002.

passing = cross the 7th and 8th pair, two passings, twist the
8th pair once, a picot at point 12, twist the 7th and 8th pair
once, cross, one passing = twist the 4th pair three times, do
not twist the 5th pair, cross, one passing = cross the 5th and
6th pair, one passing = twist the 6th pair three times, do not
twist the 7th pair, cross, one passing, stick a pin in at point 13
= cross the 7th and 8th pair, one passing = twist the 9th pair
twice, do not twist the 10th pair, cross, one passing = cross
the 10th and 11th pair, one passing, twist the 11th pair once,

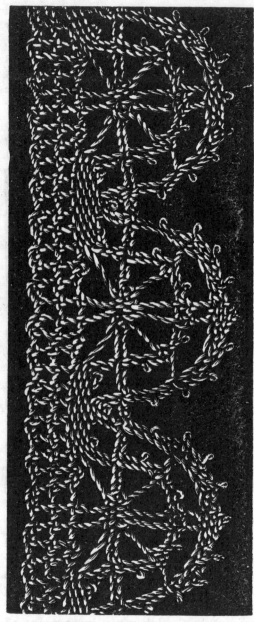

Fig. 1004. Plaited lace.
Materials: D.M.C Flax lace thread No. 16,
D.M.C Floss flax No. 16,
or D.M.C Pearl cotton No. 8, in white or écru.

a picot at point 14, do not twist the 10th pair, twist the 11th pair once, cross, one passing = cross the 9th and 10th pair, one passing = cross the 10th and 11th pair, one passing, twist the 11th pair once, a picot at point 15, do not twist the 10th pair, twist the 11th pair once, cross, one passing = cross the 9th and 10th pair, one passing = cross the 10th and 11th pair, one passing, twist the 11th pair once, a picot at point 16, do not twist the 10th pair, twist the 11th pair once, cross, one passing = cross the 9th and 10th pair, one passing = cross the 10th and 11th pair, one passing = twist the 8th pair twice, do not twist the 9th pair, cross, one passing = cross the 9th and 10th pair, one passing = cross the 10th and 11th pair, one passing, stick a pin in at point 17, do not twist the 10th pair, twist the 11th pair twice, cross, one passing = cross the 9th and 10th pair, one passing = cross the 8th and 9th pair, one passing = twist the 7th pair once, twist the 8th pair twice, cross, one passing = twist the 6th pair once,

do not twist the 7th pair, cross, one passing = do not twist
the 5th pair, twist the 6th pair three times, cross, one passing

= cross the 4th
and 5th pair, one
passing = twist
the 3d pair once,
twist the 4th pair
three times, cross,
one passing =
twist the 2nd and
3d pair once,
cross, one pass-
ing = twist the
1st and 2nd pair
once, cross, one
passing, stick a
pin in at point 18,
twist the 1st pair
twice, twist the
2nd pair once,
cross, one pass-
ing = twist the
2nd and 3d pair
once, cross, one
passing = twist
the 3d and 4th
pair once, cross,
one passing, stick
a pin in at point
19, two passings
= twist the 2nd
and 3d pair once,
cross, one pass-
ing = twist the
1st and 2nd pair
once, cross, one
passing, stick a
pin in at point 20,
twist the 1st pair
twice, twist the
2nd pair once,
cross, one pass-
ing = twist the

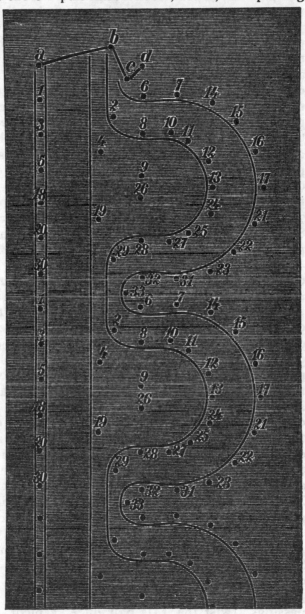

Fig. 1005.
Pattern of plaited lace figure 1004.

2nd and 3d pair once, cross, one passing = twist the 3d and
4th pair once, cross, one passing = cross the 10th and 11th
pair, one passing = cross the 9th and 10th pair, one passing
= cross the 10th and 11th pair, one passing, twist the 11th
pair once, a picot at point 21, do not twist the 10th pair,
twist the 11th pair once, cross, one passing = cross the 9th
and 10th pair, one passing = cross the 10th and 11th pair,
one passing, twist the 11th pair once, a picot at point 22, do
not twist the 10th pair, twist the 11th pair once, cross, one
passing = cross the 9th and 10th pair, one passing = cross
the 10th and 11th pair, one passing, twist the 11th pair once,
a picot at point 23, do not twist the 10th pair, twist the 11th
pair once, cross, one passing = cross the 9th and 10th pair,
one passing = twist the 7th and 8th pair once, cross, one
passing, twist the 8th pair once, a picot at point 24, twist the
7th and 8th pair once, cross, one passing = do not twist the
8th pair, twist the 9th pair twice, cross, one passing, stick a
pin in at point 25 = cross the 7th and 8th pair, one passing
= do not twist the 6th pair, twist the 7th pair three times,
cross, one passing, stick a pin in at point 26 = cross the 5th
and 6th pair, one passing = cross the 6th and 7th pair, three
passings = cross the 8th and 9th pair, two passings, twist the
9th pair once, a picot at point 27, twist the 8th and 9th pair
once, cross, one passing = crossing with the 6th, 7th, 8th and
9th pair, stick a pin in at point 28 = twist the 6th and 7th
pair once, cross, two passings = do not twist the 4th pair,
twist the 5th pair three times, cross, one passing = cross the
5th and 6th pair, one passing = cross the 6th and 7th pair,
one passing, stick a pin in at point 29, one passing = cross
the 5th and 6th pair, one passing = cross the 4th and 5th pair,
one passing = cross the 3d and 4th pair, one passing = twist
the 2nd and 3d pair once, cross, one passing = twist the 1st
and 2nd pair once, cross, one passing, stick a pin in at point
30, twist the 1st pair twice, twist the 2nd pair once, cross, one
passing = twist the 2nd and 3d pair once, cross, one passing
= twist the 3d pair once, do not twist the 4th pair, cross, one
passing = cross the 4th and 5th pair, one passing = cross the
5th and 6th pair, one passing = cross the 6th and 7th pair,
one passing = twist the 8th and 9th pair once, cross, two
passings = twist the 10th and 11th pair once, cross, two
passings, twist the 11th pair once, a picot at point 31, twist
the 10th and 11th pair once, cross, two passings = crossing
with the 8th, 9th, 10th and 11th pair, stick a pin in at point 32

= twist the 8th and 9th pair once, cross, two passings = cross the 7th and 8th pair, one passing = cross the 8th and 9th pair, one passing, stick a pin in at point 33. Repeat from the beginning.

Gold lace with figures in spot stitch and framing (figs. 1006 and 1007). — Hang on 1 pair of bobbins at points *a* and *g*, 2 pairs at points *b*, *c*, *e*, *f* and 4 threads for the framing at point *d*, in pattern fig. 1007.

Twist the 3d pair once, twist the 4th pair twice, cross, one passing, stick a pin in at point 1, two passings = twist the 2nd and 3d pair once, cross, stick a pin in at point 2, one passing = twist the 1st and 2nd pair once, cross, one passing, stick a pin in at point 3, two passings = twist the 2nd and 3d pair once, cross, stick a pin in at point 4, one passing = slip the framing threads I and II through the 5th, 4th and 3d pair twisted once = twist the 7th pair twice, twist the 8th pair once, cross, one passing, stick a pin in at point 5, two passings = twist the 8th and 9th pair once, cross, stick a pin in at point 6, one passing = twist the 9th and 10th pair once, cross, one passing, stick a pin in at point 7, two passings = twist the 8th and 9th pair once, cross, stick a pin in at point 8, one passing = slip the framing threads IV and III through the 6th, 7th and 8th pair twisted once = twist the 5th and 6th pair once, cross, one passing, stick a pin in at point 9, one passing = twist the 4th pair once, twist the 5th pair twice, cross, one passing, stick a pin in at point 10, one passing = twist the 6th pair twice, twist the 7th pair once, cross, one passing, stick a pin in at point 11, one passing = twist the 5th and 6th pair twice, cross, one passing, stick a pin in at point 12, two passings = eight times spot stitch, see fig. 989, with the 4th and 5th pair = twist the 3d and 4th pair once, cross, one passing, stick a pin in at point 13, two passings = twist the 4th pair once, twist the 5th pair twice, cross, eight times spot stitch = eight times spot stitch with the 6th and 7th pair = twist the 7th and 8th pair once, cross, one passing, stick a pin in at point 14, two passings = twist the 6th pair twice, twist the 7th pair once, cross, eight times spot stitch = twist the 5th and 6th pair once, cross, one passing, stick a pin in at point 15, two passings = twist the 4th pair once, twist the 5th pair twice, cross, stick a pin in at point 16, two passings = twist the 6th pair twice, twist the 7th pair once, cross, stick a pin in at point 17, two passings = twist the 5th and 6th pair twice, cross, stick a pin in at point 18, two passings = slip the framing threads II and I through the 3ᵈ, 4ᵗʰ and 5ᵗʰ pair once twisted = twist the 2ⁿᵈ and 3ᵈ pair

Fig. 1006. Gold lace with figures in spot stitch and framing.
Materials: D.M.C Embroidery gold thread and D.M.C Gold cord, or D.M.C Gold chiné, écru and gold, and D.M.C Turkish gold cord.

once, cross, stick a pin in at point 19, one passing = twist the 1ˢᵗ pair twice, twist the 2ⁿᵈ pair once, cross, one passing, stick a pin in at point 20, two passings = twist the 2ⁿᵈ and

Fig. 1007. Pattern for gold lace figure 1006.

3ᵈ pair once, cross, stick a pin in at point 21, one passing =
twist the 3ᵈ pair twice, twist the 4ᵗʰ pair once, cross, one
passing, stick a pin in at point 22, two passings = twist the

4th pair twice, twist the 5th pair once, cross, one passing, stick a pin in at point 23, two passings = twist the 2nd and 3^d pair once, cross, stick a pin in at point 24, one passing = twist the 1st and 2nd pair once, cross, stick a pin in at point 25, twist the 1st pair twice, do not twist the 2nd pair, cross, twist the 1st pair once, twist the 2nd pair twice, cross,

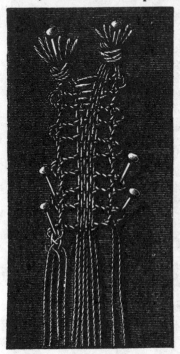

stick a pin in at point 26, twist the 1st pair twice, do not twist the 2nd pair, cross, twist the 1st pair once, twist the 2nd pair twice, cross, stick a pin in at point 27, twist the 1st pair twice, do not twist the 2nd pair, cross, twist the 1st pair once, twist the 2nd pair twice, cross, stick a pin in at point 28, twist the 1st pair twice, do not twist the 2nd pair, cross, twist the 1st pair once, twist the 2nd pair twice, cross, stick a pin in at point 29, twist the 1st pair twice, do not twist the 2nd pair, cross, twist the 1st pair once, twist the 2nd pair twice, cross, stick a pin in at point 30, twist the 1st pair twice, do not twist the 2nd pair, cross, twist the 1st pair once, twist the 2nd pair twice, cross, stick a pin in at point 31, twist the 1st pair twice, do not twist the 2nd pair, cross = twist the 2nd and 3^d pair once, cross, stick a pin in at point 32, one passing = slip the framing

Fig. 1008.
Straight cloth braid.

threads III and IV through the 8th, 7th and 6th pair, twisted once = twist the 8th and 9th pair once, cross, stick a pin in at point 33, one passing = twist the 9th pair once, twist the 10th pair twice, cross, one passing, stick a pin in at point 34, two passings = twist the 8th and 9th pair once, cross, stick a pin in at point 35, one passing = twist the 7th pair once, twist the 8th pair twice, cross, one passing, stick a pin in at point 36, two passings = twist the 6th pair once, twist the 7th pair twice, cross, one passing, stick a pin in at point 37, two passings = twist the 8th and 9^{tb} pair once, cross, stick a pin in at point 38, one passing = twist the 9th and 10th pair once, cross, stick a pin in at point 39, do not twist the 9th pair,

twist the 10th pair twice, cross, twist the 9th pair twice, twist
the 10th pair once, cross, stick a pin in at point 40, do not
twist the 9th pair, twist the 10th pair twice, cross, twist the 9th
pair twice, twist the 10th pair once, cross, stick a pin in at
point 41, do not twist the 9th pair, twist the 10th pair twice,
cross, twist the 9th pair twice, twist the 10th pair once, cross,
stick a pin in at point 42, do not twist the 9th pair, twist the

10th pair twice, cross, twist the 9th pair
twice, twist the 10th pair once, cross,
stick a pin in at point 43, do not twist
the 9th pair, twist the 10th pair twice,
cross, twist the 9th pair twice, twist the
10th pair once, cross, stick a pin in at
point 44, do not twist the 9th pair, twist
the 10th pair twice, cross, twist the 9th
pair twice, twist the 10th pair once, cross,
stick a pin in at point 45, do not twist
the 9th pair, twist the 10th pair twice,
cross = twist the 8th and 9th pair once,
cross, stick a pin in at point 46, one
passing = cross the framing threads I
and II with the threads III and IV and
repeat from the beginning.

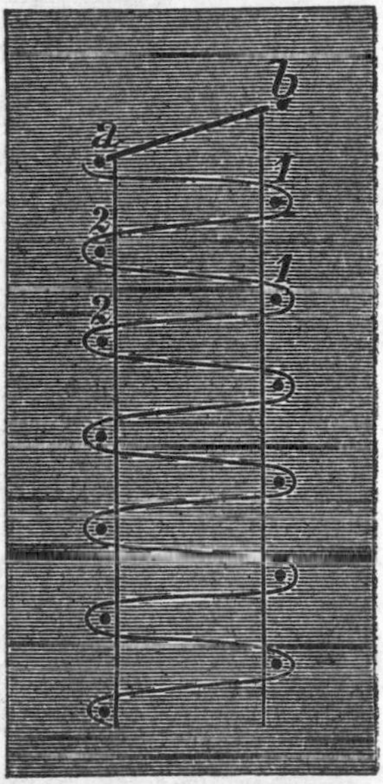

Fig. 1009.
Pattern for straight braid,
figure 1008.

Pillow lace braids. — The braids of
which Russian lace is composed, see
fig. 1012, may be quite plain or more
or less richly decorated and worked in
various colours.

We give examples in figure 1008 and
figure 1010, of plain straight and wavy "cloth braids" worked
in one colour.

Straight cloth braid (figs. 1008 and 1009). — Hang on
3 pairs of bobbins at points a and b, in pattern fig. 1009.

Twist the 2nd pair twice, do not twist the 3d pair, cross,
one passing = cross the 3d and 4th pair, one passing = cross
the 4th and 5th pair, one passing = twist the 5th and 6th pair
twice, cross, one passing, stick a pin in at point 1, twist the 5th
pair once, twist the 6th pair twice, cross, one passing = do not
twist the 4th pair, twist the 5th pair twice, cross, one passing
= cross the 3d and 4th pair, one passing = cross the 2nd and 3d
pair, one passing = twist the 1st and 2nd pair twice, cross, one
passing, stick a pin in at point 2, twist the 1st pair twice, twist
the 2nd pair once, cross, one passing. Repeat from the beginning.

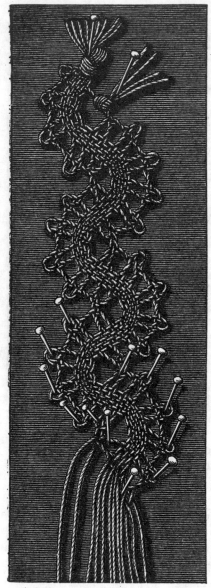

Fig. 1010.
Waved cloth braid.

Waved cloth braid (figs. 1010 and 1011). – Hang on 4 pairs of bobbins at point a and 2 pairs at point b, in pattern figure 1011.

Do not twist the 4th pair, twist the 5th pair twice, cross, one passing = cross the 3^d and 4th pair, one passing = cross the 2nd and 3^d pair, one passing = twist the 1st and 2nd pair twice, cross, one passing, stick a pin in at point 1, twist the 1st pair twice, twist the 2nd pair once, cross, one passing = twist the 2nd pair twice, do not twist the 3^d pair, cross, one passing = cross the 3^d and 4th pair, one passing = cross the 4th and 5th pair, one passing = cross the 3^d and 4th pair, one passing = cross the 2nd and 3^d pair, one passing = twist the 1st and 2nd pair twice, cross, one passing, stick a pin in at point 2, twist the 1st pair twice, twist the 2nd pair once, cross, one passing = twist the 2nd pair twice, do not twist the 3^d pair, cross, one passing = cross the 3^d and 4th pair, one passing = cross the 4th and 5th pair, one passing = cross the 3^d and 4th pair, one passing = cross the 2nd and 3^d pair, one passing = twist the 1st and 2nd pair twice, cross, one passing, stick a pin in at point 3, twist the 1st pair twice, twist the 2nd pair once, cross, one passing = twist the 2nd pair twice, do not twist the 3^d pair, cross, one passing = cross the 3^d and 4th pair, one passing = cross the 4th and 5th pair, one passing = cross the 3^d and 4th pair, one passing = cross the 2nd and 3^d pair, one passing = twist the 1st and

2ⁿᵈ pair twice, cross, one passing, stick a pin in at point 4, twist the 1ˢᵗ pair twice, twist the 2ⁿᵈ pair once, cross, one passing = twist the 2ⁿᵈ pair twice, do not twist the 3ᵈ pair, cross, one passing = cross the 3ᵈ and 4ᵗʰ pair, one passing = cross the 4ᵗʰ and 5ᵗʰ pair, one passing = twist the 5ᵗʰ pair twice, do not twist the 6ᵗʰ pair, cross, one passing, stick a pin in at point 5 (left of the 5ᵗʰ pair) = do not twist the 4ᵗʰ pair, twist the 5ᵗʰ pair twice, cross, one passing = cross the 3ᵈ and 4ᵗʰ pair, one passing = cross the 2ⁿᵈ and 3ᵈ pair, one passing = twist the 1ˢᵗ and 2ⁿᵈ pair twice, cross, one passing, stick a pin in at point 6 (on the right of the 2ⁿᵈ pair) = twist the 2ⁿᵈ pair twice, do not twist the 3ᵈ pair, cross, one passing = cross the 3ᵈ and 4ᵗʰ pair, one passing = cross the 4ᵗʰ and 5ᵗʰ pair, one passing = twist the 5ᵗʰ and 6ᵗʰ pair twice, cross, one passing, stick a pin in at point 7, twist the 5ᵗʰ pair once, twist the 6ᵗʰ pair twice, cross, one passing = do not twist the 4ᵗʰ pair, twist the 5ᵗʰ pair twice, cross, one passing = cross the 3ᵈ and 4ᵗʰ pair, one passing = cross the 2ⁿᵈ and 3ᵈ pair, one passing = cross the 3ᵈ and 4ᵗʰ pair, one passing = cross the 4ᵗʰ and 5ᵗʰ pair, one passing = twist the 5ᵗʰ and 6ᵗʰ pair twice, cross, one passing, stick a pin in at point 8, twist the 5ᵗʰ pair once, twist the 6ᵗʰ pair

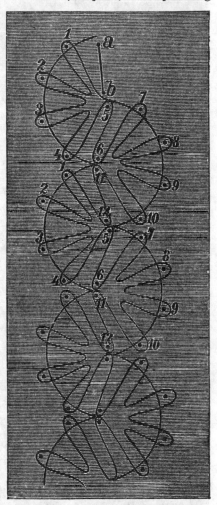

Fig. 1011.
Pattern for waved cloth braid figure 1010.

twice, cross, one passing = do not twist the 4ᵗʰ pair, twist the 5ᵗʰ pair twice, cross, one passing = cross the 3ᵈ and 4ᵗʰ pair, one passing = cross the 2ⁿᵈ and 3ᵈ pair, one passing = cross the 3ᵈ and 4ᵗʰ pair, one passing = cross the 4ᵗʰ and 5ᵗʰ

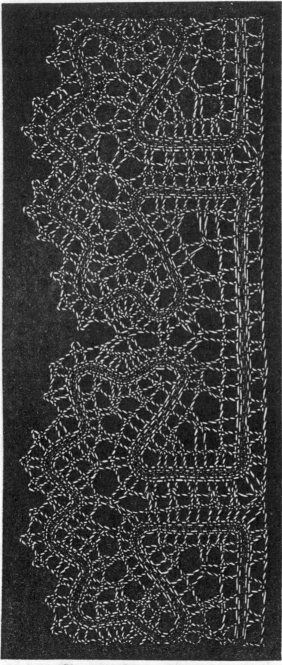

Fig. 1012. Russian braid lace.

pair, one passing = twist the 5th and 6th pair twice, cross, one passing, stick a pin in at point 9, twist the 5th pair once, twist the 6th pair twice, cross, one passing = do not twist the 4th pair, twist the 5th pair twice, cross, one passing = cross the 3d and 4th pair, one passing = cross the 2nd and 3d pair, one passing = cross the 3d and 4th pair, one passing = cross the 4th and 5th pair, one passing = twist the 5th and 6th pair twice, cross, one passing, stick a pin in at point 10, twist the 5th pair once, twist the 6th pair twice, cross, one passing = do not twist the 4th pair, twist the 5th pair twice, cross, one passing = cross the 3d and 4th pair, one passing = cross the 2nd and 3d pair, one passing = do not twist the 1st pair, twist the 2nd pair twice, cross, one passing, stick a pin in at point 11 (on the right of the 2nd pair) = twist the 2nd pair twice, do not twist the 3d pair, cross, one passing =

cross the 3d and 4th pair, one passing = cross the 4th and 5th pair, one passing = twist the 5th and 6th pair twice, cross one passing, stick a pin in at point 12 (left of the 5th pair). Repeat from the beginning.

Russian braid lace (figs. 1012, 1013,

Fig. 1013.
How to connect the braids.

1014). = "Russian" lace, so-called, differs from the pillow laces we have been describing in that it is entirely composed of one or more narrow braids which form the whole pattern. Our pattern is made of a single braid

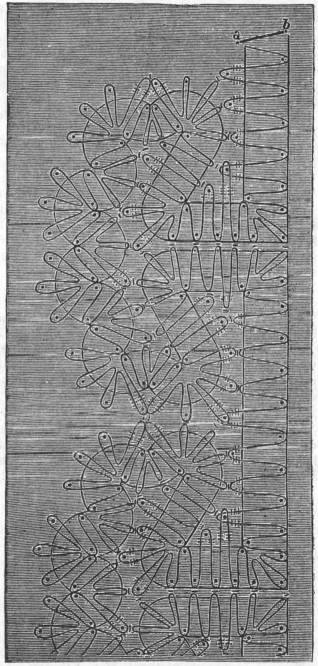

Fig. 1014. Pattern for lace with braid figure 1012.

47

which runs about in straight and curved lines, the curves and
the straight lines connected together by small loops of thread.

To explain clearly how this kind of lace is made we have
shewn in figs. 1008 to 1011, a straight and a waved braid in
process of making, with the pattern and description. We
advise our readers to practise making these braids before
attempting the lace itself.

For the lace in two colours, as directed for fig. 1012, the
middle pair of bobbins should be filled with a coloured thread.

In the pattern of the lace you will notice the waved lines
by the help of which you will see the change of braids.

The places where the work should be fastened to a finished
braid are marked by little lines on the pattern.

For this take one bobbin of the pair nearest the finished
work, catch hold of the thread with a crochet needle, draw a
loop through the picot of the finished braid and slip the
second bobbin of the pair through this loop and then draw
up the threads.

Fig. 1013 shews how to proceed. There in *a* we see a picot
of a braid finished, in *b* the loop of thread drawn through the
picot by the first bobbin and in *c* the thread of the second
bobbin of the pair slipped through the loop of thread.

The drawing further shews the places where the picots are
to come, marked by little strokes. These strokes indicate how
many times to twist the bobbins that form the picot; in cases
where the picot is made as we described for the straight and
waved braids we have made no special marks.

Patterns of needlework. — Besides the different kinds
of work described above a great choice of patterns for pillow
laces will be found in the publication: *Pillow Laces I,* of the
D.M.C Library. (*)

Fringe with Tassels and Crochet Footing.

Needlework Trimmings

In the foregoing chapters we have taught how the different kinds of embroideries and laces are made. To complete this Encyclopedia we will now give our readers a few directions as to the decoration and trimming of needlework.

Embroideries that require no lining can be bordered with a hem or a small fringe; whilst those that are lined may be edged with cord, narrow gimp or braid.

For very handsome embroideries, heavy fringes and tassels at the corners look best, the finer embroideries look best edged with lace.

In any case the trimming must not be more important than the work, but rather shew it off by a tasteful simplicity.

Hems. — A hem is the best finish for all such pieces of needlework as are likely to be subject to frequent washing. Hems are of various kinds and may be divided into openwork hems, hems with ornamental stitches, hems with picots or scallops.

For the first a few horizontal threads must be drawn out, see the chapter on "Openwork on Linen".

A very good effect is obtained by ornamenting a hem with embroidery stitches in some colour, in the same shade as the stuff; these stitches can be varied indefinitely according to the taste and skill of the worker; in flat stitch and button-hole stitch, plait stitch and crossed back stitch are all suitable; in fact almost any of the stitches described in the chapters on "Embroidery upon White Stuff" and "Linen Embroidery".

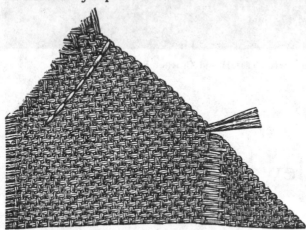

Fig. 1015. Stitched seam for forming the corner of a hem. Inside.

With regard to narrow hems it is best to ornament them with, either crochet, tatting, needle-made or lace picots for which all the necessary directions will be found in the different chapters of this book.

How to form the corners of hems (figs. 1015 and 1016). — The beauty of a hem depends greatly on a neat and well shaped corner. After drawing out the necessary number of threads — or marked the place for the hem by a coloured tacking thread — fold the stuff over in the corners diagonally, the right side inside, and starting from the folded edge, back stitch the double stuff together as the engraving shews.

Fig. 1016. Corner finished. Outside.

The little seam must be the width of the intended hem, must be at right angles with the folded edge and stop about five threads within the outside edge of the stuff: cut off the corner, left of the seam, turn the stuff inside out and lay the hem, turning in the edge from where the back-stitched seam stops and proceed with the hem-stitching. Figure 1016 shews the corner completed, from the outside.

Hem ornamented with picots (figs. 1017, 1018, 1019, 1020, 1021). — The edge of the hem must be thickly overcast, as shewn in figure 1017.

Figure 1018 shews the thread carried from left to right, forming a little loop, which may be held with a pin, then the thread is taken back to the middle of the loop and twisted round it forming a little picot, which can be secured preliminarily by a second pin; then tighten the thread and fill the space between the two pins with three or five Russian stitches, fig. 1019, only instead of simply crossing the threads you pick up the thread before passing to the next stitch.

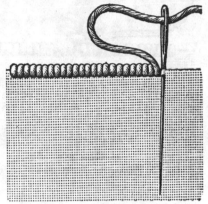

Fig. 1017. Hem with picots.
Overcasting a selvedge or hem.

These picots may be a few stitches apart, as they are in figures 1020 and 1021, or set quite close together.

A slightly twisted thread is the best material to use for this, for instance, D.M.C Pearl cotton (Coton perlé), or D.M.C Embroidery cotton (Coton à broder), in Cardinal red 304. (*)

Hem edged with button-hole scallops (fig. 1022). — Any one who can do button-holing will find no difficulty in making these scallops. They should be worked from right to left, as explained in the chapter on "Needle-made Laces". They may be executed in several colours, every three, that is, in a different one.

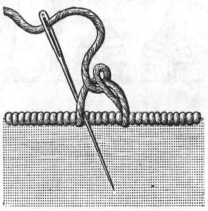

Fig. 1018. Hem with picots.
Formation of the little top picot.

Moderately twisted threads, such as D.M.C Embroidery cotton (Coton à broder), D.M.C Pearl cotton (Coton perlé) or D.M.C Alsatia are the best materials to use for these scallops.

Hem with picots in crochet and point stitch (fig. 1023). Before laying the hem make a row of detached cross stitches,

(*) This number indicates a colour on the colour cards of the articles stamped with the D.M.C trade mark, These cards can be consulted at all the mercers' and needlework shops.

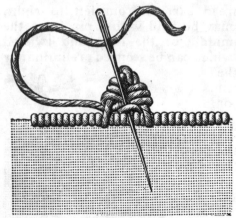

Fig. 1019. Hem with picots.
How to make the cross stitch to fill the picot.

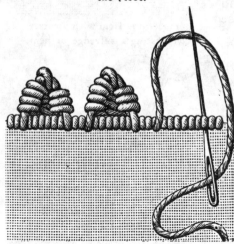

Fig. 1020. Hem with picots.
Two picots completed and passage of the needle to the next picot.

Fig. 1021. Hem with picots.
Series of picots finished. Natural size.
Materials: D.M.C Pearl cotton No. 5, in Cardinal red 304.

then sew down the hem with overcasting stitches.

The crochet picots along the edge are made as follows: 1 plain stitch on the edge of the hem, 5 chain, 1 bar on the first chain stitch, repeat from the beginning.

For the cross stitches and the crochetwork use D.M.C Pearl cotton (Coton perlé) No. 5, in Garnet red 326.

Hem with crochet picots and a row of openwork (fig. 1024). — The row of openwork is done with D.M.C Pearl cotton (Cotton perlé) No. 8, in Saffron yellow 727, the little reversed bars are done in darning stitches, fig. 748.

The crochet picots worked with the same thread, require 1 bar on the edge of the hem, 3 chain stitches and 3 bars at the top of the bar beneath, 1 bar on the hem and so on.

Openwork hem ornamented with a small crochet edging (fig. 1025). After making a hem with a single row of openwork, according to the directions given for figures 730 and 731, make the little crochet edging in four rows.

1st row — 1 plain stitch on the edge, 2 chain, 1 plain on the edge, 2 chain and so on.

2nd row — 1 plain with 3 chain on the 2 chain of the row beneath,

3d row — 1 plain with 4 chain on the 3 chain of the row beneath.

4th row — 1 plain on the 4 chain of the row beneath with 1 chain, 1 picot and 1 chain between.

According to the stuff use either white or écru D.M.C Alsatian thread (Fil d'Alsace) Nos. 3o to 5o, or D.M.C Flax lace thread Nos. 20 to 40.

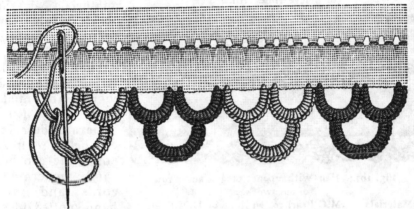

Fig. 1022. Hem edged with button-hole scallops.

Materials: D.M.C Embroidery cotton, D.M.C Pearl cotton, or D.M.C Alsatia, in Indigo blue 322 and Mandarin yellow 742. (*)

The mounting of embroideries. — Mounting a piece of embroidery either on wood or metal is a difficult thing to do, and requires skill and practice, we therefore advise our readers to employ an upholsterer for the purpose or have it done in a shop because a fine piece of work may be entirely spoilt by bad mounting.

The lining of needlework. — If a plain stuff lining is all that is required it presents little difficulty and your workers can do it for themselves. The lining should be soft and supple, of the same colour as the stuff on which the embroidery is done, or one that goes well with it. It must be cut straight to the thread, turned in at the edges, carefully laid on and

(*) See at the end of the last chapter the tables of the sizes and colours of the cotton, flax and silk articles, mark D.M.C.

tacked down. The two layers of stuff are then hemmed together all round, and the hem finally hidden by a thick cord or gimp which forms the outside finish.

Fig. 1023. Hem with picots in crochet and point stitch.
Materials: D.M.C Pearl cotton No. 5, in Garnet red 326 or Mauve violet 316. (*)

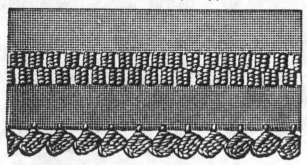

Fig. 1024. Hem with crochet picots and a row of openwork.
Materials: D.M.C Pearl cotton No. 8 or D.M.C Floss flax or flourishing thread No. 8, in Saffron yellow 727 or Locust-bean brown 357. (*)

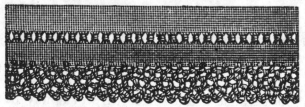

Fig. 1025. Openwork hem ornamented with a small crochet edging.
Materials: D.M.C Alsatian thread Nos. 30 to 50, or D.M.C Flax lace thread Nos. 20 to 40, in white or écru. (*)

Cords. — It is useful to know how to make cords of all kinds in case of need; as one can then make them of the same materials as the work itself and secure perfect uniformity of colour.

The easiest cords to make are those which are made with the little apparatus described below; next come the crochet and macramé cords and the hand-knotted ones.

Apparatus for making cords. To be recommended to all workers. It consists of one big wheel mounted on a little pillar with a stand, which by means of a cord sets in motion three little wheels mounted on the same stand.

The big wheel has a handle to it and the way to mount the cord on the little wheels is indicated upon it. For the apparatus to work regularly the cord round the wheels must be stretched very tight.

(*) See at the end of the last chapter the tables of the sizes and colours of the cotton, flax and silk articles, mark D.M.C.

On each little wheel there is a metal hook which serves to hold the threads of which the cord is to be made.

To make a cord without any one to help you a little board with metal hooks is necessary which you screw to the table and which holds the threads at the other end.

Figure 1026 shews how to set the wheel in motion once the threads are stretched.

How to make the cord (fig. 1026). — The simplest cord you can made with this apparatus consists of two threads. You make a loop at one end of each thread and fix it on to the little wheels and fasten the opposite ends to the hooks in

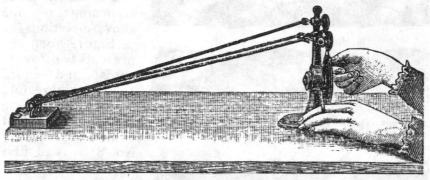

Fig. 1026. How to make the cords.

the little board screwed to the table, then pull the apparatus back till the threads are tightly stretched. Then you turn the handle from left to right or from right to left according to the twist of the thread used, until the two threads begin to twist slightly. Then unhook one thread from the little wheel and hook it on to the one on which the second thread is fastened, and turn the handle the reverse way until the cord is finished.

Cords consisting of three threads are made the same way using the three little wheels.

With two such instruments you can make cords of four, five and six threads and thicker cords can be made by hooking several threads together on to each little wheel.

Cords made of cotton threads (figs. 1027 and 1028). — For heavy embroideries intended for furniture and cushions, thick cords made of cotton threads are most suitable, of these we give a series in figures 1027 and 1028.

Figure 1027 represents three cords made of two threads

of D.M.C Pearl cotton (Cotton perlé) No. 1. These are twisted first from left to right, then from right to left.

For the fine cord the threads are taken single, for the next size, double, and for the thickest quadruple.

The cords in figure 1028 are made in the same way with three threads of 3 different shades.

Cords made of cotton or flax and of metal threads

(figs. 1029, 1030, 1031). — Some kinds of coloured embroideries require fine cords made of brilliant or metal threads which can be easily made according to the above directions.

Fig. 1027. Cords in two-stranded cotton threads.
Materials: D.M.C Pearl cotton No. 1, in Old gold 680 and Raspberry red 3685.

Figure 1029 represents two double cords, and figure 1030 two threefold cords made of one and two threads of D.M.C Pearl cotton No. 8, twisted first from left to right, and figure 1031 two cords made of a single and of a double thread of gold and silver, twisted first from right to left.

Fig. 1028. Cords in three-stranded cotton threads.
Materials: D.M.C Pearl cotton No. 1,
in Yellow green 733, Dawn red 360 and Indigo
blue 312.

Hand-knotted cord

(figs. 1032, 1033, 1034, 1035, 1036). — Here the fingers play the part of a crochet needle.

The cord consists of a chain of loops tightly drawn and is perfectly simple and easy to make,

Join two ends of thread together; take one of the ends in the left hand, fig. 1032, and make a loop with it, passing it over the right hand, raising the forefinger and stretching out the thread with the left hand.

Then holding the outstretched thread with the left hand,

put your left forefinger into the loop which is on the right forefinger and draw the thread coming from the left hand and behind the loop back towards you, fig. 1033.

At the moment when the left forefinger comes back with the new loop, let the one on the right forefinger slip, and the end with the knots passes between the thumb and the third finger of the left hand whilst the right hand tightens the knot, fig, 1034.

In figure 1035 representing the fourth position of the hands, you are shewn how the forefinger of the right hand lifts up the thread and draws it through the loop on the left hand; the end will therefore also at once pass into the right hand and the left will tighten the knot.

By thus alternately tightening the right knot and then the left this pretty cord is easily made.

Figure 1036 shews the same on a rather larger scale. It can also be made in two colours.

Macramé cord (fig. 1037). — This is made with D.M.C Knotting cotton (Fil

Fig. 1029. Cords in two-stranded cotton or flax threads. Materials: D.M.C Pearl cotton No. 8 or D.M.C Floss flax No. 16.

Fig. 1030. Cords in three-stranded cotton or flax threads. Materials: D.M.C Pearl cotton No. 8 or D.M C Floss flax No. 16.

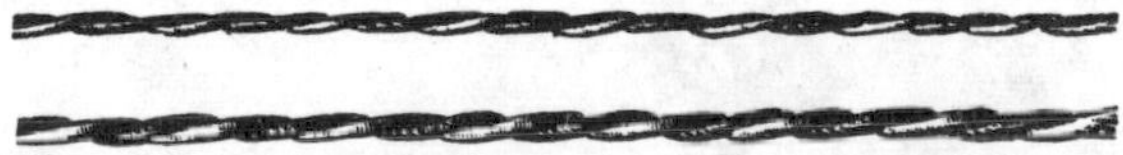

Fig. 1031. Cords in two-stranded metal threads. Materials: D.M.C Gold and silver embroidery threads.

à pointer) No. 15, the length of the threads depends on the length of braid required; they should any way be wound on macramé shuttles, see fig. 613.

Leave ends 4 inches long at the top, which are afterwards tied together in a knot and fastened to the macramé cushion. Knot three light threads from left to right on to the cord *a,* three dark ones on to the cord *b* and the same on to the cord *a* also, to the right of the light knots. Take a third cord *c,* add on three light and three dark threads, and knot these new threads also over the *b* and *a* cords.

Close the ring by knotting these twelve threads over cord *c,* and continue the work by knotting them over the *b* and *a* cords and so on.

The result is a cord which is hollow inside with stripes running round from right to left.

Crochet cord (fig. 1038 and 1039). — This has the advantage of being extremely simple and easy to make. Figure

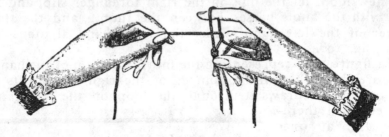

Fig. 1032. Hand-knotted cord. First position of the hands.

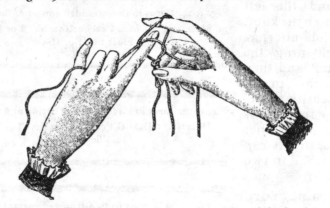

Fig. 1033. Hand-knotted cord. Second position of the hands.

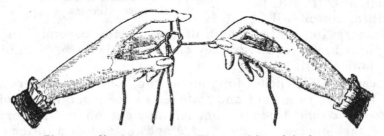

Fig. 1034. Hand-knotted cord. Third position of the hands.

1039 gives a clear explanation rendering further directions almost unnecessary.

Begin with 4 chain, close the ring and make 1 single in each chain stitch and one in each single, placing them on the back loops of the stitches beneath.

Contrary to ordinary crochet this is done not from the outside to the inside but the reverse.

Braids. — Embroideries intended for furniture, screens, &c., require only a very simple trimming.

Coarse cords or better still flat braids are best for this purpose. These braids ought to be neither too elaborate as to pattern nor too many coloured; simple patterns and quiet colours are preferable.

Braids may be classed under five headings, as follows:

1º Embroidered braids;
2º Crochet braids;
3º Tatted braids;
4º Macramé braids;
5º Lace braids.

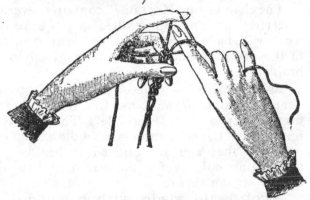

Fig. 1035. Hand-knotted cord.
Fourth position of the hands.

Fig. 1036.
Hand-knotted cord.

Materials:
D.M.C Knotting cotton Nos. 10 to 30, D.M.C Flax thread for knitting Nos. 4 to 20, or D.M.C Pearl cotton Nos. 1, 3, 5 or 8. (*)

Embroidered braids. — Woven linen or canvas braids ornamented with a little cross stitch or stroke stitch work of the colour of the principal embroidery are best for trimming articles liable to be washed. Such braids are very strong and suitable for objects in constant use. The chapter on "Linen Embroidery" contains pretty patterns for such braids.

Crochet braids. — These composed of chain and single stitches, bars in the form of

(*) See at the end of the last chapter the tables of the sizes and colours of the cotton, flax and silk articles, mark D.M.C.

rings and scallops on a close braid are a good imitation of gimp and braiding. They should be made of strongly twisted thread, of medium size. (See also the fringe footings, figs. 1047. 1049 and 1050, as well as the Bosnian crochet braids, p. 316).

Tatted braids. — These though very delicate are strong. They can be embellished by wheels or lace stitches in gold or silver thread. The simplest pattern, chains of little rings, for instance, make a pretty and effective little braid which can be further varied in different ways.

Macramé braids. — Macramé lends itself particularly well to the making of braids and admits of turning corners without any difficulty.

The chapter on "Macramé" contains several patterns and any one skilled in the kind of work will have no difficulty in turning most of the grounds and fringes there given into braids.

Lace braids. — These can be made with 4 and 6 pairs of bobbins; the best pattern for the purpose is "Eternelle". The chapter on "Pillow Laces" contains a whole series of grounds that can be utilised as braids by taking one subject for the width and using a very strong thread.

Fig. 1037.
Macramé cord.

Picot braid made with bobbins (fig. 1040). — For edging fine delicate embroideries on silk or velvet use the little braid figure 1040, made with D.M.C Embroidery gold thread (Or fin à broder) No. 20.

It consists of a plait with picots made alternately right and left after each passing.

How to make joins in braids. — These have to be as

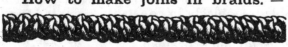

invisible as possible. If the pattern contain big figures the joins should be made

Fig. 1038. Crochet cord.

at the end of a figure so that there may be no interruption in the pattern.

Turning corners. — Following the angle required, the braid must be folded and sewn with back-stitches in a diagonal line pressed down on the right side with the thimble and the fold on the wrong side cut off.

Fringes. — Fringe is always the most natural trimming for stuff articles of all kinds and there are many ways of making it.

The simplest fringes are those produced by unravelling the horizontal threads of the stuff after overcasting the edge. Such stuff fringes can be made more interesting by introducing coloured threads or tassels between, or knotting the disengaged threads together in patterns. Here we may remind our readers of the knotted fringes (see the chapter on "Macramé"), the fringes with crochet footings, and those made with bobbins.

We give a series of different fringes, beginning with the simplest, the one above referred to, made by unravelling the stuff itself.

Small fringe differently ornamented (figs. 1041, 1042, 1043, 1044). — Figure 1041 represents a narrow fringe formed solely by the ravellings of the stuff. After overcasting the edge draw out the horizontal threads. Figure 1042 represents the same fringe with the addition of a red thread between each cluster. These red

Fig. 1039.
Making the crochet cord.

Fig. 1040. Picot braid made with bobbins.

threads are knotted alternately over one and two groups of the threads of the stuff.

Figure 1043 represents a fringe knotted in two rows. The knots are all made with two clusters of threads. In the second row you divide the bunches of thread that hang from the knots of the first row, take half a bunch from the right and half from the left and knot them together so that the knots come between those of the row above.

Lastly figure 1044 represents a fringe with tassels. After overcasting the edge, as shewn in figure 1041, fasten on little tassels eight threads of the stuff or four clusters apart. Then take a thick mesh of loose thread, fasten it to the edge by a knot made with an auxiliary thread, fold back the two parts of the mesh and draw them together $\frac{3}{8}$ of an inch below the edge with a different coloured thread.

It is needless to remark that in process of working the un-ravelled threads do not all remain as long as they were at first; these inequalities must be rectified as directed in the chapter on "Macramé", as they spoil the appearance of the fringe.

Abanian fringe (fig. 1045). — The edge of the linen is here strengthened by a row of chain stitches alike on both

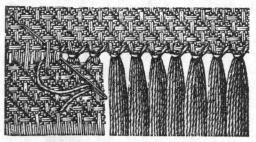

Fig. 1041. Little fringe made with the unravelled threads of the stuff.

sides, which are at once ornamental and useful.

Before making these chain stitches you must of course first unravel the necessary depth of the stuff for the fringe, in this case about 6 inches.

Then having made the chain stitches along the edge to prevent its un-ravelling further, twist the freed threads together two and two into little cords, and knot tassels on to the ends, fig. 1045. These tassels should be made of D.M.C Special stranded cotton (Mouliné spécial) or D.M.C Floss flax (Lin floche); both materials make very handsome full tassels.

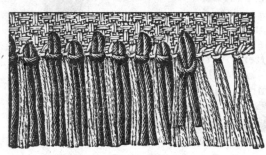

Fig. 1042.
Little fringe with coloured threads.

Tasseled fringe on net canvas (fig. 1046). — This is a pretty variety of fringe, made on net canvas with tassels hung on to the overcast bars which form the conclusion to the stroke stitch pattern of the border. Begin by drawing out the necessary number of woof threads for the depth of the fringe, leaving if the length of your stuff permit, a full edge about an inch deep below the drawn out threads : this greatly facilitates the subsequent work of stretching and overcasting the warp threads. Once the stuff is prepared overcast three double threads of the warp very closely to a depth of $\frac{3}{4}$ of an inch (1st detail on the left). This done pass to the next three double threads and knot them firmly to the first cluster before overcasting it in its turn to the same depth as the first.

The 2nd detail of figure 1046 shews 3 bars finished and the 4th begun, as well as the transverse bars that start from the latter.

In the 3d detail the 4 bars are connected by a few overcasting stitches which form a collecting knot beneath which, with two double threads, you make a double knot through which you slip a bunch of threads which you fold over and secure by a few twists of threads. This tassel should be cut rather short (detail 4 on the right).

Fig. 1043.
Little knotted fringe in two rows.

For the little tassels and the stroke stitch embroidery use D.M.C Special stranded cotton (Mouliné spécial), for the overcast bars D.M.C Pearl cotton (Coton perlé).

Formation of the corners. — When the threads of the stuff round a square piece of work are drawn out empty spaces result in the corners ; these spaces should be filled up by one or more clusters

Fig. 1044.
Little fringe with tassels.

of the drawn out threads, then the corners are ornamented like the fringe and gently rounded off.

Fringe with two rows of tassels and crochet footing (figs. 1047 and 1048). — D.M.C Pearl cotton (Coton perlé)

No. 3, used double serves as braid for the footing of this fringe which is crocheted in D.M.C Pearl cotton (Coton perlé) No. 5, in plain stitches. The double threads form short and long loops, to which the little tassels, made of D.M.C Special stranded cotton (Mouliné spécial) No. 25, are afterwards fastened.

Figure 1048 explains the work, which is done from right to left. On the double thread of D.M.C Pearl cotton (Coton perlé) No. 3, make first 8 plain stitches = turn the work = 3 plain on the first 3 plain (insert the needle always into the two little loops of the underneath stitches and work over

Fig. 1045. Albanian fringe.
Materials: D.M.C Special stranded cotton or D.M.C Floss flax, in Turkish red 321 Morocco red 3328 or Garnet red 3367.

the double thread), 5 plain over the double thread = * turn the work = 3 plain on the 3 stitches beneath, make a short loop with the double thread over a slip of cardboard 1 ½ inch wide, 1 chain = turn the work = 3 plain on the 3 stitches beneath, 5 plain over the double thread = turn the work = 3 plain on the 3 plain, 5 plain over the double thread = turn the work = 3 plain on the 3 plain, 5 plain over the double thread = turn the work = 3 plain on the 3 plain, make a long loop with the double thread over a slip of cardboard 2 ½ inches wide, 1 chain = turn the work = 3 plain on the 3 plain, 5 plain over the double thread = turn the work = 3 plain on the 3 plain, 5 plain over the double thread = turn the work = 3 plain on the 3 plain, 5 plain over the double thread; repeat from * and go on making one short and one long loop on side of the close braid.

Each of these loops consists of 2 double threads: these threads are to be twisted separately from right to left, then the two ends are joined and they are turned from left to right thus forming a cord (see also the explanatory engraving, fig. 1048). To the ends of this cord knot on with an auxiliary

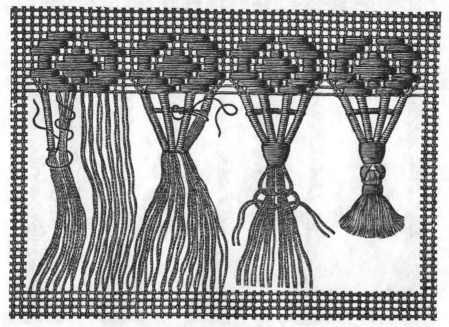

Fig. 1046. Fringe with tassels on net canvas.
Materials: D.M.C Special stranded cotton and D.M.C Pearl cotton.

thread by the middle a bunch of about 32 threads of D.M.C Special stranded cotton (Mouliné spécial) (*) 2 ¾ inches long; fold back the two ends and finish the little tassels by tying them round at the top.

Fringe with a row of tassels and crochet footing (fig. 1049). This is made in two colours. As padding for the footing use D.M.C Pearl cotton (Coton perlé) No. 3, taken

---

(*) See at the end of the last chapter the tables of the sizes and colours of the cotton, flax and silk articles, mark D.M.C. — The French names, in brackets, are those stamped on the labels of the D.M.C articles.

double, for the crochet D.M.C Pearl cotton (Coton perlé) No. 5, in Moss green 470; the tassels and the ornamental stitches require a loose material, D.M.C Special stranded cotton (Mouliné spécial) No. 14, in Garnet red 3367.

The close braid is worked in rows to and fro, of 6 plain stitches and 1 chain to turn; the stitches are set in the 2 loops of the stitches underneath.

Fig. 1047. Fringe with two rows of tassels and crochet footing.

Materials: D.M.C Pearl cotton Nos. 3 and 5 and D.M.C Special stranded cotton No. 25, in Locust bean brown 759, Bronze yellow 768 or Greenish grey 599.

On one side of this braid make — always over a slip of cardboard — loops ⅝ of an inch long, on the other side loops three times that length.

The little loops are secured at the top by a row of chain stitches done in crochet, in D.M.C Pearl cotton (Coton perlé) No. 5, Garnet red 3367. Taking two double loops on the hook, join them by 1 plain stitch, 4 chain, 1 plain on the next 2 loops, 4 chain, and so on. The long double loops at the bottom are likewise separated two by two, and have tassels of 25 to 30 red threads knotted with green thread fastened to them.

The braid formed of plain crochet is lastly ornamented with 4 rows of running stitches in inverted order, worked in red.

Fringe with balls and crochet footing (fig. 1050). — For the padding of this fringe take three threads of D.M.C Pearl cotton (Coton perlé) (*) No. 3, in Saffran yellow 725. The

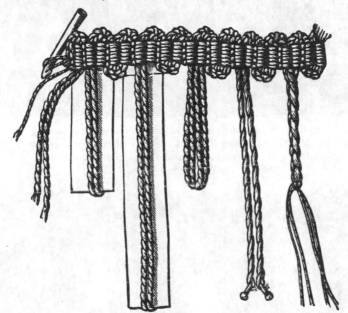

Fig. 1048. Detail of figure 1047.

braid takes seven rows of plain stitches, made with D.M.C Pearl cotton (Coton perlé) No. 5, in Locust-bean brown 303, and worked to and fro with 1 chain stitch for returning. The stitches are set in the two loops of the stitches beneath.

At the top the little triple loops formed by the yellow padding threads measure ⅜ of an inch, the pendent loops, of which three are also made the same length, measure 1 ¼ of an inch and 1 ¾ of an inch. The loops of the same length are

(*) See at the end of the last chapter the tables of the sizes and colours of the cotton, flax and silk articles, mark D.M.C. — The French names, in brackets, are those stamped on the labels of the D.M.C articles.

joined together in threes at the bottom by a ball made of
D.M.C Special stranded cotton (Mouliné spécial) No. 25, in
Locust-bean brown 3o3. (See fig. 1o69).

The little loops at the top are left empty.

Fig. 1049. Fringe with a row of tassels and crochet footing.
Materials: D.M.C Pearl cotton Nos. 3 and 5, in Moss green 470, and D.M.C
Special stranded cotton No. 14 and D.M.C Pearl cotton No. 5,
in Garnet red 3367.

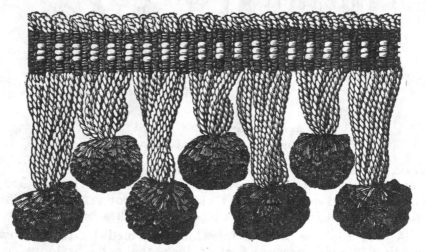

Fig. 1050. Fringe with balls and crochet footing.
Materials: D.M.C Pearl cotton No. 5 and D.M.C Special stranded cotton No. 25,
in Locust-bean brown 303, and D.M.C Pearl cotton No. 3,
in Saffron yellow 725.

The crochet braid is ornamented with three rows of running
stitches one above the other.

Knotted ball fringe (figs. 1051, 1052, 1053, 1054, 1055). —
Quite a special kind of knotted fringe as regards execution
and effect is represented in figure 1051.

The details of the pattern consist of knotted threads cut
and then threaded like beads to form the different parts.

The knots are of two kinds, little double and big double
ones. The former are plain knots made with one thread, as
shewn in figure 1052; these cut two by two count as little
double knots; the length of thread between the knots must
not be more than that taken up by one knot.

The big double knots begin with a plain knot, to which
three more plain ones are added, interlaced by a 4th so as
to form a single big knot, see fig. 1053, you then finish with

Fig. 1051. Knotted ball ringe.
Materials : D.M.C Embroidery cotton No. 3 or D.M.C Pearl cotton No. 1,
in Turkish red 321 and Black fast dye 310, or in Azure blue 3325
and Locust-bean brown 357. (*)

one plain knot. Quite close to this you make a second double
knot, then cut the thread and the big double knot is completed.

The footing of the fringe consists of a braid made of flat
knots, knotted over 4 padding threads and it is on to this
braid that the knotted figures above described are attached.
It is best to begin with the big single tassel first. After making
enough big and little double knots with red and black cotton,
take red cotton to make a small single knot, thread a coarse

_____

(*) See at the end of the last chapter the tables of the sizes and colours of
the cotton, flax and silk articles, mark D.M.C.

tapestry needle with it and string on 14 little double knots in black cotton and 8 big double ones in red cotton; then press them all tightly together towards the bottom and finish the whole with a small single knot. Leaving a space of ⅜ of an inch between, make another small single knot, string on 6 little double knots in red cotton, press them together and

Fig. 1052.   Fig. 1053.
Making the little double knots.   Making the big double knots.

end up with a small single knot, then fasten the finished tassel on to the braid, again leaving ⅜ of an inch of cotton free. The next tassel is 16 double knots distant in the braid.

The little intermediate figures with two tassels are also in ▾red cotton. After making a single big knot, string on 2 big

Fig. 1054. Making the big tassel.

double knots in red cotton and 5 small double ones in black, press them together and finish up with a single small knot.

Leaving an interval of ⅜ of an inch between, make 2 small single knots quite close together and a third ⅜ of an inch distant. Then string on 5 little double knots in black cotton

Fig. 1055. Making the little double pendants.

and 2 big double ones in red, press the knots together and finish the ball by one big single knot, and cut the thread. For fastening this ball to the braid take red cotton again, make a small single knot and string on 5 little double knots in red, then pass the cotton between the 2 little knots close together in the middle of the little tasse and end with a small single knot.

Lastly fasten this double tassel on to the braid, exactly

in the middle between the two big tassels, leaving ⅜ of an inch of cotton free above it.

Between these figures come the little balls consisting of 8 small double knots in black, which must be fastened to the braid.

Fig. 1056. Fringe and footing made on a lace pillow.

Materials — For the fringe : D.M.C Special stranded cotton No. 25, in Mignonette green 750; for the bobbin braid : D.M.C Pearl cotton No. 5, in Old gold 729 and Raspberry red 3687. (*)

Slightly twisted materials, such as D.M.C Pearl cotton (Coton perlé) Nos. 1 and 3 and D.M.C Embroidery cotton (Coton à broder) No. 3, are the best for this fringe.

Fringe and footing made on a lace pillow (figs. 1056 and 1057). — Hang on to the pattern, fig. 1057, at *a,* 3 fleecy threads of a green shade and at *b,* 3 pairs of bobbins, each pair containing a yellow and a pink thread.

* Twist the 1st pair from right to left, slip the green threads through = twist the 2nd pair from right to left, slip the green threads through = twist the 3d pair from right to left, slip the green threads, stick a pin in at point 1 = twist the 3d pair from right to left, slip the green threads = twist the 2nd pair from right to left, slip the green threads = twist the 1st pair from right to left, slip the green threads, stick a pin in at point 2 ** = repeat twice from * to ** = *** twist the 1st pair from right to left, slip the green threads = twist the 2nd pair from right to left, slip the green threads = twist the 3d pair from right to left, slip the green threads, stick a pin in at point 3

Fig. 1057.

Pattern for the bobbin fringe figure 1056.

(*) See at the end of the last chapter the tables of the sizes and colours of the cotton, flax and silk articles, mark D.M.C.

= twist the 3d pair from right to left, slip the green threads
= twist the 2nd pair from right to left, slip the green threads
= twist the 1st pair from right to left, slip the green threads,

stick a pin in at point 4 **** = repeat twice from *** to **** and begin again from the beginning.

Fig. 1058. Scalloped fringe made on a lace pillow.

Materials — For the fringe: D.M.C Special stranded cotton No. 25, in Saffron yellow 726 and Golden green 581;
For the bobbin braid: D.M.C Pearl cotton No. 5, in Saffron yellow 726 and Scabious violet 394.

Scalloped fringe made on a lace pillow (figs. 1058 and 1059). — Hang on to the pattern figure 1059, at *a*, 2 fleecy yellow threads and at *b*, 2 pairs of bobbins (one filled with yellow thread, the other with violet).

Fig. 1059.
Pattern for the fringe figure 1058.

Twist the 1st pair from left to right, slip the 2 yellow threads = twist the 2nd pair from right to left, slip the 2 yellow threads, stick a pin in at point 1 = twist the 2nd pair from right to left, slip the 2 yellow threads, = twist the 1st pair from left to right, slip the 2 yellow threads, stick a pin in at point 2 ** = repeat 6 times from * to ** = fasten on two green fleecy threads at point *c* = twist the 1st pair from left to right, slip the 2 yellow and the 2 green threads = twist the 2nd pair from right to left, slip the 2 yellow and the 2 green threads, stick a pin in at point 3 = twist the 2nd pair from right to left, slip the 2 yellow and the 2 green threads = twist the 1st pair from left to right, slip the 2 yellow and the 2 green threads, stick a pin in at point 2 and fasten the 2 yellow threads on one side = repeat 6 times from * to ** = add the yellow thread = twist the 1st pair from left to right, slip the 2 green and the 2 yellow threads = twist the 2nd pair from right to left, slip the 2 green threads and the 2 yellow, stick a pin in at point 3 = twist the 2nd pair from right to left, slip the 2 green threads and the 2 yellow

= twist the 1st pair from left to right, slip the 2 green threads and the 2 yellow, stick a pin in at point 2 = put the green threads aside and continue the fringe with the yellow ones.

When all the fringe is made cut the connecting threads quite close to the scallops.

Double rowed scalloped fringe made on a pillow (figs. 1060 and 1061). — Hang on a soft dark yellow thread at point *a* of the pattern figure 1061, two soft red threads at point *b* and 2 pairs of bobbins with light yellow cotton at point *c*.

* Twist the 1st pair from left to right, slip the yellow thread and the red ones = twist the 2nd pair from left to right, slip the yellow thread and the red ones stick a pin in at point 1 = twist the 2nd pair from left to right, slip the yellow and the red threads = twist the 1st pair from left to right, slip the yellow and red threads, stick

Pig 1060. Double rowed scalloped fringe made on a pillow.
Materials — For the fringe : D.M.C Special stranded cotton No. 14, in Old gold 679 and Cardinal red 347 ;
For the bobbin braid: D.M.C Pearl cotton No. 5, in Old gold 729. (*)

a pin in at point 2 to hold the yellow thread and a pin at point 3 to hold the red threads ; repeat 8 times from * and continue the work in the same way.

When the fringe is taken off the lace pillow, cut the long yellow loops.

Fringe in two horizontal rows made on a pillow (figs. 1062 and 1063). — Hang on to the pattern figure 1063, at point *a*, 4 soft threads of light violet and 6 pairs of shuttles at point *b* (the 1st, 2nd, 5th and 6th pair with light yellow on them, the 3d and 4th with dark yellow).

Twist the 1st pair from right to left, slip the violet threads = twist the 2nd pair from right to left, slip the violet threads

---

(*) See at the end of the last chapter the tables of the sizes and colours of the cotton, flax and silk articles, mark D.M.C.

= twist the 3ᵈ pair from right to left, slip the violet threads =
twist the 4ᵗʰ pair from left to right, slip the violet threads =
twist the 5ᵗʰ pair from left to right, slip the violet threads =

Fig. 1061.
Pattern for the fringe,
figure 1060.

twist the 6ᵗʰ pair from left to right, slip the violet threads, stick a pin in at point 1 = twist the 6ᵗʰ pair from left to right, slip the violet threads = twist the 5ᵗʰ pair from left to right, slip the violet threads = twist the 4ᵗʰ pair from left to right, slip the violet threads = twist the 3ᵈ pair from right to left, slip the violet threads = twist the 2ⁿᵈ pair from right to left, slip the violet threads = twist the 1ˢᵗ pair from right to left, slip the violet threads, stick a pin in at point 2 to hold the 2 first violet threads and stick a pin in as well at point 3 to hold the 2 last violet threads.

Repeat from the beginning.

Balls for gimp trimmings (figs. 1064, 1065, 1066, 1067, 1068, 1069). — Begin by preparing a certain number of rounds of cardboard with holes in the middle, fig. 1064, put two together and cover them with very close stitches, fig. 1065, made in D.M.C Special stranded cotton (Mouliné spécial) or D.M.C Floss flax (Lin floche).

When the whole circumference of the card is covered, slip the scissors in between the two rounds and cut all the threads at the outside edge, fig. 1066; draw a thread through between the two rounds, wind it several times very tightly round the threads, fig. 1067, fasten it off with a knot and leave long enough ends to tie the ball on with later on; this done you make a snip in the cards, fig. 1068, pull them out and the ball is finished, as seen in figure 1069.

Tassels. — The corners of cushions and pieces of work of different kinds are often ornamented with tassels. These, whether plain or fancy, should harmonise with the article they are intended for. Little tassels are made without any accessories, whilst the big ones are made on a wooden shape.

The following are a few specimens of more or less handsome ones made in different ways.

Plain tassel (figs. 1070, 1071, 1072, 1073). — To make the plain tassel represented in figure 1073, a wooden shape

Fig. 1062.. Fringe in two horizontal rows made on a pillow.
Materials — For the fringe: D.M.C Special stranded cotton No. 14, in Old violet 3545;
For the bobbin braid: D.M.C Pearl cotton No. 5, in Mandarin yellow 746 and 741. (*)

is used on which bunches of soft cotton are knotted. This wooden shape consists of a ball or disc, joined together by a little round bar, the whole perforated. At the bottom end of the bar a big mesh of stranded cotton is fastened to serve as body to the tassel.

The wooden ball is covered with meshes of thread the two ends of which hang down round the bar; they are connected by plain crochet stitches, fig. 1071, and fastened at the top of the ball. (See fig. 1072.) After arranging these threads equally all round, knot them between the ball and the disc, cut them all the same length at the bottom and the tassel is finished.

So as to be better able to fasten

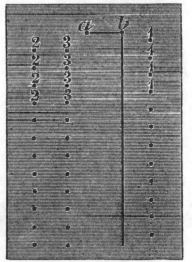

Fig. 1063.
Pattern for the fringe, figure 1062.

(*) See at the end of the last chapter the tables of the sizes and colours of the cotton, flax and silk articles, mark D.M.C.

on the tassel to the work, a little cord or braid should be attached to the head of the ball.

The materials to be used are, for the meshes, a loose thread,

Fig. 1064.
Ball for gimp trimming. Circular piece of cardboard.

Fig. 1065.
Ball for gimp trimming. Cardboard round partly overcast.

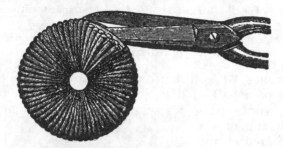

Fig. 1066.
Ball for gimp trimming. How to cut the threads.

Fig. 1067.
Ball or gimp trimming. Preparing the tie.

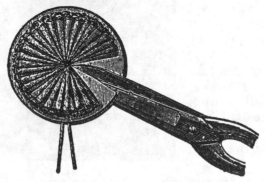

Fig. 1068.
Ball for gimp trimming. Cutting away the cardboard rounds.

Fig. 1069.
Ball completed with the tie.

D.M.C Special stranded cotton (Mouliné spécial), or D.M.C Floss flax (Lin floche) ; for the crochet work, the braid and the neck of the tassel, a moderately twisted thread D.M.C Pearl cotton (Coton perlé) or D.M.C Alsatia in a different colour.

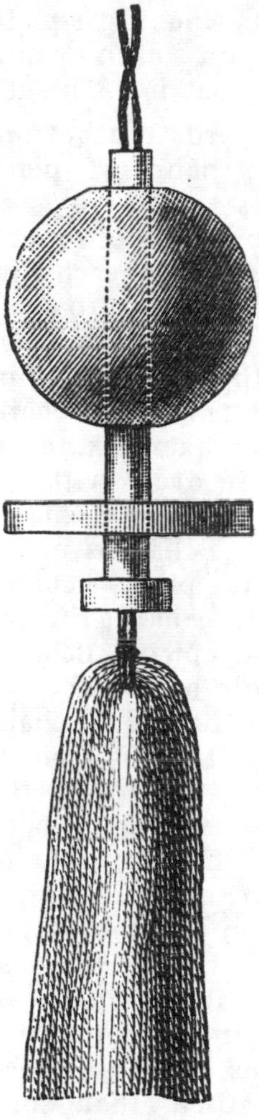

Tassel ornamented with crochet work (figs. 1074, 1075, 1076, 1077). — The body of the tassel is made of D.M.C Special stranded cotton (Mouliné spécial) No. 25, in light grey on a wooden mould.

The neck-tie, the trimming of the head of the tassel and the drops are in crochet in D.M.C Silver embroidery thread (Argent fin) No. 20.

The crochet work should be begun from the neck and consists of plain stitches. Begin with 9 chain, then : make 18 rows of plain stitches going and 17 returning, for which you only take the back loops of the stitches beneath. This neck-tie is fastened by little stitches round the meshes below the ball.

The net that covers the ball is formed by to rows of looped chain stitches which are explained by figures 1075, 1076 and 1077.

These looped chain stitches are made as follows : crochet one very loose chain stitch, then make 1 plain stitch over the single thread at the bottom of the chain stitch ;

Fig. 1070.
Wooden mould for tassel.

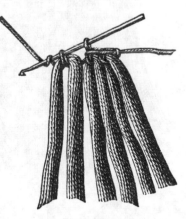

Fig. 1071.
How to unite the bunches of threads.

two of these looped chain stitches make one little scallop, which is joined in the first row to the band of chain stitches by 2 plain stitches, see fig. 1076.

Each row of 9 scallops begins with 2 plain stitches and ends with 1 single stitch on the 1st plain stitch. From the 2nd to the 10th row the 2 plain stitches are made on the looped chain stitches of the row beneath, see fig. 1077.

After the 10th row of scallops make one row of plain stitches, making 1 plain stitch on each chain stitch, that is 18 in all.

Fig. 1072. How to make the tie the tassel.

Towards the bottom of the hand of plain stitches add 3 rows of scallops made of looped chain stitches; each row should number 10 scallops. In the 3d row, after the plain stitch in the first looped chain stitch, make a kind of pendant drop with: 1 chain, 1 picot, 3 chain, 1 picot, 3 chain, 1 picot, 3 chain, 1 picot, 3 chain, 1 picot, 3 chain, 1 picot, 3 chain, 3 picots, 1 chain, 1 double bar on the 2nd of the 3 preceding chain stitches, 1 chain, 1 picot, 1 chain, 1 bar on the 2nd of the 3 next chain, then 5 times: 1 chain, 1 picot, 1 chain and 1 plain on the 2nd of the next 3 chain, the last time make 1 single on the plain stitch that terminates the 1st looped chain stitch, then continue the scallops.

Macramé tassel (figs. 1078 and 1079). — The ornaments of this tassel, worked in D.M.C Embroidery gold thread (Or fin à broder) are first the pendant drops, of which five short and five long are wanted for each tassel; they are connected at the top by a network of flat knots. Length of the threads of D.M.C Embroidery gold thread (Or fin a broder) (*) No. 20: 60 and 50 inches.

Begin with the round figure at the bottom, fasten a cord to carry the knots on to the cushion. then make a double bar, knotting on to it 5 threads more. Regard this double bar as the middle; add 2 similar bars more to it on the right and left, then take all the threads and with the 6 inside threads make 2 flat knots over 4 threads, then add the 6 outside threads and make 4 flat knots over the 10 threads, after the 2nd knot add a looped picot on the right and left, see detail fig. 1079. The threads are divided and tightened on each side by a flat knot, then knot two double bars with each half of the threads and finish off the bars with a flat knot.

This done, collect all the threads with flat knots. After the 2nd, 5th, 8th and 11th flat knot add a looped picot on each side.

Fig. 1073. Tassel completed.

Decrease the number of threads in working by cutting them off until there are only six left.

The five short pendants consist of the five-barred figure only a the bottom, with 10 flat knots above it broken by 2

(*) See at the end of the last chapter the tables of the sizes and colours of the cotton, flax and silk articles, mark D.M.C. — The French names, in brackets· are those stamped on the labels of the D.M.C articles.

picots. When all the pendants are made they are fastened on to the macramé cushion, a long and a short one alternately, $\frac{5}{8}$ of an inch apart, then you make the net cap of 10 rows of flat knots in inverted order over the tassel.

The tassel is made over a wooden mould, without a neck-tie, in D.M.C Special stranded cotton (Mouliné spécial) No. 25, in Old gold 729. After the 10th row make two more with the knots one above the other and fasten all the threads 10 the head of the tassel. Finally, with 4 threads, make a round cord of waved knots. fig. 562; the other threads are fastened off inside by invisible stitches.

Tassel with a double row of smaller tassels (figs. 1080 and 1081). — This tassel intended as a finish to articles trimmed with fringes figures 1047 or 1049, require a pear-shaped wooden mould which has to be covered with a crochet cap made of D.M.C Pearl cotton (Coton perlé) No. 5, in Blue grey 591.

Fig. 1074.
Tassel ornamented with crochet work.
Materials — For the body of the tassel : D.M.C Special stranded cotton No. 25, in Ash grey 762 ; for the crochet : D.M.C Silver embroidery thread No. 20.

Begin the crochet cap at the lower end of the mould by a ring of 5 chain stitches, on which make to crochet increasing or according to the shape of the

10 plain stitches, then continue decreasing the number of stitches the mould. The plain stitches are always to be placed in the

two top loops of the stitches of the preceding row As the tassel gets narrower towards the top, the crochet cap ends finally in a round cord, consisting of 6 plain stitches. The little tassels are fastened round the mould by a row of chain and single stitches. After fastening on the thread to the crochet cap at the right place for the upper row of tassels, make 12 chain stitches, then take a mesh of about 20 threads of D.M.C Special stranded cotton (Mouliné spécial) (*) No. 14, in Drab green 692, place it on the last 5 chain stitches, skip these 5 and crochet 6 single stitches on the 2nd and 7th of the 12 chain so that the Drab green mesh resting on the loop formed by the 5 chain, seems suspended to a cord, see fig. 1081. Finally make another chain and another plain stitch on the 2nd stitch of the cap and repeat the above all round the mould.

Fig. 1075. Making the looped chain stitches. Detail of tassel figure 1074.

Fig. 1076. Making the first row of looped chain stitches. Detail of tassel figure 1074.

The original from which the engraving is taken has twelve small tassels in the upper row and twenty-five in the lower. The loops of the lower are longer; they number 18 chain and 12 single stitches; the meshes are blue.

When these rows are

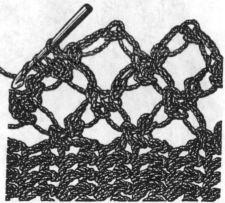

Fig. 1077. Making the next rows of looped chain stitches. Detail of tassel figure 1074.

(*) See at the end of the last chapter the tables of the sizes and colours of the cotton, flax and silk articles, mark D.M.C. — The French names, in brackets, are those stamped on the labels of the D.M.C articles.

finished, the meshes are folded back on both sides and knotted: the Drab green with blue and the blue with yellow cotton.

In conclusion make a big ball, fig. 1069, of D.M.C

Fig. 1079.
Making a pendant for
the tassel figure 1078.

Fig. 1078. Macramé tassel.
Material: D.M.C Gold thread for embroidery No. 20
and D.M.C Special stranded cotton No. 25,
in Old gold 729.

Special stranded cotton (Mouliné spécial) No. 14, in Drab green 692, and fasten it at the bottom of the mould to the little ring of chain stitches to make the two rows of little tassels stand out and give the whole a wider circumference at the bottom.

Lace trimmings. — Fine embroideries on linen or cambric

are mostly trimmed with lace sewn on plain or full according to its quality and character.

Embroidered laces and those made with braid are sewn on

Fig. 1080. Tassel with a double row of smaller tassels.
Materials: D.M.C Pearl cotton No. 5, in Blue grey 591 or Cardinal red 347, and D.M.C Special stranded cotton No. 14, in Drab green 692 and Blue grey 591 or Old gold 729 and Cardinal red 347. (*)

with overcasting stitches; crochet and knitted ones with a stitch set carefully in every loop.

(*) See at the end of the last chapter the tables of the sizes and colours of the cotton, flax and silk articles, mark D.M.C.

Formation of the corners. — In hand-knitted laces, the same as in those made with the needle, corners can be prepared in advance; otherwise sufficient fulness must

Fig. 1081. How to fasten on the tassels.

be allowed for and gathered in, to turn the corners so that the outside edge may not be drawn in but lie quite flat all round.

Head piece after Holbein.

Miscellaneous directions

Having exhausted all the subjects which formed the purpose of the present publication it remains for us to add a few words as to the manner of copying, arranging and transforming the designs and on the different processes it is useful to know: the right application of which is often essential to the complete success of a piece of work whatever that work may be.

Whilst it is a good thing to know how to adapt a design to the space at your disposal, it is often useful to know how to give a piece of lace that slight stiffness which marks the new, and, in the case of embroideries that require the help of paste to know the ingredients that should be used and how to prepare them.

Ordinary tracing. — To get a reproduction of a design lay a sheet of vegetable paper or tracing linen on the design. Fasten the two together at the four corners with fine pins that they may not get shifted if you are interrupted in your work. As it is difficult to fit them together again exactly, then go over all the lines of the pattern with a pencil or better still with a brush dipped in Indian ink or colour.

In the absence of proper tracing paper use a sheet of ordinary paper and trace the pattern against the window pane.

If you want to take the pattern of a piece of lace or embroidery fix it on a board and lay a sheet of glass or gelatine paper upon it and on this the sheet of vegetable paper or tracing linen, pasted down at the four corners. In this manner you can follow the outlines of the lace or embroidery without injuring it.

To take off a pattern by rubbing. — To take the pattern direct from a piece of embroidery lay it, right side up, on a board or table and cover it with a sheet of rather soft white paper. The paper must neither be too thick to take a clear impression of the marks made upon it, nor too thin as the rubbing might tear it. Fasten it firmly down upon the work with drawing pins or small nails and pass a special kind of wax backwards and forwards over the paper, or in default of the wax, a tin spoon or silver coin.

The outlines will not of course, in any case, be very clearly marked upon the paper and will have to be supplemented and strengthened afterwards by going over them with a pencil. The process is a very rapid one but has the disadvantage of flattening the relief of the embroidery or lace that is copied.

Transferring a pattern direct on to the stuff. — The simplest way of transferring a pattern on to a transparent stuff is the following: begin by going over all the lines of the drawing with Indian ink so as to make them thick and distinct and tacking the tracing with large stitches on to the back of the stuff. Then dilute some very dark powdered indigo with water in a glass with a small pinch of sugar and powdered gum arabic, and using this as ink, trace the pattern that shines through on to the stuff with a brush or a fine slightly split pen.

The tracing must be very slight for if some time elapse before the embroidery is done, the lines get so firmly fixed in the stuff that one washing will not obliterate them, moreover the tracing ink makes the work disagreeably sticky.

Copying by means of oiled paper. — Another rather expeditious way of reproducing patterns on to thin and especially on to smooth, glossy stuffs is by means of a special kind of tinted paper, called autographic paper, strongly impregnated with a coloured oily substance.

You place this paper, which is to be had at every stationery shop, between this pattern and the stuff, having previously fastened the latter, perfectly straight by the line of the thread, on to a board with drawing-pins. When you have likewise fitted the two papers exactly together, go over all the lines of the pattern carefully with a blunt pencil, or better still, the point of a bone crochet needle or the back of a folder, pressing lightly on your implement so as not to tear the paper pattern.

By the pressure exercised on the two sheets the oily substance of the coloured paper is discharged on to the stuff beneath, so that when it is removed all the traced lines are imprinted upon the stuff.

This blue tracing paper can however only be used for transferring patterns to washing materials as satin and all other silken textures are stained by it.

Pouncing patterns upon stuff. — The preceding ways of copying cannot be indiscriminately used; they are not applicable, in the case of thick stuffs such as cloth, velvet and plush, for these, pouncing is the only means available.

The pattern having been traced on vegetable paper is pricked through. You lay it on a piece of cloth, or felt and with a special needle, see fig. 967, prick out all the lines of the drawing. Several sheets of paper can be laid one upon another and pricked through at the same time if desired, but in this case the paper must be very thin or the patterns will not be clear.

In the case of a complicated pattern with very fine lines the needles you prick with must also be very fine. Every line must be carefully followed and the holes which should be clear and round not set too far apart.

When the pricking is done rub the wrong side of the vegetable paper over with emery paper so as to remove the edges formed round the little holes by the pricking.

Then fasten down paper and stuff firmly together with drawing pins to prevent their shifting during the process of pouncing, otherwise you are very likely to find double and confused lines on your stuff when you take off the paper, which are not so easy to get rid of afterwards.

When the pattern has thus been pricked out, dip the pouncing implement, resembling a little drumstick, stuffed and covered with cloth, into powdered charcoal for light stuff, or powdered chalk for dark, and rub it lightly over the whole surface of the pattern. By this rubbing the powder penetrates to the stuff through the prickings, tracing the pattern upon it.

In the case of a running pattern with recurring figures replace the paper at the point where the pouncing leaves off and where the lines should meet. This must be carefully done so that the joins cannot be detected.

When the pouncing is finished and the paper removed you proceed to draw or rather paint in the pattern with water-colour paints.

Four colours are all that are wanted for the purpose black, blue, white and yellow. On a smooth surface the painting may be done with a pen but a small sable-hair brush is preferable under all circumstances. The rougher and more hairy the stuff, the finer the brush should be in order that the colour may sink in well between the fibres.

Before beginning the painting gently blow away all the superfluous powder from the surface of the stuff.

Preparation of the stuffs and subdivision of the patterns. — We know many draughtsmen, artists in their line as long as they had to exercise their art on paper, but who have found themselves confronted by real difficulties when they had to transfer their compositions to stuff.

We shall therefore call our readers' attention, as far as possible, to certain precautions to be taken in tracing patterns, going back for that purpose to one of the initial operations, namely the pricking.

In the first place the paper to be pricked should be large enough for there to be a clear margin of from $1\frac{1}{2}$ to 2 inches outside the actual pattern so that the pouncing implement may never come in contact with the stuff covered by the paper.

In the case of a square and symmetrical pattern, fold it in four and prick the four parts all at once; if on the contrary the pattern consist of detached subjects, each subject or the entire pattern must be pricked separately.

In transferring patterns to stuff never divide out the ground first with chalk, lead pencil or charcoal as it is hardly possible entirely to obliterate such lines which often spoil the whole after effect of a piece of work.

Before beginning the tracing divide your stuff into four, then determine how wide a margin you wish to have outside the pattern, for it is quite an exceptional thing to carry the work right up to the edge.

Stuffs that will take a bend such as all linen and cotton textures can be folded in four like the paper, and the folds pinched and pressed down so that the lines may remain clear and distinct until the tracing is done. Having thus divided your stuff into quarters fold the corners over diagonally so that any motives to be worked in them may be correctly placed by the aid of the fold.

As regards how to divide the stuff into equal parts, most of our readers know how to make these cross lines on paper with pencil and ruler, but not perhaps on stuff. It suffices to fold the stuff over so that the outside thread of the warp or cut edge run parallel with the woof edge which marks the angle of the fold-over.

By the double folding the ground is divided into eight parts. To arrange for the outside border or margin is easy enough if, supposing it to be a linen napkin or table-cloth, it is to have an openwork border, as then the straight line produced by the drawing out of the threads will serve as a guide for tracing the pattern straight to the line of the stuff. It is often better however not to draw out the threads for an openwork border till the pattern has been traced. If you do not wish or are not able to draw out threads to mark the pattern and your stuff admits of the threads being counted follow the directions explained by figure 154.

Cloth, silken materials, velvet and plush cannot be marked in this way by folding, some will not take a bend and others that will would be injured thereby.

All these should be mounted in a frame before the tracing is done and the ground be then marked out in the following way: take a strong thread, make a knot at one end, stick a pin through it and tighten the knot round the pin: then with a pair of compasses divide one of the sides into two equal parts, plant the pin with the knot in the middle and repeat the same operation on the opposite side, and plant a second pin there by means of which you stretch the thread; carry other threads across horizontally and diagonally from corner to corner and your ground will be correctly marked out with no marks left upon it, when, after the pouncing is done you remove the threads and pins. Before finishing the pouncing of a pattern see that it is the right size for the purpose it is intended for.

Supposing you are tracing a border with a corner, you should measure the length it will occupy and then by a very light pouncing you can mark the points from which the pattern will have to be repeated. It may be that a gap will be left in the middle, which, if not too wide, can be got rid of without altering the pattern by pushing the whole a little further in and so lessening the distance between the corners.

Should the gap however be too wide for this, you will have to make a supplementary centre design to fill up the interval. The same thing would be necessary in the case of having to shorten a pattern.

To transpose and repeat patterns by means of two mirrors (fig. 1082). — We have referred above to the frequent necessity of adapting patterns to the spaces available; these changes which occasionally require the assistance of a draughtsman are greatly facilitated, especially in the case of

Fig. 1082. How to transpose and repeat a straight pattern by means of two mirrors

cross stitch embroidery by the use of two unframed mirrors, called "Penelope mirrors", which adroitly placed, according to the following directions, give surprising results.

If you want to utilize one piece only of a straight border, to magnify it, or form a corner or centre piece with it, place the mirror in the two former cases straight across; in the two latter, diagonally across, at the point where the pattern is to be interrupted, either doubled or reversed and it will be reflected in the mirror under the required conditions.

To form a square, use two mirrors, join them together on the right side where the diagonal lines meet and you have the square as shewn in figure 1082.

You cannot use just any part of a pattern for reproduction: it is only after a few preliminary essays that you can fix upon the most suitable with which to form corners or a centre, as some motives do not lend themselves to favourable changes.

A few experiments made with the help of a mirror will make our readers understand the importance of these directions better than a long explanation.

How to reproduce patterns by means of squares and modify their dimensions and proportions (figs. 1083 and 1084). — Cases occur in which a pattern has to be subjected to still greater modifications than have been already dealt with.

For example, you want to embroider a running ground on a piece of stuff not large enough for the motive in question, or the pattern is too small for the piece of stuff it is to fill. If you cannot draw you would have either to have recourse to a draughtsman or give up the pattern you had chosen. The following directions, if carefully followed, will relieve you from all difficulty.

Take a piece of checked paper, which you can prepare for yourself, if necessary; reproduce the pattern upon it or make the squares on the pattern direct, as seen in figure 1083. Take a second sheet of vegetable paper, mark it out in squares, a quarter, a third or half the size of those on the first sheet. Thus if one side of a square measure $\frac{3}{4}$ of an inch and you want to reduce your pattern by a third the sides of the new squares must only measure $\frac{1}{2}$ an inch, see fig. 1084. In the same way if you want to increase the pattern by a third the sides of the squares must be made to measure one inch. Then follow square by square the lines of the pattern, extending or contracting them, according to whether the pattern is to be enlarged or reduced.

To copy a pattern direct on to an embroidered model and at the same time modify it in the way we have just explained, proceed as follows:

Fasten the embroidery on a board, stretching it equally in all directions; then measure the length of the pattern, divide the inches by the number of units corresponding with the proportions you wish to give to the copy, subdivide any fractions of inches there may be over and make your division by the measure you adopted; take a pair of compasses, separate the points wide enough for the opening to answer to the distance obtained by the division; plant a pin with a thread to it, at the place indicated by the point of the compass, and repeat the operation along one whole side of the embroidery and, if possible a little beyond, so that the pins may not injure it. Then carry the threads across to the opposite side in perfectly straight lines and plant pins with threads to form a second layer of threads across the first, thus marking out the whole surface in squares.

Needless to say that this plan could not be followed in the case of a piece of work mounted in a frame but with a little invention a way to plant the pins without injuring the embroidery will be devised.

Fig. 1083. Pattern prepared for copying or modifying.

How to reduce a pattern in the width (figs. 1085, 1086, 1087). — A pattern has frequently to be elongated in certain proportions without its being possible to alter the width. In this case long or narrow squares are made according to the general shape of the pattern to be reproduced.

Figure 1085 represents a pattern for D.M.C Superfine braids (Lacets superfins) in its original proportions; in figure 1086, the squares are made half as long again as they were originally and the pattern is expanded; in figure 1987, the squares are compressed, the vertical lines being made closer together by one third.

By these means all the difficulties of copying are simplified, they enable those who are least practised in the art of drawing to undertake these modifications, and we feel sure that few apt workers know so little of drawing as not to be able to copy the contents of a square.

To prepare the paste for fixing embroideries and for appliqué work. — It may perhaps seem strange to devote a special paragraph to such an apparently simple thing. It is

Fig. 1084. Pattern reduced.

however by no means unimportant, t or badly prepared paste can completely ruin a piece of work begun under the best conditions, besides wasting a quantity of costly materials.

Put into a vessel with a concave bottom some wheaten, not rice, starch, add just enough water to dissolve the starch and stir it with a wooden spoon till all the little grains have disappeared.

Meanwhile put about $\frac{1}{4}$ of a pint of pure water on to boil, when it is boiling put in a pinch of powdered resin, about the size of a dried pea, and pour the starch in gradually, stirring all the time. Let the mixture boil for a few seconds and then take it off the fire and continue to stir until it cools to prevent little lumps forming in it.

This kind of paste causes no spots and does not affect even the most delicate colours because it contains no acidity. In winter it will keep for several days but in hot weather it soon begins to ferment and must on no account then be used,

Fig. 1085. Pattern for braiding. Natural size.

Fig. 1086. Pattern, fig. 1085, kept the same in height but expanded in width.

Fig. 1087. Pattern, fig. 1085, kept the same in height but contracted in width.

Gum arabic should never be used for embroidery or appliqué work, because the saline substances it contains are apt to make spots in the stuff.

How to impart stiffness to new needlework. — In the chapter on "Needle-made laces", pag. 632, we said that new work of that kind had to be ironed.

The way in which the ironing is done is by no means an indifferent matter.

Having taken the lace off its foundation, lay it, face downwards, on fine white flannel; then dip a piece of very highly dressed new organdie muslin into water, take it out as soon as it is soaked, gently squeeze out the superfluous water, that no drops may fall from it and dab all over the wrong side of the lace with this kind of pad and pass a hot iron over it moving the iron slowly so that the moisture imparted to the lace by the organdie pad may evaporate gradually.

Not until you are sure the lace is quite dry should it be taken off the board.

We know of no better way than this of giving lace that almost imperceptible degree of stiffness which often alone distinguishes new from old. Water alone does not stiffen the threads sufficiently and it is difficult even with carefully diluted starch to hit upon exactly the right consistency whereas the wetted organdie muslin supplies just the needful degree.

Embroidered network can be treated in the same manner and should be damped in the frame on the wrong side and only taken off when quite dry.

We also recommend embroidery on linen being similarly treated. But when the linen is very creased cover it with a damp cloth, by preference a towel dipped in water, and then wrung out, and iron on that.

Knitted and crochet work should be pinned out on the ironing board dabbed over with a wet pad of organdie and then ironed.

How to wash ordinary lace. — Wind it round a cylindrical bottle and cover it entirely with white muslin tacked on with a few stitches.

Immerse the bottle in a saucepan full of cold water with a small piece of household soap and if the lace is very dirty, a pinch of soda in it and let it boil for an hour, pouring off the water as it gets dirty and adding clean. To prevent the bottle getting knocked about too violently by the boiling water it is as well to fill it half full of sand before winding on the lace.

When the water remains quite clean take the bottle out and rinse it well in cold water to get rid of the soap and then take the lace off and let it dry.

How to wash fine lace. — The process is the same as the above only that as valuable lace it not often washed it is generally yellower than the commoner kinds and often very fragile.

Therefore if stained or greasy it should be put to soak for some hours, or even days, in a bath of the best olive oil. This restores that softness and smoothness to the threads of the lace which wear and time have impaired. After the oil bath it can be washed on a bottle as already explained.

How to stiffen lace. — When the washed lace is perfectly dry dip it in thin starch made as follows.

Take some pure wheaten starch, divide it into two portions, dissolve both in cold water, then boil one portion in boiling water and when it has so far cooled as to have ceased to steam stir the cold starch into it and dilute the whole with cold water to the consistency of thick cream.

If the lace is to be tinted mix a few drops of coffee with the water or instead of water dilute the starch with a weak decoction of China tea or guimauve: the coffee gives the lace a dark cream colour; the tea or the guimauve a pale greenish hue.

Dip the lace in this preparation of starch and squeeze out gently, without wringing, the superfluous liquid, then lay it flat on one hand and beat it for a few minutes with the other to work the starch well in, repeat this whole process twice and then roll the lace in a fine white cloth and leave it there till you are ready to iron or pin it out as the case may be.

To iron lace. — After leaving the lace for a couple or hours in the dry cloth, iron it if machine-made, or pin it out if it be needle-made, or net-guipure.

Before ironing lace take it in your left hand, hold it by the footing and with the right hand pull out all the picots along the edge of the piece you are going to iron, to an equal length, then lay it out flat on an ironing-board covered with white flannel and iron it with a moderately hot iron. Hold the iron on the lace as long as it is damp; when you move the iron on, the part it has just left should be perfectly dry.

Should you by chance have creased the lace in ironing, dab the creases over with a fine sponge dipped in water containing a few drops of the starch used for stiffening the lace and pass the iron over it again.

After the first ironing pull the lace out crossways and lengthways, from right to left and from left to right and pass the iron over it once more. This gets rid of the artificial stiffness caused by the first ironing and makes it soft and pliant like new lace.

How to pin out lace. — In order to do this in a thoroughly satisfactory manner you should provide yourself with a wooden drum about 12 inches high and 24 inches in diameter, because it has to be large enough to rest upon the knees. The outside circumference of the wood must be padded and covered with grey or white ticking.

The pins must be the same size as the picots, very fine ones will be wanted for Valenciennes and needle point lace and coarser ones for other kinds, but they must be of white metal as steel pins rust and would spoil the lace. Cover the cylinder with blue paper (less trying for the eyes than white), then take only just as much lace out of the damp cloth as you think you will be able to pin out before it gets dry, keeping the rest covered up.

Lay the lace upon the drum and pin the footing down first in a straight line, sticking the pins in pretty closely and at equal distances apart; then pin down each picot separately, taking care not to open them if they have kept their original shape and to twist them round if they had got untwisted.

If you cannot get all the pins stuck in before the lace dries, damp the picots with a sponge as you go along Never stick pins in to parts that are dry as you risk tearing the picots and thereby destroying the worth of perhaps very valuable lace.

Raised lace has to be stamped out from the wrong side with a lace awl, a kind of bone hook made for the purpose. Some professional lace-cleaners stamp out even Valenciennes lace in this way, but we regard it as a mistake, seeing that it is by nature a perfectly flat lace.

Leave the lace you have pinned out on the cylinder until you have gone the whole round, whether it is part of a length you are repairing, or a piece that has been washed and has to be perfectly dry before it is taken off.

Cover up the lace as you go along and slip each piece as it is finished into a blue paper bag that the whole may be equally clean.

In conclusion our advice is that lace-washing should only be undertaken when you are fairly safe from interruption, as the pinning out more especially requires to be finished off out of hand.

How to wash coloured embroideries. — The best soap to use for the purpose is the finest quality of Marseilles soap. Above all avoid soda, washing powders and chloride of line.

Wash quickly and without much rubbing in a hot lather of soap, and rinse in several plentiful changes of cold water, squeeze out the water without wringing, and iron on the wrong side with a moderately hot iron. On no account leave wet pieces of embroidery heaped one upon another. If the foundation of the embroidery be of coarse linen or any other thick stuff, stretch it out between two linen cloths, wrong side up, and iron it so.

It sometimes happens that owing to inadequate rinsing after a first washing the ground of the embroidery is stained by the excess of colouring matter in the materials. A few more rinsings in an abundance of cold water will generally remedy this, which moreover by careful attention to our instructions can always be avoided.

Should you wish slightly to tone down the whiteness of washed stuffs follow the directions given with regard to tinting lace, that is dip them in a weak decoction of coffee or China tea.

To wash a piece of work on a foundation of washing silk, follow the instructions given above with certain added precautions; such as using very soft and tepid water, quick drying without wringing and calandering instead of ordinary ironing.

Materials. — We stated in the preface that we had made a special point of facilitating the choice of materials and colours to our readers by indicating the most suitable kinds and numbers at the foot of each engraving. This has been done throughout; but all these directions would have been incomplete without the tables we have appended to these pages which enable every one to choose the number and colour they want without having the materials before them.

The strokes, in the comparative tables, that accompany each number, indicate exactly the size of the corresponding thread, thus, if you want to decide what number of thread to buy, you take a fibre of the desired size, lay it, stretching it slightly, on the strokes placed against the numbers, and stop at the one that corresponds to the pattern.

As regards the colours, the names and shades of which have been classed with the utmost care and which offer such a rich choice in all the different kinds, we have only indicated those in our explanations which matching best together are in consequence the most classical.

We feel justified in reminding the public that if we have recommended the D.M.C mark preferably to every other, a long experience has proved to us that the articles bearing that mark are of a quite superior quality and offer an exceptional variety of sizes and colours, without which it is impossible to execute really artistic works.

We conclude this chapter with a recommendation of great importance to our readers, never to begin a piece of work of any considerable size or importance without providing themselves in advance with all the materials necessary to complete it, for it is often difficult, if not impossible, to match the colours exactly later on, the shades of the same being liable to vary from one dyeing to another.

Persons desiring further information regarding matters treated in this volume or to know where the materials mentioned in it are to be obtained are requested to apply to the house of TH. DE DILLMONT, MULHOUSE (Alsace), which will furnish them without delay with all the needful instructions.

List of the special Articles
of COTTON, FLAX and SILK
for embroidery, sewing, knitting, crochet, and in general all needlework
manufactured and put on sale with the trade mark

D·M·C

Cotton : Alsatian thread (Fil d'Alsace). — Cotton lace thread (Fil à dentelle). — Demi-Alsatian (Demi-Alsace). — Tiers-Alsatian (Tiers-Alsace). — Bell thread (Fil à la cloche). — Embroidery cottons (Cotons à broder). — Embroidery cottons special quality (Cotons à broder qualité spéciale). — Pearl cotton (Coton perlé). — Shaded pearl cotton (Perlé ombré). — Chiné for crochet, knitting, &c. — Special stranded cotton (Mouliné spécial). — Floss Crochet (Crochet floche). — Crochet cotton 6 cord (Cordonnet 6 fils). — Special crochet cotton (Cordonnet qualité spéciale). — Crochet cotton, Bell mark (Cordonnet à la cloche). — Crochet cotton (Coton pour crochet). — Knitting cotton (Coton à tricoter). — Fluted cotton (Coton cannelé). — Hosiery cotton (Coton pour bonneterie). — Felting cotton (Coton à feutrer). — Stranded cotton 8 threads (Mouliné 8 fils). — Darning cotton (Coton à repriser). — Darning cotton special quality (Coton à repriser qualité spéciale). — Sewing cottons superior quality and good quality (Cotons à coudre qualité supérieure et bonne qualité). — Sewing cottons and Bell tacking cottons (Cotons à coudre et à bâtir à la cloche). — Best 6 cord Sewing-Machine cotton (Câblé 6 fils pour machines à coudre). — « Alsa » Brilliant sewing and machine twist — Marking cotton (Coton à marquer). — Marking cotton special quality (Coton à marquer qualité spéciale). — Knotting cotton (Fil à pointer). — Alsatian crochet cotton (Câblé d'Alsace). — Knitting cotton, Bell mark (Retors pour mercerie). — Knitting cotton, Bell mark, special quality (Retors spécial pour mercerie). — « Alsatia » Brilliant twist for knitting and crochet — Alsatian twist special quality (Retors d'Alsace qualité spéciale). — Superfine braid and braid Ist quality (Lacet superfin d'Alsace et Lacet Ire qualité). — Cotton twists for industrial purposes (Retors de coton pour l'industrie).

Flax threads : Floss flax or flourishing thread (Lin floche).
— Stranded flax thread (Lin mouliné). — Flax thread for
knitting and crochet (Lin pour tricoter et crocheter). — Flax
lace thread (Lin pour dentelles).

Washing silk : Persian silk (Soie de Perse).

Gold and Silver : Gold and silver embroidery threads (Or
et Argent fins pour la broderie).

These articles are made in all sizes in écru, white, black
and all colours.

They are to be had in embroidery and haberdashery
shops, &c. ; but the variety of articles manufactured by the
SOCIÉTÉ ANONYME DOLLFUS-MIEG & Cⁱᵉ, bearing the D.M.C
trade mark, is so great that it is impossible for even the best
furnished shops to keep them all in stock.

But as houses that are in connection with this firm or its
agents are able to procure any of the D.M.C articles in small
consignments, customers can always be supplied through them
with what they require.

Table giving in alphabetical order the names with colour card for the dyeing of the COTTON and

COLOURS	Ultra-dark	Very dark	Dark	Medium	Light	Very light	Ultra-light
Blacks :							
Black fast dye	310						
Greenish black		473					
Jet black		681					
Blues :							
Ashy blue				448			
Azure blue					3325	775	
Blue fast dye	849.850	820.796	797	798	799	800	821
Campanula blue	859	860	861	862.863	864		
China blue		481	482	483	484	485	
Cornflower blue		791	792	793	794	795	
Drake's neck blue		3305	3306	3307	3308	3309	
French blue		337	338	339	340	341	
Gentian blue		476	477	478	479	480	
Greenish blue		525	526	527	528	529	
Greyish blue			870	871	872	873	
Indigo blue	939.823	336	311	312	322	334	
Lapis Lazuli blue		342	333	343	344	345	
Navy blue		505	506	507	508	509	
Navy blue	885	886	887				
Old blue		929	930	931	932	933	
Pale blue					668		
Peacock blue		805	806	807	808	809	
Periwinkle blue		3355	3356	3357	3358	3359	
Sky blue		847.515	516	517	518	519	747.848
Solid blue		824	825	826	813	827	828
Tender blue						709	
Ultramarine			682	683			
Very dark blue		3665					
Bronzes :							
Gilt bronze		585	586	587	588	589	
Yellow bronze		764	765	766	767	768	769
Browns :							
Brown fast dye		3371					
Brown of dead leaves		615	616	617	618	619	
Cachou brown		433	434	435	436	437.738	739
Chamois brown		416	417	324	418	419	
Chesnut brown	852	403	404	405	406	407	
Cinnamon brown		660	661	662	663	664	
Copper brown		880.881	882	883	884		
Drab brown				3440		3442	

COLOURS	Ultra-dark	Very dark	Dark	Medium	Light	Very light	Ultra-light
Greyish brown		837	838	839	840.841	842	
Havana brown		454	455	456	457	458	
Leather brown		430	431	302	432	325	
Locust-bean brown		354	355	303	356	357.758	759
Mahogany brown		300	400	301	401	402.771	772
Myrtle brown				463			
Negro's head brown	938.898	801					
Old brown		3674	3675	3451	3452	3453	
Otter brown		438	439	440	441	442	
Puce brown		459					
Red brown		918	919	920	921	922.923	
Rust brown		3310	3311	3312	3313	3314	
Violet brown	888						
Greens :							
Beetle green	895	3345	3346	3347	3348	3349	3373
Bottle green		491	492	493	494	495	
Bright green		897.785	786	787	788	789	
Bronze green		669	670	671	672	673	
Copper green		829	830	831	832	833.834	
Cypress green	802	856	803				
Drab green		689	690	691	692	693	
Emerald green		555	556	557	558	559	
Green of Duck's plumage		545	546	547	548	549	
Golden green	901	580	581	582	583	584	774
Ivy green		500	501	502	503	504	
Malachite green		560	561	562	563	564	
Meadow green	857	858.699	700	701	702	703.854	855
Metallic green		465	466	467			
Mignonette green				750	751	752	
Moss green	934.935	936.937	468.469	470	471	472	773
Myrtle green		535	536	537	538	539	
Olive green		510	511	512	513	514	
Pale green		3362	3363	3364	3365	3366	
Paroquet green		904	905	906	907	908	
Parrot green		694	695	696	697	698	
Pistachio green	890	319	367	320	368	369	770
Russian green			499				
Tender green						710	
Verdigris			474	475			
Water green				713	714	715	
Yellow green		730.731	732	733	734	735.736	737

Table giving in alphabetical order the names with colour card for the dyeing of the COTTON and

COLOURS	Ultra-dark	Very dark	Dark	Medium	Light	Very light	Ultra-light
Greys :							
Ash grey	..853..	..413..	..317..	..414..	..318..	..415..	..762..
Beaver grey	..843..	844.645	.646..	..647..	..648..	..649..	....
Blue grey		.590.	..591..	..592..	..593..	..594..	..757..
Brown grey	865.866	408.867	..409..	..410..	..411..	..412..	....
Cream grey				..810..	..811..	..812..	....
Dove grey		3368..	3369..	3330.	3331.	3370..	
Dust grey		3630..	3631..	3632.	3633.	3634..	
Felt grey		.635..	..636..	..637..	..638..	..639..	
Flax grey				716..	..717.		
Greenish grey		.595..	..596..	..597..	..598..	..599..	
Hay grey		.520..	..521..	..522..	..523..	..524..	
Hazel-nut grey	..868..	869.420	.421..	..422..	..423..	..424..	
Iron grey		3600..	.3601..	.3602.	.3603.	.3604..	
Lead grey	..876..	877.378	..379..	..380..	..381..	..382..	
Lilac grey		3332..	3333..	3334.	3335.	3336..	
Lime-tree grey		.391..	..392..	..393..	..330..	..331..	
Mignonette grey		.924..	..925..	..926..	..927..	..928..	
Mourning grey		.655..	..656..	.657..	..658..	..659..	
Mouse grey		.425.	..426..	..427..	..428..	..429..	
Neutral grey		.620..	..621..	..622..	..623..	..624..	
Pearl grey		.625..	..626..	..627..	..628..	..629..	
Smoke grey	878.879	.640..	..641..	..642..	..643..	..644..	..822..
Steel grey		3650..	3651..	3652.	3653.	3654..	
Ticking grey		.387..	..388..	..323..	..389..	..390..	
Tinder grey		.329..	..383..	..384..	..385..	..386..	
Twine grey			..460..	..461..	..462..		
Wood grey	874.875	.610..	..611..	..612..	..613..	..614..	804.851
Lilac:							
Lilac grey		.313..	..398..	..314..	..328..	..399..	..753..
Pinks:							
Briar rose pink		.570..	..571..	..572..	..573..	..574..	....
Bright pink		.565..	..566..	..567..	..568..	..569..	..784..
Geranium pink			..891..	..892..	..893..	..894..	
Old pink		3704..	3705..	3706..	3707.	3708..	
Rose fast dye		3350..	3351..	3352..	3353.	3354 903	.3372..
Tender pink					..899..	3326 776	818.819
Reds :							
Bordeaux red	..845..	846.496	....	....	....	....	....

To prevent mistakes we request that the numbers and in
The brilliant cottons and the linen articles are dyed after

COLOURS	Ultra-dark	Very dark	Dark	Medium	Light	Very light	Ultra-light
Cardinal red		346	347	304	305	348	
Cherry red		3315	3316	3317	3318	3319	
Cornelian red			449	450			
Dawn red	835	836.360	306	361	332	362	763
Etruscan red		3337	3338	3339	3340	3341	
Garnet red		358	359 3367	326	309	335	
Geranium red	817.349		350	351	352	353	754
Mandarin red		3342	3343	3344			
Morocco red				3327	3328	3329 760	761.896
Orange red			900				
Raspberry red		3684	3685	3686	3687	3688	3689
Red currant red		3605	3606	3607	3608	3609	
Scarlet	902.814	815.816	498	464			
Turkish red				321			
Vermillion red				666			
Violets:							
Amethyst		3320	3321	3322	3323	3324	
Bishop's violet		914	915	916	917		
Mauve violet		375	315	376	316	377	778
Old violet		3540	3541	3542	3543	3544	3545
Pansy violet		530	531	532	533	534	
Plum violet		550	551	552	553	554	755
Purple violet		723	724				
Scabious violet		394	327	395	396	397	756
Violet		889					
Wine-Lees Violet		370	371	372	373	374	
Yellows:							
Cream yellow				711	712		
Golden yellow		779	780.781	782	783		
Leather yellow			720	721	722		
Lemon yellow			307	445	446		
Maize yellow		575	576	577	578	579	
Mandarin yellow		740	741	742.743	744	745	746
Ochre yellow					676	677	777
Old gold		728 678	679	680	729		
Orange yellow		443	444				
Rust yellow		363	364	308	365	366	
Saffron yellow			725	726	727	748	749

COLOURS	Ultra-dark	Very dark	Dark	Medium	Light	Very light	Ultra-light
Black :							
Black............	1187						
Blues :							
Delft blue	1246	1245	1244	1243	1242	1241	
Indigo blue......	1013	1012	1307	1011 1306	1010	1305	1009
Navy blue	1240	1239	1238	1237	1236	1235 1413	
Peacock blue	1221 1194	1193	1192	1191	1190	1189	1431 1188
Sky blue	1212	1102	1395 1101	1100 1394	1099 1393	1098	1392 1256
Steel blue		1107	1106	1105	1104	1103	
Ultramarine	1381 1294	1293	1058 1057	1056 1055	1380 1054	1379 1053	1378 1052
Browns :							
Cachou brown....	1017	1016	1015	1014	1205	1432 1292	1291
Cinnamon brown			1153	1152	1215	1151	
Drab brown		1446 1124	1123	1122	1121	1270	1120
Havana brown...	1304	1303	1085	1084 1083	1082	1081	1211
Otter brown.....	1047	1046	1045	1044	1043	1042 1209	1441 1440
Rust brown.....		1158	1157	1156	1155	1229	1154 1401
Tender brown...			1051	1050	1049	1048	
Greens :							
Beetle green....		1223	1200	1397	1199	1396	1311
Bottle green	1390	1341	1340	1339	1338	1337	1336
Bronze green	1097	1096	1095	1094	1093	1092	1445
Golden green	1302	1301 1146	1145 1144	1386 1143	1385 1261	1142	1300 1384
Ivy green........	1184	1183	1182	1181	1416 1314	1415 1313	1312 1414
Meadow green...		1347	1346	1345 1344	1343	1421 1342	1420
Mignonette green	1025	1024 1023	1022 1021	1020	1019 1018	1425 1207	1206
Moss green......		1131	1130	1129	1128	1213	
Myrtle green	1141	1140	1139	1228	1295	1138	1137
Olive green......		1198	1197	1196	1195 1284	1434	1222 1433
Paroquet green...	1377	1376	1375 1374	1373 1372	1371 1370	1369	
Sportsman's green	1290	1289	1288	1287	1430 1286	1285	1429
Yellow green	1280	1279	1278 1277	1404 1276	1403 1275	1402 1274	1273
Greys :							
Blue grey........		1216	1167	1166	1165	1164	1299
Greenish grey ...			1180	1179	1178	1177	

To prevent mistakes we request that the numbers and in

COLOURS	Ultra-dark	Very dark	Dark	Medium	Light	Very light	Ultra-light
Hazel-nut grey		1358	1357	1356	1355	1354	
Pearl grey		1208	1034	1033	1310	1032	1309
Lilac :							
Old lilac		1080	1079	1078	1225	1077	1076
Pinks :							
Bright pink	1335	1334	1333	1332	1407 1331	1330 1406	1329 1405
Old pink	1008	1007	1006	1005 1004	1003	1002	1001
Tender pink	1320	1319	1400 1234	1233 1399	1283	1232	1231 1398
Reds :							
Bright red					1368		
Cherry red	1063	1062	1321	1061 1439	1210	1060	1059
Copper red		1135	1134	1444	1133 1443	1227 1442	1132
Crimson red			1185				
Geranium red	1328	1327	1326	1325	1419 1324	1323	1322 1418
Old red	1041	1040 1039	1038 1037	1383 1036	1382 1255	1035 1254	1253
Purple red			1110	1108			
Raspberry red		1150	1149	1148 1438	1147 1437	1214	1436 1435
Red currant red	1091	1090	1089	1088	1087	1086	1417
Violets :							
Heliotrope	1163	1282	1281	1424 1162	1423 1161	1422	1160
Pansy violet		1353	1352	1351 1428	1350 1427	1349	1426 1348
Scabious violet			1203	1202	1230	1201	
Violet	1252	1251	1250	1249	1410 1248	1409 1247	1408
Whites :							
Blueish white							1186
Cream white						1308	1220
Snow white							1219
Yellows :							
Brown yellow	1367	1366	1365	1364 1363	1362 1361	1360	1359
Golden yellow	1031	1030	1029	1318 1412	1317	1316	1315 1411
Maize yellow	1075	1074	1073	1072 1389	1071	1388 1070	1387 1069
Old gold	1170	1169	1168	1217	1259	1258	1257
Orange yellow	1119	1118 1117	1116 1115	1114	1113 1112	1111	1260 1391
Straw yellow	1298	1297 1296	1269 1268	1267 1266	1265 1264	1263	1262

no case the names of the colours be quoted in an order.

Names and numbers enumerated on the colour card for the dyeing of the SHADED PEARL COTTON and CHINÉ bearing the D.M.C trade mark.

SHADED COLOURS	Nos	SHADED COLOURS	Nos
Blue	...50..	Black and white	...88..
Blue and white	...78..	Black and yellow	...83..
Blue and yellow	...71..	Black and red	...87..
Blue and pink	...70..		
Blue and green	...84..	Orange	...51..
Blue and old gold	...72..	Light pink	...62..
Dark blue and green	...86..	Pink and green	...79..
Blue fast dye	...93..	Rose	...89..
Blue, yellow and green	...74..		
Light blue	...67..	Geranium red	...96..
Mid blue	...91..	Light red	...64..
		Raspberry red	...99..
Brown	...61..	Red	...57..
Brown and red	...75..		
Rust brown	...100..	Beetle green	...92..
Terra	...69..	Brown green	...94..
		Green	...60..
Tartan	...77..	Green and yellow	...76..
Tartan	...82..	Green and black	...85..
		Green and pink	...59..
Grey	...53..	Green and red	...56..
Grey and yellow	...54..	Green and violet	...58..
Grey and pink	...73..	Light green	...63..
Grey and green	...80..		
Silver grey	...97..	Old gold	...68..
		Light mauve	...65..
Golden yellow	...98..	Violet	...52..
Light yellow	...66..	Violet mauve	...95..
Orange yellow	...90.	Violet and yellow	...55..

MIXED SHADES	Nos	MIXED SHADES	Nos
Dark blue and white	...13..	Black and pink	...21..
Dark blue and yellow	...12..	Black and red	...23..
Light blue and white	...17..		
		Red and white	...14..
Brown and white	...18..	Red and light blue	...15..
		Red and dark blue	...22..
Yellow and white	...10..	Red and green	...16..
Black and white	...20..		
Black and yellow	...19..	Violet and white	...11..

Table giving the numbers and sizes of the Cotton articles bearing the D.M.C trade mark.

150 DMC 80 MÈT.

ALSATIAN THREAD, DEMI-ALSATIAN
(Fil d'Alsace, Demi-Alsace)
TIERS-ALSATIAN
and COTTON LACE THREAD 9 cord
(Tiers-Alsace et Fil à dentelle, 9 brins)

30 ——————————————
36 ——————————————
40 ——————————————
50 ——————————————
60 ——————————————
70 ——————————————
80 ——————————————
90 ——————————————
100 —————————————
110 —————————————
120 —————————————
130 —————————————
140 —————————————
150 —————————————
160 —————————————
180 —————————————
200 —————————————
250 —————————————
300 —————————————
400 —————————————
500 —————————————
600 —————————————
700 —————————————

DMC — DOLLFUS – MIEG & Cie – MULHOUSE-BELFORT

MACHINE THREAD
(Fil pour machines)

10 ——————————————
12 ——————————————
16 ——————————————
20 ——————————————
24 ——————————————
30 ——————————————
36 ——————————————
40 ——————————————
50 ——————————————
60 ——————————————
70 ——————————————
80 ——————————————
90 ——————————————
100 —————————————
120 —————————————
150 —————————————
180 —————————————
200 —————————————

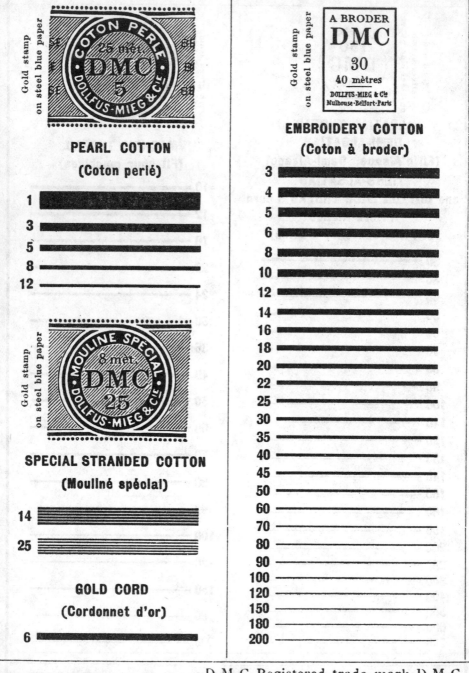

PEARL COTTON

(Coton perlé)

SPECIAL STRANDED COTTON

(Mouliné spécial)

GOLD CORD

(Cordonnet d'or)

EMBROIDERY COTTON

(Coton à broder)

D.M.C Registered trade mark D.M.C

of the **Flax** and **Silk** articles
bearing the **D.M.C** trade mark.

FLAX LACE THREAD

(Lin pour dentelles)

6	
12	
16	
20	
25	
30	
35	
40	
45	
50	
60	
70	

PERSIAN SILK
(Washing)
(Sole de Perse)

SUPERFINE BRAIDS

(Lacets superfins d'Alsace)

Nᵒˢ	Widths	Width In m/m
1	⊢⊣	$^3/_4$
1 $^1/_2$	⊢⊣	1
2	⊢⊣	$1\,^1/_4$
3	⊢⊣	$1\,^1/_2$
4	⊢⊣	2
5	⊢⊣	3
6	⊢⊣	$3\,^1/_2$
7	⊢⊣	4
8	⊢⊣	$4\,^1/_2$
9	⊢⊣	5
10	⊢⊣	$5\,^1/_2$
12	⊢⊣	$6\,^1/_2$
14	⊢⊣	8
16	⊢⊣	9
18	⊢⊣	10
20	⊢⊣	12
24	⊢⊣	13
28	⊢⊣	16
32	⊢⊣	19

— Beware of imitations.

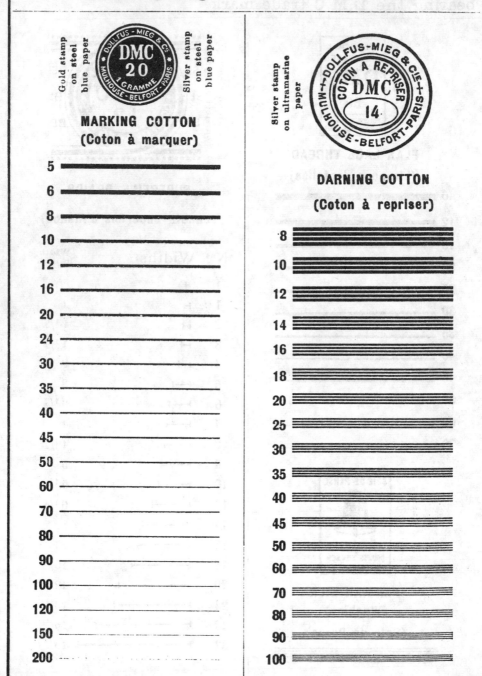

MARKING COTTON

(Coton à marquer)

Gold stamp on steel blue paper

Silver stamp on steel blue paper

5
6
8
10
12
16
20
24
30
35
40
45
50
60
70
80
90
100
120
150
200

DARNING COTTON

(Coton à repriser)

Silver stamp on ultramarine paper

8
10
12
14
16
18
20
25
30
35
40
45
50
60
70
80
90
100

Cotton articles bearing the D.M.C trade mark.

KNITTING COTTON

Bell mark

(Retors pour mercerie)

6

10

12

15

20

25

30

35

40

50

OR FIN D·M·C
25 mètres Nº 30

**EMBROIDERY GOLD
AND SILVER THREADS
(washing)
(Or et Argent fins pour
la broderie)**

20

30

40

**RETORS SPÉCIAL
POUR
MERCERIE
Nº 25
DMC
50 grammes
DOLLFUS-MIEG & Cⁱᵉ
Mulhouse-Belfort-Paris**

KNITTING COTTON

Bell mark

Special quality

(Retors spécial pour mercerie)

10

12

15

20

25

30

35

50

TURKISH GOLD CORD

(Ganse turque)

Écru and gold

6

12

— Beware of imitations.

ALSATIAN TWIST

(Retors d'Alsace)

5 ————————————————

8 ————————————————

10 ————————————————

12 ————————————————

16 ————————————————

20 ————————————————

30 ————————————————

40 ————————————————

50 ————————————————

60 ————————————————

80 ————————————————

100 ————————————————

FELTING COTTON

(Coton à feutrer)

25 ————————————————

KNITTING COTTON

(Coton à tricoter)

6 ━━━━━━━━━━━━━━━━

8 ━━━━━━━━━━━━━━━━

10 ━━━━━━━━━━━━━━━

12 ━━━━━━━━━━━━━━

14 ━━━━━━━━━━━━━

16 ━━━━━━━━━━━━

18 ━━━━━━━━━━━

20 ━━━━━━━━━━

25 ━━━━━━━━━

30 ————————————

35 ————————————

40 ————————————

50 ————————————

EMBROIDERY COTTON
special quality
for monograms and cambric

(Coton à broder surfin)

100 ————————————————

Cotton articles bearing the D.M.C trade mark.

Silver stamp on steel blue paper

« ALSATIA »

15	━━━━━━━━
20	━━━━━━━━
25	━━━━━━━━
30	━━━━━━━━
40	━━━━━━━━

Black stamp on grey paper

KNOTTING COTTON
(Fil à pointer)

10	━━━━━━━━
15	━━━━━━━━
20	━━━━━━━━
30	━━━━━━━━

Gold stamp on white paper

« ALSA »

40 ━━━━━━━━

MADEIRA EMBROIDERY COTTON
(Coton à broder Madeira)

This article is made
in Nos 16 to 200
corresponding with those of
Embroidery Cotton.

Silver stamp on ultramarine paper

FLOSS CROCHET COTTON
(Crochet floche)

25 ━━━━━━━━

GOLD CHINÉ
(Chiné d'or)

In red, blue, green, black
and écru.

30 ━━━━━━━━

— Beware of imitations.

LIN
POUR
TRICOTER
ET
CROCHETER
DMC
Nº 25
50 grammes
DOLLFUS-MIEG & Cⁱᵉ
Mulhouse-Belfort-Paris

Gold stamp on steel blue paper

FLAX THREAD
FOR KNITTING AND CROCHET
(Lin pour tricoter et crocheter)

3
4
6
8
10
12
14
16
20
25
30
35
40
45
50
60
70

LIN
FLOCHE
DMC
50
40 mètres
DOLLFUS-MIEG & Cⁱᵉ
Mulhouse-Belfort-Paris

Gold stamp on steel blue paper

FLOSS FLAX (Lin floche)

3
5
6
8
10
12
16
20
25
30
35
40
50
60
70
100
150

LIN
MOULINÉ
DMC
8 mètres
DOLLFUS-MIEG & Cⁱᵉ
Mulhouse-Belfort-Paris

Gold stamp on steel blue paper

STRANDED FLAX
(Lin mouliné)

D.M.C Registered trade mark D.M.C

Cotton articles bearing the D.M.C trade mark.

Silver stamp on garnet red paper

COTON FLOCHE
A BRODER
Qualté spéciale
DMC
25
40 mètres
DOLLFUS-MIEG & Cie
Mulhouse·Belfort·Paris

Silver stamp on steel blue paper

DOLLFUS - MIEG & Cie
CORDONNET 6 FILS
DMC
50
25 GRAMMES
MULHOUSE - BELFORT - PARIS

FLOSS EMBROIDERY COTTON

Special quality

(Coton floche à broder

Qualité spéciale)

6	
8	
10	
12	
14	
16	
18	
20	
25	
30	
35	
40	
50	
60	
70	
80	
90	
100	
110	
120	

CROCHET COTTON and

CROCHET COTTON Bell mark

(Cordonnet 6 fils

et Cordonnet à la Cloche)

1	
1½	
2	
2½	
3	
4	
5	
10	
15	
20	
25	
30	
40	
50	
60	
70	
80	
90	
100	
120	
150	
200	

— Beware of imitations.

D·M·C Library

In order to encourage and develop the taste for needlework of all kinds and to make the use of the numerous articles specially manufactured by them for sewing and embroidery more widely known, the Société anonyme Dollfus-Mieg & Cie have issued a series of publications forming a complete library in itself, which treats with every form and description of needlework.

Each album consists of a series of unpublished and very varied patterns, accompanied by an explanatory text with the assistance of which it will be found easy to execute even the most complicated designs.

Although in artistic value, in the selection of the patterns and the care expended on the execution, these publications surpass every thing till now produced of the kind, they are sold at a price greatly below their value; that they could be produced under such favourable conditions is due solely to the size of the editions and the object in view.

All needlework publications are edited in French and German, and some in English. As the text however is but of secondary importance while the designs are the principal feature, all these works can be used to great advantage even in the countries where other languages are spoken than those in which they are edited.

Further on will be found a list of these publications, which are to be had of all booksellers, mercers and embroidery shops, or, if necessary, direct from the publisher Th. de Dillmont, Mulhouse (Alsace).

———

Albums for Cross-Stitch Embroidery
By Th. de Dillmont
(Albums de Broderies au Point de Croix)

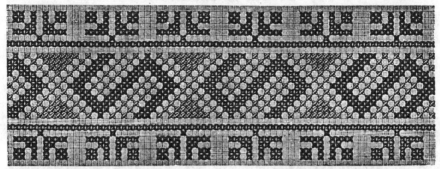

FIGURE 231 OF ALBUM I, REDUCED IN SIZE.

FIGURE 79 OF ALBUM II, REDUCED IN SIZE.

FIGURE 148 OF ALBUM III, REDUCED IN SIZE.

ALBUM I:
32 plates with 278 designs and a treatise on embroidery.
In-4°. Artistic cover. Price : **1/3**

ALBUM II:
40 plates with 136 coloured designs, comprising several
alphabets and a treatise on embroidery. In-4°. Artistic cover.
Price............. **2/—**

ALBUM III:
40 plates with 182 designs, without text. In-4°. Artistic cover.
Price............. **1/3**

These albums are edited in **French** and **German**.

Motifs for Coptic Embroidery

(CHRISTIAN ART IN EGYPT)

By Th. de Dillmont.

(Motifs de Broderie copte)

In 3 parts, each containing 3o plates, one coloured,
with explanatory text and artistic cover. In-4°.

Each part, Price : **2/—**

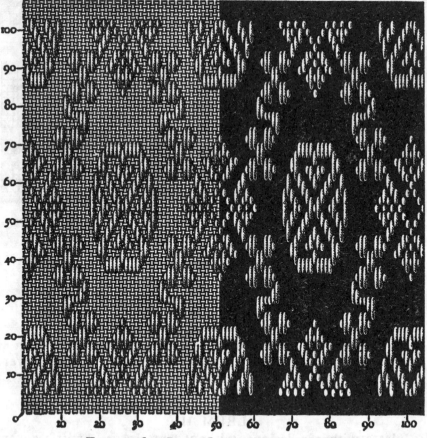

Figure 69, Part I, reduced in size.

The three parts are edited in **French** and **German**.

FIGURE 7, PART II, REDUCED IN SIZE.

FIGURE 24, PART III, REDUCED IN SIZE.

The three parts are edited in **French** and **German**.

French Net-work

By Th. de Dillmont.

(Le Filet-Richelieu)

Album in-4°, containing 3o plates with explanatory text.
Artistic cover. Price : **2/—**

FIGURE 84 OF THE ALBUM, REDUCED IN SIZE.

FIGURE 85 OF THE ALBUM, REDUCED IN SIZE.

This album is edited in **French** and **German**.

NET-WORK EMBROIDERY
(La Broderie sur Lacis)

Ist and IInd Series, each composed of 20 plates with explanatory text. In-4°. Polychrome cover.

Price of each series : **1/3**

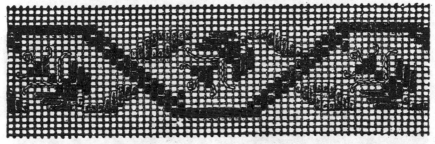

FIGURE 2, Ist SERIES, REDUCED IN SIZE.

The two Series are edited in **French** and **German**.

THE EMBROIDERER'S ALPHABET

Bound in-16mo................ Price : **5**^{d}

Album containing 82 coloured plates composed of alphabets, monograms and patterns for counted stitch embroideries, followed by 10 plates of monograms and festoons with tracings for white embroidery.

BORDER FROM PLATE 68.

This album is edited in **English, French, German** and **Italian**

The same album, bound in-8° (edited in **French, German** and **Russian**)....... Price : **10**^{d}

Macramé (Le Macramé)

By Th. de Dillmont.

Album in-4°, containing 32 plates with explanatory text.
Polychrome cover. Price : 2/—

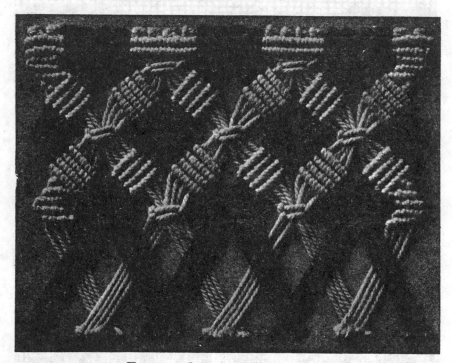

FIGURE 152, REDUCED IN SIZE.

The word « Macramé », of Arabic origin, serves to designate a certain kind of work, produced by the knotting or plaiting together of threads.

Completely forgotten for a long while this kind of work reappeared only a few years ago as a novelty and soon took an important place in the domain of needlework, owing to the variety of patterns it can be executed in and the durability of the objects produced in it.

This album is edited in **French** and **German**.

Knitting (Le Tricot)

By Th. de Dillmont.

Two parts, containing the first **72**, the second **63** patterns for knitting and a detailed description of the patterns.

Artistic cover. In-4°. Price of each part : **2/—**

FIGURE 53, PART I.

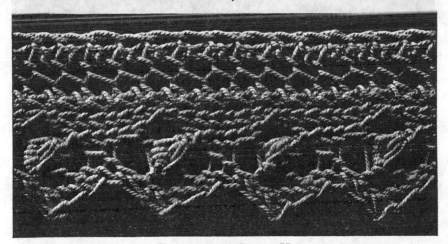

FIGURE 47, PART II.

These albums are edited in **French** and **German**.

New Patterns in Old Style

By Emilie Bach.

**Work divided into two parts each of which
includes 12 plates,
accompanied by an explanatory text and figures. In-4°.**

Price of each part : **3/—**

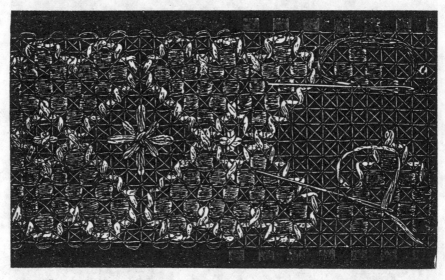

INSERTION WITH NETWORK GROUND, REDUCED IN SIZE.

These albums are edited in **English.**

Works of various kinds
(Recueil d'Ouvrages divers)

Album in-4°, containing 35 plates with 242 engravings and explanatory text. Price : **1/8**

STRIPE IN BUTTON-HOLE AND FISHBONE STITCH, REDUCED IN SIZE.

Alphabets and Monograms
BY TH. DE DILLMONT.
(Alphabets et Monogrammes)

Album in-4° (oblong shape), with gilt edges, composed of 60 plates with explanatory text. Price : **1/3**

LETTER J, PLATE 59.   LETTER N, PLATE 60.

These albums are edited in **French** and **German**.

Crochet Work, Ist and IInd Series

By Th. de Dillmont.

(Le Crochet)

Two albums in-4°, containing the first 64, the second 57 patterns for crochet work and a detailed description of the patterns. Artistic cover. Price of each series : **2/—**

FIGURE 61, Ist SERIES.

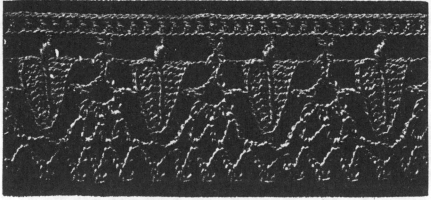

FIGURE 33, IInd SERIES.

The Ist and IInd Series are edited in **French** and **German**.

Crochet Work, IIIrd Series

An album in large octavo, containing 14 plates with a great variety of patterns for crochet work and an explanatory text with figures. Artistic cover .... Price : **10** ^{d.}

FIGURE ON PLATE IX.

The IIIrd Series are edited in **English, French, German** and **Italian.**

Flat-Stitch Embroidery

BY TH. DE DILLMONT.

(La Broderie au Passé)

Album in-4°, containing 20 plates with tracings for reproducing the patterns, explanatory text and polychrome cover.
Price.......... **2/—**

FIGURE 21, REDUCED IN SIZE.

This album is edited in **French** and **German.**

Embroidery on Net

Containing 28 pages of text with explanatory figures
and 20 plates with patterns for embroidery on net, printed on
fine paper. In-8⁰. Price : **5** ᵈ·

PART OF PLATE **XV**, REDUCED IN SIZE.

Cross Stitch · New Designs

I**st** SERIES

Album in-8⁰, containing 24 coloured plates, composed of
grounds, borders and various motifs for cross-stitch
embroideries .... Price : **2½** ᵈ·

These albums are edited in **English**, **French** and **German**.

Cross Stitch · New Designs

IInd and IIIrd SERIES

Two albums in large octavo, each containing 20 coloured plates
composed of grounds, borders and various motifs
for cross-stitch embroideries........ Price of each series: **4 d.**

SUBJECT ON PLATE 18 OF THE IInd SERIES.

BORDER FROM PLATE 16 OF THE IInd SERIES.
(DESIGNS REDUCED IN SIZE.)

These albums are edited in **English, French, German**
and **Italian.**

Motifs for Embroideries

Iˢᵗ and IIⁿᵈ **SERIES**. — Two albums in-8°, each containing 32 coloured plates, composed of grounds, borders, floral designs, &c., also a series of tracings to facilitate reproducing and enlarging the patterns. Price of each series...... **1/—**

IIIʳᵈ and IVᵗʰ **SERIES**. — Two albums in large octavo, each containing 20 coloured plates, composed of various designs in modern style, for embroidery on counted threads. Price of each series .... **6ᵈ.**

GROUND ON PLATE I OF THE IIIʳᵈ SERIES, REDUCED IN SIZE.

The Iˢᵗ Series are edited in **French** and **German**.

Motifs for Embroideries

PLATE 4 OF THE IInd SERIES, REDUCED IN SIZE.

The IInd, IIIrd and IVth Series are edited in **English, French, German** and **Italian**.

Motifs for Embroideries, Vth Series

Album in large octavo, containing 15 coloured plates with numerous models for embroidery. A text with explanatory figures facilitates the reproduction of the models and a series of tracings of the plates contained in the album completes this publication .... Price : **7**½^{d.}

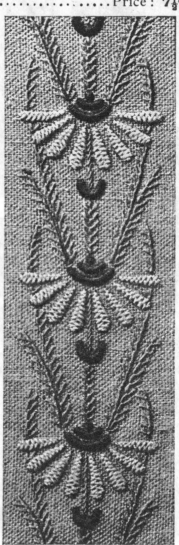

FIGURES ON PLATES II AND III, REDUCED IN SIZE.

This album is edited in **English, French, German and Italian**.

Teneriffe Lace Work

An album in-8°, of 20 plates containing a great variety of patterns for wheels, borders and lace, preceded by a text with explanatory figures to facilitate the execution of this kind of work. Artistic cover................ Price : **3 ½ d.**

FIGURE ON PLATE XI.

Teneriffe lace is a kind of work long known in Southern and Central America under the name of Brazilian or Bolivian lace. It is an imitation of a kind of needlework cultivated in Spain in the 16th and 17th centuries and known as "Sols" (Sun lace).

This album is edited in **English, French, German** and **Italian.**

DRAWN THREAD WORK, Ist Series

Album in-8°, containing 55 pages of text with explanatory figures and 20 plates with 31 patterns for openwork on linen.
Price........... 5ᵈ.

FIGURE ON PLATE VIII, REDUCED IN SIZE.

This album is edited in **English, French, German**
and **Italian**.

POINT LACE
(La Dentelle Renaissance)

Album in-8°, containing 76 pages of text with explanatory figures, 10 plates without text and 10 patterns on cambric for executing the designs reproduced on these plates. Price : **1/3**

FIGURE ON PLATE II, REDUCED IN SIZE.

This album is edited in **French, German** and **Italian**.

Irish Crochet Lace

Album in large octavo,
containing 5o pages of text with numerous explanatory figures
and 7 plates of patterns for Irish crochet lace, to which are
added tracings on linen for reproducing the patterns
illustrated on the plates .... Price : **1/5**

FIGURE ON PLATE VI.

This album is edited in **English, French, German**
and **Italian.**

Marking Stitch, I^st Series

Album in-8°,

containing 12 coloured plates composed of alphabets,
monograms and patterns for counted stitch embroideries.

Price..................... 1^d.

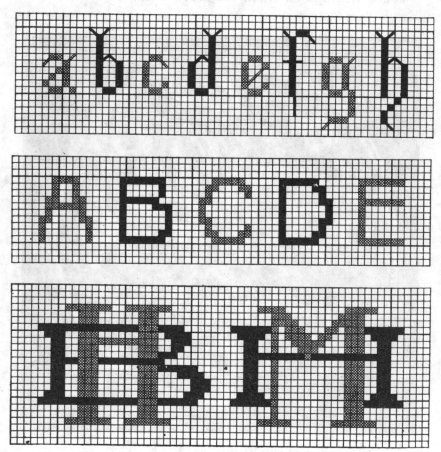

LETTERS AND MONOGRAMS OF THE ALBUM.

This album is edited in **English, French, German, Italian, Spanish** and **Russian.**

Pillow Laces, Ist Series

(Les Dentelles aux Fuseaux)

Octavo volume,
containing 176 pages of text, with numerous explanatory
illustrations, 8 plates, with patterns of laces, insertions and
braids and 55 tracings for executing the
different patterns described in the book.......... Price : **2/2**

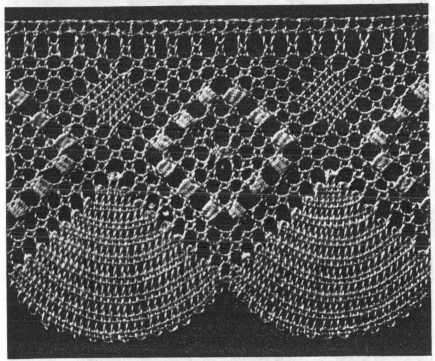

FIGURE ON PLATE VII.

This album is edited in **French** and **German**.

Embroidery on Tulle, Ist Series

Album in large octavo, containing 16 plates printed in black and 8 plates in colours, with numerous patterns of laces, edgings, insertions and powderings, preceded by an explanatory text with figures........................ Price : **10** d.

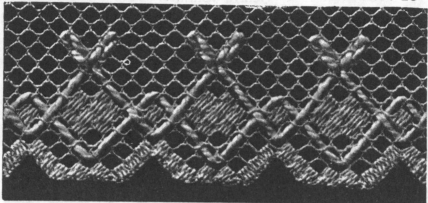

FIGURE ON PLATE III.

Hardanger Embroideries

Album in large octavo, containing 36 plates composed of a number of patterns for openwork embroidery on counted threads; 20 pages of text with explanatory figures accompany the plates.................................... Price : **8** d.

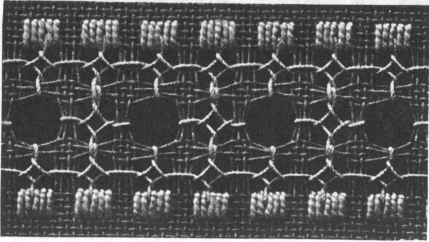

PART OF PLATE XXXVI.

These albums are edited in **English, French, German and Italian.**

Drawn thread Work, IInd Series
(Les Jours sur Toile)

Pamphlet in-8°, consisting of 11 pages of text with explanatory figures and 32 plates besides the text containing patterns for openwork a number of which may be executed in embroidery on net.............................. Price : **8**^{d.}

FIGURE ON PLATE XVI, REDUCED IN SIZE.

This album is edited in **French** and **German**.

Needle-made Laces, Ist Series

Album in large octavo, containing 15 plates comprising numerous designs for laces, as well as a series of patterns for their execution, the whole preceded by a text with explanatory figures............................... Price: **1/−**

FIGURES ON PLATES I AND V, REDUCED IN SIZE.

This album is edited in **English, French, German** and **Italian**.